THE NORTON MIX:
SOCIOLOGY

GENERAL EDITORS

Nathan Palmer
COORDINATING EDITOR
Georgia Southern University

Tanya Gladney
University of St. Thomas

Erica Hunter
State University of New York–Albany

Fernando I. Rivera
University of Central Florida

THE NORTON MIX:
SOCIOLOGY

A CUSTOM TEXTBOOK AND READER

Sociology 1

Professor Mark Jepson

Fall 2013

UCLA

NORTON
CUSTOM
W. W. NORTON & COMPANY, INC.
NEW YORK • LONDON

W. W. NORTON & COMPANY has been independent since its founding in 1923, when William Warder Norton and Mary D. Herter Norton first published lectures delivered at the People's Institute, the adult education division of New York City's Cooper Union. The firm soon expanded its program beyond the Institute, publishing books by celebrated academics from America and abroad. By midcentury, the two major pillars of Norton's publishing program—trade books and college texts—were firmly established. In the 1950s, the Norton family transferred control of the company to its employees, and today—with a staff of four hundred and a comparable number of trade, college, and professional titles published each year—W. W. Norton & Company stands as the largest and oldest publishing house owned wholly by its employees.

Editor: Karl Bakeman
Custom editor: Katie Hannah
Project editors: Kate Feighery and Melissa Atkin
Production managers, College: Ashley Horna and Diana Spiegle
Custom assistant editor: Erica Wnek
Custom editorial assistants: Elizabeth Dana and Sophie Hagen
Editorial assistant: Alicia Gonzalez-Gross
Managing editor: Marian Johnson
Copyeditor: Letta Wren Page
Design director: Rubina Yeh
Book designers: Joan Greenfield, Hope Miller Goodell, and Kiss Me I'm Polish
Text permissions manager: Megan Jackson
Text permissions editor: Nancy Rodwan
Photo permissions manager: Trish Marx
Photo permissions editor: Stephanie Romeo
Composition: Westchester Publishing Services
Manufacturing: RR Donnelley

ISBN 978-0-393-90725-4

W. W. Norton & Company, Inc., 500 Fifth Avenue, New York, N.Y. 10110
www.wwnorton.com
W. W. Norton & Company Ltd., Castle House, 75/76 Wells Street, London W1T 3QT

CONTENTS

Politics and Power

Class and Inequality

Race, Gender and Sexuality

Social Change

CONTENTS

DUNCAN WATTS

The Myth of Common Sense

from *Everything Is Obvious* Once You Know the Answer*

You never hear "What we need here is *LESS* common sense!" Instead, politicians, educators, and coworkers all bemoan its absence and call for a return to it. How can something so obvious—so common—be so hard to find? In this article Duncan Watts explores why common sense appears so obvious but is so ineffective at solving social problems.

COMMON SENSE IS SO ORDINARY THAT WE TEND TO NOTICE IT only when it's missing, but it is absolutely essential to functioning in everyday life. Common sense is how we know what to wear when we go to work in the morning, how to behave on the street or the subway, and how to maintain harmonious relationships with our friends and coworkers. It tells us when to obey the rules, when to quietly ignore them, and when to stand up and challenge the rules themselves. It is the essence of social intelligence, and is also deeply embedded in our legal system, in political philosophy, and in professional training.

For something we refer to so often, however, common sense is surprisingly hard to pin down.[1] Roughly speaking, it is the loosely organized set of facts, observations, experiences, insights, and pieces of received wisdom that each of us accumulates over a lifetime, in the course of encountering, dealing with, and learning from, everyday situations. Beyond that, however, it tends to resist easy classification. Some common-sense knowledge is very general in nature—what the American anthropologist Clifford Geertz called an "ancient tangle of received practices, accepted beliefs, habitual judgments, and untaught emotions."[2] But common sense can also refer to more specialized knowledge, as with the everyday working knowledge of a professional, such as a doctor, a lawyer, or an engineer, that develops over years of training and experience. In his address to the annual meeting of the American Sociological Society in Chicago in 1946, Carl Taylor, then president of the association, put it as well as anyone:

> By common sense I mean the knowledge possessed by those who live in the midst and are a part of the social situations and processes which sociologists seek to understand. The term thus used may be synonymous with folk knowledge, or it may be the knowledge possessed by engineers, by the practical politicians, by those who gather and publish news, or by others who handle or work with and must interpret and predict the behavior or persons and groups.[3]

Taylor's definition highlights two defining features of common sense that seem to differentiate it from other kinds of human knowledge, like science or mathematics. The first of these features is that unlike formal systems of knowledge, which are fundamentally theoretical, common sense is overwhelmingly *practical*, meaning that it is more concerned with providing answers to questions than in worrying about how it came by the answers. From the perspective of common sense, it is good enough to know that something is true, or that it is the way of things. One does not need to know why in order to benefit from the knowledge, and arguably one is better off not worrying about it too much. In contrast with theoretical knowledge, in other words, common sense does not reflect on the world, but instead attempts to deal with it simply "as it is."[4]

The second feature that differentiates common sense from formal knowledge is that while the power of formal systems resides in their ability to organize their specific findings into logical categories described by general principles, the power of common sense lies in its ability to deal with every concrete situation on its own terms. For example, it is a matter of common sense that what we wear or do or say in front of our boss will be different from how we behave in front of our friends, our parents, our parents' friends, or our friends' parents. But whereas a formal system of knowledge would try to derive the appropriate behavior in all these situations from a single, more general "law," common sense just "knows" what the appropriate thing to do is in any particular situation, without knowing how it knows it.[5] It is largely for this reason, in fact, that commonsense knowledge has proven so hard to replicate in computers—because, in contrast with theoretical knowledge, it requires a relatively large number of rules to deal with even a small number of special cases. Let's say, for example, that you wanted to program a robot to navigate the subway. It seems like a relatively simple task. But as you would quickly discover, even a single component of this task such as the "rule" against asking for another person's subway seat turns out to depend on a complex variety of other rules—about seating arrangements on subways in particular, about polite behavior in public in general, about life in crowded cities, and about general-purpose norms of courteousness, sharing, fairness, and ownership—that at first glance seem to have little to do with the rule in question.

Attempts to formalize commonsense knowledge have all encountered versions of this problem—that in order to teach a robot to imitate even a limited range of human behavior, you would have to, in a sense, teach it *everything* about the world. Short of that, the endless subtle distinctions between the things that matter, the things that are supposed to matter but don't, and the things that may or may not matter depending on other things, would always eventually trip up even the most sophisticated robot. As soon as it encountered a situation that was slightly different from those you had programmed it to handle, it would have no idea how to behave. It would stick out like a sore thumb. It would always be screwing up.[6]

People who lack common sense are a bit like the hapless robot in that they never seem to understand what it is that they should be paying attention to, and they never seem to understand what it is that they don't understand. And for exactly the same reason that programming robots is hard, it's surprisingly hard to explain to someone lacking in common sense what it is that they're doing wrong. You can take them back through various examples of when they said or did the wrong thing, and perhaps they'll be able to avoid making exactly those errors again. But as soon as anything is different, they're effectively back to square one. We had a few cadets like that at the academy:* otherwise perfectly intelligent, competent people who just couldn't seem to figure out how to play the game. Everyone knew who they were, and everyone could see that they just didn't get it. But because it wasn't exactly clear what it was that they didn't get, we were unable to help them. Bewildered and overwhelmed, most of them eventually left.

NOT COMMON AT ALL

As remarkable as it is, common sense exhibits some mysterious quirks, one of the most striking of which is how much it varies over time, and across cultures. Several years ago, for example, an enterprising group of economists and anthropologists set out to test how different cultures play a particular kind of game, called an ultimatum game. The game goes something like this: First, pick two people and give one of them $100. That person then has to propose a split of the money between himself and the other player, ranging from offering them the whole amount to nothing at all. The other player then gets to accept the deal or reject it. If the second player accepts the deal, they get what they were offered and both players go on their merry way. But if they reject the offer, neither player gets anything; hence the "ultimatum."

In hundreds of these experiments conducted in industrialized societies, researchers had already demonstrated that most players propose a fifty-fifty split, and offers of less than $30 are typically rejected. Economists find this behavior surprising because

---

* Watts attended the Australian Defence Force Academy as an undergraduate.

it conflicts with their standard notion of economic rationality. Even a single dollar, the reasoning goes, is better than nothing at all, so from a strictly rational perspective, recipients ought to accept any offer above zero. And knowing this, rational "proposers" ought to offer the least they can get away with—namely, one dollar. Of course, a moment's thought quickly suggests why people play the way they do—namely that it doesn't seem fair to exploit a situation just because you can. Recipients being offered less than a third therefore feel taken advantage of and so opt to walk away from even a substantial sum of money in order to teach miserly proposers a lesson. And anticipating this response, proposers tend to offer what they assume the recipient will consider a fair split.

If your reaction to this breakthrough insight is that economists need to get out a little more, then you're not alone. If anything seems like common sense, it's that people care about fairness as well as money—sometimes even more so. But when the experimenters replicated the game in fifteen small-scale preindustrial societies across five continents, they found that people in different societies have very different ideas about what counts as fair. At one extreme, the Machiguenga tribe of Peru tended to offer only about a quarter of the total amount, and virtually no offers were refused. At the other extreme, the Au and Gnau tribes of Papua New Guinea tended to make offers that were even better than fifty-fifty, but surprisingly these "hyperfair" offers tended to get rejected just as frequently as unfair offers.[7]

What explains these differences? As it turns out, the Au and Gnau tribes had long-established customs of gift exchange, according to which receiving a gift obligates the receiver to reciprocate at some point in the future. Because there was no equivalent of the ultimatum game in the Au or Gnau societies, they simply "mapped" the unfamiliar interaction onto the most similar social exchange they could think of—which happened to be gift exchange—and responded accordingly. Thus what might have seemed like free money to a Western participant looked to an Au or Gnau participant very much like an unwanted obligation. The Machiguenga, by contrast, live in a society in which the only relationship bonds that carry any expectation of loyalty are with immediate family members. When playing the ultimatum game with a stranger, therefore, Machiguenga participants—again mapping the unfamiliar onto the familiar—saw little obligation to make fair offers, and experienced very little of the resentment that would well up in a Western player upon being presented with a split that was patently unequal. To them, even low offers were seen as a good deal.

Once you understand these features of Au, Gnau, and Machiguenga cultures, their puzzling behavior starts to seem entirely reasonable—commonsense even. And that's exactly what it was. Just as we reflexively regard fairness and reciprocity as common-sense principles in our world that should be respected in general, and should be defended when violated without good reason, so the people of the fifteen preindustrial societies have their own implicit set of understandings about how the world is supposed to work. Those understandings might be different from ours. But once they have been accepted, their commonsense logic works in exactly the same way as ours does. It is simply what any reasonable person would do if they had grown up in that culture.

What these results reveal is that common sense is "common" only to the extent that two people share sufficiently similar social and cultural experiences. Common sense, in other words, depends on what the sociologist Harry Collins calls collective tacit knowledge, meaning that it is encoded in the social norms, customs, and practices of the world.[8] According to Collins, the acquisition of this type of knowledge can be learned only by participating in society itself—and that's why it is so hard to teach to machines. But it also means that even among humans, what seems reasonable to one might seem curious, bizarre, or even repugnant to another. For example, as Clifford Geertz, the anthropologist, has described, the treatment of hermaphroditic children has varied dramatically across different times and cultures. The Romans abhorred and killed them; the Greeks tolerated them; the Navajo revered them; and the east African Pokot tribe regarded them simply as "mistakes," to be kept around or discarded in the same way they might keep or throw out a flawed pot.[9] Likewise, practices including human slavery, sacrifice, cannibalism, foot binding, and female genital mutilation that are reviled in most contemporary cultures have all been (and in some cases, still are) considered entirely legitimate in different times and places.

Another important consequence of the socially embedded nature of common sense is that disagreements over matters of common sense can be surprisingly difficult to resolve. For example, it may seem remarkable to people who have grown up with the impression that New York is a crime-ridden cesspool, or at the very least a cold, hard-edged city full of people you can't trust, that, according to a recent news story, there is a small cadre of Manhattan residents who don't lock their doors. As the article makes clear, most people in the city think that the "no lock people" are crazy. As one woman said, "I live in a high-rise with a doorman, I've been there fifteen years, and I've never heard of a burglary in the building. But that has absolutely nothing to do with it—it's common sense [to lock your door]." Yet the only thing that seems shocking to the people who don't lock their doors is that anyone else would be shocked by it.[10]

What's curious about this story is that the language of the people involved almost precisely mirrors the experiences of Geertz, who noted in his study of witchcraft in Java that "when the whole family of a Javanese boy tells me that the reason he has fallen out of a tree and broken his leg is that the spirit of his deceased grandfather pushed him out because some ritual duty toward the grandfather has been inadvertently overlooked, that, so far as they are concerned, is the beginning, the middle, and the end of the matter: it is precisely what they think has occurred, it is all they think has occurred, and they are puzzled only at my puzzlement at their lack of puzzlement." Disagreements over matters of common sense, in other words, are hard to resolve because it's unclear to either side on what grounds one can even conduct a reasonable argument. Whether the issue is a Western anthropologist discussing witchcraft with preindustrial tribes in Indonesia, New Yorkers disagreeing about door locks, or the

NRA disagreeing with the Brady Campaign over the sorts of guns that Americans ought to be able to buy, whatever it is that people believe to be a matter of common sense, they believe it with absolute certainty. They are puzzled only at the fact that others disagree.[11]

SOME RESERVATIONS

That what is self-evident to one person can be seen as silly by another should give us pause about the reliability of common sense as a basis for understanding the world. How can we be confident that what we believe is right when someone else feels equally strongly that it's wrong—especially when we can't articulate why we think we're right in the first place? Of course, we can always write them off as crazy or ignorant or something and therefore not worth paying attention to. But once you go down that road, it gets increasingly hard to account for why we ourselves believe what we do. Consider, for example, that since 1996 support among the general public for allowing same-sex couples to marry has almost doubled, from 25 percent to 45 percent.[12] Presumably those of us who changed our minds over this period do not think that we were crazy fourteen years ago, but we obviously think that we were wrong. So if something that seemed so obvious turned out to be wrong, what else that we believe to be self-evident now will seem wrong to us in the future?

Once we start to examine our own beliefs, in fact, it becomes increasingly unclear even how the various beliefs we espouse at any given time fit together. Most people, for example, consider their own views about politics to be derived from a single coherent worldview: "I'm a moderate liberal" or "I'm a diehard conservative," and so on. If that were true, however, then one would expect that people who identify as liberals would tend to espouse the "liberal" perspective on most matters, and that conservatives would espouse a consistently different view. Yet research finds that regardless of whether people identify themselves as liberals or conservatives, what they think about any one issue, like, say, abortion, has relatively little relation to what they believe about other issues, such as the death penalty or illegal immigration. In other words, we have the impression that our particular beliefs are all derived from some overarching philosophy, but the reality is that we arrive at them quite independently, and often haphazardly.[13]

The same difficulty of reconciling what, individually, appear to be self-evident beliefs shows up even more clearly in the aphorisms that we invoke to make sense of the world. As sociologists are fond of pointing out, many of these aphorisms appear to be direct contradictions of each other. Birds of a feather flock together, but opposites attract. Absence indeed makes the heart grow fonder, but out of sight is out of mind. Look before you leap, but he who hesitates is lost. Of course, it is not necessarily the case that these beliefs are contradictory—because we invoke different aphorisms in different circumstances. But because we never specify the conditions under which one aphorism applies versus another, we have no way of describing what it is that we really think or why we think it. Common sense, in other words, is not so much a worldview as a grab bag of logically inconsistent, often contradictory beliefs, each of which seems right at the time but carries no guarantee of being right any other time.

THE MISUSE OF COMMON SENSE

The fragmented, inconsistent, and even self-contradictory nature of common sense does not generally present a problem in our everyday lives. The reason is that everyday life is effectively broken up into small problems, grounded in very specific contexts that we can solve more or less independently of one another. Under these circumstances, being able to connect our thought processes in a logical manner isn't really the point. It doesn't really matter that absence makes the heart grow fonder in one situation, and that out of sight is out of mind in the next. In any given situation we know the point we're trying to make, or the decision we want to support, and we choose the appropriate piece of commonsense wisdom to apply to it. If we had to explain how all our explanations, attitudes, and commonsense beliefs fit together, we would encounter all kinds of inconsistencies and contradictions. But because our experience of life rarely forces us to perform this task, it doesn't really matter how difficult it would be.

Where it does start to matter, however, is when we use common sense to solve problems that are *not* grounded in the immediate here and now of everyday life—problems that involve anticipating or managing the behavior of large numbers of people, in situations that are distant from us either in time or space. This may sound like an unlikely thing to do, but in fact we do it all the time. Whenever we read a newspaper and try to understand events playing out in some foreign country—the Israel-Palestine conflict, the unfolding insurgency in Iraq, or the seemingly endless conflict in Afghanistan—we are implicitly using our commonsense reasoning to infer the causes and explanations of the events we're reading about. Whenever we form an opinion about financial reform or healthcare policy, we are implicitly using our commonsense reasoning to speculate about how different rules and incentives will affect the various parties' behavior. And whenever we argue about politics or economics or the law, we are implicitly using our commonsense reasoning to reach conclusions about how society will be affected by whatever policy or proposal is being debated.

In none of these cases are we using our common sense to reason about how we should behave in the here and now. Rather, we are using it to reason about how other people behaved—or will behave—in circumstances about which we have at best an incomplete understanding. At some level we understand that the world is complicated, and that everything is somehow connected to everything else. But when we read some story about reforming the healthcare system, or about banker bonuses, or about the Israel-Palestine conflict, we don't try to understand how all these different problems fit together. We just focus on the one little piece of the huge underlying tapestry of the world that's being presented to us at that moment, and form our opinion accordingly. In this way, we can flip through the newspaper while drinking our morning cup of coffee and develop twenty different opinions about twenty different topics without breaking a sweat. It's all just common sense.

It may not matter much, of course, what conclusions ordinary citizens reach about the state of the world in the privacy of their own homes, based on what they're reading in the newspaper or arguing about with their friends. So it may not matter much that the way we reason about the problems of the world is poorly suited to the nature of the problems themselves. But ordinary citizens are not the only ones who apply commonsense reasoning to social problems. When policy makers sit down, say, to design some scheme to alleviate poverty, they invariably rely on their own commonsense ideas about why it is that poor people are poor, and therefore how best to help them. As with all commonsense explanations, it is likely that everyone will have his or her own views, and that these views will be logically inconsistent or even contradictory. Some may believe that people are poor because they lack certain necessary values of hard work and thrift, while others may think they are genetically inferior, and others still may attribute their lack of wealth to lack of opportunities, inferior systems of social support, or other environmental factors. All these beliefs will lead to different proposed solutions, not all of which can be right. Yet policy makers empowered to enact sweeping plans that will affect thousands or millions of people are no less tempted to trust their intuition about the causes of poverty than ordinary citizens reading the newspaper.

A quick look at history suggests that when common sense is used for purposes beyond the everyday, it can fail spectacularly. As the political scientist James Scott writes in *Seeing Like a State*, the late nineteenth and early twentieth centuries were characterized by pervasive optimism among engineers, architects, scientists, and government technocrats that the problems of society could be solved in the same way that the problems of science and engineering had been solved during the Enlightenment and the industrial revolution. According to these "high modernists," the design of cities, the management of natural resources, even the business of running an entire economy were all within the scope of "scientific" planning. As one of the undisputed high priests of modernism, the architect Le Corbusier, wrote in 1923, "the plan is generator; without it poverty, disorder, willfulness reign supreme."[14]

Naturally, the high modernists didn't describe what they were doing as an exercise in using their common sense, preferring instead to clothe their ambitions in the language of science. But as Scott points out, this scientific aura was a mirage. In reality there was no science of planning—just the opinions of individual planners who relied on their intuition to speculate about how their plans would play out in the real world. No one doubts that men like Le Corbusier were brilliant and original thinkers. Nevertheless, the outcomes of their plans, like Soviet collectivization or Le Corbusier's Brasilia, were often disastrous; and some of them, like the social engineering of Nazism or apartheid in South Africa, are now regarded among the great evils of the twentieth century. Moreover, even when these plans did succeed, they often did so in spite of themselves, as individuals on the ground figured out ways to create a reasonable outcome by ignoring, circumventing, or even undermining the plan itself.[15]

Looking back, it may seem as if the failures of high modernism—whether centrally planned economies or centrally designed cities—are a thing of the past, a product of a naïve and simplistic belief in science that we have since outgrown. Yet politicians, bureaucrats, architects, and regulators continue to make essentially the same mistake all the time. As the economist William Easterly has argued, the foreign aid community has been dominated for the past fifty years by large, bureaucratic organizations that are in turn run by powerful individuals whose ideas about what should and should not work inevitably play a large role in determining how resources will be devoted. Just as with the high modernists before them, these "planners," as Easterly calls them, are well-meaning and intelligent people who are often passionately devoted to the task of helping the people of the developing world. Yet in spite of the trillions of dollars of aid that planners have devoted to economic development, there is shockingly little evidence that the recipients are better off for it.[16]

Closer to home, and over roughly the same period of time, urban planners in the United States have repeatedly set out to "solve" the problem of urban poverty and have repeatedly failed. As the journalist and urban activist Jane Jacobs put it fifty years ago, "There is a wistful myth that if only we had enough money to spend—the figure is usually put at a hundred billion dollars—we could wipe out all our slums in ten years.... But look what we have built with the first several billions: Low-income projects that have become worse centers of delinquency, vandalism and general social hopelessness than the slums they were supposed to replace."[17] It is ironic that around the same time that Jacobs reached this conclusion, work began on the Robert Taylor Homes in Chicago, the largest public housing project ever built. And sure enough, as the sociologist Sudhir Venkatesh describes in *American Project*, what started out as a high-minded and carefully thought-out plan to help inner-city, largely African American families rise up into the middle class became a debacle of dilapidated buildings, overcrowded apartments and playgrounds, concentrated poverty, and eventually gang violence.[18]

The large scale and disruptive nature of economic and urban development plans make them especially prone to failure, but many of the same criticisms have been leveled at government plans to improve public education, reform healthcare services, manage public resources, design local regulations, or decide foreign policy.[19] Nor are governments alone in suffering from extreme planning failures. Corporations are rarely as large as governments, so their failures tend not to attract the same kind of scrutiny—although the near collapse of the financial system in 2008–2009 comes close. There are also so many more corporations than governments that it's always possible to find success stories, thereby perpetuating the view that the private sector is better at planning than the government sector. But as a number of management scholars have shown in recent years, corporate plans—whether strategic bets, mergers and acquisitions, or marketing campaigns—also fail frequently, and for much the same reasons that government plans do.[20] In all these cases, that is, a small number of people sitting in conference rooms are using their own commonsense intuition to predict, manage, or manipulate the behavior of thousands or millions of distant and diverse people whose motivations and circumstances are very different from their own.[21]

The irony of all this is that even as we observe the mistakes of politicians, planners, and others, our reaction is not to criticize common sense, but instead to demand more of it. At the World Economic Forum meeting in Davos in early 2009, for example, in the darkest depths of global financial crisis, one indignant audience member announced to the audience, "What we need now is a return to common sense!" It's an appealing notion, and drew loud applause at the time, but I couldn't help wondering what it was that he meant by it. After all, two years earlier at the 2007 Davos meeting, much the same mix of businesspeople, politicians, and economists were congratulating one another on having generated astonishing levels of wealth and unprecedented stability of the financial sector. Did anyone suspect that they had somehow taken leave of their common sense? And if not, then how exactly would it help to return to it? If anything, in fact, what the history of financial crises, both before and after the advent of high-technology trading, ought to teach us is that—like truth in war—it is common sense, not computer models, that is the first casualty of a financial mania.[22] And much the same is true of failures in politics, business, and marketing. Bad things happen not because we forget to use our common sense, but rather because the incredible effectiveness of common sense in solving the problems of everyday life causes us to put more faith in it than it can bear.

TOO MUCH INTUITION

But if common sense is so bad at dealing with complex social phenomena like political conflicts, healthcare economics, or marketing campaigns, why are its shortcomings not more obvious to us? After all, when it comes to the physical world, we also have plenty of intuition that we use to solve everyday problems—think of all the intuitive physics that is required to chase down and catch a fly baseball. But unlike in the social world, we have learned over time that our "commonsense physics" is easily tripped up. For example, common sense tells us that heavy objects fall under the force of gravity. But consider the following: A man stands on a perfectly flat plain holding a bullet in his left hand and a pistol, loaded with an identical bullet, in his right. Holding both pistol and bullet at the same height, he simultaneously fires the gun and drops the bullet. Which bullet will hit the ground first? Elementary high school physics will tell you that in fact the two bullets will hit the ground at exactly the *same* time. But even knowing this, it is hard not to think that the bullet from the gun is somehow kept up for longer by its velocity.

The physical world is filled with examples like this that defy commonsense reasoning. Why does water spiral down the toilet in opposite directions in the northern and southern hemispheres? Why do you see more shooting stars after midnight? And when floating ice melts in a glass, does the water level go up or down? Even if you really do understand the physics behind some of these questions, it is still easy to get them wrong, and they're nothing compared to the really strange phenomena of quantum mechanics and relativity. But as frustrating as it can be for physics students, the consistency with which our commonsense physics fails us has one great advantage for human civilization: It forces us to do science. In science, we accept that if we want to learn how the world works, we need to test our theories with careful observations and experiments, and then trust the data no matter what our intuition says. And as laborious as it can be, the scientific method is responsible for essentially all the gains in understanding the natural world that humanity has made over the past few centuries.

But when it comes to the human world, where our unaided intuition is so much better than it is in physics, we rarely feel the need to use the scientific method. Why is it, for example, that most social groups are so homogeneous in terms of race, education level, and even gender? Why do some things become popular and not others? How much does the media influence society? Is more choice better or worse? Do taxes stimulate the economy? Social scientists are endlessly perplexed by these questions, yet many people feel as though they could come up with perfectly satisfactory explanations themselves. We all have friends, most of us work, and we generally buy things, vote, and watch TV. We are constantly immersed in markets, politics, and culture, and so are intimately familiar with how they work—or at least that is how it seems to us. Unlike problems in physics, biology, and so on, therefore, when the topic is human or social behavior, the idea of running expensive, time-consuming "scientific" studies to figure out what we're pretty sure we already know seems largely unnecessary.

HOW COMMON SENSE FAILS US

Without a doubt, the experience of participating in the social world greatly facilitates our ability to understand it. Were it not for the intimate knowledge of our own thought processes, along with countless observations of the words, actions, and explanations of others—both experienced in person and also learned remotely—the vast intricacies of human behavior might well be inscrutable. Nevertheless, the combination of intuition, experience, and received wisdom on which we rely to generate commonsense explanations of the social world also disguises certain errors of reasoning that are every bit as systematic and pervasive as the errors of commonsense physics. These errors fall into three broad categories.

The first type of error is that when we think about why people do what they do, we invariably focus on factors like incentives, motivations, and beliefs, of which we are consciously aware. As sensible as it sounds, decades of research in psychology and cognitive science have shown that this view of human behavior encompasses just the tip of the proverbial iceberg. It doesn't occur to us, for example, that the music playing in the background can influence our choice of wine in the liquor store, or that the font in which a statement is written may make it more or less believable; so we don't factor these details into our anticipation of how people will react. But they do matter, as do many other apparently trivial or seemingly irrelevant factors. In fact, it is probably impossible to anticipate everything that might be relevant to a given situation. The result is that no matter how carefully we try to put ourselves in someone else's shoes, we are likely to make serious mistakes when predicting how they'll behave anywhere outside of the immediate here and now.

If the first type of commonsense error is that our mental model of individual behavior is systematically flawed, the second type is that our mental model of collective behavior is even worse. The basic problem here is that whenever people get together in groups—whether at social events, workplaces, volunteer organizations, markets, political parties, or even as entire societies—they interact with one another, sharing information, spreading rumors, passing along recommendations, comparing themselves to their friends, rewarding and punishing each other's behaviors, learning from the experience of others, and generally influencing one another's perspectives about what is good and bad, cheap and expensive, right and wrong. As sociologists have long argued, these influences pile up in unexpected ways, generating collective behavior that is "emergent" in the sense that it cannot be understood solely in terms of its component parts. Faced with such complexity, however, commonsense explanations instinctively fall back on the logic of individual action. Sometimes we invoke fictitious "representative individuals" like "the crowd," "the market," "the workers," or "the electorate," whose actions stand in for the actions and interactions of the many. And sometimes we single out "special people," like leaders, visionaries, or "influencers" to whom we attribute all the agency. Regardless of which trick we use, however, the result is that our explanations of collective behavior paper over most of what is actually happening.

The third and final type of problem with commonsense reasoning is that we learn less from history than we think we do, and that this misperception in turn skews our perception of the future. Whenever something interesting, dramatic, or terrible happens—Hush Puppies become popular again, a book by an unknown author becomes an international best seller, the housing bubble bursts, or terrorists crash planes into the World Trade Center—we instinctively look for explanations. Yet because we seek to explain these events only after the fact, our explanations place far too much emphasis on what actually happened relative to what might have happened but didn't. Moreover, because we only try to explain events that strike us as sufficiently interesting, our explanations account only for a tiny fraction even of the things that do happen. The result is that what appear to us to be causal explanations are in fact just stories—descriptions of what happened that tell us little, if anything, about the mechanisms at work. Nevertheless, because these stories have the form of causal explanations, we treat them as if they have predictive power. In this way, we deceive ourselves into believing that we can make predictions that are impossible, even in principle.

Commonsense reasoning, therefore, does not suffer from a single overriding limitation but rather from a combination of limitations, all of which reinforce and even disguise one another. The net result is that common sense is wonderful at *making sense* of the world, but not necessarily at understanding it. By analogy, in ancient times, when our ancestors were startled by lightning bolts descending from the heavens, accompanied by claps of thunder, they assuaged their fears with elaborate stories about the gods, whose all-too-human struggles were held responsible for what we now understand to be entirely natural processes. In explaining away otherwise strange and frightening phenomena in terms of stories they did understand, they were able to make sense of them, effectively creating an illusion of understanding about the world that was enough to get them out of bed in the morning. All of which is fine. But we would not say that our ancestors "understood" what was going on, in the sense of having a successful scientific theory. Indeed, we tend to regard the ancient mythologies as vaguely amusing.

What we don't realize, however, is that common sense often works just like mythology. By providing ready explanations for whatever particular circumstances the world throws at us, commonsense explanations give us the confidence to navigate from day to day and relieve us of the burden of worrying about whether what we think we know is really true, or is just something we happen to believe. The cost, however, is that we think we have understood things that in fact we have simply papered over with a plausible-sounding story. And because this illusion of understanding in turn undercuts our motivation to treat social problems the way we treat problems in medicine, engineering, and science, the unfortunate result is that common sense actually inhibits our understanding of the world.

* * *

Real explanations of the social world will require us to examine what it is about our common sense that misleads us into thinking that we know more than we do.[23]

END NOTES

1. Although the nature and limitations of common sense are discussed in introductory sociology textbooks (according to Mathisen [1989], roughly half of the sociology texts he surveyed contained references to common sense), the topic is rarely discussed in sociology journals. See, however, Taylor (1947), Stouffer (1947), Lazarsfeld (1949), Black (1979), Boudon (1988a), Mathisen (1989), Bengston and Hazzard (1990), Dobbin (1994), and Klein (2006) for a variety of perspectives by sociologists. Economists have been even less concerned with common sense than sociologists, but see Andreozzi (2004) for some interesting remarks on social versus physical intuition.

2. See Geertz (1975, p.6).

3. Taylor (1947, p. 1).

4. Philosophers in particular have wondered about the place of common sense in understanding the world, with the tide of philosophical opinion going back and forth on the matter of how much respect common sense ought to be given. In brief, the argument seems to have been about the fundamental reliability of experience itself; that is, when is it acceptable to take something—an object, an experience, or an observation—for granted, and when must one question the evidence of one's own senses? On one extreme were the radical skeptics, who posited that because all experience was, in effect, filtered through the mind, nothing at all could be taken for granted as representing some kind of objective reality. At the other extreme were philosophers like Thomas Reid, of the Scottish Realist School, who were of the opinion that any philosophy of nature ought to take the world "as it is." Something of a compromise position was outlined in America at the beginning of the nineteenth century by the pragmatist school of philosophy, most prominently William James and Charles Saunders Peirce, who emphasized the need to reconcile abstract knowledge of a scientific kind with that of ordinary experience, but who also held that much of what passes for common sense was to be regarded with suspicion (James 1909, p 193). See Rescher (2005) and Mathisen (1989) for discussions of the history of common sense in philosophy.

5. It should be noted that commonsense reasoning also seems to have backup systems that act like general principles. Thus when some commonsense rule for dealing with some particular situation fails, on account of some previously unencountered contingency, we are not completely lost, but rather simply refer to this more general covering rule for guidance. It should also be noted, however, that attempts to formalize this backup system, most notably in artificial intelligence research, have so far been unsuccessful (Dennett 1984); thus, however it works, it does not resemble the logical structure of science and mathematics.

6. See Minsky (2006) for a discussion of common sense and artificial intelligence.

7. For a description of the cross-cultural Ultimatum game study, see Henrich et al. (2001). For a review of Ultimatum game results in industrial countries, see Camerer, Loewenstein, and Rabin (2003).

8. See Collins (2007). Another consequence of the culturally embedded nature of commonsense knowledge is that what it treats as "facts"—self-evident, unadorned descriptions of an objective reality—often turn out to be value judgments that depend on other seemingly unrelated features of the socio-cultural landscape. Consider, for example, the claim that "police are more likely to respond to serious than non-serious crimes." Empirical research on the matter has found that indeed they do—just as common sense would suggest—yet as

the sociologist Donald Black has argued, it is also the case that victims of crimes are more likely to classify them as "serious" when the police respond to them. Viewed this way, the seriousness of a crime is determined not only by its intrinsic nature—robbery, burglary, assault, etc.—but also by the circumstances of the people who are the most likely to be attended to by the police. And as Black noted, these people tend to be highly educated professionals living in wealthy neighborhoods. Thus what seems to be a plain description of reality—serious crime attracts police attention—is, in fact, really a value judgment about what counts as serious; and this in turn depends on other features of the world, like social and economic inequality, that would seem to have nothing to do with the "fact" in question. See Black (1979) for a discussion of the conflation of facts and values. Becker (1998, pp. 133–34) makes a similar point in slightly different language, noting that "factual" statements about individual attributes—height, intelligence, etc.—are invariably relational judgments that in turn depend on social structure (e.g., someone who is "tall" in one context may be short in another; someone who is poor at drawing is not considered "mentally retarded" whereas someone who is poor at math or reading may be). Finally, Berger and Luckman (1966) advance a more general theory of how subjective, possibly arbitrary routines, practices, and beliefs become reified as "facts" via a process of social construction.

9. See Geertz (1975).

10. See Wadler (2010) for the story about the "no lock people."

11. For the Geertz quote, see Geertz (1975, p. 22). For a discussion of how people respond to their differences of opinions, and an intriguing theoretical explanation of their failure to converge on a consensus view, see Sethi and Yildiz (2009).

12. See Gelman, Lax, and Phillips (2010) for survey results documenting Americans' evolving attitudes toward same-sex marriage.

13. It should be noted that political professionals, like politicians, pundits, and party officials, do tend to hold consistently liberal or conservative positions. Thus, Congress, for example, is much more polarized along a liberal-conservative divide than the general population (Layman et al. 2006). See Baldassari and Gelman (2008) for a detailed discussion of how political beliefs of individuals do and don't correlate with each other. See also Gelman et al. (2008) for a more general discussion of common misunderstanding about political beliefs and voting behavior.

14. Le Corbusier (1923, p. 61).

15. See Scott (1998).

16. For a detailed argument about the failures of planning in economic development, particularly with respect to Africa, see Easterly (2006). For an even more negative viewpoint of the effect of foreign aid in Africa, see Moyo (2009), who argues that it has actually hurt Africa, not helped. For a more hopeful alternative viewpoint see Sachs (2006).

17. See Jacobs (1961, p. 4).

18. See Venkatesh (2002).

19. See Ravitch (2010) for a discussion of how popular, commonsense policies such as increased testing and school choice actually undermined public education. See Cohn (2007) and Reid (2009) for analysis of the cost of health care and possible alternative models. See O'Toole (2007) for a detailed discussion on forestry management, urban planning, and other failures of government planning and regulation. See Howard (1997) for a discussion and numerous anecdotes of the unintended consequences of government regulations. See Easterly (2006) again for some interesting remarks on nation-building and political

interference, and Tuchman (1985) for a scathing and detailed account of US involvement in Vietnam. See Gelb (2009) for an alternate view of American foreign policy.

20. See Barbera (2009) and Cassidy (2009) for discussion of the cost of financial crises. See Mintzberg (2000) and Raynor (2007) for overviews of strategic planning methods and failures. See Knee, Greenwald, and Seave (2009) for a discussion of the fallibility of media moguls; and McDonald and Robinson (2009), and Sorkin (2009) for inside accounts of investment banking leaders whose actions precipitated the recent financial crisis. See also recent news stories recounting the failed AOL-Time Warner merger (Arango 2010), and the rampant, ultimately doomed growth of Citigroup (Brooker 2010).

21. Clearly not all attempts at corporate or even government planning end badly. Looking back over the past few centuries, in fact, overall conditions of living have improved dramatically for a large fraction of the world's populations—evidence that even the largest and most unwieldy political institutions do sometimes get things right. How are we to know, then, that common sense isn't actually quite good at solving complex social problems, failing no more frequently than any other method we might use? Ultimately we cannot know the answer to this question, if only because no systematic attempt to collect data on relative rates of planning successes and failures has ever been attempted—at least, not to my knowledge. Even if such an attempt had been made, moreover, it would still not resolve the matter, because absent some other "uncommon sense" method against which to compare it, the success rate of commonsense-based planning would be meaningless. A more precise way to state my criticism of commonsense reasoning, therefore, is not that it is universally "good" or "bad," but rather that there are sufficiently many examples where commonsense reasoning has led to important planning failures that it is worth contemplating how we might do better.

22. For details of financial crises throughout the ages, see Mackay (1932), Kindleberger (1978), and Reinhart and Rogoff (2009).

23. There are, of course, several overlapping traditions in philosophy that already take a suspicious view of what I am calling common sense as their starting point. One way to understand the entire project of what Rawls called political liberalism (Rawls 1993), along with the closely related idea of deliberative democracy (Bohman 1998; Bohman and Rehg 1997), is, in fact, as an attempt to prescribe a political system that can offer procedural justice to all its members without presupposing that any particular point of view—whether religious, moral, or otherwise—is correct. The whole principle of deliberation, in other words, presupposes that common sense is not to be trusted, thereby shifting the objective from determining what is "right" to designing political institutions that don't privilege any one view of what is right over any other. Although this tradition is entirely consistent with the critiques of common sense that I raise, my emphasis is somewhat different. Whereas deliberation simply assumes incompatibility of commonsense beliefs and looks to build political institutions that work anyway, I am more concerned with the particular types of errors that arise in commonsense reasoning.

BIBLIOGRAPHY

Andreozzi, Luciano. 2004. "A Note on Paradoxes in Economics." *Kyklos* 57 (1):3–20.

Arango, Tim. 2010. "How the AOL-Time Warner Merger Went So Wrong." *New York Times*, Jan. 10.

Baldassari, Delia, and Andrew Gelman. 2008. "Partisans Without Constraint: Political Polarization and Trends in American Public Opinion." *American Journal of Sociology* 114 (2):408–46.

Barbera, Robert 2009. *The Cost of Capitalism: Understanding Market Mayhem and Stabilizing Our Economic Future.* New York: McGraw-Hill.

Becker, Howard S. 1998. *Tricks of the Trade: How to Think About Your Research While You're Doing it.* Chicago: University of Chicago Press.

Bengston, William F., and John W. Hazzard. 1990. "The Assimilation of Sociology in Common Sense: Some Implications for Teaching." *Teaching Sociology* 18 (1):39–45.

Berger, Peter L., and Thomas Luckman. 1966. *The Social Construction of Reality.* New York: Anchor Books.

Black, Donald. 1979. "Common Sense in the Sociology of Law." *American Sociological Review* 44 (1):18–27.

Blass, Thomas. 2009. *The Man Who Shocked the World: The Life and Legacy of Stanley Milgram.* New York: PublicAffairs Books.

Bohman, James. 1998. "Survey Article: The Coming of Age of Deliberative Democracy." *Journal of Political Philosophy* 6:400–425.

Bohman, James, and William Rehg. 1997. *Deliberative Democracy: Essays on Reason and Politics.* Cambridge, MA: MIT Press.

Boudon, Raymond. 1988a. "Common Sense and the Human Sciences." *International Sociology* 3 (1):1–22.

Brooker, Katrina. 2010. "Citi's Creator, Alone with His Regrets." "*New York Times,* Jan. 2.

Camerer, Colin F., George Loewenstein, and Matthew Rabin. 2003. *Advances in Behavioral Economics.* Princeton, NJ: Princeton University Press.

Cassidy, John. 2009. *How Markets Fail: The Logic of Economic Calamities,* New York: Farrar, Straus and Giroux.

Cohn, Jonathan. 2007. *Sick: The Untold Story of America's Health Care Crisis—and the People Who Pay the Price.* New York: HarperCollins.

Collins, Harry. 2007. "Bicycling on the Moon: Collective Tacit Knowledge and Somatic-Limit Tacit Knowledge." *Organization Studies* 28 (2):257.

Corbusier, Le. 1923. "Towards a New Architecture." Trans. F. Etchells. New York: Dover. First published as Vers une Architecture.

Dennett, Daniel C. 1984. "Cognitive Wheels: The Frame Problem of AI." In *Minds, Machines and Evolution,* ed. C. Hookaway. Cambridge, UK: Cambridge University Press.

Dobbin, Frank. 1994. "Cultural Models of Organization: The Social Construction of Rational Organizing Principles." In *The Sociology of Culture: Emerging Theoretical Perspectives,* ed. D. Crane. Oxford: Basil Blackwell.

Easterly, William. 2006. *The White Man's Burden: Why the West's Efforts to Aid the Rest Have Done So Much Ill and So Little Good.* New York: Penguin.

Geertz, Clifford. 1975. "Common Sense as a Cultural System." *The Antioch Review* 33 (1):5–26.

Gelb, Leslie. 2009. *Power Rules: How Common Sense Can Rescue American Foreign Policy.* New York: Harper Collins.

Gelman, Andrew, David Park, Boris Shor, et al. 2008. *Red State, Blue State, Rich State, Poor State: Why Americans Vote the Way They Do.* Princeton, NJ: Princeton University Press.

Gelman, Andrew, Jeffrey Lax, and Justin Phillips. 2010. "Over Time, a Gay Marriage Groundswell." *New York Times,* August 21.

Henrich, Joseph, Robert Boyd, Samuel Bowles, et al. 2001. "In Search of Homo Economicus: Behavioral Experiments in 15 Small-Scale Societies." *American Economic Review* 91 (2):73–78.

Howard, Philip K. 1997. *The Death of Common Sense*. New York: Warner Books.

Jacobs, Jane. 1961. *The Life and Death of Great American Cities*. New York: Random House.

James, William. 1909. *Pragmatism*. New York: Longmans, Green and Co.

Kindleberger, Charles. 1978. *Manias, Panics, and Crashes: A History of Financial Crises*. New York: Basic Books.

Klein, Lisl. 2006. "Applied Social Science: Is It Just Common Sense?" *Human Relations* 59 (8):1155–72.

Knee, Jonathan A., Bruce C. Greenwald, and Ava Seave. 2009. *The Curse of the Mogul: What's Wrong with the World's Leading Media Companies*. New York: Portfolio.

Layman, Geoffrey C., Thomas M. Carsey, and Juliana M. Horowitz. 2006. "Party Polarization in American Politics: Characteristics, Causes, and Consequences." *Annual Review of Political Science* 9: 83–110.

Lazarsfeld, Paul F. 1949. "The American Soldier—An Expository Review." *Public Opinion Quarterly* 13 (3):377–404.

Mackay, Charles. 1932. *Extraordinary Popular Delusions and the Madness of Crowds*. Boston: L.C. Page & Company.

Mathisen, James A. 1989. "A Further Look at 'Common Sense' in Introductory Sociology." *Teaching Sociology* 17 (3):307–15.

McDonald, Lawrence G., and Patrick Robinson. 2009. *A Colossal Failure of Common Sense: The Inside Story of the Collapse of Lehman Brothers*. New York: Crown Business.

Milgram, Stanley. 1969. *Obedience to Authority*. New York: Harper and Row.

Milgram, Stanley, and John Sabini. 1983. "On Maintaining Social Norms: A Field Experiment in the Subway." In *Advances in Environmental Psychology*, ed. Andrew Baum, Jerome E. Singer, and S. Valins. Hillsdale, NJ: Lawrence Erlbaum Associates.

Milgram, Stanley. 1992. *The Individual in a Social World*. Second ed. New York: McGraw Hill.

Minsky, Marvin. 2006. *The Emotion Machine*. New York: Simon & Schuster.

Mintzberg, Henry. 2000. *The Rise and Fall of Strategic Planning*. Upper Saddle River, NJ: Pearson Education.

Moyo, Dambias. 2009. *Dead Aid: Why Aid Is Not Working and How There Is Another Way for Africa*. New York: Farrar, Straus and Giroux.

O'Toole, Randal. 2007. *Best-Laid Plans: How Government Planning Harms Your Quality of Life, Your Pocketbook, and Your Future*. Washington, D.C.: Cato Institute.

Ramirez, Anthony, and Jennifer Medina. 2004. "Seeking a Favor, and Finding It, Among the Strangers on a Train." *New York Times*, Sept. 14.

Ravitch, Diane. 2010. "The Death and Life of the Great American School System." New York: Basic Books.

Rawls, John. *The John Dewey Essays in Philosophy, #4: Political Liberalism*. New York: Columbia University Press, 1993.

Raynor, Michael. 2007: *The Strategy Paradox: Why Committing to Success Leads to Failure*. New York: Doubleday.

Reid, T. R. 2009. "The Healing of America: A Global Quest for Better, Cheaper, and Fairer Health Care." New York: Penguin.

Reinhart, Carmen M., and Kenneth Rogoff. 2009. *This Time Is Different: Eight Centuries of Financial Folly.* Princeton, NJ: Princeton University Press.

Rescher, Nicholas. 2005. *Common-Sense: A New Look at Old Tradition.* Milwaukee, WI: Marquette University Press.

Sachs, Jeffrey. 2006. *The End of Poverty: Economic Possibilities for Our Time.* New York: Penguin.

Scott, James C. 1998. *Seeing Like a State: How Certain Schemes to Improve the Human Condition Have Failed.* New Haven, CT: Yale University Press.

Sethi, Rajiv, and Muhamet Yildiz. 2009. "Public Disagreement." In *MIT Department of Economics Working Paper Series.* Cambridge, MA.

Sorkin, Andrew Ross. 2009a. *Too Big to Fail: The Inside Story of How Wall Street and Washington Fought to Save the Financial System from Crisis—and Themselves,* New York: Viking Adult.

Stouffer, Samuel A. 1947. "Sociology and Common Sense: Discussion." *American Sociological Review* 12 (1):11–12.

Taylor, Carl C. 1947. "Sociology and Common Sense." *American Sociological Review* 12 (1):1–9.

Tuchman, Barbara W. 1985. *The March of Folly: From Troy to Vietnam.* New York: Ballantine Books.

Venkatesh, Sudhir. 2002. *American Project: The Rise and Fall of a Modern Ghetto.* Cambridge, MA: Harvard University Press.

Wadler, Joyce. 2010. "The No Lock People." *New York Times,* Jan. 13.

STUDY QUESTIONS

1. Watts argues that common sense is extremely helpful at _____, but terrible at _____.

2. Why are disagreements on matters of "common sense" hard to resolve? How do these disagreements typically end?

3. Many students read this piece and can see how people they know are victims of common sense, but the real opportunity to learn from **sociology** is to examine how you think and how it affects how you live your life. Reflect on your own worldview. What common sense beliefs do you hold that are based on inaccuracies, mythology, or ideas that are only true when we look at a situation one piece at a time?

4. Do an Internet search of the term common sense. Click the links and scan the articles. Based on your findings, who is most likely to use the idea of common sense to support a point of view? How do such people use the term? When you look from link to link do you see any contradictory examples?

C. WRIGHT MILLS

From *The Sociological Imagination*

I f you're taking an introductory **sociology** course, you're likely to hear about "the **sociological imagination**" early and often. In this excerpt, the influential sociologist C. Wright Mills describes what it means to look at the world through the eyes of a social analyst. To be truly curious about the world, Mills argues, you must consider history, biography, and **social structure**. Such curiosity will result in a new understanding of the world and your place in it. Do you think you have a sociological imagination? If not, what would it take to begin to exercise one?

NOWADAYS MEN OFTEN FEEL THAT THEIR PRIVATE LIVES ARE A series of traps. They sense that within their everyday worlds, they cannot overcome their troubles, and in this feeling, they are often quite correct: What ordinary men are directly aware of and what they try to do are bounded by the private orbits in which they live; their visions and their powers are limited to the close-up scenes of job, family, neighborhood; in other milieux, they move vicariously and remain spectators. And the more aware they become, however vaguely, of ambitions and of threats which transcend their immediate locales, the more trapped they seem to feel.

Underlying this sense of being trapped are seemingly impersonal changes in the very structure of continent-wide societies. The facts of contemporary history are also facts about the success and the failure of individual men and women. When a society is industrialized, a peasant becomes a worker; a feudal lord is liquidated or becomes a businessman. When classes rise or fall, a man is employed or unemployed; when the rate of investment goes up or down, a man takes new heart or goes broke. When wars happen, an insurance salesman becomes a rocket launcher; a store clerk, a radar man; a wife lives alone; a child grows up without a father. Neither the life of an individual nor the history of a society can be understood without understanding both.

Yet men do not usually define the troubles they endure in terms of historical change and institutional contradiction. The well-being they enjoy, they do not usually impute to the big ups and downs of the societies in which they live. Seldom aware of the intricate connection between the patterns of their own lives and the course of world history, ordinary men do not usually know what this connection means for the kinds of men they are becoming and for the kinds of history-making in which they might take part. They do not possess the quality of mind essential to grasp the interplay of man and society, of biography and history, of self and world. They cannot cope with their personal troubles in such ways as to control the structural transformations that usually lie behind them.

Surely it is no wonder. In what period have so many men been so totally exposed at so fast a pace to such earthquakes of change? That Americans have not known such catastrophic changes as have the men and women of other societies is due to historical facts that are now quickly becoming "merely history." The history that now affects every man is world history. Within this scene and this period, in the course of a single generation, one sixth of mankind is transformed from all that is feudal and backward into all that is modern, advanced, and fearful. Political colonies are freed; new and less visible forms of imperialism installed. Revolutions occur; men feel the intimate grip of new kinds of authority. Totalitarian societies rise, and are smashed to bits—or succeed fabulously. After two centuries of ascendancy, capitalism is shown up as only one way to make society into an industrial apparatus. After two centuries of hope, even formal democracy is restricted to a quite small portion of mankind. Everywhere in the underdeveloped world, ancient ways of life are broken up and vague expectations become urgent demands. Everywhere in the overdeveloped world, the means of authority and of violence become total in scope and bureaucratic in form. Humanity itself now lies before us, the super-nation at either pole concentrating its most coordinated and massive efforts upon the preparation of World War Three.

The very shaping of history now outpaces the ability of men to orient themselves in accordance with cherished values. And which values? Even when they do not panic, men often sense that older ways of feeling and thinking have collapsed and that newer beginnings are ambiguous to the point of moral stasis. Is it any wonder that ordinary men feel they cannot cope with the larger worlds with which they are so suddenly confronted? That they cannot understand the meaning of their epoch for their own lives? That—in defense of selfhood—they become morally insensible, trying to remain altogether private men? Is it any wonder that they come to be possessed by a sense of the trap?

———————

It is not only information that they need—in this Age of Fact, information often dominates their attention and overwhelms their capacities to assimilate it. It is not only the skills of reason that they need—although their struggles to acquire these often exhaust their limited moral energy.

What they need, and what they feel they need, is a quality of mind that will help them to use information and to develop reason in order to achieve lucid summations of what is going on in the world and of what may be happening within themselves. It is this quality, I am going to contend, that journalists and scholars, artists and publics, scientists and editors are coming to expect of what may be called the sociological imagination.

1

The sociological imagination enables its possessor to understand the larger historical scene in terms of its meaning for the inner life and the external career of a variety of individuals. It enables him to take into account how individuals, in the welter of their daily experience, often become falsely conscious of their social positions. Within that welter, the framework of modern society is sought, and within that framework the psychologies of a variety of men and women are formulated. By such means the personal uneasiness of individuals is focused upon explicit troubles and the indifference of publics is transformed into involvement with public issues.

The first fruit of this imagination—and the first lesson of the social science that embodies it—is the idea that the individual can understand his own experience and gauge his own fate only by locating himself within his period, that he can know his own chances in life only by becoming aware of those of all individuals in his circumstances. In many ways it is a terrible lesson; in many ways a magnificent one. We do not know the limits of man's capacities for supreme effort or willing degradation, for agony or glee, for pleasurable brutality or the sweetness of reason. But in our time we have come to know that the limits of "human nature" are frighteningly broad. We have come to know that every individual lives, from one generation to the next, in some society; that he lives out a biography, and that he lives it out within some historical sequence. By the fact of his living he contributes, however minutely, to the shaping of this society and to the course of its history, even as he is made by society and by its historical push and shove.

The sociological imagination enables us to grasp history and biography and the relations between the two within society. That is its task and its promise. To recognize this task and this promise is the mark of the classic social analyst. And it is the signal of what is best in contemporary studies of man and society.

No social study that does not come back to the problems of biography, of history and of their intersections within a society has completed its intellectual journey. Whatever the specific problems of the classic social analysts, however limited or however broad the features of social reality they have examined, those who have been imaginatively aware of the promise of their work have consistently asked three sorts of questions:

1. What is the structure of this particular society as a whole? What are its essential components, and how are they related to one another? How does it differ from other varieties of social order? Within it, what is the meaning of any particular feature for its continuance and for its change?

2. Where does this society stand in human history? What are the mechanics by which it is changing? What is its place within and its meaning for the development of humanity as a whole? How does any particular feature we are examining affect, and how is it affected by, the historical period in which it moves? And this period—what are its essential features? How does it differ from other periods? What are its characteristic ways of history-making?

3. What varieties of men and women now prevail in this society and in this period? And what varieties are coming to prevail? In what ways are they selected and formed, liberated and repressed, made sensitive and blunted? What kinds of "human nature" are revealed in the conduct and character we observe in this society in this period? And what is the meaning for "human nature" of each and every feature of the society we are examining?

Whether the point of interest is a great power state or a minor literary mood, a family, a prison, a creed—these are the kinds of questions the best social analysts have asked. They are the intellectual pivots of classic studies of man in society—and they are the questions inevitably raised by any mind possessing the sociological imagination. For that imagination is the capacity to shift from one perspective to another—from the political to the psychological; from examination of a single family to comparative assessment of the national budgets of the world; from the theological school to the military establishment; from considerations of an oil industry to studies of contemporary poetry. It is the capacity to range from the most impersonal and remote transformations to the most intimate features of the human self—and to see the relations between the two. Back of its use there is always the urge to know the social and historical meaning of the individual in the society and in the period in which he has his quality and his being.

That, in brief, is why it is by means of the sociological imagination that men now hope to grasp what is going on in the world, and to understand what is happening in themselves as minute points of the intersections of biography and history within society. In large part, contemporary man's self-conscious view of himself as at least an outsider, if not a permanent stranger, rests upon an absorbed realization of social relativity and of the transformative power of history. The sociological imagination is the most fruitful form of this self-consciousness. By its use men whose mentalities have swept only a series of limited orbits often come to feel as if suddenly awakened in a house with which they had only supposed themselves to be familiar. Correctly or incorrectly, they often come to feel that they can now provide themselves with adequate summations, cohesive assessments, comprehensive orientations. Older decisions that once appeared sound now seem to them products of a mind unaccountably dense. Their capacity for astonishment is made lively again. They acquire a new way of thinking, they experience a transvaluation of values: in a word, by their reflection and by their sensibility, they realize the cultural meaning of the social sciences.

2

Perhaps the most fruitful distinction with which the sociological imagination works is between "the personal troubles of milieu" and "the public issues of social structure." This distinction is an essential tool of the sociological imagination and a feature of all classic work in social science.

Troubles occur within the character of the individual and within the range of his immediate relations with others; they have to do with his self and with those limited areas of social life of which he is directly and personally aware. Accordingly, the statement and the resolution of troubles properly lie within the individual as a biographical entity and within the scope of his immediate milieu—the social setting that is directly open to his personal experience and to some extent his willful activity. A trouble is a private matter: values cherished by an individual are felt by him to be threatened.

Issues have to do with matters that transcend these local environments of the individual and the range of his inner life. They have to do with the organization of many such milieux into the institutions of an historical society as a whole, with the ways in which various milieux overlap and interpenetrate to form the larger structure of social and historical life. An issue is a public matter: some value cherished by publics is felt to be threatened. Often there is a debate about what that value really is and about what it is that really threatens it. This debate is often without focus if only because it is the very nature of an issue, unlike even widespread trouble, that it cannot very well be defined in terms of the immediate and everyday environments of ordinary men. An issue, in fact, often involves a crisis in institutional arrangements, and often too it involves what Marxists call "contradictions" or "antagonisms."

In these terms, consider unemployment. When, in a city of 100,000, only one man is unemployed, that is his personal trouble, and for its relief we properly look to the character of the man, his skills, and his immediate opportunities. But when in a nation of 50 million employees, 15 million men are unemployed, that is an issue, and we may not hope to find its solution within the range of opportunities open to any one individual. The very structure of opportunities has collapsed. Both the correct statement of the problem and the range of possible solutions require us to consider the economic and political institutions of the society, and not merely the personal situation and character of a scatter of individuals.

Consider war. The personal problem of war, when it occurs, may be how to survive it or how to die in it with honor; how to make money out of it; how to climb into the higher safety of the military apparatus; or how to contribute to the war's termination. In short, according to one's values, to find a set of milieux and within it to survive the war or make one's death in it meaningful. But the structural issues of war have to do with its causes; with what types of men it throws up into command; with its effects upon economic and political, family and religious institutions, with the unorganized irresponsibility of a world of nation-states.

Consider marriage. Inside a marriage a man and a woman may experience personal troubles, but when the divorce rate during the first four years of marriage is 250 out of every 1,000 attempts, this is an indication of a structural issue having to do with the institutions of marriage and the family and other institutions that bear upon them.

Or consider the metropolis—the horrible, beautiful, ugly, magnificent sprawl of the great city. For many upper-class people, the personal solution to 'the problem of the city' is to have an apartment with private garage under it in the heart of the city, and forty miles out, a house by Henry Hill, garden by Garrett Eckbo, on a hundred acres of private land. In these two controlled environments—with a small staff at each end and a private helicopter connection—most people could solve many of the problems of personal milieux caused by the facts of the city. But all this, however splendid, does not solve the public issues that the structural fact of the city poses. What should be done with this wonderful monstrosity? Break it all up into scattered units, combining residence and work? Refurbish it as it stands? Or, after evacuation, dynamite it and build new cities according to new plans in new places? What should those plans be? And who is to decide and to accomplish whatever choice is made? These are structural issues; to confront them and to solve them requires us to consider political and economic issues that affect innumerable milieux.

In so far as an economy is so arranged that slumps occur, the problem of unemployment becomes incapable of personal solution. In so far as war is inherent in the nation-state system and in the uneven industrialization of the world, the ordinary individual in his restricted milieu will be powerless—with or without psychiatric aid—to solve the troubles this system or lack of system imposes upon him. In so far as the family as an institution turns women into darling little slaves and men into their chief providers and unweaned dependents, the problem of a satisfactory marriage remains incapable of purely private solution. In so far as the overdeveloped megalopolis and the overdeveloped automobile are built-in features of the overdeveloped society, the issues of urban living will not be solved by personal ingenuity and private wealth.

––––––––––

What we experience in various and specific milieux, I have noted, is often caused by structural changes. Accordingly, to understand the changes of many personal milieux we are required to look beyond them. And the number and variety of such structural changes increase as the institutions within which we live become more embracing and more intricately connected with one another. To be aware of the idea of social structure and to use it with sensibility is to be capable of tracing such linkages among a great variety of milieux. To be able to do that is to possess the sociological imagination.

STUDY QUESTIONS

1. What does the **sociological imagination** enable its possessor to do?

2. What is the difference between "troubles" and "issues"? How can knowing the difference help us analyze a situation?

3. Mills says that the "first lesson" of the sociological imagination is both "terrible" and "magnificent." What does he mean? In what ways do your own knowledge of history and your own place in the world seem both terrible and magnificent?

4. Choose a **culture** to describe (it could be your fraternity/sorority, the group of actors and other theater types you hang out with, a regional group such as Southerners or Westerners, or some other culture). With your group in mind, answer the questions Mills outlines as those asked by the "imaginatively aware." Discuss with your classmates what you learned about this culture in the process.

MITCHELL DUNEIER

From *Sidewalk*

I f you've ever walked through certain areas of New York City, you've seen the sidewalk vendors selling books, pashmina shawls, and winter caps. If you were thinking like a **sociologist**, you might have wondered what those vendors' lives were like. Sociologist Mitchell Duneier's **ethnography** of people who make a living selling merchandise on the streets of the city provides an enlightening look at **urban** life. In this introduction to his book *Sidewalk*, the author describes his methods in obtaining information. Before you begin reading, jot down what you think are the characteristics of a person who sells knock-off watches on the street; after you finish, review your list and consider how your views might have changed.

HAKIM HASAN IS A BOOK VENDOR AND STREET INTELLECTUAL AT the busy intersection of Eighth Street, Greenwich Avenue, and the Avenue of the Americas—aka Sixth Avenue. He is a sturdy and stocky five-foot-seven African American, forty-two years old. In the winter, he wears Timberland boots, jeans, a hooded sweatshirt, a down vest, and a Banana Republic baseball cap.

One Thursday in February 1996, an African-American man in his mid-thirties came up to Hakim's table and asked for a copy of Alice Walker's book *The Same River Twice*, about her experiences in turning her novel *The Color Purple* into a movie. Hakim was all sold out, but said he would get some more in stock soon.

"When you get some, you let me know," said the man, who worked delivering groceries.

"I'll let you know."

"Because, you see, not only that," said the man, "I've got a friend that loves to read."

"Male or female?" asked Hakim.

"Female. She's like this: when she gets a book in her hand, in another hour it's finished. In other words—like, with me, I'll read maybe . . . five chapters, then I'll put it down 'cause I gotta do something, then maybe I'll come back to it. But with her, she gets into it and goes through the whole book like that. Boom. And she puts it on the shelf and it's just like brand-new. Like, when it's her birthday or what-have-you, I buy her books, because that's one of the things that she likes. I bought the book *Waiting to Exhale* in paperback, right? Listen to this: when I approached her with the book, the movie was coming out and she said, 'You late! I been read that book!'"

Hakim laughed. "I think she had a point."

"I said, 'Better late than never.' I wish I read that book before I seen the movie. Now, you can tell me this, Hakim: is it the same thing in the paperback as the hardcover?"

"Yeah, it's just different print."

"Just different print? Okay. Well, when you get the other book by Alice Walker, you let me know."

The man made a motion to leave, but then he continued talking.

"Because, you see, what happens is that there are a lot of females . . . authors that are coming out that are making their voices heard. More so than ever black. Even Alice Walker says something about this. It goes deep, man."

"Yeah, I'm gonna read that book by Alice Walker," said Hakim. "I'm gonna read it today."

"Oh, you're gonna read it today?" the man asked, laughing.

"I just finished two books over the weekend. I read at least one book a week," said Hakim.

"I try to tell my son that," said the deliveryman. "If you read one book a week, man, you don't know how much knowledge you can get."

Hakim doesn't just name titles. He knows the contents. I have observed the range and depth of his erudition impress scholars, and have seen him show great patience with uneducated people who are struggling with basic ideas and don't know much about books. He might sit for hours without having a single customer step up to his table; other times the table becomes a social center where men and women debate into the night.

For two years, I lived around the corner from where Hakim sets up. Almost every day, whenever I had time to amble about on the block, I'd visit and listen to the conversations taking place at his table.

At first, Hakim sold what he called "black books," works exclusively by or about blacks. In later years, he became romantically involved with a Filipina book vendor named Alice, who carried used paperback classics and *New York Times* best-sellers, and they merged their vending tables. Now they are on their own again, working side by side. Alice is the only woman who works outside on Sixth Avenue every day, and she has practically raised her daughters and granddaughters there. Whereas Alice tends to be "about business," local residents, workers, and visitors come to Hakim to discuss topics of all kinds, from burning issues of the day to age-old questions.

———————

Not long after we met, I asked Hakim how he saw his role.

"I'm a public character," he told me.

"A what?" I asked.

"Have you ever read Jane Jacobs's *The Death and Life of Great American Cities?*" he asked. "You'll find it in there."

I considered myself quite familiar with the book, a classic study of modern urban life published in 1961, and grounded in the author's observations of her own neighborhood, Greenwich Village. But I didn't recall the discussion of public characters. Nor did I realize that Hakim's insight would figure in a central way in the manner in which I would come to see the sidewalk life of this neighborhood. When I got home, I looked it up:

> The social structure of sidewalk life hangs partly on what can be called self-appointed public characters. A public character is anyone who is in frequent contact with a wide circle of people and who is sufficiently interested to make himself a public character. A public character need have no special talents or wisdom to fulfill his function—although he often does. He just needs to be present, and there need to be enough of his counterparts. His main qualification is that he *is* public, that he talks to lots of different people. In this way, news travels that is of sidewalk interest.[1]

Jacobs had modeled her idea of the public character after the local shopkeepers with whom she and her Greenwich Village neighbors would leave their spare keys. These figures could be counted on to let her know if her children were getting out of hand on the street, or to call the police if a strange-looking person was hanging around for too long: "Storekeepers and other small businessmen are typically strong proponents of peace and order," Jacobs explained. "They hate broken windows and holdups."[2] She also modeled the public character after persons like herself, who distributed petitions on local political issues to neighborhood stores, spreading local news in the process.

Although the idea is meaningful to anyone who has lived in an urban neighborhood where people do their errands on foot, Jacobs did not define her concept except to say, "A public character is anyone who is . . . sufficiently interested to make himself a public character." To clarify, we may consider her opening observation that the social structure "hangs partly" on the public characters. What Jacobs means is that the social context of the sidewalk is patterned in a particular way because of the presence of the public character: his or her actions have the effect of making street life safer, stabler, and more predictable. As she goes on to explain, this occurs because the public character has "eyes upon the street."

Following Jacobs, urban theorists have emphasized what city dwellers in pedestrian areas like Greenwich Village have always known: sidewalk life is crucial because the sidewalk is *the* site where a sense of mutual support must be felt *among strangers* if they are to go about their lives there together. Unlike most places in the United States, where people do their errands in cars, the people of Greenwich Village do many, if not most, of their errands by walking. The neighborhood's sidewalk life matters deeply to residents and visitors alike. Jacobs emphasized that social contact on the sidewalks must take place within a context of mutual respect for appropriate limits on interaction and intimacy. This made for interactive pleasantness, adding up to "an almost unconscious assumption of general street support when the chips are down."[3] The Village's "eyes upon the street," in Jacobs's famous dictum, indicated that residents and strangers were safe and consequently produced safety in fact.

Greenwich Village looked very different forty years ago, when Jane Jacobs was writing her classic book. Much of the architecture remains, and many people still live the way Jacobs's descriptions suggest; but there is another, more marginal population on these streets: poor black men who make their lives on the Village sidewalks. The presence of such people today means that pedestrians handle their social boundaries *in situ*, whereas, in the past, racial segregation and well-policed skid-row areas kept the marginal at bay.

In this book, I will offer a framework for understanding the changes that have taken place on the sidewalk over the past four decades. In asking *why* the sidewalk life has changed in this affluent neighborhood, I provide the context and point of departure for my research. It has changed because the concentration of poverty in high poverty zones has produced social problems of a magnitude that cannot be contained by even the most extreme forms of social control and exclusion. Many people living and/or working on Sixth Avenue come from such neighborhoods. Some were among the first generation of crack users, and so were affected by the war on those who use the drug and the failure of prisons to help them prepare for life after released. Some, under new workfare rules, have lost their benefits when they refused to show up to work as "the Mayor's slave."

In asking *how* the sidewalk life works today, I begin by looking at the lives of the poor (mainly) black men who work and/or live on the sidewalks of an upper-middle-class neighborhood. Unlike Hakim, who has an apartment in New Jersey, magazine vendors like Ishmael Walker are without a home; the police throw their merchandise, vending tables, clothes, and family photos in the back of a garbage truck when they leave the block to relieve themselves. Mudrick Hayes and Joe Garbage "lay shit out" on the ground (merchandise retrieved from the trash) to earn their subsistence wages. Keith Johnson sits in his wheelchair by the door of the automated teller machine and panhandles.

How do these persons live in a moral order? How do they have the ingenuity to do so in the face of exclusion and stigmatization on the basis of race and class? How does the way they do so affront the sensibilities of the working and middle classes? How do their acts intersect with a city's mechanisms to regulate its public spaces?

The people making lives on Sixth Avenue depend on one another for social support. The group life upon which their survival is contingent is crucial to those who do not rely on religious institutions or social service agencies. For some of these people, the informal economic life is a substitute for illegal ways of supporting excessive drug use. For others, informal modes of self-help enable them to do things most citizens seek to achieve by working: to support families, others in their community, or themselves. For still others, the informal economy provides a forum where they can advise, mentor, and encourage one another to strive to live in accordance with standards of moral worth.

Yet the stories of these sidewalks cannot ultimately serve as sociological romance, celebrating how people on the streets "resist" the larger structures of society. The social order these relationships carve out of what seems to be pure chaos, powerful as its effects are, still cannot control many acts that affront the sensibilities of local residents and passersby. How can we comprehend types of behavior such as sidewalk sleeping, urinating in public, selling stolen goods, and entangling passersby in unwanted conversations? What factors engender and sustain such behavior? How can we understand the processes that lead many people to regard those who engage in such acts as "indecent"? How do the quantity and quality of their "indecency" make them different from conventional passersby?

One of the greatest strengths of firsthand observation is also its greatest weakness. Through a careful involvement in people's lives, we can get a fix on how their world works and how they see it. But the details can be misleading if they distract us from the forces that are less visible to the people we observe but which influence and sustain the behaviors.[4] How do economic, cultural, and political factors contribute to make these blocks a habitat—a place where poor people can weave together complementary elements to organize themselves for subsistence? And how do such forces contribute to bringing these men to the sidewalk in the first place?

I look at all these aspects of sidewalk life in a setting where government retrenchment on welfare is keenly felt, as is the approbation of influential business groups. When government does assume responsibility in the lives of people like these, it attempts to eradicate them from the streets or to shape their behavior. These "social controls"—e.g., cutting down on the space for vending or throwing vendors' belongings in the back of garbage trucks—are the intended and unintended results of what has become the most influential contemporary idea about deviance and criminality: the "broken windows" theory, which holds that minor signs of disorder lead to serious crime. What are the consequences of this theory, its assumptions, and the formal social controls to which it has led?

In trying to understand the sidewalk life, I refer to an area of about three city blocks. Here we can see the confluence of many forces: some global (deindustrialization), some national (stratification of race and class and gender), some local (restrictive and punitive policies toward street vendors). Here, also, are blocks which can be studied in light of Jane Jacobs's earlier account and which contain the kinds of social problems that have become iconic in representations of the city's "quality of life" crisis. My visits to some other New York neighborhoods[5] and some other American cities suggest that they, too, have tensions surrounding inequalities and cultural differences in dense pedestrian areas. Across the country, liberals have voted to elect moderate, "law and order" mayors, some of them Republican. Whereas disorderly-conduct statutes were once enough, anti-panhandling statutes have been passed in Seattle, Atlanta, Cincinnati, Dallas, Washington, D.C., San Francisco, Santa Barbara, Long Beach, Philadelphia, New Haven, Raleigh, and Baltimore.

Yet New York City and Greenwich Village are unique in a multitude of ways. I certainly cannot hope to account for life in the majority of places, which have not seen severe sidewalk tensions in dense pedestrian districts; even many places that *have* seen such tensions are different from Greenwich Village.[6] Nor can I hope to show how the sidewalk works in low-income neighborhoods where the majority of tense sidewalk interactions occur among members of the same class or racial group. In the end, I must leave it to readers to test my observations against their own, and hope that the concepts I have developed to make sense of this neighborhood will prove useful in other venues.

———————

I gained entrée to this social world when I became a browser and customer at Hakim's table in 1992. Through my relationship with him, I came to know others in the area. He introduced me to unhoused and formerly unhoused people who scavenge and sell on the street, as well as other vendors who compete with him for sidewalk space and access to customers. These relations then led me to panhandlers, some of whom also sometimes scavenge and vend.

Once I was in the network, contacts and introductions took place across the various spheres. Eventually, I worked as a general assistant—watching vendors' merchandise while they went on errands, buying up merchandise offered in their absence, assisting on scavenging missions through trash and recycling bins, and "going for coffee." Then I worked full-time as a magazine vendor and scavenger during the summer of 1996, again for three days a week during the summer of 1997 and during part of the fall of 1997. I also made daily visits to the blocks during the summer of 1998, often for hours at a time, and worked full-time as a vendor for two weeks in March 1999, when my research came to an end.

Although in race, class, and status I am very different from the men I write about, I was myself eventually treated by them as a fixture of the blocks, occasionally referred to as a "scholar" or "professor," which is my occupation. My designation was Mitch.

This seemed to have a variety of changing meanings, including: a naïve white man who could himself be exploited for "loans" of small change and dollar bills; a Jew who was going to make a lot of money off the stories of people working the streets; a white writer who was trying to "state the truth about what was going on."

My continual presence as a vendor provided me with opportunities to observe life among the people working and/or living on the sidewalk, including their interactions with passersby. This enabled me to draw many of my conclusions about what happens on the sidewalk from incidents I myself witnessed, rather than deriving them from interviews. Often I simply asked questions while participating and observing.

Sometimes, when I wanted to understand how the local political system had shaped these blocks, I did my interviews at the offices of Business Improvement Districts, politicians, and influential attorneys. I also questioned police officers, pedestrians, local residents, and the like. I carried out more than twenty interviews with people working the sidewalk in which I explicitly asked them to tell me their "story." These sessions, held on street corners, in coffee shops, and on subway platforms, lasted between two and six hours. I paid the interviewees fifty dollars when their sessions were over, as compensation for time they could have spent selling or panhandling. Throughout the book, I try to be clear about the kind of research from which a quotation has been culled.

After I had been observing on the block for four years, Ovie Carter, an African-American photojournalist who has been taking pictures of the inner city for three decades, agreed to take photographs to illustrate the things I was writing about. He visited the blocks year-round and came to know the people in the book intimately. Ovie's photographs helped me to see things that I had not noticed, so that my work has now been influenced by his.

After three years passed, I believed I had a strong sense of the kinds of events and conversations that were typical on the blocks. In the next two years of this research, my field methods evolved to the point where intense use was made of a tape recorder. The tape recorder was on throughout my days on the block, usually kept in a milk crate under my vending table. People working and/or living on the sidewalk became accustomed to the machine and, after being exposed to it over a period of weeks, came to talk in ways that I determined to be like the talk I had heard before. Since the machine was taping on a public street, I hoped that I was not violating any expectation of privacy if it picked up the words of people who couldn't efficiently be informed that it was on. I have since received permission to quote almost all the people who were taped without their knowledge. When names are used, they are real ones, and I do so with consent. In those few cases when this is not possible (such as incidents involving police officers whose speech was recorded by my microphone without their knowing it), I have not used names at all or have indicated that a name is false.

I am committed to the idea that the voices of the people on Sixth Avenue need to be heard. To that end, my goal has been to assure the reader that what appears between quotation marks is a reasonably reliable record of what was said. (Some quotes have been edited slightly to make them more concise.) When the best I could do was rely on my memory or notes, quotation marks are not used. I have come to believe that this is perhaps especially necessary when a scholar is writing about people who occupy race and class positions widely divergent from his or her own, for the inner meanings and logics embodied in language that is distinctive to those positions can easily be misunderstood and misrepresented if not accurately reproduced. Furthermore, the increasingly popular practice of creating composite characters, and combining events and quotations sometimes occurring months or years apart, is *not* employed here. No characters have been combined. No events have been reordered.

Some of the people on the street volunteered to "manage" the taping by themselves, leaving the tape recorder on while wearing it in their pocket or resting it on their table when I was away from the scene or out of town. Such acts demonstrated the desire of persons in the book to ask their own questions, have their own topics addressed and recognized, and enable me to hear some things that went on when I could not be present. Sometimes they used the machine to interview one another and gave me the tapes. (In the pages that follow, I indicate when I rely upon such a source.) Given the knowledge Hakim had of both Jane Jacobs's work (which he inspired me to reread) and the life of these sidewalks, I asked him to respond to this book. He took time out of his daily grind as a vendor to write an afterword.

There was another way in which the vendors, scavengers, and panhandlers worked with me as collaborators. I invited some of them to classes to teach my students, in both Santa Barbara and Wisconsin. And I asked all of them to judge my own "theories" of the local scene when the book was complete, though always indicating that, while respecting their interpretations, I would not be bound by them. Throughout the book, it is I who have selected the material presented, and I take responsibility for the interpretations that go along with that material. For twenty-one people who figure prominently on the blocks, I have now made a commitment to return the advance and a share of any royalties or other forms of income that the book might yield.

Like all observers, I have my subjectivities. I know that scrupulous adherence to rules of method will not lead necessarily to objective truth. I believe that what is most important is that I try to help the reader recognize the lens through which the reality is refracted. I have written a statement on method to that end, and throughout the book I endeavor to explain my procedures for selecting data and my own biases and uncertainties about the inferences I draw.

Fieldwork is presumed to require trust. But one never can know for certain that he or she has gained such trust, given the absence of any agreed-upon indicator of what "full" trust would look like. In this case, I think, some level of trust was shown by people's readiness to provide access to information, settings, and activities of the most intimate sort. They sometimes revealed illegal activities or actions which, if others knew of them, might result in violent retribution.

But as I will explain, there were times when the trust I thought I had developed was nothing more than an illusion: deep suspicion lingered despite an appearance of trust. In some cases, perhaps it always will. Surely it takes more than goodwill to transcend distrust that comes out of a complex history. Though participant observers often remark on the rapport they achieve and how they are seen by the people they write about, in the end it is best to be humble about such things, because one never really knows.

NOTES

1. Jane Jacobs, *The Death and Life of Great American Cities* (New York: Vintage, 1961), p. 68.
2. Ibid., p. 47.
3. Ibid., p. 56.
4. For an excellent statement, see Stephen Steinberg, "The Urban Villagers: Thirty Years Later," remarks prepared for a plenary session at meeting of the Eastern Sociology Society, Boston, March 25, 1993.
5. For an excellent collection of ethnographies of the East Village, see Janet L. Abu-Lughod, *From Urban Village to "East Village": The Battle for New York's Lower East Side* (Cambridge: Blackwell, 1994); for an excellent ethnography of the political culture of Corona, with reference to quality-of-life discourse among working-class blacks in Queens, see Steven Gregory, *Black Corona: Race and the Politics of Place in an Urban Community* (Princeton, N.J.: Princeton University Press, 1988).
6. For a comprehensive analysis, see Lyn H. Lofland, *The Public Realm* (Hawthorne, N.Y.: Aldine De Gruyter, 1998).

STUDY QUESTIONS

1. What is a public character? In what ways does Hakim Hasan qualify as a public character?

2. How has sidewalk life changed in the last forty years, according to Duneier? What factors contributed to these changes?

3. Summarize Duneier's **research methods**. How did he get his information? How thorough and reliable would you judge it to be?

4. Duneier employed fieldwork to get the information he wanted from his subjects. What are some other ways he might have gathered information? Discuss the importance of **qualitative** versus **quantitative** research. What are the strengths and weaknesses of each?

ERVING GOFFMAN

Performances

from *The Presentation of Self in Everyday Life*

J ust who do you think you are? And, who do you want other people to think you are? As Erving Goffman notes, each of us performs as we want to be seen. That is, we are acting in a way that reflects how we see ourselves and how we think others see us. Goffman explores how our sense of **self** is constructed by the performances we give and by the **fronts** we wear like masks. As you read be thinking of what you do to construct in the minds of others the perception of who you are.

BELIEF IN THE PART ONE IS PLAYING

WHEN AN INDIVIDUAL PLAYS A PART HE IMPLICITLY REQUESTS his observers to take seriously the impression that is fostered before them. They are asked to believe that the character they see actually possesses the attributes he appears to possess, that the task he performs will have the consequences that are implicitly claimed for it, and that, in general, matters are what they appear to be. In line with this, there is the popular view that the individual offers his performance and puts on his show "for the benefit of other people." It will be convenient to begin a consideration of performances by turning the question around and looking at the individual's own belief in the impression of reality that he attempts to engender in those among whom he finds himself.

At one extreme, one finds that the performer can be fully taken in by his own act; he can be sincerely convinced that the impression of reality which he stages is the real reality. When his audience is also convinced in this way about the show he puts on—and this seems to be the typical case—then for the moment at least, only the sociologist or the socially disgruntled will have any doubts about the "realness" of what is presented.

At the other extreme, we find that the performer may not be taken in at all by his own routine. This possibility is understandable, since no one is in quite as good an observational position to see through the act as the person who puts it on. Coupled with this, the performer may be moved to guide the conviction of his audience only as a means to other ends, having no ultimate concern in the conception that they have of him or of the situation. When the individual has no belief in his own act and no ultimate concern with the beliefs of his audience, we may call him cynical, reserving the term "sincere" for individuals who believe in the impression fostered by their own performance. It should be understood that the cynic, with all his professional disinvolvement, may obtain unprofessional pleasures from his masquerade, experiencing a kind of gleeful spiritual aggression from the fact that he can toy at will with something his audience must take seriously.[1]

It is not assumed, of course, that all cynical performers are interested in deluding their audiences for purposes of what is called "self-interest" or private gain. A cynical individual may delude his audience for what he considers to be their own good, or for the good of the community, etc. For illustrations of this we need not appeal to sadly enlightened showmen such as Marcus Aurelius or Hsun Tzǔ.[2] We know that in service occupations practitioners who may otherwise be sincere are sometimes forced to delude their customers because their customers show such a heartfelt demand for it. Doctors who are led into giving placebos, filling station attendants who resignedly check and recheck tire pressures for anxious women motorists, shoe clerks who sell a shoe that fits but tell the customer it is the size she wants to hear—these are cynical performers whose audiences will not allow them to be sincere. Similarly, it seems that sympathetic patients in mental wards will sometimes feign bizarre symptoms so that student nurses will not be subjected to a disappointingly sane performance.[3] So also,

---

[1] Perhaps the real crime of the confidence man is not that he takes money from his victims but that he robs all of us of the belief that middle-class manners and appearance can be sustained only by middle class people. A disabused professional can be cynically hostile to the service relation his clients expect him to extend to them, the confidence man is in a position to hold the whole "legit" world in this contempt. [All notes are those of the author unless otherwise indicated.]

[2] Marcus Aurelius Antoninus (121–180 C.E.) was a Roman emperor and Stoic philosopher. Hsun Tzǔ (312–230 B.C.E.) was a Chinese philosopher. [Ed.]

[3] See Taxel, p. 4. Harry Stack Sullivan has suggested that the tact of institutionalized performers can operate in the other direction, resulting in a kind of *noblesse-oblige* sanity. See his "Socio-Psychiatric Research," *American Journal of Psychiatry*, X, pp. 987–88. "A study of 'social recoveries'

when inferiors extend their most lavish reception for visiting superiors, the selfish desire to win favor may not be the chief motive; the inferior may be tactfully attempting to put the superior at ease by simulating the kind of world the superior is thought to take for granted.

I have suggested two extremes: an individual may be taken in by his own act or be cynical about it. These extremes are something a little more than just the ends of a continuum. Each provides the individual with a position which has its own particular securities and defenses, so there will be a tendency for those who have traveled close to one of these poles to complete the voyage. Starting with lack of inward belief in one's role, the individual may follow the natural movement described by Park:

> It is probably no mere historical accident that the word person, in its first meaning, is a mask. It is rather a recognition of the fact that everyone is always and everywhere, more or less consciously, playing a role . . . It is in these roles that we know each other; it is in these roles that we know ourselves.[4]

> In a sense, and in so far as this mask represents the conception we have formed of ourselves—the role we are striving to live up to—this mask is our truer self, the self we would like to be. In the end, our conception of our role becomes second nature and an integral part of our personality. We come into the world as individuals, achieve character, and become persons.[5]

This may be illustrated from the community life of Shetland.[6] For the last four or five years the island's tourist hotel has been owned and operated by a married couple of crofter origins. From the beginning, the owners were forced to set aside their own conceptions as to how life ought to be led, displaying in the hotel a full round of middle-class services and amenities. Lately, however, it appears that the managers have become less cynical about the performance that they stage; they themselves are becoming middle class and more and more enamored of the selves their clients impute to them.

Another illustration may be found in the raw recruit who initially follows army etiquette in order to avoid physical punishment and eventually comes to follow the

---

in one of our large mental hospitals some years ago taught me that patients were often released from care because they had learned not to manifest symptoms to the environing persons; in other words, had integrated enough of the personal environment to realize the prejudice opposed to their delusions. It seemed almost as if they grew wise enough to be tolerant of the imbecility surrounding them, having finally discovered that it was stupidity and not malice. They could then secure satisfaction from contact with others, while discharging a part of their cravings by psychotic means."

[4] Robert Ezra Park, *Race and Culture* (Glencoe, Ill.: The Free Press, 1950), p. 249.
[5] *Ibid.*, p. 250.
[6] Shetland Isle study.

rules so that his organization will not be shamed and his officers and fellow soldiers will respect him.

As suggested, the cycle of disbelief-to-belief can be followed in the other direction, starting with conviction or insecure aspiration and ending in cynicism. Professions which the public holds in religious awe often allow their recruits to follow the cycle in this direction, and often recruits follow it in this direction not because of a slow realization that they are deluding their audience—for by ordinary social standards the claims they make may be quite valid—but because they can use this cynicism as a means of insulating their inner selves from contact with the audience. And we may even expect to find typical careers of faith, with the individual starting out with one kind of involvement in the performance he is required to give, then moving back and forth several times between sincerity and cynicism before completing all the phases and turning-points of self-belief for a person of his station. Thus, students of medical schools suggest that idealistically oriented beginners in medical school typically lay aside their holy aspirations for a period of time. During the first two years the students find that their interest in medicine must be dropped that they may give all their time to the task of learning how to get through examinations. During the next two years they are too busy learning about diseases to show much concern for the persons who are diseased. It is only after their medical schooling has ended that their original ideals about medical service may be reasserted.[7]

While we can expect to find natural movement back and forth between cynicism and sincerity, still we must not rule out the kind of transitional point that can be sustained on the strength of a little self-illusion. We find that the individual may attempt to induce the audience to judge him and the situation in a particular way, and he may seek this judgment as an ultimate end in itself, and yet he may not completely believe that he deserves the valuation of self which he asks for or that the impression of reality which he fosters is valid. Another mixture of cynicism and belief is suggested in Kroeber's discussion of shamanism:

> Next, there is the old question of deception. Probably most shamans or medicine men, the world over, help along with sleight-of-hand in curing and especially in exhibitions of power. This sleight-of-hand is sometimes deliberate; in many cases awareness is perhaps not deeper than the foreconscious. The attitude, whether there has been repression or not, seems to be as toward a pious fraud. Field ethnographers seem quite generally convinced that even shamans who know that they add fraud nevertheless also believe in their powers, and especially in those of other shamans: they consult them when they themselves or their children are ill.[8]

---

[7] H. S. Becker and Blanche Greer, "The Fate of Idealism in Medical School," *American Sociological Review*, 23, pp. 50–56.

[8] A. L. Kroeber, *The Nature of Culture* (Chicago: University of Chicago Press, 1952), p. 311.

FRONT

I have been using the term "performance" to refer to all the activity of an individual which occurs during a period marked by his continuous presence before a particular set of observers and which has some influence on the observers. It will be convenient to label as "front" that part of the individual's performance which regularly functions in a general and fixed fashion to define the situation for those who observe the performance. Front, then, is the expressive equipment of a standard kind intentionally or unwittingly employed by the individual during his performance. For preliminary purposes, it will be convenient to distinguish and label what seem to be the standard parts of front.

First, there is the "setting," involving furniture, décor, physical layout, and other background items which supply the scenery and stage props for the spate of human action played out before, within, or upon it. A setting tends to stay put, geographically speaking, so that those who would use a particular setting as part of their performance cannot begin their act until they have brought themselves to the appropriate place and must terminate their performance when they leave it. It is only in exceptional circumstances that the setting follows along with the performers; we see this in the funeral cortège, the civic parade, and the dreamlike processions that kings and queens are made of. In the main, these exceptions seem to offer some kind of extra protection for performers who are, or who have momentarily become, highly sacred. These worthies are to be distinguished, of course, from quite profane performers of the peddler class who move their place of work between performances, often being forced to do so. In the matter of having one fixed place for one's setting, a ruler may be too sacred, a peddler too profane.

In thinking about the scenic aspects of front, we tend to think of the living room in a particular house and the small number of performers who can thoroughly identify themselves with it. We have given insufficient attention to assemblages of sign-equipment which large numbers of performers can call their own for short periods of time. It is characteristic of Western European countries, and no doubt a source of stability for them, that a large number of luxurious settings are available for hire to anyone of the right kind who can afford them. One illustration of this may be cited from a study of the higher civil servant in Britain:

> The question how far the men who rise to the top in the Civil Service take on the "tone" or "color" of a class other than that to which they belong by birth is delicate and difficult. The only definite information bearing on the question is the figures relating to the membership of the great London clubs. More than three-quarters of our high administrative officials belong to one or more clubs of high status and considerable luxury, where the entrance fee might be twenty guineas or more, and the annual subscription from twelve to twenty guineas. These institutions are of the upper class (not even of the upper-middle) in their premises, their equipment, the style of living practiced

there, their whole atmosphere. Though many of the members would not be described as wealthy, only a wealthy man would unaided provide for himself and his family space, food and drink, service, and other amenities of life to the same standard as he will find at the Union, the Travellers', or the Reform.[9]

Another example can be found in the recent development of the medical profession where we find that it is increasingly important for a doctor to have access to the elaborate scientific stage provided by large hospitals, so that fewer and fewer doctors are able to feel that their setting is a place that they can lock up at night.[1]

If we take the term "setting" to refer to the scenic parts of expressive equipment, one may take the term "personal front" to refer to the other items of expressive equipment, the items that we most intimately identify with the performer himself and that we naturally expect will follow the performer wherever he goes. As part of personal front we may include: insignia of office or rank; clothing; sex, age, and racial characteristics; size and looks; posture; speech patterns; facial expressions; bodily gestures; and the like. Some of these vehicles for conveying signs, such as racial characteristics, are relatively fixed and over a span of time do not vary for the individual from one situation to another. On the other hand, some of these sign vehicles are relatively mobile or transitory, such as facial expression, and can vary during a performance from one moment to the next.

It is sometimes convenient to divide the stimuli which make up personal front into "appearance" and "manner," according to the function performed by the information that these stimuli convey. "Appearance" may be taken to refer to those stimuli which function at the time to tell us of the performer's social statuses. These stimuli also tell us of the individual's temporary ritual state, that is, whether he is engaging in formal social activity, work, or informal recreation, whether or not he is celebrating a new phase in the season cycle or in his life-cycle. "Manner" may be taken to refer to those stimuli which function at the time to warn us of the interaction role the performer will expect to play in the oncoming situation. Thus a haughty, aggressive manner may give the impression that the performer expects to be the one who will initiate the verbal interaction and direct its course. A meek, apologetic manner may give the impression that the performer expects to follow the lead of others, or at least that he can be led to do so.

We often expect, of course, a confirming consistency between appearance and manner; we expect that the differences in social statuses among the interactants will be expressed in some way by congruent differences in the indications that are made of an expected interaction role. This type of coherence of front may be illustrated by the following description of the procession of a mandarin through a Chinese city:

---

[9] H. E. Dale, *The Higher Civil Service of Great Britain* (Oxford: Oxford University Press, 1941), p. 50.
[1] David Solomon, "Career Contingencies of Chicago Physicians" (unpublished Ph.D. dissertation, Department of Sociology, University of Chicago, 1952), p. 74.

Coming closely behind...the luxurious chair of the mandarin, carried by eight bearers, fills the vacant space in the street. He is mayor of the town, and for all practical purposes the supreme power in it. He is an ideal-looking official, for he is large and massive in appearance, whilst he has that stern and uncompromising look that is supposed to be necessary in any magistrate who would hope to keep his subjects in order. He has a stern and forbidding aspect, as though he were on his way to the execution ground to have some criminal decapitated. This is the kind of air that the mandarins put on when they appear in public. In the course of many years' experience, I have never once seen any of them, from the highest to the lowest, with a smile on his face or a look of sympathy for the people whilst he was being carried officially through the streets.[2]

But, of course, appearance and manner may tend to contradict each other, as when a performer who appears to be of higher estate than his audience acts in a manner that is unexpectedly equalitarian, or intimate, or apologetic, or when a performer dressed in the garments of a high position presents himself to an individual of even higher status.

In addition to the expected consistency between appearance and manner, we expect, of course, some coherence among setting, appearance, and manner.[3] Such coherence represents an ideal type that provides us with a means of stimulating our attention to and interest in exceptions. In this the student is assisted by the journalist, for exceptions to expected consistency among setting, appearance, and manner provide the piquancy and glamor of many careers and the salable appeal of many magazine articles. For example, a *New Yorker* profile on Roger Stevens (the real estate agent who engineered the sale of the Empire State Building) comments on the startling fact that Stevens has a small house, a meager office, and no letterhead stationery.[4]

In order to explore more fully the relations among the several parts of social front, it will be convenient to consider here a significant characteristic of the information conveyed by front, namely, its abstractness and generality.

However specialized and unique a routine is, its social front, with certain exceptions, will tend to claim facts that can be equally claimed and asserted of other, somewhat different routines. For example, many service occupations offer their clients a performance that is illuminated with dramatic expressions of cleanliness, modernity, competence, and integrity. While in fact these abstract standards have a different significance in different occupational performances the observer is encouraged to stress the abstract similarities. For the observer this is a wonderful, though sometimes disastrous, convenience. Instead of having to maintain a different pattern of expectation and responsive treatment for each slightly different performer and performance,

---

[2] J. Macgowan, *Sidelights on Chinese Life* (Philadelphia: Lippincott, 1908), p. 187.

[3] Cf. Kenneth Burke's comments on the "scene-act-agent ratio," *A Grammar of Motives* (New York: Prentice-Hall, 1945), pp. 6–9.

[4] E. J. Kahn, Jr., "Closings and Openings," *The New Yorker,* February 13 and 20, 1954.

he can place the situation in a broad category around which it is easy for him to mobilize his past experience and stereo-typical thinking. Observers then need only be familiar with a small and hence manageable vocabulary of fronts, and know how to respond to them, in order to orient themselves in a wide variety of situations. Thus in London the current tendency for chimney sweeps[5] and perfume clerks to wear white lab coats tends to provide the client with an understanding that the delicate tasks performed by these persons will be performed in what has become a standardized, clinical confidential manner.

There are grounds for believing that the tendency for a large number of different acts to be presented from behind a small number of fronts is a natural development in social organization. Radcliffe-Brown has suggested this in his claim that a "descriptive" kinship system which gives each person a unique place may work for very small communities, but, as the number of persons becomes large, clan segmentation becomes necessary as a means of providing a less complicated system of identifications and treatments.[6] We see this tendency illustrated in factories, barracks, and other large social establishments. Those who organize these establishments find it impossible to provide a special cafeteria, special modes of payment, special vacation rights, and special sanitary facilities for every line and staff status category in the organization, and at the same time they feel that persons of dissimilar status ought not to be indiscriminately thrown together or classified together. As a compromise, the full range of diversity is cut at a few crucial points, and all those within a given bracket are allowed or obliged to maintain the same social front in certain situations.

In addition to the fact that different routines may employ the same front, it is to be noted that a given social front tends to become institutionalized in terms of the abstract stereotyped expectations to which it gives rise, and tends to take on a meaning and stability apart from the specific tasks which happen at the time to be performed in its name. The front becomes a "collective representation" and a fact in its own right.

When an actor takes on an established social role, usually he finds that a particular front has already been established for it. Whether his acquisition of the role was primarily motivated by a desire to perform the given task or by a desire to maintain the corresponding front, the actor will find that he must do both.

Further, if the individual takes on a task that is not only new to him but also unestablished in the society, or if he attempts to change the light in which his task is viewed, he is likely to find that there are already several well-established fronts among which he must choose. Thus, when a task is given a new front we seldom find that the front it is given is itself new.

*   *   *

---

[5] See Mervyn Jones, "White as a Sweep," *The New Statesman and Nation*, December 6, 1952.
[6] A. R. Radcliffe-Brown, "The Social Organization of Australian Tribes," *Oceania*, I, 440.

STUDY QUESTIONS

1. What are settings and how do we use them to communicate who we are? It may be helpful to think about how a particular profession is communicated with setting.

2. What does Goffman mean when he says that personal **fronts** can become "collective representations"?

3. How do you communicate to the world around you who you are? Discuss your personal front (in both manner and appearance) and the settings you use to present it. Your answer should demonstrate your understanding of these terms.

4. Go to a public place like a park, college student union, or shopping mall with a notebook and a pen. Watch and wait for a pair of people to meet. Write down how you see people presenting themselves when they see someone they know in public. What physical and nonphysical cues do they give one another?

KARI LERUM

"Precarious Situations" in a Strip Club: Exotic Dancers and the Problem of Reality Maintenance

What do a gynecologist and a stripper have in common? Both **occupations** require the professional to create a reality and then maintain it. When an occupation requires clients to be exposed or vulnerable or there is a possibility of misperceived intimacy, the practitioner must carefully create a reality that protects both him- or herself and the client. For instance, when a doctor has to see you naked, he or she works hard to set a mood of professionalism and scientific objectivity. In this essay Kari Lerum explores how exotic dancers create a reality that is emotional and intimate, but has clear boundaries.

IN HER CLASSIC ARTICLE, "BEHAVIOR IN PRIVATE PLACES: SUStaining Definitions of Reality in Gynecological Examinations" (1970), Joan Emerson uses the example of a gynecological exam to demonstrate how social order can prevail even when a social situation is rife with contradictions. In this article, I use Emerson's work as a reference point for another contradictory social situation: a contemporary strip club. The point of this comparison is to examine some similarities and differences in how "reality" is created, threatened, and maintained in each setting, and to gain insight into how specific social conditions impact the process of reality maintenance.

DEFINING REALITY IN A PRECARIOUS SITUATION

Emerson explains that the process of undergoing a gynecological exam can bring about two diametrically opposed messages: (1) the gynecological exam is *sexual and/or intimate* because it involves the (female) patient's genitals being touched by a (male) physician, and (2) the gynecological exam is merely a *routine, scientific procedure*; therefore the exam is completely free of sexual or emotional meaning. Such contradictory messages create what Emerson calls "the problem of reality maintenance"; a problem that is particularly acute for the people most invested in maintaining a certain understanding of reality. In Emerson's case, those people are the gynecologists—since they (as well as most medical experts) base their professional legitimacy upon behaving in a scientific, professional manner, they have tremendous incentive to project an objective, detached image, while extinguishing any threats to this image.

For gynecologists, a contradictory image takes root when their client considers the following question: "Is this *truly* just a professional routine, or is it a sexual and/or intimate act?" Interestingly, in my research of the commercial sex industry, including field work as a waitress in a strip club,[1] I have seen the reverse question arise among clients of sex workers; that is, "Is this *truly* a sexual and/or intimate act, or is it just a professional routine?" In both cases these questions cast doubt on the definition of reality projected by the worker, thus jeopardizing their control over clients.

It is within these questioning moments, suspended between contradictory definitions of what is "really" going on, that Emerson sees a "precarious situation." The situation is precarious because the pendulum of meaning could easily swing either way; if it swings in favor of the worker's definition, the worker succeeds in performing her or his transaction with professional and personal integrity intact. If, however, the pendulum swings in favor of any contradictory definition, the routine is disrupted and the worker's grip on the situation is loosened.

To some extent, this problem is embedded everywhere; all social situations contain symbols or messages that people may interpret in numerous ways. However, this only becomes a problem when new perceptions of reality conflict with institutionalized ones. If people perceive an institution to have meaning contradictory to its "purpose," people are left with no established pattern, or guide, for behavior. Lacking any clear definition of what is "really" going on, the situation becomes one of confusion; people may get nervous and perplexed, and their behavior becomes unpredictable.

This is an unsettling possibility for anyone engaged in an activity requiring the full cooperation of others such as performing a gynecological exam or performing a

---

[1] As part of my dissertation research, during 1998–1999 I spent six months working as a strip club waitress.

private "lap dance"[2] at a strip club. While at first glance these two actions may seem to have little in common—the first being an unpleasant but necessary medical procedure performed on a woman for "her own good"; the second being an unnecessary act performed primarily on men simply because it "feels good"—workers in both situations face strikingly similar problems of reality maintenance.

In both cases, the medical worker and the sex worker perform actions that their clients may interpret in contradictory ways. Due to the precarious situation that this brings, a considerable amount of effort on the part of workers is needed to ensure client cooperation. Initially, the desired definitions of reality appear as opposites— medical workers want their actions understood as *standardized* and *non-intimate* while sex workers want their actions understood as *intimate* and *non-standardized*. However, in both cases workers also occasionally find it useful to intentionally project contradictory messages, or counterthemes. For example, the gynecologist occasionally includes a few personal (non-standardized) touches to keep the patient from feeling humiliated and dehumanized; the sex worker occasionally reminds the customer of his customer (standardized) role as a way to squelch any expectations that their relationship will carry on outside of work boundaries. As a result, skillful workers in both fields alternate between themes of standardized professionalism and personalized intimacy as it suits their immediate needs.

The point of these maneuvers is to get clients to succumb to the worker's definition of reality, thus allowing the worker to complete a successful transaction. However, since both transactions involve objects or behaviors with deeply symbolic meanings (for the gynecological exam, exposure to genitals = sexual intimacy; for the lap dance, sexual intimacy = a "real" relationship), convincing people to think otherwise is not an easy task. Reality maintenance in these circumstances requires considerable skill and collective effort; it is a process that works best when it is invisible to the client. As Emerson (1970) writes, successful reality maintenance creates the feeling that "reality seems to be out there before we arrive on the scene."

Due to the symbolic and contradictory meanings found in both gynecological exams and lap dancing, many of the ways that the medical worker's definition of reality is maintained in a gynecological exam also work toward maintaining the sex worker's definition of reality in a strip club. However, a number of structural and interactional factors make the process of reality maintenance in the strip club more precarious.

---

[2] In contrast to a stage dance, where dancers perform for the entire audience and sometimes collect tips, lap dances are performed for the enjoyment of one customer and must be individually paid for. For most exotic dancers, the lap dance is the primary source of income.

FACTORS THAT EXACERBATE PRECARIOUS SITUATIONS

Perhaps the most important factor that impacts the management of a precarious situation is that of institutional legitimacy. Unlike the gynecological business, whose legitimacy is protected by massive institutions like the American Medical Association and the U.S. government, the social and legal legitimacy of exotic dancing is far shakier and subject to regional, state, and local variation.

This lack of institutional legitimacy in many strip club settings leads to a number of related problems, including the likelihood of intrusive troublemakers. Namely, a strip club's projection of reality is subject to constant and serious threat from troublemakers such as police officers, jealous lovers, and misguided customers (imagine a jealous husband or a police officer busting up a gynecological exam). All of these intrusions interfere with normal business, sometimes requiring workers to halt operations.

In addition to serious troublemakers, clients in strip clubs are generally less predictable and cooperative than clients in gynecological exams. In part, this lack of customer predictability is due to the nature of the business: One-on-one interactions with customers require the worker to individually tailor her approach. However, workers who provide other intimate, individually tailored services (such as hair styling, massage, counseling, or even gynecological exams) do not generally face uncooperative customers, so it is clear that the problem again stems from a lack of social legitimacy. In other words, customers might simply not see the worker as "legitimate"; thus an internalized sense of respect for the worker is lacking.

Additionally, the stigmatized work of selling and performing exotic dances may pose unique emotional requirements. As opposed to working within an arena built on emotional detachment (such as medicine), sex work requires the simultaneous *encouragement* of and *containment* of highly charged emotions. This, in addition to managing the stigma of sex work, may require more emotional labor for the sex practitioner in both managing her own and her customers' emotions. This in turn may make the process of reality maintenance more precarious.

Finally, the gendered, service-oriented nature of female erotic dancing might give customers the idea that control and power is in their hands rather than in the workers'. Since the broader culture still deems men more legitimately powerful than women, women in many occupations face problems of establishing interactional legitimacy. This combined with a culture of customer service (where the customer is allegedly "always right"), makes for a situation where worker control is not guaranteed.

In sum, with a lack of institutional, social, and interactional legitimacy, erotic dancers (and sex workers in general) cannot take their control for granted. Not only is their work itself often precarious legally, but on an interactional level, control over the definition of the situation must be continuously negotiated. Thus, in these settings, workers are more challenged in maintaining their definition of the situation.

MAINTAINING REALITY IN A STRIP CLUB

Despite differences in legitimacy, in both the gynecological examining room and the strip club, a successful reality maintenance campaign involves a practiced performance using several techniques. These techniques fall into two steps of reality maintenance: (1) *setting the mood* (setting and maintaining an overall message or atmosphere), and (2) *enforcing the rules* (enacting and enforcing that message with individual clients). When both levels of reality maintenance are employed, the likelihood of client cooperation increases.

Setting the Mood

The creation of an overall "mood" or atmosphere is accomplished through the use of several techniques, images, and props, all of which work in concert. In gynecological exams, an atmosphere of *objectivity, rationality,* and *standardization* is projected by normalizing and routinizing the exam, donning medical uniforms, and downplaying any emotional content. In the strip club where I worked (referred to here as "Club X"), an atmosphere of *excitement, intrigue,* and *exclusivity* was accomplished by heightening clients' emotions, making them believe that the experience was fun, sexy, exclusive, and slightly taboo, although also legitimate and professional. In both settings, workers intentionally influence the content and tone of clients' emotions. In one setting, the worker maintains control by making sure the client does not blush; in another setting, the worker maintains control by making sure the client *does.*

At Club X, the goal of making clients both emotionally "charged up" *and* compliant to workers' wishes was first accomplished by routinizing and standardizing the club's "mood." This was achieved by manipulating the appearance, language, and behavior of staff members, the images projected, the music and lighting, and the DJ's announcements.

On a typical night at Club X, the DJ had the greatest immediate influence over the mood; thus this person's routine was key for reality maintenance. The DJ was responsible for controlling the television channel (linked to five TV monitors in the club), as well as the light level of the club and, of course, the music. Each DJ had their unique style (one favored loud music, another kept the light level low), but all DJs had to ultimately comply with the company CEO's standards—the club could not be "too" dark, "too" loud, and the music had to stay fairly upbeat.

The DJ was also the official "voice" of the club; his or her words and tone influenced the mood and acted as a vocal tour guide for customers, encouraging them to see the experience from the club's point of view. One such viewpoint was that the experience was exciting and fun, similar to a sporting event. This message was made most explicit once an hour, when the DJ announced that it was time for the "Texas Teaser." All the dancers (sometimes numbering over thirty) gathered on the front stage, smiling, posing, and flirting with the customers on the floor, while the DJ goaded the crowd:

> Just *look* at all those gorgeous ladies! Guys, what do you say?! Take your hands out of your pockets and show some appreciation! On the count of three I want you to all shout as loud as you can, and the guy who makes the most noise will get a *free pass* to the club!! One . . . Two . . . Threeeee!!!! [The crowd goes wild, some young men standing on their seats, yelling, and pumping their arms in the air.]

These exuberant displays of concentrated emotion might have resulted in a loss of control for the workers, but interestingly, it rarely did. Rather, customers seemed to clearly understand that this game was not serious and that the workers controlled the rules. This understanding was reinforced immediately after the contest—the dancers would descend from the stage, flood the floor, and choose a customer for a "free" dance (while the DJ explained that they must buy a second dance). Since not every customer could get chosen for this free dance, and since the choosing process was up to the dancer, in a matter of moments the customers' demeanor shifted from noisy swaggering to humble anticipation (or dread). If a customer was overlooked this would sometimes turn to embarrassment; as one young man said to me, laughing and pointing to his friend, "Look at him, he was sitting there waiting on the couch, but no one wanted to give him a dance!"

In addition to the vulnerability that comes with waiting to be chosen, customers were also put in their place by the DJ, who routinely teased them by questioning both their heterosexual virility ("What are ya, a bunch of wussies?! What's wrong with you, don't ya like naked chicks?!") and their manners ("Didn't your mother teach you any manners?! Show some appreciation and buy a dance. And buy that lady a drink while you're at it.").

During all this excitement and teasing, an implicit message of professionalism and customer service was also projected by workers. One way this was demonstrated was in the standardized dress of staff members. Just as medical professionals and staff wear specific and unique clothing to both distinguish themselves from their patients and to project a certain (detached) message, the dancers and staff of Club X also used clothing as a method of intentional reality maintenance. One obvious use of this method was found in the rule that all staff members—including waitresses, doormen, bartenders, DJs, floor managers, and the parking lot attendant—wear the same uniform: a white tuxedo shirt, black slacks, and black shoes. The one variation in this uniform was that male staff members (essentially, everyone except the waitresses) were additionally required to wear a bow tie. As a fellow waitress explained to me, this dress code was established because "some of the waitresses were wearing really short skirts . . . but they [the management] wanted us to look classier."

This "professional" and sexually de-emphasized dress code for staff members also created a distinct contrast to the dancers—all of whom wore costumes meant to symbolize and create a sexually alluring image. None of the dancers wore identical outfits, and these outfits often changed by the night (and sometimes two or three times on the same night), but most of them fell within a narrow range of variability, ranging from short tight dresses to lingerie and g-string panties. These differences between the dancers' and staff members' costumes are not unlike the costume differences found within medical staff ranks where each variation symbolizes a difference in the person's status and role. However, in the strip club setting, costume variety between dancers and staff members also served to simultaneously portray a seemingly contradictory mixture of messages.

Another mood-shaping tool in Club X were the TV monitors. When I first began working at this club, every night brought a variety of soundless video images. Many of these images were of male sporting events, but sometimes the DJ would decide to watch the news, cartoons, or the Nature channel. Scrolling across these images were club advertisements such as "Welcome to Club X!," "$5 table dances; $12 couch dances, and $20 VIP dances!" and "If you've been overcharged, contact a manager." While these messages seemed congruent with images of football, race cars, and wrestling, the image of Dan Rather discussing Middle East politics made for a comically ironic fit. Eventually, these contradictory video messages stirred higher management to create new rules about acceptable video images. At one employee meeting, the general manager of Club X was particularly upset about the showing of cartoons, inspiring him to instigate a "no cartoon" rule.

> Absolutely no cartoons! That drives me crazy! No more cartoons! You wanna know why? Cuz cartoons make you think of kids. When I see cartoons, I think of my kids. It makes me miss my kids, I wish I could see them more often. So if you've got some pervert in here, spending three, four hundred dollars, and he sees cartoons up on the TV, he's going to think of his kids, feel like shit, and he's going to leave. So no more cartoons!

In other words, the point of these televised images was to encourage a specific mood as well as to sustain customers' attention by keeping them entranced and undistracted by their external emotional ties.[3]

The language of the staff also shaped the club's mood. Just as the use of clinical terms in a gynecological office creates an atmosphere of emotional and sexual detachment, the language at Club X was used to create an atmosphere that was sexually exciting as well as professional and polite. The DJ would routinely describe a dancer as a "beautiful showgirl" or a "hottie," but the language in this club was generally not sexually explicit. Rather, body parts were euphemized or avoided altogether. As a

---

[3] Interestingly, pornography was rarely shown at Club X. During my six months of work, I only saw it shown twice. On both occasions, dancers complained loudly, calling these images lewd and disgusting.

result, the club could be distinguished as a "gentlemen's club" rather than as "pornographic" or "raunchy."

The language of waitresses and doormen also served to create an atmosphere of exclusivity and politeness to both customers and dancers. Club X advertised that it gave *every* customer "VIP" treatment, and staff members were instructed to treat dancers with old-fashioned respect (at least in front of customers). For instance, when a dancer was found sitting with a customer, waitresses were trained to formally ask the customer, "Would you like to buy the lady a drink?" As Emerson puts it, such scripted language serves to "embody intentional themes." In other words, by routinizing worker behavior, specific messages can be reliably portrayed to customers. Thus, by consistently referring to dancers as "ladies," the message was sent that—although this was a place where one could get rowdy and receive good service—this was a place where one had to be polite to dancers.

In both the gynecological examining room and in the strip club, the work routine also includes similar specialized work areas—a table in the examining room; a couch in the strip club. Both also have "chaperones" (either a floor manager or a nurse) whose presence serves to discourage deviations from the intended reality.

Although the DJ was a heavyweight in creating the initial "mood," Club X's reality relied on the cooperation of all employees. Management was aware of this need for cooperation, judging by the messages staff members received such as a sign in the break-room which read: "T.E.A.M.—together everyone achieves more." Here the point of working together was to create a reality that was "respectable," service-oriented, and profitable. This emphasis on professional customer service is evident from the following quote from the general manager of Club X:

> Our competitors turned up the music, turned down the lights, and let the hand jobs fly . . . but that's not the kind of operation I'm running here . . . we need to stress service and entertainment. . . . When people go to a restaurant, they don't go there for the service, but it is what brings them back. So when customers come in, take care of them . . . be friendly, say, "Hey how's it going? If you see a girl you'd like, just let me know, and I'll get her for you." You know, take care of them.

From the worker's point of view, the ideal result of all these images, routines, and props is to prevent situations from becoming precarious—to barrage the client with consistent implicit (and sometimes explicit) messages, asserting that "this is how it's done here," and hoping for client cooperation.

Enforcing the Rules

Once the mood is set, a secondary process of enforcement is sometimes necessary. In both Emerson's observations of the gynecological exam and my own at Club X, rule enforcement was typically accomplished by simply instructing uninitiated clients (as well as co-workers) about their expected roles. In both settings, workers expect obedience and passivity from clients. And just as the physician guides the patient through the precarious scene by taking the initiative, controlling the encounter, and carefully monitoring the patient's reactions, so does the exotic dancer.

At Club X, once a dancer got a customer to agree to a dance, she was responsible for guiding the client into his or her proper role. While some role expectations were basic and mandatory (e.g., "no touching" and "keep your hands by your sides"), other role expectations were subtler—requiring the dancer to strategically combine her messages.

For instance, when an ambivalent customer conceded to a dance, dancers often found it useful to interact with the customer in a way that made him (or her) feel special and "really" cared for, yet also aware that the feeling came with a price. After getting paid, a dancer sometimes gave her customer a friendly hug and kiss on the cheek, reinforcing the message that she really did care about him. With younger male customers (who were notoriously "cheap" and who might have been embarrassed about paying for a temporary girlfriend), dancers would frequently walk with them hand-in-hand, leading them to the cash machine, but looking like high school kids going steady. With such shy, young, "cheap," emotionally sensitive, or uninitiated customers, subtle emotional management was often required.

For the hostile or uncooperative customer, rule enforcement relied upon the threat of physical force from male employee "chaperones." The primary chaperone at Club X was the floor manager, but all employees (especially male employees) were expected to jump in if trouble started. This club also had an informal enforcement team, composed of a few men who were allegedly not employees, but who were frequent visitors and known as "friends of the club." As one veteran waitress explained to me, these "friends" "watch out for the girls and pitch in if they're needed."

Fortunately, the majority of customers accepted the reality of Club X and played along with the expected rules: that is, they applauded the dancers on stage, stood up and yelled when the DJ told them to do so, accepted all "free" dances, sat passively while a private dance was performed on them, and then graciously paid the previously negotiated price (mostly ranging from ten to forty dollars, with the average being twenty dollars a dance). However, some customers remained mystified or shy observers, some were arrogantly skeptical of the rules, and others became aggressive or hostile.

In one case, Nicki[4] had just finished two lap dances and had successfully collected her fee, but as she turned to leave the customer reached his hand up inside of her underwear and squeezed her buttock. Nicki became very upset and immediately told Aaron, who was working as the doorman. As Aaron later told me the story, he "told the guy to get the fuck out of here" before he "beat the shit out of him." The threat worked, and the deviant customer departed.

Other, perhaps even more troublesome intruders were jealous lovers of dancers, delusional customers who refused to accept that they could not have a "real"

---

[4] All names have been changed.

relationship with their favorite dancer, as well as customers who were simply belligerent and looking for a fight. Due to the highly explosive nature of these situations, staff members had to stay alert and immediately call for help if needed—even if this involved asking for help from another set of troublesome intruders, the police.

Despite their role as potential protectors, the most precarious situations often arose with the entrance of the police. Since this club was in a suburban area where strip clubs were a highly contentious political issue, police officers occasionally stopped by to make their presence known and to monitor the club's activities. When this happened, Club X's reality was severely interrupted. Word would quickly spread throughout the club that the police were there. If there was enough lead time, special red lights would flash behind the bar to warn workers that the police were coming. The manager would then put on a friendly face, greet the officers at the door, and give them a tour of the facility. While business appeared to continue, with waitresses serving drinks, the music continuing, and the DJ introducing each dancer as she appeared on stage, the money exchange would essentially halt; dancers would quit performing lap dances and sit quietly next to their customers or with each other. Sometimes, if a dancer was not notified quickly enough of the threat, she would get caught in the middle of an illegal lap dance[5] and be ticketed. The heart of the entire business (lap dances) would not resume until the departure of the police.

Although far less frequent, precarious situations also rose from the actions of dancers. Often coming from dancers who had previously worked in more sexually lenient clubs, their deviations came in the form of intimacy transgressions—in other words, they went "too far" with their customers. In my six months of work at Club X, there were several cases of dancers who were chastised and sanctioned by other dancers for such transgressions.

For example, Tasha, a dancer at Club X who routinely grabbed at men's genitals through their trousers, was overwhelmingly disliked by the other dancers and staff. As one waitress told me, "You know who I really don't like? Tasha. She's really not classy; that's when I hate working here, when it feels like a whorehouse." It probably was no coincidence that Tasha did not last long as a Club X dancer; without the respect of the other dancers and staff members, negotiation of precarious situations becomes far more difficult.

In some cases, the initiation of a new dancer or the sanctioning of an established dancer simply involved a cold shoulder. But many times the punishment of inappropriate behavior was more direct. In one case, Janessa—a dancer with experience at several other clubs around the United States—was surrounded by several dancers in the

---

[5] Strip clubs within this police jurisdiction are subject to a "four-foot" rule; that is, erotic dances performed closer than four feet away from the patron are against the law. The problem is, it is virtually impossible for a dancer to make any money unless she dances closer than four feet.

dressing room and scolded for putting her crotch in a customer's face. Janessa left her shift early, crying.

In another case, a veteran Club X dancer lashed out at a newer dancer who she felt had gone "too far." The verbal explosion (below) was witnessed by several other dancers and staff:

> I'm fucking old school! Remember how much shit you gave me when I started working here?! [directed at another veteran dancer, who nods her head.] That Regina girl's letting people grab her and shit and only charging twelve dollars! If she wants to do that she should put her ass on the street!! I'm fucking old school. She needs to be taught.

The newer dancer also took a verbal shot or two, but the veteran had publicly and definitively made her point. The manager then quickly intervened, taking both dancers into her office for a private "consultation."

If a manager directly witnessed an intimacy transgression, the dancer would risk harsher penalties. Officially, each dancer was allowed two warnings about such behavior, and on the third offense they would get "termed" (i.e., their independent business contract with the club would be terminated). In one case, a new dancer, Cyndi, performed stage shows that were more sexually graphic than the norm (which other dancers described as "gross"). She was also observed on a number of occasions physically groping the genitals of her customers (through their clothing)—which is against both the club's rules and the state's laws. In her short time at the club, Cyndi had already received two warnings. I observed Cyndi's third offense: She was on a female customer's lap, fondling her breast, and kissing her on the lips. It was the kissing more than anything that shocked the rest of the dancers and staff, since kissing in these circumstances was seen as outrageously intimate. The floor manager was notified and Cyndi was immediately termed.

In all of these examples, it is clear that when a dancer heightened her sexual intimacy with customers, the club's (as well as the dancers') definition of reality was threatened. These actions made the club more at risk of legal sanctions, increased customers' expectations (which subsequently created more competition between dancers), and threatened the "high class" aim of Club X. In an atmosphere where workers were greatly invested in distancing themselves from prostitutes, most dancers and staff members were personally offended by such behavior.

CONCLUSIONS

Comparing Emerson's observations on gynecological exams with my own observations of Club X leads to a number of insights about reality maintenance. One is simply that the process of creating and maintaining reality in both situations is strikingly similar. However, by examining the contrasting points of each case, one also finds that different settings create the need for different techniques. The most relevant contrasts are the *level of institutionalized legitimacy* and the *required amount of client management*. It seems that the higher the social legitimacy of an industry, and the lower the need to constantly monitor and manage one's customers, the lower the threat of a precarious situation. In such a situation, the worker's power is assured and automatic client compliance is likely. In contrast, lower social legitimacy combined with a "high maintenance" customer results in a more precarious situation that needs constant monitoring, manipulation, and rule enforcement.

While rule enforcement at Club X occasionally required the threat of physical force, the vast majority of this enforcement was enacted through the skillful manipulation of messages. Emerson claims that if one pays better attention to the interplay between implicit and explicit messages, then a richer understanding of reality maintenance will emerge. Unlike gynecological exams, contradictory *explicit* messages are the key to reality maintenance at Club X. In other words, in order for the sex workers in this context to "pull it off," a simultaneous explicit expression of both professionalism and intimacy was not only possible, but necessary to maintain control.

In sum, strip clubs and gynecological exam rooms are both infused with contradictory messages, which can result in precarious definitions of the situation. In a sense, both are getting away with highly "intimate" acts in a commercial setting. However, Club X is doing so with a lack of social and legal legitimacy, making it more dependent on the efforts of individual workers to create a reality where business can be done.

REFERENCE

Emerson, J. P. (1970). "Behavior in Private Places: Sustaining Definitions of Reality in Gynecological Examinations." In P. Dreitsel (ed.), *Recent Sociology* (pp. 74–97). New York: Macmillan.

STUDY QUESTIONS

1. How do strip clubs control or "set the mood" to maximize their profitability? Provide evidence from the text to support your answers.

2. In what ways are the messages sent to clients at a strip club contradictory? Why does this increase the need to maintain reality by enforcing rules?

3. What reality is created and maintained in a classroom? That is, how do educators set the mood for learning and what rules do they enforce to maintain this reality?

4. Think of another "precarious situation" where maintaining a certain reality is really important. Pick something where either the client or the practitioner is vulnerable. How is a reality created and maintained with mood setting and rule enforcement?

C. J. PASCOE

Dude, You're a Fag:
Adolescent Male Homophobia

From *Dude, You're a Fag: Masculinity and Sexuality in High School*

T urn on the TV, listen to the radio, or just eavesdrop, and before long, you're bound to hear a guy use a phrase like, "You're such a fag!" "No homo," or "That's gay." But while this casual **homophobia** is rampant, Americans increasingly support same-sex **marriage** and sexual-orientation equality. What can explain this disconnect? In this article, C. J. Pascoe sets out to discover why homophobic terms are so common and what they actually mean to the young men who use them.

THE SUN SHONE BRIGHT AND CLEAR OVER RIVER HIGH'S ANNUAL Creative and Performing Arts Happening, or CAPA. During CAPA the school's various art programs displayed students' work in a fairlike atmosphere. The front quad sported student-generated computer programs. Colorful and ornate chalk art covered the cement sidewalks. Tables lined with student-crafted pottery were set up on the grass. Tall displays of students' paintings divided the rear quad. To the left of the paintings a television blared student-directed music videos. At the rear of the back quad, a square, roped-off area of cement served as a makeshift stage for drama, choir, and dance performances. Teachers released students from class to wander around the quads, watch performances, and look at the art. This freedom from class time lent the day an air of excitement because students were rarely allowed to roam the campus without a hall pass, an office summons, or a parent/faculty escort. In honor of CAPA, the school district bussed in elementary school students from the surrounding grammar schools to participate in the day's festivities.

Running through the rear quad, Brian, a senior, yelled to a group of boys visiting from the elementary schools, "There's a faggot over there! There's a faggot over there! Come look!" Following Brian, the ten-year-olds dashed down a hallway. At the end of the hallway Brian's friend Dan pursed his lips and began sashaying toward the little boys. As he minced, he swung his hips exaggeratedly and wildly waved his arms. To the boys Brian yelled, "Look at the faggot! Watch out! He'll get you!" In response, the ten-year-olds raced back down the hallway screaming in terror. Brian and Dan repeated this drama throughout the following half hour, each time with a new group of young boys.

Making jokes like these about faggots was central to social life at River High. Indeed, boys learned long before adolescence that faggots were simultaneously predatory and passive and that they were, at all costs, to be avoided. Older boys repeatedly impressed upon younger ones through these types of homophobic rituals that whatever they did, whatever they became, however they talked, they had to avoid becoming a faggot.

Feminist scholars of masculinity have documented the centrality of homophobic insults and attitudes to masculinity (Kimmel 2001; Lehne 1998), especially in school settings (Burn 2000; Kimmel 2003; Messner 2005; Plummer 2001; G. Smith 1998; Wood 1984). They argue that homophobic teasing often characterizes masculinity in adolescence and early adulthood and that antigay slurs tend to be directed primarily at gay boys. This chapter both expands on and challenges these accounts of relationships between homophobia and masculinity. Homophobia is indeed a central mechanism in the making of contemporary American adolescent masculinity. A close analysis of the way boys at River High invoke the faggot as a disciplinary mechanism makes clear that something more than simple homophobia is at play in adolescent masculinity. The use of the word *fag* by boys at River High points to the limits of an argument that focuses centrally on homophobia. Fag is not only an identity linked to homosexual boys but an identity that can temporarily adhere to heterosexual boys as well. The fag trope is also a racialized disciplinary mechanism.

Homophobia is too facile a term with which to describe the deployment of *fag* as an epithet. By calling the use of the word *fag* homophobia—and letting the argument stop there—previous research has obscured the gendered nature of sexualized insults (Plummer 2001). Invoking homophobia to describe the ways boys aggressively tease each other overlooks the powerful relationship between masculinity and this sort of insult. Instead, it seems incidental, in this conventional line of argument, that girls do not harass each other and are not harassed in this same manner. This framing naturalizes the relationship between masculinity and homophobia, thus obscuring that such harassment is central to the formation of a gendered identity for boys in a way that it is not for girls.

Fag is not necessarily a static identity attached to a particular (homosexual) boy. Fag talk and fag imitations serve as a discourse with which boys discipline themselves and each other through joking relationships. Any boy can temporarily become a fag in a given social space or interaction. This does not mean that boys who identify as or are perceived to be homosexual aren't subject to intense harassment. Many are. But becoming a fag has as much to do with failing at the masculine tasks of competence, heterosexual prowess, and strength or in any way revealing weakness or femininity as it does with a sexual identity. This fluidity of the fag identity is what makes the specter of the fag such a powerful disciplinary mechanism. It is fluid enough that boys police their behaviors out of fear of having the fag identity permanently adhere and definitive enough so that boys recognize a fag behavior and strive to avoid it.

An analysis of the fag discourse also indicates ways in which gendered power works through racialized selves. The fag discourse is invoked differently by and in relation to white boys' bodies than it is by and in relation to African American boys' bodies. While certain behaviors put all boys at risk for becoming temporarily a fag, some behaviors can be enacted by African American boys without putting them at risk of receiving the label. The racialized meanings of the fag discourse suggest that something more than simple homophobia is involved in these sorts of interactions. It is not that gendered homophobia does not exist in African American communities. Indeed, making fun of "negro faggotry seems to be a rite of passage among contemporary black male rappers and filmmakers" (Riggs 1991, 253). However, the fact that "white women and men, gay and straight, have more or less colonized cultural debates about sexual representation" (Julien and Mercer 1991, 167) obscures varied systems of sexualized meanings among different racialized ethnic groups (Almaguer 1991). Thus far male homophobia has primarily been written about as a racially neutral phenomenon. However, as D. L. King's (2004) recent work on African American men and same-sex desire pointed out, homophobia is characterized by racial identities as well as sexual and gendered ones.

WHAT IS A FAG? GENDERED MEANINGS

"Since you were little boys you've been told, 'Hey, don't be a little faggot,'" explained Darnell, a football player of mixed African American and white heritage, as we sat on a bench next to the athletic field. Indeed, both the boys and girls I interviewed told me that *fag* was the worst epithet one guy could direct at another. Jeff, a slight white sophomore, explained to me that boys call each other fag because "gay people aren't really liked over here and stuff." Jeremy, a Latino junior, told me that this insult literally reduced a boy to nothing, "To call someone *gay* or *fag* is like the lowest thing you can call someone. Because that's like saying that you're nothing."

Most guys explained their or others' dislike of fags by claiming that homophobia was synonymous with being a guy. For instance, Keith, a white soccer-playing senior, explained, "I think guys are just homophobic." However, boys were not equal-opportunity homophobes. Several students told me that these homophobic insults applied only to boys and not to girls. For example, while Jake, a handsome white senior, told me that he didn't like gay people, he quickly added, "Lesbians, okay, that's *good*." Similarly Cathy, a popular white cheerleader, told me, "Being a lesbian is accepted because guys think, 'Oh that's cool.'" Darnell, after telling me that boys were warned about becoming faggots, said, "They [guys] are fine with girls. I think it's the guy part that they're like ewwww." In this sense it was not strictly homophobia but a gendered homophobia that constituted adolescent masculinity in the culture of River High. It is clear, according to these comments, that lesbians were "good" because of their place in heterosexual male fantasy, not necessarily because of some enlightened approach to same-sex relationships. A popular trope in heterosexual pornography depicts two women engaging in sexual acts for the purpose of male titillation. The boys at River High are not unique in making this distinction; adolescent boys in general dislike gay men more than they dislike lesbians (Baker and Fishbein 1998). The fetishizing of sex acts between women indicates that using only the term *homophobia* to describe boys' repeated use of the word *fag* might be a bit simplistic and misleading.

Girls at River High rarely deployed the word *fag* and were never called fags. I recorded girls uttering *fag* only three times during my research. In one instance, Angela, a Latina cheerleader, teased Jeremy, a well-liked white senior involved in student government, for not ditching school with her: "You wouldn't 'cause you're a faggot." However, girls did not use this word as part of their regular lexicon. The sort of gendered homophobia that constituted adolescent masculinity did not constitute adolescent femininity. Girls were not called dykes or lesbians in any sort of regular or systematic way. Students did tell me that *slut* was the worst thing a girl could be called. However, my field notes indicate that the word *slut* (or its synonym *ho*) appeared one time for every eight times the word *fag* appeared.

Highlighting the difference between the deployment of *gay* and *fag* as insults brings the gendered nature of this homophobia into focus. For boys and girls at River High *gay* was a fairly common synonym for "stupid." While this word shared the sexual origins of *fag*, it didn't *consistently* have the skew of gender-loaded meaning. Girls and boys often used *gay* as an adjective referring to inanimate objects and male or female people, whereas they used *fag* as a noun that denoted only unmasculine males. Students used *gay* to describe anything from someone's clothes to a new school rule that they didn't like. For instance, one day in auto shop, Arnie pulled out a large older version of a black laptop computer and placed it on his desk. Behind him Nick cried, "That's a gay laptop! It's five inches thick!" The rest of the boys in the class laughed at Arnie's outdated laptop. A laptop can be gay, a movie can be gay, or a group of people can be gay. Boys used *gay* and *fag* interchangeably when they referred to other boys, but *fag* didn't have the gender-neutral attributes that *gay* frequently invoked.

Surprisingly, some boys took pains to say that the term *fag* did not imply sexuality. Darnell told me, "It doesn't even have anything to do with being gay." Similarly, J. L., a white sophomore at Hillside High (River High's cross-town rival), asserted, "*Fag*, seriously, it has nothing to do with sexual preference at all. You could just be calling somebody an idiot, you know?" I asked Ben, a quiet, white sophomore who wore heavy-metal T-shirts to auto shop each day, "What kind of things do guys get called a fag for?" Ben answered, "Anything . . . literally, anything. Like you were trying to turn a wrench the wrong way, 'Dude, you're a fag.' Even if a piece of meat drops out of your sandwich, 'You fag!'" Each time Ben said, "You fag," his voice deepened as if he were imitating a more masculine boy. While Ben might rightly *feel* that a guy could be called a fag for "anything . . . literally, anything," there were actually specific behaviors that, when enacted by most boys, could render them more vulnerable to a *fag* epithet. In this instance Ben's comment highlights the use of *fag* as a generic insult for incompetence, which in the world of River High, was central to a masculine identity. A boy could get called a fag for exhibiting any sort of behavior defined as unmasculine (although not necessarily behaviors aligned with femininity): being stupid or incompetent, dancing, caring too much about clothing, being too emotional, or expressing interest (sexual or platonic) in other guys. However, given the extent of its deployment and the laundry list of behaviors that could get a boy in trouble, it is no wonder that Ben felt a boy could be called fag for "anything." These nonsexual meanings didn't replace sexual meanings but rather existed alongside them.

One-third (thirteen) of the boys I interviewed told me that, while they might liberally insult each other with the term, they would not direct it at a homosexual peer. Jabes, a Filipino senior, told me, "I actually say it [*fag*] quite a lot, except for when I'm in the company of an actual homosexual person. Then I try not to say it at all. But when I'm just hanging out with my friends I'll be like, 'Shut up, I don't want to hear you any more, you stupid fag.'" Similarly J. L. compared homosexuality to a disability, saying there was "no way" he'd call an actually gay guy a fag because "there's people who are the retarded people who nobody wants to associate with. I'll be so nice to those guys, and I hate it when people make fun of them. It's like, 'Bro do you realize that they can't help that?' And then there's gay people. They were born that way." According to this group of boys, gay was a legitimate, or at least biological, identity.

There was a possibility, however slight, that a boy could be gay and masculine (Connell 1995). David, a handsome white senior dressed smartly in khaki pants and a white button-down shirt, told me, "Being gay is just a lifestyle. It's someone you choose to sleep with. You can still throw around a football and be gay." It was as if David was justifying the use of the word *fag* by arguing that gay men could be men if they tried but that if they failed at it (i.e., if they couldn't throw a football) then they deserved to be called a fag. In other words, to be a fag was, by definition, the opposite of masculine, whether the word was deployed with sexualized or nonsexualized meanings. In explaining this to me, Jamaal, an African American junior, cited the explanation of the popular rap artist Eminem: "Although I don't like Eminem, he had a good definition of it. It's like taking away your title. In an interview they were like, 'You're always capping on gays, but then you sing with Elton John.' He was like 'I don't mean gay as in gay.'" This is what Riki Wilchins (2003) calls the "Eminem Exception. Eminem explains that he doesn't call people 'faggot' because of their sexual orientation but because they're weak and unmanly" (72). This is precisely the way boys at River High used the term *faggot*. While it was not necessarily acceptable to be gay, at least a man who was gay could do other things that would render him acceptably masculine. A fag, by the very definition of the word, could not be masculine.

This distinction between fag as an unmasculine and problematic identity and gay as a possibly masculine, although marginalized, sexual identity is not limited to a teenage lexicon; it is reflected in both psychological discourses and gay and lesbian activism. Eve Sedgwick (1995) argues that in contemporary psychological literature homosexuality is no longer a problem for men so long as the homosexual man is of the right age and gender orientation. In this literature a homosexual male must be an adult and must be masculine. Male homosexuality is not pathologized, but gay male *effeminacy* is. The lack of masculinity is the problem, not the sexual practice or orientation. Indeed, the edition of the *Diagnostic and Statistical Manual of Mental Disorders* (a key document in the mental health field) that erased homosexuality as a diagnosis in the 1970s added a new diagnosis in its wake: Gender Identity Disorder. According to Sedgwick, the criteria for diagnosis are different for girls and boys. A girl has to actually assert that she is a boy, indicating a psychotic disconnection with reality, whereas a boy need only display a preoccupation with female activities. The policing of boys' gender orientation and of a strict masculine identity for gay men is also reflected in gay culture itself. The war against fags as the specter of unmasculine manhood appears in gay male personal ads in which men look for "straight-appearing, straight-acting men." This concern with both straight and gay men's masculinity not only reflects teenage boys' obsession with hypermasculinity but also points to the conflict at the heart of the contemporary "crisis of masculinity" being played out in popular, scientific, and educational arenas.

BECOMING A FAG: FAG FLUIDITY

"The ubiquity of the word *faggot* speaks to the reach of its discrediting capacity" (Corbett 2001, 4). It's almost as if boys cannot help shouting it out on a regular basis—in the hallway, in class, or across campus as a greeting. In my fieldwork I was amazed by the way the word seemed to pop uncontrollably out of boys' mouths in all kinds of situations. To quote just one of many instances from my field notes: two boys walked out of the PE locker room, and one yelled, "Fucking faggot!" at no one in particular. None of the other students paid them any mind, since this sort of thing happened so frequently. Similar spontaneous yelling of some variation of the word *fag*, seemingly apropos of nothing, happened repeatedly among boys throughout the school. This and repeated imitations of fags constitute what I refer to as a "fag discourse."

Fag discourse is central to boys' joking relationships. Joking cements relationships among boys (Kehily and Nayak 1997; Lyman 1998) and helps to manage anxiety and discomfort (Freud 1905). Boys both connect with one another and manage the anxiety around this sort of relationship through joking about fags. Boys invoked the specter of the fag in two ways: through humorous imitation and through lobbing the epithet at one another. Boys at River High imitated the fag by acting out an exaggerated "femininity" and/or by pretending to sexually desire other boys. As indicated by the introductory vignette in which an older boy imitated a predatory fag to threaten little boys, male students at River High linked these performative scenarios with a fag identity. They also lobbed the *fag* epithet at each other in a verbal game of hot potato, each careful to deflect the insult quickly by hurling it toward someone else. These games and imitations made up a fag discourse that highlighted the fag not as a static but rather as a fluid identity that boys constantly struggled to avoid.

In imitative performances the fag discourse functioned as a constant reiteration of the fag's existence, affirming that the fag was out there; boys reminded themselves and each other that at any moment they could become fags if they were not sufficiently masculine. At the same time these performances demonstrated that the boy who was invoking the fag was *not* a fag. Emir, a tall, thin African American boy, frequently imitated fags to draw laughs from other students in his introductory drama class. One day Mr. McNally, the drama teacher, disturbed by the noise outside the classroom, turned to the open door, saying, "We'll shut this unless anyone really wants to watch sweaty boys playing basketball." Emir lisped, "I wanna watch the boys play!" The rest of the class cracked up at his imitation. No one in the class actually thought Emir was gay, as he purposefully mocked both same-sex sexual desire (through pretending to admire the boys playing basketball) and an effeminate gender identity (through speaking with a lisp and in a high-pitched voice). Had he said this in all seriousness, the class most likely would have responded in stunned silence. Instead, Emir reminded them he was masculine by immediately dropping the fag act. After imitating a fag, boys assure others that they are not a fag by instantly becoming masculine again after the performance. They mock their own performed femininity and/or same-sex desire, assuring themselves and others that such an identity deserves derisive laughter.

Boys consistently tried to force others into the fag position by lobbing the *fag* epithet at each other. One day in auto shop, Jay was rummaging through a junk-filled car in the parking lot. He poked his head out of the trunk and asked, "Where are Craig and Brian?" Neil responded with "I think they're over there," pointing, then thrusting his hips and pulling his arms back and forth to indicate that Craig and Brian might be having sex. The boys in auto shop laughed. This sort of joke temporarily labeled both Craig and Brian as faggots. Because the fag discourse was so familiar, the other boys immediately understood that Neil was indicating that Craig and Brian were having sex. However, these were not necessarily identities that stuck. Nobody actually thought Craig and Brian were homosexuals. Rather, the fag identity was fluid—certainly an identity that no boy wanted but that most boys could escape, usually by engaging in some sort of discursive contest to turn another boy into a fag.

In this way the fag became a hot potato that no boy wanted to be left holding. One of the best ways to move out of the fag position was to thrust another boy into that position. For instance, soon after Neil made the joke about Brian having sex with Craig, Brian lobbed the *fag* epithet at someone else, deflecting it from himself, by initiating a round of a favorite game in auto shop, the "cock game." Brain said quietly, looking at Josh, "Josh loves the cock," then slightly louder, "Josh loves the cock." He continued saying this until he was yelling, "JOSH LOVES THE COCK!" The rest of the boys laughed hysterically as Josh slunk away, saying, "I have a bigger dick than all you motherfuckers!" These two instances show how the fag could be mapped, for a moment, onto one boy's body and how he, in turn, could attach it to another boy, thus deflecting it from himself. In the first instance Neil made fun of Craig and Brian for simply hanging out together. In the second instance Brian went from being a fag to making Josh into a fag through the "cock game." Through joking interactions boys moved in and out of the fag identity by discursively creating another as a fag.

Given the pervasiveness of fag jokes and the fluidity of the fag identity, it is difficult for boys to consistently avoid the brand. As Ben stated, it almost seemed that a boy could get called a fag for "anything." But most readily acknowledged that there were spaces, behaviors, and bodily comportments that made one more likely to be subject to the fag discourse, such as bodily practices involving clothing and dancing.

According to boys at River, fags cared about the style of their clothes, wore tighter clothes, and cared about cleanliness. Nils explained to me that he could tell that a guy was a fag by the way he dressed: "Most guys wear loose-fitting clothing, just kind of baggy. They [fags] wear more tight clothes. More fashionable, I guess." Similarly, nonfags were not supposed to care about dirtying their clothes. Auto shop was a telling example of this. Given that the boys spent two hours working with greasy car parts, they frequently ended up smudged and rumpled by the end of class. While in the front of the classroom there was a room boys could change in, most of them opted not to change out of their school clothes, with a few modifying their outfits by taking their shirts off and walking around in their "beaters." These tank tops were banned at River High because of their association with gang membership. Auto shop was the one place on campus where boys could wear them with impunity. Like most of the boys in auto shop, Ben never changed out of his jeans or heavy-metal T-shirts. After working on a particularly oily engine he walked in to the classroom with grease stains covering his pants. He looked down at them, made a face, and walked toward me laughing, waving his hands around with limp wrists, and lisping in a high-pitched singsong voice, "I got my good panths all dirty!" Ben's imitation indicated that only a fag would actually care about getting his clothes dirty. "Real" guys didn't care about their appearance; thus it didn't matter if they were covered in grease stains. Of course, to not care about one's clothes, or to make fun of those who care about their clothes, ironically, is to also care about one's appearance. In this sense, masculinity became the carefully crafted appearance of not caring about appearance.

Indeed, the boys' approach to clothing and cleanliness mirrored trends in larger society and the ascendance of the "metrosexual." *Metrosexual* is the recently coined label for straight men who care about their appearance, meticulously piecing together outfits, using product in their hair, and even making manicure appointments (for clear polish, of course). Because these sorts of grooming practices are associated with gay men, straight men developed a new moniker to differentiate themselves from other straight men and from gay men.

Dancing was another practice that put a boy at risk of being labeled a fag. Often boys would jokingly dance together to diffuse the sexualized and feminized meanings embedded in dancing. At dances white boys frequently held their female dates tightly, locking their hips together. The boys never danced with one another unless they were joking or trying to embarrass one another. The examples of boys jokingly dancing together are too numerous to discuss, but the following example was particularly memorable. Lindy danced behind her date, Chris. Chris's friend Matt walked up and nudged Lindy aside, imitating her dance moves behind Chris. As Matt rubbed his hands up and down Chris's back, Chris turned around and jumped back, startled to see Matt there instead of Lindy. Matt cracked up as Chris turned red and swore at his friend.

A similar thing happened at CAPA as two of the boys from the band listened to another band play swing music. These two boys walked toward each other and began to ballroom-dance. Within a second or two they keeled over in laughter, hitting each other and moving away. This ritualized dance, moving closer and then apart, happened again and again when music played at River High. Boys participated in this ritualized exchange to emphasize that indeed they weren't fags.

When boys were forced to dance with one another, as in classroom activities, this sort of joking escalated. In the drama class Mr. McNally walked the students through an exercise that required them to stand so close to each other that most parts of their bodies touched. He instructed the students to stand in two circles on the stage, with each person on the outer circle directly behind someone in the inner circle. He began to play a haunting instrumental song with no vocals. As the song continued Mr. McNally told the students in the inner circle to close their eyes and let their bodies go limp, while still standing. He instructed the students in the outer circle to move the person in front through an interpretive dance, following his lead as he moved the student in front of him. As the music continued, most of the students in the outer circle watched Mr. McNally's movements intently, trying their best to mirror his actions. The result was an intimate and beautiful puppet-and-puppeteer-like dance with the student in back moving the student in front through slow, fluid poses. Instead of following Mr. McNally's movements like the rest of the class, one pair of white sophomores, Liam and Jacob, barely touched. Jacob stood in back of Liam and, instead of gently holding Liam's wrist with their full arms touching as the other students did, picked up Liam's wrist with two fingers as if picking up something repulsive and flung Liam's hand to its destination. He made jokes with Liam's arm, repeatedly flinging it up against Liam's chest in a movement that indicated Liam was "retarded." The jokes continued as the students switched places, so that the inner circle became the outer circle, with Liam now "in control" of Jacob. Liam placed Jacob's hand against his forehead as if saluting, made his arms flap like birds, and used Jacob's finger to poke at his eyes, all the while, unlike the other students, never letting the majority of his body touch Jacob's. At the end of the exercise Mr. McNally asked for the students' feedback. One of the girls said, a little embarrassed, "I hate to say it, but it was almost sexual." To which Mr. McNally responded, "Yeah, it's full physical contact," at which point Liam and Jacob took two steps apart from one another. Even though the entire class was assigned to touch one another simultaneously, Jacob and Liam had a hard time following the instructions because it was so dangerous to actually "dance" together like this. Even in a class situation, in the most nonsuspect of interactions, the fag discourse ran deep, forbidding boys to touch one another.

The constant threat of the fag regulated boys' attitudes toward their bodies in terms of clothing, dancing, and touching. Boys constantly engaged in repudiatory rituals to avoid permanently inhabiting the fag position. Boys' interactions were composed of competitive joking through which they interactionally created the constitutive outside and affirmed their positions as subjects.

* * *

REFRAMING HOMOPHOBIA

Homophobia is central to contemporary definitions of adolescent masculinity. Unpacking multilayered meanings that boys deploy through their uses of homophobic language and joking rituals makes clear that it is not just homophobia but a gendered and racialized homophobia. By attending to these meanings, I reframe the discussion as a fag discourse rather than simply labeling it as homophobia. The fag is an "abject" (Butler 1993) position, a position outside masculinity that actually constitutes masculinity. Thus masculinity, in part, becomes the daily interactional work of repudiating the threatening specter of the fag.

The fag extends beyond a static sexual identity attached to a gay boy. Few boys are permanently identified as fags; most move in and out of fag positions. Looking at fag as a discourse in addition to a static identity reveals that the term can be invested with different meanings in different social spaces. *Fag* may be used as a weapon with which to temporarily assert one's masculinity by denying it to others. Thus the fag becomes a symbol around which contests of masculinity take place.

* * *

The *fag* epithet, when hurled at other boys, may or may not have explicit sexual meanings, but it always has gendered meanings. When a boy calls another boy a fag, it means he is not a man but not necessarily that he is a homosexual. The boys at River High knew that they were not supposed to call homosexual boys fags because that was mean. This, then, has been the limited success of the mainstream gay rights movement. The message absorbed by some of these teenage boys was that "gay men can be masculine, just like you." Instead of challenging gender inequality, this particular discourse of gay rights has reinscribed it. Thus we need to begin to think about how gay men may be in a unique position to challenge gendered as well as sexual norms. The boys in the drama performances show an alternative way to be teenage boys, which is about playing with gender, not just enforcing gender duality based on sexual meanings.

STUDY QUESTIONS

1. Why does Pascoe doubt the word "fag," as used by the high school men she studies, is based solely in **homophobia**?

2. What role does "the fag" serve in the social construction of **gender**? As an abject social position, how does "the fag" define masculinity and enforce gender normativity?

3. How are the words "fag," "gay," and "homo" used in your social circles? Do you notice differences in the use of such terms when students who identify as gay or lesbian are present?

4. Watch Dalton Conley's interview with C. J. Pascoe on the Norton Sociology YouTube channel (http://bit.ly/cjpascoe). Describe the policy recommendations Pascoe makes; how might they reduce homophobic harassment in high schools and on university campuses?

ELIJAH ANDERSON

The Mating Game

From *Code of the Street: Decency, Violence,
and the Moral Life of the Inner City*

The decline in manufacturing jobs and the flight to suburban areas have left the **inner city** in peril. The consequences are not only **economic**, but also **social—poverty** and lack of hope have affected how the inner-city youth practice their **sexuality** and mate selection. In this chapter from his best-selling book, *Code of the Street*, Elijah Anderson reveals the process that boys and girls in the inner city use to rationalize their sexual behaviors. This selection will help you learn about the role societal circumstances play in determining individual outcomes such as mating and teen pregnancy. When you've read it, you may be able to answer the question some raise about why the poor continue to have children out of wedlock.

THE PROBLEM OF TEENAGE PREGNANCY IN THE INNER CITY DRAWS as much attention and expressions of puzzlement from the wider community as do the problems of drugs and violence. These kinds of behavior appear to work against everything for which decent young Americans strive: education, good jobs, a stable household, and middle-class values. Yet they make sense of a sort in the world of the street and in relation to the code that dominates it. * * * This chapter looks at what young people, both decent and street, face as they grow up and find one another in this same world. It needs to be made clear that for these teenagers the benefits they perceive as deriving from their sexual behavior outweigh the risks. Their outlook on sex and pregnancy, like their outlook on violence, is strongly affected by their perceived options in life, and their sexual behavior follows rules very much shaped by the code of the street. Such perceptions are formed by the fortunes of immediate peers, family, and others with whom the youths identify. Among teenagers one of the most important factors working against pregnancy is their belief that they have something to lose by becoming parents at an early age; many believe they have something to gain.

THE SOCIAL CONTEXT

* * *

Working poor residents, for social purposes, distinguish values they see as decent from those they associate with the street. Generally, decency is a highly regarded personal quality, and the assigning of a street orientation to a person is usually deeply discrediting. In the impoverished neighborhood the meanings of the terms sometimes overlap, compete, and even support one another; their interaction is highly complex. In fact, though, these distinctions operate more or less to identify social polarities; and particularly among the young their social referents may be used to distinguish the socially "lame" from the "hip."

* * *

Many youths observe the would-be legitimate role models around them and tend to find them unworthy of emulation. Conventional hard work seems not to have paid off for the old, and the relatively few hardworking people of the neighborhood appear to be struggling to survive. At the same time unconventional role models beckon the youths to a thriving underground economy, which promises "crazy" money, along with a certain thrill, power, and prestige. Streetwise and severely alienated young men can easily deal in the drug trade, part-time or full-time. They may even draw their intimate female counterparts along with them, "hooking them up," and smoothly initiating them into prostitution.

Given that persistent poverty is so widespread in the neighborhood, for many residents, particularly the young, values of decency and law abidingness are more easily compromised. Needing money badly, these people feel social pressure and see the chance for making sometimes huge sums outside their front door. Because of all the vice and crime in the neighborhood, those who can leave tend to do so, isolating the very poor and the working poor even more. This exodus further demoralizes neighborhood residents and makes them more vulnerable to a number of ills, including rising drug use and teenage pregnancy.

The manufacturing jobs that used to provide opportunities for young people in inner-city neighborhoods and strongly, although indirectly, supported values of decency and conventionality have largely vanished from the economy, replaced by thousands of low-paying service jobs often located in the suburbs, beyond the reach of poor neighborhoods. These changes have damaged the financial health of the inner city and undermined the quality of available role models. The trust and perceptions of decency that once prevailed in the community are increasingly absent. In their place, street values, represented by the fast life, violence, and crime, become more prominent.

The consequences of these changes can be illustrated by their effect on one of the community's most important institutions, the relationship between old heads and young boys. The old head was once the epitome of decency in inner-city neighborhoods. Thanks to a vibrant manufacturing economy, he had relatively stable means. His acknowledged role in the community was to teach, support, encourage, and, in effect, socialize young men to meet their responsibilities regarding work, family life, the law, and common decency. Young boys and single men in their late teens or twenties had confidence in the old head's ability to impart practical advice. Very often he played surrogate father to those who needed his attention and moral support.

But as meaningful employment becomes increasingly scarce for young men of the neighborhood and the expansion of the drug culture offers opportunities for quick money, the old head is losing prestige and authority. Streetwise boys are concluding that his lessons about life and work ethic are no longer relevant, and a new role model is emerging. The embodiment of the street, this man is young, often a product of the street gang, and indifferent, at best, to the law and traditional values.

Traditional female role models, often paragons of decency, have also suffered decreased authority. Mature women, often grandmothers themselves, once effectively served the community as auxiliary parents who publicly augmented and supported the relationship between parent and child. These women would discipline children and act as role models for young women, exerting a certain degree of social control. As the neighborhoods grow ever more drug infested, ordinary young mothers and their children are among the most obvious casualties. The traditional female old head becomes stretched and overburdened; her role has become more complicated as she often steps in as a surrogate mother for her grandchildren or a stray neighborhood child.

These women universally lament the proliferation of drugs in the community, the "crack whores" who walk the neighborhood, the sporadic violence that now and then claims innocent bystanders. The open-air drug sales, the many pregnant girls, the incivility, the crime, the many street kids, and the diminished number of upstanding (as the residents say) role models make it difficult for old and young alike to maintain a positive outlook, to envision themselves beyond the immediate situation. As neighborhood deterioration feeds on itself, decent law-aiding people become increasingly demoralized; many of those who are capable leave, while some succumb to the street.

This is the social context in which the incidence of teenage pregnancy must be seen, complicated by peer pressure, ignorance, passion, luck, intent, desire for conquest, religion, love, and even deep hostility between young men and women. It is nothing less than the cultural manifestation of persistent urban poverty.

* * *

The lack of family-sustaining jobs denies many young men the possibility of forming an economically self-reliant family, the traditional American mark of manhood. Partly in response, many young black men form strong attachments to peer groups that emphasize sexual prowess as proof of manhood, with babies as evidence. These groups congregate on street corners, boasting about their sexual exploits and deriding conventional family life. They encourage this orientation by rewarding members who are able to get over the sexual defenses of women. For many the object is to hit and run while maintaining personal freedom and independence from conjugal ties; when they exist, the ties should be on the young man's terms. Concerned with immediate gratification, some boys want babies to demonstrate their ability to control a girl's mind and body.

A sexual game emerges as girls are lured by the (usually older) boys' vague but convincing promises of love and sometimes marriage. At the same time the "fast" adolescent street orientation presents early sexual experience and promiscuity as a virtue. But when the girls submit, they often end up pregnant and abandoned. However, for many such girls who have few other perceivable options, motherhood, accidental or otherwise, becomes a rite of passage to adulthood. Although an overwhelming number may not be actively trying to have babies, many are not actively trying to prevent having them. One of the reasons for this may be the strong fundamentalist religious orientation of many poor blacks, which emphasizes the role of fate in life. If something happens, it happens; if something was meant to be, then let it be, and "God will find a way." With the dream of a mate, a girl may be indifferent to the possibility of pregnancy, even if it is not likely that pregnancy will lead to marriage. So the pregnant girl can look forward to a certain affirmation, particularly after the baby arrives—if not from the father, then from her peer group, from her family, from the Lord.

Thus, if it becomes obvious that the young father's promises are empty, the young woman has a certain amount of help in settling for the role of single parent. A large part of her identity is provided by the baby under her care and guidance, and for many street-oriented girls there is no quicker way to grow up. Becoming a mother can be a strong play for authority, maturity, and respect, but it is also a shortsighted and naïve gamble because the girl often fails to realize that her life will be suddenly burdened and her choices significantly limited.

In these circumstances outlook, including a certain amount of education, wisdom, and mentoring from decent role models, becomes extremely important. The strong, so-called decent family, often with a husband and wife, sometimes with a strong-willed single mother helped by close relatives and neighbors, may instill in girls a sense of hope. These families can hope to reproduce the relatively strong family form, which is generally regarded in the neighborhood as advantaged. The two parents or close kin are known as hard workers, striving to have something and strongly emphasizing the work ethic, common decency, and social and moral responsibility. Though the pay may be low, the family often can count on a regular income, giving its members the sense that decent values have paid off for them.

A girl growing up in such a family, or even living in close social and physical proximity to some, may have strong support from a mother, a father, friends, and neighbors who not only care very much whether she becomes pregnant but are also able to share knowledge about negotiating life beyond the confines of the neighborhood. The girl may then approach social mobility or at least delay pregnancy. In these circumstances she has a better chance to cultivate a positive sense of the future and a healthy self-respect; she may come to feel she has a great deal to lose by becoming an unwed parent.

Contributing strongly to this outlook are ministers, teachers, parents, and upwardly mobile peers. At times a successful older sister sets a standard and expectations for younger siblings, who may attempt to follow her example. The community and the decent family help place the successful one high in the sibling hierarchy by praising her achievements. At the very least, such support groups can strongly communicate their expectations that the girl will do something with her life other than have a baby out of wedlock—that is, they subscribe to and seek to pass on middle-class values.

Although the basic sexual codes of inner-city youths may not differ fundamentally from those of other young people, the social, economic, and personal consequences of adolescent sexual conduct vary profoundly for different social classes. Like all adolescents, inner-city youths are subject to intense, hard-to-control urges. Sexual relations, exploitive and otherwise, are common among middle-class teenagers as well, but most middle-class youths take a stronger interest in their future and know what a pregnancy can do to derail it. In contrast, many inner-city adolescents see no future that can be derailed—no hope for a tomorrow much different from today—hence they see little to lose by having a child out of wedlock.

Sexual conduct among these young people is to a large extent the product of the meshing of two opposing drives, that of the boys and that of the girls. For a variety of reasons tied to the socioeconomic situation, their goals are often diametrically opposed, and sex becomes a contest between them. As was noted above, to many boys sex is an important symbol of local social status; sexual conquests become so many notches on one's belt. Many of the girls offer sex as a gift in bargaining for the attentions of a young man. As boys and girls try to use each other to achieve their own ends, the reality that emerges sometimes approximates their goals, but it often brings frustration and disillusionment and perpetuates or even worsens their original situation.

Each sexual encounter generally has a winner and a loser. The girls have a dream, the boys a desire. The girls dream of being carried off by a Prince Charming who will love them, provide for them, and give them a family. The boys often desire either sex without commitment or babies without responsibility for them. It becomes extremely difficult for the boys, in view of their employment prospects, to see themselves taking on the responsibilities of conventional fathers and husbands. Yet they know what the girls want and play that role to get sex. In accepting a boy's advances, a girl may think she is maneuvering him toward a commitment or that her getting pregnant is the nudge he needs to marry her and give her the life she wants. What she does not see is that the boy, despite his claims, is often incapable of giving her that life, for in reality he has little money, few prospects for earning much, and no wish to be tied to a woman who will have a say in what he does. His loyalty is to his peer group and its norms. When the girl becomes pregnant, the boy tends to retreat from her, although, with the help of pressure from her family and peers, she may ultimately succeed in getting him to take some responsibility for the child.

SEX: THE GAME AND THE DREAM

To many inner-city male youths, the most important people in their lives are members of their peer groups. They set the standards for conduct, and it is important to live up to those standards, to look good in their eyes. The peer group places a high value on sex, especially what middle-class people call casual sex. But though sex may be casual in terms of commitment to the partner, it is usually taken quite seriously as a measure of the boy's worth. A young man's primary goal is thus to find as many willing females as possible. The more "pussy" he gets, the more esteem accrues to him. But the young man not only must "get some"; he also must prove he is getting it. This leads him to talk about girls and sex with any other young man who will listen. Because of the implications sex has for their local social status and esteem, the young men are ready to be regaled with graphic tales of one another's sexual exploits.

* * *

In many instances the game plays on the dream that many inner-city girls harbor from their early teenage years. The popular love songs they listen to, usually from the age of seven or eight, are imbued with a wistful air, promising love and ecstasy to someone "just like you." This dream involved having a boyfriend, a fiancé, or a husband and the fairy-tale prospect of living happily ever after with one's children in a nice house in a good neighborhood—essentially the dream of the middle-class American lifestyle, complete with nuclear family. It is nurtured by daily watching of television soap operas, or "stories," as the women call them. The heroes and heroines may be white and upper middle class, but such characteristics only make them more attractive. Many girls dream of becoming the comfortable middle-class housewife portrayed on television, even though they see that their peers can only approximate that role.

When a girl is approached by a boy, her faith in the dream clouds her view of the situation. A romantically successful boy has a knack for knowing just what is on a girl's mind, what she wants from life, and how she hopes to obtain it. The young man's age—he may be four or five years older than the girl—gives him an authoritative edge and makes his readiness to "settle down" more credible. By enacting this role, he can shape the interaction, calling up the resources he needs to play the game successfully. He fits himself to be the *man* she wants him to be, but this identity may be exaggerated and temporary, maintained only until he gets what he wants. Essentially, he shows her the side of himself that he knows she wants to see, that represents what she wants in a man. For instance, he will sometimes "walk through the woods" with the girl: he might visit at her home and go to church with her family or even do "manly" chores around her house, showing that he is an "upstanding young man." But all of this may only be part of his game, and after he gets what he wants, he may cast off this aspect of his presentation and reveal something of his true self, as he flits to other women and reverts to behavior more characteristic of his everyday life—that which is centered on his peer group.

*   *   *

At times, however, a boy earnestly attempts to *be* a dream man, with honorable intentions of "doing right" by the young woman, of marrying her and living happily ever after according to their version of middle-class propriety. But the reality of his poor employment prospects makes it hard for him to follow through.

Unable to realize his vision of himself as the young woman's provider in the American middle-class tradition, which the peer group often labels "square," the young man may become even more committed to his game. In his ambivalence he may go so far as to make plans with the girls, including going house-hunting and shopping for furniture. A twenty-three-year-old woman who at seventeen became a single parent of a baby girl said this:

> Yeah, they'll [boys will] take you out. Walk you down to Center City, movies, window shops. [laughs] They point in the window, "Yeah, I'm gonna get you this. Wouldn't you like this? Look at that nice livin' room set." Then they want to take you to his house, go to his room: "Let's go over to my house, watch some TV." Next thing you know, your clothes is off and you in bed havin' sex, you know.

Such shopping trips carry important psychological implications for the relationship, serving as a salve that heals wounds and erases doubt about the young man's intentions. The young woman may report to her parents or friends about her last date or shopping trip, describe the furniture they priced and the supposed payment terms. She continues to have hope, which he fuels by "going with" her, letting her and others know that she is his "steady"—though for him to maintain status within his peer group, she should not be his only known girl. For the young man, however, making plans and successive shopping trips may be elements of the game—often nothing more than a stalling device to keep the girl hanging on so that he can continue to receive her social sexual favors.

* * *

During this emotional turmoil the young girl may well become careless about birth control, which is seen by the community, especially the males, as being her responsibility. She may believe the boy's rap, becoming convinced that he means what he says about taking care of her, that her welfare is his primary concern. Moreover, she wants desperately to believe that if she becomes pregnant, he will marry her or at least be more obligated to her than to others he has been "messing with." Perhaps all he needs is a little nudge. The girl may think little about the job market and the boy's prospects. She may underestimate peer-group influences and the effect of other "ladies" that she knows or suspects are in his life. If she is in love, she may be sure that a child and the profound obligation a child implies will forge such a strong bond that all the other issues will go away. Her thinking is often clouded by the prospect of winning at the game of love. Becoming pregnant can be a way to fulfill the persistent dream of bliss.

For numerous women, when the man turns out to be unobtainable, just having his baby is enough. Sometimes a woman seeks out a popular and "fine," or physically attractive, young man in hopes that his good looks will grace her child, resulting in a "prize"—a beautiful baby. Moreover, becoming pregnant can become an important part of the competition for the attentions or even delayed affections of a young man—a profound, if socially shortsighted, way of making claims on him.

PREGNANCY

Up to the point of pregnancy, given the norms of his peer group, the young man could simply be said to be messing around. Pregnancy suddenly introduces an element of reality into the relationship. Life-altering events have occurred, and the situation is usually perceived as serious. The girl is pregnant, and he could be held legally responsible for the child's long-term financial support. If the couple were unclear about their intentions before, things may now crystallize. She now considers him seriously as a mate. Priorities begin to emerge in the boy's mind. He has to decide whether to claim the child as his or to shun the woman who has been the object of his supposed affections.

To own up to a pregnancy is to go against the peer-group street ethic of hit and run. Other street values at risk of being flouted include the subordination of women and freedom from formal conjugal ties, and some young men are not interested in "taking care of somebody else" when it means having less for themselves. In this social context of persistent poverty, they have come to devalue the conventional marital relationship, viewing long-term ties with women as a burden and children as even more of one. Moreover, a young man wants to "come as I want and go as I please," indulging important values of freedom and independence. Accordingly, from the perspective of the street peer group, any such male-female relationship should be on the man's terms. Thus, in understanding the boy's relationship to the girl, his attitudes toward his limited financial ability and his need for personal freedom should not be underestimated.

Another important attitude of the street group is that most girls have multiple sexual partners. Whether or not this claim is true in a particular case, a common working conception says it holds for young women in general. It is a view with which many young men approach females, initially assuming they are socially and morally deficient, though many are willing to adjust their view as they start to "deal" with the woman and to get to know her intimately. The double standard is at work, and for any amount of sexual activity women are more easily discredited than men.

* * *

At the insistence of her family and for her own peace of mind, the young woman wants badly to identify the father of her child. When the baby is born, she may, out of desperation, arbitrarily designate a likely young man as the father; at times it may be simply a lover who is gainfully employed. As I have mentioned, there may be genuine doubt about paternity. This atmosphere often produces charges and countercharges; the appointed young man usually either denies responsibility and eases himself out of the picture or accepts it and plays his new role of father part-time.

In the past, before welfare reform, the young woman sometimes had an incentive not to identify the father, even though she and the local community knew whose baby it was, for a check from the welfare office was much more dependable than the irregular support payments of a sporadically employed youth. With today's new welfare reality, there is much more incentive to publicly identify the father and try hard to hold him accountable. Moreover, the new welfare laws give sexually active young people pause and will likely work to decrease the long-term incidence of out-of-wedlock teenage pregnancy. In this new context sanctions are more strongly applied, if not on moral grounds, then for financial and legal considerations. In these circumstances the young man has greater incentive to do right by the young woman and to try out the role of husband and father, often acceding to the woman's view of the matter and working to establish a family.

* * *

A strongly related important defense against youthful pregnancy is the "decent" inner-city family unit. Two parents, together with the extended network of cousins, aunts, uncles, grandparents, nieces, and nephews, can form a durable team, a viable support group engaged to fight in a committed manner the problems confronting inner-city teenagers, including street violence, drugs, crime, pregnancy, and poverty.

This unit, when it does endure, tends to be equipped with a survivor's mentality. Its weathering of a good many storms has given it wisdom and strength. As has been argued throughout this volume, the parents are generally known in the community as decent, but more than this, they tend to be strict on their children; they impose curfews and tight supervision, demanding to know their children's whereabouts at all times. Determined that their offspring will not become casualties of the inner-city environment, they scrutinize their children's associates, rejecting those who seem to be "no good" and encouraging others who seem on their way to "amount to something."

By contrast, in domestic situations where there is only one adult—say, a woman with two or three teenage daughters—the dwelling may be viewed, superficially at least, as an unprotected nest. The local street boys may be attracted to the home as a challenge, just to test it out, to see if they can get over by charming or seducing the women who live there. In such a setting a man—the figure the boys are prepared to respect—is not there to keep them in line. Girls in this vulnerable situation may become pregnant earlier than those living in homes more closely resembling nuclear families. A young man made the following comments:

> I done seen where four girls grow up under their mama. The mama turn around and she got a job between 3 P.M. and 11 P.M. These little kids, now they grow up like this. Mama working three to eleven o'clock at night. They kinda raise theyself. What they know? By the time they get thirteen or fourteen, they trying everything under the sun. And they ain't got nobody to stop 'em. Mama gone. Can't nobody else tell 'em what to do. Hey, all of 'em pregnant by age sixteen. And they do it 'cause they wanta get out on they own. They can get they own baby, they get they own [welfare] check, they get they own apartment. They wanta get away from Mama.

THE BABY CLUB

In the absence of a strong family unit, a close-knit group of "street girls" often fills a social, moral, and family void in the young girl's life. With the help of her peers and sometimes older siblings and the usually very limited supervision of parents, after a certain age she primarily raises herself. On the street she plays seemingly innocent games, but through play she becomes socialized into a peer group. Many of these neighborhood "street kids" are left to their own devices, staying out late at night, sometimes until one or two in the morning, even on school nights. By the age of ten or twelve, many are aware of their bodies and, according to some residents, are beginning to engage in sexual relations, with very little knowledge about their bodies and even less about the long-term consequences of their behavior.

* * *

As the babies arrive, the peer group takes on an even more provocative feature: the early play and social groups develop into "baby clubs." The girls give one another social support, praising each other's babies. But they also use their babies to compete, on the premise that the baby is an extension of the mother and reflects directly on her. This competition, carried on at social gatherings such as birthday parties, weddings, church services, and spontaneous encounters of two or more people, often takes the form of comparing one baby to another. First the baby's features are noted, usually along the lines of "spoiledness," texture of hair, skin color, and grooming and dress, as well as general "cuteness." To enhance her chances at such competitions and status games, the young mother often feels the need to dress her baby in the latest and most expensive clothes that fit (rather than in a size larger, which the baby can grow into): a fifty-dollar sweater for a three-month-old or forty-dollar Reebok sneakers for a six-month-old. This status-oriented behavior provokes criticism from more mature people, including mothers and grandmothers. As one forty-five-year-old grandmother said,

> Oh, they can't wait until check day [when welfare checks arrive] so they can go to the store. I listen at 'em, talking about what they gon' buy *this* time. [They say,] "Next time my check come, I'm gon' buy my baby this, I'm gon' buy my baby that." And that's exactly what they will do—expensive stores, too. The more expensive, the better; some will buy a baby an expensive outfit that the baby only gon' wear for a few months. I seen a girl go . . . went out, and she paid, I think she paid forty-five dollars for a outfit. I think the baby was about six weeks old. Now, how long was that child gon' wear that outfit? For that kind of money. They do these silly, silly things.

And as a twenty-three-year-old woman college graduate from the community (who did not become pregnant) said,

> Once there was a sale at the church at Thirteenth and Beaufort. A friend of mine had some baby clothes for sale. They were some cute clothes, but they weren't new. They were sweat suits, older things. The young girls would just pass them by. Now, the older women, the grandmothers, would come by and buy them for their grandchildren. But the girls, sixteen or seventeen, had to have a decked-out baby. No hand-me-downs. Some would pay up to forty dollars for a pair of Nike sneakers. They go to Carl's [a downtown children's boutique]. And the babies sometimes are burning up in the clothes, but they dress them up anyway. The baby is like a doll in some ways. They [young mothers] sometimes do more to clothe the baby than to feed the baby.

But this seeming irresponsibility of the young mother evolves in a logical way. For a young woman who fails to secure a strong commitment from a man, a baby becomes a partial fulfillment of the good life. The baby club deflects criticism of the young mothers and gives them a certain status. "Looking good" negates the generalized notion that a teenage mother has messed up her life, and amid this deprivation nothing is more important than to show others you are doing all right.

* * *

In this way, welfare and persistent poverty have affected the norms of the ghetto culture, such as the high value placed on children. "The check" has thus had an important impact on domestic relations between young men and women. In the past, the young woman could count not only on the public aid but also on a serious interest on the young man's part after the baby arrived. And, very often, the honest man was discouraged from marrying the young woman for fear of putting the check in jeopardy. In the Reverend Mosby's day the young man frequently took at least a fatherly interest in his child, and the girl's father and the rest of the extended family could at times be expected to encourage the boy to become an honest man, thus creating dynamic tension between the requirements of welfare on the one hand and pressure from the family to do right on the other. The welfare check, in some instances, has served to bond the young man with the woman, without the benefit of wedlock—in effect uniting them in the regular expectation of the welfare check. In the impoverished conditions of the inner city, when the check arrives, the young man may expect his share, even though he and the young woman do not reside under the same roof. If a new suitor emerges—and one frequently does—there are sometimes arguments, and even violence, over who has rights to the check, as various individuals voice their claims.

With the advent of welfare reform, more young women and men are inclined to pause, to be more circumspect in their sexual habits, in large part because the check is no longer to be counted on. Babies may become less significant symbols of status, but they will continue to be important symbols of passage to adulthood, of being a grown woman, and of being a man. Most young mothers and fathers, I believe, do not have babies just for the check, but in structurally impoverished areas, the regular cash the check provides is not unimportant. In the past it perhaps was a question less of whether the girl was going to have children than of when, for she often saw herself as having little to lose and much to gain by becoming pregnant, and this remains true in a social sense. In the new climate of welfare reform, however, there is more of an impetus for young men and women to take greater responsibility for their personal lives and, in turn, to have fewer babies out of wedlock. But the jury is still out on this.

THE GOOD MAN AND THE NOTHIN'

In their small, intimate groups, the women draw distinctions between "the nothin'" and the "good man." The nothin' is a "a man who is out to use every women he can for himself. He's somethin' like a pimp. Don't care 'bout nobody but himself." One older single mother, who now considers herself wiser, said,

> I know the difference now between a nothin' and a good man. I can see. I can smell him. I can just tell a nothin' from the real thing. I can just look at a guy sometimes, you know, the way he dresses. You know, the way he carries himself. The way he acts, the

way he talks. I can tell the bullshitter. Like, you know, "What's up, baby?" You know. "What's you want to do?" A nice guy wouldn't say, "What's you want to do?" A nice guy wouldn't say, "What's up, baby? What's goin' on?" Actin' all familiar, tryin' to give me that line. Saying, "You want a joint? You wan' some 'caine?" Hollerin' in the street, you know. I can tell 'em. I can just smell 'em.

In this social climate the good man, who would aspire to play the role of the decent daddy of old, is considerate of his mate and provides for her and her children, but at the same time he runs the risk of being seen as a pussy by the women as well as by his peer group. This inversion in the idea of the good man underscores the ambivalent position of girls squeezed between their middle-class dreams and the ghetto reality. As one woman said with a laugh, "There are so many sides to the bad man. We see that, especially in this community. We see more bad men than we do good. I see them [inner-city girls] running over that man if he's a wimp, ha-ha."

* * *

OF MEN AND WOMEN, MOTHERS AND SONS

The relationship between the young man and woman undergoes a basic change during pregnancy; once the baby is born, it draws on other social forces, most notably their families. The role of the girl's family has been discussed. The boy's family is important in a different way. There is often a special bond between a mother and her grown son that competes with the claims of his girlfriend. The way this situation is resolved has considerable consequences for the family and its relationship to the social structure of the community. In teenage pregnancy among the poor, the boy's mother often plays a significant role, while that of his father, if he is present at all, is understated. Depending on the woman's personality, her practical experience in such matters, and the girl's family situation, the mother's role may be subtle or explicit. At times she becomes deeply involved with the young woman, forming a female bond with her that is truly motherly, involving guidance, protection, and control.

* * *

If the child clearly resembles the alleged father physically, there may be strong pressure for the boy to claim the child and assume his responsibilities. This may take a year or more, since the resemblance may initially be less apparent. But when others begin to make comments such as "Lil' Tommy look like Maurice just spit him out [is his spitting image]," the boy's mother may informally adopt the child into her extended family and signal others to do the same. She may see the child regularly and develop a special relationship with its mother. Because of her social acknowledgment of her son's paternity, the boy himself is bound to accept the child. Even if he does not claim the child legally, in the face of the evidence he will often acknowledge "having something to do with him." As one informant said, "If the baby look just like him, he should admit to himself that that's his. Some guys have to wait till the baby grow up a little to see if the baby gon' look like him 'fore they finally realize that was his'n. Because yours should look like you, you know, should have your features and image."

Here the young man informally acknowledging paternity may feel some pressure to take care of his own. But owing to his limited employment and general lack of money, he feels that he "can only do what he can" for his child. Many young men enact the role of father part-time. A self-conscious young man may be spied on the street carrying a box of Pampers, the name used generically for all disposable diapers, or cans of Similac—baby formula—on the way to see his child and its mother. As the child ages, a bond may develop, and the young man may take a boy for a haircut or shopping for shoes or clothes. He may give the woman token amounts of money. Such gestures of support suggest a father providing for his child. In fact, however, they often come only sporadically and—an important point—in exchange for the woman's favors, social or sexual. Such support may thus depend upon the largesse of the man and may function as a means of controlling the woman.

If the woman "gets papers" on the man, or legalizes his relationship to the child, she may sue for regular support—what people call "going downtown on him." If her case is successful, the young man's personal involvement in making child support payments may be eliminated: the money may simply be deducted from his salary, if he has one. Sometimes the woman's incentive for getting papers may emerge when the young man lands a good job, particularly one with a major institution that includes family benefits. While sporadically employed, the youth may have had no problem with papers, but when he finds a steady job, he may be served with a summons. In some cases, especially if they have two or three children out of wedlock by different women, young men lose the incentive to work, for much of their pay will go to someone else. After the mother of his four children got papers on him and he began to see less and less of his pay, one of my informants quit his job and returned to the street corner and began to hustle drugs.

* * *

As jobs become scarce for young black men, their success as breadwinners and traditional husbands declines. The notion is that with money comes control of the domestic situation. Without money or jobs, many men are unable to play house to their satisfaction. It is much easier and more fun to stay home and "take care of Mama," some say, when taking care consists of "giving her some change for room and board," eating good food, and being able "to come as I want and to go as I please." Given the present state of the economy, such an assessment of their domestic outlook appears in many respects adaptive.

SEX, POVERTY, AND FAMILY LIFE

In conclusion, the basic factors at work here are youth, ignorance, the culture's receptiveness to babies, and the young man's attempt to prove his manhood through sexual conquests that often result in pregnancy. These factors are exacerbated by persistent urban poverty. In the present hard times a primary concern of many inner-city residents is to get along as best they can. In the poorest communities the primary financial sources are low-paying jobs, crime—including drugs—and public assistance. Some of the most desperate people devise a variety of confidence games to separate others from their money.

* * *

Although middle-class youths and poor youths may have much in common sexually, their level of practical education differs. The ignorance of inner-city girls about their bodies astonishes the middle-class observer. Many have only a vague notion about birth control until after they have their first child—and sometimes not even then. Parents in this culture are extremely reticent about discussing sex and birth control with their children. Many mothers are ashamed to talk about it or feel they are in no position to do so, since they behaved the same way as their daughters when they were young. Education thus emerges as a community health problem, but most girls come in contact with community health services only when they become pregnant—sometimes many months into their pregnancies.

A baby could in cold economic terms be considered an asset, which is without doubt an important factor behind exploitative sex and out-of-wedlock babies, though this seems to be changing. Public assistance was one of the few reliable sources of money, low-income jobs are another, and, for many people, drugs are yet another. The most desperate people thus feed on one another. Babies and sex were once more commonly used for income than they are now; women continue to receive money from welfare for having babies, and men sometimes act as prostitutes to pry the money from them.

The lack of gainful employment today not only keeps the entire community in a pit of poverty but also deprives young men of the traditional American way of proving their manhood—by supporting a family. They must thus prove themselves in other ways. Casual sex with as many women as possible, impregnating one or more, and getting them to have his baby brings a boy the ultimate in esteem from his peers and makes him a man. Casual sex is therefore fraught with social significance for the boy who has little or no hope of achieving financial stability and hence cannot see himself taking care of a family.

The meshing of these forces can be clearly seen. Trapped in poverty, ignorant of the long-term consequences of their behavior but aware of the immediate benefits, adolescents engage in a mating game. The girl has her dream of a family and a home, of a good man who will provide for her and her children. The boy, knowing he cannot be that family man, because he has few job prospects, yet needing to have sex to achieve manhood in the eyes of his peer group, pretends to be the decent and good man and so persuades the girl to give him sex and perhaps a baby. He may then abandon her, and she realizes he was not the good man, after all, but rather a nothin' out to exploit her. The boy has gotten what he wanted, but the girl learns that she has gotten something, too. The baby may bring her a certain amount of praise, (in the past) a steady welfare check, and a measure of independence. Her family often helps out as best they can. As she becomes older and wiser, she can use her income to turn the tables, attracting her original man or other men.

In this inner-city culture people generally get married for love and to have something. But this mind-set presupposes a job, the work ethic, and, perhaps most of all, a persistent sense of hope for an economic future. When these social factors are present, the more wretched elements of the ethnographic portrait presented here begin to lose their force, slowly becoming neutralized. For many of those who are caught in the web of persistent urban poverty and become unwed mothers and fathers, however, there is little hope for a good job and even less for a future of conventional family life.

STUDY QUESTIONS

1. Why are **values** of decency and law abidingness for the young more easily compromised in the **inner city**?

2. What is the response of young black men to the lack of **family**-sustaining jobs?

3. Discuss the "mating game." How do the poor differ from the **middle class**?

4. List and discuss three factors in the mating game that might be prevalent in both inner-city and middle-class neighborhoods.

HOWARD BECKER

Culture: A Sociological View

We think of **culture** primarily as art, classical music, or some portrayal of a native tribe in a documentary. In this reading, though, Howard Becker discusses the sociological view of culture as a system of shared meanings that make **society** function. As you read, think about your understanding of culture, including what it is, how it changes, how it affects your everyday interaction with others, and how it impacts your relationship with the social structure.

I WAS FOR SOME YEARS WHAT IS CALLED A SATURDAY NIGHT MUSIcian, making myself available to whoever called and hired me to play for dances and parties in groups of varying sizes, playing everything from polkas through mambos, jazz, and imitations of Wayne King.[1] Whoever called would tell me where the job was, what time it began, and usually would tell me to wear a dark suit and a bow tie, thus ensuring that the collection of strangers he was hiring would at least look like a band because they would all be dressed more or less alike. When we arrived at work we would introduce ourselves—the chances were, in a city the size of Chicago (where I did much of my playing), that we were in fact strangers—and see whom we knew in common and whether our paths had ever crossed before. The drummer would assemble his drums, the others would put together their instruments and tune up, and when it was time to start the leader would announce the name of a song and a key—"Exactly Like You" in B flat, for instance—and we would begin to play. We not only began at the same time, but also played background figures that fit the melody someone else was

"Culture: A Sociological View" by Howard S. Becker from *The Yale Review*, 71, Summer 1982. Copyright © 1982 by *The Yale Review*. Reproduced with permission of Blackwell Publishing Ltd.

---

[1] American bandleader (1901–85), known for playing waltzes.

playing and, perhaps most miraculously, ended together. No one in the audience ever guessed that we had never met until twenty minutes earlier. And we kept that up all night, as though we had rehearsed often and played together for years. In a place like Chicago, that scene might be repeated hundreds of times during a weekend.

What I have just described embodies the phenomenon that sociologists have made the core problem of their discipline. The social sciences are such a contentious bunch of disciplines that it makes trouble to say what I think is true, that they all in fact concern themselves with one or another version of this issue—the problem of collective action, of how people manage to act together. I will not attempt a rigorous definition of collective action here, but the story of the Saturday night musicians can serve as an example of it. The example might have concerned a larger group—the employees of a factory who turn out several hundred automobiles in the course of a day, say. Or it might have been about so small a group as a family. It needn't have dealt with a casual collection of strangers, though the ability of strangers to perform together that way makes clear the nature of the problem. How do they do it? How do people act together so as to get anything done without a great deal of trouble, without missteps and conflict?

We can approach the meaning of a concept by seeing how it is used, what work it is called on to do. Sociologists use the concept of *culture* as one of a family of explanations for the phenomenon of concerted activity; I will consider some of the others below, in order to differentiate culture from them. Robert Redfield defined culture as "conventional understandings made manifest in act and artifact." The notion is that the people involved have a similar idea of things, understand them in the same way, as having the same character and the same potential, capable of being dealt with in the same way; they also know that this idea is shared, that the people they are dealing with know, just as they do, what these things are and how they can be used. Because all of them have roughly the same idea, they can all act in ways that are roughly the same, and their activities will, as a result, mesh and be coordinated. Thus, because all those musicians understood what a Saturday night job at a country club consisted of and acted accordingly, because they all knew the melody and harmony of "Exactly Like You" and hundreds of similar songs, because they knew that the others knew this as they knew it, they could play that job successfully. The concept of culture, in short, has its use for sociologists as an explanation of those musicians and all the other forms of concerted action for which they stand.

I said that culture was not the only way sociologists explain concerted action. It often happens, for example, even in the most stable groups and traditional situations, that things happen which are not fully or even partly covered by already shared understandings. That may be because the situation is unprecedented—a disaster of a kind that has never occurred before—or because the people in the group come from such a variety of backgrounds that, though they all have some idea about the matter at hand and all speak a common language, they do not share understandings. That can easily happen in stratified societies, in ethnically differentiated societies, in situations where different occupational groups meet. Of course, people in such situations will presumably share some understandings which will form the basis of discussion and mediation as they work out what to do. If the Saturday night musicians had not shared as much knowledge as they did, they would have sat down to discuss what kind of music they would play, sketched out parts, and so on. They would have had to negotiate, a process I will consider more fully below.

Culture, however, explains how people act in concert when they *do* share understandings. It is thus a consequence (in this kind of sociological thinking) of the existence of a group of acting people. It has its meaning as one of the resources people draw on in order to coordinate their activities. In this it differs from most anthropological thinking in which the order of importance is reversed, culture leading a kind of independent existence as a system of patterns that make the existence of larger groups possible.

Most conceptions of culture include a great deal more than the spare definition I offered above. But I think, for reasons made clear later, that it is better to begin with a minimal definition and then to add other conditions when that is helpful.

Many people would insist that, if we are to call something culture, it must be traditional, of long standing, passed on from generation to generation. That would certainly make the concept unavailable as an explanation of the Saturday night musician. While we might conceivably say that these men were engaging in a traditional cultural activity, since a tradition of musicians playing for the entertainment of others goes back centuries and the American tradition of professional musicians playing for dances and parties is decades old, they were not doing it the way people who play for peasant parties in Greece or Mexico do, playing songs their grandparents played, perhaps on the same instruments. No, they were playing songs no more than twenty or thirty years old, songs their grandfathers never knew; in fact, few of their grandfathers had been musicians in whatever countries they came from, and, by becoming musicians themselves, these men were doing something untraditional in their families (and usually something not desired by their families either). They, of course, had learned to do many of the things they were doing from others who were slightly older, as I had learned many of the tricks of being a weekend musician when I was fifteen from people as old as seventeen or eighteen, who had in turn learned them from still older people. But, still, they did not know how to do what they were doing because it was traditional.

Many other people would insist that, if we are to call something culture, it must be part of a larger *system*, in which the various parts not only cohere in the sense of being noncontradictory, but, more than that, harmonize in the sense of being different versions of the same underlying themes. Such people would not use the term "culture" to describe the patterns of cooperation of the weekend musicians unless those patterns were also reflected in the music they played, the clothing they wore, the way they spent their leisure time, and so on. But none of that was true because they were not just musicians, and much of what they did reflected understandings they had acquired by participating in other social arenas in which the musicians' culture was irrelevant and vice versa. Nor, in any event, did they play what they might have played if they had been free to express their cultural understandings, for what they played was largely what they were paid to play (polkas on Friday, mambos on Saturday).

And many people would insist that my example is misleading to begin with, for the kinds of coherence that constitute "real" culture occur only at the level of the whole society. But if we connect culture to activities people carry on with one another, then we have to ask what all the members of a whole society do, or what they all do together, that requires them to share these general understandings. There are such things, but I think they tend to be rather banal and not at the level usually meant in discussions of general cultural themes. Thus, we all use the money of our society and know how many of the smaller units make one of the larger ones. Less trivially, we probably share understandings about how to behave in public, the things Edward T. Hall and Erving Goffman have written about—how close to stand to someone when we talk or how much space someone is entitled to in a public place, for example. But, even if for the sake of the argument we imagine that some substantial body of such materials exists, as it might in a relatively undifferentiated or rural society, that would not help us understand how the weekend musicians did their trick, and we would need some other term for what they were able to do and the web of shared understandings they used to do it.

Other people have other requirements for what can be called culture, all of which can be subjected to similar criticisms. Some think that culture, to be "really" culture, must be built in some deep way into the personalities of the people who carry it; others require that culture consist of "basic values," whatever might be meant by that. In neither case would the activities of the Saturday night musicians qualify as culture, however, if those definitional requirements were observed.

Normally, of course, we can define terms any way we want, but in the case of culture, several things seem to limit our freedom. The two most important are the quasi ownership of the term by anthropologists and the ambiguity of the word with respect to the problem of "high culture," to which I will return later. Anthropologists and most other people regard culture as anthropology's key concept and assume that the discipline is therefore entitled to make the definition. But anthropologists do not agree on a definition of culture; indeed, they differ spectacularly among themselves, as a famous compendium by Alfred Kroeber and Clyde Kluckhohn demonstrates. That did not dissuade Kroeber and Talcott Parsons from assigning a jurisdictional agreement (like those by which the building trades decide how much of the work carpenters can do and where electricians must take over) giving "culture" to anthropology and "society" to sociology. But the social sciences, unlike the building trades, have not respected the deal their leaders made.

Which of these additional criteria, if any, should be incorporated into the definition of culture I have already given? Do we need any of them? Do we lose anything by using the most minimal definition of culture, as the shared understandings that people use to coordinate their activities? I think not. We have an inclusive term which describes not only the Saturday night musicians and the way they accomplish their feat of coordination, but all the other combinations of attributes that turn up in real life, raising questions about when they go together and when they do not.

Much depends on what kind of archetypal case you want the definition to cover, since a small Stone Age tribe living at the headwaters of the Amazon, which has never been in contact with European civilization, is obviously quite different from such typical products of twentieth-century urban America as the weekend musicians. The kinds of collective action required in the two situations differ enormously and, consequently, the kinds of shared understandings participants can rely on vary concomitantly. Many anthropologists have a kind of temperamental preference for the simplicity, order, and predictability of less complicated societies, in which everyone knows what everyone else is supposed to do, and in which there is a "design for living." If you share that preference, then you can turn culture into an honorific term by denying it to those social arrangements which do not "deserve" it, thereby making a disguised moral judgment about those ways of life. But that leaves a good part of modern life, not just the Saturday night musicians, out of the culture sphere altogether.

How does culture—shared understanding—help people to act collectively? People have ideas about how a certain kind of activity might be carried on. They believe others share these ideas and will act on them if they understand the situation in the same way. They believe further that the people they are interacting with believe that they share these ideas too, so everyone thinks that everyone else has the same idea about how to do things. Given such circumstances, if everyone does what seems appropriate, action will be sufficiently coordinated for practical purposes. Whatever was under way will get done—the meal served, the child dealt with, the job finished, all well enough so that life can proceed.

The cultural process, then, consists of people doing something in line with their understanding of what one might best do under the given circumstances. Others, recognizing what was done as appropriate, will then consult their notions of what might be done and do something that seems right to them, to which others in return will respond similarly, and so on. If everyone has the same general ideas in mind, and does something congruent with that image or collection of ideas, then what people do will fit together. If we all know the melody and harmony of "Exactly Like You," and improvise accordingly, whatever comes out will sound reasonable to the players and listeners, and a group of perfect strangers will sound like they know what they are doing.

Consider another common situation. A man and woman meet and find each other interesting. At some stage of their relationship, they may consider any of a variety of ways of organizing their joint activities. Early on, one or the other might propose that they "have a date." Later, one or the other might, subtly or forthrightly, suggest that they "spend the night together." Still later, they might try "living together." Finally, they might decide to "get married." They might skip some of these stages and they might not follow that progression, which in contemporary America is a progression of increasingly formal commitment. In other societies and at other times, of course, the stages and the relationships would differ. But, whatever their variety, insofar as there are names for these relationships and stages, and insofar as most or all of the people in a society know those names and have an idea of what they imply as far as continuing patterns of joint activity are concerned, then the man and woman involved will be able to organize what they do by referring to those guideposts. When one or the other suggests one of these possibilities, the partner will know, more or less, what is being suggested without requiring that every item be spelled out in detail, and the pair can then organize their daily lives, more or less, around the patterns suggested by these cultural images.

What they do from day to day will of course not be completely covered by the details of that imagery, although they will be able to decide many details by consulting it together and adapting what it suggests to the problem at hand. None of these images, for instance, really establishes who takes the garbage out or what the details of their sexual activity may be, but the images do, in general, suggest the kind of commitments and obligations involved on both sides in a wide range of practical matters.

That is not the end of the matter, though. Consider a likely contemporary complication: the woman, divorced, has small children who live with her. In this case, the couple's freedom of action is constrained, and no cultural model suggests what they ought to do about the resulting difficulties. The models for pairing and for rearing children suggest incompatible solutions, and the partners have to invent something. They have to improvise.

This raises a major problem in the theory of culture I am propounding. Where does culture come from? The typical cultural explanation of behavior takes the culture as given, as preexisting the particular encounter in which it comes into play. That makes sense. Most of the cultural understandings we use to organize our daily behavior are there before we get there and we do not propose to change them or negotiate their details with the people we encounter. We do not propose a new economic system every time we go to the grocery store. But those understandings and ways of doing things have not always been there. Most of us buy our food in supermarkets today, and that requires a different way of shopping from the corner grocery stores of a generation ago. How did the new culture of supermarkets arise?

One answer is that the new culture was imposed by the inventors of the concept, the owners of the new stores which embodied it. They created the conditions under which change was more or less inevitable. People might have decided not to shop in supermarkets and chain stores, but changing conditions of urban life caused so many of them to use the new markets that the corner grocery, the butcher shop, the poultry and fish stores disappeared in all but a few areas. Once that happened, supermarkets became the only practical possibility left, and people had to invent new ways of serving themselves.

So, given new conditions, people invent culture. The way they do it was suggested by William Graham Sumner a century ago in *Folkways*. We can paraphrase him in this way. A group finds itself sharing a common situation and common problems. Various members of the group experiment with possible solutions to those problems and report their experiences to their fellows. In the course of their collective discussion, the members of the group arrive at a definition of the situation, its problems and possibilities, and develop a consensus as to the most appropriate and efficient ways of behaving. This consensus thenceforth constrains the activities of individual members of the group, who will probably act on it, given the opportunity. In other words, new situations provoke new behavior. But people generally find themselves in company when dealing with these new situations, and since they arrive at their solutions collectively, each assumes that the others share them. The beginnings of a new shared understanding thus come into play quickly and easily.

The ease with which new cultural understandings arise and persist varies. It makes a difference, for one thing, how large a group is involved in making the new understandings. At one extreme, as I have noted, every mating couple, every new family, has to devise its own culture to cover the contingencies of daily interaction. At the other, consider what happens during industrialization when hundreds of thousands—perhaps millions—of people are brought from elsewhere to work in the new factories. They have to come from elsewhere because the area could not support that many people before industrialization. As a result, the newcomers differ in culture from the people already there, and they differ as well in the role they play in the new industries, usually coming in at the bottom. When industrialization takes place on a large scale, not only does a new culture of the workplace have to be devised but also a new culture of the cities in which they all end up living—a new experience for everyone involved.

The range of examples suggests, as I mean it to, that people create culture continuously. Since no two situations are alike, the cultural solutions available to them are only approximate. Even in the simplest societies, no two people learn quite the same cultural material; the chance encounters of daily life provide sufficient variation to ensure that. No set of cultural understandings, then, provides a perfectly applicable solution to any problem people have to solve in the course of their day, and they therefore must remake those solutions, adapt their understandings to the new situation in the light of what is different about it. Even the most conscious and determined effort to keep things as they are would necessarily involve strenuous efforts to remake and reinforce understandings so as to keep them intact in the face of what was changing.

There is an apparent paradox here. On the one hand, culture persists and ante-dates the participation of particular people in it; indeed, culture can be said to shape the outlooks of people who participate in it. But cultural understandings, on the other hand, have to be reviewed and remade continually, and in the remaking they change.

This is not a true paradox, however: the understandings last *because* they change to deal with new situations. People continually refine them, changing some here and some there but never changing all of them at once. The emphasis on basic values and coherence in the definition of culture arises because of this process. In making the new versions of the old understandings, people naturally rely on what they already have available, so that consciously planned innovations and revolutions seem, in historical perspective, only small variations on what came before.

To summarize, how culture works as a guide in organizing collective action and how it comes into being are really the same process. In both cases, people pay attention to what other people are doing and, in an attempt to mesh what they do with those others, refer to what they know (or think they know) in common. So culture is always being made, changing more or less, acting as a point of reference for people engaged in interaction.

What difference does it make that people continually make culture in the way I have described? The most important consequence is that they can, as a result, cooperate easily and efficiently in the daily business of life, without necessarily knowing each other very well.

Most occupations, for example, operate on the premise that the people who work in them all know certain procedures and certain ways of thinking about and respond-ing to typical situations and problems, and that such knowledge will make it possible to assemble them to work on a common project without prior team training. Most professional schools operate on the theory that the education they offer provides a basis for work cooperation among people properly trained anywhere. In fact, people probably learn the culture which makes occupational cooperation possible in the workplace itself. It presents them with problems to solve that are common to people in their line of work, and provides a group of more experienced workers who can suggest solutions. In some occupations, workers change jobs often and move from workplace to workplace often (as do the weekend musicians), and they carry what they have learned elsewhere with them. That makes it easy for them to refine and update their solutions frequently, and thus to develop and maintain an occupational culture. Work-ers who do not move but spend their work lives in one place may develop a more idio-syncratic work culture, peculiar to that place and its local problems—a culture of IBM or Texas Instruments or (because the process is not limited to large firms) Joe's Diner.

At a different level of cooperative action, Goffman has described cultural under-standings which characterize people's behavior in public. For instance, people obey a norm of "civil inattention," allowing each other a privacy which the material circumstances, of, say, waiting for a bus do not provide. Since this kind of privacy is what Americans and many others find necessary before they can feel comfortable and safe in public (Hall has shown how these rules differ in other cultures), these understandings make it possible for urban Americans to occupy crowded public spaces without making each other uneasy. The point is not trivial, because violations of these rules are at least in part responsible for the currently common fear that some public areas are "not safe," quite apart from whatever assaults have taken place in them. Most people have no personal knowledge of the alleged assaults, but they experience violation of what might be called the "Goffman rules" of public order as the prelude to danger and do not go to places which make them feel that way.

Cultural understandings, if they are to be effective in the organization of public behavior, must be very widely held. That means that people of otherwise varying class, ethnic, and regional cultures must learn them routinely, and must learn them quite young, because even small children can disrupt public order very effectively. That requires, in turn, substantial agreement among people of all segments of the society on how children should be brought up. If no such agreement exists or if some of the people who agree in principle do not manage to teach their children the necessary things, public order breaks down, as it often does.

In another direction, cultural understandings affect and "socialize" the internal experiences people have. By applying understandings they know to be widely accepted to their own perhaps inchoate private experiences, people learn to define those internal experiences in ways which allow them to mesh their activities relevant to those topics with those of others with whom they are involved. Consider the familiar example of falling in love. It is remarkable that one of the experiences we usually consider private and unique—falling in love—actually has the same character for most people who experience it. That is not to say that the experience is superficial, but rather that when people try to understand their emotional responses to others, one available explanation of what they feel is the idea, common in Western culture, of romantic love. They learn that idea from a variety of sources, ranging from the mass media to discussion with their peers, and they learn to see their own experiences as embodiments of it. Because most people within a given culture learn to experience love in the same way from the same sources, two people can become acquainted and successfully fall in love with each other—not an easy trick.

Because shared cultural understandings make it easy to do things in certain ways, moreover, their existence favors those ways of doing things and makes other ways of achieving the same end, which might be just as satisfactory to everyone involved, correspondingly less likely. Random events, which might produce innovations desirable to participants, occur infrequently. In fact, even when the familiar line of activity is not exactly to anyone's liking, people continue it simply because it is what everyone knows and knows that everyone else knows, and thus is what offers the greatest likelihood of successful collective action. Everyone knows, for instance, that it would be better to standardize the enormous variety of screw threads in this country, or to convert the United States to the metric system. But the old ways are the ones we know, and, of course, in this instance, they are built into tools and machines which would be difficult and costly to change. Many activities exhibit that inertia, and they pose a problem that sociologists have been interested in for many years: which elements of a society or culture are most likely to change? William Fielding Ogburn, for instance, proposed sixty years ago that material culture (screw threads) changed more quickly than social organization, and that the resultant "lag" could be problematic for human society.

A final consequence: the existence of culture makes it possible for people to plan their own lives. We can plan most easily for a known future, in which the major organizational features of society turn out to be what we expected them to be and what we made allowances for in our planning. We need, most importantly, to predict the actions of other people and of the organizations which consist of their collective actions. Culture makes those actions, individual and collective, more predictable than they would otherwise be. People in traditional societies may not obey in every detail the complex marriage rules held out to them, but those rules supply a sufficiently clear guide for men and women to envision more or less accurately when they will marry, what resources will be available to them when they do, and how the course of their married life will proceed.

In modern industrial societies, workers can plan their careers better when they know what kinds of work situations they will find themselves in and what their rights and obligations at various ages and career stages will be. Few people can make those predictions successfully in this country anymore, which indicates that cultural understandings do not always last the twenty or thirty years necessary for such predictability to be possible. When that happens, people do not know how to prepare themselves for their work lives and do not receive the benefits of their earlier investments in hard work. People who seemed to be goofing off or acting irrationally, for example, sometimes make windfall profits as the work world comes to need just those combinations of skills and experiences that they acquired while not following a "sensible" career path. As technical and organizational innovations make new skills more desirable, new career lines open up which were not and could not have been predicted ten years earlier. The first generation of computer programmers benefited from that kind of good luck, as did the first generation of drug researchers, among others.

In every society, some of the understandings we have been talking about are thought to be more important, more noble, more imbued with the highest aspirations or achievements of that society. For hundreds of years, Western societies have given that kind of privileged position to what some regard as "high culture" and what others regard as "culture" without a qualifying adjective—art, reflective thought, philosophy.

These pursuits are generally opposed to more manual occupations and to those connected with industry and commerce, although the growth of science and the commercialization of art in more recent times have created substantial areas of ambiguity. It seems obvious, without Thorstein Veblen to point it out, that these judgments reflect the relative prestige of those segments of society which more often engage in or patronize those pursuits. They are the hobbies, the playthings of political and religious leaders as well as of people of power and privilege in general, and it is a good sociological question whether they receive their *mana* from the power of those interested in them or whether they lend some portion of that *mana* to those supporters.

How do these areas of cultural understanding differ from the more mundane examples I addressed earlier? They have a better reputation, of course, but is the basis for that reputation discernible in them or could any set of concerns and activities achieve that special estate? That is an enormously complicated question which I am not going to answer in a few words. It is enough to ask, from the point of view assumed here, what kinds of activities, pursued by whom, follow from the existence of these understandings. Who can do what together as a result of their existence?

One answer is that, in Western societies originally at least, culturally reputable activities are carried on by specialists who make a profession of them. Those professions gather around them a special world—a network of people who collaborate in the production, distribution, and celebration of "high" culture—and that collaboration is made possible by the kinds of cultural understandings I have been discussing throughout this paper.

In addition, the people who cooperate in these ventures regard the work they do as having special value. "Art" is an honorific category, a word applied to productions that a society decides to treat as especially valuable. A great deal of work that seems to share the observable qualities of what comes to be called high art never earns that distinction, and that suggests the difference does not lie in the *work* so honored but rather in the process of *honoring*. We can easily observe, furthermore, that the same objects and events earn the label of "art" on some occasions and not others, often migrating back and forth across the dividing line as fashions change. (I have discussed these matters at length in *Art Worlds*.)

High culture, then, consists of work recognized as belonging to an honored category of cultural understandings by the people who have the power to make that determination and to have it accepted by others. We may be able to devise systematic criteria that will identify work of superior quality, but it is unlikely that the work we can distinguish in that way will be the same as the work legitimated as high culture by the institutions that make the decision for any society.

Thinking of high culture this way suggests the levelling impulse contained in most systematic sociological analysis. Basic social processes, such as the development of common ways of looking at things, usually cross the honorific lines drawn in a society. Discussing culture in this fashion may seem awkward or impudent, but the warrant for doing it comes from the increased understanding the procedure gives us of the processes that lie under all our activities, honorable and otherwise.

STUDY QUESTIONS

1. According to Becker, what are the most important things limiting our ability to define **culture**?

2. Define the cultural process and give an example of it.

3. Write your own definition of culture. How is it similar to and different from Becker's definition?

4. Visit the American Sociological Association's Section on Culture (www.asanet .org/sections/culture.cfm). Read the section's mission statement, then go to the section webpage and read one or more of the Section on Culture's newsletters. Share what you learn with your classmates. Why would a sociological group specifically want to have a culture section?

JULIET B. SCHOR

The Changing World of Children's Consumption

Are advertisers programming our children to shop? In her book *Born To Buy* Juliet B. Schor presents a host of research suggesting that children as young as six recognize corporate brands and influence how their parents spend up to $1 trillion annually on consumer goods. Schor **correlates** this consumption-focused childhood with many negative outcomes. Before you begin reading, recall what advertisements you saw often as a child. What kind of influence do you think you had over **family** purchases? As you read, consider how this focus on material goods has affected children, childhood, and the natural **environment**.

> *A nation of kids and they Drive purchases; Kids influence 62% of family SUV and minivan purchases! Nickelodeon owns 50% of the K2–11 GRP's [Gross Rating Points] in Kids' Commercial TV.*
>
> —From a Nickelodeon ad, with a smiling kid in an SUV

THE TYPICAL AMERICAN CHILD IS NOW IMMERSED IN THE CONsumer marketplace to a degree that dwarfs all historical experience. At age one, she's watching *Teletubbies* and eating the food of its "promo partners" Burger King and McDonald's. Kids can recognize logos by eighteen months, and before reaching their second birthday, they're asking for products by brand name. By three or three and a half, experts say, children start to believe that brands communicate their personal qualities, for example, that they're cool, or strong, or smart. Even before starting school, the likelihood of having a television in their bedroom is 25 percent, and their viewing time is just over two hours a day. Upon arrival at the schoolhouse steps, the typical first grader can evoke 200 brands. And he or she has already accumulated an unprecedented number of possessions, beginning with an average of seventy new toys a year.

By age six and seven, girls are asking for the latest fashions, using nail polish, and singing pop music tunes. The day after the dELIA*s clothing catalogue arrives in the mail, marketers report that "everyone brings their catalog to school" to talk about the products in it. (When I wrote those words dELIA*s was hot; when they appear in print, who knows? Trends move at the speed of light in this world.) Eight-year-old boys are enjoying Budweiser commercials (the consistent favorite ad for this age group), World Wrestling Entertainment, and graphically violent video games. Schools routinely ban the toy fads that sweep the market, from Power Rangers to Pokémon, on the grounds that they lead to fights, antisocial behavior, and disruption. The average eight to thirteen year old is watching over three and a half hours of television a day. American children view an estimated 40,000 commercials annually. They also make approximately 3,000 requests for products and services each year.

As kids age, they turn to teen culture, which is saturated with violence, alcohol, drugs, and guns. Teen media depict a manipulated and gratuitous sexuality, based on unrealistic body images, constraining gender stereotypes, and, all too frequently, the degradation of women. The dominant teen culture is also rife with materialism and preaches that if you're not rich, you're a loser. Adolescents are subjected to unremitting pressure to conform to the market's definition of cool. MTV has been the global leader in promoting these values, and its worldview has become pervasive among youth. And now, teen culture has migrated down to younger children. Eight and nine year olds watch MTV and BET (Black Entertainment Television), reality shows, and other prime-time fare ostensibly aimed at teens and adults. Marketers are deliberately investing children's culture with the themes and sensibilities that have worked with teens. As Betsy Frank, head of research for MTV Networks, explained, "If something works for MTV, it will also work for Nickelodeon." It's a widespread process, known as tweening.

THE MARKETING JUGGERNAUT

This commercialization of childhood is being driven by a number of factors, including broad social trends. But underlying them all is a marketing juggernaut characterized by growing reach, effectiveness, and audacity. One clue to the marketing mentality is industry language. It's a war out there. Those at whom ads are directed are "targets." When money is committed to an ad campaign it is referred to as "going against the target." Printed materials are called "collateral." Impromptu interviews with consumers are "intercepts." The industry is heavily into the metaphor of biological warfare, as in the terms "viral marketing" and "sending out a virus." Other conventions include "converting [a kid] into a user" (a phrase from drug culture), delivering the "eyeballs," and becoming "top of mind." There's not much doubt about who's winning this war either. When Nickelodeon tells its advertisers that it "owns kids aged 2–12," the boast is closer to the mark than most of us realize.

The companies' successes are partly attributable to their enormous outlays of money. James McNeal, the nation's most influential estimator of the size of the children's market, has calculated that by 2004, total advertising and marketing expenditures directed at children reached $15 billion, a stunning rise from the mere $100 million in television advertising spent in 1983.

Researchers have chopped up the 52 million plus children in the age-twelve-and-under demographic into discrete age, gender, ethnic, and product segments, each with tailored messages. Nearly every segment warrants a yearly conference. For those who want to capture Hispanic youth, there's the Annual Hispanic KidPower meeting, which promises to unlock the special secrets of the most rapidly growing market segment in the country. The Annual KidPower Food and Beverage conference teaches participants how to sell more junk food to kids. There are conferences devoted to teens, to tweens, to Latin America, Asia, and Europe. African American children sometimes get special attention, as do themes such as girl power or technology. Hundreds of representatives of the client companies come to hear the latest findings about what kids are up to from researchers, psychologists, and ad agency reps. At one conference, I was treated to the pitch of the Gepetto Group, which created a simulated safari video, *The Nature of Kids*. The animals, of course, are children, defined as "nature's most elusive creature." The narrator has a British colonial accent, to conjure up images of safari suit and pith helmet. The kids slink through the jungle on all fours, guzzling soda and eating toaster pop-ups, speaking their own commercially inspired lingo. They're a species apart. But have no fear. Gepetto, the intrepid hunter, can help. It has snared and dissected these strange creatures we call our children and is ready to sell that information to anyone with cash to spend. Its representative promises to teach the client "how to get a grip on cool all the time" or do an assessment of kids' innermost dreams, aspirations, and fears.

Other companies have less elaborate come-ons but offer similar messages. Their workshop titles include "Emotional Branding: Maximizing the Appeal of Your Brand to Hispanic Youth," "Purchasing Power: Capturing Your Share of the Tween Wallet," and "Seeing the World Through Kids' Eyes: An Intimate Peek into the Minds and Hearts of Kids." Companies promise to "create an experience so engaging that the consumer won't have another option but to pay attention to it."

The growth of specialized kid expertise is made possible by a deluge of industry-generated research. Companies have created scores of surveys, polls, and other research instruments. They've gone anthropological, using ethnographic methods that scrutinize the most intimate details of children's lives. Marketers are videotaping children in their private spaces, providing in-depth analysis of the rituals of daily life. They are taking to the streets, to stores, and even into schools to observe and record. Researchers are paying adults whom kids trust, such as coaches, clergy, and youth workers, to elicit information from them. Online, they're offering money, products, and prizes directly to kids in return for saleable consumer information.

Once the research has been done, message crafting begins. Ads depict kid-friendly worlds free of annoying parents and teachers. They rely on "attitude" and use increasing daring in terms of shock value or sexuality. There's a growing sense of license. Marketing is also being delivered in new ways, as stealth, guerrilla, and peer-to-peer techniques have taken hold. Companies enlist children to market to each other at school, in chat rooms, on playgrounds, even inside their homes. Marketing to children is occurring almost everywhere—at market festivals, concerts, and public schools, which have been a major staging ground for advertisers in the past decade. Trusted social institutions, such as the Girl Scouts and Boys and Girls Clubs, are teaming up with marketers. When the *Los Angeles Times* decided to create a children's version of its well-known book fair, it turned, tellingly, to a marketing group. All the while, the industry claims that it is empowering kids and promoting their self-esteem.

A recent poll by the Center for a New American Dream reveals that children are well aware, and even critical, of these efforts. Among those aged nine to fourteen, 63 percent expressed concern that there is too much advertising that tries to get kids to buy things, 74 percent say "it's too bad you have to buy certain things to be cool," and 81 percent believe that "lots of kids place way too much importance on buying things." Fifty-seven percent agree that they sometimes feel they spend too much time trying to "get their parents to buy you things rather than doing fun things with them." And the same fraction worry that "advertising that tries to get kids to buy things causes trouble between kids and parents."

THE EXPLOSION OF YOUTH SPENDING

Companies are advertising because kids are buying. Every half-second, somewhere in the world another Barbie is sold. More than 120 million kids worldwide have watched Children's Television Workshop. McDonald's, despite its current woes, still manages to attract 8 percent of the American population every day, and a fifth of its business is in Happy Meals. Whether it's music, food, movies, video games, apparel, footwear, toys, television, sports, school supplies, retailing, e-tailing, health and beauty products, consumer electronics, entertainment, or travel, there is now a thriving children's market segment.

Children's purchasing power has risen rapidly. McNeal reports that children aged four to twelve made $6.1 billion in purchases in 1989, $23.4 billion in 1997, and $30.0 billion in 2002, an increase of 400 percent. The number one spending category, at a third of the total, is for sweets, snacks, and beverages. Toys are number two and apparel is growing fast. Older kids, aged twelve to nineteen, spend even more: they accounted for $170 billion of personal spending in 2002, or a weekly average of $101 per person. This teen market is important because the children's market tracks it, and because trends and styles now migrate quickly from adolescents to kids. Teens have become a leading indicator for tween and child behavior.

Children are becoming shoppers at an earlier age. Six to twelve year olds are estimated to visit stores two to three times per week and to put six items into the shopping cart each time they go. Eighty percent of them shop regularly with their parents, a change necessitated by the decline of stay-at-home mothers. But kids are also going solo. McNeal estimates that one in four make trips to stores alone before they enter elementary school and that the median age for independent trips is eight. Youthful shoppers are now often buying for family needs, particularly in single-parent households. The proliferation of children in stores is also leading to changes in retail environments. In 1996, the world's first mall catering exclusively to children opened in Alpharetta, Georgia. It has been enormously successful, and its "kids' village" concept has been copied around the country. Expect one on your local interstate before too long.

"KID-FLUENCE"

The more children shop, the more voice they have in parental purchases. In the industry, this is called the influence market, and it is enormous. McNeal estimates that children aged four to twelve directly influenced $330 billion of adult purchasing in 2004 and "evoked" another $340 billion. And he believes that influence spending is growing at 20 percent per year. Global estimates for tween influence topped $1 trillion in 2002. That persuasive power is why Nickelodeon, the number one television channel for kids, has had Ford Motor Company, Target, Embassy Suites, and the Bahamas Ministry of Tourism as its advertisers. (This explains why your child has been asking for an SUV, a vacation in the Bahamas, and a Robert Graves teapot.)

Children's influence is being driven by a number of factors, including changes in parenting style. Older generations were more authoritarian, believing that they knew what was best for their kids. The famous "children should be seen and not heard" adage also meant that parents made most buying decisions. Baby boom and later generations of parents have been far more willing to give voice and choice, to see consumer decisions as "learning opportunities." (Cheerios or Fruit Loops? Cherry Popsicle or grape?) As one marketer explained to me, "When I was a kid I got to pick the color of the car. Kids nowadays get to pick the car." While that may be an exaggeration, there is little doubt that parental attitudes have changed markedly. One industry estimate finds that 67 percent of car purchases by parents are influenced by children. Marketers have put tremendous effort into discovering just how far kid influence has permeated into household purchasing dynamics and for what types of products. And what they have found is that for a growing array of expenditures, children, not parents, are making choices.

What's more, kids' opinions are solicited from the earliest ages. According to a consumer panel run by New York agency Griffin Bacal, 100 percent of the parents of children aged two to five agreed that their children have a major influence on their food and snack purchases. For video and book choices, the rate of major influence was 80 percent, and for restaurants, clothes, and health and beauty products, it stood at 50 percent. The Roper Youth Report has found that among six and seven year olds, 30 percent choose their own grocery store food items, 15 percent choose their toys and games, and 33 percent make fast food and candy decisions. As kids age, their influence grows.

Food is an area where influence marketing and the decline of parental control has been most pronounced. Consider the case of Fruit Roll-ups, a phenomenally successful snack food represented by Saatchi and Saatchi's Kid Connection. When the product was introduced, the ads had both kid and mom appeal. For moms, they called attention to the fruit aspect of the snack. But over time, the agency realized that this "dual messaging" was unnecessary. As a former Saatchi employee explained to me: "For years we used to say 10 percent fruit juice. And finally we're just like, okay, forget it. Who are we kidding? . . . That was also a conscious effort to move toward direct kid marketing and not even worrying about Mom. Just take her out of the equation because the nag factor is so strong on something like that, that you can just take advantage of that."

Parental time pressure and longer working hours have also driven this trend. Time-starved households have become easy prey for marketers, whose research shows that parents who spend less time with their children will spend more money on them. "Guilt money," as they call it, came up in almost all my discussions about why kids have so much influence now. Research done by one of my students is consistent with this view. She found that parents who spent more hours working bought more discretionary items such as toys, videos, and books for their children. This effect is in addition to the fact that the additional income from working more also leads to more spending. By contrast, parents who spent more time with their children bought fewer of these items. The amount of extra spending was larger for mothers than fathers. And it was greater for toys than for other items. In higher-income families, spending was even more sensitive to time spent with children. These results do not show that parental guilt is motivating purchases, but marketers' belief in the power of guilt, and their ability to exploit it, remains strong.

Time pressure operates in other ways as well. Parents have less time to cajole kids to eat products they don't like or to return rejected purchases to stores. This is part of why 89 percent of parents of tweens report that they ask their children's opinions about products they are about to buy for them. Kids are also technologically savvy and eagerly seek out consumer information. Many parents now believe that their children know more about products and brands than they do, and they rely on that knowledge.

"BONDED TO BRANDS"

These days, when kids ask, they ask for particular brands. A 2001 Nickelodeon study found that the average ten year old has memorized 300 to 400 brands. Among eight to fourteen year olds, 92 percent of requests are brand specific, and 89 percent of kids agree that "when I find a brand I like, I tend to stick with it." A 2000 Griffin Bacal study found that nearly two-thirds of mothers thought their children were brand aware by age three, and one-third said it happened at age two. Kids have clear brand preferences, they know which brands are cool, they covet them, and they pay attention to the ads for them. Today's tweens are the most brand-conscious generation in history.

The increased salience of brands is a predictable outcome of kids' greater exposure to ads. Companies spend billions to create positive brand associations for their products, attempting to connect them with culturally valued images, feelings, and sensibilities. This is especially true in the youth marketplace, where so many of the products are hardly differentiable without the labels. There's a copycat sameness to sodas, fast food, candy, athletic shoes, jeans, and even music and films. And in light of that, companies have to work overtime to establish brand identity and loyalty. They turn brands into "signs," pure symbolic entities, detached from specific products and functional characteristics. This has been a winning strategy, and youth have eagerly embraced an ethic of labels and logos. But brand value is a hard quality to sustain, especially in today's super-competitive environment. The intensification of what scholars Robert Goldman and Stephen Papson have dubbed "sign wars," that is, corporate competition centered on images, has led to an ever-accelerating spiral of changing symbolism and brand vulnerability. And that vulnerability fuels marketing innovation and sometimes desperation.

In what industry insiders call the "kidspace," much of the action has been in what is called brand extension. Products are inserted into a vast matrix of other products. There's the Pokémon TV program, the collectible cards, the handheld electronic game, Pokémon toys at the fast food outlet, Pokémon versions of classic board games, Pokémon clothing, school supplies, plastic cups, backpacks, Pokémon everything and anything. Indeed, the process of extensive branding has become a profoundly normalized part of children's lives. It's now a lack of branding that's out of the ordinary. One of my friends explained to me that her son, a five year old with sophisticated musical tastes, was baffled by the fact that there was no "Talking Heads" stuff—no show, no toys, no logo, no nothing. What was going on, he wondered, with this band he liked so much?

Increasingly the brands kids want aren't just any brands. They crave designer duds and luxury items. By the mid-1990s, parents and buyers reported a sea change as girls aged six to ten became more fashion and label conscious. They wanted trendy styles like platform shoes and black clothing. They started asking for Hilfiger and Donna Karan labels. The designers claim that "kids are driving the trend," but they have been advertising heavily to them. Meanwhile, children's lines have sprung up at fashion houses such as Armani and Calvin Klein. Burberry opened Burberry Kids, and Abercrombie & Fitch, the current bad boy of youth apparel, became tweens' favorite brand. Upscaling has gone beyond designer clothes. By the end of the 1990s, Marianne Szymanski, founder of the Toy Research Institute, reported that "kids are starting to want more expensive toys like computer software, cell phones, VCRs, e-mail, stereos, bedroom microwaves (for making popcorn while they watch movies in their own 'bedroom theater'). And guess what? Parents are buying all these items." Kids are also amassing far more toys than ever before. The number of toys sold annually rose 20 percent between 1995 and 2000. The United States, despite having only 4.5 percent of the world's population, now consumes 45 percent of global toy production.

Consumer experiences are also going luxe, and they're often more adult-like. The London salon MiniKin Kinder offers eight year olds its "Princess Treat," with haircut, manicure, and minifacial. Even cosmetic surgery has begun to reach down into childhood, according to journalist Alissa Quart, who reports that the year between elementary and middle schools is becoming a popular time for aesthetic enhancements for eyes, lips, chins, and ears. For those seeking the ultimate experience, FAO Schwartz offered birthday sleepover parties at a price of $17,500, and they were booked solid. Restaurateurs report that "crayons just won't do it anymore." Now they're providing menus attached to Magna Doodle sets, watercolor paint boxes, and Chinese carryout boxes with chopsticks, fortune cookies, and toys. In perhaps the most dramatic example of restaurant upscaling to come along yet, in 2002 McDonald's gave away Madame Alexander dolls, full-sized versions of which go for $50, with its Happy Meals.

REAL-LIFE MONOPOLY

The commercialization of childhood is certainly being driven by the fact that kids have more money and more say, the explanation most marketers articulate. But there's another side to what scholars Shirley and Joe Kincheloe have insightfully called the "Corporate Construction of Childhood." It's the growing scope, market power, and political influence wielded by the small number of megacorporations that sell most of what kids buy. Far from being a consumers' mecca ruled by diverse and rich choices, children's consumer culture is marked by bigness and sameness. Four companies now dominate the children's media and entertainment market almost entirely. There's Disney, with its global reach, anodyne cultural products, and long history of racial and sexual stereotyping. Number two is Viacom, king of cool, whose MTV Networks is the parent company's most profitable division, whose annual revenue in 2001 exceeded $3 billion. We have MTV to thank for shows such as *Beavis and Butthead*, which has been accused of inspiring copycat antics that led to real-life death and destruction. (Viacom also published this book.[1]) Rupert Murdoch's News Corp is the parent to Fox, which has brought us such contributions to youth culture as *Fear Factor*. And finally, there's AOL Time Warner, owners of WB, Cartoon Network, *Sports Illustrated for Kids*, and DC Comics. In 2002, the company announced it would begin showing paid sponsorship on its CNN-branded school news broadcast, but backed down after criticism. In the midst of these behemoths, PBS is overmatched, and anyway, it has joined up with Nickelodeon (Viacom) to infiltrate the "educational" market.

In the toy category, it's Mattel and Hasbro, which together have gobbled up virtually all the other toy companies. Playskool, Fisher-Price, Parker Brothers, Milton Bradley, Tonka Trucks, Tyco, Hot Wheels, American Girl, Cabbage Patch Dolls, Tinker Toys, Avalon Hill, Wizards of the Coast, and Mr. Potato Head are all owned by the big two. In early 2002, eight of the top-selling ten toys belonged to these two companies. Video games are dominated by a small number of producers—Nintendo, Sony, and Microsoft among them. The big-two model prevails in other markets as well. In candy it's M&M and Hershey. In soft drinks it's Coke and Pepsi. In fast food McDonald's and Burger King. Philip Morris (the tobacco giant, renamed Altria) owns Kraft with its Lunchables product, kids' second favorite lunch choice after pizza, as well as Nabisco and Post cereals. Frito-Lay is part of PepsiCo, as are Tropicana, Gatorade, and Quaker Oats. PepsiCo tries to retain a wholesome oatmeal image with the venerable Quaker on the box, but it's the same company that sells Cap'n Crunch's Choco Donuts cereal. Throughout the world of children's products, the markets are dominated by a few powerful companies.

This matters for a number of reasons. One is that with monopoly comes uniformity. Economic theory predicts that when two opponents face off, the winning strategy for both entails their becoming almost identical. This model explains why gas stations congregate at intersections, why Democrats and Republicans cleave to the political center, and why Coke and Pepsi are hard to tell apart with a blindfold. What it means for consumers is that true variety and diversity of products is hard to find. If you want greasy pizza, sugared drinks, plastic toys, and violent programming for your kids, no problem. It's the other stuff that's missing.

Monopoly also means bigger profits and market power for producers and less value and influence for consumers. That's standard economic reasoning. Finally, many of these companies have spent the past two decades stockpiling money and political

---

[1] That is, Schor's book, *Born to Buy*, from which this selection is taken. It was published in 2004 by Scribner, then owned by Viacom, now owned by CBS.

influence. At the end of the 1970s, the Federal Trade Commission was investigating practices in children's advertising and didn't like what it saw. It advocated a ban on advertising sugared products to kids, as well as an end to commercials aimed at children under age eight. Today, such a stance seems almost inconceivable, given the tremendous growth in political influence enjoyed by media corporations and food processors. Philip Morris gave more than $9 million in soft money to the two political parties between 1995 and 2002 ($7.8 million of it went to Republicans). AOL Time Warner gave more than $4 million (nearly equally divided). Disney contributed $3.6 million. Coca-Cola gave $2.3 million (mostly to the Republicans). The U.S. Sugar Corporation is also among the top "Double Givers." Two decades of corporate monies have eroded the regulatory, legislative, and judicial environment, making it far harder to protect children.

PLAYING LESS AND SHOPPING MORE

Memories shape adult views of childhood. Many in my generation—the baby boomers—have vivid recollections of endless hours of unsupervised, spontaneous play. We remember outdoor activities such as pick-up games on an empty sandlot. Many of us had a "gang" (in the wholesome sense) of neighborhood kids, often of mixed age and sex, who met up after school. When I was a kid, we would get obsessed with particular games, often ones we invented ourselves. There was plenty of traditional indoor play as well, such as house, war, and board games. We made concoctions, played dress-up, built forts, and fought with our siblings. Sometimes we even watched television.

We were lucky. Earlier generations of children spent much of their time working, on farms, in factories, and in domestic service. Paid child labor wasn't eliminated in this country until the 1920s. Baby boomers also escaped the sobering effects of depression and war. And we were a group of girls who were unusually liberated, both because we were allowed out on our own and because we were increasingly excused from household work. Children born in the late 1940s and afterward had more carefree, play-oriented upbringings with less family responsibility than the generations that preceded them. It was a childhood experience that took many decades to achieve, and unfortunately, the era was short-lived. In recent years, children's unsupervised time has declined. They spend more hours in worklike activities. More of daily life is structured by commercial and consumer activities than was true for previous generations.

Large-scale studies of children's time use are rare. In 1997, the Panel Survey of Income Dynamics conducted a major survey on children and their environments, and gathered data on how they spend their time. The "Child Development Supplement" was a nationally representative sample with more than 3,500 children from approximately 2,400 households. Time use was measured through a daily activity diary. The data show that time spent in leisure and unstructured play is limited. After subtracting eating, sleeping, personal care, schooling, studying, day care, shopping, and household work, only 25 percent of children's time remains discretionary. For six to twelve year olds, the fraction is a percentage point lower. (See Table 1.)

How do children spend that time? While three to five year olds still play a considerable amount, what study authors Sandra Hofferth and John Sandberg define as play comprises only about ten hours per week for the six-to-twelve age group, lower than school hours (thirty-three), and fewer than the thirteen hours spent watching television as a primary activity. Nine to twelve year olds play fewer than nine hours a week. There are other play-oriented activities during discretionary time, such as art and hobbies, measured at one hour, and "outdoors," at thirty-five minutes.

There is a widespread belief that in comparison with the past, today's children are harried, sped up, herded into productive activities, and less able to be kids. Book titles such as *The Hurried Child* and *The Over-Scheduled Child* reveal these social anxieties. Investigation of time-use patterns two decades ago suggests these worries may not be misplaced. In comparison to 1981, today's children spend more hours in school, and they spend more time on homework. They spend a lot less time visiting others and having household conversations. And their passive leisure time has fallen.

TABLE 1. Weekly Time Children Spend in Various Activities, 1981–1997
(in hours and minutes)

	Ages 3–5		Ages 6–8		Ages 9–12		All Ages	
	1981	1997	1981	1997	1981	1997	1981	1997
Household work	2:09	2:20	2:49	2:07	5:18	3:42	3:46	2:49
Shopping	2:35	3:44	0:59	2:38	1:57	2:24	1:52	2:53
Personal care	6:18	8:32	6:13	7:53	6:21	7:53	6:18	8:05
Eating	9:43	9:24	9:08	8:05	8:13	7:23	8:52	8:13
Sleeping	77:19	76:11	70:04	70:49	65:36	67:24	70:01	71:07
School	14:30	12:05	27:52	32:46	29:02	34:03	24:45	26:48
Studying	0:25	0:36	0:52	2:08	3:22	3:41	1:53	2:16
Visiting	2:58	3:04	3:40	2:48	3:48	2:40	3:32	2:50
Sports	1:31	4:08	6:01	5:13	4:51	6:33	4:15	5:25
Outdoors	0:13	0:37	0:28	0:30	0:46	0:36	0:32	0:35
Art activities	0:28	1:12	0:21	0:45	0:22	0:54	0:23	0:57
Playing	25:50	17:21	14:58	11:10	7:24	8:54	14:30	12:12
Television	15:14	13:52	15:55	12:54	20:01	13:36	17:35	13:29
Reading	0:29	1:24	0:59	1:09	1:03	1:14	0:53	1:16
Household conversations	0:37	0:48	1:07	0:30	0:53	0:27	0:53	0:35
Other passive leisure	2:59	2:35	1:58	1:33	3:24	2:19	2:53	2:11
Day care	0:10	7:30	0:12	1:33	0:18	0:24	0:14	2:57

Source: Hofferth and Sandberg (2001b, Table 2).

They also have somewhat less free time. These trends may help to explain why there are now stress management workshops for kindergartners and why marketing studies report that one of the major problems articulated by kids today is that they want less pressure, less overload, and more time to relax.

Contemporary children also do far more shopping. In 1997, the average child aged six to twelve spent more than two and a half hours a week shopping, a full hour more than in 1981. Children are frequent visitors to the grocery store and the pharmacy. They run errands to the dry cleaners and accompany parents to the mall. They spent as much time shopping as visiting, twice as much time shopping as reading or going to church, and five times as much as playing outdoors. They spent half as much time shopping as playing sports. More children go shopping each week (52 percent) than read (42 percent), go to church (26 percent), participate in youth groups (25 percent), play outdoors (17 percent), or spend time in household conversation (32 percent).

POSTMODERN CHILDHOOD: THE ELECTRONIC GENERATION

The change that has attracted most attention is kids' heavy involvement with electronic media, prompting some to posit a new, postmodern childhood, driven by television, Internet, video games, movies, and videos. To see the magnitude of these changes, we need to move beyond the diary data, which focus mainly on television, to more detailed surveys of media use.

One such study is the Kaiser Family Foundation's 1999 *Kids & Media @ the Millennium*, a high-quality, large-scale survey that combined a time diary with questions about yesterday's media viewing. It found that daily television viewing for two to eighteen year olds was two hours and forty-six minutes, plus an additional twenty-eight minutes watching videotapes. Viewing is most intense at ages eight to thirteen, when television takes up three hours and thirty-seven minutes a day, plus an additional twenty-nine minutes with videotapes. That's nearly thirty hours per week. The averages conceal wide variations, because there is a substantial group of very heavy watchers: 27.5 percent of kids aged eight to thirteen report more than five hours a day of TV viewing.

These estimates accord with most surveys of media use, including Nielsen's, but are much higher than traditional time diaries, which yield average viewing times of only thirteen to fourteen hours per week. One reason for the difference is that the diaries focus on primary activities, and television is often watched while doing other things. For example, in the Kaiser study, 42 percent of respondents reported that in their house, the television was on "most of the time." In 60 percent of households the television is on during meals.

When we combine all types of media—video games, computers, music, radio, and print—media time almost doubles. The average American child is estimated to spend five hours and twenty-nine minutes a day with media, for a weekly total of more than thirty-eight hours. About forty-five minutes a day is spent with print media. Forty-six percent of eight to thirteen year olds report total media exposure (which double counts media being used simultaneously) of more than seven hours per day. (See Tables 2 and 3.)

Television viewing varies significantly by race, income, and parental education, with the racial variations being most pronounced. For example, among eight to eighteen year olds, white children watch an average of two hours and forty-seven minutes a day, Hispanic children watch three hours and fifty minutes, and black children watch four hours and forty-one minutes of television a day. All three groups also watch an additional thirty minutes of video. In households with lower incomes, there is more television watching, especially among younger children. And in households where

TABLE 2. Average Daily Time Exposed to Each Medium (in hours and minutes)

	Ages 2–7	Ages 8–13
Total media exposure	4:17	8:08
Television	1:59	3:37
Taped TV shows	0:03	0:20
Videotapes (commercial)	0:26	0:29
Movies	0:02	0:26
Video games	0:08	0:32
Print media	0:45	0:50
Radio	0:24	0:35
CDs and tapes	0:21	0:47
Computer	0:07	0:32

Source: Kaiser Family Foundation (1999, Table 8-A).

TABLE 3. Amount of Daily Media Exposure and Media Use (in hours and minutes)

	Total exposure	Person hour
All ages	6:32	5:29
Ages 2–7	4:17	3:34
Ages 8–13	8:08	6:47

Note: Total exposure is the sum of the amount of time children spend with each type of media, which includes double-counting. Person hours adjusts exposure time to avoid double-counting and represents total daily time spent with media.
Source: Kaiser Family Foundation (1999, Table 7).

parents have lower educational levels, viewing times are higher, especially among younger children.

HOW CHILDREN ARE FARING

The conservative take on the trends I've described is that we've produced a generation of couch potato kids, scarfing down chips and soda, driving their parents crazy about those hundred-dollar sneakers. They're spoiled, unable to delay gratification, and headed for trouble. An alternate view stresses the enormous accomplishments of young people today, their volunteer spirit, resiliency, and tolerance. Setting aside these value judgments, what do we know about how children are doing? The past fifteen to twenty years have witnessed big changes in what kids have been eating, drinking, watching, and doing. How are they faring?

Let's start with child nutrition. Historically, poverty has been the major culprit in malnutrition and poor diet. And despite the nation's wealth, we have significant levels of poverty-induced hunger and malnutrition. In 1999, 16.9 percent of children were subject to what is called "food insecurity" and did not have adequate food to live active, healthy lives. Millions of American children still go hungry. But now there's a new problem with food. Diets have gotten far out of line with recommended nutritional standards. Most kids are eating the wrong foods, and too many of them. A 1997 study found that 50 percent of children's calories are from added fat and sugar, and the diets of 45 percent of children failed to meet any of the standards of the USDA's food pyramid. Children eat excessive quantities of advertised food products and not enough fruits, vegetables, and fiber. Among children aged six to twelve, only 12 percent have a healthy diet, and 13 percent eat a poor diet. The rest are in the "needs improvement" category.

As has been widely reported, rates of youth obesity are skyrocketing. Using the eighty-fifth percentile Body Mass Index as a cutoff, about 25 percent of American youth are now overweight or obese. By the stiffer ninety-fifth percentile criterion, 15 percent of children are obese. Since 1980, obesity rates for children have doubled, and those for teens have tripled. Weight-related diseases, such as type II diabetes and hypertension, are rising rapidly. Alongside the rise in obesity is excessive concern with thinness and body image and a host of eating disorders. Record numbers of girls are on diets, and they are beginning to diet at an increasingly young age.

Other forms of consumption are similarly troubling. Kids are smoking, drinking alcohol, and taking illegal drugs at alarming rates. As early as the eighth grade, more than 7 percent of kids are regular smokers, and that number nearly triples by twelfth grade. Despite the tobacco settlement, more than 2,000 children and teens still start smoking every day, a third of whom will die of smoking-related causes. In the eighth grade, 14 percent of kids report that they have taken five alcoholic drinks in a row within the past two weeks. By the twelfth grade, twice as many answer affirmatively. Half of all high schoolers report that they currently drink alcohol. And 12 percent of eighth graders report that they have used illegal drugs within the past thirty days. Among twelfth graders, that percentage rises to 25 percent.

Children and youth are increasingly suffering from emotional and mental health problems. A study published in the *Pediatrics Journal* found that rates of emotional and behavioral problems among children aged four to fifteen soared between 1979 and 1996. Rates of anxiety and depression went from negligible to 3.6 percent; attention deficit hyperactivity disorder rose from 1.4 percent to 9.2 percent. Estimates of major depression are as high as 8 percent for adolescents. In recent decades, suicide rates have climbed, and suicide is now the fourth leading cause of death among ten to fourteen year olds. Suicide rates are highest among racial minorities. In 2001, the annual survey of incoming college freshmen by the University of California at Los Angeles found that self-reports of physical and emotional health reached their worst level in the sixteen years the questions had been asked.

The large-scale MECA study (Methods for the Epidemiology of Child and Adolescent Mental Disorders) yields similar findings. It found that 13 percent of kids aged nine to seventeen suffer from anxiety, 6.2 percent have mood disorders, 10.3 percent have disruptive disorders, and 2 percent suffer from substance abuse. Taken together, about 21 percent of this age group had a "diagnosable mental or addictive disorder with at least minimum impairment." Eleven percent had a significant functional impairment, and 5 percent were reported to have an extreme functional impairment. (See Table 4.)

Conclusions from the 1997 Child Development Supplement, which included children aged three to twelve, are also cause for concern. Although parents reported that their children were generally happy and healthy, one in five said that they were fearful or anxious, unhappy, sad, depressed, or withdrawn. Two in five reported that their children were impulsive, disobedient, or moody. All told, nearly 50 percent had at least one of these problems. This survey also asked about the quality of relationships between children and parents. It found that only 59 percent of parents reported that their relationships with their school-aged children are "extremely or very close," and only 57 percent reported engaging in very warm behaviors with their child several times a week. (Warm behaviors are defined as hugging, joking, playing, and telling them they love them.)

Taken together, these findings are not comforting. They show that American children are worse off today than they were ten or twenty years ago. This conclusion is especially notable when we consider that during the past fifteen years, child poverty fell substantially, from a high of 22 percent in the late 1980s to its current rate of 16 percent. The decline in child poverty should have led to improvements in measures of distress, because child poverty is correlated with adverse physical and psychological

TABLE 4. Youth Mental and Addictive Disorders Children and Adolescents Age 9–17

	Percentage of Youth, Ages 9–17
Anxiety disorders	13.0
Mood disorders	6.2
Disruptive disorders	10.3
Substance use disorders	2.0
Any disorder	20.9

Source: Data cited in U.S. Office of the Surgeon General (1999, Table 3-1).

health outcomes. The deterioration of the well-being indicators suggests that some powerful negative factors are undermining children's well-being.

One of them may be the upsurge in materialist values. Children's top aspiration now is to be rich, a more appealing prospect to them than being a great athlete, or a celebrity, or being really smart, the goals of earlier eras. Forty-four percent of kids in fourth through eighth grades now report that they daydream "a lot" about being rich. And nearly two-thirds of parents report that "my child defines his or her self-worth in terms of the things they own and wear more than I did when I was that age."

Psychologists have found that espousing these kinds of materialist values undermines well-being, leading people to be more depressed, anxious, less vital, and in worse physical health. Among youth, those who are more materialistic are more likely to engage in risky behaviors. In the light of these findings, the survey data are worrisome. One of the few large national surveys of children's materialism found that more than a third of all children aged nine to fourteen would rather spend time buying things than doing almost anything else, more than a third "really like kids that have very special games or clothes," more than half agree that "when you grow up, the more money you have, the happier you are," and 62 percent say that "the only kind of job I want when I grow up is one that gets me a lot of money." To understand how and why American children got this way, it's time to take a stroll down Madison Avenue.[2]

STUDY QUESTIONS

1. What kinds of annual conferences are held for advertisers who hope to influence children? How do the advertisers hope children will influence their parents?

2. What does the redefining of childhood in materialistic terms mean for the natural **environment**? Overconsumption of natural resources is central to the envi-

---

[2] Street in New York City famed as a location for advertising agencies.

ronmental crisis of today. How will a generation of children raised in the consumer **culture** Schor describes affect the natural environment?

3. This article was written in 2002. Many of the brands, fads, and consumer trends have changed. Can you update this article? What products, clothing, movies, video games, and experiences are popular with children today? List examples for toddlers, tweens, and high schoolers. Do you feel nostalgic toward any of the products or programs Schor mentions?

4. Watch a half hour of programming on one of the children's television networks that has advertisements (public television won't work here). Create a list of all the products or services advertised and take notes on how they were presented. After you've collected a half hour's worth of data, analyze your notes for trends or common themes. Also note the differences between products targeted at adults (e.g. cars) and products targeted at children.

JEFFREY REIMAN

The Sources of Crime

From *The Rich Get Richer and the Poor Get Prison*

The United States imprisons more people than any other **industrialized** country. We spend more on **criminal justice** and yet have, by far, the highest **crime** rate in the world. Why should this be the case? In his book *The Rich Get Richer and the Poor Get Prison*, Jeffrey Reiman argues that we as a **society** don't control crime well, we make excuses for our failure to reduce crime, and we ignore crime's true sources. The following excerpt from that book examines the known causes of crime and suggests what might be done—if only someone will do it!

---

* * *

ON JULY 23, 1965, PRESIDENT LYNDON JOHNSON SIGNED AN EXECU-
tive order establishing the President's Commission on Law Enforcement and Administration of Justice to investigate the causes and nature of crime, to collect existing
knowledge about our criminal justice system, and to make recommendations about
how that system might better meet "the challenge of crime in a free society." The commission presented its report to the president early in 1967, thick with data and recommendations. Because we are a nation higher on commissions than on commitments, it
should come as no surprise that, for all the light cast on the crime problem by the
President's Commission, little heat has been generated and—aside from the massive imprisonment binge—virtually no profound changes in criminal justice policy
have taken place in the 39 years since the report was issued.

During this period, however, more and more money has been poured into crime control, with bleak results. When the commission wrote, it estimated that more than $4 billion was being spent annually at the national, state, and local levels to pay for police, courts, and Correctional facilities in the fight against crime.[1] Since that time, the violent crime rate climbed from 200 per 100,000 in the population in 1965 to 465 in 2004, and the property crime rate went from 2,249 to 3,517 per 100,000.[2] The annual cost to the public of this brand of domestic tranquility was more than $167 billion by 2001, with 2.3 million persons employed by the criminal justice system. Taking inflation into account, this represents real growth of more than 600 percent in criminal justice spending since 1965, and 165 percent since 1982.[3] And this doesn't even count the more than $100 billion spent each year on private security.[4] Dollar for dollar, crime control is hardly an impressive investment—that is, if you think you are investing in crime reduction.

Multiplying almost as fast as crime and anticrime dollars are excuses for our failure to reduce crime significantly in the face of increased expenditure, personnel, research, and knowledge.

* * *

KNOWN SOURCES OF CRIME

There are many things that we do know about the sources of crime. Note that I have said *sources* rather than *causes* because the kind of knowledge we have is far from the precise knowledge that a physicist has about how some event *causes* another. We know that poverty, slums, and unemployment are *sources* of street crime. We know that they breed alienation from social institutions, and that they reduce the likely rewards of going straight. But, we do not fully understand how they *cause* crime, because we know as well that many, if not most, poor, unemployed slum dwellers do not engage in street crime. Yet, to say that this means we do not know that poverty and the other conditions discussed below are sources of violent crime is like saying that we do not know that a bullet in the head is deadly because some people survive or because we do not fully understand the physiological process that links the wound with the termination of life.

Poverty

Those youngsters who figure so prominently in arrest statistics are not drawn equally from all economic strata. Although there is much reported and even more unreported crime among middle-class youngsters, the street crime attributed to this age group that makes our city streets a perpetual war zone is largely the work of poor inner-city youth. This is the group at the lowest end of the economic spectrum. This is a group among whom unemployment hovers around 25 percent, with *under*employment (the percentage of persons either jobless or with part-time, low-wage jobs) still higher. This is a group with no realistic chance (for any but a rare individual) to enter college or amass sufficient capital (legally) to start a business or to get into the high-wage, skilled job markets. We know that poverty is a *source* of crime, and yet we do virtually nothing to improve the life chances of the vast majority of the inner-city poor. They are as poor as ever and are facing cuts in welfare and other services.

That poverty is a source of crime is not refuted by the large and growing amount of white-collar crime that I shall document later. In fact, poverty contributes to crime by creating need, while, at the other end of the spectrum, wealth can contribute to crime by unleashing greed. Some criminologists have argued that economic inequality itself worsens crimes of the poor and of the well-off by increasing the opportunities for the well-off and increasing the humiliation of the poor.[5] And inequality has worsened in recent years.

The gap between rich and poor worsened during the 1980s and 1990s. In 1970, the poorest fifth of the nation's families received 5.5 percent of the aggregate income, and the richest fifth received 41.6 percent. In 1980, the share of the poorest fifth was 5.3 percent of aggregate income, and that of the richest fifth was 41.1 percent. By 2004, the share of the poorest fifth had declined to 3.4 percent, while that of the richest fifth had risen to 50.1 percent. In the period from 1980 to 2002, the share of the top 5 percent rose from 14.6 to 20.8 percent. By 2004, the number of poor Americans was 37 million (about 1 in 8 Americans), up from 30.1 million in 1990, and from 25.2 million in 1980.[6] And, due to cuts in welfare,

> from 1995 to 1997, despite continued economic growth, the average incomes of the poorest 20 percent of female-headed households fell . . . an average of $580 per family. Among the poorest 10 percent of female-headed families with children, income fell an average of $810 between 1995 and 1997.[7]

Moreover, these developments were the predictable outcome of the Reagan administration's strategy of fighting inflation by cutting services to the poor while reducing the taxes of the wealthy. In September 1982, a group of 34 prominent economists sharply criticized Reagan's economic policy as extremely regressive in its impact on our society, redistributing wealth and power from the middle class and the poor to the rich, and shifting more of the tax burden away from business and onto low- and middle-income consumers.[8] In that same month, a study released by the Urban Institute concluded that "the Reagan administration's policies are not only aiding upper-income families at the expense of the working poor, but also are widening the gulf between affluent and poorer regions of the country."[9] The study maintained that the combined effect of the administration's tax and social service spending cuts was "to penalize working families near the poverty line who receive some federal benefits . . . creating 'major work disincentives.'"

Edward Wolff writes that the

equalizing trends of the 1930s–1970s reversed sharply in the 1980s. The gap between the haves and have-nots is greater now than at any time since 1929. The sharp increase in inequality since the late 1970s has made wealth distribution in the United States more unequal than in what used to be perceived as the class-ridden societies of northwestern Europe.[10]

By 2004, 17 percent of American children were living in poverty, with 33 percent of black children and 28 percent of Latino children living in families below the poverty level, compared with 10 percent of white children.[11]

The tax cuts recently enacted by President George W. Bush had much the same effect because 25 percent of the benefits went to those with incomes in the top 1 percent, and nearly 50 percent of the benefits went to those with incomes in the top 10 percent. Using data from the Congressional Budget Office (CBO), the nonpartisan Center on Budget and Policy Priorities calculated that "the top one percent of households (whose incomes average nearly $1.2 million) will receive an average tax cut of approximately $40,990 in 2004"—a figure "more than 40 times the average tax break for those in the middle fifth of the income distribution." They further note that between 1979 and 2001,

> the average after-tax income of the top one percent of households rose by a stunning $409,000, or 139 percent, after adjusting for inflation. This dwarfed the $6,300, or 17 percent, average increase among the middle fifth of the population, over this 22-year period, and the $1,100, or 8 percent, increase among the bottom fifth of the population.[12]

Furthermore, as unemployment has gone up and down over the past decades, unemployment at the bottom of society remains strikingly worse than the national average. For example, over the past 35 years, black unemployment has remained slightly more than twice the rate of white unemployment. In 1967, when 3.4 percent of white workers were unemployed, 7.4 percent of black workers were jobless. By 2000, when overall unemployment was about 4 percent, 3.5 percent of white workers were unemployed and 7.6 percent of blacks were. Among those in the crime-prone ages of 16 to 19, 11.4 percent of white youngsters and 24.7 percent (almost one in every four) black youngsters were jobless.[13] The pattern held true for the economic slump starting in 2002, and for all of 2003—when the overall unemployment rate was 6 percent—the white jobless rate was 5.2 percent and the black rate was almost 11 percent.[14]

In his important book, *A Theory of Justice,* John Rawls—the late Harvard moral and political philosopher called by some the John Stuart Mill of the twentieth century—argued for a principle of economic justice called the *difference principle.*[15] According to this principle, economic inequalities are unjust unless they work to maximize the share of the worst-off group in society, say, by providing incentives that increase production overall.[16] This implies that the inequalities are only just if reducing them would further reduce the share of the worst-off group. This is as egalitarian as a distributive principle can be without simply insisting on equal shares for everyone.

In a later work, *Justice as Fairness: A Restatement*, Rawls compares two models of society, "property-owning democracy" and "welfare-state capitalism."[17] A property-owning democracy is a capitalist society governed by the difference principle along with other principles that guarantee equal liberty, in both form and substance, and fair equality of opportunity. Welfare-state capitalism is a capitalist society where equal liberties are guaranteed formally in the law, but little is done to guarantee their substance, that is, to make sure that people have adequate means to exercise those liberties. Moreover, in welfare-state capitalism, economic and other inequalities are limited only by the existence of a social safety net, providing for the basic needs of those at the bottom of society.

Rawls characterizes the difference principle as a principle of reciprocity. Its requirement that inequalities work to the maximum advantage of the worst off means that the greater than equal economic benefits for the better off are matched by increased benefits for those at the bottom of society. Moreover, the principle guaranteeing the substance of equal liberties requires that, where necessary, the government intervene to make sure that economic inequalities are not reducing the equal liberties of the poor to empty legal forms, or giving the rich disproportionate influence on political decisions. Rawls contends that citizens of a property-owning democracy, even the poorest citizens, will feel allegiance to the society because they will see that, though others are doing better, those others are only doing better on terms that also improve the shares of those who are less well off. By contrast, writes Rawls, in a capitalist welfare state, "there may develop a discouraged and depressed underclass many of whose members are chronically dependent on welfare. This underclass feels left out and does not participate in the public political culture."[18]

Can there be any doubt that Rawls is describing the United States here? Is there any wonder why a society that does no more than provide for the most basic needs of its poorest members (when it even does that much!)[19] also finds that those individuals commit crimes? Rawls's analysis shows us that economic inequality may result in crime, not simply from need, but by producing an impoverished class that feels "left out" of society and thus does not develop allegiance to its major institutions.

Writes Todd Clear, professor of criminal justice at Rutgers University, "Let's start investing in things that really reduce crime: good schools, jobs and a future for young parents and their children."[20] Why don't we?

Prison

We know that prison produces more criminals than it cures. We know that more than 70 percent of the inmates in the nation's prisons or jails are not there for the first time. A study from the Bureau of Justice Statistics indicates that, of inmates released in 1994, 67.5 percent were rearrested within three years, "almost exclusively for a felony or serious misdemeanor."[21] We know that prison inmates are denied autonomy and privacy and are subjected to indignities and acts of violence as regular features of their confinement, all of which is heightened by overcrowding. As of the last day of 2004, 24 state prison systems were operating above the most generous measure of their reported capacity; the federal prison system was operating at 40 percent above capacity.[22] A study of prisons in four Midwestern states found that about one-fifth of male inmates reported "a pressured or forced sex incident while incarcerated. About nine percent of male inmates reported that they had been raped."[23]

The predictable result, as delineated by Robert Johnson and Hans Toch in *The Pains of Imprisonment*, "is that the prison's survivors become tougher, more pugnacious, and less able to feel for themselves and others, while its nonsurvivors become weaker, more susceptible, and less able to control their lives."[24] Prisoners are thus bereft of both training and capacity to handle daily problems in competent and socially constructive ways, inside or outside of prison. The organization Stop Prison Rape reports, "Upon release, male prisoner rape survivors may bring with them emotional scars and learned violent behavior that continue the cycle of harm. Feelings of rage can be suppressed until release, when survivors may engage in violent, antisocial behavior."[25] According to a Human Rights Watch report entitled "No Escape: Male Rape in U.S. Prisons," "[T]he only way to avoid the repetition of sexual abuse, many prisoners assert, is to strike back violently." The report quotes a victim of prison rape saying, "People start to treat you right, once you become deadly."[26] In this way, prison makes inmates a greater harm to society than they were when they entered.

Once on the outside, burdened with the stigma of a prison record and rarely trained in a marketable skill, they find few opportunities for noncriminal employment open to them. Nor does this affect all groups in America alike. According to Professor Michael Tonry, author of *Malign Neglect: Race, Crime and Punishment in America*, "By affecting so many young black men, American criminal laws have further undermined the black family and made it harder for black men to get an education and find good jobs." A recent study by the Sentencing Project indicates that the enormous number of African American men who have been convicted of felonies, and therefore deprived of their right to vote, is "having a profound [negative!] impact on the black community's ability to participate in the political process."[27]

What's more, because so much of the recent increase in imprisonment has been of inner-city black men who were involved in families and who had at least part-time legitimate employment at the time of their arrest and incarceration, social scientists are beginning to study the ways in which massive imprisonment is undermining the family and other community institutions, depriving children of male role models, and depriving women of potential husbands and support. Several criminologists have found limited evidence suggesting that massive imprisonment may weaken inner-city institutions of informal social control *and thus lead to more crime in the long run*. Others argue that high levels of incarceration can weaken the stigma and thus the deterrent value of punishment in prison, and massive incarceration can strengthen ties between prison gangs and offenders on the street.[28]

Can we honestly act as if we do not know that our prison system (including our failure to ensure a meaningful postrelease noncriminal alternative for the ex-con) is a source of crime? Should we really pretend, then, that we do not *know* why ex-cons turn to crime? Recidivism does not happen because ex-cons miss their alma mater. In fact, if prisons are supposed to deter people from crime, one would expect that ex-prisoners would be the most deterred, because the deprivations of prison are more real to them than to the rest of us. Recidivism is thus a doubly poignant testimony to the job that prison does in preparing its graduates for crime, yet we do little to change the nature of prisons or to provide real services to ex-convicts.

In his 2004 State of the Union Address, President Bush seemed to indicate that he understood at least a small part of the recidivism problem when he discussed the 600,000 inmates released back into society each year. He said, "We know from long experience that if they can't find work, or a home, or help, they are much more likely to commit more crimes and return to prison." His proposed Prisoner Re-entry Initiative would expand job training and placement, and help with transitional housing and mentoring. But the $300 million he proposed to spend over four years, divided into the 2,400,000 inmates who would be released over that period, amounts to about $125 per inmate. That is hardly enough to ensure that America is "the land of the second chance—and when the gates of the prison open, the path ahead should lead to a better life."[29] (Two years later, the Republican-led U.S. Congress has not scheduled hearings on this bill.)

Guns

President Bush noted in 2001, "In America, a teenager today is more likely to die from a gunshot than from all natural causes of death combined."[30] Our firearm death rate is higher by far than that of any other modern nation. And, because the fatality rate for robberies using a gun is three times higher than for robberies with knives and ten times higher than for robberies with other weapons, countries like Italy and Australia that have robbery rates comparable to the United States' have far fewer robberies that end up as homicides.[31]

Speaking about the extraordinary spate of deadly violence that we had in the late 1980s and early 1990s, Garen Wintemute puts it bluntly: "the entire increase in homicide in the United States through 1993 was attributable to firearm homicide."[32] Increasingly, this was due to highly lethal semiautomatic pistols (during the same period, the percentage of homicides with regular revolvers declined significantly). Hospitals reported an increase in gunshot wounds per victim, and in the size of bullets removed. This phenomenon is closely linked to trends in handgun production. Starting in the late 1980s, American gun manufacturers started producing "high capacity, medium-caliber semiautomatic pistols that were also very inexpensive." Almost all were produced "by a small group of manufacturers in Southern California."[33]

Gary Kleck estimates that, by 1990, the civilian stock of guns in the United States had passed the 200 million mark. This estimate is corroborated by a 1993 report from the Bureau of Alcohol, Tobacco, and Firearms, which estimated 200 million guns, about 1 percent of which were assault rifles. They also note that the "number of large caliber pistols produced annually increased substantially after 1986."[34] A more recent review by the nonpartisan National Research Council suggests that by 1999, the civilian gun stock climbed to 258 million. The United States has 925 guns for every 1,000 people, with about 43 percent of households owning at least one.[35]

The President's Crime Commission reported that, in 1965, "5,600 murders, 34,700 aggravated assaults and the vast majority of the 68,400 armed robberies were committed by means of firearms. All but 10 of 278 law enforcement officers murdered during the period 1960–65 were killed with firearms." The commission concluded almost 40 years ago that

> more than one-half of all willful homicides and armed robberies, and almost one-fifth of all aggravated assaults, involve use of firearms. As long as there is no effective gun-control legislation, violent crimes and the injuries they inflict will be harder to reduce than they might otherwise be.[36]

The situation has worsened since the commission's warning. The FBI states, "In 1975, 66 percent of murders of persons (aged 15 to 19) were attributable to guns, while in 1992 the figure rose to 85 percent. This increase supports the theory that today's high-school-aged youths are exposed to an environment that includes guns."[37] The Office of Juvenile Justice reports, "By 1997, the homicide rate for 15- to 24-year-olds was 15.2 per 100,000, which is higher than the combined total homicide rate of eleven industrialized nations," and goes on to point out, "Firearms were the weapons of choice in nearly two-thirds of all murders."[38]

Furthermore, guns kill and maim outside of crime as well. "Every 14 minutes someone in America dies from a gunshot wound. Slightly more than half of those deaths are suicides, about 44 percent are homicides and 4 percent are unintentional shootings."[39] The Centers for Disease Control report that in 1997, "32,436 deaths resulted from firearm-related injuries, making such injuries the second leading cause of injury mortality in the United States after motor-vehicle-related incidents," and, further, that "an estimated 64,207 persons sustained nonfatal firearm-related injuries."[40] Guns also take a grave and worsening toll among our children. According to a report from the Children's Defense Fund, nearly 50,000 children were killed by guns between 1979 and 1991.[41]

In the face of facts like these—indeed, in the face of his own nearly fatal shooting by a would-be assassin—President Reagan refused to support any legislative attempts to control the sale of handguns.[42] His successor, President George H. W. Bush, followed suit.[43] On Thanksgiving Day 1993, Bush's successor, Bill Clinton, signed into law the so-called Brady Bill, which goes only so far as imposing a five-day waiting period for gun purchases to enable checks to see whether would-be gun purchasers have criminal records. The Brady Law leaves it to the states to enforce the waiting period and to get their police to make a "reasonable effort" to conduct the background checks. However, the bill provides no sanctions for states that do not comply, and it leaves it effectively up to the states to provide funding for the checks and to determine what is a "reasonable effort."[44] From 1994, when the Brady Law went into effect, until 2003, over 1.1 million applications for firearms have been rejected, but as Blumstein notes, "it is not known how many of those customers eventually bought guns from an unregulated source."[45] Moreover, while the Brady Law prohibits sales of guns to individuals with prior felony convictions, the sad fact is that, as different studies show, between half and three-quarters of those arrested for crimes involving weapons had *no prior felony conviction.*[46]

Can we believe that our leaders sincerely want to cut down on violent crime and the injuries it produces when they oppose even as much as *registering* guns or *licensing* gun owners, much less actually restricting the sale and movement of guns as a matter of national policy? Can we really believe that if guns were less readily available, violent criminals would simply switch to other weapons to commit the same number of crimes and do the same amount of damage? Is there a weapon other than the handgun that works as quickly, that allows its user so safe a distance, or that makes the criminal's physical strength (or speed or courage, for that matter) irrelevant? Could a bank robber hold a row of tellers at bay with a switchblade? Studies indicate that, if gun users switched to the next deadliest weapon—the knife—and attempted the same number of crimes, we could still expect *two-thirds fewer fatalities* because the fatality rate of the knife is roughly one-third that of the gun. In other words, even if guns were eliminated and the number of crimes held steady, we could expect to save as many as two out of every three persons who are now the victims of firearm homicide.

Drugs

Finally, the United States has an enormous drug abuse and addiction problem. There is considerable evidence, however, that our attempts to cure it are worse than the disease itself. Consider first heroin. Some people think this drug is out of fashion and no longer widely used. Far from it! Its use is widespread and persistent. The number of heroin users is hard to estimate because we only know about the ones who get caught and because there is a large but unknown number of individuals who (contrary to popular mythology) shoot up occasionally without becoming addicts, a practice known as "chipping." In his book, *The Heroin Solution*, Arnold Trebach suggests that this number may be as high as 3.5 million.[47] For 1999, the Office of National Drug Control Policy estimated about 1 million chronic heroin users and another 140,000 to 600,000 occasional users. The number of chronic users decreased earlier in the 1990s, "Perhaps due to the AIDS epidemic and increased incarceration, but that decrease had largely abated by the latter part of the decade, perhaps because new users were attracted by the availability of high-quality low-cost heroin."[48]

As shocking as these numbers may be, it must be at least as shocking to discover that there is little evidence proving that heroin is a *dangerous* drug. James Q. Wilson, a defender of the prohibition of heroin and other drugs, admits that "there are apparently no specific pathologies—serious illnesses or physiological deterioration—that are known to result from heroin use per se."[49] On the basis of available scientific evidence, there is every reason to suspect that we do our bodies more damage, more *irreversible* damage, by smoking cigarettes and drinking liquor than by using heroin. Most of the physical damage associated with heroin use is probably attributable to the trauma of withdrawal, a product not so much of heroin as of its occasional unobtainability.

It remains the case that most drug arrests are for marijuana use or possession, and that marijuana is a relatively safe drug.[50] The 1988 surgeon general's report lists tobacco as a more dangerous drug than marijuana.[51] According to the findings and conclusions of Francis Young, administrative law judge for the Drug Enforcement Administration, there are no documented marijuana user fatalities ("despite [its 5,000-year-]long history of use and the extraordinarily high numbers of social smokers, there are simply no credible medical reports to suggest that consuming marijuana has caused a single death"!), and no amount of marijuana that a person could possibly eat or smoke would constitute a lethal dose. By contrast, aspirin overdoses cause hundreds of deaths a year.[52]

Regarding the illicit drugs that can cause death from overdose, the dangers have been blown wildly out of proportion. Trebach points out that, although federal authorities documented 2,177 deaths from the most popular illicit drugs in 1985, between 400,000 and 500,000 people died from alcohol and tobacco during that same year. He adds that 59 children aged 17 and under died from drug overdoses in 1987, while "408 American children (from infants through the age of 14) were murdered by their parents in 1983"![53]

It might be said that the evil of drugs such as heroin is that they are *addicting*, because this is a bad thing even if the addicting substance is not itself harmful. It is hard to deny that the image of a person enslaved to a chemical is ugly and repugnant to our sense that the dignity of human beings lies in their capacity to control their destinies. More questionable, however, is whether this is, in the case of adults, anybody's business but their own. Even so, suppose we agree that addiction is an evil worthy of prevention. Doesn't that make us hypocrites? What about all our other addictions? What about cigarette smoking, which, unlike heroin, contributes to cancer and heart disease? Nicotine's addictiveness—according to former Surgeon General C. Everett Koop—is similar to that of heroin, and *more addicting than cocaine,* more likely to addict the new user, and more difficult to quit once addicted.[54] What about the roughly

15 million alcoholics in the nation working their way through their livers and into their graves? What about the people who cannot get started without a caffeine fix in the morning and those who, once started, cannot slow down without their alcohol fix in the evening? What of the folks who can't face daily life without their Prozac? Are they not all addicts?[55]

Suffice it to say, then, at the very least, our attitudes about heroin are inconsistent and irrational, and there is reason to believe they are outrageous and hypocritical. Even if this were not so, even if we could be much more certain that heroin addiction is a disease worth preventing, the fact would remain that the "cure" we have chosen is worse than the disease. We *know* that treating the possession of heroin as a criminal offense produces more crime than it prevents.

Alfred Blumstein provides a useful categorization of the relationship between drugs and crime:

- *Pharmacological/psychological consequences:* The chemical properties of the drug directly cause criminal activity.
- *Economic/compulsive crimes:* Drug users commit crimes to get money to support their habit.
- *Systemic crime:* Crime, violence, and corruption are committed as part of the regular means of doing business in the drug industry because there is no regulation and because formal dispute-resolution mechanisms are unavailable.[56]

About the pharmacological consequences of drugs, says Blumstein, the drug "that has the strongest pharmacological effect is alcohol.... Heroin is a downer, so heroin doesn't do much. And there hasn't been shown to be much pharmacological effect of the other serious drugs on crime, not anything comparable to that of alcohol, which has been shown to be a strong stimulator of violence."[57] PCP tends to be one of the only other drugs to have a pharmacological link to violence. High doses of cocaine and methamphetamine can lead to some psychoses that include paranoia and delusion, which can lead to violence. But most of the violence associated with drugs falls under the second and third of Blumstein's categories. As for systemic crime, we have already seen the link between the crack trade and the murder epidemic of the late 1980s and early 1990s. Both systemic crimes and the economic/compulsive crimes that are engaged in by drug users to support their habits are due to the fact that drugs are so costly, and that is due to the fact that the drugs are illegal.

Prior to 1914, when anyone could go into a drugstore and purchase heroin and other opiates the way we buy aspirin today, hundreds of thousands of upstanding, law-abiding citizens were hooked.[58] Opiate addiction is not in itself a *cause* of crime. If anything, it is a pacifier.[59] There is, writes Trebach, "nothing in the pharmacology, or physical and psychological impact, of the drug that would propel a user to crime."[60] Nor is there anything about heroin itself that makes it extremely costly. The heroin for which an addict pays $100 or more a day could be produced legally at a cost of a few cents for a day's supply. However, once sale or possession of heroin is made a serious criminal offense, a number of consequences follow. First, the prices go up because those who supply it face grave penalties, and those who want it want it bad. Second, because the supply (and the quality) of the drug fluctuates, depending on how vigorously the agents of the law try to prevent it, the addict's life is continuously unstable. Addicts live in constant uncertainty about the next fix and must devote much of their wit and energy to getting it and to getting enough money to pay for it. They do not, then, fit easily into the routines of a nine-to-five job, even if they could get one that would pay enough to support their habits. Finally, all the difficulties of securing the drug add up to an incentive to be not merely a user of heroin but a dealer as well, because this both earns money and makes one's own supply more certain. Addicts thus have an incentive to find and encourage new addicts, which they would not have if heroin were legally and cheaply available. If we add to this the fact that heroin addiction has remained widespread, and possibly even increased in spite of all our law enforcement efforts, can we doubt that the cure is worse than the disease? Can we doubt that the cure is a *source* of crime?

Says former Washington, D.C., Police Chief Maurice Turner,

> If you see an addict going through withdrawal, he's in some kind of damn pain.... When they get pretty well strung out, they have about a $100- to $120-a-day habit. When they get that type of habit, they're going to have to steal approximately six times that much [because fences don't pay list price].[61]

Professor Blumstein agrees that "you need money to buy drugs, so the higher the price of the drug, the greater the incentive to commit the crime."[62] The result is a recipe for large-scale and continual robbery and burglary, which would not exist if the drug were available legally. A recent study by Anglin and Speckart of the relationship between narcotics use and crime concludes that there is "strong evidence that there is a strong causal relationship, at least in the United States, between addiction to narcotics and property crime levels."[63]

Do a little arithmetic. Suppose that there are half a million addicts with $100-a-day habits. And let's make some conservative assumptions about these addicts. Suppose that they fill their habits only 250 days a year (sometimes they're in jail or in the hospital). Suppose that they have to steal for half their drug needs, and that they must steal three times the dollar value of what they need because they must convert their booty into cash through a fence. (These conservative assumptions are similar to those made in a report of the U.S. Department of Health, Education, and Welfare, entitled *Social Cost of Drug Abuse,* estimating the amount of theft in which heroin addicts had to engage to support their habits in 1974.)[64] If you've done your arithmetic, you have seen that our half-million addicts need to steal $18,750,000,000 a year to support their habits. This is more than the $16.1 billion that the FBI estimates as the loss due to property crimes during 2004,[65] and it doesn't even take into consideration theft by those addicted to other drugs, such as crack cocaine.

The Bureau of Justice Statistics reports that, in 1997, roughly one of every six prisoners—19 percent of state inmates, 15 percent of federal inmates—said that they had committed their current offense in order to get money for drugs.[66] Because heroin doesn't produce crime through its pharmacological effects, and because it is so costly only because it's illegal, it is not the "disease" of heroin addiction but its "cure" that leads to property crime. *It is our steadfast refusal to provide heroin through legal sources that, for a significant number of the approximately 1 million heroin addicts, translates a physical need for a drug into a physical need to steal billions of dollars worth of property a year.*

Against this conclusion, it is sometimes countered that studies show that a large proportion of criminal heroin addicts were criminals before they were addicts. Such studies would only refute the claim that the illegality of heroin is a source of crime if the claim was that heroin addiction turns otherwise law-abiding citizens into thieves. Rather, the claim is that the illegality of heroin (and, thus, its very high price) places addicts in situations in which they *must* engage in theft, continually and at a high level, to keep a step ahead of the pains of withdrawal. Anglin and Speckart affirm that "while involvement in property crime activities generally precedes the addiction career, after addiction occurs the highly elevated property crime levels demonstrated by addicts appear to be regulated by similarly high narcotics use levels."[67] Thus, even for addicts who already were criminals, heroin addiction increases the amount they need to steal and works to make them virtually immune to attempts to wean them from a life of crime. Consequently, even if all heroin addicts were criminals before they were addicts, the illegality of heroin would still be a source of crime because of the increased pressure it places on the addict to steal a lot and to steal often. Much the same reasoning applies to other illegal addictive drugs.

Recently, attention has shifted from heroin to "crack," a highly addictive derivative of cocaine. The Office of National Drug Control Policy (ONDCP) reports that there were 2.8 million hard-core cocaine users in 1999.[68] Having learned nothing from our experience with heroin, we have applied to cocaine and crack the same policy that failed with heroin, with predictable results. A report from the ONDCP indicates that in 2000, Americans spent $64 billion on these illegal drugs: "$36 billion on cocaine, $10 billion on heroin, $5.4 billion on methamphetamine, $11 billion on marijuana, and $2.4 billion on other substances."[69] Because the price per pure gram of cocaine and of heroin has generally gone down between 1980 and the present, we can only conclude that, for all the hoopla of the war on drugs, not to mention the enormous increase in the number of persons sent to prison for drug offenses, there is a plentiful supply and these drugs remain popular.

According to the ONDCP, during the decade of the 1990s, "cocaine users consumed somewhere between 270 and 450 metric tons of pure cocaine each year," while "heroin users consumed 14 metric tons at the beginning and end of the decade."[70] According to an earlier United Nations estimate, illicit drugs account for some $400 billion worldwide, nearly one-tenth of world trade in all products![71] The General Accounting Office reports that U.S. efforts to reduce cultivation of drug crops in

Bolivia and Colombia "have been almost entirely ineffective and the cultivation of drug crops has increased dramatically in both countries."[72] This caps a long history of failure, starting with President Richard Nixon's (successful) attempt to pressure Turkey into eradicating local cultivation of poppies (the source of opium and thus of heroin, an opium derivative) in 1971 and continuing with both Reagan's and Bush Sr.'s largely futile attempts to pressure foreign countries to reduce domestic production of narcotic substances. Even when such pressure works, it serves only to displace production elsewhere. And when the pressure lets up, production rebounds.

In spite of three U.S.-led international drug wars since 1971, worldwide illicit opium production rose from 990 tons in 1971 to 4,200 tons in 1989 and 4,500 tons in 2002. Andean coca leaf (the source of cocaine and thus of crack) production went from 319,200 metric tons in 1990 down to 294,400 in 2002, but UN estimates of total world cocaine manufacture increased from 774 metric tons in 1990 to 800 in 2002.[73] Likewise, attempts to use the U.S. Coast Guard and Navy to interdict cocaine coming into the United States by sea have failed to put a dent in the traffic. After all, America has over 88,000 miles of coastline.[74] *The Wall Street Journal* reports that a kilogram of cocaine that cost between $55,000 and $65,000 in 1981 cost between $20,000 and $40,000 in 1987.[75] The National Narcotics Intelligence Consumers' Committee reports cocaine prices as low as $10,500 per kilogram in 1994.[76] In a summary of these trends, a 2004 ONDCP report indicated "very sharp (roughly 70 percent) price declines during the 1980s through 1989" and "gradual declines during the 1990s," with occasional years of price increases. Prices continued declining through 2003, "reaching all-time lows that are roughly 12 to 21 percent below prices in 1999. Cumulatively, powder cocaine prices have declined by roughly 80 percent since 1981," and "purity-adjusted prices were at or near all-time lows in 2003."[77] All of this testifies to the general failure of our costly "war on drugs" to make these drugs harder to obtain—a conclusion endorsed by the conservative American Enterprise Institute in a 2005 book on drug policy.[78]

In 1988, the *National Law Journal* surveyed 181 chief prosecutors or their top drug deputies throughout the United States and reported that "nearly two-thirds of the country's top state and local prosecutors say they are having little to no impact in the fight against illegal narcotics."[79] The American Enterprise Institute study stated that "on the whole, then, there is now less reason than ever to believe that current policies are an efficient and effective response to the problem of illicit drugs."[80] This failing drug war cost federal, state, and local governments approximately $33 billion in 1999, up nearly $5 billion from 1994.[81] The National Drug Control Budget alone is $12.1 billion for fiscal year 2005.[82]

To that must be added the *nonfinancial* costs, such as increased violence among competing drug traffickers and increased corruption among law enforcement officials on the front line in the drug war. The year 1988 saw the nation's capital reach and overtake its annual homicide record, with all experts attributing the surge in murders to the struggle to capture the lucrative drug market.[83] *The New York Times* reports that "researchers say there are now more than 100 cases each year in state and Federal courts in which law enforcement officials are charged or implicated in drug corruption."[84] Says William Green, assistant commissioner for internal affairs at the U.S. Customs Service, "The money that's being offered by the drug dealers is so big it is just hard to visualize."[85] The Mollen Commission report on police corruption in New York City found "willful blindness" to corruption throughout the police department, resulting in networks of rogue officers who dealt in drugs and preyed on black and Hispanic neighborhoods.[86]

In sum, we have an antidrug policy that is failing at its own goals and succeeding only in adding to crime. First, there are the heroin and crack addicts, who must steal to support their habits. Then, there are the drug merchants who are offered fabulous financial incentives to provide illicit substances to a willing body of consumers. This in turn contributes to the high rate of inner-city murders and other violence as drug gangs battle for the enormous sums of money available. Next, there are the law enforcement officials who, after risking their lives for low salaries, are corrupted by nearly irresistible amounts of money. Finally, there are the otherwise law-abiding citizens who are made criminals because they use cocaine, a drug less harmful than tobacco, and those who are made criminals because they use marijuana, a drug that is safer than alcohol and less deadly than aspirin.

Much of the recent dramatic growth in our prison population (documented above) is the result of the hardening of drug enforcement policy starting in the Reagan years and continuing into the present: In 1968 there were 162,000 drug arrests nationwide, in 1977 there were 569,000, and in 1989 there were 1,150,000 drug arrests.[87] In 2004 there were more than 1.7 million drug arrests, and the Bureau of Justice Statistics reports that 55 percent of federal inmates were serving sentences for drug violations in 2003.[88] The absolute numbers are even more striking. In 2003, federal prisons held 86,972 drug offenders, compared to 30,470 in 1990.[89] On the state level, there were less than 20,000 drug offenders in state prisons in 1990, but by 2000, there were over 250,000.[90] Because numerous studies show that arrested drug dealers in inner-city neighborhoods are quickly replaced, it was apparent from the start that this policy would have little success in reducing the availability of illicit drugs.[91]

All this is occurring at a time when there is increasing evidence that what does work to reduce substance abuse is public education. Because this has succeeded in reducing alcohol and tobacco consumption and, in some cases, marijuana and cocaine consumption as well, it's time that we take the money we are wasting in the "war on drugs" and spend it on public education instead. Because that would be far less costly than the "war," this would leave over money to fight a more effective war against muggers and rapists rather than recreational drug users. Evidence from the 11 states that decriminalized marijuana possession in the 1970s suggests that decriminalization does not lead to increased use. And President Clinton's former surgeon general,

Joycelyn Elders, recommended that we study seriously the possibility of decriminalizing drugs as a means to reducing violence, noting that "other countries had decriminalized drug use and had reduced their crime rates without increasing the use of narcotics."[92] Baltimore Mayor Kurt Schmoke has called for consideration of decriminalization, and so has Jerry Wilson, former chief of police of Washington, D.C. (where 42 percent of murders were drug-related in 1990).[93] A draft of a report commissioned by the American Medical Association recommended legalization of marijuana and decriminalization of other illicit drugs. The report was shelved when some doctors "expressed outrage at its recommendation."[94] Some form of decriminalization of marijuana, heroin, and cocaine would reduce the criminalization of otherwise law-abiding users; it would drive down the price of drugs, which would reduce the need for addicts to steal, and reduce as well the incentives to drug traffickers and smugglers to ply their trades and to find new users; and it would free up personnel and resources for a more effective war against the crimes that people fear most.

In the face of all this, it is hard not to share the frustration expressed by Norval Morris, former dean of the University of Chicago Law School: "It is trite but it remains true that the main causes of crime are social and economic. The question arises whether people really care. The solutions are so obvious. *It's almost as if America wished for a high crime rate.*"[95] If this is so, then *the system's failure is only in the eye of the victim: For those in control, it is a roaring success!*

WHAT WORKS TO REDUCE CRIME

Surveying the programs that might contribute to reducing crime, criminologist Elliott Currie concludes that "four priorities seem especially critical: preventing child abuse and neglect, enhancing children's intellectual and social development, providing support and guidance to vulnerable adolescents, and working extensively with juvenile offenders." About these programs, Currie observes that "the best of them work, and they work remarkably well given how limited and underfunded they usually are."[96] A study entitled *Diverting Children from a Life of Crime: Measuring Costs and Benefits,* issued in June 1996 by the Rand Corporation, concluded,

> Programs that try to steer the young from wrongdoing—the training of parents whose children often misbehave, for example, or incentives to graduate from high school— are far more cost-effective in preventing crime over the long term than are mandatory sentences that imprison repeat adult offenders for long periods.[97]

A more recent report from the Rand Corporation, entitled *Investing in Our Children: What We Know and Don't Know about the Costs and Benefits of Early Childhood Interventions,* reached a similar conclusion. Evaluating nine programs in which early interventions were targeted at disadvantaged children, the study concludes that such programs lead to decreased criminal activity and save taxpayer dollars at the same time.[98] Similar results were found for Head Start programs: "At age 27, those who participated [in Head Start programs as children] had lower arrest rates, higher education rates, earned more money, [and] were more likely to be homeowners and less likely to receive social services."[99]

The National Treatment Improvement Study, "the largest study of its kind, which followed more than 5,300 clients in programs funded by the federal Center for Substance Abuse Treatment," concludes that

> drug and alcohol treatment programs significantly reduced substance use, crime, and homelessness.... Use of most illicit substances in the year after treatment entry declined about 50 percent compared with the year before.... Arrest rates fell substantially in the sample—from 48 percent to 17 percent.[100]

And a study by the Rand Corporation Drug Policy Research Center, entitled *Controlling Cocaine: Supply versus Demand Programs,* found that "[t]reatment is seven times more cost-effective than domestic drug enforcement in reducing cocaine use and 15 times more cost-effective in reducing the social costs of crime and lost productivity."[101] The study also concluded that "treatment is the most effective way to reduce violent crime."[102]

A recent review of more than 500 crime-prevention program evaluations yielded a list of what works. Among the programs that appear effective in reducing crime, the report lists family therapy and parent training for delinquent and at-risk adolescents; teaching of social competency skills in schools, and coaching of high-risk youth in "thinking skills"; vocational training for older male ex-offenders; extra police patrols in high-crime hot spots; monitoring of high-risk repeat offenders by specialized police forces as well as incarceration; rehabilitation programs with risk-focused treatments for convicted offenders; and therapeutic community treatment for drug-using offenders in prisons.[103]

In short, there is a growing body of knowledge showing that early childhood intervention, drug treatment, and numerous other programs can work to reduce crime. As Professor Blumstein observed, "If you intervene early, you not only save the costs of incarceration, you also save the costs of crime and gain the benefits of an individual who is a taxpaying contributor to the economy."[104] But, as Peter Greenwood, author of the Rand Corporation Study, *Diverting Children from a Life of Crime,* says, "The big policy question is, Who will act on this?"[105]

FURTHER READINGS

Chambliss, William. *Power, Politics, and Crime.* Boulder, CO: Westview Press, 1999.

Christie, Nils. *Crime Control as Industry: Toward Gulags, Western Style?* 3rd ed. London: Routledge, 2000.

Conklin, John. *Why Crime Rates Fell.* Boston: Allyn & Bacon, 2003.

Currie, Elliott. *Crime and Punishment in America.* New York: Henry Holt, 1998.

Diaz, Tom. *Making a Killing: The Business of Guns in America.* New York: New Press, 1999.

Dyer, Joel. *The Perpetual Prisoner Machine: How America Profits from Crime.* Boulder, CO: Westview Press, 2000.

Irwin, John, and James Austin. *It's about Time: America's Imprisonment Binge,* 3rd ed. Belmont, CA: Wadsworth, 2000.

Kappeler, Victor, Mark Blumberg, and Gary Potter. *The Mythology of Crime and Criminal Justice,* 4th ed. Long Grove, IL: Waveland, 2005.

Mauer, Marc, and Meda Chesney-Lind. *Invisible Punishment: The Collateral Consequences of Mass Imprisonment.* New York: New Press/W. W. Norton, 2002.

Messerschmidt, J. *Capitalism, Partriarchy and Crime.* Totowa, NJ: Rowman & Littlefield, 1985.

Quinney, Richard. *Class, State and Crime.* New York: Longman, 1997.

Ross, Jeffrey, and Stephen Richards. *Convict Criminology.* Belmont, CA: Wadsworth, 2002.

Shelden, Randall. *Controlling the Dangerous Classes: A Critical Introduction to the History of Criminal Justice.* Boston: Allyn & Bacon, 2001.

NOTES

1. *Challenge,* p. 35.
2. *Sourcebook 2003,* Table 3.106; and *UCR 2004,* pp. 11, 41.
3. BJS, *Justice Expenditures and Employment in the U.S., 1999,* NCJ191746, February 2002, p. 1; and BJS, *Justice Expenditures and Employment in the U.S., 2001,* NCJ202792, May 2004, p. 1.
4. Private security is one of the fastest growing industries in the nation. For 1990, expenditure on private security was $52 billion, and the number of people employed in some form of private security work was "more than 1.5 million people, outnumbering police officers by a 2:1 margin. In that year, more than 2.6 percent of the workforce was employed in the private security industry, double the percentage it was in 1970. The latest figures show that this ratio is now about 3:1, with more than $100 billion, dwarfing law enforcement expenditures [on police] of around $40 billion." Randall Shelden, *Controlling the Dangerous Classes* (Boston: Allyn & Bacon, 2001), p. 280.
5. See, for example, John Braithwaite, "Poverty, Power, and White-Collar Crime," in *White-Collar Crime Reconsidered,* ed. Kip Schlegel and David Weisburd (Boston: Northeastern University Press, 1992), pp. 78–107.
6. *StatAbst—2004–5,* Table 672, p. 447; *StatAbst—1972,* Table 528, p 324; Carmen DeNavas-Walt, Bernadette Proctor, and Cheryl Hill Lee, U.S. Census Bureau, *Current Population Reports,* P60-229, *Income, Poverty & Health Insurance Coverage in the United States; 2004* (Washington, DC: U.S. Government Printing Office, 2005).
7. Kathy Sawyer, "Poorest Families Are Losing Ground," *The Washington Post,* August 22, 1999, p. A7. The article goes on to point out that a "report from the House Ways and Means Committee . . . acknowledged that the poorest families are losing ground."
8. *The Washington Post,* September 6, 1982, p. 2; the report was issued by the Full Employment Action Council (a coalition of religious, civil rights, and union groups) and the National Policy Exchange (an economic research and educational organization).
9. *The Washington Post,* September 14, 1982, pp. 1, 4.

10. Edward Wolff, *Top Heavy: A Study of the Increasing Inequality of Wealth in America* (New York: Twentieth Century Fund Press, 1995), p. 2.

11. National Center for Children in Poverty at Columbia University, "Who Are America's Poor Children?" *www.nccp.org/pub_cpt05b.html.*

12. David Kamin and Isaac Shapiro, "Studies Shed New Light on Effects of Administration's Tax Cuts," Center on Budget and Policy Priorities, 2004, *www.cbpp.org/8-25-04tax.htm.*

13. *StatAbst—2001*, p. 386, Table 598. See also *"Racial Gulf:* Blacks' Hopes, Raised by '68 Kerner Report, Are Mainly Unfulfilled," *The Wall Street Journal*, February 26, 1988, pp. 1, 9; and "Today's Native Sons," *Time*, December 1, 1986, pp. 26–29.

14. *StatAbst—2004–5*, p. 393, Table 603; and John Berry, "Jobless Rate Rose to 6% in November," *The Washington Post*, December 7, 2002, pp. E1, E2.

15. John Rawls, *A Theory of Justice* (Cambridge, MA: Harvard University Press, 1971; rev. ed., 1999).

16. See ch. 4, n. 52 below (and accompanying text) for more on this principle of distributive justice.

17. John Rawls, *Justice as Fairness: A Restatement* (Cambridge, MA: Harvard University Press, 2001), pp. 138–40.

18. Rawls, *Justice as Fairness*, p. 146. Note that Rawls is not using the term *underclass* in the technical sense in which it is used in some sociological literature. For him, it simply refers to the economically worst-off group in a society, and emphasizes their likely sense of exclusion.

19. An article in the *American Journal of Public Health* in March 1998 reported on the Third National Health and Nutrition Examination Survey (NHANES III), the most comprehensive health examination survey in the United States, which found that 10 million Americans, including 4 million children, suffer from hunger; see K. Alaimo et al., "Food Insufficiency Exists in the United States: Results from the Third National Health and Nutrition Examination Survey (NHANES III)," *American Journal of Public Health* 88, no. 3 (March 1998): 419–26.

20. Todd R. Clear, "'Tougher' Is Dumber," *The New York Times*, December 4, 1993, p. 21.

21. BJS, *Recidivism of Prisoners Released in 1994*, NCJ 193427, June 2002, p. 1.

22. BJS, *Prisoners in 2004*, p. 7.

23. Stop Prison Rape (STP), *Prisoner Rape Factsheet, www.spr.org.*

24. Robert Johnson and Hans Toch, "Introduction," in *The Pains of Imprisonment*, ed. Robert Johnson and Hans Toch (Beverly Hills, CA: Sage, 1982), pp. 19–20.

25. STP, *Prisoner Rape Factsheet.*

26. Human Rights Watch, "No Escape: Male Rape in U.S. Prisons," *www.hrw.org/reports /2001/prison.*

27. Fox Butterfield, "More Blacks in Their 20's Have Trouble with the Law," *The New York Times*, October 5, 1995, p. A18; and Pierre Thomas, "Study Suggests Black Male Prison Rate Impinges on Political Process," *The Washington Post*, January 30, 1997, p. A3. See Jeffrey Reiman, "Liberal and Republican Arguments against the Disenfranchisement of Felons," *Criminal Justice Ethics* 24, no. 1 (Winter–Spring 2005): 3–18.

28. James P. Lynch and William J. Sabol, "Prison Use and Social Control," U.S. Department of Justice, Office of Justice Programs, *Policies, Processes, and Decisions of the Criminal Justice System*, vol. 3 of *Criminal Justice 2000*, pp. 7–44; Conklin, *Why Crime Rates Fell*, pp. 83–84; and Todd Clear, "The Problem with 'Addition by Subtraction,'" in *Invisible Punishment: The*

Collateral Consequences of Mass Imprisonment, ed. Mark Mauer and Meda Chesney-Lind (New York: New Press, 2002).

29. State of the Union Message, January 21, 2004, as provided by the Republican National Committee, *www.gop.com.*

30. Bush, "Remarks by the President on Project Safe Neighborhoods."

31. Philip J. Cook and Jens Ludwig, *Gun Violence: The Real Costs* (New York: Oxford University Press, 2000), pp. 15, 34, 35.

32. Garen Wintemute, "Guns and Gun Violence," in Blumstein and Wallman, *The Crime Drop in America,* p. 52.

33. Wintemute, "Guns and Gun Violence," pp. 54–57.

34. Gary Kleck, *Point Blank: Guns and Violence in America* (New York: Aldine de Gruyter, 1991), p. 17. Kleck's estimate of the number of guns is supported by the Bureau of Alcohol, Tobacco, and Firearms, which calculated 200 million in 1990 (cited in Albert Reiss and Jeffrey Roth, eds., *Understanding and Preventing Violence* [Washington, DC: National Academy Press, 1993], p. 256). See also BJS, *Guns Used in Crime,* NCJ-148201, July 1995, pp. 3, 6.

35. National Research Council, *Firearms and Violence: A Critical Review,* Committee to Improve Research Information and Data on Firearms, ed. Charles Wellford, John Pepper, and Carol Petrie, Committee on Law and Justice, Division of Behavioral and Social Sciences and Education (Washington, DC: National Academies Press, 2005), pp. 57–58.

36. *Challenge,* p. 239 (emphasis added).

37. *UCR–1995,* p. 36.

38. Office of Juvenile Justice and Delinquency Prevention, "Fact Sheet," February 1999, no. 93, *www.ncjrs.org/jjfact.htm.*

39. Don Colburn and Abigail Trafford, "Guns at Home: Doctors Target Growing Epidemic of Violence," *The Washington Post Health,* October 12, 1993, p. 12.

40. National Center for Injury Prevention and Control, "Nonfatal and Fatal Firearm-Related Injuries: United States, 1993–1997," November 19, 1999, *www.cdc.gov/mmwr/preview /mmwrhtml/mm4845a1.htm.*

41. Barbara Vobejda, "Children's Defense Fund Cites Gun Violence," *The Washington Post,* January 21, 1994, p. A3.

42. Presidential news conference, June 16, 1981; see also "Reagan Denounces Gun Control Laws," *The Washington Post,* May 7, 1983, p. A8.

43. "Whenever there is a crime involving a firearm, there are various groups, some of them quite persuasive in their logic, that think you can ban certain kinds of guns, and I am not in that mode" (George H. W. Bush, quoted in George Will, "Playing with Guns," *Newsweek,* March 27, 1989, p. 78).

44. Pierre Thomas, "Brady Gun Law Contains No Penalties, Little Money for States," *The Washington Post,* December 3, 1993, p. A3.

45. BJS, *Background Checks for Firearm Transfers, 2003,* NCJ 204428, September 2004, p. 1; and Blumstein, "The Recent Rise and Fall of American Violence," p. 5.

46. Lawrence W. Sherman, "Reducing Gun Violence: What Works, What Doesn't, What's Promising," *NIJ Perspectives on Crime and Justice: 1999–2000 Lecture Series,* NCJ 184245, March, 2001, p. 74.

47. Arnold S. Trebach, *The Heroin Solution* (New Haven, CT: Yale University Press, 1982), pp. 3–24, 246.

48. Office of National Drug Control Policy, *What America's Users Spend on Illegal Drugs,* NCJ 192334, December 2001, pp 8, 1.

49. Quoted in Doug Bandow, "War on Drugs or War on America?" p. 246.

50. Marvin D. Miller, National Organization for the Reform of Marijuana Laws, testimony at the Hearings on Proposals to Legalize Drugs held by the House Select Committee on Narcotics Abuse and Control, September 29, 1988, pp. 12–13; *UCR–2004,* pp. 178, 180.

51. Miller, testimony, p. 19.

52. U.S. Department of Justice, Drug Enforcement Administration, Opinion and Recommended Ruling, Findings of Fact, Conclusions of Law and Decision of Administrative Law Judge Francis L. Young, in the Matter of MARIJUANA RESCHEDULING PETITION, Docket no. 86–22, September 6, 1988, pp. 56–57.

53. Arnold S. Trebach, Testimony at the Hearings on Proposals to Legalize Drugs Held by the House Select Committee on Narcotics Abuse and Control, September 29, 1988 (Washington, DC: U.S. Government Printing Office, 1988), pp. 11–12. Doug Bandow of the Cato Institute confirms Trebach's numbers:

> *Tobacco kills roughly 390,000 people annually and alcohol is responsible for some 150,000 deaths a year. . . . In contrast, all illicit drugs combined account for about 5,000 deaths, most of which, as explained below, are caused by the effects of prohibition. For 100,000 users, tobacco kills 650, alcohol 150, heroin 80, and cocaine 4. (Bandow, "War on Drugs or War on America?" p. 245)*

In a footnote, the author mentions that these figures have been reduced to reflect only the drug use, not the effects of prohibition.

54. Surgeon General C. Everett Koop quoted, and reports on the relative addictiveness of cigarettes and cocaine, in Bandow, "War on Drugs or War on America?" p. 249.

55. "The largest study ever made of drug abuse in this country shows that two widely available legal drugs—alcohol and the tranquilizer Valium—are responsible for the greatest amount of drug-related illness, the government reported yesterday." Stuart Auerbach, "2 Drugs Widely Abused," *The Washington Post,* July 9, 1976, p. A1.

56. Blumstein, "Why Is Crime Falling—or Is It?," p. 13.

57. "A LEN Interview with Professor Alfred Blumstein of Carnegie Mellon University," *Law Enforcement News* 21, no. 422 (April 30, 1995): p. 11.

58. Troy Duster, *The Legislation of Morality: Law, Drugs, and Moral Judgment* (New York: Free Press, 1970), pp. 3, 7, inter alia.

59. Cf. Philip C. Baridon, *Addiction, Crime, and Social Policy* (Lexington, MA: Lexington Books, 1976), pp. 4–5.

60. Trebach, *The Heroin Solution,* p. 246.

61. Quoted in Doug Bandow, "War on Drugs or War on America?" p. 250.

62. "A LEN interview with Professor Alfred Blumstein of Carnegie Mellon University," p. 11.

63. M. Douglas Anglin and George Speckart, "Narcotics Use and Crime: A Multisample, Multimethod Analysis," *Criminology* 26, no. 2 (1988): 226.

64. U.S. Department of Health, Education, and Welfare, Public Health Service, National Institute on Alcohol Abuse and Alcoholism, Special Action Office for Drug Abuse Prevention, *Social Cost of Drug Abuse* (Washington, DC: U.S. Government Printing Office, 1974), pp. 20–21.

65. *UCR–2004,* p. 42.

66. Christoper Mumola, *Substance Abuse and Treatment, State and Federal Prisoners, 1997*, Bureau of Justice Statistics Special Report NCI 172871, January 1997, p. 5.

67. Anglin and Speckart, "Narcotics Use and Crime," p. 197.

68. Office of National Drug Control Policy (ONDCP), *What America's Users Spend on Illegal Drugs*, December (Washington, DC: Office of National Drug Control Policy, 2001), p. 1.

69. Ibid., p. 2.

70. Ibid., p. 18.

71. "U.S. Anti-drug Effort Criticized," *The Washington Post*, November 12, 1988, p. A15.

72. Ibid.

73. McCoy and Block, "U.S. Narcotics Policy: An Anatomy of Failure," p. 3; and United Nations Office on Drugs and Crime, *Global Illicit Drug Trends 2003* (New York: United Nations, 2003), pp. 8 and 23, *www.unodc.org/unodc/global_illicit_drug_trends.html.*

74. Bandow, "War on Drugs or War on America?" p. 244; and BJS, *Drugs, Crime, and the Justice System*, December 1992, p. 44.

75. "Cocaine Down: Signs Indicate That America's Cocaine Habit Is Easing," *The Wall Street Journal*, July 20, 1987, p. 21.

76. National Narcotics Intelligence Consumers' Committee, *The NNICC 1994: The Supply of Illegal Drugs to the United States*, DEA-95051 August (Washington, DC: NNICC, 1995), p. 1.

77. ONDCP, *The Price and Purity of Illicit Drugs: 1981 through the Second Quarter of 2003*, NCJ 207768, November 2004, pp. v–vi.

78. David Boyum and Peter Reuter, *An Analytic Assessment of U.S. Drug Policy* (Washington, DC: AEI Press, 2005). "Yet despite the incarceration of hundreds of thousands of drug dealers and steadfast attempts to stop overseas cultivations and trafficking, drugs have become substantially cheaper, casting doubt on the effectiveness of this strategy" (p. 2).

79. "Prosecutors Admit: No Victory in Sight," *National Law Journal*, August 8, 1988, p. S-2.

80. Boyum and Reuter, *An Analytic Assessment of U.S. Drug Policy*, p. 2.

81. BJS Fact Sheet, *Drug Data Summary*, NCJ-167246, February 1998.

82. ONDCP, *National Drug Control Strategy*, February (Washington, DC: Office of National Drug Control Policy, 2005), p. 61.

83. "Drug Wars Push D.C. to Brink of Homicide Record: Police Efforts Futile as Turf Disputes Raise 1988 Slaying Total to 285," *The Washington Post*, October 26, 1988, p. A1. By year's end the record was soundly broken, with the number of murders reaching 372! And the carnage continued: In 1991, there were 482 homicides in the nation's capital; *UCR–1991*, p. 64.

84. "Enemy Within: Drug Money Is Corrupting the Enforcers," pp. A1, A12.

85. Ibid.

86. Clifford Krauss, "2-Year Corruption Inquiry Finds a 'Willful Blindness' in New York's Police Dept," *The New York Times*, July 7, 1994, p. A1.

87. Bandow, "War on Drugs or War on America?" p. 243; and McCoy and Block, "U.S. Narcotics Policy," p. 6.

88. *UCR 2004*, p 280; and BJS, *Prisoners in 2004*, p. 10.

89. BJS, *Prisoners in 2001*, p. 14; and BJS, *Prisoners in 2004*, p. 10.

90. Boyum and Reuter, *An Analytic Assessment of U.S. Drug Policy*, p. 10.

91. Michael Tonry, "Racial Politics, Racial Disparities, and the War on Crime," *Crime & Delinquency 40*, no. 4 (October 1994): 487.

92. BJS, *Correctional Populations in the U.S., 1992*, p. 31; Surgeon General Joycelyn Elders's statement was reported in *International Herald Tribune*, December 8, 1993, p. 1. She reiter-

ated the suggestion after "reviewing many studies," and even after President Clinton's opposition to the idea was reported. "Elders Reiterates Her Support for Study of Drug Legalization," *The Washington Post*, January 15, 1994, p. A8.

93. Jerry V. Wilson, "Our Wasteful War on Drugs," *The Washington Post*, January 18, 1994, p. A20.

94. Christopher Wren, "A.M.A. Shelves Disputed Report on Drugs," *The New York Times*, June 23, 1996, p. A22.

95. *Time*, June 30, 1975, p. 17 (emphasis added).

96. Currie, *Crime and Punishment in America*, pp. 81, 98.

97. Fox Butterfield, "Intervening Early Costs Less than '3-Strikes' Laws, Study Says," *The New York Times*, June 23, 1996, p. A24.

98. Peter W. Greenwood, "Costs and Benefits of Early Childhood Intervention," OJJDP Fact Sheet no. 94, February (Washington, DC: U.S. Department of Justice, Office of Juvenile Justice and Delinquency Prevention, 1999).

99. Steven Donziger, ed., *The Real War on Crime: The Report of the National Criminal Justice Commission* (New York: HarperPerenniel, 1966), p. 216.

100. "Federally Funded Drug and Alcohol Programs Found Effective in Reducing Drug Use, Crime, Homelessness," *Psychiatric Services* 47, no. 11 (November 1996): 1280.

101. *The National Report on Substance Abuse* 8, no. 15 (July 1, 1994): p. 2.

102. Rand Corporation Press Release, *www.ndsn.org/JULY94/RAND.html*.

103. Lawrence Sherman et al., "Preventing Crime: What Works, What Doesn't, What's Promising," *NIJ Research in Brief*, NIJ171676, July (Washington, DC: National Institute of Justice, 1988).

104. Quoted in Butterfield, "Intervening Early Costs Less than '3-Strikes' Laws," p. A24.

105. Ibid. For an extensive list of promising programs aimed at reducing crime, see Donziger, *The Real War on Crime*, app. B. StopViolence.com, "Resources for a Just Peace," *http://stopviolence.com*, contains a growing collection of information about nonrepressive responses to crime and violence.

STUDY QUESTIONS

1. What are the known sources of **crime**? Why does Reiman make a distinction between *sources* and *causes* of crime?

2. Why does prison make its inmates a greater menace to **society**?

3. Given Reiman's findings, why do you think the U.S. **government** spends more money on incarcerating people than on preventing child abuse and neglect? If you were in charge, what kinds of policy decisions would you make?

4. Locate an **organization** that is trying to reduce crime in your area through **education** and outreach programs. What services do these organizations provide? Do you think they are effective? Based on what you learned from reading this selection, what could be done to help this organization?

D. L. ROSENHAN

On Being Sane in Insane Places

Are you sane? How do you know? Can you, simply by looking at a person, know he or she is sane? D. L. Rosenhan set out to answer the last question by planting sane people, referred to as "pseudopatients," into mental hospitals around the country. The pseudopatients were diagnosed with and treated for mental illnesses even though they had never really experienced any psychological issues before admission to the hospital. As you read this piece think about what terms like *sane* and *insane* really mean and how we can tell one from the other.

IF SANITY AND INSANITY EXIST, HOW SHALL WE KNOW THEM?

The question is neither capricious nor itself insane. However much we may be personally convinced that we can tell the normal from the abnormal, the evidence is simply not compelling. It is commonplace, for example, to read about murder trials wherein eminent psychiatrists for the defense are contradicted by equally eminent psychiatrists for the prosecution on the matter of the defendant's sanity. More generally, there are a great deal of conflicting data on the reliability, utility, and meaning of such terms as "sanity," "insanity," "mental illness," and "schizophrenia" (*1*). Finally, as early as 1934, Benedict suggested that normality and abnormality are not universal (*2*). What is viewed as normal in one culture may be seen as quite aberrant in another. Thus, notions of normality and abnormality may not be quite as accurate as people believe they are.

"On Being Sane in Insane Places" by D. L. Rosenhan from *Science*, New Series, Vol. 179, No. 4070 (Jan. 19, 1973). Used by permission of the American Association for the Advancement of Science.

To raise questions regarding normality and abnormality is in no way to question the fact that some behaviors are deviant or odd. Murder is deviant. So, too, are hallucinations. Nor does raising such questions deny the existence of the personal anguish that is often associated with "mental illness." Anxiety and depression exist. Psychological suffering exists. But normality and abnormality, sanity and insanity, and the diagnoses that flow from them may be less substantive than many believe them to be.

At its heart, the question of whether the sane can be distinguished from the insane (and whether degrees of insanity can be distinguished from each other) is a simple matter: do the salient characteristics that lead to diagnoses reside in the patients themselves or in the environments and contexts in which observers find them? From Bleuler, through Kretchmer, through the formulators of the recently revised *Diagnostic and Statistical Manual* of the American Psychiatric Association, the belief has been strong that patients present symptoms, that those symptoms can be categorized, and, implicitly, that the sane are distinguishable from the insane. More recently, however, this belief has been questioned. Based in part on theoretical and anthropological considerations, but also on philosophical, legal, and therapeutic ones, the view has grown that psychological categorization of mental illness is useless at best and downright harmful, misleading, and pejorative at worst. Psychiatric diagnoses, in this view, are in the minds of the observers and are not valid summaries of characteristics displayed by the observed (3–5).

Gains can be made in deciding which of these is more nearly accurate by getting normal people (that is, people who do not have, and have never suffered, symptoms of serious psychiatric disorders) admitted to psychiatric hospitals and then determining whether they were discovered to be sane and, if so, how. If the sanity of such pseudopatients were always detected, there would be prima facie evidence that a sane individual can be distinguished from the insane context in which he is found. Normality (and presumably abnormality) is distinct enough that it can be recognized wherever it occurs, for it is carried within the person. If, on the other hand, the sanity of the pseudopatients were never discovered, serious difficulties would arise for those who support traditional modes of psychiatric diagnosis. Given that the hospital staff was not incompetent, that the pseudopatient had been behaving as sanely as he had been outside of the hospital, and that it had never been previously suggested that he belonged in a psychiatric hospital, such an unlikely outcome would support the view that psychiatric diagnosis betrays little about the patient but much about the environment in which an observer finds him.

This article describes such an experiment. Eight sane people gained secret admission to 12 different hospitals (6). Their diagnostic experiences constitute the data of the first part of this article; the remainder is devoted to a description of their experiences in psychiatric institutions. Too few psychiatrists and psychologists, even those who have worked in such hospitals, know what the experience is like. They rarely talk about it with former patients, perhaps because they distrust information coming from the previously insane. Those who have worked in psychiatric hospitals are likely to have adapted so thoroughly to the settings that they are insensitive to the impact of that experience. And while there have been occasional reports of researchers who submitted themselves to psychiatric hospitalization (7), these researchers have commonly remained in the hospitals for short periods of time, often with the knowledge of the hospital staff. It is difficult to know the extent to which they were treated like patients or like research colleagues. Nevertheless, their reports about the inside of the psychiatric hospital have been valuable. This article extends those efforts.

PSEUDOPATIENTS AND THEIR SETTINGS

The eight pseudopatients were a varied group. One was a psychology graduate student in his 20's. The remaining seven were older and "established." Among them were three psychologists, a pediatrician, a psychiatrist, a painter, and a housewife. Three pseudopatients were women, five were men. All of them employed pseudonyms, lest their alleged diagnoses embarrass them later. Those who were in mental health professions alleged another occupation in order to avoid the special attentions that might be accorded by staff, as a matter of courtesy or caution, to ailing colleagues (8). With the exception of myself (I was the first pseudopatient and my presence was known to the hospital administrator and chief psychologist and, so far as I can tell, to them alone), the presence of pseudopatients and the nature of the research program was not known to the hospital staffs (9).

The settings were similarly varied. In order to generalize the findings, admission into a variety of hospitals was sought. The 12 hospitals in the sample were located in five different states on the East and West coasts. Some were old and shabby, some were quite new. Some were research-oriented, others not. Some had good staff-patient ratios, others were quite understaffed. Only one was a strictly private hospital. All of the others were supported by state or federal funds or, in one instance, by university funds.

After calling the hospital for an appointment, the pseudopatient arrived at the admissions office complaining that he had been hearing voices. Asked what the voices said, he replied that they were often unclear, but as far as he could tell they said "empty," "hollow," and "thud." The voices were unfamiliar and were of the same sex as the pseudopatient. The choice of these symptoms was occasioned by their apparent similarity to existential symptoms. Such symptoms are alleged to arise from painful concerns about the perceived meaninglessness of one's life. It is as if the hallucinating person were saying, "My life is empty and hollow." The choice of these symptoms was also determined by the *absence* of a single report of existential psychoses in the literature.

Beyond alleging the symptoms and falsifying name, vocation, and employment, no further alterations of person, history, or circumstances were made. The significant events of the pseudopatient's life history were presented as they had actually occurred. Relationships with parents and siblings, with spouse and children, with people at work and in school, consistent with the aforementioned exceptions, were described as they were or had been. Frustrations and upsets were described along with joys and satisfactions. These facts are important to remember. If anything, they strongly biased the subsequent results in favor of detecting sanity, since none of their histories or current behaviors were seriously pathological in any way.

Immediately upon admission to the psychiatric ward, the pseudopatient ceased simulating *any* symptoms of abnormality. In some cases, there was a brief period of mild nervousness and anxiety, since none of the pseudopatients really believed that they would be admitted so easily. Indeed, their shared fear was that they would be immediately exposed as frauds and greatly embarrassed. Moreover, many of them had never visited a psychiatric ward; even those who had, nevertheless had some genuine fears about what might happen to them. Their nervousness, then, was quite appropriate to the novelty of the hospital setting, and it abated rapidly.

Apart from that short-lived nervousness, the pseudopatient behaved on the ward as he "normally" behaved. The pseudopatient spoke to patients and staff as he might ordinarily. Because there is uncommonly little to do on a psychiatric ward, he attempted to engage others in conversation. When asked by staff how he was feeling, he indicated that he was fine, that he no longer experienced symptoms. He responded to instructions from attendants, to calls for medication (which was not swallowed), and to dining-hall instructions. Beyond such activities as were available to him on the admissions ward, he spent his time writing down his observations about the ward, its patients, and the staff. Initially these notes were written "secretly," but as it soon became clear that no one much cared, they were subsequently written on standard tablets of paper in such public places as the dayroom. No secret was made of these activities.

The pseudopatient, very much as a true psychiatric patient, entered a hospital with no foreknowledge of when he would be discharged. Each was told that he would have to get out by his own devices, essentially by convincing the staff that he was sane. The psychological stresses associated with hospitalization were considerable, and all but one of the pseudopatients desired to be discharged almost immediately after being admitted. They were, therefore, motivated not only to behave sanely, but to be paragons of cooperation. That their behavior was in no way disruptive is confirmed by nursing reports, which have been obtained on most of the patients. These reports uniformly indicate that the patients were "friendly," "cooperative," and "exhibited no abnormal indications."

THE NORMAL ARE NOT DETECTABLY SANE

Despite their public "show" of sanity, the pseudopatients were never detected. Admitted, except in one case, with a diagnosis of schizophrenia (*10*), each was discharged with a diagnosis of schizophrenia "in remission." The label "in remission" should in no way be dismissed as a formality, for at no time during any hospitalization had any question been raised about any pseudopatient's simulation. Nor are there any indications in the hospital records that the pseudopatient's status was suspect. Rather, the evidence is strong that, once labeled schizophrenic, the pseudopatient was stuck with that label. If the pseudopatient was to be discharged, he must naturally be "in remission"; but he was not sane, nor, in the institution's view, had he ever been sane.

The uniform failure to recognize sanity cannot be attributed to the quality of the hospitals, for, although there were considerable variations among them, several are considered excellent. Nor can it be alleged that there was simply not enough time to observe the pseudopatients. Length of hospitalization ranged from 7 to 52 days, with an average of 19 days. The pseudopatients were not, in fact, carefully observed, but this failure clearly speaks more to traditions within psychiatric hospitals than to lack of opportunity.

Finally, it cannot be said that the failure to recognize the pseudopatients' sanity was due to the fact that they were not behaving sanely. While there was clearly some tension present in all of them, their daily visitors could detect no serious behavioral consequences—nor, indeed, could other patients. It was quite common for the patients to "detect" the pseudopatients' sanity. During the first three hospitalizations, when accurate counts were kept, 35 of a total of 118 patients on the admissions ward voiced their suspicions, some vigorously. "You're not crazy. You're a journalist, or a professor [referring to the continual note-taking]. You're checking up on the hospital." While most of the patients were reassured by the pseudopatient's insistence that he had been sick before he came in but was fine now, some continued to believe that the pseudopatient was sane throughout his hospitalization (*11*). The fact that the patients often recognized normality when staff did not raises important questions.

Failure to detect sanity during the course of hospitalization may be due to the fact that physicians operate with a strong bias toward what statisticians call the type 2 error (*5*). This is to say that physicians are more inclined to call a healthy person sick (a false positive, type 2) than a sick person healthy (a false negative, type 1). The reasons for this are not hard to find: it is clearly more dangerous to misdiagnose illness than health. Better to err on the side of caution, to suspect illness even among the healthy.

But what holds for medicine does not hold equally well for psychiatry. Medical illnesses, while unfortunate, are not commonly pejorative. Psychiatric diagnoses, on the contrary, carry with them personal, legal, and social stigmas (*12*). It was therefore important to see whether the tendency toward diagnosing the sane insane could be reversed. The following experiment was arranged at a research and teaching hospital whose staff had heard these findings but doubted that such an error could occur in their hospital. The staff was informed that at some time during the following 3 months, one or more pseudopatients would attempt to be admitted into the psychiatric hospital. Each staff member was asked to rate each patient who presented himself at admissions or on the ward according to the likelihood that the patient was a pseudopatient. A 10-point scale was used, with a 1 and 2 reflecting high confidence that the patient was a pseudopatient.

Judgments were obtained on 193 patients who were admitted for psychiatric treatment. All staff who had had sustained contact with or primary responsibility for the patients—attendants, nurses, psychiatrists, physicians, and psychologists—were asked to make judgments. Forty-one patients were alleged, with high confidence, to be pseudopatients by at least one member of the staff. Twenty-three were considered suspect by at least one psychiatrist. Nineteen were suspected by one psychiatrist *and* one other staff member. Actually, no genuine pseudopatient (at least from my group) presented himself during this period.

The experiment is instructive. It indicates that the tendency to designate sane people as insane can be reversed when the stakes (in this case, prestige and diagnostic acumen) are high. But what can be said of the 19 people who were suspected of being "sane" by one psychiatrist and another staff member? Were these people truly "sane," or was it rather the case that in the course of avoiding the type 2 error the staff tended to make more errors of the first sort—calling the crazy "sane"? There is no way of knowing. But one thing is certain: any diagnostic process that lends itself so readily to massive errors of this sort cannot be a very reliable one.

THE STICKINESS OF PSYCHODIAGNOSTIC LABELS

Beyond the tendency to call the healthy sick—a tendency that accounts better for diagnostic behavior on admission than it does for such behavior after a lengthy period of exposure—the data speak to the massive role of labeling in psychiatric assessment. Having once been labeled schizophrenic, there is nothing the pseudopatient can do to overcome the tag. The tag profoundly colors others' perceptions of him and his behavior.

From one viewpoint, these data are hardly surprising, for it has long been known that elements are given meaning by the context in which they occur. Gestalt psychology made this point vigorously, and Asch (*13*) demonstrated that there are "central" personality traits (such as "warm" versus "cold") which are so powerful that they markedly color the meaning of other information in forming an impression of a given personality (*14*). "Insane," "schizophrenic," "manic-depressive," and "crazy" are probably among the most powerful of such central traits. Once a person is designated abnormal, all of his other behaviors and characteristics are colored by that label. Indeed, that label is so powerful that many of the pseudopatients' normal behaviors were overlooked entirely or profoundly misinterpreted. Some examples may clarify this issue.

Earlier I indicated that there were no changes in the pseudopatient's personal history and current status beyond those of name, employment, and, where necessary, vocation. Otherwise, a veridical description of personal history and circumstances was offered. Those circumstances were not psychotic. How were they made consonant with the diagnosis of psychosis? Or were those diagnoses modified in such a way as to bring them into accord with the circumstances of the pseudopatient's life, as described by him?

As far as I can determine, diagnoses were in no way affected by the relative health of the circumstances of a pseudopatient's life. Rather, the reverse occurred: the perception of his circumstances was shaped entirely by the diagnosis. A clear example of such translation is found in the case of a pseudopatient who had had a close relationship with his mother but was rather remote from his father during his early childhood. During adolescence and beyond, however, his father became a close friend, while his relationship with his mother cooled. His present relationship with his wife was characteristically close and warm. Apart from occasional angry exchanges, friction was minimal. The children had rarely been spanked. Surely there is nothing especially pathological about such a history. Indeed, many readers may see a similar pattern in their own experiences, with no markedly deleterious consequences. Observe, however, how such a history was translated in the psychopathological context, this from the case summary prepared after the patient was discharged.

> This white 39-year-old male ... manifests a long history of considerable ambivalence in close relationships, which begins in early childhood. A warm relationship with his mother cools during his adolescence. A distant relationship to his father is described as becoming very intense. Affective stability is absent. His attempts to control emotionality with his wife and children are punctuated by angry outbursts and, in the case of the children, spankings. And while he says that he has several good friends, one senses considerable ambivalence embedded in those relationships also ...

The facts of the case were unintentionally distorted by the staff to achieve consistency with a popular theory of the dynamics of a schizophrenic reaction (15). Nothing of an ambivalent nature had been described in relations with parents, spouse, or friends. To the extent that ambivalence could be inferred, it was probably not greater than is found in all human relationships. It is true the pseudopatient's relationships with his parents changed over time, but in the ordinary context that would hardly be remarkable—indeed, it might very well be expected. Clearly, the meaning ascribed to his verbalizations (that is, ambivalence, affective instability) was determined by the diagnosis: schizophrenia. An entirely different meaning would have been ascribed if it were known that the man was "normal."

All pseudopatients took extensive notes publicly. Under ordinary circumstances, such behavior would have raised questions in the minds of observers, as, in fact, it did among patients. Indeed, it seemed so certain that the notes would elicit suspicion that elaborate precautions were taken to remove them from the ward each day. But the precautions proved needless. The closest any staff member came to questioning these notes occurred when one pseudopatient asked his physician what kind of medication he was receiving and began to write down the response. "You needn't write it," he was told gently. "If you have trouble remembering, just ask me again."

If no questions were asked of the pseudopatients, how was their writing interpreted? Nursing records for three patients indicate that the writing was seen as an aspect of their pathological behavior. "Patient engages in writing behavior" was the daily nursing comment on one of the pseudopatients who was never questioned about his writing. Given that the patient is in the hospital, he must be psychologically disturbed. And given that he is disturbed, continuous writing must be a behavioral manifestation of that disturbance, perhaps a subset of the compulsive behaviors that are sometimes correlated with schizophrenia.

One tacit characteristic of psychiatric diagnosis is that it locates the sources of aberration within the individual and only rarely within the complex of stimuli that surrounds him. Consequently, behaviors that are stimulated by the environment are commonly misattributed to the patient's disorder. For example, one kindly nurse found a pseudopatient pacing the long hospital corridors. "Nervous, Mr. X?" she asked. "No, bored," he said.

The notes kept by pseudopatients are full of patient behaviors that were misinterpreted by well-intentioned staff. Often enough, a patient would go "berserk" because he had, wittingly or unwittingly, been mistreated by, say, an attendant. A nurse coming upon the scene would rarely inquire even cursorily into the environmental stimuli of the patient's behavior. Rather, she assumed that his upset derived from his pathology, not from his present interactions with other staff members. Occasionally, the staff might assume that the patient's family (especially when they had recently visited) or other patients had stimulated the outburst. But never were the staff found to assume that one of themselves or the structure of the hospital had anything to do with a patient's behavior. One psychiatrist pointed to a group of patients who were sitting outside the cafeteria entrance half an hour before lunchtime. To a group of young residents he indicated that such behavior was characteristic of the oral-acquisitive nature of the syndrome. It seemed not to occur to him that there were very few things to anticipate in a psychiatric hospital besides eating.

A psychiatric label has a life and an influence of its own. Once the impression has been formed that the patient is schizophrenic, the expectation is that he will continue to be schizophrenic. When a sufficient amount of time has passed, during which the patient has done nothing bizarre, he is considered to be in remission and available for discharge. But the label endures beyond discharge, with the unconfirmed expectation that he will behave as a schizophrenic again. Such labels, conferred by mental health professionals, are as influential on the patient as they are on his relatives and friends, and it should not surprise anyone that the diagnosis acts on all of them as a self-fulfilling prophecy. Eventually, the patient himself accepts the diagnosis, with all of its surplus meanings and expectations, and behaves accordingly (5).

The inferences to be made from these matters are quite simple. Much as Zigler and Phillips have demonstrated that there is enormous overlap in the symptoms presented by patients who have been variously diagnosed (16), so there is enormous overlap in the behaviors of the sane and the insane. The sane are not "sane" all of the time. We lose our tempers "for no good reason." We are occasionally depressed or anxious, again for no good reason. And we may find it difficult to get along with one or another person—again for no reason that we can specify. Similarly, the insane are not always insane. Indeed, it was the impression of the pseudopatients while living with them that they were sane for long periods of time—that the bizarre behaviors upon which their diagnoses were allegedly predicated constituted only a small fraction of their total behavior. If it makes no sense to label ourselves permanently depressed on the basis of an occasional depression, then it takes better evidence than is presently available to label all patients insane or schizophrenic on the basis of bizarre behaviors or cognitions. It seems more useful, as Mischel (17) has pointed out, to limit our discussions to *behaviors*, the stimuli that provoke them, and their correlates.

It is not known why powerful impressions of personality traits, such as "crazy" or "insane," arise. Conceivably, when the origins of and stimuli that give rise to a behavior are remote or unknown, or when the behavior strikes us as immutable, trait labels regarding the *behaver* arise. When, on the other hand, the origins and stimuli are known and available, discourse is limited to the behavior itself. Thus, I may hallucinate because I am sleeping, or I may hallucinate because I have ingested a peculiar drug. These are termed sleep-induced hallucinations, or dreams, and drug-induced hallucinations, respectively. But when the stimuli to my hallucinations are unknown, that is called craziness, or schizophrenia—as if that inference were somehow as illuminating as the others.

THE EXPERIENCE OF PSYCHIATRIC HOSPITALIZATION

The term "mental illness" is of recent origin. It was coined by people who were humane in their inclinations and who wanted very much to raise the station of (and the public's sympathies toward) the psychologically disturbed from that of witches and "crazies" to one that was akin to the physically ill. And they were at least partially successful, for the treatment of the mentally ill *has* improved considerably over the years. But while treatment has improved, it is doubtful that people really regard the mentally ill in the same way that they view the physically ill. A broken leg is something one recovers from, but mental illness allegedly endures forever (18). A broken leg does not threaten the observer, but a crazy schizophrenic? There is by now a host of evidence that attitudes toward the mentally ill are characterized by fear, hostility, aloofness, suspicion, and dread (19). The mentally ill are society's lepers.

That such attitudes infect the general population is perhaps not surprising, only upsetting. But that they affect the professionals—attendants, nurses, physicians, psychologists, and social workers—who treat and deal with the mentally ill is more disconcerting, both because such attitudes are self-evidently pernicious and because they are unwitting. Most mental health professionals would insist that they are sympathetic toward the mentally ill, that they are neither avoidant nor hostile. But it is more likely that an exquisite ambivalence characterizes their relations with psychiatric patients, such that their avowed impulses are only part of their entire attitude. Negative attitudes are there too and can easily be detected. Such attitudes should not surprise us. They are the natural offspring of the labels patients wear and the places in which they are found.

Consider the structure of the typical psychiatric hospital. Staff and patients are strictly segregated. Staff have their own living space, including their dining facilities, bathrooms, and assembly places. The glassed quarters that contain the professional staff, which the pseudopatients came to call "the cage," sit out on every dayroom. The staff emerge primarily for caretaking purposes—to give medication, to conduct a therapy or group meeting, to instruct or reprimand a patient. Otherwise, staff keep to themselves, almost as if the disorder that afflicts their charges is somehow catching.

So much is patient-staff segregation the rule that, for four public hospitals in which an attempt was made to measure the degree to which staff and patients mingle, it was necessary to use "time out of the staff cage" as the operational measure. While it was not the case that all time spent out of the cage was spent mingling with patients (attendants, for example, would occasionally emerge to watch television in the dayroom), it was the only way in which one could gather reliable data on time for measuring.

The average amount of time spent by attendants outside of the cage was 11.3 percent (range, 3 to 52 percent). This figure does not represent only time spent mingling with patients, but also includes time spent on such chores as folding laundry, supervising patients while they shave, directing ward cleanup, and sending patients to off-ward activities. It was the relatively rare attendant who spent time talking with patients or playing games with them. It proved impossible to obtain a "percent mingling time" for nurses, since the amount of time they spent out of the cage was too brief. Rather, we counted instances of emergence from the cage. On the average, daytime nurses emerged from the cage 11.5 times per shift, including instances when they left the ward entirely (range, 4 to 39 times). Late afternoon and night nurses were even less available, emerging on the average 9.4 times per shift (range, 4 to 41 times). Data

TABLE 1. Self-Initiated Contact by Pseudopatients with Psychiatrists and Nurses and Attendants, Compared to Contact with Other Groups.

| | Psychiatric hospitals | | University campus (nonmedical) | University medical center | | |
| | | | | Physicians | | |
Contact	(1) Psychiatrists	(2) Nurses and attendants	(3) Faculty	(4) "Looking for a psychiatrist"	(5) "Looking for an internist"	(6) No additional comment
Responses						
Moves on, head averted (%)	71	88	0	0	0	0
Makes eye contact (%)	23	10	0	11	0	0
Pauses and chats (%)	2	2	0	11	0	10
Stops and talks (%)	4	0.5	100	78	100	90
Mean number of questions answered (out of 6)	*	*	6	3.8	4.8	4.5
Respondents (No.)	13	47	14	18	15	10
Attempts (No.)	185	1283	14	18	15	10

* Not applicable.

on early morning nurses, who arrived usually after midnight and departed at 8 a.m., are not available because patients were asleep during most of this period.

Physicians, especially psychiatrists, were even less available. They were rarely seen on the wards. Quite commonly, they would be seen only when they arrived and departed, with the remaining time being spent in their offices or in the cage. On the average, physicians emerged on the ward 6.7 times per day (range, 1 to 17 times). It proved difficult to make an accurate estimate in this regard, since physicians often maintained hours that allowed them to come and go at different times.

The hierarchical organization of the psychiatric hospital has been commented on before (20), but the latent meaning of that kind of organization is worth noting again. Those with the most power have least to do with patients, and those with the least power are most involved with them. Recall, however, that the acquisition of role-appropriate behaviors occurs mainly through the observation of others, with the most powerful having the most influence. Consequently, it is understandable that attendants not only spend more time with patients than do any other members of the staff—that is required by their station in the hierarchy—but also, insofar as they learn from their superiors' behavior, spend as little time with patients as they can. Attendants are seen mainly in the cage, which is where the models, the action, and the power are.

I turn now to a different set of studies, these dealing with staff response to patient-initiated contact. It has long been known that the amount of time a person spends with you can be an index of your significance to him. If he initiates and maintains eye contact, there is reason to believe that he is considering your requests and needs. If he pauses to chat or actually stops and talks, there is added reason to infer that he is individuating you. In four hospitals, the pseudopatient approached the staff member with a request which took the following form: "Pardon me, Mr. [or Dr. or Mrs.] X, could you tell me when I will be eligible for grounds privileges?" (or ". . . when I will be presented at the staff meeting?" or ". . . when I am likely to be discharged?"). While the content of the question varied according to the appropriateness of the target and the pseudopatient's (apparent) current needs the form was always a courteous and relevant request for information. Care was taken never to approach a particular member of the staff more than once a day, lest the staff member become suspicious or irritated. In examining these data, remember that the behavior of the pseudopatients was neither bizarre nor disruptive. One could indeed engage in good conversation with them.

The data for these experiments are shown in Table 1, separately for physicians (column 1) and for nurses and attendants (column 2). Minor differences between these four institutions were overwhelmed by the degree to which staff avoided continuing contacts that patients had initiated. By far, their most common response consisted of either a brief response to the question, offered while they were "on the move" and with head averted, or no response at all.

The encounter frequently took the following bizarre form: (pseudopatient) "Pardon me, Dr. X. Could you tell me when I am eligible for grounds privileges?" (physician) "Good morning, Dave. How are you today?" (Moves off without waiting for a response.)

It is instructive to compare these data with data recently obtained at Stanford University. It has been alleged that large and eminent universities are characterized by faculty who are so busy that they have no time for students. For this comparison, a young lady approached individual faculty members who seemed to be walking purposefully to some meeting or teaching engagement and asked them the following six questions.

1. "Pardon me, could you direct me to Encina Hall?" (at the medical school: "...to the Clinical Research Center?").
2. "Do you know where Fish Annex is?" (there is no Fish Annex at Stanford).
3. "Do you teach here?"
4. "How does one apply for admission to the college?" (at the medical school: "...to the medical school?").
5. "Is it difficult to get in?"
6. "Is there financial aid?"

Without exception, as can be seen in Table 1 (column 3), all of the questions were answered. No matter how rushed they were, all respondents not only maintained eye contact, but stopped to talk. Indeed, many of the respondents went out of their way to direct or take the questioner to the office she was seeking, to try to locate "Fish Annex," or to discuss with her the possibilities of being admitted to the university.

Similar data, also shown in Table 1 (columns 4, 5, and 6), were obtained in the hospital. Here too, the young lady came prepared with six questions. After the first question, however, she remarked to 18 of her respondents (column 4), "I'm looking for a psychiatrist," and to 15 others (column 5), "I'm looking for an internist." Ten other respondents received no inserted comment (column 6). The general degree of cooperative responses is considerably higher for these university groups than it was for pseudopatients in psychiatric hospitals. Even so, differences are apparent within the medical school setting. Once having indicated that she was looking for a psychiatrist, the degree of cooperation elicited was less than when she sought an internist.

POWERLESSNESS AND DEPERSONALIZATION

Eye contact and verbal contact reflect concern and individuation; their absence, avoidance and depersonalization. The data I have presented do not do justice to the rich daily encounters that grew up around matters of depersonalization and avoidance. I have records of patients who were beaten by staff for the sin of having initiated verbal contact. During my own experience, for example, one patient was beaten in the presence of other patients for having approached an attendant and told him, "I like you." Occasionally, punishment meted out to patients for misdemeanors seemed so excessive that it could not be justified by the most radical interpretations of psychiatric canon. Nevertheless, they appeared to go unquestioned. Tempers were often short. A patient who had not heard a call for medication would be roundly excoriated, and the morning attendants would often wake patients with, "Come on, you m——f——s, out of bed!"

Neither anecdotal nor "hard" data can convey the overwhelming sense of powerlessness which invades the individual as he is continually exposed to the depersonalization of the psychiatric hospital. It hardly matters *which* psychiatric hospital—the excellent public ones and the very plush private hospital were better than the rural and shabby ones in this regard, but, again, the features that psychiatric hospitals had in common overwhelmed by far their apparent differences.

Powerlessness was evident everywhere. The patient is deprived of many of his legal rights by dint of his psychiatric commitment (*21*). He is shorn of credibility by virtue of his psychiatric label. His freedom of movement is restricted. He cannot initiate contact with the staff, but may only respond to such overtures as they make. Personal privacy is minimal. Patient quarters and possessions can be entered and examined by any staff member, for whatever reason. His personal history and anguish is available to any staff member (often including the "grey lady" and "candy striper" volunteer) who chooses to read his folder, regardless of their therapeutic relationship to him. His personal hygiene and waste evacuation are often monitored. The water closets may have no doors.

At times, depersonalization reached such proportions that pseudopatients had the sense that they were invisible, or at least unworthy of account. Upon being admitted, I and other pseudopatients took the initial physical examinations in a semipublic room, where staff members went about their own business as if we were not there.

On the ward, attendants delivered verbal and occasionally serious physical abuse to patients in the presence of other observing patients, some of whom (the pseudopatients) were writing it all down. Abusive behavior, on the other hand, terminated quite abruptly when other staff members were known to be coming. Staff are credible witnesses. Patients are not.

A nurse unbuttoned her uniform to adjust her brassiere in the presence of an entire ward of viewing men. One did not have the sense that she was being seductive. Rather, she didn't notice us. A group of staff persons might point to a patient in the dayroom and discuss him animatedly, as if he were not there.

One illuminating instance of depersonalization and invisibility occurred with regard to medications. All told, the pseudopatients were administered nearly 2100 pills, including Elavil, Stelazine, Compazine, and Thorazine, to name but a few. (That such a variety of medications should have been administered to patients presenting identical symptoms is itself worthy of note.) Only two were swallowed. The rest were either pocketed or deposited in the toilet. The pseudopatients were not alone in this. Although I have no precise records on how many patients rejected their medications, the pseudopatients frequently found the medications of other patients in the toilet before they deposited their own. As long as they were cooperative, their behavior and the pseudopatients' own in this matter, as in other important matters, went unnoticed throughout.

Reactions to such depersonalization among pseudopatients were intense. Although they had come to the hospital as participant observers and were fully aware that they did not "belong," they nevertheless found themselves caught up in and fighting the process of depersonalization. Some examples: a graduate student in psychology asked his wife to bring his textbooks to the hospital so he could "catch up on his homework"—this despite the elaborate precautions taken to conceal his professional association. The same student, who had trained for quite some time to get into the hospital, and who had looked forward to the experience, "remembered" some drag races that he had wanted to see on the weekend and insisted that he be discharged by that time. Another pseudopatient attempted a romance with a nurse. Subsequently, he informed the staff that he was applying for admission to graduate school in psychology and was very likely to be admitted, since a graduate professor was one of his regular hospital visitors. The same person began to engage in psychotherapy with other patients—all of this as a way of becoming a person in an impersonal environment.

THE SOURCES OF DEPERSONALIZATION

What are the origins of depersonalization? I have already mentioned two. First are attitudes held by all of us toward the mentally ill—including those who treat them—attitudes characterized by fear, distrust, and horrible expectations on the one hand, and benevolent intentions on the other. Our ambivalence leads, in this instance as in others, to avoidance.

Second, and not entirely separate, the hierarchical structure of the psychiatric hospital facilitates depersonalization. Those who are at the top have least to do with patients, and their behavior inspires the rest of the staff. Average daily contact with psychiatrists, psychologists, residents, and physicians combined ranged from 3.9 to 25.1 minutes, with an overall mean of 6.8 (six pseudopatients over a total of 129 days of hospitalization). Included in this average are time spent in the admissions interview, ward meetings in the presence of a senior staff member, group and individual psychotherapy contacts, case presentation conferences, and discharge meetings. Clearly, patients do not spend much time in interpersonal contact with doctoral staff. And doctoral staff serve as models for nurses and attendants.

There are probably other sources. Psychiatric installations are presently in serious financial straits. Staff shortages are pervasive, staff time at a premium. Something has to give, and that something is patient contact. Yet, while financial stresses are realities, too much can be made of them. I have the impression that the psychological forces that result in depersonalization are much stronger than the fiscal ones and that the addition of more staff would not correspondingly improve patient care in this regard. The incidence of staff meetings and the enormous amount of record-keeping on patients, for example, have not been as substantially reduced as has patient contact. Priorities exist, even during hard times. Patient contact is not a significant priority in the traditional psychiatric hospital, and fiscal pressures do not account for this. Avoidance and depersonalization may.

Heavy reliance upon psychotropic medication tacitly contributes to depersonalization by convincing staff that treatment is indeed being conducted and that further patient contact may not be necessary. Even here, however, caution needs to be exercised in understanding the role of psychotropic drugs. If patients were powerful rather than powerless, if they were viewed as interesting individuals rather than diagnostic entities, if they were socially significant rather than social lepers, if their anguish truly and wholly compelled our sympathies and concerns, would we not *seek* contact with them, despite the availability of medications? Perhaps for the pleasure of it all?

THE CONSEQUENCES OF LABELING AND DEPERSONALIZATION

Whenever the ratio of what is known to what needs to be known approaches zero, we tend to invent "knowledge" and assume that we understand more than we actually do. We seem unable to acknowledge that we simply don't know. The needs for diagnosis and remediation of behavioral and emotional problems are enormous. But rather than acknowledge that we are just embarking on understanding, we continue to label patients "schizophrenic," "manic-depressive," and "insane," as if in those words we had captured the essence of understanding. The facts of the matter are that we have known for a long time that diagnoses are often not useful or reliable, but we have nevertheless continued to use them. We now know that we cannot distinguish insanity from sanity. It is depressing to consider how that information will be used.

Not merely depressing, but frightening. How many people, one wonders, are sane but not recognized as such in our psychiatric institutions? How many have been needlessly stripped of their privileges of citizenship, from the right to vote and drive to that of handling their own accounts? How many have feigned insanity in order to avoid the criminal consequences of their behavior, and, conversely, how many would rather stand trial than live interminably in a psychiatric hospital—but are wrongly thought to be mentally ill? How many have been stigmatized by well-intentioned, but nevertheless erroneous, diagnoses? On the last point, recall again that a "type 2 error" in psychiatric diagnosis does not have the same consequences it does in medical diagnosis. A diagnosis of cancer that has been found to be in error is cause for celebration. But psychiatric diagnoses are rarely found to be in error. The label sticks, a mark of inadequacy forever.

Finally, how many patients might be "sane" outside the psychiatric hospital but seem insane in it—not because craziness resides in them, as it were, but because they are responding to a bizarre setting, one that may be unique to institutions which harbor nether people? Goffman (4) calls the process of socialization to such institutions "mortification"—an apt metaphor that includes the processes of depersonalization that have been described here. And while it is impossible to know whether the pseudopatients' responses to these processes are characteristic of all inmates—they were, after all, not real patients—it is difficult to believe that these processes of socialization to a psychiatric hospital provide useful attitudes or habits of response for living in the "real world."

SUMMARY AND CONCLUSIONS

It is clear that we cannot distinguish the sane from the insane in psychiatric hospitals. The hospital itself imposes a special environment in which the meanings of behavior can easily be misunderstood. The consequences to patients hospitalized in such an environment—the powerlessness, depersonalization, segregation, mortification, and self-labeling—seem undoubtedly counter-therapeutic.

I do not, even now, understand this problem well enough to perceive solutions. But two matters seem to have some promise. The first concerns the proliferation of community mental health facilities, of crisis intervention centers, of the human potential movement, and of behavior therapies that, for all of their own problems, tend to avoid psychiatric labels, to focus on specific problems and behaviors, and to retain the individual in a relatively non-pejorative environment. Clearly, to the extent that we refrain from sending the distressed to insane places, our impressions of them are less likely to be distorted. (The risk of distorted perceptions, it seems to me, is always present, since we are much more sensitive to an individual's behaviors and verbalizations than we are to the subtle contextual stimuli that often promote them. At issue here is a matter of magnitude. And, as I have shown, the magnitude of distortion is exceedingly high in the extreme context that is a psychiatric hospital.)

The second matter that might prove promising speaks to the need to increase the sensitivity of mental health workers and researchers to the *Catch 22* position of psychiatric patients. Simply reading materials in this area will be of help to some such workers and researchers. For others, directly experiencing the impact of psychiatric hospitalization will be of enormous use. Clearly, further research into the social psychology of such total institutions will both facilitate treatment and deepen understanding.

I and the other pseudopatients in the psychiatric setting had distinctly negative reactions. We do not pretend to describe the subjective experiences of true patients. Theirs may be different from ours, particularly with the passage of time and the necessary process of adaptation to one's environment. But we can and do speak to the relatively more objective indices of treatment within the hospital. It could be a mistake, and a very unfortunate one, to consider that what happened to us derived from malice or stupidity on the part of the staff. Quite the contrary, our overwhelming impression of them was of people who really cared, who were committed and who were uncommonly intelligent. Where they failed, as they sometimes did painfully, it would be more accurate to attribute those failures to the environment in which they, too, found themselves than to personal callousness. Their perceptions and behavior were controlled by the situation, rather than being motivated by a malicious disposition. In a more benign environment, one that was less attached to global diagnosis, their behaviors and judgments might have been more benign and effective.

REFERENCES AND NOTES

1. P. Ash, *J. Abnorm. Soc. Psychol.* 44, 272 (1949); A. T. Beck, *Amer. J. Psychiat.* 119, 210 (1962); A. T. Boisen, *Psychiatry* 2, 233 (1938); N. Kreitman, *J. Ment. Sct.* 107, 876 (1961); N. Kreitman, P. Sainsbury, J. Morrisey, J. Towers, J. Scrivener, *ibid.*, p. 887; H. O. Schmitt and C. P. Fonda, *J. Abnorm. Soc. Psychol.* 52, 262 (1956); W. Seeman, *J. Nerv. Ment. Dis.* 118, 541 (1953). For an analysis of these artifacts and summaries of the disputes, see J. Zubin, *Annu. Rev. Psychol.* 18, 373 (1967); L. Phillips and J. G. Draguns, *ibid.* 22, 447 (1971).

2. R. Benedict, *J. Gen. Psychol.* 10, 59 (1934).

3. See in this regard H. Becker, *Outsiders: Studies in the Sociology of Deviance* (Free Press, New York, 1963); B. M. Braginsky, D. D. Braginsky, K. Ring, *Methods of Madness: The Mental Hospital as a Last Resort* (Holt, Rinehart & Winston, New York, 1969); G. M. Crocetti and P. V. Lemkau, *Amer. Social. Rev.* 30, 577 (1965); E. Goffman, *Behavior in Public Places* (Free Press, New York, 1964); R. D. Laing, *The Divided Self: A Study of Sanity and Madness* (Quadrangle, Chicago, 1960) → D. L. Phillips, *Amer. Sociol. Rev.* 28, 963 (1963); T. R. Sarbin, *Psychol. Today* 6, 18 (1972); E. Schur, *Amer. J. Sociol.* 75, 309 (1969); T. Szasz, *Law, Liberty and Psychiatry* (Macmillan, New York, 1963); *The Myth of Mental Illness: Foundations of a Theory of Mental Illness* (Hoeber-Harper, New York, 1963). For a critique of some of these views, → W. R. Gove, *Amer. Sociol. Rev.* 35, 873 (1970).

4. E. Goffman, *Asylums* (Doubleday, Garden City, N.Y., 1961).

5. T. J. Scheff, *Being Mentally Ill: A Sociological Theory* (Aldine, Chicago, 1966).

6. Data from a ninth pseudopatient are not incorporated in this report because, although his sanity went undetected, he falsified aspects of his personal history, including his marital status and parental relationships. His experimental behaviors therefore were not identical to those of the other pseudopatients.

7. A. Barry, *Bellevue Is a State of Mind* (Harcourt Brace Jovanovich, New York, 1971); I. Belknap, *Human Problems of a State Mental Hospital* (McGraw-Hill, New York, 1956); W. Caudill, F. C. Redlich, H. R. Gilmore, E. B. Brody, *Amer. J. Orthopsychiat.* 22, 314 (1952); A. R. Goldman, R. H. Bohr, T. A. Steinberg, *Prof. Psychol.* 1, 427 (1970); unauthored, *Roche Report* 1 (No. 13), 8 (1971).

8. Beyond the personal difficulties that the pseudopatient is likely to experience in the hospital, there are legal and social ones that, combined, require considerable attention before entry. For example, once admitted to a psychiatric institution, it is difficult, if not impossible, to be discharged on short notice, state law to the contrary notwithstanding. I was not

sensitive to these difficulties at the outset of the project, nor to the personal and situational emergencies that can arise, but later a writ of habeas corpus was prepared for each of the entering pseudopatients and an attorney was kept "on call" during every hospitalization. I am grateful to John Kaplan and Robert Bartels for legal advice and assistance in these matters.

9. However distasteful such concealment is, it was a necessary first step to examining these questions. Without concealment, there would have been no way to know how valid these experiences were; nor was there any way of knowing whether whatever detections occurred were a tribute to the diagnostic acumen of the staff or to the hospital's rumor network. Obviously, since my concerns are general ones that cut across individual hospitals and staffs, I have respected their anonymity and have eliminated clues that might lead to their identification.

10. Interestingly, of the 12 admissions, 11 were diagnosed as schizophrenic and one, with the identical symptomatology, as manic-depressive psychosis. This diagnosis has a more favorable prognosis, and it was given by the only private hospital in our sample. On the relations between social class and psychiatric diagnosis, see A. deB. Hollingshead and F. C. Redlich, *Social Class and Mental Illness: A Community Study* (Wiley, New York, 1958).

11. It is possible, of course, that patients have quite broad latitudes in diagnosis and therefore are inclined to call many people sane, even those whose behavior is patently aberrant. However, although we have no hard data on this matter, it was our distinct impression that this was not the case. In many instances, patients not only singled us out for attention, but came to imitate our behaviors and styles.

12. J. Cumming and E. Cumming, *Community Ment. Health* 1, 135 (1965); A. Farina and K. Ring, *J. Abnorm. Psychol.* 70, 47 (1965); H. E. Freeman and O. G. Simmons, *The Mental Patient Comes Home* (Wiley, New York, 1963); W J. Johannsen, *Ment. Hygiene* 53, 218 (1969); A. S. Linsky, *Soc. Psychiat.* 5, 166 (1970).

13. S. E. Asch, *J. Abnorm. Soc. Psychol.* 41, 258 (1946); *Social Psychology* (Prentice-Hall, New York, 1952).

14. See also I. N. Mensh and J. Wishner, *J. Personality* 16, 188 (1947); J. Wishner, *Psychol. Rev.* 67, 96 (1960); J. S. Bruner and R. Tagiuri, in *Handbook of Social Psychology*, G. Lindzey, Ed. (Addison-Wesley, Cambridge, Mass., 1954), vol. 2, pp. 634–654; J. S. Bruner, D. Shapiro, R. Tagiuri, in *Person Perception and Interpersonal Behavior*, R. Tagiuri and L. Petrullo, Eds. (Stanford Univ. Press, Stanford, Calif., 1958), pp. 277–288.

15. For an example of a similar self-fulfilling prophecy, in this instance dealing with the "central" trait of intelligence, see R. Rosenthal and L. Jacobson, *Pygmalion in the Classroom* (Holt, Rinehart & Winston, New York, 1968).

16. E. Zigler and L. Phillips, *J. Abnorm. Soc. Psychol.* 63, 69 (1961). See also R. K. Freudenberg and J. P. Robertson, *A.M.A. Arch. Neurol. Psychiatr.* 76, 14 (1956).

17. W. Mischel, *Personality and Assessment* (Wiley, New York, 1968).

18. The most recent and unfortunate instance of this tenet is that of Senator Thomas Eagleton.

19. T. R. Sarbin and J. C. Mancuso, *J. Clin. Consult. Psychol.* 35, 159 (1970); T. R. Sarbin, *Ibid.* 31, 447 (1967); J. C. Nunnally, Jr., *Popular Conceptions of Mental Health* (Holt, Rinehart & Winston, New York, 1961).

20. A. H. Stanton and M. S. Schwartz, *The Mental Hospital: A Study of Institutional Participation in Psychiatric Illness and Treatment* (Basic, New York, 1954).

21. D. B. Wexler and S. E. Scoville, *Ariz. Law Rev.* 13, 1 (1971).

22. I thank W. Mischel, E. Orne, and M. S. Rosenhan for comments on an earlier draft of this manuscript.

STUDY QUESTIONS

1. When the pseudopatients in the study were released, what was their diagnosis and what does this tell us about being labeled as mentally ill?

2. What do you make of the fact that the other patients could tell that the researchers were faking their illness? Why were the medical staff more likely to assume illness and the patients less likely to assume illness?

3. Imagine that you have just been diagnosed, in error, with a mental illness and have been forced into a mental hospital. How would you go about proving your sanity? What does this scenario tell you about how sanity is socially constructed?

4. Assume for a moment that we really are unable to diagnose mental illness—that normal or sane cannot be distinguished from abnormal or insane. How would this change the medical industry, the legal justice system, and all our other **social institutions**?

BRUCE WESTERN AND CHRISTOPHER WILDEMAN

The Black Family and Mass Incarceration

The United States has one of the highest incarceration rates in the world. Inequality in the rate of incarceration for young African American males is astounding and, as Bruce Western and Christopher Wildeman report in this article, it has had a profoundly negative effect on the black **family**. In this age of "individual responsibility" for the elimination of social problems, we need to understand the result social policies of mass incarceration have on the well-being of African American families.

TODAY, WE READ DANIEL PATRICK MOYNIHAN'S 1965 REPORT, *THE Negro Family: The Case For National Action*, with a sense of lost opportunity. The report drew attention to the problems of chronic idleness, addiction, and serious violence in minority urban neighborhoods of concentrated poverty. Moynihan traced these problems to the breakdown of the African American family. High nonmarital birth rates, divorce and separation, and single-parenthood, in Moynihan's analysis, all contributed to ghetto poverty, crime, and other dislocations. Although Moynihan did not offer a detailed policy solution, he understood that the social problems of the urban poor stood in the way of the historic promise of full African American citizenship demanded by the civil rights movements.

Sounding the alarm over ghetto poverty in 1965, Moynihan named a social problem and suggested a direction for its solution. Viewed in hindsight, the report marked a fork in the road. Many of the social problems Moynihan identified have subsequently worsened. Joblessness among young, black, noncollege men climbed through the 1960s and 1970s. Crime rates and rates of single-parenthood also escalated. While Moynihan called for increased social investment to avert the problems of crime and poverty, public policy turned instead in a punitive direction, massively expanding the role of the criminal justice system. By the early 2000s, more than a third of young black noncollege men were incarcerated. Among black men younger than forty, there were nearly twice as many prison records as bachelor's degrees. The spectacular growth of the American penal system has transformed the institutional context of urban poverty in a way that was wholly unexpected by Moynihan or other students of social policy of his time.

In this article, we describe the main contours of the American prison boom and its effect on the lives and structure of poor African American families. We argue that in the wake of the Moynihan Report, economic conditions among the ghetto poor continued to deteriorate. Instead of a movement for social investment in the urban poor that Moynihan supported, politics turned to the right. Political currents flowed to law and order and away from rehabilitative criminal justice policy. Retribution and incapacitation were embraced as the main objectives of criminal punishment. As a result, the prison population ballooned through the 1980s and 1990s, producing astonishing incarceration rates among young African American men. Although family breakdown was not the immediate cause of the American prison boom, mass incarceration has had potentially profound effects on the family life of those caught in the web of the criminal justice system. Research is still in its infancy, but we conclude by describing what we see as the most important questions linking mass incarceration to the family life of America's urban poor.

POLITICAL AND ECONOMIC ROOTS OF THE PRISON BOOM

Mass imprisonment of the late 1990s can be traced to two basic shifts in politics and economics. The growth of harsh sentencing policies and a punitive approach to drug control began with a rightward shift in American politics, first visible at the national level in the mid-1960s. Barry Goldwater's ill-fated presidential run in 1964 was pivotal (Beckett 1997; Gest 2001). Goldwater, in accepting the Republican nomination, warned that crime and disorder were threats to human freedom, and freedom must be "balanced so that liberty lacking order will not become the license of the mob and of the jungle." The Republican campaign of 1964 linked the problem of street crime to civil rights protest and the growing unease among whites about racial violence.

Although Goldwater was roundly defeated by Lyndon B. Johnson, conservatives within the Republican Party had brought to the national stage a new kind of politics.

Historically, responsibilities for crime control were divided mostly between state and local agencies. The Republicans had placed the issue of crime squarely on the national agenda. What is more, by treating civil rights protest as a strain of social disorder, veiled connections were drawn between the crime problem, on one hand, and black social protest, on the other.

The social problem of crime became a reality as rates of murder and other violent crimes escalated in the decade following the 1964 election. Throughout the 1960s, urban riots in Los Angeles, New York, Newark, Detroit, and dozens of other cities provided a socially ambiguous mixture of disorder and politics. Despite Goldwater's defeat, support grew for the new law and order message, particularly among southern whites and northern working-class voters of Irish, Italian, and German descent who turned away from the Democratic Party in the 1970s (Edsall and Edsall 1991).

Elevated crime rates and the realigned race relations of the post—civil rights period provided a receptive context for the law and order themes of the Republican Party. In state politics, Republican governors and legislators increased their representation through the South and West and placed themselves in the vanguard of the movements for mandatory minimum sentences, sentence enhancements for repeat offenders, and expanded prison capacity (Western 2006; Davey 1998; Jacobs and Carmichael 2001). Quantitative analyses show that incarceration rates grew fastest under Republican governors and state legislators (Western 2006, chap. 3).

Although Republicans were quick to promote prison expansion and tough new criminal sentences, Democrats also came to support punitive criminal justice policy. Perhaps the clearest signal that Democrats too were tough on crime was sent by President Clinton's Violent Crime Control and Law Enforcement Act (1994). The Clinton crime bill earmarked $9.9 billion for prison construction and added life terms for third-time federal felons (Windelsham 1998, 104–7). By the 1990s, Democrats and Republicans had come to support the sentencing policies and capital construction campaigns that grew the penal population.

Shifts in politics and policy, however, are only half the story. The newly punitive system of criminal sentencing would have had largely symbolic significance but for the ready supply of chronically idle young men that came to swell the nation's prisons and jails. Urban deindustrialization eroded the labor market for unskilled young men while punitive politics gained momentum in the 1970s and 1980s. Wilson's (1987) study of *The Truly Disadvantaged* provides the classic analysis. The decline of manufacturing industry employment in the Midwest and the Northeast coupled with the exodus of middle class and working-class blacks from inner cities produced pockets of severe unemployment in poor urban neighborhoods.

From 1969 to 1979, central cities recorded enormous declines in manufacturing and blue collar employment. New York, for example, lost 170,000 blue-collar jobs through the 1970s, another 120,000 jobs were shed in Chicago, and blue-collar employment in Detroit fell by 90,000 jobs (Kasarda 1989, 29). For young black men in metropolitan areas, employment rates fell by 30 percent among high school dropouts and nearly 20 percent among high school graduates. Job loss was only a third as large among young noncollege whites (Bound and Holzer 1993, 390).

Variation in imprisonment is closely linked to variation in wages and employment. Weekly earnings for young low-education men declined through the 1980s and 1990s while imprisonment rates were rising. Among black men, unemployment increased steeply with declining education. One study estimates that if wages and employment had not declined among low-education men since the early 1980s, growth in prison admission rates would have been reduced by as much as 25 percent by 2001 (Western, Kleykamp, and Rosenfeld 2004).

The urban deindustrialization that produced the raw material for the prison boom was as much a failure of institutions as a failure of markets. Large job losses in the mid-1970s and early 1980s were concentrated in unionized industries (Farber and Western 2001). De-unionization thus joined manufacturing decline to drive down the incomes of unskilled inner city workers. Besides unemployment insurance, which provided only temporary assistance, few social programs were available to supplement the incomes or retrain or mobilize young able-bodied men into new jobs. The welfare system was also poorly equipped to handle the social problems linked to male unemployment. Drug addiction, petty offending, and public idleness all afflicted the neighborhoods of concentrated disadvantage.

Idle young men in poor minority neighborhoods supplied a large share of the inmates that drove the prison boom. The path from concentrated economic disadvantage to mass imprisonment runs partly through the mechanism of crime, but policy also played a vital role. At any given point in time, crime among young disadvantaged men is higher than in the rest of the population. For example, the murder rates—victimization and offending—are about twenty-five times higher for black men aged eighteen to twenty-four than for white men aged twenty-five and older (Pastore and Maguire 2006). Violent crime is also a more serious problem in poor communities than affluent ones (e.g., Sampson 1987; see also the review of Braithwaite 1979). The criminal involvement of young, economically disadvantaged men makes them more likely at a given point in time to go to prison than others who are less involved in crime.

Crime cannot explain, however, why disadvantaged young men were so much more likely to go to prison by the end of the 1990s than two decades earlier. Indeed, survey data show that poor male youth were much less involved in crime at the height of the prison boom, in 2000, than at its inception, in 1980. To explain the growing risk of imprisonment over time, the role of policy is decisive. Because the system of criminal sentencing had come to rely so heavily on incarceration, an arrest in the late 1990s was far more likely to lead to prison time than at the beginning of the prison boom in 1980 (Blumstein and Beck 1999).

The drug trade holds a special place in this story. The drug trade itself became a source of economic opportunity in the jobless ghetto. Ethnographers paint striking pictures of how the inner-city drug trade becomes a focal point for the problems of economic disadvantage, violence, and state control. Sudhir Venkatesh and Steven Levitt (2000) describe how drug trafficking thrived in the vacuum of legitimate employment in Chicago's South Side neighborhoods. Chicago youth spoke to Venkatesh and Levitt of their "gang affiliation and their drive to earn income in ways that resonated with representations of work in the mainstream corporate firm. Many approached [gang] involvement as an institutionalized path of socioeconomic mobility for down-and-out youth" (p. 447). In Elijah Anderson's (1999) account, violence follows the drug trade as crime becomes a voracious force in the poor neighborhoods of Philadelphia:

> Surrounded by violence and by indifference to the innocent victims of drug dealers and users alike, the decent people are finding it harder and harder to maintain a sense of community. Thus violence comes to regulate life in the drug-infested neighborhoods and the putative neighborhood leaders are increasingly the people who control the violence. (p. 134)

The picture drawn by the ethnographic research is of poor neighborhoods, chronically short of legitimate work and embedded in a violent and illegal market for drugs. High rates of joblessness and crime, and a flourishing street trade in illegal drugs, combined with harsher criminal penalties and intensified urban policing to produce high incarceration rates among young unskilled men in inner cities. In the twenty-five years from 1980, the incarceration rate tripled among white men in their twenties, but fewer than 2 percent were behind bars by 2004. Imprisonment rates for young black men increased less quickly, but one in seven were in custody by 2004. Incarceration rates are much higher among male high school dropouts in their twenties. Threefold growth in the imprisonment of young white male dropouts left 7 percent in prison or jail by 2004. The incarceration rate for young low-education black men rose by 22 points in the two decades after 1980. Incredibly, 34 percent of all young black male high school dropouts were in prison or jail on an average day in 2004, an incarceration rate forty times higher than the national average (Western 2006, chap. 1).

Tough sentences for drug and repeat offenders, strict policing and prosecution of drug traffic and public order offending, and unforgiving parole supervision broadened the use of imprisonment from its traditional focus on serious crime. Certainly sentences increased for serious crime, and this contributed to incarceration rates too. For example, time served for murderers increased from five to eleven years, from 1980 to 1996 (Blumstein and Beck 1999, 36). But growth in the share of less serious offenders in state prison increased much more rapidly (Blumstein and Beck 1999, 24, 37). Growth in the numbers of drug offenders, parole violators, and public order offenders reflects the use of penal policy as a surrogate social policy, in which a troublesome and unruly population is increasingly managed with incarceration.

MASS INCARCERATION

The scale of the penal system is usually measured by an incarceration rate. The incarceration rate records the number of people in prison or jail on a given day per 100,000 of the population. Figure 1 compares the United States's incarceration rate in 2004 to the incarceration rates of the long-standing democracies of Western Europe. The penal systems of Western Europe locked up, on average, about 100 per 100,000. The United States by contrast incarcerated more than seven times the European average, with an incarceration rate of more than 700 per 100,000.

The contemporary scale of criminal punishment is also historically unusual. Although we do not have long time series of the total penal population of prison and jail inmates, data on the state and federal prison populations extend back to 1925. The time series in Figure 2 shows that between 1925 and 1973, the fraction of the U.S. population in state and federal prison varied in a narrow range of around 100 per 100,000—close to the total incarceration rates in Western Europe. Beginning in 1974, the prison population began to grow, and the incarceration rate increased continu-

FIGURE 1. Incarceration Rates per One Hundred Thousand Residents, United States and Western Europe, 2004

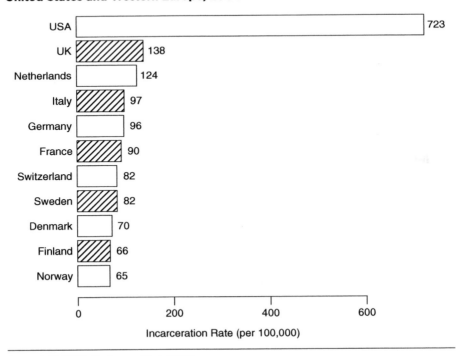

Source: Aebi (2005); Harrison and Beck (2006).

FIGURE 2. U.S. State and Federal Imprisonment Rates, 1925–2005; U.S. Prison and Jail Incarceration Rates, 1983–2005

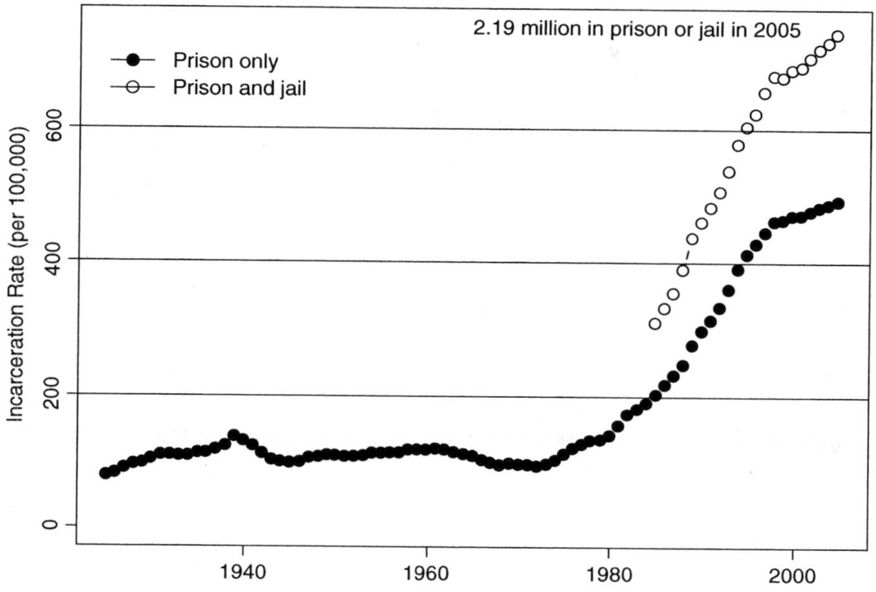

Source: Maguire and Pastore (2007).

ously for the next three decades. By 2005, nearly 2.2 million people were in custody, either in prison for felony convictions or in local jails awaiting trial or serving short sentences. These figures do not fully reflect the contemporary correctional population. In 2005, another 784,000 men and women were under community supervision on parole, while 4.1 million people were on probation. The total population under correctional supervision thus includes more than 7 million people, or about 3.1 percent of all U.S. adults (Glaze and Bonczar 2006).

The broad significance of the penal system for American social inequality results from extreme social and economic disparities in incarceration. More than 90 percent of all prison and jail inmates are men. Women's incarceration rates have increased more quickly than men's since 1980, but much higher rates persist for men, leaving women to contend with raising children while their partners cycle in and out of jail. These men are young, of working age, many with small children. About two-thirds of state prisoners are over eighteen years old but under age thirty-five. With this age pattern, only a small number of people are incarcerated at any point in time, but many more pass through the penal system at some point in their lives.

Incarceration is also concentrated among the disadvantaged. High incarceration rates among low-status and minority men are unmistakable. The 1997 survey of state and federal prisoners shows that state inmates average less than eleven years of schooling. A third were not working at the time of their incarceration, and the average wage of the remainder is much lower than that of other men with the same level of education. African Americans and Hispanics also have higher incarceration rates than whites, and together the two groups account for about two-thirds of the state prison population.

The black-white difference in incarceration rates is especially striking. Black men are eight times more likely to be incarcerated than whites, and large racial disparities can be seen for all age groups and at different levels of education. The large black-white disparity in incarceration is unmatched by most other social indicators. Racial disparities in unemployment (two to one), nonmarital childbearing (three to one), infant mortality (two to one), and wealth (one to five) are all significantly lower than the eight to one black-white ratio in incarceration rates (see Western 2006). If white men were incarcerated at the same rate as blacks, there would be more than 6 million people in prison and jail, and more than 5 percent of the male working-age population would be incarcerated.

Age, race, and educational disparities concentrate imprisonment among the disadvantaged. Figure 3 shows trends in incarceration rates for young black and white

FIGURE 3. The Percentage of Men, Aged Twenty-Two to Thirty, in Prison or Jail by Race and Education

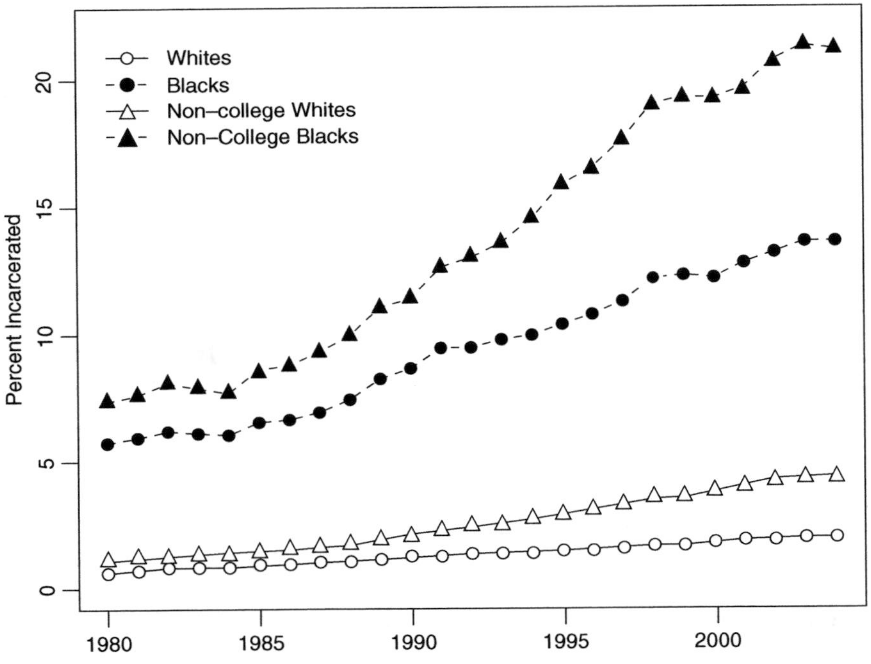

Source: Authors' tabulations, following Western (2006, 17).

men with different levels of schooling. From 1980 to 2004, the percentage of young white men in prison or jail increased from 0.6 to 1.9 percent. Among young white men with only a high school education, incarceration rates were about twice as high. At the dawn of the prison boom, in 1980, the incarceration rate for young black men, 5.7 percent, was more than twice as high as that for low-education whites. By 2004, 13.5 percent of black men in their twenties were in prison or jail. Incarceration rates were higher in the lower half of the education distribution. More than one in five young noncollege black men were behind bars on a typical day in 2004.

Incarceration rates offer a snapshot of the extent of penal confinement. Time series of incarceration rates tell us how the extent of penal confinement has shifted historically. We can also study, not the level of incarceration at a point in time, but how the risk of incarceration accumulates over an individual's life. This kind of life course analysis asks what is the likelihood an individual will go to prison by age twenty-five, thirty, or thirty-five. Instead of providing a snapshot of the risk of incarceration, this analysis describes a typical biography.

The life course perspective provides a compelling account of social integration. In this account, the passage to adulthood is a sequence of well-ordered stages that affect life trajectories long after the early transitions are completed. In modern times, arriving at adult status involves moving from school to work, then to marriage, to establishing a home and becoming a parent. Completing this sequence without delay promotes stable employment, marriage, and other positive life outcomes. The process of becoming an adult thus influences success in fulfilling adult roles and responsibilities.

As an account of social integration, life course analysis has attracted the interest of students of crime and deviance. Criminologists point to the normalizing effects of life course transitions. Steady jobs and good marriages build social bonds that keep would-be offenders in a daily routine. They enmesh men who are tempted by crime in a web of supportive social relationships. Strong family bonds and steady work restrict men's opportunities for antisocial behavior and offer them a stake in normal life. For persistent lawbreakers, the adult roles of spouse and worker offer a pathway out of crime (Sampson and Laub 1993; Warr 1998; Hagan 1993). Those who fail to secure the markers of adulthood are more likely to persist in criminal behavior. This idea of a normalizing, integrative life path offers a powerful alternative to claims that criminality is a stable trait possessed by some but absent in others. Above all else, the life course account of crime is dynamic, describing how people change as their social context evolves with age.

Imprisonment significantly alters the life course. Working life is disrupted as workers with prison records try to find jobs from employers who are deeply suspicious of applicants with criminal records. The stigma of a prison record also creates legal barriers to skilled and licensed occupations, rights to welfare benefits, and voting rights (Holzer 1996; Pager 2003; Uggen and Manza 2002). Ex-prisoners are also less likely to get married or cohabit with the mothers of their children (Lopoo and Western 2005). By eroding opportunities for employment and marriage, incarceration may also lead ex-inmates back to a life of crime. The volatility of adolescence may last well into midlife for men serving prison time. In short, imprisonment is a turning point in which young crime-involved men acquire a new status involving diminished life chances.

To place the risks of imprisonment in the context of the life course, we report new estimates of the cumulative risks of imprisonment by age thirty to thirty-four, for five-year birth cohorts born through the postwar period (see Table 1). Because most inmates enter prison for the first time before age thirty-five, these cumulative risks of imprisonment roughly describe lifetime risks of imprisonment. We emphasize that these lifetime risks of incarceration are for imprisonment, as opposed to jail incarceration. Imprisonment here describes a sentence of twelve months or longer for a felony conviction, now about twenty-eight months of time served, at the median.

The oldest cohort was born just after World War II, and its members reached their midthirties in 1979, just at the takeoff of the prison boom. In this group, just over 1 percent of whites and 9 percent of blacks would go to prison. As incarceration rates climbed through the 1980s, lifetime imprisonment risks also increased. The big jump in imprisonment separates men born in the 1950s and earlier from those born in the 1960s and later. The pervasive presence of the criminal justice system in the lives of African American men only emerges among those born since the mid-1960s who were reaching their midthirties from the end of the 1990s. Like the long time series of incarceration rates, these figures on postwar birth cohorts underscore the historic novelty of mass incarceration. Only through the 1990s did the penal system figure prominently in the lives of young black men.

Like incarceration rates, lifetime risks of imprisonment are also steeply stratified by education. We report cumulative risks of imprisonment for men who have had at least some college education and for all those with just a high school education. Among those with just a high school education, we separate high school dropouts and high school graduates. We report figures for all noncollege men because—particularly for African Americans—those without college education have remained an approximately constant proportion of the population. Educational attainment has increased across birth cohorts chiefly because the proportion of high school dropouts has declined.

Lifetime risks of imprisonment among black men with little schooling are particularly striking. For noncollege African American men, about 12 percent of those born just after the war would ultimately go to prison. For those born thirty years later, reaching their thirties in 2005, at least 36 percent would serve prison time. The latter figure is actually a slight underestimate, because those born 1975 to 1979 have not been exposed to the risk of imprisonment for as long as the older cohorts.

At the very bottom of the education distribution, among high school dropouts, prison time has become extraordinarily prevalent. For black male dropouts born since the mid-1960s, 60 to 70 percent go to prison. For this very poorly schooled segment of the population, serving time in prison has become a routine life event on the pathway through adulthood. Indeed, we need only go back several decades to find a time when incarceration was not pervasive in the lives of young black men with little schooling.

TABLE 1. Cumulative Risk of Imprisonment by Age Thirty to Thirty-Four by Race and Education for Men Born 1945 through 1949 to 1975 through 1979 (in Percentages)

	1945-1949	1950-1954	1955-1959	1960-1964	1965-1969	1970-1974	1975-1979
White men							
High school dropouts	4.2	7.2	8.0	8.0	10.5	14.8	15.3
High school only	0.7	2.0	2.1	2.5	4.0	3.8	4.1
All noncollege	1.8	2.9	3.2	3.7	5.1	5.1	6.3
Some college	0.7	0.7	0.6	0.8	0.7	0.9	1.2
All men	1.2	1.9	2.0	2.2	2.8	2.8	3.3
Black men							
High school dropouts	14.7	19.6	27.6	41.6	57.0	62.5	69.0
High school only	10.2	11.3	9.4	12.4	16.8	20.3	18.0
All noncollege	12.1	14.1	14.7	19.9	26.7	30.9	35.7
Some college	4.9	3.5	4.3	5.5	6.8	8.5	7.6
All men	9.0	10.6	11.5	15.2	20.3	22.8	20.7

Source: Data sources and methods are described in Pettit and Western (2004).

Note: Estimates for the cohorts born after 1969 are based on data from the 2004 Survey on Inmates of States and Federal Correctional Facilities.

Detailed figures on the racial and educational differences in imprisonment also show another pattern. While lifetime risks of imprisonment grew threefold for men without a college education, imprisonment among the college-educated less than doubled. In short, most of the growth in imprisonment was concentrated among those with little schooling. At the same time, racial disparities in imprisonment risks, while large, did not increase significantly. The figures thus indicate that in the period of the prison boom, class inequality in incarceration clearly increased, but racial inequality did not. Because racial disparities in imprisonment were so large to begin with, however, the prison boom produced extraordinarily high rates of incarceration among young noncollege black men.

From a life course perspective, we can compare imprisonment to other significant life events that are commonly thought to mark the path through young adulthood. Life course researchers have previously studied college graduation, military service, and marriage as key milestones that move young men forward in life to establishing a household and a steady job. Comparing imprisonment to these life events suggests how the pathway through adulthood has been changed by the prison boom.

The risks of each life event are different for blacks and whites, but racial differences in imprisonment greatly overshadow any other inequality. By their early thirties, whites are more than twice as likely to hold a bachelor's degree compared with blacks, whereas blacks are about 50 percent more likely to have served in the military. However, black men in their early thirties are about seven times more likely than whites to have a prison record. Indeed, recent birth cohorts of black men are more likely to have prison records (22.4 percent) than military records (17.4 percent) or bachelor's degrees (12.5 percent). The share of the population with prison records is particularly striking among noncollege men. Whereas few noncollege white men have prison records, nearly a third of black men with less than a college education have been to prison. Noncollege black men in their early thirties in 1999 were more than twice as likely to be ex-felons as veterans (see Table 2).

By 1999, imprisonment had become a common life event for black men that sharply distinguished their pathway through adulthood from that of white men. David Garland coined the term "mass imprisonment" to refer to the high rate of incarceration in the contemporary United States. In Garland's definition, mass imprisonment has two characteristics. First, he writes, "mass imprisonment implies a rate of imprisonment . . . that is markedly above the historical and comparative norm for societies of this type" (Garland 2001, 1). Indeed, we have seen that the rate of incarceration in the United States by the late 1990s was far higher than in Western Europe and without precedent in U.S. history. Second, Garland argues, the demographic concentration of imprisonment produces not the incarceration of individual offenders, but the "systematic imprisonment of whole groups of the population" (Garland 2001, 2).

The empirical markers of mass imprisonment are more slippery in this case. When will the incarceration rate be high enough to imprison, not the individual, but the group? The picture painted by the statistics in this article helps us answer this

TABLE 2. Percentage of Non-Hispanic Black and White Men, Born 1965 to 1969, Experiencing Life Events by 1999

Life Event	Whites	Blacks
All men		
Prison incarceration	3.2	22.4
Bachelor's degree	31.6	12.5
Military service	14.0	17.4
Marriage	72.5	59.3
Noncollege men		
Prison incarceration	6.0	31.9
High school diploma/GED	73.5	64.4
Military service	13.0	13.7
Marriage	72.8	55.9

Source: Pettit and Western (2004).

Note: The incidence of all live events except prison incarceration were calculated from the 2000 Census. To make the incarceration risks comparable to census statistics, the estimates are adjusted to describe the percentage of men, born 1965 to 1969, who have ever been imprisoned and survived to 1999.

question. Not only did incarceration become common among young black men at the end of the 1990s, but its prevalence also exceeded that of other life events that we usually associate with passage through the life course. More than college graduation or military service, incarceration has come to typify the biographies of African American men born since the late 1960s.

MASS INCARCERATION AND FAMILY LIFE

As imprisonment became common for low-education black men by the end of the 1990s, the penal system also became familiar to poor minority families. By 1999, 30 percent of noncollege black men in their midthirties had been to prison, and through incarceration, many were separated from their wives, girlfriends, and children. Women and children in low-income urban communities now routinely cope with absent husbands and fathers lost to incarceration and adjust to their return after release. Poor single men detached from family life are also affected, bearing the stigma of a prison record in the marriage markets of disadvantaged urban neighborhoods.

Discussions of the family life of criminal offenders typically focus on the crime-suppressing effects of marriage, not the effects of incarceration on family life. Researchers find that marriage offers a pathway out of crime for men with histories of delinquency. Not a wedding itself, but marriage in the context of a warm, stable, and constructive relationship, offers the antidote to crime (Sampson and Laub 1993; Laub, Nagin, and Sampson 1998). Wives and family members in such relationships provide the web of obligations and responsibilities that restrains young men and reduces their contact with the male friends whose recreations veer into antisocial behavior (Warr 1998).

The prison boom places the link between crime and marriage in a new light. If a good marriage is important for criminal desistance, what is the effect of incarceration on marriage? The connections between incarceration, marriage, and the family are also implicated in the larger story of rising urban inequality. In the past three decades, American family life was transformed by declining marriage rates and growth in the number of single-parent households. Marriage rates fell among women from all class backgrounds. Between 1970 and 2000, the share of white women aged twenty-five to thirty-four who were married declined from more than 80 percent to just over 60 percent. Marriage rates for African American women halved from 60 to around 30 percent. The decline in marriage propelled growth in the number of single-parent households, although this effect was confined to those with little education (Ellwood and Jencks 2004). The share of college-educated women who were single mothers remained constant at around 5 percent between 1970 and 2000, while the fraction of single mothers among low-education white women increased from 8 to 18 percent. Trends were most dramatic among black women. In 1970, about one-third of low-education black women were single parents, but the number increased to more than 50 percent in the next thirty years. By 2000, stable two-parent households became relatively rare, especially among African Americans with little schooling (Western 2006, chap. 1).

Poverty researchers closely followed the changing shape of American families. Growing numbers of female-headed families increased the risks of enduring poverty for women and children. Growing up poor also raised a child's risk of school failure, poor health, and delinquency. Writing in the mid-1980s, William Julius Wilson (1987) traced the growth in the number of female-headed black families to the shrinking number of "marriageable men" in poor urban areas. The shortage of suitable husbands in ghetto neighborhoods was driven by two processes. High rates of male incarceration and mortality tilted the gender ratio, which made it harder for poor urban women to find partners. These effects were small, however, compared to the high rate of joblessness that left few black men in inner cities able to support a family. Many studies later examined the impact of men's employment on marriage rates and found that the unemployed are less likely to be married and that joblessness can increase chances of divorce or separation (e.g., Lichter, LeClere, and McLaughlin 1991; McLanahan and Casper 1995; Blau, Kahn, and Waldfogel 2000). Studies of the effects of employment dominated research on marriage among the disadvantaged, and the idea that incarceration destabilized family life was undeveloped.

To study the family ties of prisoners, we begin by simply describing the levels of marriage and fatherhood in the penal population. Figure 3 compares rates of marriage and fatherhood in the penal population to those for men who are not incarcerated.

Levels of marriage are measured for noninstitutional men and male prison and jail inmates, aged twenty-two to thirty, in 2000. Rates of fatherhood are the percentage of noninstitutional men and male state prisoners, aged thirty-three to forty, who had children by 1997 to 1998.

Marriage rates among prison and jail inmates are very low compared to those on the outside. White male inmates in their twenties are less than half as likely to be married as young white noninstitutional men of the same age. The incarceration gap in marriage is also large for black and Hispanic men. The general level of marriage is highest for Hispanics, but in this case, inmates are only half as likely to be married as their counterparts in the noninstitutional population. Although marriage rates are lowest for black men, only 11 percent of young black inmates are married, compared to a marriage rate of 25 percent among young black men outside of prison and jail. In short, marriage rates among male prisoners in their twenties are only around half as high as in the free population.

Although marriage is uncommon among prisoners, they are just as likely as other men to have children. Figure 3 shows the percentage of men who have ever had children by their late thirties. The prevalence of fatherhood among prisoners is almost identical to that on the outside. For example, 73 percent of noninstitutional black men have had children by their late thirties, compared to 70 percent of black male prisoners of the same age. Male fertility rates among prisoners and nonprisoners are also very similar for whites and Hispanics.

The combination of high incarceration rates with a large proportion of fathers among inmates means many children now have incarcerated fathers. Data from surveys of prison and jail inmates can be used to calculate the numbers of children with fathers in prison or jail. A time series for 1980 to 2000 shows that the total number of children with incarcerated fathers increased sixfold from about 350,000 to 2.1 million, nearly 3 percent of all children nationwide in 2000. Among whites, the fraction of children with a father in prison or jail is relatively small—about 1.2 percent in 2000. The figure is about three times higher (3.5 percent) for Hispanics. Among African Americans, more than a million, or one in eleven, black children had a father in prison or jail in 2000. The numbers are higher for younger children: by 2000, 10.4 percent of black children under age ten had a father in prison or jail. Just as incarceration has become a normal life event for disadvantaged young black men, parental incarceration has become commonplace for their children.

To better gauge the impact of mass incarceration on children, we report the cumulative risks that one of their parents will be sent to prison. We also report these risks of parental incarceration for black and white children of parents at different levels of education. Just as lifetime risks of imprisonment help describe the life course of adults, cumulative risks of parental imprisonment tell us about the early life course of children.

These figures include incarceration among mothers as well as fathers. The rapid growth in incarceration among women is reflected in these figures. Although incarceration rates among mothers are much lower than those for fathers, the effects of maternal imprisonment on parental separation from children are relatively large. Whereas just under half of fathers were living with their children at the time they were sent to prison, nearly two-thirds of mothers sent to prison were living with their children (Mumola 2000, 3).

Table 3 reports the risks of parental imprisonment by age fourteen for children born in 1978 and 1990 (see Wildeman forthcoming). Among white children born in 1978 who reached their teenage years in the early 1990s, around 2 percent experienced a parent being sent to prison. Among African American children born in the same year, around 14 percent had a parent sent to prison by age fifteen. Twelve years later, among children born in 1990, about a quarter of all black children had a parent sent to prison. Indeed, the proportion of black children who had a mother sent to prison (a relatively rare event) nearly equaled the proportion of white children who had a father sent to prison.

The children of low-education parents were far more exposed to the criminal justice system than the population in general. These estimates indicate that among children born in the late 1970s to noncollege African American parents, about one in seven had a parent sent to prison by the time they reached their teenage years. Just over a decade later, more than a quarter of the children of noncollege black parents experienced parental imprisonment. For black children whose parents dropped out

TABLE 3. Cumulative Risks of Paternal and Maternal Imprisonment for Children Born in 1978 and 1990, by Parents' Race and Education (in Percentages)

	Whites		Blacks	
	Maternal	Paternal	Maternal	Paternal
Born 1978				
All	0.2	2.1	1.4	13.4
High school dropout	0.2	4.0	1.9	21.4
High school graduate	0.2	2.0	0.9	9.9
All noncollege	0.2	2.8	1.5	15.1
Some college	0.2	1.4	1.2	7.1
Born 1990				
All	0.6	3.6	3.2	24.5
High school dropout	1.0	7.1	5.0	49.4
High school graduate	0.7	4.7	2.6	20.0
All noncollege	0.8	5.5	3.6	24.5
Some college	0.3	1.7	2.6	13.2

Source: Sources, methods, and figures are reported in Wildeman (forthcoming).

of high school, around half had a parent sent to prison by the early 2000s. Just as imprisonment had become a normal life event for young black male dropouts, so had parental imprisonment become normal for their children.

The prevalence of marriage and fatherhood among prison and jail inmates tells us something about the incapacitation effect of incarceration. Men behind bars cannot fully play the role of father and husband. Single incarcerated men are unlikely to get married while they are locked up. On the outside, the incapacitation effect takes the form of lopsided gender ratios of poor communities. For example, in the high-incarceration neighborhoods of Washington, D.C., there are only sixty-two men for every one hundred women (Braman 2004, 86). Studying U.S. counties, William Sabol and James Lynch (1998) quantify the effects of the removal of men to prison. After accounting for educational attainment, welfare receipt, poverty, employment, and crime, Sabol and Lynch find that the doubling of the number of black men admitted to prison between 1980 and 1990 is associated with a 19 percent increase in the number of families headed by black women.

The incapacitation effect captures only part of the impact of the prison boom on marriage. In Wilson's terms, incarceration also damages men's marriageability. Wilson (1987, 83–92) traced declining marriage rates among the ghetto poor to the increasing inability of young disadvantaged black men to support families. Incarceration erodes men's economic desirability even more. Incarceration reduces men's wages, slows the rate of wage growth, increases unemployment, and shortens job tenure. If a poor employment record damages the marriage prospects of single men and contributes to the risk of divorce among those who are married, the economic effects of incarceration will decrease the likelihood of marriage among men who have been to prison and jail.

Wilson (1987) measured marriageability mostly by employment, but a man's criminal record also signals his ability to care and provide for his family. While poor women care about men's economic status, they also worry about men's honesty and respectability. Edin's (2000) ethnographic interviews showed that these noneconomic concerns weighed heavily on low-income women in metropolitan Philadelphia. The women Edin interviewed were deeply distrustful of men. The respondents were often reluctant to marry or develop romantic relationships because they viewed men's marital infidelity as inevitable. Some women's trust in men was shaken by boyfriends who spent household savings on drugs or drink and neglected children in their care.

This wariness was compounded by the men's low social status. For the women in Edin's sample, marriage offered a route to respectability, but "marriage to an economically unproductive male means . . . permanently taking on his very low status" (Edin 2000, 29). Elijah Anderson (1999, 153) makes a similar point in the opposite way, by describing the dreams of teenage girls in ghetto neighborhoods, a "dream of living happily ever after with one's children in a nice house in a good neighborhood—essentially the dream of the middle-class American lifestyle." In these cases, it is the social status of jobless men, their lack of esteem, as much as their material resources, which limits their appeal as husbands.

If reliability and reputation measure the noneconomic aspects of marriageability, incarceration has likely eroded the pool of marriageable men. Just as the stigma of incarceration confers disadvantage in the labor market, it also undermines a man's prospects in the marriage market. Men in trouble with the authorities cannot offer the respectability that many poor women seek from their partners. A prison record—the official stamp of criminality—can convey trouble to mothers looking for a stable home. For example, Edin's (2000, 28) interviews described women's aversion to drug dealing, even when it provided a couple with income: "Mothers fear that if their man gets involved in drug dealing, he might stash weapons, drugs, or drug proceeds in the household, that the violence of street life might follow him into the household." Because marriage offers a way of enhancing status, the trouble foreshadowed by a prison record may be even more repellent than chronic unemployment.

The stigma of incarceration also strains existing relationships. Erving Goffman (1963, 30) describes stigma's contagious quality, suffusing personal relationships: "In general the tendency for a stigma to spread from the stigmatized individual to his close connections provides a reason why such relations tend either to be avoided or to be terminated where existing." Braman's (2004) fieldwork in Washington, D.C., provides empirical support. The high prevalence of incarceration, he finds, does little to reduce its stigmatic effect. Braman describes the experience of Louisa, whose husband Robert was arrested on an old armed robbery charge after a lengthy period out of prison and in recovery from drug addiction. The couple

> had come to think and present themselves as morally upstanding citizens and churchgoers. Because of this, Louisa felt the stigma of her husband's most recent incarceration all the more intensely. She began to avoid friends and family, not wanting to talk about Robert's incarceration and lying to them when she did. (p. 170)

Louisa came to withdraw from her extended family and grappled with depression during Robert's incarceration. Braman argues that the stigma of incarceration is even more severe for family members than the offender, because wives and children live and work outside the prison, exposed to the condemnation of neighbors and other community members.

The separation imposed by incarceration also weighs heavily on relationships. Interviews with ex-offenders suggest that the friendships underlying romantic relationships are diluted by time apart. Often women become more independent and self-sufficient while their partners are incarcerated (Nurse 2002, 109). Just as Edin's (2000) female respondents distrusted men's commitment, Ann Nurse (2002) reports that individuals in her Californian sample of juvenile offenders were constantly suspicious of the fidelity of their wives and girlfriends. Often, these fears were well-founded, and many romantic relationships failed while men were incarcerated (see also Edin, Nelson, and Paranal 2004, 62).

Quantitative analysis of survey data is generally consistent with the field research. Black single men are especially likely to remain unmarried if they have prison records. The gap in marriage rates between black noninmates and ex-inmates is estimated to be anywhere from 20 to 200 percent. Survey data point more strongly to the destabilizing effects of incarceration on couples. Consider an analysis of the Fragile Families Survey of Child Wellbeing—a survey of poor urban couples with infant children. The survey shows that men who are living with the mothers of their newborn children are three times more likely to separate within the year if they have a history of incarceration (Western 2006, chap. 7).

UNANSWERED QUESTIONS

Moynihan traced the dilapidated state of the black family of the early 1960s to the burdens of slavery and a history of discrimination. In the early 2000s, however, the family life of poor African Americans in urban neighborhoods of concentrated poverty is also strained by mass incarceration. Emerging only in the closing years of the 1990s, mass incarceration has routinely drawn young noncollege black men and their families into the orbit of the penal system.

While a handful of ethnographic studies are beginning to shed light on the effects of incarceration on the family life of the urban poor, and several quantitative studies have examined the effects of incarceration on marriage and divorce, research is still in its infancy. We close our discussion by describing what we see as the central research questions and offering some hypotheses for understanding the family life of the urban poor in the era of mass incarceration.

How does incarceration affect family violence and other victimization?

In many cases, violent husbands and fathers are removed from households by incarceration. Survey data indicate that men who have been incarcerated are much more likely to have violent relationships with their partners, even if they were incarcerated for nonviolent offenses. From this perspective, mass incarceration may have significantly reduced family violence and other conflict in poor households. On the other hand, removing a father from the household may also open the door to other adult males who also pose a risk to poor women and their children. If children are at greater risk of abuse, for example, when a nonbiological adult male begins living in the household, mass incarceration may contribute to victimization rather than reduce it. What is more, returning prisoners may present more of a risk of family violence as a consequence of their incarceration. Very little is known about the patterns of violence and abuse that follow the removal of a parent from a family by incarceration. In assessing the effects of incarceration on the lives of poor families, this question is perhaps paramount.

What are the financial consequences of incarceration for poor families?

Research shows that incarceration is associated with reductions in employment and earnings of ex-prisoners after release (Western 2006; see the review of Western, Kling, and Weiman 2001). The annual earnings of ex-prisoners are about 40 percent lower than before imprisonment, controlling for changes in age, work experience, and schooling. The economic penalties of incarceration for ex-prisoners, however, do not necessarily translate into economic losses for their families. If men going to prison are only weakly connected to their families or make little financial contribution to their household, their earnings loss while incarcerated and poor job prospects after release may have little effect on the family economy.

A parent in prison may also impose a direct financial burden, however. The costs of visiting far-flung facilities, accepting collect calls, and retaining legal representation all add to the financial strains of poor families. The extent of these costs is largely unknown. The economic effect of mass incarceration on families is thus fundamentally an empirical question. Research on the pay and employment of ex-prisoners suggests that the economic effects of mass incarceration on families may be large, but this hinges on the strength of the connection between crime-involved men and their families before and after incarceration.

What are the effects of incarceration on the supervision and socialization of children?

As with the question of economic effects, much turns here on the involvement of incarcerated fathers in their families before they were sent to prison. If fathers were not highly involved, the effects of incarceration would be quite small. Inmate surveys show that nearly half of state prisoners who are fathers were living with at least some of their children at the time of their incarceration. For those children, incarceration contributes to family breakup. Poor fathers, even if nonresident, frequently maintain some kind of supportive relationship with their partners and children. For these children, paternal incarceration likely involves the loss of an adult figure that could play some role in the supervision and socialization of children.

We have seen that rates of maternal incarceration are much lower, but incarcerated mothers are more likely to be living with their children at the time of imprisonment. Again, the effects of imprisonment depend on the quality of the relationship between parent and child, and here relatively little is known. While the loss of a parent to the criminal justice system likely affects the socialization of children, children's aspirations and sense of self-worth are likely to be affected by the stigma of imprisonment. Although Goffman (1963) writes about the contagious character of social stigma, few studies have examined how children may be affected in their peer groups or at school (though see Comfort 2002).

We have argued here that the emergence of mass imprisonment has transformed the institutional context of America's urban poor. In this sense, this new era of mass incarceration adds another chapter to Moynihan's original analysis of urban poverty and its social correlates. The data suggest that the prison boom has been massively corrosive for family structure and family life, but much work remains to be done. In the background of this research agenda is the key question of the durability of urban poverty in the era of mass incarceration. If pervasive imprisonment undermines family life and disrupts the developmental path of children into young adulthood, the inequalities produced by mass incarceration may be exceptionally enduring. If the children of the prison boom are at greater risk of poverty and violence and are more involved in crime themselves, they too will risk following their parents into prison. Under these circumstances, the inequalities of mass incarceration will be sustained not just over a lifetime, but from one generation to the next.

ACKNOWLEDGMENTS

This research was supported by grants from the National Science Foundation, the Russell Sage Foundation, and a Guggenheim Fellowship.

REFERENCES

Aebi, Marcelo. 2005. *Council of Europe annual penal statistics.* Strasbourg, France: Council of Europe.

Anderson, Elijah. 1999. *Code of the street: Decency, violence, and the moral life of the inner city.* New York: Norton.

Beckett, Katherine. 1997. *Making crime pay: Law and order in contemporary American politics.* New York: Oxford University Press.

Blau, Francine D., Lawrence M. Kahn, and Jane Waldfogel. 2000. Understanding young women's marriage decisions: The role of labor and marriage market conditions. *Industrial and Labor Relations Review* 53:624–47.

Blumstein, Alfred, and Allen J. Beck. 1999. Population growth in U.S. prisons, 1980–1996. In *Crime and justice: Prisons,* vol. 26, ed. Michael Tonry and Joan Petersilia, 17–62. Chicago: University of Chicago Press.

Bound, John, and Harry Holzer. 1993. Industrial shifts, skill levels, and the labor market for white and black men. *Review of Economics and Statistics* 75:387–96.

Braithwaite, John. 1979. *Inequality, crime and public policy.* London: Routledge.

Braman, Donald S. 2004. *Doing time on the outside: Incarceration family life in urban America.* Ann Arbor: University of Michigan Press.

Comfort, Megan. 2002. Papa's house: The prison as domestic and social satellite. *Ethnography* 3:467–99.

Davey, Joseph D. 1998. *The politics of prison expansion: Winning elections by waging war on crime.* Westport, CT: Praeger.

Edin, Kathy. 2000. Few good men: Why poor mothers don't marry or remarry. *American Prospect* 11:26–31.

Edin, Katherine, Timothy Nelson, and Rechelle Paranal, 2004. Fatherhood and incarceration as potential turning points in the criminal careers of unskilled men. In *Imprisoning America: The social effects of mass incarceration*, ed. Mary Patillo, David Weiman, and Bruce Western, 46–75. New York: Russell Sage Foundation.

Edsall, Thomas B., and Mary D. Edsall. 1991. *Chain reaction: The impact of race, rights, and taxes on American politics*. New York: Norton.

Ellwood, David, and Christopher Jencks. 2004. The uneven spread of single-parent families: What do we know? Where do we look for answers? In *Social inequality*, ed. Katherine Neckerman, 3–77. New York: Russell Sage Foundation.

Farber, Henry S., and Bruce Western. 2001. Accounting for the decline of unions in the private sector, 1973–1998. *Journal of Labor Research* 22:459–86.

Garland, David. 2001. Introduction: The meaning of mass imprisonment. In *Mass imprisonment: Social causes and consequences*, ed. David Barland, 1–3. Thousand Oaks, CA: Sage.

Gest, Ted. 2001. *Crime and politics: Big government's erratic campaign for law and order*. New York: Oxford University Press.

Glaze, Lauren E., and Thomas P. Bonczar. 2006. *Probation and parole in the United States, 2005*. Washington, DC: U.S. Department of Justice.

Goffman, Erving. 1963. *Stigma: Notes on the management of spoiled identity*. Englewood Cliffs, NJ: Prentice Hall.

Hagan, John. 1993. The social embeddedness of crime and unemployment. *Criminology* 31:465–91.

Harrison, Paige M., and Allen J. Beck. 2006. Prison and jail inmates at midyear 2005. Bureau of Justice Statistics Bulletin. NCJ 208801. Washington, DC: U.S. Department of Justice.

Holzer, Harry J. 1996. *What employers want: Job prospects for less-educated workers*. New York: Russell Sage Foundation.

Jacobs, David, and Jason T. Carmichael. 2001. The politics of punishment across time and space: A pooled time-series analysis of imprisonment rates. *Social Forces* 80:61–91.

Kasarda, Jack. 1989. Urban industrial transition and the underclass. *The Annals of the American Academy of Political and Social Sciences* 501:26–47.

Laub, John H., Daniel S. Nagin, and Robert J. Sampson. 1998. Trajectories of change in criminal offending: Good marriages and desistance processes. *American Sociological Review* 63:225–38.

Lichter, Daniel T., Felicia B. LeClere, and Diane K. McLaughlin. 1991. Local marriage markets and the marital behavior of black and white women. *American Journal of Sociology* 96:843–67.

Lopoo, Leonard M., and Bruce Western. 2005. Incarceration and the formation and stability of marital unions. *Journal of Marriage and the Family* 65:721–34.

Maguire, Kathleen, and Ann L. Pastore, eds. 2007. *Sourcebook of criminal justice statistics*. http://www.albany.edu/sourcebook/ (accessed December 2007).

McLanahan, Sara, and Lynne Casper. 1995. Growing diversity and inequality in the American family. In *State of the union, America in the 1990s: Social trends*, ed. Reynolds Farley, 1–46. New York: Russell Sage Foundation.

Mumola, Christopher. 2000. *Incarcerated parents and their children*. Washington, DC: U.S. Department of Justice.

Nurse, Ann M. 2002. *Fatherhood arrested: Parenting from within the juvenile justice system*. Nashville, TN: Vanderbilt University Press.

Pager, Devah. 2003. The mark of a criminal record. *American Journal of Sociology* 108:937–75.

Pastore, Ann L., and Kathleen Maguire, eds. 2006. *Sourcebook of criminal justice statistics*. http://www.albany.edu/sourcebook/ (accessed December 2007).

Pettit, Becky, and Bruce Western. 2004. Mass imprisonment and the life course: Race and class inequality in U.S. incarceration. *American Sociological Review* 69:151–69.

Sabol, William J., and James P. Lynch. 1998. Assessing the longer-run consequences of incarceration: Effects on families and unemployment. Paper Presented at the 20th annual conference of the Association for Public Policy and Analysis, New York.

Sampson, Robert. 1987. Urban black violence: The effect of male joblessness and family disruption. *American Journal of Sociology* 93:348–82.

Sampson, Robert J., and John H. Laub. 1993. *Crime in the making: Pathways and turning points through life*. Cambridge, MA: Harvard University Press.

Uggen, Christopher, and Jeff Manza. 2002. Democratic contraction? Political consequences of felon disenfranchisement in the United States. *American Sociological Review* 67:777–803.

Venkatesh, Sudhir A., and Steven D. Levitt. 2000. Are we a family or a business? History and disjuncture in the urban American street gang. *Theory and Society* 29:427–62.

Warr, Mark. 1998. Life-course transitions and desistance from crime. *Criminology* 36:183–216.

Western, Bruce. 2006. *Punishment and inequality in America*. New York: Russell Sage Foundation.

Western, Bruce, Meredith Kleykamp, and Jake Rosenfeld. 2004. Crime, punishment, and American inequality. In *Social inequality*, ed. Katherine Neckerman, 771–96. New York: Russell Sage Foundation.

Western, Bruce, Jeffrey R. Kling, and David F. Weiman. 2001. The labor market consequences of incarceration. *Crime and Delinquency* 47:410–27.

Wildeman, Christopher. Forthcoming. Parental imprisonment, the prison boom, and the concentration of childhood disadvantage. *Demography*.

Wilson, William Julius. 1987. *The truly disadvantaged: The inner city, the underclass and public policy*. Chicago: University of Chicago Press.

Windelsham, Lord. 1998. *Politics, punishment and populism*. New York: Oxford University Press.

STUDY QUESTIONS

1. List some of the consequences of mass incarceration for black **families**.

2. Please discuss the **incapacitation** effect of incarceration on young children.

3. Has the mass incarceration of young black men affected your family or families you know? Discuss or write a journal entry.

4. Watch an episode of MSNBC's show "Lockup"(www.msnbc.msn.com/id/2711 8605/). Do you see any situations similar to the ones exposed in the reading? Please discuss.

MAX WEBER

The Spirit of Capitalism

From *The Protestant Ethic and the Spirit of Capitalism*

The accumulation of profit is the main purpose of **capitalism**. In this classic piece, the influential **sociologist** Max Weber defines what he means by the "spirit of capitalism" and analyzes the process by which capitalism became the staple of modern **society** (particularly American society). Weber argues that greed has always been with us, but that modern capitalism uniquely prizes the making of money as an end in itself. Pay attention to how Weber lays out his belief that the roles of faith, economic change, and individualism led to the rise of capitalism.

IN THE TITLE OF THIS STUDY IS USED THE SOMEWHAT PRETENtious phrase, the *spirit* of capitalism. What is to be understood by it? The attempt to give anything like a definition of it brings out certain difficulties which are in the very nature of this type of investigation.

If any object can be found to which this term can be applied with any understandable meaning, it can only be an historical individual, i.e. a complex of elements associated in historical reality which we unite into a conceptual whole from the standpoint of their cultural significance.

Such an historical concept, however, since it refers in its content to a phenomenon significant for its unique individuality, cannot be defined according to the formula *genus proximum, differentia specifica*[1] but it must be gradually put together out of the individual parts which are taken from historical reality to make it up. Thus the final and definitive concept cannot stand at the beginning of the investigation,

---

[1] That is, it cannot be defined by how it differs from something else.

but must come at the end. We must, in other words, work out in the course of the discussion, as its most important result, the best conceptual formulation of what we here understand by the spirit of capitalism, that is the best from the point of view which interests us here. This point of view (the one of which we shall speak later) is, further, by no means the only possible one from which the historical phenomena we are investigating can be analysed. Other standpoints would, for this as for every historical phenomenon, yield other characteristics as the essential ones. The result is that it is by no means necessary to understand by the spirit of capitalism only what it will come to mean to *us* for the purposes of our analysis. This is a necessary result of the nature of historical concepts which attempt for their methodological purposes not to grasp historical reality in abstract general formulæ, but in concrete genetic sets of relations which are inevitably of a specifically unique and individual character.

Thus, if we try to determine the object, the analysis and historical explanation of which we are attempting, it cannot be in the form of a conceptual definition, but at least in the beginning only a provisional description of what is here meant by the spirit of capitalism. Such a description is, however, indispensable in order clearly to understand the object of the investigation. For this purpose we turn to a document of that spirit which contains what we are looking for in almost classical purity, and at the same time has the advantage of being free from all direct relationship to religion, being thus, for our purposes, free of preconceptions.

> Remember, that *time* is money. He that can earn ten shillings a day by his labour, and goes abroad, or sits idle, one half of that day, though he spends but sixpence during his diversion or idleness, ought not to reckon *that* the only expense; he has really spent, or rather thrown away, five shillings besides.
>
> Remember, that *credit is* money. If a man lets his money lie in my hands after it is due, he gives me the interest, or so much as I can make of it during that time. This amounts to a considerable sum where a man has good and large credit, and makes good use of it.
>
> Remember, that money is of the prolific, generating nature. Money can beget money, and its offspring can beget more, and so on. Five shillings turned is six, turned again it is seven and threepence, and so on, till it becomes a hundred pounds. The more there is of it, the more it produces every turning, so that the profits rise quicker and quicker. He that kills a breeding-sow, destroys all her offspring to the thousandth generation. He that murders a crown, destroys all that it might have produced, even scores of pounds.
>
> Remember this saying, *The good paymaster is lord of another man's purse.* He that is known to pay punctually and exactly to the time he promises, may at any time, and on any occasion, raise all the money his friends can spare. This is sometimes of great use. After industry and frugality, nothing contributes more to the raising of a young man in the world than punctuality and justice in all his dealings; therefore never keep borrowed money an hour beyond the time you promised, lest a disappointment shut up your friend's purse for ever.

The most trifling actions that affect a man's credit are to be regarded. The sound of your hammer at five in the morning, or eight at night, heard by a creditor, makes him easy six months longer; but if he sees you at a billiard-table, or hears your voice at a tavern, when you should be at work, he sends for his money the next day; demands it, before he can receive it, in a lump.

It shows, besides, that you are mindful of what you owe; it makes you appear a careful as well as an honest man, and that still increases your credit.

Beware of thinking all your own that you possess, and of living accordingly. It is a mistake that many people who have credit fall into. To prevent this, keep an exact account for some time both of your expenses and your income. If you take the pains at first to mention particulars, it will have this good effect: you will discover how wonderfully small, trifling expenses mount up to large sums; and will discern what might have been, and may for the future be saved, without occasioning any great inconvenience.

For six pounds a year you may have the use of one hundred pounds, provided you are a man of known prudence and honesty.

He that spends a groat a day idly, spends idly above six pounds a year, which is the price for the use of one hundred pounds.

He that wastes idly a groat's worth of his time per day, one day with another, wastes the privilege of using one hundred pounds each day.

He that idly loses five shillings' worth of time, loses five shillings, and might as prudently throw five shillings into the sea.

He that loses five shillings, not only loses that sum, but all the advantage that might be made by turning it in dealing, which by the time that a young man becomes old, will amount to a considerable sum of money.

It is Benjamin Franklin who preaches to us in these sentences, the same which Ferdinand Kürnberger satirizes in his clever and malicious *Picture of American Culture* as the supposed confession of faith of the Yankee. That it is the spirit of capitalism which here speaks in characteristic fashion, no one will doubt, however little we may wish to claim that everything which could be understood as pertaining to that spirit is contained in it. Let us pause a moment to consider this passage, the philosophy of which Kürnberger sums up in the words, "They make tallow out of cattle and money out of men." The peculiarity of this philosophy of avarice appears to be the ideal of the honest man of recognized credit, and above all the idea of a duty of the individual toward the increase of his capital, which is assumed as an end in itself. Truly what is here preached is not simply a means of making one's way in the world, but a peculiar ethic. The infraction of its rules is treated not as foolishness but as forgetfulness of duty. That is the essence of the matter. It is not mere business astuteness, that sort of thing is common enough, it is an ethos. *This* is the quality which interests us.

When Jacob Fugger, in speaking to a business associate who had retired and who wanted to persuade him to do the same, since he had made enough money and should let others have a chance, rejected that as pusillanimity and answered that "he (Fugger) thought otherwise, he wanted to make money as long as he could," the spirit of his statement is evidently quite different from that of Franklin. What in the former case was an expression of commercial daring and a personal inclination morally neutral, in the latter takes on the character of an ethically coloured maxim for the conduct of life. The concept spirit of capitalism is here used in this specific sense, it is the spirit of modern capitalism. For that we are here dealing only with Western European and American capitalism is obvious from the way in which the problem was stated. Capitalism existed in China, India, Babylon, in the classic world, and in the Middle Ages. But in all these cases, as we shall see, this particular ethos was lacking.

Now, all Franklin's moral attitudes are coloured with utilitarianism. Honesty is useful, because it assures credit; so are punctuality, industry, frugality, and that is the reason they are virtues. A logical deduction from this would be that where, for instance, the appearance of honesty serves the same purpose, that would suffice, and an unnecessary surplus of this virtue would evidently appear to Franklin's eyes as unproductive waste. And as a matter of fact, the story in his autobiography of his conversion to those virtues, or the discussion of the value of a strict maintenance of the appearance of modesty, the assiduous belittlement of one's own deserts in order to gain general recognition later, confirms this impression. According to Franklin, those virtues, like all others, are only in so far virtues as they are actually useful to the individual, and the surrogate of mere appearance is always sufficient when it accomplishes the end in view. It is a conclusion which is inevitable for strict utilitarianism. The impression of many Germans that the virtues professed by Americanism are pure hypocrisy seems to have been confirmed by this striking case. But in fact the matter is not by any means so simple. Benjamin Franklin's own character, as it appears in the really unusual candidness of his autobiography, belies that suspicion. The circumstance that he ascribes his recognition of the utility of virtue to a divine revelation which was intended to lead him in the path of righteousness, shows that something more than mere garnishing for purely egocentric motives is involved.

In fact, the *summum bonum*[2] of this ethic, the earning of more and more money, combined with the strict avoidance of all spontaneous enjoyment of life, is above all completely devoid of any eudæmonistic, not to say hedonistic, admixture. It is thought of so purely as an end in itself, that from the point of view of the happiness of, or utility to, the single individual, it appears entirely transcendental and absolutely irrational. Man is dominated by the making of money, by acquisition as the ultimate purpose of his life. Economic acquisition is no longer subordinated to man as the means for the satisfaction of his material needs. This reversal of what we should call the natural relationship, so irrational from a naïve point of view, is evidently as definitely a leading principle of capitalism as it is foreign to all peoples not under capitalistic influence. At the same time it expresses a type of feeling which is closely connected with certain religious ideas. If we thus ask, *why* should "money be made out of men," Benjamin

---

[2] Greatest good (Latin).

Franklin himself, although he was a colourless deist, answers in his autobiography with a quotation from the Bible, which his strict Calvinistic father drummed into him again and again in his youth: "Seest thou a man diligent in his business? He shall stand before kings" (Prov. xxii. 29). The earning of money within the modern economic order is, so long as it is done legally, the result and the expression of virtue and proficiency in a calling; and this virtue and proficiency are, as it is now not difficult to see, the real Alpha and Omega of Franklin's ethic, as expressed in the passages we have quoted, as well as in all his works without exception.

And in truth this peculiar idea, so familiar to us to-day, but in reality so little a matter of course, of one's duty in a calling, is what is most characteristic of the social ethic of capitalistic culture, and is in a sense the fundamental basis of it. It is an obligation which the individual is supposed to feel and does feel towards the content of his professional activity, no matter in what it consists, in particular no matter whether it appears on the surface as a utilization of his personal powers, or only of his material possessions (as capital).

Of course, this conception has not appeared only under capitalistic conditions. On the contrary, we shall later trace its origins back to a time previous to the advent of capitalism. Still less, naturally, do we maintain that a conscious acceptance of these ethical maxims on the part of the individuals, entrepreneurs or labourers, in modern capitalistic enterprises, is a condition of the further existence of present-day capitalism. The capitalistic economy of the present day is an immense cosmos into which the individual is born, and which presents itself to him, at least as an individual, as an unalterable order of things in which he must live. It forces the individual, in so far as he is involved in the system of market relationships, to conform to capitalistic rules of action. The manufacturer who in the long run acts counter to these norms, will just as inevitably be eliminated from the economic scene as the worker who cannot or will not adapt himself to them will be thrown into the streets without a job.

Thus the capitalism of to-day, which has come to dominate economic life, educates and selects the economic subjects which it needs through a process of economic survival of the fittest. But here one can easily see the limits of the concept of selection as a means of historical explanation. In order that a manner of life so well adapted to the peculiarities of capitalism could be selected at all, i.e. should come to dominate others, it had to originate somewhere, and not in isolated individuals alone, but as a way of life common to whole groups of men. This origin is what really needs explanation. Concerning the doctrine of the more naïve historical materialism, that such ideas originate as a reflection or superstructure of economic situations, we shall speak more in detail below. At this point it will suffice for our purpose to call attention to the fact that without doubt, in the country of Benjamin Franklin's birth (Massachusetts), the spirit of capitalism (in the sense we have attached to it) was present before the capitalistic order. There were complaints of a peculiarly calculating sort of profit-seeking in New England, as distinguished from other parts of America, as early as

1632. It is further undoubted that capitalism remained far less developed in some of the neighbouring colonies, the later Southern States of the United States of America, in spite of the fact that these latter were founded by large capitalists for business motives, while the New England colonies were founded by preachers and seminary graduates with the help of small bourgeois, craftsmen and yeomen, for religious reasons. In this case the causal relation is certainly the reverse of that suggested by the materialistic standpoint.

But the origin and history of such ideas is much more complex than the theorists of the superstructure suppose. The spirit of capitalism, in the sense in which we are using the term, had to fight its way to supremacy against a whole world of hostile forces. A state of mind such as that expressed in the passages we have quoted from Franklin, and which called forth the applause of a whole people, would both in ancient times and in the Middle Ages have been proscribed as the lowest sort of avarice and as an attitude entirely lacking in self-respect. It is, in fact, still regularly thus looked upon by all those social groups which are least involved in or adapted to modern capitalistic conditions. This is not wholly because the instinct of acquisition was in those times unknown or undeveloped, as has often been said. Nor because the *auri sacra fames,* the greed for gold, was then, or now, less powerful outside of bourgeois capitalism than within its peculiar sphere, as the illusions of modern romanticists are wont to believe. The difference between the capitalistic and precapitalistic spirits is not to be found at this point. The greed of the Chinese Mandarin, the old Roman aristocrat, or the modern peasant, can stand up to any comparison. And the *auri sacra fames* of a Neapolitan cab-driver or *barcaiuolo,*[3] and certainly of Asiatic representatives of similar trades, as well as of the craftsmen of southern European or Asiatic countries, is, as anyone can find out for himself, very much more intense, and especially more unscrupulous than that of, say, an Englishman in similar circumstances.

The universal reign of absolute unscrupulousness in the pursuit of selfish interests by the making of money has been a specific characteristic of precisely those countries whose bourgeois-capitalistic development, measured according to Occidental standards, has remained backward. As every employer knows, the lack of *coscienziosità*[4] of the labourers of such countries, for instance Italy as compared with Germany, has been, and to a certain extent still is, one of the principal obstacles to their capitalistic development. Capitalism cannot make use of the labour of those who practise the doctrine of undisciplined *liberum arbitrium,*[5] any more than it can make use of the business man who seems absolutely unscrupulous in his dealings with others, as we can learn from Franklin. Hence the difference does not lie in the degree of development of any impulse to make money. The *auri sacra fames* is as old as the history of

---

[3] Boatman (Italian).
[4] Conscientiousness (Italian).
[5] Free will (Latin).

man. But we shall see that those who submitted to it without reserve as an uncontrolled impulse, such as the Dutch sea-captain who "would go through hell for gain, even though he scorched his sails", were by no means the representatives of that attitude of mind from which the specifically modern capitalistic spirit as a mass phenomenon is derived, and that is what matters. At all periods of history, wherever it was possible, there has been ruthless acquisition, bound to no ethical norms whatever. Like war and piracy, trade has often been unrestrained in its relations with foreigners and those outside the group. The double ethic has permitted here what was forbidden in dealings among brothers.

Capitalistic acquisition as an adventure has been at home in all types of economic society which have known trade with the use of money and which have offered it opportunities, through *commenda*,[6] farming of taxes, State loans, financing of wars, ducal courts and office-holders. Likewise the inner attitude of the adventurer, which laughs at all ethical limitations, has been universal. Absolute and conscious ruthlessness in acquisition has often stood in the closest connection with the strictest conformity to tradition. Moreover, with the breakdown of tradition and the more or less complete extension of free economic enterprise, even to within the social group, the new thing has not generally been ethically justified and encouraged, but only tolerated as a fact. And this fact has been treated either as ethically indifferent or as reprehensible, but unfortunately unavoidable. This has not only been the normal attitude of all ethical teachings, but, what is more important, also that expressed in the practical action of the average man of pre-capitalistic times, pre-capitalistic in the sense that the rational utilization of capital in a permanent enterprise and the rational capitalistic organization of labour had not yet become dominant forces in the determination of economic activity. Now just this attitude was one of the strongest inner obstacles which the adaptation of men to the conditions of an ordered bourgeois-capitalistic economy has encountered everywhere.

The most important opponent with which the spirit of capitalism, in the sense of a definite standard of life claiming ethical sanction, has had to struggle, was that type of attitude and reaction to new situations which we may designate as traditionalism. In this case also every attempt at a final definition must be held in abeyance. On the other hand, we must try to make the provisional meaning clear by citing a few cases. We will begin from below, with the labourers.

One of the technical means which the modern employer uses in order to secure the greatest possible amount of work from his men is the device of piece-rates. In agriculture, for instance, the gathering of the harvest is a case where the greatest possible intensity of labour is called for, since, the weather being uncertain, the difference between high profit and heavy loss may depend on the speed with which the harvesting can be done. Hence a system of piece-rates is almost universal in this case. And

---

[6] A medieval method of financing maritime trading.

since the interest of the employer in a speeding-up of harvesting increases with the increase of the results and the intensity of the work, the attempt has again and again been made, by increasing the piece-rates of the workmen, thereby giving them an opportunity to earn what is for them a very high wage, to interest them in increasing their own efficiency. But a peculiar difficulty has been met with surprising frequency: raising the piece-rates has often had the result that not more but less has been accomplished in the same time, because the worker reacted to the increase not by increasing but by decreasing the amount of his work. A man, for instance, who at the rate of 1 mark per acre mowed 2½ acres per day and earned 2½ marks, when the rate was raised to 1.25 marks per acre mowed, not 3 acres, as he might easily have done, thus earning 3.75 marks, but only 2 acres, so that he could still earn the 2½ marks to which he was accustomed. The opportunity of earning more was less attractive than that of working less. He did not ask: how much can I earn in a day if I do as much work as possible? but: how much must I work in order to earn the wage, 2½ marks, which I earned before and which takes care of my traditional needs? This is an example of what is here meant by traditionalism. A man does not "by nature" wish to earn more and more money, but simply to live as he is accustomed to live and to earn as much as is necessary for that purpose. Wherever modern capitalism has begun its work of increasing the productivity of human labour by increasing its intensity, it has encountered the immensely stubborn resistance of this leading trait of pre-capitalistic labour. And today it encounters it the more, the more backward (from a capitalistic point of view) the labouring forces are with which it has to deal.

Another obvious possibility, to return to our example, since the appeal to the acquisitive instinct through higher wage-rates failed, would have been to try the opposite policy, to force the worker by reduction of his wage-rates to work harder to earn the same amount than he did before. Low wages and high profits seem even today to a superficial observer to stand in correlation; everything which is paid out in wages seems to involve a corresponding reduction of profits. That road capitalism has taken again and again since its beginning. For centuries it was an article of faith, that low wages were productive, i.e. that they increased the material results of labour so that, as Pieter de la Cour, on this point, as we shall see, quite in the spirit of the old Calvinism, said long ago, the people only work because and so long as they are poor.

But the effectiveness of this apparently so efficient method has its limits. Of course the presence of a surplus population which it can hire cheaply in the labour market is a necessity for the development of capitalism. But though too large a reserve army may in certain cases favour its quantitative expansion, it checks its qualitative development, especially the transition to types of enterprise which make more intensive use of labour. Low wages are by no means identical with cheap labour. From a purely quantitative point of view the efficiency of labour decreases with a wage which is physiologically insufficient, which may in the long run even mean a survival of the unfit. The present-day average Silesian mows, when he exerts himself to the full, little more than two-thirds as much land as the better paid and nourished Pomeranian or Mecklenburger, and the Pole, the further East he comes from, accomplishes progressively less than the German. Low wages fail even from a purely business point of view wherever it is a question of producing goods which require any sort of skilled labour, or the use of expensive machinery which is easily damaged, or in general wherever any great amount of sharp attention or of initiative is required. Here low wages do not pay, and their effect is the opposite of what was intended. For not only is a developed sense of responsibility absolutely indispensable, but in general also an attitude which, at least during working hours, is freed from continual calculations of how the customary wage may be earned with a maximum of comfort and a minimum of exertion. Labour must, on the contrary, be performed as if it were an absolute end in itself, a calling. But such an attitude is by no means a product of nature. It cannot be evoked by low wages or high ones alone, but can only be the product of a long and arduous process of education. Today, capitalism, once in the saddle, can recruit its labouring force in all industrial countries with comparative ease. In the past this was in every case an extremely difficult problem. And even today it could probably not get along without the support of a powerful ally along the way, which, as we shall see below, was at hand at the time of its development.

What is meant can again best be explained by means of an example. The type of backward traditional form of labour is today very often exemplified by women workers, especially unmarried ones. An almost universal complaint of employers of girls, for instance German girls, is that they are almost entirely unable and unwilling to give up methods of work inherited or once learned in favour of more efficient ones, to adapt themselves to new methods, to learn and to concentrate their intelligence, or even to use it at all. Explanations of the possibility of making work easier, above all more profitable to themselves, generally encounter a complete lack of understanding. Increases of piece-rates are without avail against the stone wall of habit. In general it is otherwise, and that is a point of no little importance from our view-point, only with girls having a specifically religious, especially a Pietistic, background. One often hears, and statistical investigation confirms it, that by far the best chances of economic education are found among this group. The ability of mental concentration, as well as the absolutely essential feeling of obligation to one's job, are here most often combined with a strict economy which calculates the possibility of high earnings, and a cool self-control and frugality which enormously increase performance. This provides the most favourable foundation for the conception of labour as an end in itself, as a calling which is necessary to capitalism: the chances of overcoming traditionalism are greatest on account of the religious upbringing. This observation of present-day capitalism in itself suggests that it is worth while to ask how this connection of adaptability to capitalism with religious factors may have come about in the days of the early development of capitalism. For that they were even then present in much the same form can be inferred from numerous facts. For instance, the dislike and the persecution which

Methodist workmen in the eighteenth century met at the hands of their comrades were not solely nor even principally the result of their religious eccentricities, England had seen many of those and more striking ones. It rested rather, as the destruction of their tools, repeatedly mentioned in the reports, suggests, upon their specific willingness to work as we should say to-day.

However, let us again return to the present, and this time to the entrepreneur, in order to clarify the meaning of traditionalism in his case.

Sombart, in his discussions of the genesis of capitalism, has distinguished between the satisfaction of needs and acquisition as the two great leading principles in economic history. In the former case the attainment of the goods necessary to meet personal needs, in the latter a struggle for profit free from the limits set by needs, have been the ends controlling the form and direction of economic activity. What he calls the economy of needs seems at first glance to be identical with what is here described as economic traditionalism. That may be the case if the concept of needs is limited to traditional needs. But if that is not done, a number of economic types which must be considered capitalistic according to the definition of capital which Sombart gives in another part of his work, would be excluded from the category of acquisitive economy and put into that of needs economy. Enterprises, namely, which are carried on by private entrepreneurs by utilizing capital (money or goods with a money value) to make a profit, purchasing the means of production and selling the product, i.e. undoubted capitalistic enterprises, may at the same time have a traditionalistic character. This has, in the course even of modern economic history, not been merely an occasional case, but rather the rule, with continual interruptions from repeated and increasingly powerful conquests of the capitalistic spirit. To be sure the capitalistic form of an enterprise and the spirit in which it is run generally stand in some sort of adequate relationship to each other, but not in one of necessary interdependence. Nevertheless, we provisionally use the expression spirit of (modern) capitalism to describe that attitude which seeks profit rationally and systematically in the manner which we have illustrated by the example of Benjamin Franklin. This, however, is justified by the historical fact that that attitude of mind has on the one hand found its most suitable expression in capitalistic enterprise, while on the other the enterprise has derived its most suitable motive force from the spirit of capitalism.

But the two may very well occur separately. Benjamin Franklin was filled with the spirit of capitalism at a time when his printing business did not differ in form from any handicraft enterprise. And we shall see that at the beginning of modern times it was by no means the capitalistic entrepreneurs of the commercial aristocracy, who were either the sole or the predominant bearers of the attitude we have here called the spirit of capitalism. It was much more the rising strata of the lower industrial middle classes. Even in the nineteenth century its classical representatives were not the elegant gentlemen of Liverpool and Hamburg, with their commercial fortunes handed down for generations, but the self-made parvenus of Manchester and Westphalia, who often rose from very modest circumstances. As early as the sixteenth century the situation was similar; the industries which arose at that time were mostly created by parvenus.

The management, for instance, of a bank, a wholesale export business, a large retail establishment, or of a large putting-out enterprise dealing with goods produced in homes, is certainly only possible in the form of a capitalistic enterprise. Nevertheless, they may all be carried on in a traditionalistic spirit. In fact, the business of a large bank of issue cannot be carried on in any other way. The foreign trade of whole epochs has rested on the basis of monopolies and legal privileges of strictly traditional character. In retail trade—and we are not here talking of the small men without capital who are continually crying out for Government aid—the revolution which is making an end of the old traditionalism is still in full swing. It is the same development which broke up the old putting-out system, to which modern domestic labour is related only in form. How this revolution takes place and what is its significance may, in spite of the fact these things are so familiar, be again brought out by a concrete example.

Until about the middle of the past century the life of a putter-out was, at least in many of the branches of the Continental textile industry, what we should to-day consider very comfortable. We may imagine its routine somewhat as follows: The peasants came with their cloth, often (in the case of linen) principally or entirely made from raw material which the peasant himself had produced, to the town in which the putter-out lived, and after a careful, often official, appraisal of the quality, received the customary price for it. The putter-out's customers, for markets any appreciable distance away, were middlemen, who also came to him, generally not yet following samples, but seeking traditional qualities, and bought from his warehouse, or, long before delivery, placed orders which were probably in turn passed on to the peasants. Personal canvassing of customers took place, if at all, only at long intervals. Otherwise correspondence sufficed, though the sending of samples slowly gained ground. The number of business hours was very moderate, perhaps five to six a day, sometimes considerably less; in the rush season, where there was one, more. Earnings were moderate; enough to lead a respectable life and in good times to put away a little. On the whole, relations among competitors were relatively good, with a large degree of agreement on the fundamentals of business. A long daily visit to the tavern, with often plenty to drink, and a congenial circle of friends, made life comfortable and leisurely.

The form of organization was in every respect capitalistic; the entrepreneur's activity was of a purely business character; the use of capital, turned over in the business, was indispensable; and finally, the objective aspect of the economic process, the book-keeping, was rational. But it was traditionalistic business, if one considers the spirit which animated the entrepreneur: the traditional manner of life, the traditional rate of profit, the traditional amount of work, the traditional manner of regulating the relationships with labour, and the essentially traditional circle of customers and the manner of attracting new ones. All these dominated the conduct of the business, were at the basis, one may say, of the *ethos* of this group of business men.

Now at some time this leisureliness was suddenly destroyed, and often entirely without any essential change in the form of organization, such as the transition to a unified factory, to mechanical weaving, etc. What happened was, on the contrary, often no more than this: some young man from one of the putting-out families went out into the country, carefully chose weavers for his employ, greatly increased the rigour of his supervision of their work, and thus turned them from peasants into labourers. On the other hand, he would begin to change his marketing methods by so far as possible going directly to the final consumer, would take the details into his own hands, would personally solicit customers, visiting them every year, and above all would adapt the quality of the product directly to their needs and wishes. At the same time he began to introduce the principle of low prices and large turnover. There was repeated what everywhere and always is the result of such a process of rationalization: those who would not follow suit had to go out of business. The idyllic state collapsed under the pressure of a bitter competitive struggle, respectable fortunes were made, and not lent out at interest, but always reinvested in the business. The old leisurely and comfortable attitude toward life gave way to a hard frugality in which some participated and came to the top, because they did not wish to consume but to earn, while others who wished to keep on with the old ways were forced to curtail their consumption.

And, what is most important in this connection, it was not generally in such cases a stream of new money invested in the industry which brought about this revolution—in several cases known to me the whole revolutionary process was set in motion with a few thousands of capital borrowed from relations—but the new spirit, the spirit of modern capitalism, had set to work. The question of the motive forces in the expansion of modern capitalism is not in the first instance a question of the origin of the capital sums which were available for capitalistic uses, but, above all, of the development of the spirit of capitalism. Where it appears and is able to work itself out, it produces its own capital and monetary supplies as the means to its ends, but the reverse is not true. Its entry on the scene was not generally peaceful. A flood of mistrust, sometimes of hatred, above all of moral indignation, regularly opposed itself to the first innovator. Often—I know of several cases of the sort—regular legends of mysterious shady spots in his previous life have been produced. It is very easy not to recognize that only an unusually strong character could save an entrepreneur of this new type from the loss of his temperate self-control and from both moral and economic shipwreck. Furthermore, along with clarity of vision and ability to act, it is only by virtue of very definite and highly developed ethical qualities that it has been possible for him to command the absolutely indispensable confidence of his customers and workmen. Nothing else could have given him the strength to overcome the innumerable obstacles, above all the infinitely more intensive work which is demanded of the modern entrepreneur. But these are ethical qualities of quite a different sort from those adapted to the traditionalism of the past.

And, as a rule, it has been neither dare-devil and unscrupulous speculators, economic adventurers such as we meet at all periods of economic history, nor simply great financiers who have earned through this change, outwardly so inconspicuous, but nevertheless so decisive for the penetration of economic life with the new spirit. On the contrary, they were men who had grown up in the hard school of life, calculating and daring at the same time, above all temperate and reliable, shrewd and completely devoted to their business, with strictly bourgeois opinions and principles.

One is tempted to think that these personal moral qualities have not the slightest relation to any ethical maxims, to say nothing of religious ideas, but that the essential relation between them is negative. The ability to free oneself from the common tradition, a sort of liberal enlightenment, seems likely to be the most suitable basis for such a business man's success. And to-day that is generally precisely the case. Any relationship between religious beliefs and conduct is generally absent, and where any exists, at least in Germany, it tends to be of the negative sort. The people filled with the spirit of capitalism to-day tend to be indifferent, if not hostile, to the Church. The thought of the pious boredom of paradise has little attraction for their active natures; religion appears to them as a means of drawing people away from labour in this world. If you ask them what is the meaning of their restless activity, why they are never satisfied with what they have, thus appearing so senseless to any purely worldly view of life, they would perhaps give the answer, if they know any at all: "to provide for my children and grandchildren." But more often and, since that motive is not peculiar to them, but was just as effective for the traditionalist, more correctly, simply: that business with its continuous work has become a necessary part of their lives. That is in fact the only possible motivation, but it at the same time expresses what is, seen from the viewpoint of personal happiness, so irrational about this sort of life, where a man exists for the sake of his business, instead of the reverse.

Of course, the desire for the power and recognition which the mere fact of wealth brings plays its part. When the imagination of a whole people has once been turned toward purely quantitative bigness, as in the United States, this romanticism of numbers exercises an irresistible appeal to the poets among business men. Otherwise it is in general not the real leaders, and especially not the permanently successful entrepreneurs, who are taken in by it. In particular, the resort to entailed estates and the nobility, with sons whose conduct at the university and in the officers' corps tries to cover up their social origin, as has been the typical history of German capitalistic parvenu families, is a product of later decadence. The ideal type of the capitalistic entrepreneur, as it has been represented even in Germany by occasional outstanding examples, has no relation to such more or less refined climbers. He avoids ostentation and unnecessary expenditure, as well as conscious enjoyment of his power, and is embarrassed by the outward signs of the social recognition which he receives. His manner of life is, in other words, often, and we shall have to investigate the historical significance of just this important fact, distinguished by a certain ascetic tendency, as appears clearly enough in the sermon of Franklin which we have quoted. It is, namely, by no means exceptional, but rather the rule, for him to have a sort of modesty which is essentially more honest than the reserve which Franklin so shrewdly recommends. He gets nothing out of his wealth for himself, except the irrational sense of having done his job well.

But it is just that which seems to the pre-capitalistic man so incomprehensible and mysterious, so unworthy and contemptible. That anyone should be able to make it the sole purpose of his life-work, to sink into the grave weighed down with a great material load of money and goods, seems to him explicable only as the product of a perverse instinct, the *auri sacra fames*.

At present under our individualistic political, legal, and economic institutions, with the forms of organization and general structure which are peculiar to our economic order, this spirit of capitalism might be understandable, as has been said, purely as a result of adaptation. The capitalistic system so needs this devotion to the calling of making money, it is an attitude toward material goods which is so well suited to that system, so intimately bound up with the conditions of survival in the economic struggle for existence, that there can to-day no longer be any question of a necessary connection of that acquisitive manner of life with any single *Weltanschauung*.[7] In fact, it no longer needs the support of any religious forces, and feels the attempts of religion to influence economic life, in so far as they can still be felt at all, to be as much an unjustified interference as its regulation by the State. In such circumstances men's commercial and social interests do tend to determine their opinions and attitudes. Whoever does not adapt his manner of life to the conditions of capitalistic success must go under, or at least cannot rise. But these are phenomena of a time in which modern capitalism has become dominant and has become emancipated from its old supports. But as it could at one time destroy the old forms of mediæval regulation of economic life only in alliance with the growing power of the modern State, the same, we may say provisionally, may have been the case in its relations with religious forces. Whether and in what sense that was the case, it is our task to investigate. For that the conception of money-making as an end in itself to which people were bound, as a calling, was contrary to the ethical feelings of whole epochs, it is hardly necessary to prove. The dogma *Deo placere vix potest*[8] which was incorporated into the canon law and applied to the activities of the merchant, and which at the time (like the passage in the gospel about interest)[9] was considered genuine, as well as St. Thomas's character-

---

[7] Worldview (German).

[8] A merchant can rarely please God (Latin).

[9] Most biblical prohibitions on charging interest come not in the gospels but in the Old Testament (as in Deuteronomy 23:19).

ization of the desire for gain as *turpitudo*[1] (which term ever included unavoidable and hence ethically justified profit-making) already contained a high degree of concession on the part of the Catholic doctrine to the financial powers with which the Church had such intimate political relations in the Italian cities, as compared with the much more radically anti-chrematistic views of comparatively wide circles. But even where the doctrine was still better accommodated to the facts, as for instance with Anthony of Florence the feeling was never quite overcome, that activity directed to acquisition for its own sake was at bottom a *pudendum*[2] which was to be tolerated only because of the unalterable necessities of life in this world.

Some moralists of that time, especially of the nominalistic school accepted developed capitalistic business forms as inevitable, and attempted to justify them, especially commerce, as necessary. The *industria* developed in it they were able to regard, though not without contradictions, as a legitimate source of profit, and hence ethically unobjectionable. But the dominant doctrine rejected the spirit of capitalistic acquisition as *turpitudo*, or at least could not give it a positive ethical sanction. An ethical attitude like that of Benjamin Franklin would have been simply unthinkable. This was, above all the attitude of capitalistic circles themselves. Their life-work was, so long as they clung to the tradition of the Church, at best something morally indifferent. It was tolerated, but was still, even if only on account of the continual danger of collision with the Church's doctrine on usury, somewhat dangerous to salvation. Quite considerable sums, as the sources show, went at the death of rich people to religious institutions as conscience money, at times even back to former debtors as *usura*[3] which had been unjustly taken from them. It was otherwise, along with heretical and other tendencies looked upon with disapproval, only in those parts of the commercial aristocracy which were already emancipated from the tradition. But even sceptics and people indifferent to the Church often reconciled themselves with it by gifts, because it was a sort of insurance against the uncertainties of what might come after death, or because (at least according to the very widely held latter view) an external obedience to the commands of the Church was sufficient to insure salvation. Here the either non-moral or immoral character of their action in the opinion of the participants themselves comes clearly to light.

Now, how could activity, which was at best ethically tolerated, turn into a calling in the sense of Benjamin Franklin? The fact to be explained historically is that in the most highly capitalistic centre of that time, in Florence of the fourteenth and fifteenth centuries, the money and capital market of all the great political Powers, this attitude was considered ethically unjustifiable, or at best to be tolerated. But in the backwoods small bourgeois circumstances of Pennsylvania in the eighteenth century, where

---

[1] Dishonorable (Latin).

[2] Shame (Latin).

[3] Interest (Latin).

business threatened for simple lack of money to fall back into barter, where there was hardly a sign of large enterprise, where only the earliest beginnings of banking were to be found, the same thing was considered the essence of moral conduct, even commanded in the name of duty. To speak here of a reflection of material conditions in the ideal superstructure would be patent nonsense. What was the background of ideas which could account for the sort of activity apparently directed toward profit alone as a calling toward which the individual feels himself to have an ethical obligation? For it was this idea which gave the way of life of the new entrepreneur its ethical foundation and justification.

The attempt has been made, particularly by Sombart, in what are often judicious and effective observations, to depict economic rationalism as the salient feature of modern economic life as a whole. Undoubtedly with justification, if by that is meant the extension of the productivity of labour which has, through the subordination of the process of production to scientific points of view, relieved it from its dependence upon the natural organic limitations of the human individual. Now this process of rationalization in the field of technique and economic organization undoubtedly determines an important part of the ideals of life of modern bourgeois society. Labour in the service of a rational organization for the provision of humanity with material goods has without doubt always appeared to representatives of the capitalistic spirit as one of the most important purposes of their life-work. It is only necessary, for instance, to read Franklin's account of his efforts in the service of civic improvements in Philadelphia clearly to apprehend this obvious truth. And the joy and pride of having given employment to numerous people, of having had a part in the economic progress of his home town in the sense referring to figures of population and volume of trade which capitalism associated with the word, all these things obviously are part of the specific and undoubtedly idealistic satisfactions in life to modern men of business. Similarly it is one of the fundamental characteristics of an individualistic capitalistic economy that it is rationalized on the basis of rigorous calculation, directed with foresight and caution toward the economic success which is sought in sharp contrast to the hand-to-mouth existence of the peasant, and to the privileged traditionalism of the guild craftsman and of the adventurers' capitalism, oriented to the exploitation of political opportunities and irrational speculation.

It might thus seem that the development of the spirit of capitalism is best understood as part of the development of rationalism as a whole, and could be deduced from the fundamental position of rationalism on the basic problems of life. In the process Protestantism would only have to be considered in so far as it had formed a stage prior to the development of a purely rationalistic philosophy. But any serious attempt to carry this thesis through makes it evident that such a simple way of putting the question will not work, simply because of the fact that the history of rationalism shows a development which by no means follows parallel lines in the various departments of life. The rationalization of private law, for instance, if it is thought of as a logical simplification and rearrangement of the content of the law, was achieved in the highest hitherto known degree in the Roman law of late antiquity. But it remained most backward in some of the countries with the highest degree of economic rationalization, notably in England, where the Renaissance of Roman Law was overcome by the power of the great legal corporations, while it has always retained its supremacy in the Catholic countries of Southern Europe. The worldly rational philosophy of the eighteenth century did not find favour alone or even principally in the countries of highest capitalistic development. The doctrines of Voltaire are even to-day the common property of broad upper, and what is practically more important, middle-class groups in the Romance Catholic countries. Finally, if under practical rationalism is understood the type of attitude which sees and judges the world consciously in terms of the worldly interests of the individual ego, then this view of life was and is the special peculiarity of the peoples of the *liberum arbitrium,* such as the Italians and the French are in very flesh and blood. But we have already convinced ourselves that this is by no means the soil in which that relationship of a man to his calling as a task, which is necessary to capitalism, has pre-eminently grown. In fact, one may—this simple proposition, which is often forgotten should be placed at the beginning of every study which essays to deal with rationalism—rationalize life from fundamentally different basic points of view and in very different directions. Rationalism is an historical concept which covers a whole world of different things. It will be our task to find out whose intellectual child the particular concrete form of rational thought was, from which the idea of a calling and the devotion to labour in the calling has grown, which is, as we have seen, so irrational from the standpoint of purely eudæmonistic self-interest, but which has been and still is one of the most characteristic elements of our capitalistic culture. We are here particularly interested in the origin of precisely the irrational element which lies in this, as in every conception of a calling.

STUDY QUESTIONS

1. What does Weber mean by "traditionalism"? How are wages related to profits? What does Weber say has the greatest chance of overcoming traditionalism?

2. Describe the process by which **capitalism** came to dominate **economic** life.

3. Weber's main thesis is that the Protestant ethic was related to the rise of capitalism. List some of the aspects of the Protestant faith that are related to some of the main economic philosophies of capitalism and discuss whether they are becoming more or less socially important.

4. Is there room for another economic system in the United States? Discuss as a group.

NADA EL SAWY

Yes, I Follow Islam,
But I'm Not A Terrorist

What does a terrorist look like? Even years after the September 11 terrorist attacks many still believe that most Muslims are terrorists or at the very least religious fanatics. Many Muslim Americans have faced severe **prejudice** and **discrimination**, and some have been victimized by hate crimes just for being Muslim. In this essay, written a month after the attacks, Nada El Sawy tries to educate her readers about her beliefs, and calls upon others to learn about the beauty and peacefulness of Islam. As you read this piece think of the ways that Muslim Americans still face **stereotypes**.

AS AN EGYPTIAN-AMERICAN AND A MUSLIM, I'VE ALWAYS BEEN dismayed by the way Islam has been generally misrepresented in the media and misunderstood by most Americans. Since the tragic events of Sept. 11. Islam has been in the spotlight, and though leaders such as President George W. Bush and New York Mayor Rudolph Giuliani have made a concerted effort to distinguish it from terrorism, some people still aren't getting the message.

I am a graduate student in journalism, often assigned to write articles about current events. The day after the terrorist attacks I headed out to Brooklyn to cover a story about an Islamic school that had been pelted with rocks and bloody pork chops in the hours after the World Trade Center towers collapsed. Whoever committed this act knew enough about Islam to know that pork is forbidden, but apparently little else about Islamic beliefs. "I wish people would stop calling us terrorists," one sixth grader told me.

When I read about Osama bin Laden or groups like the Egyptian Islamic Jihad, I want to tell them, "You're giving Islam a bad name!" I want to show people that the religion I know is one that calls for patience, harmony and understanding.

Islam may be the world's second largest religion, but in the United States, home to about 6 million of its followers, it remains a mystery. Americans seem to believe that backpacking through Europe or keeping up with the news gives them an understanding of everything about the cultures, religions and traditions that differ from their own. While I'm heartened by the sincere curiosity of some, like the stylist who asked me about my beliefs as he trimmed my hair, most people still have a long way to go.

I have yet to meet anyone—who isn't either especially well read, a religion major or a Muslim—who can accurately describe Islamic beliefs. Many people find it fascinating that I worship Allah without understanding that "Allah" is simply the Arabic word for God. Muslims use the word only because the universal teachings of Islam have been preserved in the Arabic language.

I can recall a Thanksgiving dinner with family friends several years ago when the host offered a small prayer. As we all held hands, he started with the customary thanks for the food, family and friends. Then he proceeded to say, "And thank you to God—or whoever else you choose to worship, may it be Allah . . ." He meant well, but I remember flinching. He and his family had traveled to the Middle East, taken pictures of Muslims praying, read about the cultures they were visiting, but none of it had led to a clear understanding of Islam.

I'm not surprised when classmates confront me with the charge that Muslims around the world are killing in the name of religion. I'm careful not to mention the many Muslims who have been killed in places like Kosovo, Indonesia and Palestine. I don't want to respond with that kind of foolish rebuttal because I abhor the senseless murder of all human beings.

The truth is, fanaticism can spring from misguided excess in any religion, and Muslims who kill in the name of their beliefs are not true Muslims. Aggression is not a tenet of our religion, but rather something that is condemned except in self-defense. The Quran states: "Fight in the cause of Allah those who fight you, but commit no aggression; for Allah loves not transgressors" (al-Baqarah 2:190).

If few people understand that Islam is a peaceful religion, even fewer know how beautiful it can be. When I studied in Cairo during my junior year of college, my grandmother had a religion teacher come to her house every week to teach us the Quran. Hearing him chant the verses was like listening to breathtaking music. There is also an element of poetry in a Muslim's everyday life. One says "Allah" or "ma sha'a Allah" ("as God wills") upon seeing something beautiful, like a sunset or a newborn baby. Whenever family members or friends part, one says, "La illah illa Allah" ("there is only one God") and the other responds, "Muhammad rasoul Allah" ("Muhammad is God's prophet").

To me, informing people about these wonderful aspects of Islam is a pleasure, not a burden. There are signs that Americans may be ready to learn. I was moved recently when I saw a woman on the subway reading a book about Islam to her young daughter. She explained that she was teaching herself, as well as her daughter. If more people take that approach, there will come a day when fanaticism is no longer equated with faith, and Muslims aren't seen as terrorists but as human beings.

STUDY QUESTIONS

1. Why does the author think that many non-Muslim Americans are uninformed about the **religion** of Islam?

2. What consequences do Muslim Americans face because of the public's misperceptions of their faith and the assumption that all Muslims are terrorists?

3. Barack Obama's critics and opponents during his campaign in 2008 asserted that he was really a Muslim despite evidence—and his own assertion—that he was a Christian. Regardless of your political views, why do you think opponents used the assertion to hurt Obama's run to become president? What does it mean about how Americans view Muslims if we use religion as a tool to discredit our political opponents?

4. Many people have suggested that because of the terrorist attacks on 9/11 we should aggressively screen Muslims at the airport. The logic here is that, because the hijackers who flew planes into the Twin Towers were all Muslim men, we should assume all Muslims are terrorists. In 1995 Timothy McVeigh blew up a rented moving truck full of explosives in front of the Alfred P. Murrah Federal Building in Oklahoma City, killing 168 people. In 2010 Joseph Stack III flew a plane into a federal Internal Revenue Service building in Austin, Texas, killing two people and injuring many more. Both of these men were white non-Muslims. Discuss whether we should aggressively screen all white, non-Muslim men who rent moving trucks or attempt to fly planes.

MARVIN HARRIS

India's Sacred Cow

n certain instances, for example when we travel abroad, we tend to use our own cultural background to make sense of the cultural practices of the place we are visiting. Some of the cultural practices seem strange, sometimes irrational. It takes a **sociological imagination** to dig deeper and understand that **culture** is how we adapt to the **environment** and the world around us. Marvin Harris traces the history of one cultural practice that may seem strange to Westerners to its logical end in this interesting selection.

NEWS PHOTOGRAPHERS THAT CAME OUT OF INDIA DURING THE famine of the late 1960s showed starving people stretching out bony hands to beg for food while sacred cattle strolled behind undisturbed. The Hindu, it seems, would rather starve to death than eat his cow or even deprive it of food. The cattle appear to browse unhindered through urban markets eating an orange here, a mango there, competing with people for meager supplies of food.

By Western standards, spiritual values seem more important to Indians than life itself. Specialists in food habits around the world like Fred Simons at the University of California at Davis consider Hinduism an irrational ideology that compels people to overlook abundant, nutritious foods for scarcer, less healthful foods.

What seems to be an absurd devotion to the mother cow pervades Indian life. Indian wall calendars portray beautiful young women with bodies of fat white cows, often with milk jetting from their teats into sacred shrines.

Cow worship even carries over into politics. In 1966 a crowd of 120,000 people, led by holy men, demonstrated in front of the Indian House of Parliament in support of the All-Party Cow Protection Campaign Committee. In Nepal, the only contemporary Hindu kingdom, cow slaughter is severely punished. As one story goes, the car driven by an official of a United States agency struck and killed a cow. In order to avoid the international incident that would have occurred when the official was arrested for murder, the Nepalese magistrate concluded that the cow had committed suicide.

Many Indians agree with Western assessments of the Hindu reverence for their cattle, the zebu, or *Bos indicus*, a large-humped species prevalent in Asia and Africa. M. N. Srinivas, an Indian anthropologist, states: "Orthodox Hindu opinion regards the killing of cattle with abhorrence, even though the refusal to kill vast numbers of useless cattle which exist in India today is detrimental to the nation." Even the Indian Ministry of Information formerly maintained that "the large animal population is more a liability than an asset in view of our land resources." Accounts from many different sources point to the same conclusion: India, one of the world's great civilizations, is being strangled by its love for the cow.

The easy explanation for India's devotion to the cow, the one most Westerners and Indians would offer, is that cow worship is an integral part of Hinduism. Religion is somehow good for the soul, even it if sometimes fails the body. Religion orders the cosmos and explains our place in the universe. Religious beliefs, many would claim, have existed for thousands of years and have a life of their own. They are not understandable in scientific terms.

But all this ignores history. There is more to be said for cow worship than is immediately apparent. The earliest Vedas, the Hindu sacred texts from the second millennium B.C., do not prohibit the slaughter of cattle. Instead, they ordain it as part of sacrificial rites. The early Hindus did not avoid the flesh of cows and bulls; they ate it at ceremonial feasts presided over by Brahman priests. Cow worship is a relatively recent development in India; it evolved as the Hindu religion developed and changed.

This evolution is recorded in royal edicts and religious texts written during the last 3,000 years of Indian history. The Vedas from the first millennium B.C. contain contradictory passages, some referring to ritual slaughter and others to a strict taboo on beef consumption. A. N. Bose, in *Social and Rural Economy of Northern India*, 600 B.C.–200 A.D., concludes that many of the sacred-cow passages were incorporated into the texts by priests of a later period.

By 200 A.D. the status of Indian cattle had undergone a spiritual transformation. The Brahman priesthood exhorted the population to venerate the cow and forbade them to abuse it or to feed on it. Religious feasts involving the ritual slaughter and consumption of livestock were eliminated and meat eating was restricted to the nobility.

By 1000 A.D., all Hindus were forbidden to eat beef. Ahimsa, the Hindu belief in the unity of all life, was the spiritual justification for this restriction. But it is difficult to ascertain exactly when this change occurred. An important event that helped to shape the modern complex was the Islamic invasion, which took place in the eighth century A.D. Hindus may have found it politically expedient to set themselves off from the invaders, who were beefeaters, by emphasizing the need to prevent the slaughter of their sacred animals. Thereafter, the cow taboo assumed its modern form and began to function much as it does today.

The place of the cow in modern India is every place—on posters, in the movies, in brass figures, in stone and wood carvings, on the streets, in the fields. The cow is a symbol of health and abundance. It provides the milk that Indians consume in the form of yogurt and ghee (clarified butter), which contribute subtle flavors to much spicy Indian food.

This, perhaps, is the practical role of the cow, but cows provide less than half the milk produced in India. Most cows in India are not dairy breeds. In most regions, when an Indian farmer wants a steady, high-quality source of milk he usually invests in a female water buffalo. In India the water buffalo is the specialized dairy breed because its milk has a higher butterfat content than zebu milk. Although the farmer milks his zebu cows, the milk is merely a by-product.

More vital than zebu milk to South Asian farmers are zebu calves. Male calves are especially valued because from bulls come oxen, which are the mainstay of the Indian agricultural system.

Small, fast oxen drag wooden plows through late-spring fields when monsoons have dampened the dry, cracked earth. After harvest, the oxen break the grain from the stalk by stomping through mounds of cut wheat and rice. For rice cultivation in irrigated fields, the male water buffalo is preferred (it pulls better in deep mud), but for most other crops, including rainfall rice, wheat, sorghum, and millet, and for transporting goods and people to and from town, a team of oxen is preferred. The ox is the Indian peasant's tractor, thresher and family car combined; the cow is the factory that produces the ox.

If draft animals instead of cows are counted, India appears to have too few domesticated ruminants, not too many. Since each of the 70 million farms in India require a draft team, it follows that Indian peasants should use 140 million animals in the fields. But there are only 83 million oxen and male water buffalo on the subcontinent, a shortage of 30 million draft teams.

In other regions of the world, joint ownership of draft animals might overcome a shortage, but Indian agriculture is closely tied to the monsoon rains of late spring and summer. Field preparation and planting must coincide with the rain, and a farmer must have his animals ready to plow when the weather is right. When the farmer without a draft team needs bullocks most, his neighbors are all using theirs. Any delay in turning the soil drastically lowers production.

Because of this dependence on draft animals, loss of the family oxen is devastating. If a beast dies, the farmer must borrow money to buy or rent an ox at interest rates so high that he ultimately loses his land. Every year foreclosures force thousands of poverty-stricken peasants to abandon the countryside for the overcrowded cities.

If a family is fortunate enough to own a fertile cow, it will be able to rear replacements for a lost team and thus survive until life returns to normal. If, as sometimes happens, famine leads a family to sell its cow and ox team, all ties to agriculture are cut. Even if the family survives, it has no way to farm the land, no oxen to work the land, and no cows to produce oxen.

The prohibition against eating meat applies to the flesh of cows, bulls, and oxen, but the cow is the most sacred because it can produce the other two. The peasant whose cow dies is not only crying over a spiritual loss but over the loss of his farm as well.

Religious laws that forbid the slaughter of cattle promote the recovery of the agricultural system from the dry Indian winter and from periods of drought. The monsoon, on which all agriculture depends, is erratic. Sometimes, it arrives early, sometimes late, sometimes not at all. Drought has struck large portions of India time and again in this century, and Indian farmers and the zebus are accustomed to these natural disasters. Zebus can pass weeks on end with little or no food and water. Like camels, they store both in their humps and recuperate quickly with only a little nourishment.

During drought the cows often stop lactating and become barren. In some cases the condition is permanent but often it is only temporary. If barren animals were summarily eliminated, as Western experts in animal husbandry have suggested, cows capable of recovery would be lost along with those entirely debilitated. By keeping alive the cows that can later produce oxen, religious laws against cow slaughter assure the recovery of the agricultural system from the greatest challenge it faces—the failure of the monsoon.

The local Indian governments aid the process of recovery by maintaining homes for barren cows. Farmers reclaim any animal that calves or begins to lactate. One police station in Madras collects strays and pastures them in a field adjacent to the station. After a small fine is paid, a cow is returned to its rightful owner when the owner thinks the cow shows signs of being able to reproduce.

During the hot, dry spring months most of India is like a desert. Indian farmers often complain they cannot feed their livestock during this period. They maintain the cattle by letting them scavenge on the sparse grass along the roads. In the cities the cattle are encouraged to scavenge near food stalls to supplement their scant diet. These are the wandering cattle tourists report seeing throughout India.

Westerners expect shopkeepers to respond to these intrusions with the deference due a sacred animal; instead, their response is a string of curses and the crack of a long bamboo pole across the beast's back or a poke at its genitals. Mahatma Gandhi was well aware of the treatment sacred cows (and bulls and oxen) received in India. "How we bleed her to take the last drop of milk from her. How we starve her to emaciation, how we ill-treat the calves, how we deprive them of their portion of milk, how cruelly we treat the oxen, how we castrate them, how we beat them, how we overload them" [Gandhi, 1954].

Oxen generally receive better treatment than cows. When food is in short supply, thrifty Indian peasants feed their working bullocks and ignore their cows, but rarely do they abandon the cows to die. When cows are sick, farmers worry over them as they would over members of the family and nurse them as if they were children. When the rains return and when the fields are harvested, the farmers again feed their cows regularly and reclaim their abandoned animals. The prohibition against beef consumption is a form of disaster insurance for all India.

Western agronomists and economists are quick to protest that all the functions of the zebu cattle can be improved with organized breeding programs, cultivated pastures, and silage. Because stronger oxen would pull the plow faster, they could work multiple plots of land, allowing farmers to share their animals. Fewer healthy, well-fed cows could provide Indians with more milk. But pastures and silage require arable land, land needed to produce wheat and rice.

A look at Western cattle farming makes plain the cost of adopting advanced technology in Indian agriculture. In a study of livestock production in the United States, David Pimentel of the College of Agriculture and Life Sciences at Cornell University, found that 91 percent of the cereal, legume, and vegetable protein suitable for human consumption is consumed by livestock. Approximately three quarters of the arable land in the United States is devoted to growing food for livestock. In the production of meat and milk, American ranchers use enough fossil fuel to equal more than 82 million barrels of oil annually.

Indian cattle do not drain the system in the same way. In a 1971 study of livestock in West Bengal, Stewart Odend'hal [1972] of the University of Missouri found that Bengalese cattle ate only the inedible remains of subsistence crops—rice straw, rice hulls, the tops of sugar cane, and mustard-oil cake. Cattle graze in the fields after harvest and eat the remains of crops left on the ground; they forage for grass and weeds on the roadsides. The food for zebu cattle costs the human population virtually nothing. "Basically," Odend'hal says, "the cattle convert the items of little direct human value into products of immediate utility."

In addition to plowing the fields and producing milk, the zebus produce dung, which fires the hearths and fertilizes the fields of India. Much of the estimated 800 million tons of manure produced annually is collected by the farmers' children as they follow the family cows and bullocks from place to place. And when the children see the droppings of another farmer's cattle along the road, they pick those up also. Odend'hal reports that the system operates with such high efficiency that the children of West Bengal recover nearly 100 percent of the dung produced by their livestock.

From 40 to 70 percent of all manure produced by Indian cattle is used as fuel for cooking; the rest is returned to the fields as fertilizer. Dried dung burns slowly, cleanly, and with low heat—characteristics that satisfy the household needs of Indian women.

Staples like curry and rice can simmer for hours. While the meal slowly cooks over an unattended fire, the women of the household can do other chores. Cow chips, unlike firewood, do not scorch as they burn.

It is estimated that the dung used for cooking fuel provides the energy-equivalent of 43 million tons of coal. At current prices, it would cost India an extra 1.5 billion dollars in foreign exchange to replace the dung with coal. And if the 350 million tons of manure that are being used as fertilizer were replaced with commercial fertilizers, the expense would be even greater. Roger Revelle of the University of California at San Diego has calculated that 89 percent of the energy used in Indian agriculture (the equivalent of about 140 million tons of coal) is provided by local sources. Even if foreign loans were to provide the money, the capital outlay necessary to replace the Indian cow with tractors and fertilizers for the fields, coal for the fires, and transportation for the family would probably warp international financial institutions for years.

Instead of asking the Indians to learn from the American model of industrial agriculture, American farmers might learn energy conservation from the Indians. Every step in an energy cycle results in a loss of energy to the system. Like a pendulum that slows a bit with each swing, each transfer of energy from sun to plants, plants to animals, and animals to human beings involves energy losses. Some systems are more efficient than others; they provide a higher percentage of the energy inputs in a final, useful form. Seventeen percent of all energy zebus consume is returned in the form of milk, traction, and dung. American cattle raised on Western rangeland return only 4 percent of the energy they consume.

But the American system is improving. Based on techniques pioneered by Indian scientists, at least one commercial firm in the United States is reported to be building plants that will turn manure from cattle feedlots into combustible gas. When organic matter is broken down by anaerobic bacteria, methane gas and carbon dioxide are produced. After the methane is cleansed of the carbon dioxide, it is available for the same purposes as natural gas—cooking, heating, electric generation. The company constructing the biogasification plant plans to sell its product to a gas-supply company, to be piped through the existing distribution system. Schemes similar to this one could make cattle ranches almost independent of utility and gasoline companies; for methane can be used to run trucks, tractors, and cars as well as to supply heat and electricity. The relative energy self-sufficiency that the Indian peasant has achieved is a goal American farmers and industry are now striving for.

Studies like Odend'hal's understate the efficiency of the Indian cow, because dead cows are used for purposes that Hindus prefer not to acknowledge. When a cow dies, an Untouchable, a member of one of the lowest ranking castes in India, is summoned to haul away the carcass. Higher castes consider the body of the dead cow polluting; if they handle it, they must go through a rite of purification.

Untouchables first skin the dead animal and either tan the skin themselves or sell it to a leather factory. In the privacy of their homes, contrary to the teachings of Hinduism, untouchable castes cook the meat and eat it. Indians of all castes rarely acknowledge the existence of these practices to non-Hindus, but most are aware that beefeating takes place. The prohibition against beefeating restricts consumption by the higher castes and helps distribute animal protein to the poorest sectors of the population that otherwise would have no source of these vital nutrients.

Untouchables are not the only Indians who consume beef. Indian Muslims and Christians are under no restriction that forbids them beef, and its consumption is legal in many places. The Indian ban on cow slaughter is state, not national, law and not all states restrict it. In many cities, such as New Delhi, Calcutta, and Bombay, legal slaughterhouses sell beef to retail customers and to restaurants that serve steak.

If the caloric value of beef and the energy costs involved in the manufacture of synthetic leather were included in the estimate of energy, the calculated efficiency of Indian livestock would rise considerably. As well as the system works, experts often claim that its efficiency can be further improved. Alan Heston [et al., 1971], an economist at the University of Pennsylvania, believes that Indians suffer from an overabundance of cows simply because they refuse to slaughter the excess cattle. India could produce at least the same number of oxen and the same quantities of milk and manure with 30 million fewer cows. Heston calculates that only 40 cows are necessary to maintain a population of 100 bulls and oxen. Since India averages 70 cows for every 100 bullocks, the difference, 30 million cows, is expendable.

What Heston fails to note is that sex ratios among cattle in different regions of India vary tremendously, indicating that adjustments in the cow population do take place. Along the Ganges River, one of the holiest shrines of Hinduism, the ratio drops to 47 cows for every 100 male animals. This ratio reflects the preference for dairy buffalo in the irrigated sectors of the Gangetic Plains. In nearby Pakistan, in contrast, where cow slaughter is permitted, the sex ratio is 60 cows to 100 oxen.

Since the sex ratios among cattle differ greatly from region to region and do not even approximate the balance that would be expected if no females were killed, we can assume that some culling of herds does take place; Indians do adjust their religious restrictions to accommodate ecological realities.

They cannot kill a cow but they can tether an old or unhealthy animal until it has starved to death. They cannot slaughter a calf but they can yoke it with a large wooden triangle so that when it nurses it irritates the mother's udder and gets kicked to death. They cannot ship their animals to the slaughterhouse but they can sell them to Muslims, closing their eyes to the fact that the Muslims will take the cattle to the slaughterhouse.

These violations of the prohibition against cattle slaughter strengthen the premise that cow worship is a vital part of Indian culture. The practice arose to prevent the population from consuming the animal on which Indian agriculture depends. During the first millennium B.C., the Gange Valley became one of the most densely populated regions of the world.

Where previously there had been only scattered villages, many towns and cities arose and peasants farmed every available acre of land. Kingsley Davis, a population expert at the University of California at Berkeley, estimates that by 300 B.C. between 50 million and 100 million people were living in India. The forested Ganges Valley became a windswept semidesert and signs of ecological collapse appeared; droughts and floods became commonplace, erosion took away the rich topsoil, farms shrank as population increased, and domesticated animals became harder and harder to maintain.

It is probable that the elimination of meat eating came about in a slow, practical manner. The farmers who decided not to eat their cows, who saved them for procreation to produce oxen, were the ones who survived the natural disasters. Those who ate beef lost the tools with which to farm. Over a period of centuries, more and more farmers probably avoided beef until an unwritten taboo came into existence.

Only later was the practice codified by the priesthood. While Indian peasants were probably aware of the role of cattle in their society, strong sanctions were necessary to protect zebus from a population faced with starvation. To remove temptation, the flesh of cattle became taboo and the cow became sacred.

The sacredness of the cow is not just an ignorant belief that stands in the way of progress. Like all concepts of the sacred and the profane, this one affects the physical world; it defines the relationships that are important for the maintenance of Indian society.

Indians have the sacred cow, we have the "sacred" car and the "sacred" dog. It would not occur to us to propose the elimination of automobiles and dogs from our society without carefully considering the consequences, and we should not propose the elimination of zebu cattle without first understanding their place in the social order of India.

Human society is neither random nor capricious. The regularities of thought and behavior called culture are the principal mechanisms by which we human beings adapt to the world around us. Practices and beliefs can be rational or irrational, but a society that fails to adapt to its environment is doomed to extinction. Only those societies that draw the necessities of life from their surroundings without destroying those surroundings inherit the earth. The West has much to learn from the great antiquity of Indian civilization, and the sacred cow is an important part of that lesson.

REFERENCES

Gandhi, Mohandas K. 1954. *How to Serve the Cow*. Bombay: Navajivan Publishing House.

Heston, Alan, et al. 1971. "An Approach to the Sacred Cow of India," *Current Anthropology* 12, 191–209.

Odend'hal, Stewart. 1972. "Gross Energetic Efficiency of Indian Cattle in Their Environment." *Journal of Human Ecology* 1, 1–27.

STUDY QUESTIONS

1. What is the easy explanation for India's devotion to the cow? What is a more complex view?

2. Why does the author state that "human **society** is neither random nor capricious"?

3. Think about a peculiar practice from your **culture** (e.g., cosmetic plastic surgery); using Harris's narrative, write about the ways the society you live in makes a behavior rational.

4. As a group, discuss what things in your culture are comparable to the Indian sacred cow.

DAN CLAWSON, NAOMI GERSTEL, AND JILL CROCKER

Employers Meet Families: Gender, Class and Paid Work Hour Differences among U.S. Medical Workers

eople in the United States work more than people in any other industrialized country. Time has become a commodity; time available to spend with **family** has shrunk. In this article, the authors explore how **social class** and **gender** influence work schedules among medical workers. Even if you want to spend more time with your family, your social class and gender might restrict your options. As you read, consider how these factors affect your current work situation, or how it might affect you after college.

MOST TIME-USE RESEARCH USES SURVEY DATA TO FOCUS ON INDIviduals; it does not examine those individuals in the immediate social contexts—whether jobs, organizations or families—in which they operate (for some research on the context shaping work hours see Cooper 2002; Lambert 2008; Perlow 1998). This article examines not just how many hours people work, but *why* they work the hours and schedules they do. Two questions frame our project:

1. What organizational and family processes explain why people work the hours and schedules they do?
2. To what extent and in what ways are these processes tied to class and gender?

We develop two related arguments. First, extending recent scholarship that argues that flexibility is a key concept for understanding hours and schedules, we argue that it is the joint flexibility (or rigidity) of both jobs and families that explains hours and schedules. Second, these processes are tied to class and gender. Focusing on class *or* gender, prior studies demonstrate considerable inequality of paid work hours; we argue that class *and* gender operate jointly to produce inequality in work hours.

EMPLOYER AND FAMILY SCHEDULES

We consider two ideal types of employers, and two ideal types of families, and their implications for schedules and hours. Employer A insists on, and receives, total control of (at least some parts of) its employees' hours. Employer B, by contrast, begins by asking their workers what hours and schedules they want to work, and permits them to choose to the maximum extent possible. We consider as well two kinds of family responses. In Family X, whatever hours family member X1 is asked to work, "the family" is willing and able to adapt. In contrast, Family Y depends on, and insists on, Y2's availability—at least at certain specified and predictable times. Pairing these employers and families produces the four groups in Table 1, each posing distinctive challenges to families and employers.

TABLE 1. Four Real Job-Family Matches

	Job schedule	
Family schedule	**Job A: employer flexibility**	**Job B: employer rigidity**
Family flexibility	Group 1: Physicians	Group 2: EMTs
Family rigidity	Group 3: Nurses	Group 4: CNAs

1. In Group 1, both the family and the employer are prepared to adapt to the employee.
2. In Group 2, employees face inflexible employer demands, and the family adapts.
3. In Group 3, employees insist on family demands, and the employer adapts.
4. In Group 4, both the family and the employer expect the employee to meet their needs.

In the real world we don't find pure ideal types. Neither jobs nor families are entirely rigid or flexible. But—as indicated in Table 1—the four occupations in our study, designed to vary by gender and class, tend toward one of the four "ideal" cells. To understand and bring order to complexity of both our data and the real world, we simplify here, stressing the modal case and neglecting much variation. This paper focuses on physicians and nursing assistants, the groups that highlight the contrasts.

DATA AND METHODS

In contrast to prior studies, our data are multi method and multi-level, distinguishing four occupations that vary by class and gender—nursing assistants (CNAs), Emergency Medical Technicians (EMTs), physicians (MDs), and registered nurses (RNs). The groups we have chosen to study differ not only as gendered occupations, but on three dimensions typically used to theorize and operationalize class: occupation, income and education. All work in a part of New England whose characteristics closely approximate those of the U.S. as a whole.

For each occupation, we collected four kinds of data:

1. Random sampled mailed surveys (800 mailed, response 64.5%);
2. Intensive interviews ($n = 191$);
3. Observation at eight medical work organizations;
4. Documents, such as schedule records, work rules, and union contracts.

The choice of four health care occupations has both methodological and substantive advantages. A crucial methodological advantage is that employees in these occupations must be registered with the state to work legally. Consequently, we were able to obtain complete lists of all those legally certified for each of the four occupations—making it possible to draw a true random sample. The substantive advantages of studying health care occupations are equally compelling. Not only is health care part of the growing 24/7 service sector, but it is probably the area that has seen the most contestation around hours of work. We are not arguing that what characterizes health care must apply, without modification, to all sectors of the economy, but many of the processes we analyze are likely to operate in some fashion in other sectors. Moreover, studying a limited number of intermeshing occupations and organizations, rather than a simple random sample drawn from all occupations, allows us to analyze the organizational contexts that shape work hours, rather than confining our analysis to the effects of individual characteristics.

RESULTS

Group 1: Physicians

Male physicians (68% of all physicians) are the closest approximation of Group 1. Medical doctors, especially (though not only) those in private practice, have much autonomy organizing their schedules and their families are willing and able to adapt to professional demands.

Overall, physicians worked long hours, averaging 50 h a week. Physicians are pushed towards long hours by their residency training, by their often massive debt from medical school, by a differential reward for additional hours ("If I worked 80% of my current hours, my pay would be 50%"), by patients' needs ("People don't choose when they get sick, and you have to take care of them when they're sick"), and by a wish to maintain high incomes ("[I]f I wanted to see less [*sic*] patients I would see less patients. The problem is your income takes a hit.").

These constraints were significant, but physicians frequently reported considerable control over their work hours. One explicitly contrasted his situation with that of other (subordinate) occupations within the office: He recently decided to not come in for a week:

> I just cancelled 5 days of appointments and went on vacation. They can't do that. They can't just decide not to come in. I can.

The fit between work hours and families is not always smooth; over half (54%) of physician fathers reported that they disagree "often or sometimes" with their spouses over hours and schedules. Nonetheless, male physicians typically had families who adapted to their work hours: only 43% of physicians' wives were employed and some of these part-time. Physicians were "public fathers," making concerted attempts to ensure they would be at their children's events (sports in particular)—planned, predictable and public. However, they participated far less in the private daily routines of their children's lives. Overall, these professional men could combine the relative flexibility of their families with the relative flexibility of their jobs to obtain hours and schedules they felt they needed and even wanted.

Group 4: Nursing Assistants

The starkest contrast with the physicians is at the other end of our class and gender spectrum: the nursing assistants. These women (89% are women, many of color) face constraints from both their employers and their families. At the nursing homes, where most nursing assistants work, employees must work at the shift times specified by the organization (7–3, 3–11, 11–7). In addition, each must work both Saturday and Sunday every other weekend, almost without exception. Explaining why she worked the hours she did, one assistant put it simply:

> I work when I do because they tell me to. I'd like to work something different; it's not my choice.

Employer demand is backed by financial necessity. When asked why they work the hours and schedules they do, the assistants used the same answer as some doctors: "for the money." But for the assistants, money is far more pressing. They are by some distance the lowest paid of our respondents: their median family income is <$20,000 a year. "Why do we work the hours we do? Poor, that's all there is to it. Just poor." Because they earn so little, nursing assistants struggle to get *enough* hours to survive. Unlike every other group, nursing assistants are more likely to complain about not being able to work enough hours, rather than working too many. The nursing home hires them for 24 or 32 h a week, and when they pick up a shift it will be paid straight time, not at overtime rates. But "if I was to only make 32 h, I'll be short of money."

While physicians often had stay-at-home wives, at one nursing home a majority of the nursing assistants were single parents. (In our survey, 49% of nursing assistants, versus 78% of physicians, were married.) To get needed income to support their families, nursing assistants often had to work a double shift, 16 h straight:

> See, my kids don't like it when I do doubles, because my 3 year old tells my mom, 'I want my mom, I want my mom' when I do doubles. . . . I'm just tired. Hopefully they'll take a nap. But I have to do what I have to do to pay my bills. . . .

This sense of constraint was a recurring theme in interviews with nursing assistants:

> That's like we complain about the policy, but, know what I'm saying, you just got to do what you got to do.
> We'll say you've got to do what you've got to do.

Many nursing assistants had such low incomes that they qualified for child care vouchers for weekdays, but since all needed to work alternate weekends, they needed to rely on family. But the family they relied on contrasted with that of physicians: they were much more likely to turn to extended kin—their mothers, ex-spouses/partners, or other kin—who sometimes made demands and sometimes were less flexible than the family and paid-care used by physicians.

CONCLUSIONS

Although our analysis here was restricted to only two groups, our larger project examines all four groups in Table 1. For female nurses, class facilitates the performance of gender: many nurses prioritize family responsibilities over time spent at work (even if it means a cut in income). Unlike nursing assistants, these women can afford to do so because of their advantaged labor market position. Finally, while male EMTs—like nursing assistants—are at a class disadvantage and experience rigid employer demands, they are able to use gender privilege to negotiate the rigid demands of work.

Most time-use studies examine the number of hours that individuals spend on various activities, including their jobs and families. Our study moves to explanation—asking why people work the hours they do. To do this requires an examination of flexibility in *both* jobs and families. To explain work hours and schedules it is necessary to consider the joint operation of class and gender—and corresponding associations with power that shape that flexibility. People dissatisfied with their work-family arrangements could of course change either their job or their family, but there are typically considerable costs in doing so, and it is important to understand the ways that the constraints differ by class and gender.

We argue that class, or material, advantage allows traditional gender responses to job hours and class disadvantage makes it more difficult to meet traditional dictates of gender. Thus, we have shown male doctors—who are often primary breadwinners—are in the privileged position of choosing how to allocate time to work and home. In contrast, female nursing assistants struggle to make ends meet, looking for supplemental work hours even if those hours make it more difficult to meet the demands of motherhood.

ACKNOWLEDGEMENTS

We gratefully acknowledge research support provided by the National Science Foundation (grant # SES-0549817), the National Association of Emergency Medical Technicians (NAEMT), the Political Economy Research Institute (PERI), and the University of Massachusetts Future of Work project.

REFERENCES

Cooper, M. (2002). Being the go-to-guy: Fatherhood, masculinity and the organization of work in the Silicon Valley. In N. Gerstel, D. Clawson, & R. Zussman (Eds.), *Families at work: Expanding the bounds* (pp. 5–31). Nashville: Vanderbilt University Press.

Perlow, L. (1998). Boundary control: The social ordering of work and family in a High Tech Corporation. *Administrative Science Quarterly, 43*, 328–357.

Lambert, S. (2008). Passing the buck: Labor flexibility practices that transfer risk onto hourly workers. *Human Relations, 61*, 1203–1227.

STUDY QUESTIONS

1. Discuss some of the differences between doctors and assistants in their explanations for working their chosen hours and schedules.

2. What are the authors' findings about the influence of **social class** and **gender** on how workers decide to allocate the amount of time they spend working?

3. Do you think your social class and/or gender influenced your decision to choose your current academic major? Explain.

4. Talk to your parent(s) or caregiver(s) about their career choices and decisions to become parents. Do the men and women characterize their choices differently? Discuss your findings with a student who comes from a different family structure than your own.

BARBARA EHRENREICH

Maid to Order: The Politics of Other Women's Work

Who is going to clean up this house?" With a growing number of **families** in the United States having two adults working, this question is common. The situation is even more perplexing for men and women who see themselves as feminists, who want to allow men and women in families to pursue a career equally. Who then will have time for the housework? In this piece Barbara Ehrenreich talks about her experience as an undercover maid and explores how a servant **economy** is related to **patriarchy**.

IN LINE WITH GROWING CLASS POLARIZATION, THE CLASSIC posture of submission is making a stealthy comeback. "We scrub your floors the old-fashioned way," boasts the brochure from Merry Maids, the largest of the residential-cleaning services that have sprung up in the last two decades, "on our hands and knees." This is not a posture that independent "cleaning ladies" willingly assume—preferring, like most people who clean their own homes, the sponge mop wielded from a standing position. In her comprehensive 1999 guide to homemaking, *Home Comforts*, Cheryl Mendelson warns: "Never ask hired housecleaners to clean your floors on their hands and knees; the request is likely to be regarded as degrading." But in a society in which 40 percent of the wealth is owned by 1 percent of households while the bottom 20 percent reports negative assets, the degradation of others is readily purchased. Kneepads entered American political discourse as a tool of the sexually subservient, but employees of Merry Maids, The Maids International, and other corporate cleaning services spend hours every day on these kinky devices, wiping up the drippings of the affluent.

I spent three weeks in September 1999 as an employee of The Maids International in Portland, Maine, cleaning, along with my fellow team members, approximately sixty houses containing a total of about 250 scrubbable floors—bathrooms, kitchens, and entryways requiring the hands-and-knees treatment. It's a different world down there below knee level, one that few adults voluntarily enter. Here you find elaborate dust structures held together by a scaffolding of dog hair; dried bits of pasta glued to the floor by their sauce; the congealed remains of gravies, jellies, contraceptive creams, vomit, and urine. Sometimes, too, you encounter some fragment of a human being: a child's legs, stamping by in disgust because the maids are still present when he gets home from school; more commonly, the Joan & David-clad feet and electrolyzed calves of the female homeowner. Look up and you may find this person staring at you, arms folded, in anticipation of an overlooked stain. In rare instances she may try to help in some vague, symbolic way, by moving the cockatoo's cage, for example, or apologizing for the leaves shed by a miniature indoor tree. Mostly, though, she will not see you at all and may even sit down with her mail at a table in the very room you are cleaning, where she would remain completely unaware of your existence unless you were to crawl under that table and start gnawing away at her ankles.

Housework, as you may recall from the feminist theories of the Sixties and Seventies, was supposed to be the great equalizer of women. Whatever else women did—jobs, school, child care—we also did housework, and if there were some women who hired others to do it for them, they seemed too privileged and rare to include in the theoretical calculus. All women were workers, and the home was their workplace—unpaid and unsupervised, to be sure, but a workplace no less than the offices and factories men repaired to every morning. If men thought of the home as a site of leisure and recreation—a "haven in a heartless world"—this was to ignore the invisible female proletariat that kept it cozy and humming. We were on the march now, or so we imagined, united against a society that devalued our labor even as it waxed mawkish over "the family" and "the home." Shoulder to shoulder and arm in arm, women were finally getting up off the floor.

In the most eye-catching elaboration of the home-as-workplace theme, Marxist feminists Maria Rosa Dallacosta and Selma James proposed in 1972 that the home was in fact an economically productive and significant workplace, an extension of the actual factory, since housework served to "reproduce the labor power" of others, particularly men. The male worker would hardly be in shape to punch in for his shift, after all, if some woman had not fed him, laundered his clothes, and cared for the children who were his contribution to the next generation of workers. If the home was a quasi-industrial workplace staffed by women for the ultimate benefit of the capitalists, then it followed that "wages for housework" was the obvious demand.

But when most American feminists, Marxist or otherwise, asked the Marxist question *cui bono?*[1] they tended to come up with a far simpler answer—men. If women were the domestic proletariat, then men made up the class of domestic exploiters, free to lounge while their mates scrubbed. In consciousness-raising groups, we railed against husbands and boyfriends who refused to pick up after themselves, who were unaware of housework at all, unless of course it hadn't been done. The "dropped socks," left by a man for a woman to gather up and launder, joined lipstick and spike heels as emblems of gender oppression. And if, somewhere, a man had actually dropped a sock in the calm expectation that his wife would retrieve it, it was a sock heard round the world. Wherever second-wave feminism took root, battles broke out between lovers and spouses over sticky countertops, piled-up laundry, and whose turn it was to do the dishes.

The radical new idea was that housework was not only a relationship between a woman and a dust bunny or an unmade bed; it also defined a relationship between human beings, typically husbands and wives. This represented a marked departure from the more conservative Betty Friedan, who, in *The Feminine Mystique*, had never thought to enter the male sex into the equation, as either part of the housework problem or part of an eventual solution. She raged against a society that consigned its educated women to what she saw as essentially janitorial chores, beneath "the abilities of a woman of average or normal human intelligence," and, according to unidentified studies she cited, "peculiarly suited to the capacities of feeble-minded girls." But men are virtually exempt from housework in *The Feminine Mystique*—why drag them down too? At one point she even disparages a "Mrs. G.," who "somehow couldn't get her housework done before her husband came home at night and was so tired then that he had to do it." Educated women would just have to become more efficient so that housework could no longer "expand to fill the time available."

Or they could hire other women to do it—an option approved by Friedan in *The Feminine Mystique* as well as by the National Organization for Women, which she had helped launch. At the 1973 congressional hearings on whether to extend the Fair Labor Standards Act to household workers, NOW testified on the affirmative side, arguing that improved wages and working conditions would attract more women to the field, and offering the seemingly self-contradictory prediction that "the demand for household help inside the home will continue to increase as more women seek occupations outside the home." One NOW member added, on a personal note: "Like many young women today, I am in school in order to develop a rewarding career for myself. I also have a home to run and can fully conceive of the need for household help as my free time at home becomes more and more restricted. Women know [that] housework is dirty, tedious work, and they are willing to pay to have it done . . ." On the aspirations of the women paid to do it, assuming that at least some of them were bright enough to entertain a few, neither Friedan nor these members of NOW had, at the time, a word to say.

---

[1] For whose benefit? (Latin).

So the insight that distinguished the more radical, post-Friedan cohort of feminists was that when we talk about housework, we are really talking, yet again, about power. Housework was not degrading because it was manual labor, as Friedan thought, but because it was embedded in degrading relationships and inevitably served to reinforce them. To make a mess that another person will have to deal with—the dropped socks, the toothpaste sprayed on the bathroom mirror, the dirty dishes left from a late-night snack—is to exert domination in one of its more silent and intimate forms. One person's arrogance—or indifference, or hurry—becomes another person's occasion for toil. And when the person who is cleaned up after is consistently male, while the person who cleans up is consistently female, you have a formula for reproducing male domination from one generation to the next.

Hence the feminist perception of housework as one more way by which men exploit women or, more neutrally stated, as "a symbolic enactment of gender relations." An early German women's liberation cartoon depicted a woman scrubbing on her hands and knees while her husband, apparently excited by this pose, approaches from behind, unzipping his fly. Hence, too, the second-wave feminists' revulsion at the hiring of maids, especially when they were women of color: At a feminist conference I attended in 1980, poet Audre Lorde chose to insult the all-too-white audience by accusing them of being present only because they had black housekeepers to look after their children at home. She had the wrong crowd; most of the assembled radical feminists would no sooner have employed a black maid than they would have attached Confederate flag stickers to the rear windows of their cars. But accusations like hers, repeated in countless conferences and meetings, reinforced our rejection of the servant option. There already were at least two able-bodied adults in the average home—a man and a woman—and the hope was that, after a few initial skirmishes, they would learn to share the housework graciously.

A couple of decades later, however, the average household still falls far short of that goal. True, women do less housework than they did before the feminist revolution and the rise of the two-income family: down from an average of 30 hours per week in 1965 to 17.5 hours in 1995, according to a July 1999 study by the University of Maryland. Some of that decline reflects a relaxation of standards rather than a redistribution of chores; women still do two thirds of whatever housework—including bill paying, pet care, tidying, and lawn care—gets done. The inequity is sharpest for the most despised of household chores, cleaning: in the thirty years between 1965 and 1995, men increased the time they spent scrubbing, vacuuming, and sweeping by 240 percent—all the way up to 1.7 hours per week—while women decreased their cleaning time by only 7 percent, to 6.7 hours per week. The averages conceal a variety of arrangements, of course, from minutely negotiated sharing to the most cliched division of labor, as described by one woman to the Washington Post: "I take care of the inside, he takes care of the outside." But perhaps the most disturbing finding is that almost the entire increase in male participation took place between the 1970s and the mid-1980s. Fifteen years after the apparent cessation of hostilities, it is probably not too soon to announce the score: in the "chore wars" of the Seventies and Eighties, women gained a little ground, but overall, and after a few strategic concessions, men won.

Enter then, the cleaning lady as *dea ex machina*,[2] restoring tranquillity as well as order to the home. Marriage counselors recommend her as an alternative to squabbling, as do many within the cleaning industry itself. A Chicago cleaning woman quotes one of her clients as saying that if she gives up the service, "my husband and I will be divorced in six months." When the trend toward hiring out was just beginning to take off, in 1988, the owner of a Merry Maids franchise in Arlington, Massachusetts, told the *Christian Science Monitor*, "I kid some women. I say, 'We even save marriages. In this new eighties period you expect more from the male partner, but very often you don't get the cooperation you would like to have. The alternative is to pay somebody to come in. . . .'" Another Merry Maids franchise owner has learned to capitalize more directly on housework-related spats; he closes between 30 and 35 percent of his sales by making follow-up calls Saturday mornings, which is "prime time for arguing over the fact that the house is a mess." The micro-defeat of feminism in the household opened a new door for women, only this time it was the servants' entrance.

In 1999, somewhere between 14 and 18 percent of households employed an outsider to do the cleaning, and the numbers have been rising dramatically. Mediamark Research reports a 53 percent increase, between 1995 and 1999, in the number of households using a hired cleaner or service once a month or more, and Maritz Marketing finds that 30 percent of the people who hired help in 1999 did so for the first time that year. Among my middle-class, professional women friends and acquaintances, including some who made important contributions to the early feminist analysis of housework, the employment of a maid is now nearly universal. This sudden emergence of a servant class is consistent with what some economists have called the "Brazilianization" of the American economy: We are dividing along the lines of traditional Latin American societies—into a tiny overclass and a huge underclass, with the latter available to perform intimate household services for the former. Or, to put it another way, the home, or at least the affluent home, is finally becoming what radical feminists in the Seventies only imagined it was—a true "workplace" for women and a tiny, though increasingly visible, part of the capitalist economy. And the question is: As the home becomes a workplace for someone else, is it still a place where you would want to live?

Strangely, or perhaps not so strangely at all, no one talks about the "politics of housework" anymore. The demand for "wages for housework" has sunk to the status of a curio, along with the consciousness-raising groups in which women once rallied support in their struggles with messy men. In the academy, according to the feminist sociologists I interviewed, housework has lost much of its former cachet—in part,

---

[2] Goddess from a machine (Greek), someone who enters at the last minute to provide a solution.

I suspect, because fewer sociologists actually do it. Most Americans, over 80 percent, still clean their homes, but the minority who do not include a sizable fraction of the nation's opinion-makers and culture-producers—professors, writers, editors, politicians, talking heads, and celebrities of all sorts. In their homes, the politics of housework is becoming a politics not only of gender but of race and class—and these are subjects that the opinion-making elite, if not most Americans, generally prefer to avoid.

Even the number of paid houseworkers is hard to pin down. The Census Bureau reports that there were 549,000 domestic workers in 1998, up 9 percent since 1996, but this may be a considerable underestimate, since so much of the servant economy is still underground. In 1995, two years after Zoe Baird lost her chance to be attorney general for paying her undocumented nanny off the books, the Los Angeles Times reported that fewer than 10 percent of those Americans who paid a housecleaner reported those payments to the IRS. Sociologist Mary Romero, one of the few academics who retain an active interest in housework and the women who do it for pay, offers an example of how severe the undercounting can be: the 1980 Census found only 1,063 "private household workers" in El Paso, Texas, though the city estimated their numbers at 13,400 and local bus drivers estimated that half of the 28,300 daily bus trips were taken by maids going to and from work. The honesty of employers has increased since the Baird scandal, but most experts believe that household workers remain, in large part, uncounted and invisible to the larger economy.

One thing you can say with certainty about the population of household workers is that they are disproportionately women of color: "lower" kinds of people for a "lower" kind of work. Of the "private household cleaners and servants" it managed to locate in 1998, the Bureau of Labor Statistics reports that 36.8 percent were Hispanic, 15.8 percent black, and 2.7 percent "other." Certainly the association between housecleaning and minority status is well established in the psyches of the white employing class. When my daughter, Rosa, was introduced to the wealthy father of a Harvard classmate, he ventured that she must have been named for a favorite maid. And Audre Lorde can perhaps be forgiven for her intemperate accusation at the feminist conference mentioned above when we consider an experience she had in 1967: "I wheel my two-year-old daughter in a shopping cart through a supermarket . . . and a little white girl riding past in her mother's cart calls out excitedly, 'Oh look. Mommy, a baby maid.'" But the composition of the household workforce is hardly fixed and has changed with the life chances of the different ethnic groups. In the late nineteenth century, Irish and German immigrants served the northern upper and middle classes, then left for the factories as soon as they could. Black women replaced them, accounting for 60 percent of all domestics in the 1940s, and dominated the field until other occupations began to open up to them. Similarly, West Coast maids were disproportionately Japanese American until that group, too, found more congenial options. Today, the color of the hand that pushes the sponge varies from region to region: Chicanas in the Southwest,

Caribbeans in New York, native Hawaiians in Hawaii, whites, many of recent rural extraction, in Maine.

The great majority—though again, no one knows exact numbers—of paid housekeepers are freelancers, or "independents," who find their clients through agencies or networks of already employed friends and relatives. To my acquaintances in the employing class, the freelance housekeeper seems to be a fairly privileged and prosperous type of worker, a veritable aristocrat of labor—sometimes paid $15 an hour or more and usually said to be viewed as a friend or even treated as "one of the family." But the shifting ethnic composition of the workforce tells another story: this is a kind of work that many have been trapped in—by racism, imperfect English skills, immigration status, or lack of education—but few have happily chosen. Interviews with independent maids collected by Romero and by sociologist Judith Rollins, who herself worked as a maid in the Boston area in the early Eighties, confirm that the work is undesirable to those who perform it. Even when the pay is deemed acceptable, the hours may be long and unpredictable; there are usually no health benefits, no job security, and, if the employer has failed to pay Social Security taxes (in some cases because the maid herself prefers to be paid off the books), no retirement benefits. And the pay is often far from acceptable. The BLS found full-time "private household cleaners and servants" earning a median annual income of $12,220 in 1998, which is $1,092 below the poverty level for a family of three. Recall that in 1993 Zoe Baird paid her undocumented household workers about $5 an hour out of her earnings of $507,000 a year.

At the most lurid extreme there is slavery. A few cases of forced labor pop up in the press every year, most recently—in some nightmare version of globalization—of undocumented women held in servitude by high-ranking staff members of the United Nations, the World Bank, and the International Monetary Fund. Consider the suit brought by Elizabeth Senghor, a Senegalese woman who alleged that she was forced to work fourteen-hour days for her employers in Manhattan, without any regular pay, and was given no accommodations beyond a pull-out bed in her employers' living room. Hers is not a particularly startling instance of domestic slavery; no beatings or sexual assaults were charged, and Ms. Senghor was apparently fed. What gives this case a certain rueful poignancy is that her employer, former U.N. employee Marie Angelique Savane, is one of Senegal's leading women's rights advocates and had told *The Christian Science Monitor* in 1986 about her efforts to get the Senegalese to "realize that being a woman can mean other things than simply having children, taking care of the house."

Mostly, though, independent maids—and sometimes the women who employ them—complain about the peculiar intimacy of the employer-employee relationship. Domestic service is an occupation that predates the refreshing impersonality of capitalism by several thousand years, conditions of work being still largely defined by the idiosyncrasies of the employers. Some of them seek friendship and even what their maids describe as "therapy," though they are usually quick to redraw the lines once the maid is perceived as overstepping. Others demand deference bordering on servility, while a growing fraction of the nouveau riche is simply out of control. In August 1999, the *New York Times* reported on the growing problem of dinner parties being disrupted by hostesses screaming at their help. To the verbal abuse add published reports of sexual and physical assaults—a young teenage boy, for example, kicking a live-in nanny for refusing to make sandwiches for him and his friends after school.

But for better or worse, capitalist rationality is finally making some headway into this weird preindustrial backwater. Corporate cleaning services now control 25 to 30 percent of the $1.4 billion housecleaning business, and perhaps their greatest innovation has been to abolish the mistress-maid relationship, with all its quirks and dependencies. The customer hires the service, not the maid, who has been replaced anyway by a team of two to four uniformed people, only one of whom—the team leader—is usually authorized to speak to the customer about the work at hand. The maids' wages, their Social Security taxes, their green cards, backaches, and child-care problems—all these are the sole concern of the company, meaning the local franchise owner. If there are complaints on either side, they are addressed to the franchise owner; the customer and the actual workers need never interact. Since the franchise owner is usually a middle-class white person, cleaning services are the ideal solution for anyone still sensitive enough to find the traditional employer-maid relationship morally vexing.

In a 1997 article about Merry Maids, *Franchise Times* reported tersely that the "category is booming, [the] niche is hot, too, as Americans look to outsource work even at home." Not all cleaning services do well, and there is a high rate of failure among informal, mom-and-pop services. The "boom" is concentrated among the national and international chains—outfits like Merry Maids, Molly Maids, Mini Maids, Maid Brigade, and The Maids International—all named, curiously enough, to highlight the more antique aspects of the industry, though the "maid" may occasionally be male. Merry Maids claimed to be growing at 15 to 20 percent a year in 1996, and spokesmen for both Molly Maids and The Maids International told me that their firms' sales are growing by 25 percent a year; local franchisers are equally bullish. Dan Libby, my boss at The Maids, confided to me that he could double his business overnight if only he could find enough reliable employees. To this end, The Maids offers a week's paid vacation, health insurance after ninety days, and a free breakfast every morning consisting—at least where I worked—of coffee, doughnuts, bagels, and bananas. Some franchises have dealt with the tight labor market by participating in welfare-to-work projects that not only funnel employees to them but often subsidize their paychecks with public money, at least for the first few months of work (which doesn't mean the newly minted maid earns more, only that the company has to pay her less). The Merry Maids franchise in the city where I worked is conveniently located a block away from the city's welfare office.

Among the women I worked with at The Maids, only one said she had previously worked as an independent, and she professed to be pleased with her new status as a cleaning-service employee. She no longer needed a car to get her from house to house and could take a day off—unpaid of course—to stay home with a sick child without risking the loss of a customer. I myself could see the advantage of not having to deal directly with the customers, who were sometimes at home while we worked and eager to make use of their supervisory skills: criticisms of our methods, and demands that we perform unscheduled tasks, could simply be referred to the franchise owner.

But there are inevitable losses for the workers as any industry moves from the entrepreneurial to the industrial phase, probably most strikingly, in this case, in the matter of pay. At Merry Maids, I was promised $200 for a forty-hour week, the manager hastening to add that "you can't calculate it in dollars per hour" since the forty hours include all the time spent traveling from house to house—up to five houses a day—which is unpaid. The Maids International, with its straightforward starting rate of $6.63 an hour, seemed preferable, though this rate was conditional on perfect attendance. Miss one day and your wage dropped to $6 an hour for two weeks, a rule that weighed particularly heavily on those who had young children. In addition, I soon learned that management had ways of shaving off nearly an hour's worth of wages a day. We were told to arrive at 7:30 in the morning, but our billable hours began only after we had been teamed up, given our list of houses for the day, and packed off in the company car at about 8:00 A.M. At the end of the day, we were no longer paid from the moment we left the car, though as much as fifteen minutes of work—refilling cleaning-fluid bottles, etc.—remained to be done. So for a standard nine-hour day, the actual pay amounted to about $ 6.10 an hour, unless you were still being punished for an absence, in which case it came out to $5.50 an hour.

Nor are cleaning-service employees likely to receive any of the perks or tips familiar to independents—free lunches and coffee, cast-off clothing, or a Christmas gift of cash. When I asked, only one of my coworkers could recall ever receiving a tip, and that was a voucher for a free meal at a downtown restaurant owned by a customer. The customers of cleaning services are probably no stingier than the employers of independents; they just don't know their cleaning people and probably wouldn't even recognize them on the street. Plus, customers probably assume that the fee they pay the service—$25 per person-hour in the case of The Maids franchise I worked for—goes largely to the workers who do the actual cleaning.

But the most interesting feature of the cleaning-service chains, at least from an abstract, historical perspective, is that they are finally transforming the home into a fully capitalist-style workplace, and in ways that the old wages-for-housework advocates could never have imagined. A house is an innately difficult workplace to control, especially a house with ten or more rooms like so many of those we cleaned; workers may remain out of one another's sight for as much as an hour at a time. For independents, the ungovernable nature of the home-as-workplace means a certain amount of autonomy. They can take breaks (though this is probably ill-advised if the homeowner is on the premises); they can ease the monotony by listening to the radio or TV while they work. But cleaning services lay down rules meant to enforce a factorylike—or even conventlike—discipline on their far-flung employees. At The Maids, there were no breaks except for a daily ten-minute stop at a convenience store for coffee or "lunch"—meaning something like a slice of pizza. Otherwise, the time spent driving between houses was considered our "break" and the only chance to eat, drink, or (although this was also officially forbidden) smoke a cigarette. When the houses were spaced well apart, I could eat my sandwich in one sitting; otherwise it would have to be divided into as many as three separate, hasty snacks.

Within a customer's house, nothing was to touch our lips at all, not even water—a rule that, on hot days, I sometimes broke by drinking from a bathroom faucet. TVs and radios were off-limits, and we were never, ever, to curse out loud, even in an ostensibly deserted house. There might be a homeowner secreted in some locked room, we were told, ear pressed to the door, or, more likely, a tape recorder or video camera running. At the time, I dismissed this as a scare story, but I have since come across ads for devices like the Tech-7 "incredible coin-sized camera" designed to "get a visual record of your babysitter's actions" and "watch employees to prevent theft." It was the threat or rumor of hidden recording devices that provided the final capitalist-industrial touch—supervision.

What makes the work most factorylike, though, is the intense Taylorization imposed by the companies. An independent, or a person cleaning his or her own home, chooses where she will start and, within each room, probably tackles the most egregious dirt first. Or she may plan her work more or less ergonomically, first doing whatever can be done from a standing position and then squatting or crouching to reach the lower levels. But with the special "systems" devised by the cleaning services and imparted to employees via training videos, there are no such decisions to make. In The Maids' "healthy touch" system, which is similar to what I saw of the Merry Maids' system on the training tape I was shown during my interview, all cleaning is divided into four task areas—dusting, vacuuming, kitchens, and bathrooms—which are in turn divided among the team members. For each task area other than vacuuming, there is a bucket containing rags and the appropriate cleaning fluids, so the biggest decision an employee has to make is which fluid and scrubbing instrument to deploy on which kind of surface; almost everything else has been choreographed in advance. When vacuuming, you begin with the master bedroom; when dusting, with the first room off of the kitchen; then you move through the rooms going left to right. When entering each room, you proceed from left to right and top to bottom, and the same with each surface—top to bottom, left to right. Deviations are subject to rebuke, as I discovered when a team leader caught me moving my arm from right to left, then left to right, while wiping Windex over a French door.

It's not easy for anyone with extensive cleaning experience—and I include myself in this category—to accept this loss of autonomy. But I came to love the system: First, because if you hadn't always been traveling rigorously from left to right it would have been easy to lose your way in some of the larger houses and omit or redo a room. Second, some of the houses were already clean when we started, at least by any normal standards, thanks probably to a housekeeper who kept things up between our visits; but the absence of visible dirt did not mean there was less work to do, for no surface could ever be neglected, so it was important to have "the system" to remind you of where you had been and what you had already "cleaned." No doubt the biggest advantage of the system, though, is that it helps you achieve the speed demanded by the company, which allots only so many minutes per house. After a week or two on the job, I found myself moving robotlike from surface to surface, grateful to have been relieved of the thinking process.

The irony, which I was often exhausted enough to derive a certain malicious satisfaction from, is that "the system" is not very sanitary. When I saw the training videos on "Kitchens" and "Bathrooms," I was at first baffled, and it took me several minutes to realize why: There is no water, or almost no water, involved. I had been taught to clean by my mother, a compulsive housekeeper who employed water so hot you needed rubber gloves to get into it and in such Niagaralike quantities that most microbes were probably crushed by the force of it before the soap suds had a chance to rupture their cell walls. But germs are never mentioned in the videos provided by The Maids. Our antagonists existed entirely in the visible world—soap scum, dust, counter crud, dog hair, stains, and smears—and were attacked by damp rag or, in hardcore cases, by a scouring pad. We scrubbed only to remove impurities that might be detectable to a customer by hand or by eye; otherwise our only job was to wipe. Nothing was ever said, in the videos or in person, about the possibility of transporting bacteria, by rag or by hand, from bathroom to kitchen or even from one house to the next. Instead, it is the "cosmetic touches" that the videos emphasize and to which my trainer continually directed my eye. Fluff out all throw pillows and arrange them symmetrically. Brighten up stainless steel sinks with baby oil. Leave all spice jars, shampoos, etc., with their labels facing outward. Comb out the fringes of Persian carpets with a pick. Use the vacuum to create a special, fernlike pattern in the carpets. The loose ends of toilet paper and paper towel rolls have to be given a special fold. Finally, the house is sprayed with the service's signature air freshener—a cloying floral scent in our case, "baby fresh" in the case of the Mini Maids.

When I described the "methods" employed to housecleaning expert Cheryl Mendelson, she was incredulous. A rag moistened with disinfectant will not get a countertop clean, she told me, because most disinfectants are inactivated by contact with organic matter—i.e., dirt—so their effectiveness declines with each swipe of the rag. What you need is a detergent and hot water, followed by a rinse. As for floors, she judged the amount of water we used—one half of a small bucket—to be grossly inadequate and, in fact, the water I wiped around on floors was often an unsavory gray. I also ran The Maids' cleaning methods by Don Aslett, author of numerous books on cleaning techniques and self-styled "number one cleaner in America." He was hesitant to criticize The Maids directly, perhaps because he is, or told me he is, a frequent speaker at conventions of cleaning-service franchise holders, but he did tell me how he would clean a countertop: first, spray it thoroughly with an all-purpose cleaner, then let it sit for three to four minutes of "kill time," and finally wipe it dry with a clean cloth. Merely wiping the surface with a damp cloth, he said, just spreads the dirt around. But the point at The Maids, apparently, is not to clean so much as it is to create the appearance of having been cleaned, not to sanitize but to create a kind of stage setting for family life. And the stage setting Americans seem to prefer is sterile only in the metaphorical sense, like a motel room or the fake interiors in which soap operas and sitcoms take place.

But even ritual work takes its toll on those assigned to perform it. Turnover is dizzyingly high in the cleaning-service industry, and not only because of the usual challenges that confront the working poor—child-care problems, unreliable transportation, evictions, and prior health problems. As my long-winded interviewer at Merry Maids warned me, and my coworkers at The Maids confirmed, this is a physically punishing occupation, something to tide you over for a few months, not year after year. The hands-and-knees posture damages knees, with or without pads; vacuuming strains the back; constant wiping and scrubbing invite repetitive stress injuries even in the very young. In my three weeks as a maid, I suffered nothing more than a persistent muscle spasm in the right forearm, but the damage would have been far worse if I'd had to go home every day to my own housework and children, as most of my coworkers did, instead of returning to my motel and indulging in a daily after-work regimen of ice packs and stretches. Chores that seem effortless at home, even almost recreational when undertaken at will for twenty minutes or so at a time, quickly turn nasty when performed hour after hour, with few or no breaks and under relentless time pressure.

So far, the independent, entrepreneurial housecleaner is holding her own, but there are reasons to think that corporate cleaning services will eventually dominate the industry. New users often prefer the impersonal, standardized service offered by the chains, and, in a fast-growing industry, new users make up a sizable chunk of the total clientele. Government regulation also favors the corporate chains, whose spokesmen speak gratefully of the "Zoe Baird effect," referring to customers' worries about being caught paying an independent off the books. But the future of housecleaning may depend on the entry of even bigger players into the industry. Merry Maids, the largest of the chains, has the advantage of being a unit within the $6.4 billion ServiceMaster conglomerate, which includes such related businesses as TruGreen-ChemLawn, Terminix, Rescue Rooter, and Furniture Medic. Swisher International, best known as an industrial toilet-cleaning service, operates Swisher Maids in Georgia and North Carolina, and Sears may be feeling its way into the business. If large multinational firms establish a foothold in the industry, mobile professionals will be able to find the same branded and standardized product wherever they relocate. For the actual workers, the change will, in all likelihood, mean a more standardized and speeded-up approach to the work—less freedom of motion and fewer chances to pause.

The trend toward outsourcing the work of the home seems, at the moment, unstoppable. Two hundred years ago women often manufactured soap, candles, cloth, and clothing in their own homes, and the complaints of some women at the turn of the twentieth century that they had been "robbed by the removal of creative work" from the home sound pointlessly reactionary today. Not only have the skilled crafts, like sewing and cooking from scratch, left the home but many of the "white collar" tasks are on their way out, too. For a fee, new firms such as the San Francisco-based Les Concierges and Cross It Off Your List in Manhattan will pick up dry cleaning, baby-sit pets, buy groceries, deliver dinner, even do the Christmas shopping. With other firms and individuals offering to buy your clothes, organize your financial files, straighten out your closets, and wait around in your home for the plumber to show up, why would anyone want to hold on to the toilet cleaning?

Absent a major souring of the economy, there is every reason to think that Americans will become increasingly reliant on paid housekeepers and that this reliance will extend ever further down into the middle class. For one thing, the "time bind" on working parents shows no sign of loosening; people are willing to work longer hours at the office to pay for the people—housecleaners and baby-sitters—who are filling in for them at home. Children, once a handy source of household help, are now off at soccer practice or SAT prep classes; grandmother has relocated to a warmer climate or taken up a second career. Furthermore, despite the fact that people spend less time at home than ever, the square footage of new homes swelled by 33 percent between 1975 and 1998, to include "family rooms," home entertainment rooms, home offices, bedrooms, and often bathrooms for each family member. By the third quarter of 1999, 17 percent of new homes were larger than 3,000 square feet, which is usually considered the size threshold for household help, or the point at which a house becomes unmanageable to the people who live in it.

One more trend impels people to hire outside help, according to cleaning experts such as Aslett and Mendelson: fewer Americans know how to clean or even to "straighten up." I hear this from professional women defending their decision to hire a maid: "I'm just not very good at it myself" or "I wouldn't really know where to begin." Since most of us learn to clean from our parents (usually our mothers), any diminution of cleaning skills is transmitted from one generation to another, like a gene that can, in the appropriate environment, turn out to be disabling or lethal. Upper-middle-class children raised in the servant economy of the Nineties are bound to grow up as domestically incompetent as their parents and no less dependent on people to clean up after them. Mendelson sees this as a metaphysical loss, a "matter of no longer being physically centered in your environment." Having cleaned the rooms of many overly privileged teenagers in my stint with The Maids, I think the problem is a little more urgent than that. The American overclass is raising a generation of young people who will, without constant assistance, suffocate in their own detritus.

If there are moral losses, too, as Americans increasingly rely on paid household help, no one has been tactless enough to raise them. Almost everything we buy, after all, is the product of some other person's suffering and miserably underpaid labor. I clean my own house (though—full disclosure—I recently hired someone else to ready it for a short-term tenant), but I can hardly claim purity in any other area of consumption. I buy my jeans at The Gap, which is reputed to subcontract to sweatshops. I tend to favor decorative objects no doubt ripped off, by their purveyors, from scantily paid Third World craftspersons. Like everyone else, I eat salad greens just picked by migrant farm workers, some of them possibly children. And so on. We can try to minimize the pain that goes into feeding, clothing, and otherwise provisioning ourselves—by observing boycotts, checking for a union label, etc.—but there is no way to avoid it altogether without living in the wilderness on berries. Why should housework, among all the goods and services we consume, arouse any special angst?

And it does, as I have found in conversations with liberal-minded employers of maids, perhaps because we all sense that there are ways in which housework is different from other products and services. First, in its inevitable proximity to the activities that compose "private" life. The home that becomes a workplace for other people remains a home, even when that workplace has been minutely regulated by the corporate cleaning chains. Someone who has no qualms about purchasing rugs woven by child slaves in India or coffee picked by impoverished peasants in Guatemala might still hesitate to tell dinner guests that, surprisingly enough, his or her lovely home doubles as a sweatshop during the day. You can eschew the chain cleaning services of course, hire an independent cleaner at a generous hourly wage, and even encourage, at least in spirit, the unionization of the housecleaning industry. But this does not change the fact that someone is working in your home at a job she would almost certainly never have chosen for herself—if she'd had a college education, for example, or a little better luck along the way—and the place where she works, however enthusiastically or resentfully, is the same as the place where you sleep.

It is also the place where your children are raised, and what they learn pretty quickly is that some people are less worthy than others. Even better wages and working conditions won't erase the hierarchy between an employer and his or her domestic help, because the help is usually there only because the employer has "something better" to do with her time, as one report on the growth of cleaning services puts it, not noticing the obvious implication that the cleaning person herself has nothing better to do with her time. In a merely middle-class home, the message may be reinforced by a warning to the children that that's what they'll end up doing if they don't try harder in school. Housework, as radical feminists once proposed, defines a human relationship and, when unequally divided among social groups, reinforces preexisting inequalities. Dirt, in other words, tends to attach to the people who remove it—"garbagemen" and "cleaning ladies." Or, as cleaning entrepreneur Don Aslett told me with some bitterness—and this is a successful man, chairman of the board of an industrial cleaning service and frequent television guest—"The whole mentality out there is that if you clean, you're a scumball."

One of the "better" things employers of maids often want to do with their time is, of course, spend it with their children. But an underlying problem with post-nineteenth-century child-raising, as Deirdre English and I argued in our book *For Her Own Good* years ago, is precisely that it is unmoored in any kind of purposeful pursuit. Once "parenting" meant instructing the children in necessary chores; today it's more likely to center on one-sided conversations beginning with "So how was school today?" No one wants to put the kids to work again weeding and stitching; but in the void that is the modern home, relationships with children are often strained. A little "low-quality time" spent washing dishes or folding clothes together can provide a comfortable space for confidences—and give a child the dignity of knowing that he or she is a participant in, and not just the product of, the work of the home.

There is another lesson the servant economy teaches its beneficiaries and, most troublingly, the children among them. To be cleaned up after is to achieve a certain magical weightlessness and immateriality. Almost everyone complains about violent video games, but paid housecleaning has the same consequence-abolishing effect: you blast the villain into a mist of blood droplets and move right along; you drop the socks knowing they will eventually levitate, laundered and folded, back to their normal dwelling place. The result is a kind of virtual existence, in which the trail of litter that follows you seems to evaporate all by itself. Spill syrup on the floor and the cleaning person will scrub it off when she comes on Wednesday. Leave *The Wall Street Journal* scattered around your airplane seat and the flight attendants will deal with it after you've deplaned. Spray toxins into the atmosphere from your factory's smokestacks and they will be filtered out eventually by the lungs of the breathing public. A servant economy breeds callousness and solipsism in the served, and it does so all the more effectively when the service is performed close up and routinely in the place where they live and reproduce.

Individual situations vary, of course, in ways that elude blanket judgment. Some people—the elderly and disabled, parents of new babies, asthmatics who require an allergen-free environment—may well need help performing what nursing-home staff call the "ADLs," or activities of daily living, and no shame should be attached to their dependency. In a more generous social order, housekeeping services would be subsidized for those who have health-related reasons to need them—a measure that would generate a surfeit of new jobs for the low-skilled people who now clean the homes of the affluent. And in a less gender-divided social order, husbands and boyfriends would more readily do their share of the chores.

However we resolve the issue in our individual homes, the moral challenge is, put simply, to make work visible again: not only the scrubbing and vacuuming but all the hoeing, stacking, hammering, drilling, bending, and lifting that goes into creating and maintaining a livable habitat. In an ever more economically unequal culture, where so many of the affluent devote their lives to such ghostly pursuits as stock-trading, image-making, and opinion-polling, real work—in the old-fashioned sense of labor that engages hand as well as eye, that tires the body and directly alters the physical world—tends to vanish from sight. The feminists of my generation tried to bring some of it into the light of day, but, like busy professional women fleeing the house in the morning, they left the project unfinished, the debate broken off in midsentence, the noble intentions unfulfilled. Sooner or later, someone else will have to finish the job.

STUDY QUESTIONS

1. What role does Ehrenreich believe domestic labor (a.k.a. housework) plays in **gender inequality**?

2. Ehrenreich's central argument is that turning domestic labor into a franchised business creates new **power** dynamics and recreates old ones. How do **race**, citizenship, and **class** affect who becomes a maid? How has this changed over time?

3. Ehrenreich acknowledges that almost all aspects of living have been turned into for-hire services; those of us with the funds can outsource nearly any task. Write down five household tasks that you can now outsource (i.e., pay someone to do for you) and accompany each with the name of a company in your area that provides the service. What do you think life is like for the employees of those companies?

4. Do men still feel they shouldn't have to do an equal share of housework? Ehrenreich asserts that if men would pick up an equal portion of the domestic labor, there would be a lessened need for outsourcing. Create a five-question survey that will help you assess whether heterosexual men still feel they don't need to carry an equal share of household chores. Administer your survey to three friends and compare your results to classmates'.

GEORGE RITZER

The "McDonaldization" of Society

Walk into any McDonald's with money in one hand and a number written on the other one and they'll feed you without your saying a word. The food you'll get will taste exactly like it does anywhere else in the country. Stay at a chain hotel anywhere in the country, and you'll find the same beds, the same carpets, and the same powdered eggs for breakfast. Drive to the suburbs, and you'll see house after house with the same facade, same floor plan, and same mailbox. This predictability is just one quality of what George Ritzer has called the "McDonaldized Society." In this landmark piece Ritzer discusses this trend toward the increased **rationalization** of the world and the consequences of this process.

A WIDE-RANGING PROCESS OF *RATIONALIZATION* IS OCCURRING across American society and is having an increasingly powerful impact in many other parts of the world. It encompasses such disparate phenomena as fast food restaurants, TV dinners, packaged tours, industrial robots, plea bargaining and open-heart surgery on an assembly-line basis. As widespread and as important as these developments are, it is clear that we have barely begun a process that promises even more extraordinary changes (e.g., genetic engineering) in the years to come. We can think of rationalization as a historical process and rationality as the end result of that development. As an historical process, rationalization has distinctive roots in the western world. Writing in the late 19th and early 20th centuries, the great German sociologist Max Weber saw his society as the center of the ongoing process of rationalization

"The 'McDonaldization of Society'" by George Ritzer from *Journal of American Culture*, Vol. 27, No. 3 (September 2004), pages 100–107. Copyright © 2004 Wiley Periodicals Inc. Reproduced with permission from Blackwell Publishing Ltd.

and the bureaucracy as its paradigm case. The model of rationalization, at least in contemporary America, is no longer the bureaucracy, but might be better thought of as the fast food restaurant. As a result, our concern here is with what might be termed the "McDonaldization of Society." While the fast food restaurant is not the ultimate expression of rationality, it is the current exemplar for future developments in rationalization.

A society characterized by rationality is one which emphasizes *efficiency, predictability, calculability, substitution of non-human for human technology* and *control over uncertainty.* In discussing the various dimensions of rationalization, we will be little concerned with the gains already made, and yet to be realized, by greater rationalization. These advantages are widely discussed in schools and in the mass media. In fact, we are in danger of being seduced by the innumerable advantages already offered, and promised in the future, by rationalization. The glitter of these accomplishments and promises has served to distract most people from the grave dangers posed by progressive rationalization. In other words, we are ultimately concerned here with the irrational consequences that often flow from rational systems. Thus, the second major theme of this essay might be termed "the irrationality of rationality."

In spite of the emphasis here on the problems posed by rationalization, this will not be one of those pleas for a return to a less rationalized way of life. Although there is certainly room for less rationalized pockets in a rational society, in most cases we cannot, and should not, try to reverse the process of rationalization. In our rush to critique rationalization we cannot ignore its many advantages (McDonald's does offer a lot of tasty food at relatively low cost). Furthermore, we should not romanticize the "noble" life of the pre-rational society with its many problems and disadvantages. We would not, in most cases, want to recreate a life beset by these problems, even if it was possible to do so. Instead, what we need do is gain a better understanding of the process of rationalization so that we can come to exercise more and better control over it.

Although we will discuss rationalization as a distinct process, we do not want to convey the impression that it is some mystical process that is, under its own momentum, sweeping through the world altering everything and everyone in its path. There are individuals, groups and organizations that are acting in various ways to foster the development and expansion of rationalization. For a wide range of reasons, they have found it in their interest to foster rationalization. Although profit is often a powerful motive for rationalization, it does not adequately explain many rational developments in capitalist societies (e.g., in schools, religious groups) and it certainly does not explain the widespread expansion of rational systems in socialist and communist societies.

The objective through most of the rest of this essay is to examine the nature of each of the major dimensions of rationalization and to illustrate the ubiquity of the process by offering a wide range of examples for each. Not only shall we discuss each of the dimensions of rationalization—efficiency, predictability, calculability, substitution of non-human for human technology and greater control over uncertainty—we will also discuss a seemingly inevitable byproduct of rationality—the irrationality of rationality.

EFFICIENCY

The process of rationalization leads to a society in which a great deal of emphasis is placed on finding the best or optimum means to any given end. Whatever a group of people define as an end, and everything they so define, is to be pursued by attempting to find the best means to achieve the end. Thus, in the Germany of Weber's day, the bureaucracy was seen as the most efficient means of handling a wide array of administrative tasks. Somewhat later, the Nazis came to develop the concentration camp, its ovens and other devices as the optimum method of collecting and murdering millions of Jews and other people. The efficiency that Weber described in turn-of-the-century Germany, and which later came to characterize many Nazi activities, has become a basic principle of life in virtually every sector of a rational society.

The modern American family, often with two wage earners, has little time to prepare elaborate meals. For the relatively few who still cook such meals, there is likely to be great reliance on cookbooks that make cooking from scratch much more efficient. However, such cooking is relatively rare today. Most families take as their objective quickly and easily prepared meals. To this end, much use is made of pre-packaged meals and frozen TV dinners.

For many modern families, the TV dinner is no longer efficient enough. To many people, eating out, particularly in a fast food restaurant, is a far more efficient way of obtaining their meals. Fast food restaurants capitalize on this by being organized so that diners are fed as efficiently as possible. They offer a limited, simple menu that can be cooked and served in an assembly-line fashion. The latest development in fast food restaurants, the addition of drive-through windows, constitutes an effort to increase still further the efficiency of the dining experience. The family now can simply drive through, pick up its order, and eat it while driving to the next, undoubtedly efficiently organized, activity. The success of the fast food restaurant has come full circle with frozen food manufacturers now touting products for the home modeled after those served in fast food restaurants.

Increasingly, efficiently organized food production and distribution systems lie at the base of the ability of people to eat their food efficiently at home, in the fast food restaurant, or in their cars. Farms, groves, ranches, slaughter houses, warehouses, transportation systems, and retailers are all oriented toward increasing efficiency. A notable example is chicken production where they are mass bred, force fed (often with many chemicals), slaughtered on an assembly line, iced or fast frozen and shipped to all parts of the country. Some may argue that such chickens do not taste as good as the fresh-killed, local variety, but their complaints are likely to be drowned in a flood of mass-produced chickens. Then there is bacon which is more efficiently shipped, stored and sold when it is preserved by sodium nitrate, a chemical which is unfortunately thought by many to be carcinogenic. Whatever one may say about the quality or the danger of the products, the fact remains that they are all shaped by the drive for efficiency.

Once the goods have reached the marketplace they need to be purchased. Over the centuries we have witnessed an increase in the efficiency of the means of exchange. We have come a long way from the inefficient method whereby people had to bring their goats to market in order to exchange them for clothing. Since then we have gone from precious metals to coins to bills and to checking accounts, to the development of credit cards and the replacement of bills and checks by the more efficiently used plastic money and computer.

The fast food restaurant is certainly not the only place one can spend money. The center of spending is now the modern shopping center and the supermarket. These are organized in a highly efficient manner in order to aid business. Supermarkets have grown even more efficient recently with the advent of computer scanning devices which expedite the checkout process and, at the same time, make the work of stockpeople more efficient by eliminating the need to stamp prices on the items.

When our shoppers return home (in efficiently produced cars and on efficiently built roads) they are likely to enter apartments or suburban tract houses which have been efficiently constructed. Among other things, this means there is little or nothing to distinguish one apartment or house from many others. In constructing such dwellings, esthetic elements like trees or hills are likely to be leveled if they stand in the way of efficient construction.

In the morning, the parents are likely to troop off to work in a variety of occupational settings in which an effort has been made to maximize the efficiency of operation. The roots of these efforts lie in Henry Ford's assembly-line and F.W. Taylor's principles of scientific management. Both were developed at the turn of the century to be applied largely to manual work. Although blue collar work remains the focus of these efforts, many white collar and professional occupations have been made more efficient in accord with ideas that trace their roots to Ford and Taylor.

While the parents are off to work, the children are headed to schools in which the specialization of classes, the platoon system, and mass classes are all designed to increase the efficiency in which students are processed through the educational system. The small class, to say nothing of the one-to-one tutorial, are disappearing since they are inefficient.

If the family is unhappy with the efficiency that pervades virtually every facet of daily life, it might seek relief in leisure-time activities that it may assume to be immune from the process of rationalization. However, even in these areas, the principles of efficiency are omnipresent. International travel is affordable for many only through organized tours that efficiently transport large groups of tourists from one site to another. The modern amusement park is often little more than a vast, elaborate people-moving machine designed to transport people through the park and its various attractions as efficiently as possible. Campgrounds, trout farms, sporting events and night clubs are other examples of entertainment that have grown increasingly efficient.

One of the most interesting and important aspects of efficiency is that it often comes to be not a means but an end in itself. This "displacement of goals" is a major problem in a rationalizing society. We have, for example, the bureaucrats who slavishly follow the rules even though their inflexibility negatively affects the organization's ability to achieve its goals. Then there are the bureaucrats who are so concerned with efficiency that they lose sight of the ultimate goals the means are designed to achieve. A good example was the Nazi concentration camp officers who, in devoting so much attention to maximizing the efficiency of the camps' operation, lost sight of the fact that the ultimate purpose of the camps was the murder of millions of people.

PREDICTABILITY

A second component of rationalization involves the effort to ensure predictability from one place to another. In a rational society, people want to know what to expect when they enter a given setting or acquire some sort of commodity. They neither want nor expect surprises. They want to know that if they journey to another locale, the setting they enter or the commodity they buy will be essentially the same as the setting they entered or product they purchased earlier. Furthermore, people want to be sure that what they encounter is much like what they encountered at earlier times. In order to ensure predictability over time and place a rational society must emphasize such things as discipline, order, systemization, formalization, routine, consistency and methodical operation.

One of the attractions of TV dinners for modern families is that they are highly predictable. The TV dinner composed of fried chicken, mashed potatoes, green peas and peach cobbler is exactly the same from one time to another and one city to another. Home cooking from scratch is, conversely, a notoriously unpredictable enterprise with little assurance that dishes will taste the same time after time. However, the cookbook cannot eliminate all unpredictability. There are often simply too many ingredients and other variables involved. Thus the cookbook dish is far less predictable than the TV dinner or a wide array of other prepared dishes.

Fast food restaurants rank very high on the dimension of predictability. In order to help ensure consistency, the fast food restaurant offers only a limited menu. Predictable end-products are made possible by the use of similar raw materials, technologies and preparation and serving techniques. Not only the food is predictable; the physical structures, the logo, the "ambience" and even the personnel are as well.

The food that is shipped to our homes and our fast food restaurants is itself affected by the process of increasing predictability. Thus our favorite white bread is indistinguishable from one place to another. In fact, food producers have made great efforts to ensure such predictability.

On packaged tours travelers can be fairly sure that the people they travel with will be much like themselves. The planes, busses, hotel accommodations, restaurants, and at least the way in which the sites are visited are very similar from one location to another. Many people go on packaged tours *because* they are far more predictable than travel undertaken on an individual basis.

Amusement parks used to be highly unpredictable affairs. People could never be sure, from one park to another, precisely what sorts of rides, events, foods, visitors, and employees they would encounter. All of that has changed in the era of the theme parks inspired by Disneyland. Such parks seek to ensure predictability in various ways. For example, a specific type of young person is hired in these parks, and they are all trained in much the same way, so that they have a robot-like predictability.

Other leisure-time activities have grown similarly predictable. Camping in the wild is loaded with uncertainties—bugs, bears, rain, cold and the like. To make camping more predictable, organized grounds have sprung up around the country. Gone are many of the elements of unpredictability replaced by RV's, paved over parking lots, sanitized campsites, fences and enclosed camp centers that provide laundry and food services, recreational activities, television and video games. Sporting events, too, have in a variety of ways been made more predictable. The use of artificial turf in baseball makes for a more predictable bounce of a ball.

Many of the jobs, occupations and careers in which people work are among the most predictable elements of American society. This predictability is traceable to many sources, but two of the most important are scientific management and the assembly line. The principles of scientific management emphasize, among other things, that there is one, and only one, best way to do a job. The idea is for the efficiency expert to discover that one best way, then institutionalize it. Of course, the predictability that stems from the assembly line, like every other segment of the rationalization process, is not without its problems and irrationalities, especially in this case the negative effect such a system has on workers: the classic alienation of the assembly-line worker.

The technology of the assembly line, and the predictability it produces, is now being extended to many, often unlikely, domains. Even open-heart surgery by the most famous heart surgeon, Dr. Denton Cooley, is being performed in a kind of assembly-line fashion. Each day a number of patients are prepared in a number of different operating rooms, preliminary steps are taken by highly specialized personnel, Cooley arrives to perform the most delicate steps and then he moves on to the next room to perform the same steps while assistants complete the process on the preceding patient. Open-heart surgery has been turned into a highly predictable process and one that is fraught with much less uncertainty for both patient and surgeon.

CALCULABILITY OR QUANTITY RATHER THAN QUALITY

It could easily be argued that the emphasis on quantifiable measures, on things that can be counted, is *the* most defining characteristic of a rational society. Quality is notoriously difficult to evaluate. How do we assess the quality of a hamburger, or a physician, or a student? Instead of even trying, in an increasing number of cases, a rational society seeks to develop a series of quantifiable measures that it takes as surrogates for quality. This urge to quantify has given great impetus to the development of the computer and has, in turn, been spurred by the widespread use and increasing sophistication of the computer.

The fact is that many aspects of modern rational society, especially as far as calculable issues are concerned, are made possible and more widespread by the computer. We need not belabor the ability of the computer to handle large numbers of virtually anything, but somewhat less obvious is the use of the computer to give the illusion of personal attention in a world made increasingly impersonal in large part *because* of the computer's capacity to turn virtually everything into quantifiable dimensions. We have all now had many experiences where we open a letter personally addressed to us only to find a computer letter. We are aware that the names and addresses of millions of people have been stored on tape and that with the aid of a number of word processors a form letter has been sent to every name on the list. Although the computer is able to give a sense of personal attention, most people are nothing more than an item on a huge mailing list.

Our main concern here, though, is not with the computer, but with the emphasis on quantity rather than quality that it has helped foster. One of the most obvious examples in the university is the emphasis given to grades and cumulative grade point averages. With less and less contact between professor and student, there is little real effort to assess the quality of what students know, let alone the quality of their overall abilities. Instead, the sole measure of the quality of most college students is their grade in a given course and their grade point averages. Another blatant example is the emphasis on a variety of uniform exams such as SATs and GREs in which the essence of an applicant is reduced to a few simple scores and percentiles.

Within the educational institution, the importance of grades is well known, but somewhat less known is the way quantifiable factors have become an essential part of the process of evaluating college professors. For example, teaching ability is very hard to evaluate. Administrators have difficulty assessing teaching quality and thus substitute quantitative scores. Of course each score involves qualitative judgments, but this is conveniently ignored. Student opinion polls are taken and the scores are summed, averaged and compared. Those who score well are deemed good teachers while those who don't are seen as poor teachers. There are many problems involved in relying on these scores such as the fact that easy teachers in "gut" courses may well obtain high ratings while rigorous teachers of difficult courses are likely to score poorly.

While teaching ratings are important to college professors, a variety of other quantifiable dimensions are of even greater importance. Although the idea of "publish or perish" has never been a completely accurate description of the demands on academics, there is a great deal of emphasis on publications, especially at the major universities. But the quality of academic work is difficult to evaluate, so the emphasis is placed on quantitative measures of academic productivity. One crude measure is the sheer number of articles and books published. Slightly more sophisticated are efforts to weight different kinds of publications (monographs, textbooks, articles in journals of varying prestige) and come up with a total score for each academician that more adequately reflects the differential importance of various kinds of publications. A measure that is gaining increasing support is the number of times an author's works are cited by colleagues. The idea is that the higher the quality of the work, the more likely it is to be cited in colleagues' bibliographies. The fallacy is that, in addition to the general problem of simply trying to reduce quality to a single number, a relatively poor work could get a high citation rating if it is singled out by many for criticism.

In the workworld we find many examples of the effort to substitute quantity for quality. Scientific management was heavily oriented to turning everything work-related into quantifiable dimensions. Instead of relying on the "rule of thumb" of the operator, scientific management sought to develop precise measures of how much work was to be done by each and every motion of the worker. Everything that could be was reduced to numbers and all these numbers were then analyzable using a variety of mathematical formulae. The assembly line is similarly oriented to a variety of quantifiable dimensions such as optimizing the speed of the line, minimizing time for each task, lowering the price of the finished product, increasing sales and ultimately increasing profits. The divisional system pioneered by General Motors and thought to be one of the major reasons for its past success was oriented to the reduction of the performance of each division to a few, bottom-line numbers. By monitoring and comparing these numbers, General Motors was able to exercise control over the results without getting involved in the day-to-day activities of each division.

Quantitative factors are of overwhelming importance in the evaluation and success of television programming. It is the rating system which determines whether television programs will remain on the air. The problem is that there is often an inverse relationship between the quality of a show and its ratings. Shows with little to offer artistically such as *Dallas, Love Boat* and the *Dukes of Hazzard*[1] get very high ratings and remain on the air year after year, while high quality shows tend not even to get air time and, if they do, it is often on PBS and with very low ratings.

Sports in general, and baseball in particular, are dominated by an emphasis on numbers. However, in sports there is a closer relationship between quantity and quality than in many other areas of life. The earned run average of a pitcher or the batting average of a batter are fairly good measures of the quality of their play. But even here a number of intangible qualities of play do not show up. For example, a player may be very valuable, even though his statistics are not particularly good, for his ability to make a clutch play, inspire his teammates or be a leader. There are examples in sports where the mania for numbers has adversely affected the quality of the game. In professional basketball a team must shoot the ball within 24 seconds, whereas in most college games a team can take as long to shoot as necessary. This of course leads to more points in pro ball, but many worry that it has turned the game into a mindless "run and gun" activity. The strategy that used to characterize professional basketball, and still is found in college ball, tends to be lost because a team must shoot the ball in such a short period of time.

Politics offers a number of interesting examples of the substitution of quantitative for qualitative measures. Presidential candidates are obsessed by their ratings in the polls and often adjust what they say or do to what the pollsters tell them is likely to increase their ratings. Even sitting presidents (and other politicians) are highly attuned to the polls. The emphasis often seems to be on the impact on the polls of taking a specific political position rather than the qualities of that position.

In foreign policy one area in which we see an absolute mania for numbers is nuclear deterrence. Even though both the United States and the Soviet Union possess arsenals large enough to destroy each other many times over, their efforts to negotiate treaties limiting nuclear weapons often get bogged down in trying to accurately assess the "relative throw weight" of their respective nuclear arms. While accurate measures of throw weight are no doubt important, there is a tendency on both sides to get lost in the minutiae of the numbers and to lose sight of the qualitative fact that both sides have the nuclear might to destroy the other side many times over. There are many other areas, for instance plea bargains in the criminal justice system, in which a quantitative emphasis undoubtedly leads to a number of qualitatively bad decisions.

Thus, the third dimension of rationalization, calculability or the emphasis on quantity rather than quality, has wide applicability to the social world. It is a truly central, if not the central, component of a rationalizing society. To return to our favorite example, it is the case that McDonald's expends far more effort telling us how many billions of hamburgers it has sold than it does in telling us about the quality of those

---

[1] American television series of the late 1970s and early 1980s.

burgers. Relatedly, it touts the size of its product (the "Big Mac") more than the quality of the product (it is not the "Good Mac"). The bottom line in many settings is the number of customers processed, the speed with which they are processed, and the profits produced. Quality is secondary, if indeed there is any concern at all for it.

SUBSTITUTION OF NON-HUMAN TECHNOLOGY

In spite of herculean efforts, there are important limits to the ability to rationalize what human beings think and do. Seemingly no matter what one does, people still retain at least the ultimate capacity to think and act in a variety of unanticipated ways. Thus, in spite of great efforts to make human behavior more efficient, more predictable, more calculable, people continue to act in unforeseen ways. People continue to make home cooked meals from scratch, to camp in tents in the wild, to eat in old-fashioned diners, and to sabotage the assembly-lines. Because of these realities, there is great interest among those who foster increasing rationality in using rational technologies to limit individual independence and ultimately to replace human beings with machines and other technologies that lack the ability to think and act in unpredictable ways.

McDonald's does not yet have robots to serve us food, but it does have teenagers whose ability to act autonomously is almost completely eliminated by techniques, procedures, routines and machines. There are numerous examples of this including rules which prescribe all the things a counterperson should do in dealing with a customer as well as a large variety of technologies which determine the actions of workers such as drink dispensers which shut themselves off when the cup is full; buzzers, lights and bells which indicate when food (e.g., french fries) is done; and cash registers which have the prices of each item programmed in. One of the latest attempts to constrain individual action is Denny's use of pre-measured packages of dehydrated food that are "cooked" simply by putting them under the hot water tap. Because of such tools and machines, as well as the elaborate rules dictating worker behavior, people often feel like they are dealing with human robots when they relate to the personnel of a fast food restaurant. When human robots are found, mechanical robots cannot be far behind. Once people are reduced to a few robot-like actions, it is a relatively easy step to replace them with mechanical robots. Thus Burgerworld is reportedly opening a prototypical restaurant in which mechanical robots serve the food.

Much of the recent history of work, especially manual work, is a history of efforts to replace human technology with non-human technology. Scientific management was oriented to the development of an elaborate and rigid set of rules about how jobs were to be done. The workers were to blindly and obediently follow those rules and not to do the work the way they saw fit. The various skills needed to perform a task were carefully delineated and broken down into a series of routine steps that could be taught to all workers. The skills, in other words, were built into the routines rather than belonging to skilled craftspersons. Similar points can be made about the assembly-line which is basically a set of non-human technologies that have the needed steps and skills built into them. The human worker is reduced to performing a limited number of simple, repetitive operations. However, the control of this technology over the individual worker is so great and omnipresent that individual workers have reacted negatively manifesting such things as tardiness, absenteeism, turnover and even sabotage. We are now witnessing a new stage in this technological development with automated processes now totally replacing many workers with robots. With the coming of robots we have reached the ultimate stage in the replacement of human with non-human technology.

Even religion and religious crusades have not been unaffected by the spread of non-human technologies. The growth of large religious organizations, the use of Madison Avenue techniques, and even drive-in churches all reflect the incursion of modern technology. But it is in the electronic church, religion through the TV screens, that replacement of human by non-human technology in religion is most visible and has its most important manifestation.

Running for president, or any other political office, used to be a highly personal undertaking in which the objective was to see personally, and be seen by, as many voters as possible. Now we have presidential politics waged largely on the TV screens and in accord with routines developed by Madison Avenue public relations types. The technology of the TV spectacular is now being applied to the campaign appearances of presidential candidates. The candidate is most likely to interact with little more than the TV screen and when he does venture out into the real world, it is likely to be only for the images that such a trip will cast on the home screen.

CONTROL

This leads us to the fifth major dimension of rationalization—control. Rational systems are oriented toward, and structured to expedite, control in a variety of senses. At the most general level, we can say that rational systems are set up to allow for greater control over the uncertainties of life—birth, death, food production and distribution, housing, religious salvation and many, many others. More specifically, rational systems are oriented to gaining greater control over the major source of uncertainty in social life—other people. Among other things, this means control over subordinates by superiors and control of clients and customers by workers.

There are many examples of rationalization oriented toward gaining greater control over the uncertainties of life. The burgeoning of the genetic engineering movement can be seen as being aimed at gaining better control over the production of life itself. Similarly, amniocentesis can be seen as a technique which will allow the parents to determine the kind of child they will have. The efforts to rationalize food production and distribution can be seen as being aimed at gaining greater control over the problems of hunger and starvation. A steady and regular supply of food can make life itself more certain for large numbers of people who today live under the threat of death from starvation.

At a more specific level, the rationalization of food preparation and serving at McDonald's gives it great control over its employees. The automobile assembly line has a similar impact. In fact, the vast majority of the structures of a rational society exert extraordinary control over the people who labor in them. But because of the limits that still exist on the degree of control that rational structures can exercise over individuals, many rationalizing employers are driven to seek to more fully rationalize their operations and totally eliminate the worker. The result is an automated, robot-like technology over which, barring some *2001*[2] rebellion, there is almost total control.

In addition to control over employees, rational systems are also interested in controlling the customer/clients they serve. For example, the fast food restaurant with its counter, the absence of waiters and waitresses, the limited seating, and the drive-through windows all tend to lead customers to do certain things and not to do others.

IRRATIONALITY OF RATIONALITY

Although not an inherent part of rationalization, the *irrationality of rationality* is a seemingly inevitable byproduct of the process. We can think of the irrationality of rationality in several ways. At the most general level it can simply be seen as an overarching label for all the negative effects of rationalization. More specifically, it can be seen as the opposite of rationality, at least in some of its senses. For example, there are the inefficiencies and unpredictabilities that are often produced by seemingly rational systems. Thus, although bureaucracies are constructed to bring about greater efficiency in organizational work, the fact is that there are notorious inefficiencies such as the "red tape" associated with the operation of most bureaucracies. Or, take the example of the arms race in which a focus on quantifiable aspects of nuclear weapons may well have made the occurrence of nuclear war more, rather than less, unpredictable.

---

[2] *2001: A Space Odyssey*, 1968 film in which a computer gains extraordinary power.

Of greatest importance, however, is the variety of negative effects that rational systems have on the individuals who live, work and are served by them. We might say that *rational systems are not reasonable systems*. As we've already discussed, rationality brings with it great dehumanization as people are reduced to acting like robots. Among the dehumanizing aspects of a rational society are large lecture classes, computer letters, pray TV, work on the automobile assembly line, and dining at a fast food restaurant. Rationalization also tends to bring with it disenchantment leaving much of our lives without any mystery or excitement. Production by a hand craftsman is far more mysterious than an assembly-line technology where each worker does a single, very limited operation. Camping in an RV tends to suffer in comparison to the joys to be derived from camping in the wild. Overall a fully rational society would be a very bleak and uninteresting place.

In addition to being dehumanizing and disenchanting many rational systems which are supposedly constructed to help people, in the end often have very negative effects. Thus to produce massive amounts of food, producers are driven to rationalize food production in a number of ways including the use of more and more pesticides and artificial ingredients. While such rational technologies are capable of producing a lot of food, they often produce foods that are not as nourishing as their natural counterparts and, in some cases, include chemicals that may be harmful, dangerous and even fatal. McDonald's seemingly rational way of feeding people quickly and cheaply has had many unforeseen and irrational consequences such as weight gain because of the highly caloric nature of the food, increased cholesterol levels, heightened blood pressure as a result of the high salt content of the food, and it has played a key role in the destruction of the family meal and perhaps ultimately the nuclear family.

CONCLUSIONS

Rationalization, with McDonald's as the paradigm case, is occurring throughout America, and, increasingly, other societies. In virtually every sector of society more and more emphasis is placed on efficiency, predictability, calculability, replacement of human by non-human technology, and control over uncertainty. Although progressive rationalization has brought with it innumerable advantages, it has also created a number of problems, the various irrationalities of rationality, which threaten to accelerate in the years to come. These problems, and their acceleration should not be taken as a case for the return to a less rational form of society. Such a return is not only impossible but also undesirable. What is needed is not a less rational society, but greater control over the process of rationalization involving, among other things, efforts to ameliorate its irrational consequences.

STUDY QUESTIONS

1. What does Ritzer mean when he says **society** has become "McDonaldized"?

2. What are the five major components of **rationalization**?

3. What are the irrationalities of the rationality behind the McDonaldization of society?

4. Describe an aspect of your life that has been "McDonaldized" that was not discussed in the text.

C. WRIGHT MILLS

The Power Elite

I n this classic of **sociology**, C. Wright Mills (known for coining the term "the **sociological imagination**") exposes the systematic formation of the American **power elite**, its influence, and its prevalence in **society**. Although Mills wrote this piece in 1956, it remains current. Only the future will tell whether there will be a shift in the **power** structure or a continuation of the reach and influence of the power elite.

EXCEPT FOR THE UNSUCCESSFUL CIVIL WAR, CHANGES IN THE power system of the United States have not involved important challenges to its basic legitimations. Even when they have been decisive enough to be called "revolutions," they have not involved the "resort to the guns of a cruiser, the dispersal of an elected assembly by bayonets, or the mechanisms of a police state."[1] Nor have they involved, in any decisive way, any ideological struggle to control masses. Changes in the American structure of power have generally come about by institutional shifts in the relative positions of the political, the economic, and the military orders.

* * *

We study history, it has been said, to rid ourselves of it, and the history of the power elite is a clear case for which this maxim is correct. Like the tempo of American life in general, the long-term trends of the power structure have been greatly speeded up since World War II, and certain newer trends within and between the dominant

The Power Elite, 2nd Edition, by C. Wright Mills (1956). 4059 words from pp. 269, 274–278, 287–294, 296–297, 408–409. By permission of Oxford University Press, Inc.

---

[1] Cf. Elmer Davis, *But We Were Born Free* (Indianapolis: Bobbs-Merrill, 1953), p. 187.

institutions have also set the shape of the power elite and given historically specific meaning to its fifth epoch:

I. In so far as the structural clue to the power elite today lies in the political order, that clue is the decline of politics as genuine and public debate of alternative decisions—with nationally responsible and policy-coherent parties and with autonomous organizations connecting the lower and middle levels of power with the top levels of decision. America is now in considerable part more a formal political democracy than a democratic social structure, and even the formal political mechanics are weak.

The long-time tendency of business and government to become more intricately and deeply involved with each other has, in the fifth epoch, reached a new point of explicitness. The two cannot now be seen clearly as two distinct worlds. It is in terms of the executive agencies of the state that the rapprochement has proceeded most decisively. The growth of the executive branch of the government, with its agencies that patrol the complex economy, does not mean merely the "enlargement of government" as some sort of autonomous bureaucracy: it has meant the ascendancy of the corporation's man as a political eminence.

During the New Deal the corporate chieftains joined the political directorate; as of World War II they have come to dominate it. Long interlocked with government, now they have moved into quite full direction of the economy of the war effort and of the postwar era. This shift of the corporation executives into the political directorate has accelerated the long-term relegation of the professional politicians in the Congress to the middle levels of power.

II. In so far as the structural clue to the power elite today lies in the enlarged and military state, that clue becomes evident in the military ascendancy. The warlords have gained decisive political relevance, and the military structure of America is now in considerable part a political structure. The seemingly permanent military threat places a premium on the military and upon their control of men, materiel, money, and power; virtually all political and economic actions are now judged in terms of military definitions of reality: the higher warlords have ascended to a firm position within the power elite of the fifth epoch.

In part at least this has resulted from one simple historical fact, pivotal for the years since 1939: the focus of elite attention has been shifted from domestic problems, centered in the 'thirties around slump, to international problems, centered in the 'forties and 'fifties around war. Since the governing apparatus of the United States has by long historic usage been adapted to and shaped by domestic clash and balance, it has not, from any angle, had suitable agencies and traditions for the handling of international problems. Such formal democratic mechanics as had arisen in the century and a half of national development prior to 1941, had not been extended to the American handling of international affairs. It is, in considerable part, in this vacuum that the power elite has grown.

III. In so far as the structural clue to the power elite today lies in the economic order, that clue is the fact that the economy is at once a permanent-war economy and a private-corporation economy. American capitalism is now in considerable part a military capitalism, and the most important relation of the big corporation to the state rests on the coincidence of interests between military and corporate needs, as defined by warlords and corporate rich. Within the elite as a whole, this coincidence of interest between the high military and the corporate chieftains strengthens both of them and further subordinates the role of the merely political men. Not politicians, but corporate executives, sit with the military and plan the organization of war effort.

The shape and meaning of the power elite today can be understood only when these three sets of structural trends are seen at their point of coincidence: the military capitalism of private corporations exists in a weakened and formal democratic system containing a military order already quite political in outlook and demeanor. Accordingly, at the top of this structure, the power elite has been shaped by the coincidence of interest between those who control the major means of production and those who control the newly enlarged means of violence; from the decline of the professional politician and the rise to explicit political command of the corporate chieftains and the professional warlords; from the absence of any genuine civil service of skill and integrity, independent of vested interests.

The power elite is composed of political, economic, and military men, but this instituted elite is frequently in some tension: it comes together only on certain coinciding points and only on certain occasions of "crisis." In the long peace of the nineteenth century, the military were not in the high councils of state, not of the political directorate, and neither were the economic men—they made raids upon the state but they did not join its directorate. During the 'thirties, the political man was ascendant. Now the military and the corporate men are in top positions.

Of the three types of circle that compose the power elite today, it is the military that has benefited the most in its enhanced power, although the corporate circles have also become more explicitly intrenched in the more public decision-making circles. It is the professional politician that has lost the most, so much that in examining the events and decisions, one is tempted to speak of a political vacuum in which the corporate rich and the high warlord, in their coinciding interests, rule.

It should not be said that the three "take turns" in carrying the initiative, for the mechanics of the power elite are not often as deliberate as that would imply. At times, of course, it is—as when political men, thinking they can borrow the prestige of generals, find that they must pay for it, or, as when during big slumps, economic men feel the need of a politician at once safe and possessing vote appeal. Today all three are involved in virtually all widely ramifying decisions. Which of the three types seems to lead depends upon "the tasks of the period" as they, the elite, define them. Just now, these tasks center upon "defense" and international affairs. Accordingly, as we have seen, the military are ascendant in two senses: as personnel and as justifying ideology. That is why, just now, we can most easily specify the unity and the shape of the power elite in terms of the military ascendancy.

But we must always be historically specific and open to complexities. The simple Marxian view makes the big economic man the *real* holder of power; the simple liberal view makes the big political man the chief of the power system; and there are some who would view the warlords as virtual dictators. Each of these is an oversimplified view. It is to avoid them that we use the term "power elite" rather than, for example, "ruling class."[2]

In so far as the power elite has come to wide public attention, it has done so in terms of the "military clique." The power elite does, in fact, take its current shape from the decisive entrance into it of the military. Their presence and their ideology are its major legitimations, whenever the power elite feels the need to provide any. But what is called the "Washington military clique" is not composed merely of military men, and it does not prevail merely in Washington. Its members exist all over the country, and it is a coalition of generals in the roles of corporation executives, of politicians masquerading as admirals, of corporation executives acting like politicians, of civil servants who become majors, of vice-admirals who are also the assistants to a cabinet officer, who is himself, by the way, really a member of the managerial elite.

Neither the idea of a "ruling class" nor of a simple monolithic rise of "bureaucratic politicians" nor of a "military clique" is adequate. The power elite today involves the often uneasy coincidence of economic, military, and political power.

* * *

Despite their social similarity and psychological affinities, the members of the power elite do not constitute a club having a permanent membership with fixed and formal boundaries. It is of the nature of the power elite that within it there is a good

---

[2] "Ruling class" is a badly loaded phrase. "Class" is an economic term; "rule" a political one. The phrase, "ruling class," thus contains the theory that an economic class rules politically. That shortcut theory may or may not at times be true, but we do not want to carry that one rather simple theory about in the terms that we use to define our problems; we wish to state the theories explicitly, using terms of more precise and unilateral meaning. Specifically, the phrase "ruling class," in its common political connotations, does not allow enough autonomy to the political order and its agents, and it says nothing about the military as such. It should be clear to the reader by now that we do not accept as adequate the simple view that high economic men unilaterally make all decisions of national consequence. We hold that such a simple view of "economic determinism" must be elaborated by "political determinism" and "military determinism"; that the higher agents of each of these three domains now often have a noticeable degree of autonomy; and that only in the often intricate ways of coalition do they make up and carry through the most important decisions. Those are the major reasons we prefer "power elite" to "ruling class" as a characterizing phrase for the higher circles when we consider them in terms of power.

deal of shifting about, and that it thus does not consist of one small set of the same men in the same positions in the same hierarchies. Because men know each other personally does not mean that among them there is a unity of policy; and because they do not know each other personally does not mean that among them there is a disunity. The conception of the power elite does not rest, as I have repeatedly said, primarily upon personal friendship.

As the requirements of the top places in each of the major hierarchies become similar, the types of men occupying these roles at the top—by selection and by training in the jobs—become similar. This is no mere deduction from structure to personnel. That it is a fact is revealed by the heavy traffic that has been going on between the three structures, often in very intricate patterns. The chief executives, the warlords, and selected politicians came into contact with one another in an intimate, working way during World War II; after that war ended, they continued their associations, out of common beliefs, social congeniality, and coinciding interests. Noticeable proportions of top men from the military, the economic, and the political worlds have during the last fifteen years occupied positions in one or both of the other worlds: between these higher circles there is an interchangeability of position, based formally upon the supposed transferability of "executive ability," based in substances upon the co-optation by cliques of insiders. As members of a power elite, many of those busy in this traffic have come to look upon "the government" as an umbrella under whose authority they do their work.

As the business between the big three increases in volume and importance, so does the traffic in personnel. The very criteria for selecting men who will rise come to embody this fact. The corporate commissar, dealing with the state and its military, is wiser to choose a young man who has experienced the state and its military than one who has not. The political director, often dependent for his own political success upon corporate decisions and corporations, is also wiser to choose a man with corporate experience. Thus, by virtue of the very criterion of success, the interchange of personnel and the unity of the power elite is increased.

Given the formal similarity of the three hierarchies in which the several members of the elite spend their working lives, given the ramifications of the decisions made in each upon the others, given the coincidence of interest that prevails among them at many points, and given the administrative vacuum of the American civilian state along with its enlargement of tasks—given these trends of structure, and adding to them the psychological affinities we have noted—we should indeed be surprised were we to find that men said to be skilled in administrative contacts and full of organizing ability would fail to do more than get in touch with one another. They have, of course, done much more than that: increasingly, they assume positions in one another's domains.

The unity revealed by the interchangeability of top roles rests upon the parallel development of the top jobs in each of the big three domains. The interchange occurs most frequently at the points of their coinciding interest, as between regulatory agency and the regulated industry; contracting agency and contractor. And, as we shall see, it leads to co-ordinations that are more explicit, and even formal.

———————

The inner core of the power elite consists, first, of those who interchange commanding roles at the top of one dominant institutional order with those in another: the admiral who is also a banker and a lawyer and who heads up an important federal commission; the corporation executive whose company was one of the two or three leading war materiel producers who is now the Secretary of Defense; the wartime general who dons civilian clothes to sit on the political directorate and then becomes a member of the board of directors of a leading economic corporation.

Although the executive who becomes a general, the general who becomes a statesman, the statesman who becomes a banker, see much more than ordinary men in their ordinary environments, still the perspectives of even such men often remain tied to their dominant locales. In their very career, however, they interchange roles within the big three and thus readily transcend the particularity of interest in any one of these institutional milieux. By their very careers and activities, they lace the three types of milieux together. They are, accordingly, the core members of the power elite.

These men are not necessarily familiar with every major arena of power. We refer to one man who moves in and between perhaps two circles—say the industrial and the military—and to another man who moves in the military and the political, and to a third who moves in the political as well as among opinion-makers. These inbetween types most closely display our image of the power elite's structure and operation, even of behind-the-scenes operations. To the extent that there is any "invisible elite," these advisory and liaison types are its core. Even if—as I believe to be very likely—many of them are, at least in the first part of their careers, "agents" of the various elites rather than themselves elite, it is they who are most active in organizing the several top milieux into a structure of power and maintaining it.

The inner core of the power elite also includes men of the higher legal and financial type from the great law factories and investment firms, who are almost professional go-betweens of economic, political and military affairs, and who thus act to unify the power elite. The corporation lawyer and the investment banker perform the functions of the "go-between" effectively and powerfully. By the nature of their work, they transcend the narrower milieu of any one industry, and accordingly are in a position to speak and act for the corporate world or at least sizable sectors of it. The corporation lawyer is a key link between the economic and military and political areas; the investment banker is a key organizer and unifier of the corporate world and a person well versed in spending the huge amounts of money the American military establishment now ponders. When you get a lawyer who handles the legal work of investment bankers you get a key member of the power elite.

* * *

The outermost fringes of the power elite—which change more than its core—consist of "those who count" even though they may not be "in" on given decisions of consequence nor in their career move between the hierarchies. Each member of the power elite need not be a man who personally decides every decision that is to be ascribed to the power elite. Each member, in the decisions that he does make, takes the others seriously into account. They not only make decisions in the several major areas of war and peace; they are the men who, in decisions in which they take no direct part, are taken into decisive account by those who are directly in charge.

On the fringes and below them, somewhat to the side of the lower echelons, the power elite fades off into the middle levels of power, into the rank and file of the Congress, the pressure groups that are not vested in the power elite itself, as well as a multiplicity of regional and state and local interests. If all the men on the middle levels are not among those who count, they sometimes must be taken into account, handled, cajoled, broken or raised to higher circles.

* * *

The conception of the power elite and of its unity rests upon the corresponding developments and the coincidence of interests among economic, political, and military organizations. It also rests upon the similarity of origin and outlook, and the social and personal intermingling of the top circles from each of these dominant hierarchies. This conjunction of institutional and psychological forces, in turn, is revealed by the heavy personnel traffic within and between the big three institutional orders, as well as by the rise of go-betweens as in the high-level lobbying. The conception of the power elite, accordingly, does *not* rest upon the assumption that American history since the origins of World War II must be understood as a secret plot, or as a great and co-ordinated conspiracy of the members of this elite. The conception rests upon quite impersonal grounds.

There is, however, little doubt that the American power elite—which contains, we are told, some of "the greatest organizers in the world"—has also planned and has plotted. The rise of the elite, as we have already made clear, was not and could not have been caused by a plot; and the tenability of the conception does not rest upon the existence of any secret or any publicly known organization. But, once the conjunction of structural trend and of the personal will to utilize it gave rise to the power elite, then plans and programs did occur to its members and indeed it is not possible to interpret many events and official policies of the fifth epoch without reference to the power elite. "There is a great difference," Richard Hofstadter has remarked, "between locating conspiracies *in* history and saying that history *is*, in effect, a conspiracy..."[2]

The structural trends of institutions become defined as opportunities by those who occupy their command posts. Once such opportunities are recognized, men may avail themselves of them. Certain types of men from each of the dominant institutional areas, more far-sighted than others, have actively promoted the liaison before it took its truly modern shape. They have often done so for reasons not shared by their partners, although not objected to by them either; and often the outcome of their liaison has had consequences which none of them foresaw, much less shaped, and which only later in the course of development came under explicit control. Only after it was well under way did most of its members find themselves part of it and become gladdened, although sometimes also worried, by this fact. But once the co-ordination is a going concern, new men come readily into it and assume its existence without question.

So far as explicit organization—conspiratorial or not—is concerned, the power elite, by its very nature, is more likely to use existing organizations, working within and between them, than to set up explicit organizations whose membership is strictly limited to its own members. But if there is no machinery in existence to ensure, for example, that military and political factors will be balanced in decisions made, they will invent such machinery and use it, as with the National Security Council. Moreover, in a formally democratic polity, the aims and the powers of the various elements of this elite are further supported by an aspect of the permanent war economy: the assumption that the security of the nation supposedly rests upon great secrecy of plan and intent. Many higher events that would reveal the working of the power elite can be withheld from public knowledge under the guise of secrecy. With the wide secrecy covering their operations and decisions, the power elite can mask their intentions, operations, and further consolidation. Any secrecy that is imposed upon those in positions to observe high decision-makers clearly works for and not against the operations of the power elite.

There is accordingly reason to suspect—but by the nature of the case, no proof—that the power elite is not altogether "surfaced." There is nothing hidden about it, although its activities are not publicized. As an elite, it is not organized, although its members often know one another, seem quite naturally to work together, and share many organizations in common. There is nothing conspiratorial about it, although its decisions are often publicly unknown and its mode of operation manipulative rather than explicit.

It is not that the elite "believe in" a compact elite behind the scenes and a mass down below. It is not put in that language. It is just that the people are of necessity confused and must, like trusting children, place all the new world of foreign policy and strategy and executive action in the hands of experts. It is just that everyone knows somebody has got to run the show, and that somebody usually does. Others do not really care anyway, and besides, they do not know how. So the gap between the two types gets wider.

* * *

The idea of the power elite rests upon and enables us to make sense of ① the decisive institutional trends that characterize the structure of our epoch, in particular, the military ascendancy in a privately incorporated economy, and more broadly, the several coincidences of objective interests between economic, military, and political institutions; ② the social similarities and the psychological affinities of the men who occupy the command posts of these structures, in particular the increased interchangeability of the top positions in each of them and the increased traffic between these orders in the careers of men of power; ③ the ramifications, to the point of virtual totality, of the kind of decisions that are made at the top, and the rise to power of a set of men who, by training and bent, are professional organizers of considerable force and who are unrestrained by democratic party training.

Negatively, the formation of the power elite rests upon ① the relegation of the professional party politician to the middle levels of power, ② the semi-organized stalemate of the interests of sovereign localities into which the legislative function has fallen, ③ the virtually complete absence of a civil service that constitutes a politically neutral, but politically relevant, depository of brainpower and executive skill, and ④ the increased official secrecy behind which great decisions are made without benefit of public or even Congressional debate.

As a result, the political directorate, the corporate rich, and the ascendant military have come together as the power elite, and the expanded and centralized hierarchies which they head have encroached upon the old balances and have now relegated them to the middle levels of power. Now the balancing society is a conception that pertains accurately to the middle levels, and on that level the balance has become more often an affair of intrenched provincial and nationally irresponsible forces and demands than a center of power and national decision.

But how about the bottom? As all these trends have become visible at the top and on the middle, what has been happening to the great American public? If the top is unprecedentedly powerful and increasingly unified and willful; if the middle zones are increasingly a semi-organized stalemate—in what shape is the bottom, in what condition is the public at large? The rise of the power elite, we shall now see, rests upon, and in some ways is part of, the transformation of the publics of America into a mass society.

STUDY QUESTIONS

1. What does Mills mean by the **power elite**?

2. What are the three domains of the power elite? Describe the interests of the power elite.

3. Identify two nationally elected officials, research what positions they held before serving their terms, what decisions they made during their time in office, and what positions they took after their public service. Discuss your results and whether they are evidence of the continued existence of the power elite.

4. Watch the documentary *Inside Job* and discuss current examples of the power elite. If the power elite lost **power**, would they be replaced? By whom?

DAN CLAWSON

Money and Politics

The American electorate is apathetic. Historically, voter turnout is very low in the United States to the point that "nonvoters" can seem to be a party of their own. In this reading Dan Clawson discusses some of the reasons for the apathy of American voters, primarily concentrating on the influence of money on the political system. As you read think about how money influences political campaigns, electoral results, and the system of **democracy**. In the current sociopolitical landscape, do you see a possible push for publicly financed campaigns or a continuous system of corporate and big donor contributions to political races?

A BASIC CONTRADICTION OF CAPITALIST DEMOCRACIES IS THAT in the political realm each person is supposed to be equal, with one and only one vote, but in the marketplace the people with the most money are supposed to have the most impact. It is difficult or impossible to maintain a barrier between the political and economic realms. In a society with enormous disparities of wealth and income the individuals and organizations with the most money will exercise disproportionate influence both on election campaigns and on the shaping of public policy.

If political influence depends on wealth, then in the United States today the top 1 percent of the population will have more "votes" than the bottom 90 percent, and Bill

Gates by himself will have more votes than the 100 million poorest Americans.[1] In practice, every capitalist democracy has rules to limit the political influence of wealth, and in every case those with wealth nonetheless find ways to use their money to exercise disproportionate influence. In recent years campaign finance problems have generated significant public attention and controversy not only in the United States, but also in France, Germany, Japan, Italy, and numerous other societies.

The 2000 election was the closest in U.S. history. Media attention focused primarily on ballot confusion and the limited number of people who were actively excluded from voting. This is insignificant compared to the fact that half the U.S. population does not vote in major national elections (and a far higher proportion does not vote in local elections).[2] In the nineteenth century U.S. voter turnout averaged around 80 percent, but the election of 1896 realigned politics and introduced a series of changes whose intent and effect was to drastically reduce voter turnout. These included the introduction of voter registration, a system under which voters must go to city hall at least thirty days before the election to register to vote. Voter registration initially applied only in major metropolitan areas where immigrant populations were concentrated. The consequences were immediate and dramatic: voter turnout fell from 77.9 percent in 1896 to 63.9 percent in 1904 and 55.7 percent in 1912.[3] Voter turnout increased during the 1930s, but in the last 40 years turnout has declined again, such that in each presidential election for more than 20 years only about half of American adults voted. Non-voting is strongly related to education and income. Republican voter participation levels are also highly correlated with social class, but Democratic voter participation is *not* class correlated. As Walter Dean Burnham argues, "The whole range of data suggests that if there is class struggle in American politics, it is almost entirely one-sided." To put it another way, "the 'party of nonvoters' fills up approximately to the extent that the Democratic party loses coherence and drifts away from the leftward end of our narrow political spectrum."[4] If the Democratic party presents candidates and policies similar to those of the Republican party, the

---

[1] See Edward N. Wolff. "How the Pie Is Sliced: America's Growing Concentration of Wealth." *American Prospect* 22 (Summer 1995): 58–64 and his *Top Heavy: A Study of Increasing Inequality of Wealth in America and What Can Be Done about It* (New York: New Press, 1996). The top 10 percent of the U.S. population controls more than two-thirds of the nation's wealth; the top 1 percent controls 42 percent.

[2] Frances Fox Piven and Richard A. Cloward, *Why Americans Don't Vote* (New York: Pantheon, 1988).

[3] See Walter Dean Burnham, "The System of 1896: An Analysis," pp. 147–202 in Paul Kleppner et al., eds. *The Evolution of American Electoral Systems* (Westport, CT: Greenwood Press, 1981), p. 193, for figures on turnout decline. See also Burnham, *Critical Elections and the Mainsprings of American Politics* (New York: W.W. Norton & Company, 1970), and Burnham, "The Changing Shape of the American Political Universe." *American Political Science Review* 1965, vol. 59 no. 1: 7–28.

[4] Walter Dean Burnham, *The Current Crisis in American Politics* (New York: Oxford University Press, 1982), pp. 188–189.

most significant shift in voting patterns is an increase in the number of people who choose not to vote, and an increase in the class skew of voter turnout.

Why does this situation persist? Why wouldn't Democratic party candidates shift to the left and thereby motivate and mobilize the large numbers of working class people who choose not to vote? The reason is simple: at least in the U.S. system, electoral success depends heavily on campaign spending. The United States has weak political parties, which means that each candidate runs more-or-less on his or her own, and most races are heavily influenced by individual personal appeal. In most cases, neither the political parties nor alternative organizations have the organizational capacity to establish personal contact with more than a small fraction of the voters. This means that races typically rely heavily on the mass media, but candidates are *not* given any free radio or television time.[5] In congressional races, for example, congressional candidates for the House of Representatives "who headed into the final three weeks with the most in combined spending and cash on hand won 93 percent of the time."[6] Candidates (and the Democratic party) have concluded that their first priority must be to raise large sums of money; in order to do so they adopt "moderate" stands that will not offend big-money donors. As a consequence many people conclude that the difference between the two parties is not important enough to make it worthwhile voting, that both parties give priority to wealthy donors and don't care about ordinary voters. Three-quarters (77 percent) of Americans believe that members of Congress listen more to major donors from outside their state than they do to voters in the state.[7] Political insiders consider "the real campaign" to be the race for money; even during the heat of the campaign, candidates spend "at least half a day, two or three days a week, on the telephone asking for money" in addition to the time they spend at fundraising gatherings.[8]

In the current American system, the most important fundraising distinction is between "hard money" and "soft money." Legislation supposedly sets strict limits on campaign contributions: only individuals, not organizations, can give money, and they can give no more than $1,000 per candidate in an election. "Hard money" is the term used for contributions that stay within these rules. Both politicians and big donors want to evade the law. In 1979 they found a loophole in the law: donations given for "party building" or for "get out the vote drives," they argued, were not covered by existing legislation. Therefore, donors could give unlimited amounts for these activities. Not only could individuals do so, but so could corporations and unions. These donations, given outside the rules, are called "soft money."

---

[5] The presidential debates are a partial exception.

[6] *Boston Globe,* November 8, 1997, p. A26.

[7] Princeton Survey Research Associates, "Money and Politics Survey: Summary and Overview," 1997.

[8] *New York Times,* November 1, 1996, p. A1.

TABLE 1. Totals Raised, 2000 Election
(In Millions of U.S. Dollars)

	Republicans	Democrats
President	191.6	132.6
Congress	508.2	506.0
Senate	202.3	228.9
House of Representatives	305.9	277.1
Political parties	691.8	513.1
Hard money	447.4	269.9
Soft money	244.4	243.1

Source: www.opensecrets.org, based on Federal Election Commission reports.

TABLE 2. Totals by Source, 2000 Election
(In Millions of U.S. Dollars)

Source of funds	Republicans	Democrats
Business	496.0	340.3
Labor	3.8	52.4
Ideological groups	16.4	17.5
Other and unknown	112.6	60.3

Source: www.opensecrets.org.

The Democratic party's priority has been to match the Republican party in fundraising, and they have come close to doing so. In the 2000 election, for example, spending for Congress was almost exactly even, as was "soft money." The Republicans had a distinct edge in "hard money" party fundraising and in the presidential race. (See Table 1.) Other parties and candidates were far behind. In the presidential race, Ralph Nader raised only $8.7 million and Patrick Buchanan $42.7 million.

The crucial financial disparity was not between political parties, but rather between business and labor. Although 1970s data are not fully comparable to that of recent years, in 1974 business was outspent by labor (.76 to 1) but by 1980 business outspent labor by 2.66 to 1.[9] Over time the funding advantage has tilted more and more toward business; currently business outspends labor by 15 to 1. (See Table 2.) The Republicans get almost no money from labor, but today even the Democrats receive *six times* as much from business as from labor. Democratic fundraisers do not wish to lose the $52 million they received from labor, but are far more concerned to maintain the $340 million they receive from business, and this makes the Democratic party

---

[9] Gary C. Jacobson, "Money in the 1980 and 1982 Congressional Elections," pp. 38–69 in Michael J. Malbin, editor, *Money and Politics in the United States* (Chatham, NJ: Chatham House Publishers, 1984).

extremely cautious about taking any positions calling for progressive economic policies, certainly any that involve a redistribution of wealth and income. How did we get to this situation, and what are its consequences?

RULES AND HISTORY

Campaign finance reform was enacted in response to the Watergate scandals, especially the discovery that the Nixon campaign had coerced many corporations to make secret contributions of $100,000 each. The system adopted in 1974 had these key provisions:[1]

1. **Disclosure**—All contributions of $200 or more must be publicly disclosed.
2. **Donation limits**—No individual may contribute more than $1,000 per candidate per election, nor more than $25,000 per year in total. Individuals may also contribute up to $5,000 to a political action committee (PAC) and $5,000 to a political party. PACs may contribute up to $5,000 per candidate per election, with no limit on the total they may contribute to all candidates.
3. **Voluntary and by individuals**—All political contributions must come from voluntary decisions by individuals. Corporations, unions, or other associations may form PACs to collect voluntary donations from their members or employees, and may pay all the costs of operating the PAC (rent, phone, salaries for staff), but may not give the organization's money (profits for corporations, member dues for unions).
4. **Candidates unlimited**—Candidates running for office may spend unlimited amounts of their own money, thus providing an incentive to nominate candidates rich enough to finance their own election. Jon Corzine of Goldman Sachs and New Jersey won his 2000 Senate race—as a *Democrat*—on the basis of $61 million of his own money.

The campaign finance law thus limited the amount of money a donor could give but not the amount a candidate could collect. No donor may give a candidate more than a small fraction of the total amount needed to run a winning race. The intent and effect of this system is that political candidates are dependent on the capitalist class as a whole, but not on a specific individual or company. Campaign contributions are to be spent on political campaigns and campaign-related activities, but in practice this is loosely interpreted: one candidate bought a luxury car and another paid himself

---

[1] For a presentation and analysis of the rules governing campaign finance, including details not covered here, see Frank J. Sorauf, *Inside Campaign Finance: Myths and Realities* (New Haven: Yale University Press, 1992).

$57,000 in campaign funds to rent part of his home as a campaign headquarters.[2] In the past two decades Congress has not modified the law at all, but in practice the law has changed drastically; soft money is by far the most important loophole, but by no means the only one. "Soft money" eliminates the two most important provisions of the initial legislation (donation limits and voluntary individual contributions). Soft money initially involved relatively trivial amounts (an estimated $19.1 million in 1980 and $21.6 million in 1984), but expanded rapidly (to $232 million in 1996 and $463 million in 2000). Beginning with the 1992 election, soft money itself was regulated to the extent of requiring that donors be disclosed and imposing some rules on the ways it can be spent; this makes the distinction between "hard" and "soft" money problematic. The money cannot be used for a message specifically urging people to *vote* for a specific candidate, but the entire advertisement can present a candidate's views and/or attack an opponent as long as the advertisement does not specifically say "vote for [this candidate]." In recent years, further forms of evasion have been perfected and are assuming ever greater importance: if soft money is prohibited (as proposed by the McCain-Feingold legislation), these new forms of evasion will expand dramatically.

THE MONEY AND ITS EFFECTS

The amounts of money involved are enormous from the perspective of a candidate but trivial from that of a business donor. In congressional races, the candidate with more money is elected 90 percent of the time. Money is most important to challengers; incumbents can almost always raise enough to be competitive, but challengers rarely can.[3] A challenger hoping to win a seat in the House of Representatives has less than one-half of 1 percent of a chance of winning unless he or she raises at least half a million dollars; far more is required to win a Senate race. In four out of five congressional races the challenger can't raise half as much as the incumbent; only 3 percent of those races are even competitive (decided by margins of 55–45 percent or closer). In the one out of five races where the challenger spent at least half as much as the incumbent, 39 percent of the races were competitive.[4]

---

[2] *New York Times*, November 12, 1990, p. A18.

[3] Gary C. Jacobson, *Money in Congressional Elections* (New Haven: Yale University Press, 1980). See also his "The Effects of Campaign Spending in House Elections: New Evidence for Old Arguments," *American Journal of Political Science* (May 1990), Vol. 34, No. 2, pp. 334–362.

[4] Dan Clawson, Alan Neustadtl, and Denise Scott, *Money Talks: Corporate PACs and Political Influence* (New York: Basic Books, 1992), p. 203, and Dan Clawson, Alan Neustadtl, and Mark Weller, *Dollars and Votes: How Business Campaign Contributions Subvert Democracy* (Philadelphia: Temple University Press, 1998), pp. 1–4.

The current system effectively excludes any candidate that cannot raise large amounts of money. This "money primary" eliminates potential candidates as decisively as the election primaries. From the point of view of the capitalist class the system is extremely effective: unless a candidate can attract significant support from those with money, he or she is excluded from public debate and stands almost no chance of being elected. It is important to be clear that the current U.S. money-election system is an effective technology of power: media-driven campaigns, based on extensive polling, directed by highly paid political consultants, are able to beat candidates who attempt to substitute popular participation for money. This is, of course, as much a measure of the weakness of oppositional culture and organization as it is a measure of the strength of the money-election system.

Increasingly incumbents use money to win elections before voters get involved. If candidates can raise enough money well in advance, no "serious" candidate will challenge them. Senator Rudy Boschwitz wrote a secret postelection analysis explaining his campaign strategy:

> Nobody in politics (except me!) likes to raise money, so I thought the best way of discouraging the toughest opponents from running was to have a few dollars in the sock. *I believe it worked.... From all forms of fund-raising I raised $6 million plus and got 3 or 4 (maybe even 5) stories and cartoons* that irked me. In retrospect, I'm glad I had the money.[5]

This strategy is highly effective and increasingly common.[6] In March 1996 Bill Paxon, chair of the House Republican campaign committee, said, "We've been pounding on members [of Congress] to raise more money by the filing deadline; if they show a good balance, that could ward off opponents."[7] As a result many U.S. congressional races are not contested at all, or involve only token opposition. Of course it doesn't *always* work—in his next election, Boschwitz raised so much money that all the "serious" candidates refused to challenge him, and although Boschwitz outspent his opponent by 5 to 1, the opponent (maverick Paul Wellstone) won nonetheless.

Although the amounts of money look enormous to candidates, from the perspective of business profits these are small donations; business could easily contribute far more money. The advertising budget for the top 50 corporate advertisers is more than $25 billion a year. If just these 50 corporations shifted 10 percent of their advertising

---

[5] Senator Rudy Boschwitz, quoted in Brooks Jackson, *Honest Graft: Big Money and the American Political Process* (New York: Knopf, 1988), pp. 251–52.

[6] See David Epstein and Peter Zemsky, "Money Talks: Deterring Quality Challengers in Congressional Elections," *American Political Science Review* 89:295–308, and Peverill Squire "Preemptive Fund-raising and Challenger Profile in Senate Elections," *Journal of Politics* 1991, vol. 53:1150–64.

[7] Quoted in Elizabeth Drew, *Whatever it Takes: The Real Struggle for Political Power in America* (New York: Viking, 1997), pp. 19–20.

budgets into campaign finance, in a two-year election cycle they would provide more money than the cost of *both* sides of *all* the races for Congress and the presidency.[8] It is not economic constraints that keep them from doing so, but rather concerns about legitimacy and fear that such massive donations would lead to a popular reaction.

Why do large donors give? Some do so because they support the candidate's positions on the issues and hope their donation will increase the candidate's chance of winning. Most business donations, however, are given to gain "access." Critics of the campaign finance system present these donations as market transactions: a donation is given to buy a vote. As in the market, they seem to believe, direct equivalents are exchanged, the transaction is balanced, minimal trust is required, and no enduring obligations are created. The most common alternative to this market metaphor is the claim, often presented by the donors themselves, that they give selflessly to promote good government and top quality leadership. The bulk of the literature on campaign finance, *both* popular *and* academic, is framed in this fashion, with the academics attempting to test such theories.[9] Donors insist that they do not and cannot "buy" the vote of a member of Congress. As the senior vice president of a major defense contractor told me: "You certainly aren't going to be able to buy anybody for $500 or $1,000 or $10,000. It's a joke."[1] The politicians who solicit contributions agree: Representative Tony Coelho, the greatest Democratic fundraiser in the interval between Lyndon Johnson and Bill Clinton, warned contributors "Don't ever try to create the impression with me, or ever say it—if you say it, it's all over—that your money has bought you something. It hasn't."[2] Academic research supports this position, if the issue is whether there is a direct exchange of equivalents: quantitative studies that try to link donations to roll-call votes find little or no relationship.

---

[8] See Dan Clawson, Alan Neustadtl, and Mark Weller, *Dollars and Votes: How Business Campaign Contributions Subvert Democracy* (Philadelphia: Temple University Press, 1998), p. 124.

[9] For popular exposes see Philip M. Stern, *The Best Congress Money Can Buy* (New York: Pantheon, 1988) and Lars-Erik Nelson, *The Buying of the Congress* (1998). For scholarly assessments see Janet M. Grenzke, "PACs and the Congressional Supermarket: The Currency Is Complex," *American Journal of Political Science* 1989, vol. 33:1–24 and Thomas Romer and James M. Synder, Jr., "An Empirical Investigation of the Dynamics of PAC Contributions," *American Journal of Political Science* 1994, vol. 38:745–69. For a largely theoretical argument that in fact politicians extort money from innocent companies, see Fred S. McChesney, *Money for Nothing: Politicians, Rent Extraction, and Political Extortion* (Cambridge, MA: Harvard University Press, 1997).

[1] This quotation, and all other unidentified quotations from corporate executives, comes from interviews I conducted with key officials at leading companies, typically vice presidents or senior vice presidents. Informants were promised confidentiality for themselves and their companies; on this basis they permitted me to tape record the interviews. For further background on methods see Dan Clawson, Alan Neustadtl, and Denise Scott, *Money Talks: Corporate PACs and Political Influence* (New York: Basic Books, 1992) and Dan Clawson, Alan Neustadtl, and Mark Weller, *Dollars and Votes: How Business Campaign Contributions Subvert Democracy* (Philadelphia: Temple University Press, 1998).

[2] Quoted in Brooks Jackson, *Honest Graft: Big Money and the American Political Process* (New York: Knopf, 1988), p. 105.

Campaign contributions are best understood as gifts, given to create a generalized sense of obligation. Marcel Mauss wrote that "in Scandinavian and many other civilizations contracts are fulfilled and exchanges of goods are made by means of gifts."[3] These gifts, Mauss argued, are supposedly "voluntary, disinterested and spontaneous" but in fact are "obligatory and interested." A gift creates an enduring relationship, one that lasts at least until it is reciprocated. Corporations thus prefer to contribute to candidates in advance, before they have any favor to request, with the intent of creating a generalized sense of obligation. Moreover, as Mauss argued, "the presentation of a gift is an imposition of identity." Given the small size of most donations ($1,000 to $2,000 to candidates for Congress), corporations happily give to candidates for years simply on the chance that at some point in the future they may want legislation tailored to their needs. As Mauss explained, "ritualized gift giving, in any society, is a method of dealing with important but insecure relationships, whereby gifts are offered to persons or collectivities whose goodwill is needed but cannot be taken for granted."

If campaign finance donations were given simply to influence election outcomes, donors would not need to be recognized. Because donations are in reality part of a complex gift exchange system that creates networks of obligation, donors insist that they must always present the money in person. Typically they do so at a fundraising gathering and use the occasion to become acquainted with the politician and his or her staff. As the vice president of a major Texas company explained to me, "If we are making a contribution to somebody who doesn't know it, we're screwing up. . . . If we are just sending money out to somebody and they are not aware of it, we've got no business giving them a contribution because they are not doing any good." As a result, corporate government relations officials attend dozens—in some cases hundreds—of fundraisers each election cycle. The fundraiser provides an opportunity to talk to the candidate on an issue of interest to the corporation, to talk to the candidate's staff, to talk to other members of Congress (especially the leadership) who show up to support the candidate, and of course also to network with representatives of other corporations.

Even if corporations are enemies in the marketplace, they often work together in politics.[4] One corporate executive explained that his company, a pharmaceutical manufacturer, had a particularly bitter rival: "You couldn't get more competitive. We're suing each other all the time. . . . We hate each other, but I have a very good relationship with them down here [in Washington DC], and often we work together on the Hill for certain bills." Corporate executives frequently serve on a candidate's fundraising

---

[3] Marcel Mauss, *The Gift: Forms and Functions of Exchange in Archaic Societies* (New York: W. W. Norton, 1925/1967; translated by Ian Cunnison), p. xiv.

[4] See Mark Mizruchi, *The Structure of Corporate Political Action: Interfirm Relations and Their Consequences* (Cambridge, MA: Harvard University Press, 1992); Dan Clawson, Alan Neustadtl, and James Bearden. "The Logic of Business Unity," *American Sociological Review* 1986, vol. 51, no. 6, pp.797–811.

committee, and in that capacity get 5 or 10 other corporations to donate to the candidate. The solicited corporation contributes as a favor to the soliciting executive or corporation, and may do so even if they dislike the *candidate*. This process allows a corporation to be responsible (and gain credit with the candidate) for raising far more money than the corporate PAC could itself give, and yields "hard money" which can be used for any purpose (as opposed to "soft money" whose uses are restricted in various ways).

ACCESS

The purpose of giving the money, attending the fundraisers, and the networking process it facilitates, is to make it possible to gain "access" to the relevant member of Congress when the corporation wants something. "Access" is a euphemism for a process that involves much more than a chance to talk. Although the relatively small donations permitted by law are not enough to determine a member's vote on a highly visible roll call bill, the corporation uses its access to get the member to make a minor change in the wording of an obscure provision of the bill, effectively exempting the corporation from the full force of the law. For example, the Tax Reform Act of 1986 contained a provision limited to a single company, identified as a "corporation incorporated on June 13, 1917, which has its principal place of business in Bartlesville, Oklahoma." As is the case with this provision, the language in the bill typically does not identify the corporation by name (so someone reading the bill cannot tell it applies to Phillips Petroleum), nor does it give any sense of the dollar impact, nor is there any way of knowing which member of Congress inserted the provision. Many U.S. bills are hundreds of pages long, with a large fraction of the total taken up with these sorts of provisions. The consequence is that the "Tax Reform Act" doesn't really reform taxes and the "Clean Air Act" leaves the air polluted. The head of government relations at a major chemical company that is also a heavy-duty polluter told me: "I spent seven years of my life trying to stop the Clean Air Act." Nonetheless, he was perfectly willing to make corporate contributions to legislators who voted in favor of the Clean Air Act—as ultimately, almost all of them did—because "how a person votes on the final piece of legislation often is not representative of what they have done." Some of the legislators who voted for the final bill in fact helped to undermine its effectiveness: "During the process some of them were very sympathetic to some of our concerns" this executive explained.

To get the provisions they want, corporations may need to visit many representatives and may need to re-work the provision. The senior vice president of a steel manufacturer explained this process:

SOFT MONEY: THE CLINTON COFFEES

A $100,000 contribution entitled donors to attend a small-group coffee with President Clinton and other top officials, held in the White House. Selected larger donors were invited to spend the night in the White House, sleeping in the Lincoln Bedroom, and often eating breakfast with the Clintons.

Typical of the Clinton coffees is the one held May 13, 1996, with Terry Murray, president and CEO of Fleet Bank; John McCoy, chairman of Banc One; Paul Hazen, chairman and CEO of Wells Fargo Bank; and Thomas G. Labrecque, chairman and CEO of Chase Manhattan Bank, as well as Treasury Secretary Robert E. Rubin, Comptroller of the Currency Eugene A. Ludwig, Democratic National Committee Chairman Don Fowler, party Finance Chairman Marvin S. Rosen, and of course President Clinton. John P. Manning, president and CEO of Boston Capital Partners, explains that at the coffees he has attended "There was give and take on a number of business and economic issues."*

Perhaps the most unusual coffee participants were two representatives of the Cheyenne-Arapaho tribes of Oklahoma. The tribe has 11,000 members, more than 60 percent of whom were unemployed, and those with jobs earned an average annual income of $6,074. At great hardship, they came up with the $100,000 to attend a coffee and tell President Clinton about their problem: Their land was taken from them in 1883 by President Chester A. Arthur's executive order, which specified, however, that the land was to be returned to the tribe as soon as it was no longer used for military purposes. The fort was closed in 1948, but the land was never returned. The land "includes unmarked graves, ritual dance grounds and an estimated $500 million in oil and gas reserves." The tribe had earlier tried to see their U.S. senator, but had been denied a meeting. President Clinton listened to their concerns, looked them in the eye, and said "We'll see what we can do to help you." In fact, he did nothing. When they complained and went to the press the money was returned to them, but the government kept their land.[†]

* *Boston Globe*, January 25, 1997, p. A6.
† *New York Times*, August 12, 1997, p. A18.

They [members of Congress] say, "Here's what I think, here's what you think, can you rework this out so I can give you a little piece of the pie and still not screw the other 93 percent of my district who want it the other way?" And we say, "Yes, if you can just do this. It doesn't change the bill, but at least it allows us to do this." It's the fun of the game.

The senior vice president of one of the nation's largest financial companies was blunt about it:

We are not big on voting records . . . because frequently the final vote on a particular bill isn't really important. . . . Probably what's more important is what's thrashed out internally in some of the important committees in Congress. And it doesn't much matter how people vote afterwards.

Corporate executives say that essentially all members of Congress participate in this process; ultra-conservatives who insist on "no government interference with the market" will insert provisions to provide government handouts, as will well known liberals with a reputation for being "anti-business." A mid-level official at a utility company told me that "You have guys that will hold rallies right outside this building here, hold news conferences and picket lines periodically, every year," attacking the company and its policies. But once in Congress those same people cooperate with the company: "I don't want to say that they are the best friends we have in government, but you can go to them."

Individual and PAC contributions are the normal routes to "access" to ordinary members of Congress; soft money has become the route to access to national party officials and the president. President Clinton defended the White House coffees he held: "I look for ways to have genuine conversations with people. I learn things when I listen to people."[5] But the people to whom President Clinton was listening were not exactly a cross-section of the population: the price for admission to the coffees was $100,000. Reportedly, most discussions at coffees focused primarily on background and general policy, rather than on the direct insertion of loopholes, and involved CEO-level officials (as opposed to the vice presidents and managers who typically talk to members of Congress and to congressional staff). One coffee participant defended the coffees by explaining that President Clinton "really seemed to want businessmen's perspective on what he was doing on the economy, tax, health care."[6]

IDEOLOGY

Corporations also give campaign contributions for ideological reasons. A few corporations follow an almost exclusively ideological approach, and many corporations pay at least some attention to ideological concerns. An "access" strategy means that corporations contribute to incumbents, regardless of political party and generally without regard to a candidate's professed ideology (since in practice all legislators participate in this access process) or whether they even have an opponent. Ideological corporations want to change Congress and so give to pro-business challengers (in practice almost all of them Republicans) who are in tight races where contributions could influence the election outcome. The 1980 election differed from all others: a large proportion of all corporations pursued an aggressively ideological strategy for that election. If we look at corporations contributing 30 percent or more of their money to Republican challengers, more did so in 1980 than in all the other elections from 1976 to 2000 *combined*. The executive vice president of one corporation explained:

---

[5] *New York Times*, March 8, 1997, p. 9.
[6] *Boston Globe*, January 25, 1997, p. A6.

There was a genuine movement, the closest thing I've ever seen on the part of business in this country, almost a phenomenon that occurred in that year and a half or two years of that particular election. It was a genuine virtual fervor. Let's go out there and we can do it, we can change the system.

Immediately after the 1980 Republican victories, Democratic strategists (led by Representative Tony Coelho, later Al Gore's campaign chairman) aggressively re-shaped the party and went to business seeking donations for Democrats. Coelho pointed out to business executives that Democrats (at that time) still controlled the House of Representatives, and therefore "I don't think it makes good business sense for you to try to destroy us."[7] Coelho notes that in 1980 "we had our butts kicked" and is convinced that if he and others had not courted business, the Republicans "would have completed the job." As a result, most corporations reverted to predominantly access-driven contribution strategies.

The few corporations which remain ideological are furious at the access strategy of other corporations. A member of the Board of Directors of a leading manufacturer said: "I can't figure out what their motive is. I just look at it and look at it, and I just can't figure it out." Such corporations, he said, are shoving money at candidates "who don't need the money and who couldn't lose if they were caught in *flagrante delicto* with the governor's wife in the public square of the capital." In his view, "the behavior of corporate PACs is absolutely fucking disgraceful. . . . And stupid and shortsighted beyond measure."

Most corporate executives, however, prefer the current situation, where *both* major parties are strongly "pro-business" and heavily dependent on business campaign contributions. One executive, formerly a party official but now in charge of an oil company's political contributions, explained to me: "I don't do this for myself, I do it for the company. I don't really feel I have a party now. I think it is foolish for anybody in this business to profess an affiliation with a party. I don't think that is very healthy." As a result, *both* major American parties depend primarily on business for campaign contributions. For soft money donations, for example, the *Democrats* receive more than *six* times as much from corporations as from labor unions.

Republicans made huge advances in the 1994 elections and took control of both houses of Congress. The easy assumption would be that this was because business had once again mobilized as it had done in 1980, and some left analysts made such claims. Thomas Ferguson, for example, wrote that "A sea of money that had been flowing reliably to congressional Democrats and the party that controlled the White House abruptly reversed direction and began gushing in torrents to Republican

---

[7] Thomas Byrne Edsall, "Coelho Mixes Democratic Fund-Raising, Political Matchmaking." *Washington Post*, December 1, 1985, pp. A17–18. See also Edsall, "The Reagan Legacy," in *The Reagan Legacy*, edited by Sidney Blumenthal and Edsall, pp. 3–50 (New York: Pantheon), and Brooks Jackson, *Honest Graft: Big Money and the American Political Process* (New York: Knopf, 1988).

challengers."[8] In fact, however, there is no truth to this claim: corporate campaign contributions in 1994 are essentially the same as they were in every election from 1982 on. The contrast with 1980 is stark. In 1980, Republican challengers received 28.6 percent of all the money contributed by corporations; in 1994, they received only 5.7 percent.[9] The 1994 Republican victories were *not* the consequence of a massive business mobilization, nor did business fund Republican challengers in 1996—which may well explain why President Clinton was easily re-elected in 1996, and why the Republicans won so few policy changes from their 1994 victories.[1]

* * *

LESSONS

Public debate and media reports usually discuss U.S. campaign finance in terms of whether campaign contributions do or do not buy politicians' votes. This fundamentally misunderstands the way the system operates. There is little correlation between campaign contributions and high visibility roll call votes. Even for low visibility issues settled through "minor" wording changes in obscure provisions of bills, the process is much looser and more uncertain than a market transaction. The problem is not outright bribery, but rather the creation of a network of obligations; the addition of one or two or three new regulations will not significantly alter this process.

At least in the U.S. context, full public disclosure of contributions has had little effect in regulating behavior. Data on campaign contributions are publicly available on the Web,[2] but this has had few consequences for behavior. It is possible that would be different in a more class conscious society, but I know of no evidence to that effect.

Another common reform proposal, an effort to limit the size of donations to amounts so small that they would be unlikely to influence behavior, also seems unlikely to be effective. It is true that today, especially for soft money, most of the money comes from a few large donors. In 1996, of 27,596 soft money donors, 19,670 gave $1,000 or less; they were 71.3 percent of the donors but accounted for only 3.6 percent of the

---

[8] Thomas Ferguson, "GOP Money Talked: Did Voters Listen?" *The Nation* December 26, 1994, p. 792.

[9] Dan Clawson, Alan Neustadtl, and Mark Weller, *Dollars and Votes: How Business Campaign Contributions Subvert Democracy* (Philadelphia: Temple University Press, 1998), p. 160.

[1] In 1996 business did increase its contributions to Republican incumbents (since they were now the majority in Congress, and would control the key committees), but not to Republican challengers. Ibid.

[2] At the Federal Election Commission website, www.fec.gov, and at that of the non-partisan watchdog group the Center for Responsive Politics, www.crp.org.

money. On the other hand, the 487 donors who gave $100,000 or more were only 1.8 percent of the contributors but accounted for 49.9% of the money.[3] Nonetheless, the most likely effect of donation limits would be that businesses would organize to increase the number of donors, just as corporations today often contribute because another corporation asks them to do so.

Because business has vastly more resources than any other group, over time it has come to more and more fully dominate campaign finance. In 1974 labor contributed more than business, and labor opposed public financing of elections, believing its large base of small donors would give it political muscle. The advantage has steadily shifted to business, until by now it outspends labor 15 to 1. Only in the last few years has labor accepted the fact it will not be able to compete; this has led it to switch its strategy and support full public funding of campaigns.

Business is not concerned about strategies that involve imposing additional regulations. Corporations are confident they will find new loopholes faster than Congress can impose new regulations. The only reform strategy that concerns business, or that has demonstrated much potential to fundamentally alter the system, is full public financing at a level sufficient to run a viable campaign. Partial public financing will make little difference: the current U.S. presidential elections receive public financing, but candidates are permitted to raise additional sums, and that private money provides the margin of victory.

STUDY QUESTIONS

1. Define "hard" and "soft" money campaign contributions.

2. What are the causes of the increasing disparities between business and labor contributions to political campaigns. What are the effects?

3. One of the elements of campaign finance reform allowed American candidates to spend unlimited amounts of their own money to finance their own campaigns. Who are some political candidates who have funded their own campaigns?

4. Should all political campaigns in the United States be publicly financed? Why or why not? Discuss as a group.

---

[3] Dan Clawson, Alan Neustadtl, and Mark Weller, *Dollars and Votes: How Business Campaign Contributions Subvert Democracy* (Philadelphia: Temple University Press, 1998), p. 114; based on Federal Election Commission data.

G. WILLIAM DOMHOFF

Power

What is **power**? G. William Domhoff first defines and then traces the history of power. For **social scientists** power has two dimensions: collective and distributive power. That is, those with power form a strong group that can effect certain intentional outcomes, and they have an ability to be successful in conflicts with other **groups**. Domhoff uses the basic framework of power structures as a theoretical lens through which to look at American history up to the twenty-first century and draws conclusions about the interactions between the **economically** and the **politically** powerful. Domhoff organizes his essay carefully; you may find it useful to create an outline of his argument as you read.

INTRODUCTION: A DEFINITION AND BRIEF HISTORY OF POWER

POWER IS ONE OF THOSE TOUCHY SUBJECTS THAT TEND TO BE talked about indirectly or through the use of revealing words and metaphors, such as "bossy," "pushy," or "too big for their britches," or in terms of "heavy hitters," "rain makers," and people with "clout." This understanding of power is part of the general definition of the concept in the social sciences: "the capacity of some persons to produce intended and foreseen effects on others" (Wrong 1995, p. 2).

For social scientists, however, power has two intertwined dimensions. First, power is the overall capacity of a group, class, or nation to produce intended and foreseen effects. Here the stress is on power as the degree to which a "collectivity" has the technological resources, organizational forms, social morale, and cooperative mindset that are necessary to achieve its general goals. In that sense, most nations have become more powerful in recent decades because their economies are bigger, their governments better able to communicate with and influence the entire population, and their militaries more lethal. Second, the concept of power includes the ability of a group, class, or nation to be successful in conflicts with other groups, classes, or nations on issues of concern to it. Here the stress is on "power over," which is also called "distributive power," with much the same meaning as the words and metaphors mentioned in the previous paragraph as the means by which Americans discuss power.

Both collective and distributive power have the same base: *organizations*. Organizations at their most basic are simply sets of rules and roles developed so a human group can accomplish a particular purpose. Put even more simply, they are ways in which people do something together in a routine fashion. Religious ceremonies, for example, are routines that become the basis for the institutions called churches. The established routines for face-to-face economic exchanges—my sandwich for your jelly beans—become one basis for the more complex economic system of markets. Since human beings have a vast array of purposes, they have formed an appropriately large number of organizations. But only four of these organizations weigh heavily in terms of generating societal power: economic organizations, political organizations, military organizations, and religious organizations. All of them enhance the collective power of their members, but at the same time they can quickly become very hierarchical and domineering when they begin to grow larger or face an outside threat.

The early outlines of these four main bases of power can already be seen in small hunting and gathering societies when hunting parties are organized (economic organization, with meat shared equally among all members of the society), when communal gatherings are called in an attempt to defuse interpersonal disputes that threaten to rip apart the whole group (political organization, which is fundamentally about regulating human interactions within a specific territory), when the men band together to do battle with rival groups or clans (military organization), and when rituals of religious solidarity are performed to deal with the anxiety, guilt, and fear of death that have been part of daily existence for most people since the dawn of humanity (religious organization). The claim that these four main forms of collective power can become the basis for distributive power is supported by the fact that even in small-scale societies men frequently use them to exclude or subjugate women. For example, the secretive men's huts, in which religious ceremonies are carried out, often exclude women on pain of gang rape or death, and men will band together to kill women who resist changes in the social order (Gregor 1985; Sanday 1981). Generally speaking, women have had little or no power in most societies, with the exception of varying degrees of economic power that range from minor to significant, until the last 200 years in Western Europe and North America, which is a commentary on the pervasiveness of power structures in and of itself (Blumberg 1984; Mann 1986a).

Generally speaking, however, these nascent and temporary forms of organization do not become the basis for distributive power in hunting and gathering or tribal-level societies. Collective power is still ascendant because the "rank-and-file" members of those societies are able to be surprisingly and subtly vigilant against would-be power-seekers, called "bullies" in our everyday language, who are controlled through gossip, chastisement, shunning, and if necessary, assassination. Contrary to the image of these societies as lacking a power structure, an image that is embodied in the Christian idea of the Garden of Eden and the Marxist idea of primitive communism, it seems more plausible that they have an "inverted power structure" in which people are able to maintain an egalitarian social structure through the kinds of collective actions against potential dominators that are mentioned in the previous sentence (Boehm 1999).

However, when the level of organization reaches a large enough scale over a long enough period of time, a permanent division of labor develops that can further increase an organization's collective power due to a specialization of function at all of its levels. Since this division of labor makes sense in terms of collective power, it clearly increases the ability of a society to grow larger and defend itself when necessary, but it also contains the potential for a more hierarchical distribution of power because "those who occupy supervisory and coordinating positions have an immense organizational superiority over the others" (Mann 1986b, pp. 6–7). As many theorists of varying persuasions have noted, those at the top can then turn the organization into a power base for themselves due to the information and material resources they control, their ability to reshape the structure of the organization, their power to hire and fire underlings, and their opportunities to make alliances with other organizational leaders. Alliances with other organizational leaders then generate a *power structure*, a network of people and organizations that uses its combined resources to develop barriers that make it more difficult for people outside or on the bottom of these organizations to participate in the governance of the society in general (see Gaventa 1980, for an excellent synthesis of how these various processes of exclusion are carried out in the United States).

At this point ordinary members of the society are organizationally outflanked, no longer able to maintain the more informal inverted power structures that kept pre-civilized societies largely egalitarian (Boehm 1999). They become enmeshed in the everyday routines of large-scale societies called "civilizations." Indeed, sociologists sometimes use the image of a "caged" population as part of their definition of civilizations, which arose independently in five or six different places with dense networks of economic activities that generated large surpluses stored in religious institutions (Mann 1986b; Weber 1904/1958, p. 181). These religious centers then evolved into city-states that had somewhat separate religious and governmental institutions—and then into empires of domination that had large armies. Once these power bases were intertwined, they had even more potential to greatly increase collective power. This is most directly observed in the case of state and military organizations, which increased the collective power of economic organizations through activities as varied as protecting trade routes and making it possible to employ coerced or slave labor.

At the same time, and crucially in terms of understanding how distributive power came to be so important in large-scale civilizations, the mobilization of greater collective power depends on the resolution of prior questions about distributive power arrangements. Who has power over whom has to be settled within organizations, cities, or nation-states before collective power can be exercised in any useful way, as the collapse of dominant economic classes, armies, and states over the centuries amply demonstrates.

Furthermore, as the brief consideration of hunting and gathering societies implied, no one network comes first or is somehow more "basic" than the others, contrary to the warring theories of power that arose in the nineteenth century and tended to dominate theorizing for the next 150 years. For example, many theorists still claim that the economic network is the most basic one because people cannot live without food and shelter, but contrary to that claim, it also can be argued that human beings would not have survived for very long if they had not developed the religious beliefs and practices that allow them to deal with the anxieties and fears that can paralyze day-to-day work efforts. The hunters in pre-agricultural societies believed they had to be on good terms with the spirit world to be successful, and early agriculturalists believed their fields had to be blessed to be fertile, which gave an important role to shamans from the outset. In other words, it may be that shamans and religious leaders carry out the rituals that make it possible for other people to go about their daily business, which implies that religious networks are necessary for economic networks to function smoothly.

However, this does not mean that the networks are always of equal importance as power bases. At some points in history, military organizations have been more powerful; in other times and places, such as in the present-day United States, networks of economic organizations are more fully developed and important. To add further complexity, the resources provided by one type of organizational power base can be used to shape or control any of the others. Economic power can be turned into political power (think campaign contributions by corporate leaders to political candidates). Religious power can generate military power (the Iranian revolution is one example). Military power can conquer political power (the many military leaders who overthrew the established governments in numerous countries in Latin America and Southeast Asia in recent decades come to mind here). In that sense, power is like the idea of "energy" in the natural sciences: it cannot be reduced to one primary form (Russell 1938, pp. 10–11). This complexity is one of the main reasons why it is necessary to do power structure studies. Generalizations from society to society or historical epoch to historical epoch are risky if not impossible.

Finally by way of overview and introduction, no firm generalizations can be made about how the development of one of the two dimensions of power, collective and distributive, affects the other. Although collective and distributive power usually increased hand-in-hand in the first several thousand years of Western civilization, this was not always the case later on. For example, the economic transformations of the eighteenth and nineteenth centuries had a large impact on collective economic power, but none on distributive power, whereas the increased collective power of governments during the same time period actually contributed to a decrease in the distributive power of political elites, as seen in the creation of parliaments to limit the power of kings and other despots. However, once legislative branches were added to governments, Mann (1993, p. 16) finds a "surprising continuity of distributive power" in Western Europe and the United States between 1760 and 1914, despite vast increases in collective power in all four organizational networks.

But how do we study power structures in action in modern societies, such as the United States? Who has power, how do they gain it, and how do they use it?

ANALYZING POWER STRUCTURES

Power structure research, the study of the way in which power is organized and distributed in modern societies, emerged suddenly in American sociology in the 1950s from empirical research by sociologists Floyd Hunter (1953), who concluded that business elites dominated the city of Atlanta based on his detailed interviews with a wide range of citizens, and C. Wright Mills (1956), who claimed that a triumvirate of corporate executives, appointees to the executive branch of the federal government, and top military brass dominated the United States based on his study of the social backgrounds, careers, and viewpoints of people at the top of all three hierarchies (see Zweigenhaft and Domhoff 2006; Zweigenhaft and Domhoff 2011, for updates of Mills's empirical findings). For Hunter and Mills, these elites run the show with little or no influence from political parties, voluntary groups, or public opinion. Their arguments and evidence are rejected by mainstream social science theorists (called "pluralists" and "historical institutionalists"), who see the United States as a country with dispersed inequalities that is governed by shifting coalitions of interest groups or rival institutions, with room for public opinion to have an impact through political parties and lobbying efforts. They are also criticized by the Marxists, the longstanding opponents of the mainstreamers, who believe that power structures always revolve around an unending class struggle between owners and non-owners, with everything else more or less secondary. The challenges by these rival theory groups to the perspective that developed from the work of Hunter and Mills are understandable because power structure research differs fundamentally from mainstream social science and Marxism due to its assumption that power is rooted first and foremost in the kind of organizational networks discussed in the previous section.

Power structure research gradually came to be based on a combination of network analysis—more specifically, "membership network analysis"—and content analysis, and it makes use of four power indicators: (1) what organization, group, or class in the social structure under study receives the most of what people seek for and value (who benefits?); (2) what organization, group, or class is over-represented in key decision-making positions (who sits in the seats of government power?); (3) what organization, group, or class wins in the decisional arena? (who wins?); and (4) who is thought to be powerful on the basis of interviews with knowledgeable observers and peers (who has a reputation for power?). The definition of a *power structure* is thereby made more specific for research purposes: it is a network of people and organizations that stands at the top in any given city or nation on the combination of power indicators it has been possible to utilize. The straightforward methodology of mapping power networks, along with the use of the four power indicators, makes it possible for social scientists to uncover any concentration or configuration of power. They can discover that power is highly concentrated or more dispersed, depending on the degree of difference between rival organizations, groups, or classes on the power indicators. They can reveal that some organizations, groups, or classes have power on one issue, some on another issue. They can discern changes in a power structure over time by changes in the power indicators.

Once the power networks have been constructed and analyzed, the substance of the policies and ideologies preferred by leaders and factions within the power structure can be determined through content analyses of the verbal and written "output" of strategically located people or organizations in the network, that is, through the examination of speeches, policy statements, campaign literature, and proposed legislation. Content analyses are not always done in a rigorous quantitative way, but content analysis is what investigators are doing if they infer on the basis of a speech, policy statement, or abstract theoretical document that a person or organization has specific values or policy preferences (see Domhoff 2009, for a detailed statement of the methodology of power structure research).

After taking a brief look at American history, we will see what power structure research has to say about the structure, distribution, and operation of power in the contemporary United States.

THE AMERICAN POWER STRUCTURE:
PAST AND PRESENT

Several familiar and taken-for-granted aspects of American history are basic starting points in understanding the country's current power structure. First, America did not have a feudal past, so its business owners were not hindered by a rival economic network of landed aristocrats that had to be battled, assimilated, or deferred to in attempting to dominate government. In addition, the absence of a rival economic elite meant that government officials could not play off one strong economic class against another in an attempt to gain autonomy from economic networks. Second, there is no church officially endorsed ("established") by the government that can compete with economic elites, such as the long-powerful Roman Catholic Church once did in several European countries. The historical role of the fragmented religious network of churches also has been limited through the separation of church and state by the Founding Fathers, reflecting both the weak nature of the rival churches at the time and the Founders' wariness of the power battles that are often fought by new religions against a nation's established religion. True, churches have influence on specific political issues and even political parties in modern America, as shown by the civil rights movement in the South in the 1950s and 1960s, and the rise of the Christian right since the 1970s, but they never have been strong enough to have more than a limited role in the overall power structure, a topic that is also discussed later in the essay.

Third, the United States does not have a strong centralized government for a variety of historical reasons that are very familiar. The pre-revolutionary history of the United States as a set of separate colonial territories led to a federal form of government with many government functions located at the state as compared to the national level. The state level in turn ceded some of its power to the city level, at which a new type of landed elites—"place entrepreneurs"—have been able to form powerful growth coalitions to protect and enhance their interest in intensifying land use, even at the expense of much-desired neighborhood amenities and environmental degradation if necessary (Gonzalez 2005; Logan and Molotch 1987/2007). As a result, the power structures that dominate most local governments in the United States are somewhat different from the national power structure, in which real estate and development interests are a secondary factor.

The rivalries among the economic elites of the various states within the new United States were a second major reason why the American national government was limited in its scope until at least the 1930s. The Founding Fathers created a system of checks and balances at the national level that has made the powerful legislative branch of the American government very accessible to elite economic groups from all regions of the country. In particular, the plantation capitalists of the South worked very hard to keep the federal government small out of concern that it might challenge their enslavement of their African-American workforce until 1860 and their dominance of that workforce through complete segregation and random violence from 1878 to 1965. The small size of the nineteenth-century federal government meant there were powerful corporations before there was a large national government, another contrast of major importance in comparison with the stronger central governments found in many European countries before the flowering of large business enterprises (Mills 1956, p. 272). The corporate elites that arose after the Civil War thus had a big role in shaping new government institutions. With the coming of World War II and the Cold War, there was no choice but to expand the federal government dramatically, but that expansion was completely controlled by the owners and top executives of large corporations (Domhoff 1996, Chapter 6).

Finally, the lack of any dangerous rival states on American borders, along with the protection from European nations provided by the British navy throughout most of the 19th century, meant that the business owners in the United States did not have to contend with a "permanent military establishment" until World War II (see Mills 1956, Chapter 8, for an excellent historical account). The American government most certainly had an army that played a large role historically in taking territory from Native Americans, Mexico, and Spain, but it was so small after the Civil War that the increasingly ascendant corporations often created their own organizations of violence to break strikes or resist unions, or else hired private specialists in such work. The largest of the private armies in that era, the Pinkerton Detective Agency, "had more men than the U.S. Army" (Mann 1993, p. 646). The military establishment was never big enough for long enough until World War II to be considered a serious contender for power. By that time civilian traditions were long established. Presidents and the corporate leaders appointed to government positions make war in the United States, not the military leaders.

From the Social Upper Class to the Power Elite

The foregoing history of power in the United States hints at an important point that can only be explained in broad outline in what follows: rival Northern and Southern economic elites were at the center of most political disputes from 1790 to the 1970s, nearly a two-hundred year span, with a newly formed and often tenuous coalition of liberals and labor unions complicating the picture from the mid-1930s to the early 1980s by challenging both North and Southern economic elites. But such claims are very general. Is it possible to be more specific? This is where power structure research enters into the picture.

We begin with the concept of *class*, which has separate but intertwined meanings that may appear obvious when they are spelled out. There are *economic classes*, which consist of people who have a common position in the economic system, such as "business owners" or "wage earners," and *social classes*, which consist of people who interact with each other, develop in-group social organizations, and share a common lifestyle.

In the case of economic classes, however, it is critical to grasp that they also involve a relationship between two or more classes as well as a set of economic roles within the overall social structure. Class in an economic sense is therefore a two-dimensional concept, denoting both the relationship between people in different economic roles and the specific roles (owner, wage earner) within the overall relationship. To repeat the earlier example once again, this time using relational terms, the business owners are "employers" and wage earners are their "employees." This is a relationship that can be filled with antagonisms and tensions, as explained later in this essay.

The distinction between economic classes and social classes is important because class as an economic relationship is always operating as part of the social structure, but the people in any given economic role may or may not develop their own social organizations, live in the same neighborhoods, and interact socially. The degree to which a given economic class is also a social class therefore can vary widely from place to place and time to time, which matters because members of an economic class may be limited in the degree to which they can exercise political power if they do not think of themselves as being members of a social class with common interests. In Western history, members of ownership classes organized themselves more frequently into social classes than did wage-earners, and thereby developed feelings of social cohesion and common views of the world that became an important part of their social identity and ability to exercise power.

Studies of shared experiences at elite private schools, overlapping social club memberships, participation in exclusive retreats, and home ownership in high-status vacation areas demonstrate that there is a small nationwide social upper class in the United States—well less than 1% of the overall population, but the exact size is difficult to establish without being arbitrary at some point (Baltzell 1958; Baltzell 1964; Domhoff 1970; Domhoff 1974). Several of the most revealing studies that make this point focus on the social institutions and activities of women of the upper class, who direct many of the nonprofit voluntary and cultural associations that have as one primary goal trying to keep government involvement in American life at a minimum (Kendall 2002; Ostrander 1984). Generally speaking, the rituals and retreats of the upper class, including the highly ritualized nature of debutante balls, demonstrate social cohesion and class consciousness through respect for traditions and the insistence upon proper conduct (Ostrander 1980). Several of these varied social institutions also have an important role in incorporating the newly rich into the upper class, few of whom fail to take advantage of the relative openness of exclusive neighborhoods, clubs, and high-status charitable and cultural organizations to them. Expensive private schools and summer vacation areas play a similar role in socializing the children of the newly rich, thereby rejuvenating the upper class in each generation.

Another set of studies looks at the relationships among corporations, as examined most readily and objectively through an analysis of "interlocking" directorships, that is, the linking together of corporations by people who sit on two or more corporate boards of directors. These studies lead to the conclusion that the largest corporations are closely enough related to be considered a "corporate community" (e.g., Barnes and Ritter 2001; Mariolis 1975; Mizruchi 1982; Sonquist and Koenig 1975). Common stock ownership by wealthy families, along with shared bankers, accountants, and corporate lawyers, also contribute to this corporate cohesion (e.g., Burch 1972; Dunn 1980; Mintz and Schwartz 1985). Still other studies reveal there is an overlap between the directors of the interlocked corporations and membership in the interconnected social institutions that constitute the upper class, which demonstrates that the corporate community and social upper class are by and large two sides of the same coin (Domhoff, 2010, Chapters 2 and 3, for summaries of this research). In terms of the critical issue of how the social upper class/corporate community is able to organize in order to influence government, the upshot of the studies of prep schools, clubs, retreats, and debutante balls is that social cohesion facilitates political and policy cohesion when members of the upper class and corporate executives gather in more formal settings; however, it needs to be emphasized that sustained policy discussions rarely if ever happen in social settings.

Building on the studies of the upper class and corporate community, detailed tracings of the linkages among individuals, institutions, financial donations, policy proposals, and the federal government demonstrate that there are four relatively distinct, but overlapping processes through which the corporate community controls the public agenda and then wins on most issues that appear on it. In terms of the classical definition of a "party" in sociology, as the means by which a class, or coalition of groups tries to influence communal action in a planned manner, these four networks constitute the party for the intertwined social upper class and corporate community. Put another way, the two major political parties in the United States are only one part of a larger relationship between the upper class/corporate community and government. The four networks are called the *special-interest process*, the *policy-planning process*, the *opinion-shaping process*, and the *candidate-selection process*.

The special-interest process deals with the narrow and short-run policy concerns of wealthy families, specific corporations, and specific business sectors. It operates primarily through lobbyists, company lawyers, and trade associations, with a focus on congressional committees, departments of the executive branch, and regulatory agencies. This is the process that is usually discussed by the news media and those who study the American government as if it were the beginning and end of corporative influence on government. There are literally thousands of such studies that explain the hows and whys of corporate victories in this arena. Most of the time these special interests win, but sometimes one or another trade association will lose out to a coalition of liberals, labor unions, and civil rights groups (Domhoff 2010, pp. 176–179, for a discussion of wins and losses for individual corporations and specific business sectors within this process).

The policy-planning process strives to formulate policies that deal with the general interests of the corporate community. It operates through a network of foundations, think tanks, and policy-discussion groups, with a focus on the White House, relevant Congressional committees, and the high-status newspapers and opinion magazines published in New York and Washington. Historically, the most important foundations in the network were the Rockefeller Foundation, Carnegie Corporation, and Ford Foundation, but they have been joined by many others in the past four decades. Think tanks are best exemplified by one of the earliest, The Brookings Institution, founded in 1929, which has steered right and left of center in its long history, depending on political circumstances, and by the American Enterprise Institute, which came into prominence in the 1970s as an ultraconservative counterweight to the government-oriented solutions to social problems that emerged in the 1970s (Peschek 1987). The key policy-discussion groups, which bring together corporate leaders, experts from think tanks and universities, journalists, and current and former government employees for sustained consideration of specific issues, include the Council on Foreign Relations, the Committee for Economic Development, and the Conference Board (e.g., Burris 1992; Moore, Sobieraj, Whitt, Mayorova, and Beaulieu 2002; Salzman and Domhoff 1983). The corporate leaders who are members of policy-discussion groups are more likely to be tapped for government service than are other corporate leaders, suggesting that such groups are a proving grounds as well as an educational and policy-formulation forum (Useem 1980; Useem 1984). It is important to note that this network has overlapping centrist (or "moderate conservative") and rightist (ultraconservative) cliques within it that disagree with each other on many issues, while at the same time uniting to thwart liberal-labor initiatives that they see as a common threat. There are also two small overlapping organizations, consisting exclusively of CEOs, the Business Council and the Business Roundtable, that bring together the moderate and ultra-conservative perspectives they learn through their participation in other policy-planning organizations as trustees or members. Their members meet regularly with government officials (Domhoff 2010, Chapter 4).

The efforts within the special-interest and policy-planning processes are supplemented and sometimes made a little easier by a third process, the *opinion-shaping process*, which attempts to influence public opinion and keep some issues off the legislative agenda. Often drawing on policy positions, rationales, and statements developed within the policy-planning process, it operates through the very large budgets provided to the public relations departments of large corporations, general public relations firms, and many small opinion-shaping organizations, all of which focus on middle-class voluntary organizations, educational institutions, and the mass media. In discussing the opinion-shaping network, the emphasis has to be on its "attempts" to influence public opinion, not on its successes, because there is ample evidence that the American public makes up its own mind on many issues and often holds to opinions that are more liberal than those favored by the corporate community and its policy-planning network, especially on economic issues (Page and Shapiro 1992; Page 2008; Page and Jacobs 2009). The best that corporate leaders can usually do in this arena is to frame the debate on specific issues in terms of various types of crises that can only be solved with policies they prefer and to spread doubt about the soundness of any new policies they do not like.

The organizations that constitute the corporate community and its affiliated policy network provide the institutional underpinnings for the leadership group that looks out for the overlapping interests of the upper class and the corporate community. These leaders are collectively called the "power elite." As illustrated in Figure 1, they are either members of the upper class who have taken on leadership roles in the corporate community or the policy network, or they are high-level employees in corporations and corporate-connected policy-planning organizations. More formally, the power elite are the people who serve as directors or trustees in profit and nonprofit institutions controlled by the corporate community through stock ownership, financial support, or a predominant role on the board of directors. This definition includes the top-level employees who are asked to join the boards of the organizations that employ them; it has proven useful for research purposes in tracing corporate involvement in voluntary associations, the media, political parties, and government (Domhoff 2010, pp. 115–116). The concept of a power elite is also useful because it makes it possible to combine class and organizational insights into a single theoretical framework, with boards of directors providing the main formal setting in which class and organizational imperatives are discussed and integrated (DiTomaso 1980; Ostrander 1987). In that regard, power structure research is a hybrid theory that incorporates ideas that are empirically supported whatever their theoretical origins.

Power Elite Involvement in Elections

Due to the independence of public opinion and the existence of a loosely knit and often fragmented liberal-labor coalition on the one side and various conservative Christian groups on the other that have agendas of their own, it is insufficient to look to the special-interest, policy-planning, and opinion-shaping networks in order to understand how the power elite dominates federal decision-making. Elections do matter, and they could matter much more to average working people if the power elite did not have ways to exercise their influence in these arenas. This is the point at which the candidate-selection process comes into the picture. It operates first and foremost through large campaign donations, with a focus on the presidential campaigns of both major political parties and the Congressional campaigns of the Republican Party. The importance of campaign finance is especially important in the party primaries, which long ago were rightly described as a "choke point" in American politics (Heard 1960, p. 34). Then too, many individuals who work in the special-interest and opinion-shaping networks take direct roles as consultants and strategists in the campaigns of

FIGURE 1.

A Venn diagram view of how members of the power elite are drawn from three overlapping networks of people and institutions: the corporate community, the social upper class, and the policy-formation network. The power elite is circumscribed by the oval outlined in black in the middle of the three overlapping circles.

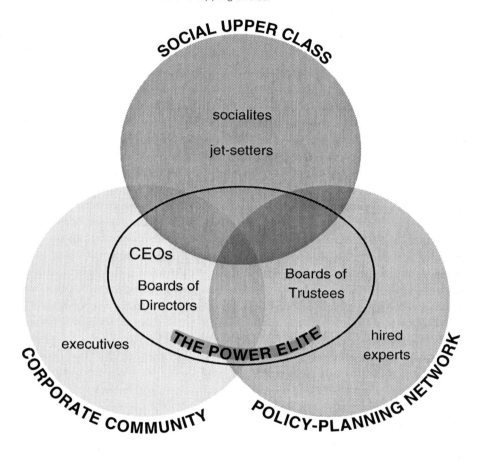

candidates in both parties. In addition, some general experts from the policy-planning network join presidential campaigns to lend them prestige and provide advice on big-picture issues concerning foreign policy or general economic trends. There also are many other ways that members of the power elite involve themselves in the careers of the politicians they favor, including employing them or paying them huge sums for speeches at the outset of their careers, or rewarding them when their political careers are over with high-paying jobs as corporate directors or as lobbyists within the special-interest process.

In discussing the candidate-selection process, it is important to stress that the electoral rules created by the Constitution and historical differences between the North and South are the main reasons why money has mattered so much in American politics compared to many European democracies. First, electing one person to a very powerful office, the presidency, which is rare in most democracies, along with the election of legislative officials from states and Congressional districts, lead to a strong tendency toward a two-party system. Moreover, a "single member district plurality system," as the American system is called, has a plurality rule that makes it unnecessary for the winning candidate to have a majority of the votes. In other words, the person with the most votes wins, even if it is well less than a majority. The American electoral system's combination of electoral districts and the need for a simple plurality, not a majority, makes it very difficult for a third party to the left of the Democrats or the right of the Republicans to get off the ground because a vote for a "leftist" or "rightist" party is in effect a vote for the person's least-preferred candidate in the mainstream party on the other side of the political spectrum (Lipset and Marks 2000; Rae 1971; Rosenstone, Behr, and Lazarus 1996). In the case of left parties, of which there have been many in the past, their votes can lead to the elections of Republicans who rarely support the interests of the low-income workers, people of color, liberal trade unionists and religious minorities who tend to favor the Democrats, as shown most recently in the presidential campaign in 2000 by Ralph Nader on the Green Party ticket. In the case of a party to the right of the Republican Party, which is incarnated in the Libertarian Party, its tiny vote totals sometimes have allowed Democrats to win senatorial seats or governorships in very close races (for example, a Senate seat in Washington in 2000, a Senate seat in South Dakota in 2002, a Senate seat in Montana in 2006, and governorships in Oregon and Wisconsin in 2002) (Miller 2002, for a good discussion from a conservative perspective).

When the electoral rules leading to a two-party system are combined with the historic division of the country into Northern and Southern regions with very different political economies, the result adds up to a situation in which the Northern industrial and financial interests controlled the Republican Party and the Southern plantation owners and merchants controlled the Democrats until the 1970s (Domhoff 1990, Chapter 9). To the degree that the liberal-labor coalition could exercise any power, it had to do so inside the Democratic Party and in the context of a bargain with the segregationist Southern Democrats, which included acquiescence in elite white domination of the low-wage labor force in the South, especially African Americans. The bargain also meant tacit acceptance of the exclusion of African Americans from craft unions and good jobs in the North in order to retain the support of the many Northern white workers who saw African Americans as racially inferior or as potential threats to their job security.

Given this state of affairs, the two major parties were such complex and confusing coalitions that it was not always clear to voters what one or the other stood for. Personalities and name recognition could matter a great deal in that context, which provided the opening for campaign finance to help boost one candidate over another. But it is necessary to add one big caveat: the candidate with the largest war chest does not always win. There are many factors that go into a winning campaign, including traditional votes for one or the other major party by parts of the electorate, or the salience of unexpected crises that swing moderates and centrists to a different party than they usually support.

Thus, the embattled and fragile liberal-labor coalition, with fewer than a majority of senators and only 100 or so seats in the House, had far less power within the Democratic Party in the post-World War II era than liberal analysts and historians usually suggest. When it came to domestic government spending, the liberal-labor coalition had to agree that the South received more than its share of the spending and subsidies created by new government programs, and that the Southern whites could exclude African Americans if they so desired (Brown 1999). On the occasions when the Northern liberals could convince the urban machine Democrats in large cities to support them on an issue in opposition to the Southerners, the Southerners joined with Northern Republicans in a highly successful *conservative voting coalition,* defined as a majority of Southern Democrats voting with a majority of Northern Republicans. This conservative voting coalition, which in effect united the Northern and Southern employers, who provided crucial support for coalition members through the candidate-selection process, was able to stop any legislation employers did not like, which usually involved issues related to control of labor markets and government regulation of business (Brady and Bullock 1980; Manley 1973; Shelley 1983).

Leaning Moderate in the 1930s, Turning Right in the 1970s

There were two critical junctures in the twentieth century that reshaped the United States and provided the major explanatory challenges for theories concerning the distribution and exercise of power in the United States. The first involved the policy responses to the Great Depression, the most important and enduring of which are the Agricultural Adjustment Act, the National Labor Relations Act, and the Social Security Act. The second concerned the right turn that began in the mid-1970s. Case studies based on new archival findings reveal the importance of the corporate-financed policy-planning network on all three of the New Deal legislative initiatives because the key ideas and institutional arrangements that they embody all came from that network (Domhoff and Webber 2011). To take the example of the Social Security Act, it was not the work of liberals, social workers, and labor leaders, as currently believed due to the fact that liberals defend it and conservatives dislike it. Instead, industrial relations experts employed by foundations, consulting firms, and think tanks, all of them funded by several of the wealthiest families and largest corporations of the 1930s, created its main outlines, served on the presidential committee that worked out the details, and testified before Congress in favor of its adoption. They then led the charge in 1937–1938 to make the act more to their liking.

Even the National Labor Relations Act, which gave a boost to labor unions and made them important power actors from the 1930s to the early 1980s, was in part the result of a series of government innovations that emerged from proposals made by the same corporate moderates who supported the Social Security Act. However, this case is more complicated because militant union leaders and Communists created the strikes and work stoppages that started the ball rolling. Then a small handful of liberal corporate lawyers and law school professors, working for the temporary National Labor Relations Board established by the president, crafted a revised set of rules and regulations to govern labor-management conflicts over union organizing, which carried the original plan several steps beyond what the moderate conservatives in the corporate community would accept. Somewhat ironically, the corporate moderates ended up leading the opposition to the legislation for which their earlier ideas provided legitimacy and respectability. Moreover, the act passed because the Southern Democrats deserted the corporate moderates in a rare act of class disloyalty on a labor issue, which was made possible by the liberal-labor coalition's willingness to exclude agricultural and domestic labor from the provisions of the act.

However, this victory for the liberal-labor coalition was in good part reversed over the next fifteen years when Southern plantation owners and their Democratic representatives in Congress found ways to hamstring the enforcement provisions of the act. This process began when the Southerners turned against the act in 1937 and 1938 due to their opposition to integrated union organizing in the South and the use of sit-down strikes in the North by the Congress of Industrial Organizations, a militant new labor federation founded by leaders of the coal miners and garment workers. The handwriting was on the wall for the union movement as early as 1939 when the Southern Democrats entered into negotiations with the ultraconservatives in the National Association of Manufacturers and the leaders of the American Federation of Labor, which was by then feeling threatened by the fast-growing Congress of Industrial Organizations. This unusual coalition then agreed upon the changes in the law that became the Taft-Hartley Act in 1947, which has numerous provisions that limit the capacity of workers to organize unions. This handwriting was temporarily obscured by the need to delay the counterattack on labor until the successful completion of World War II, by which time the American Federation of Labor tried to oppose the new legislation, but to no avail (Gross 1981).

As to the right turn in the 1970s, it was due to two intertwined factors that first manifested themselves in the 1960s. First, and most important, the civil rights movement dynamited the New Deal coalition built on the exclusion of African Americans. This unanticipated series of events was made possible by what turned out to be a surprisingly resourceful and resilient organizational base—the black churches of the South, which provided organizational skills, money, cultural and social solidarity, and courageous charismatic leadership (Morris 1984). However, the churches did not act alone. Historically black colleges and universities and the sleeping car porters union also provided power resources that power analysts of all theoretical persuasions, including power structure researchers, had overlooked. When combined with the sustained use of strategic non-violence, and with the help of a handful of white allies, most of them religious leaders and college students from the North, the result was great pressure on the political system and the passage of the Civil Rights Act of 1964 and the Voting Rights Act of 1965.

The second new ingredient in the power equation was a renewal of the corporate community's attacks on the National Labor Relations Board because a decision in 1962 by Democratic appointees reversed an earlier decision by a Republican-dominated board that favored corporations. The revised decision upheld the right of unions to bargain over outsourcing, that is, over the movement of some pieces of a larger manufacturing and assemblage process, such as the production of electrical systems or headlights for automobiles, to an independent non-union factory, often located in the South, where unions remain very weak. Interpreting the revised decision as a direct challenge to their right to manage and to invest resources when and where they pleased, moderate conservatives joined ultraconservatives within the corporate community in filing a suit that brought the matter all the way to the Supreme Court, where the corporations lost. A united corporate community then organized a very determined counteroffensive to reverse the decision within the labor board itself, a counteroffensive that would not have been successful if many white workers had not left the Democratic Party because of its eventual support for the civil rights movement.

Obtaining a reversal of the outsourcing decision necessitated a Republican president in order to ensure that all labor board appointees would be anti-union. It was victory in this battle, finally achieved a few years after the election of Richard M. Nixon to the presidency in 1968, that spelled the beginning of the end for the limited power labor unions had achieved. Within the context of civil rights militancy on the one hand and renewed capital-labor conflict on the other, the old power arrangements fractured. The fracturing began with the highly publicized abandonment of the Democratic Party by the Southern rich because it could no longer keep African Americans powerless due to the fact that they could vote against the most virulent racists in Democratic Party primaries thanks to the Voting Rights Act. They then carried a majority of already alienated middle- and low-income white Southerners into the Republican Party by focusing on their racial resentments, religious fundamentalism, and a general wariness of the federal government, which is due to its essential role in eliminating white domination of African-Americans in the South, first through the Civil War, then by the enforcement of the integration of schools mandated by the Supreme Court in 1954, and finally by the enforcement of the new civil rights laws passed in the 1960s (Carmines and Stimson 1989).

But it was not just racial conflict in the South that destroyed the New Deal coalition. It was also racial conflict in the North, as historians have demonstrated in detail by examining documents and press releases revealing that the words later used by ultraconservatives in the late 1960s were already being said quite openly by the many white trade unionists who were not prepared to share jobs or power with African Americans (e.g., Sugrue 2001; Sugrue 2008). There were a few notable exceptions, of course, and many union leaders supported the civil rights movement on legislative issues, but enough of the rank-and-file resisted integration in housing, schooling, unions, and the workplace to put the Democrats on the defensive in the North as well as the South. This point is seen most dramatically in the votes for Alabama Governor George Wallace, an avowed segregationist, in the Democratic presidential primaries as early as 1964—30% in Indiana, 34% in Wisconsin, and 47% in the former slave state of Maryland, in which he won 16 of 23 counties, the state capitol, and the ethnic neighborhoods of Baltimore (Carter 2000, p. 215). In 1972, mixing tirades against busing and welfare with revivalist religious appeals, Wallace then presaged the more coded and symbolic racial politics of the Christian Right by winning Democratic primaries in Michigan and Maryland just before he was forced to end his campaign by an assassination attempt that left him paralyzed and in excruciating pain (Carter 2000).

Nor was it simply racial conflict that led rank-and-file union members to aid unwittingly in the weakening of the labor movement at a time when it was beginning to come under siege from a corporate community intent upon asserting its right to manage on issues such as unilateral plant relocations or closings, as well as outsourcing. Many of them did not like the feminists or environmentalists either, whom they thought of as threats to their jobs and their status as respected white males. Moreover, many white union members did not like what they perceived as the anti-Americanism of the anti-war movement (e.g., Mueller 1984). Although I believe that racism was the primary issue, all of these factors contributed to the disintegration of the liberal-labor coalition and made it possible for President Nixon and his allies to attract more and more white Americans (blue collar and white collar, union and nonunion) into the Republican Party. For several reasons, then, enough white Americans of modest or low incomes switched to the Republicans to solidify a new corporate-conservative coalition that then got what it wanted from President Nixon and future Republican presidents in terms of a National Labor Relations Board that would legitimate out sourcing and in other ways continue to undercut the union movement, a story that is told in great detail by industrial relations expert James Gross (1995).

From the point of view of power structure researchers, it was these crucial power conflicts that started the decline of the union movement in the 1970s, not simply the push for freer trade and the globalization of production. This analysis is also supported by the fact that the unions have not declined nearly as far or as fast in Western Europe, where employees are far more powerful because they could develop their own political parties, thanks in fair measure to the parliamentary system of government, and at the same time organize stable unions, due to a complicated power structure in which aristocratic landed elites, established and respected government bureaucrats, and religious leaders had the ability to block the capitalist upstarts of the nineteenth and early twentieth from crushing unions (Mayer 1981; Voss 1993).

The nationwide white turn to the Republicans also made it possible for the moderate conservatives in the corporate community to make a right turn on other issues of interest to them in a context in which the streets were free of disruptions by African Americans in the inner city and anti-war protests had ended. At that point the corporate leaders in the Business Roundtable took advantage of the growing weakness of the liberal-labor coalition to deal with the new economic problems caused by spiking oil prices and inflation in a conservative way. They also used their role in the new corporate-conservative coalition to dismantle or shrink many new government social-benefit programs that had been won by the social movements of the 1960s and early 1970s (Piven and Cloward 1982/1985). We know in detail about this decision to turn right because the issues were debated in the policy-planning network, thereby making content analyses of their policy intentions possible (Jenkins and Eckert 2000; Peschek 1987). The internal tensions and disagreements over the degree to which policy should change also are revealed by the deliberations within the Committee for Economic Development, in which the majority of corporate trustees turned their backs on the moderate stances they had taken from 1960 to 1974 by saying no to permanent wage and price controls as well as to other plans for greater government involvement in the economy that would have taken the United States in the direction of the many government social insurance programs provided by Canada and countries in Western Europe (Domhoff 2010, pp. 107–111; Frederick 1981).

The right turn was solidified by the election of Ronald Reagan in 1980 in the context of rising unemployment, continuing inflation, and the Iranian hostage crisis. For the next 25 years, the power elite was united in taking a rightist direction on most issues. Even the centrist Democratic President Bill Clinton, taking the advice of advisors from Wall Street, continued the push for "free trade," which from a power point of view primarily involves agreements to ship union-wage jobs to low-wage countries, especially China, and then import the goods they make into the United States. Clinton also accepted key steps in the financial deregulation that contributed to the further concentration of the wealth and income distributions and to the economic meltdown that began in 2006-2007. As the crisis unfolded, Wall Street and the entire economics profession ignored the huge housing bubble that was frequently pointed out to them by concerned regulators and a few liberal economists. Shortly after the bubble burst and financial markets crashed, many detailed accounts appeared in the *New York Times* and *Washington Post* that explained the ways in which the investment bankers, corporate executives, and economists who controlled the Department of the Treasury and the Federal Reserve Board during the Clinton and Bush administrations actively squelched attempts by lower-level government officials to save the economy from the new cycle of booms and busts that resembled the ones that had periodically sent the country into serious crises in the nineteenth and early twentieth centuries.

How Elections Matter: 2006 and 2008

By 2006, there were no organized groups in the country that could counter the corporate-conservative coalition, which had gained complete domination of the executive, legislative, and judicial branches of the federal government with the selection of George W. Bush as president in 2000 and the continuing voter support for the Republican majorities in Congress that had existed since 1994. However, the Congressional elections in 2006 slowed the movement to the right because independent voters unexpectedly expressed a growing rejection of the war in Iraq by returning Congress to Democratic control, even though most people ignored the left-wing anti-war movement. But it wasn't just the anti-war vote that won for the Democrats, as important as it was. They also won because the various social issues that have been a major key to Republican success—the religious, morality, and gun-control issues on which social liberals and social conservatives strongly differ—were neutralized in this election because the Democrats supported candidates in socially conservative states and districts who were opposed to gun control or abortion, or who openly professed their religious faith. Finally, the Democrats won because the most incendiary social issue of them all—race—was not on the agenda in most districts or states.

The Bush Administration ignored the election results by escalating the war with the claim that it was a temporary "surge." But the troops were still in Iraq in 2008, even if they were being killed slightly less often, as the presidential elections became a burning issue. Moreover, the faltering economy headed toward a crash in the summer and fall just before the elections, leading the conservative Wall Street bankers and Ivy League economists in charge of financial policy to make unprecedented use of government monies to save the financial sector. When the ongoing war and the major economic crisis were combined with the strong campaign waged by Barack Obama and the recklessness of 72-year-old cancer survivor John McCain in putting an inexperienced and socially conservative governor from Alaska on the Republican ticket, the result was a sweeping Democratic victory in the presidential and congressional elections. In particular, the economic crisis forced white Americans in key swing states, such as Pennsylvania and Ohio, to choose between their pocketbooks and their skin color, and a slight majority of them chose their pocketbooks.

However, it is important to stress in terms of the findings from power structure research that President Obama's victory was not quite the major break with the past that was portrayed by many commentators. First, he is a biracial American with a white mother, who raised him during his early years with the help of her parents, and a Kenyan father he never knew while he was growing up. It was therefore difficult for the Republicans to convince a majority of racially sensitive voters that he was an allegedly dangerous African American leftist within the short compass of a presidential campaign. Second, Obama was raised in a completely white environment, except for a few years in Indonesia when he was under ten years old, so he is comfortable with white Americans and can put them at ease because he does not fit any of the white racial stereotypes about black Americans. In addition, he also understands and has the same style as the upper-middle and upper-class white Americans with whom he went to school after he went to live with his maternal grandparents in Honolulu, at a time when his grandfather managed a small furniture store and his grandmother had been appointed in 1970 as one of the first women to be a vice president in a large Honolulu bank. During those years President Obama attended the prestigious Punahou School, one of the wealthiest preparatory schools in the country, in which he learned an upper-class style (now called "cultural capital") and developed a network of wealthy and well-educated friends (now called "social capital").

The future president next went to Occidental College, a small liberal arts college in Los Angeles, for two years, and then moved on to Columbia University, a likely sign that he had developed bigger ambitions by this juncture. After a stint as a community organizer in Chicago, which helped earn him his alleged leftist credentials in the eyes of ultraconservatives, he went to Harvard Law School, coming back to Chicago for one summer to work as an intern in a high-status corporate law firm. After graduating from Harvard, he returned to Chicago to work for a predominantly black law firm that specialized in civil rights and real estate law, while teaching courses at the University of Chicago's highly rated law school. Except for his skin color and his father's ancestry, he is in many ways a typical—albeit highly intellectual and even tempered—upper-middle-class American lawyer who decided to go into politics, first as a representative in the Illinois state senate and then as a U.S. senator before winning the presidency.

Moreover, the future president gained the trust and support of some of the wealthiest people in Illinois while holding elective offices in the state, who helped him raise the enormous sums of money from their corporate friends that are still necessary to launch a serious national electoral campaign, even in a day when smaller sums can be raised from millions of people on the internet. (However, one of his fundraising events was hosted by a former 1960s ultra-leftist, a participant in bombing attacks on other Americans, who by the 1990s had been teaching education at a state university for several years; this fundraiser at the leftist professor's home became the major evidence for the ultraconservative effort to brand Obama as a secret leftist who hung around with terrorists.) To counter such attacks, Obama made clear during the presidential campaign that his main advisors were centrist multimillionaires and billionaires, such as Warren Buffett, the richest man in the United States in 2008, along with Wall Street financiers and experts from the policy-planning network. His top governmental appointees reflected this same preference for centrists from the corporate and financial worlds, along with traditional experts from the policy-planning networks.

However, it would be idle and foolish to try to analyze events since the 2008 election because the necessary information is not available for anything other than guesswork based on media accounts. But it can be said that most of the policy arguments since that election appear to be between moderate conservatives and ultraconservatives, with little or no influence from the liberal-labor coalition, except as reluctant supporters for a new health insurance program similar to one introduced a few years earlier by Republicans in the state of Massachusetts.

GENERAL CONCLUSIONS

The combination of economic power, policy expertise, and continuing political success makes the corporate owners and executives a *dominant economic class*, not in the sense of complete and absolute power, but in the sense that they have the power to shape the economic and political frameworks within which other groups and classes must operate. They also have won most of their policy conflicts with the liberal-labor coalition, which are best described as *class conflicts* because they concern the distribution of profits and wages, the rate and progressivity of taxation, the usefulness of labor unions, and the degree to which business should be regulated by government. The liberal-labor side wants corporations to pay higher wages to employees and higher taxes to government. It wants government to regulate a wide range of business practices and help employees to organize unions. The corporate-conservative side rejects all these policy objectives. The conflicts these disagreements generate can manifest themselves in many different ways: workplace protests, strikes, industry-wide boycotts, massive demonstrations in cities, pressure on Congress, and voting preferences, but they are not inevitable.

Despite their preponderant power in the federal government and the many useful policies it carries out for them, leaders within the corporate community are constantly critical of government because of its potential independence and its ability to aid their opponents. In particular, they are wary of the federal government due to its capacity to aid and thereby empower average Americans by (1) creating government jobs for the unemployed, (2) making government-sponsored health, unemployment, and social security benefits more inclusive and generous, (3) helping employees gain greater workplace rights and protections, and (4) supporting efforts by employees to form unions. The corporate community opposes these programs, which have been instituted in Canada and several European countries, on the grounds that they would increase taxes, impede economic growth, and limit individual freedom. However, from the perspective of power structure research, the major issue is not really taxes, government spending, or individual freedom. The deeper issue is power. In particular, all members of the corporate community and virtually all members of the policy-planning network oppose any government support for unions because unions are a potential organizational base for advocating a whole range of policies that threaten corporate power. In a phrase, *control of labor markets* is the crucial power issue in the eyes of the corporate community, which rightly worries that government policy decisions could decrease the large amount of control over labor markets it now enjoys.

Social conflict over abortion, same-sex marriage, and other social issues favored by liberals and vigorously opposed by the Christian Right are not part of this overall class conflict. Whichever way these issues are decided, they do not affect the power of the corporate community, so the mainstream policy-planning organizations funded by corporate leaders spend little or no time on them. However, hot-button social issues have been an important part of the competition between the corporate-conservative and liberal-labor coalitions in the electoral arena for the past 40 years, in which conservatives always highlight them in an attempt to win over voters who are liberal on economic and social insurance issues. Although the social issues seemed to be tamed in the 2006 and 2008 elections, with the issue of gay marriage providing the important exception, the historical record and systematic studies of past predictions by academic experts, newspaper columnists, and political pundits tell us that no one has ever made a correct prediction about the future on any issue, including social issues (Sherden 1998; Tedlock 2005).

For power structure researchers, the finding about the failure of all past predictions fits well with their open-ended and indeterminate view of history. This type of perspective once again sets them apart from pluralists and historical institutionalists on the one side—who tend to believe in gradual progress through the acceptance of liberal ideas, the increased use of rational thought, and improvements in the management and efficiency of institutions—and Marxists on the other, who believe that the inevitable collapse of capitalism and the triumph of the working class is built into the inner workings of a capitalist economy.

REFERENCES

Baltzell, E. Digby. 1958. *Philadelphia gentlemen: The making of a national upper class.* New York: Free Press.

———. 1964. *The Protestant establishment: Aristocracy and caste in America.* New York: Random House.

Barnes, Roy C. and Emily R. Ritter. 2001. "Networks of corporate interlock: 1962–1995." *Critical Sociology* 27:192–220.

Blumberg, Rae. 1984. "Women and power." Pp. 23–101 in *Sociological Theory*, edited by R. Collins. San Francisco: Jussey-Bass Publishers.

Boehm, Christopher. 1999. *Hierarchy in the forest: The evolution of egalitarian behavior.* Cambridge: Harvard University Press.

Brady, David and Charles Bullock. 1980. "Is there a conservative coalition in the House?" *Journal of Politics* 42:549–559.

Brown, Michael K. 1999. *Race, money and the American welfare state.* Ithaca: Cornell University Press.

Burch, Philip 1972. *The managerial revolution reassessed: Family control in America's large corporations.* Lexington, MA: Lexington Books.

Burris, Val. 1992. "Elite policy-planning networks in the United States." *Research in Politics and Society* 4:111–134.

Carmines, Edward G. and James A. Stimson. 1989. *Issue evolution: Race and the transformation of American politics.* Princeton, N.J.: Princeton University Press.

Carter, Dan 2000. *The politics of rage: George Wallace, the origins of the new conservatism, and the transformation of American politics.* Baton Rouge: Louisiana State University Press.

DiTomaso, Nancy. 1980. "Organizational analysis and power structure research." Pp. 255–268 in *Power Structure Research*, edited by G. W. Domhoff. Beverly Hills: Sage.

Domhoff, G. William. 1970. *The higher circles.* New York: Random House.

———. 1974. *The Bohemian Grove and other retreats: A study in ruling-class cohesiveness.* New York: Harper & Row.

———. 1990. *The power elite and the state: How policy is made in America.* Hawthorne, NY: Aldine de Gruyter.

———. 1996. *State autonomy or class dominance? Case studies on policy making in America.* Hawthorne, NY: Aldine de Gruyter.

———. 2009. "How to do power structure research." *www.whorulesamerica.net [retrieved October 5, 2011].*

———. 2010. *Who rules America? Challenges to corporate and class dominance.* New York: McGraw-Hill.

Domhoff, G. William and Michael J. Webber. 2011. *Class and power in the New Deal: Corporate moderates, Southern Democrats, and the liberal-labor coalition.* Palo Alto: Stanford University Press.

Dunn, Marvin. 1980. "The family office: Coordinating mechanism of the ruling class." Pp. 17–45 in *Power Structure Research*, edited by G. W. Domhoff. Beverly Hills: Sage.

Frederick, William. 1981. "Free market vs. social responsibility: Decision time at the CED." *California Management Review* 23:20–28.

Gaventa, John. 1980. *Power and powerlessness: Quiescence and rebellion in an Appalachian valley.* Chicago: University of Illinois Press.

Gonzalez, George. 2005. *The politics of air pollution.* Albany: State University of New York Press.

Gregor, Thomas. 1985. *Anxious pleasures: The sexual lives of an Amazonian people.* Chicago: University of Chicago Press.

Gross, James A. 1981. *The reshaping of the National Labor Relations Board.* Albany: State University of New York Press.

———. 1995. *Broken promise: The subversion of U.S. labor relations policy.* Philadelphia: Temple University Press.

Heard, Alexander. 1960. *The costs of democracy.* Chapel Hill: University of North Carolina Press.

Hunter, Floyd. 1953. *Community power structure: A study of decision makers.* Chapel Hill: University of North Carolina Press.

Jenkins, Craig and Craig Eckert. 2000. "The right turn in economic policy: Business elites and the new conservative economics." *Sociological Forum* 15:307–338.

Kendall, Diana. 2002. *The power of good deeds: Privileged women and the social reproduction of class.* Lanham, MD: Rowman & Littlefield.

Lipset, Seymour and Gary Marks. 2000. *It didn't happen here: Why socialism failed in the United States.* New York: W.W. Norton & Co.

Logan, John and Harvey Molotch. 1987/2007. *Urban fortunes: The political economy of place.* Berkeley: University of California Press.

Manley, John F. 1973. "The conservative coalition in congress." *American Behavioral Scientist* 17:223–247.

Mann, Michael. 1986a. "A crisis in stratification theory? Persons, households/families/lineages, genders, classes, and nations." Pp. 42–56 in *Gender and stratification*, edited by R. Crompton and M. Mann. Cambridge: Polity Press.

———. 1986b. *The sources of social power: A history of power from the beginning to A.D. 1760*, Vol. 1. New York: Cambridge University Press.

———. 1993. *The sources of social power: The rise of classes and nation-states, 1760–1914*, Vol. 2. New York: Cambridge University Press.

Mariolis, Peter. 1975. "Interlocking directorates and control of corporations." *Social Sciences Quarterly* 56:425–439.

Mayer, Arno. 1981. *The persistence of the old regime*. New York: Pantheon.

Miller, John J. 2002. "A third party on the right?" Pp. A27 in *New York Times*. New York.

Mills, C. Wright. 1956. *The power elite*. New York: Oxford University Press.

Mintz, Beth and Michael Schwartz. 1985. *The power structure of American business*. Chicago: University of Chicago Press.

Mizruchi, Mark. 1982. *The American corporate network, 1904–1974*. Beverly Hills: Sage Publications.

Moore, G., S. Sobieraj, J. Whitt, O. Mayorova, and D. Beaulieu. 2002. "Elite interlocks in three U.S. sectors: Nonprofit, corporate, and government." *Social Science Quarterly* 83:726–744.

Morris, Aldon D. 1984. *The origins of the civil rights movement: Black communities organizing for change*. New York: Free Press.

Mueller, John E. 1984. "Reflections on the Vietnam antiwar movement and on the curious calm at the war's end." Pp. 151–157 in *Vietnam as History: Ten Years After the Paris Peace Accords*, edited by P. Braestrup. Washington: University Press of America.

Ostrander, Susan A. 1980. "Upper-class women: Class consciousness as conduct and meaning." Pp. 73–96 in *Power Structure Research*, edited by G. W. Domhoff. Beverly Hills: Sage.

———. 1984. *Women of the upper class*. Philadelphia: Temple University Press.

———. 1987. "Elite domination in private social agencies: How it happens and how it is challenged." Pp. 85–102 in *Power Elites and Organizations*, edited by G. W. Domhoff and T. Dye. Beverly Hills: Sage.

Page, Benjamin. 2008. *The foreign policy disconnect: What Americans want from our leaders but don't get*. Chicago: University of Chicago Press.

Page, Benjamin and Lawrence Jacobs. 2009. *Class war? What Americans really think about economic inequality*. Chicago: University of Chicago Press.

Page, Benjamin and Robert Y. Shapiro. 1992. *The rational public: Fifty years of trends in Americans' policy preferences*. Chicago: University of Chicago Press.

Peschek, Joseph. 1987. *Policy-planning organizations: Elite agendas and America's rightward turn*. Philadelphia: Temple University Press.

Piven, Frances and Richard Cloward. 1982/1985. *The new class war: Reagan's attack on the welfare state and its consequences*. New York: Pantheon Books.

Rae, Douglas. 1971. *The political consequences of electoral laws*. New Haven: Yale University Press.

Rosenstone, Steven J., Roy L. Behr, and Edward H. Lazarus. 1996. *Third parties in America: Citizen response to major party failure*. Princeton, N.J.: Princeton University Press.

Russell, Bertrand. 1938. *Power: A new social analysis*. London: Allen and Unwin.

Salzman, Harold and G. William Domhoff. 1983. "Nonprofit organizations and the corporate community." *Social Science History* 7:205–216.

Sanday, Peggy. 1981. *Female power and male dominance: On the origins of sexual inequality.* New York: Cambridge University Press.

Shelley, Mack C. 1983. *The permanent majority: The conservative coalition in the United States Congress.* Tuscaloosa.: University of Alabama Press.

Sherden, William. 1998. *The fortune sellers: The big business of buying and selling predictions.* New York: John Wiley.

Sonquist, John and Thomas Koenig. 1975. "Interlocking directorates in the top U. S. corporations." *Insurgent Sociologist* 5:196–229.

Sugrue, Thomas. 2001. "Breaking through: The troubled origins of affirmative action in the workplace." Pp. 31–52 in *Color lines: Affirmative action, immigration, and civil rights options for America,* edited by J. Skrentny. Chicago: University of Chicago Press.

——. 2008. *Sweet land of liberty: The forgotten struggle for civil rights in the North.* New York: Random House.

Tedlock, Philip. 2005. *Expert political judgment: How good is it? How can we know?* Princeton: Princeton University Press.

Useem, Michael. 1980. "Which business leaders help govern?" Pp. 199–225 in *Power Structure Research,* edited by G. W. Domhoff. Beverly Hills: Sage.

——. 1984. *The inner circle: Large corporations and the rise of business political activity in the U.S. and U.K.* New York: Oxford University Press.

Voss, Kim. 1993. *The making of American exceptionalism: The Knights of Labor and class formation in the nineteenth century.* Ithaca: Cornell University Press.

Weber, Max. 1904/1958. *The Protestant ethic and the spirit of capitalism.* New York: Charles Scribner.

Wrong, Dennis. 1995. *Power: Its forms, bases, and uses.* New Brunswick: Transaction Publishers.

Zweigenhaft, Richard L. and G. William Domhoff. 2006. *Diversity in the power elite: How it happened, why it matters.* Lanham, MD: Rowman & Littlefield.

——. 2011. *The new CEOs: Women, African American, Latino, and Asian American leaders of Fortune 500 companies.* Lanham, MD: Rowman & Littlefield.

STUDY QUESTIONS

1. According to the author, what are the two dimensions and four organizational bases of **power**?

2. What four questions are asked in the power structure **network** analysis?

3. Explore an **organization**'s power structure (for example, your town, school, or fraternity/sorority) based on the Venn Diagram in Figure 1. Does it draw on the **power elite** or rely on one of the three overlapping networks more than others?

4. Should the United States have a formal separation of business and **state**? Discuss as a group.

CLAUDE S. FISCHER, MICHAEL HOUT, MARTÍN SÁNCHEZ JANKOWSKI, SAMUEL R. LUCAS, ANN SWIDLER, AND KIM VOSS

How Unequal? America's Invisible Policy Choices

From *Inequality by Design: Cracking the Bell Curve Myth*

A re you self-made? Did you earn every opportunity you've had in life? Most of us have a story of overcoming adversity, but we may not recognize the help we've had along the way. In this piece, a group of **sociologists** examines "visible policy," or social programs clearly designed to assist the disadvantaged, alongside less obvious policies like subsidies for home ownership and investment in higher **education**. As you read, think about how visible policies might help the poor less than we might hope and how invisible policies might help the **middle class** and wealthy people more than we may think.

AMERICANS CAN SIGNIFICANTLY ALTER HOW MUCH INEQUALITY there is among them. Inequality changes over time and varies from nation to nation. Such fluidity results in large measure from changes and variations in *policy.* Here we focus on several specific American policy choices that shape inequality.

Obvious redistributive programs, such as welfare spending, are not the only policies, or even the most important ones, that affect inequality. Many "invisible" practices are more significant. For example, American housing and road-building programs have largely subsidized the expansion of suburban homeownership for the middle class. Other largely unnoticed policies set the ground rules for the competition to get ahead. Just as in baseball, where the height of the pitcher's mound affects whether pitchers or batters have the advantage, so in the marketplace laws and regulations favor some competitors and disadvantage others. We saw in the last chapter that the United States has the greatest inequality in earnings among full-time workers and that that inequality has increased since 1970.

Some policies narrow inequality and some widen it. Again and again we will see that the basic dimensions of social inequality—how rich the rich are and how poor the poor are, and even who becomes rich or poor—are a result of our social and political choices. Many of our policies operate indirectly, and hence invisibly. The programs that help the poor are glaringly obvious, but those that aid the rich and middle class tend to be invisible. Obscured even more are the policies that set the rules of "the game" for the labor market. In the pages that follow, we will reveal some of the many ways that social policy shapes inequality.

We will begin by looking at one general pattern of American social policy, which is to provide, with one hand, limited direct help to some of the poor and indirectly to subsidize, with another, the middle class and the wealthy. * * * Finally, through an examination of higher education, we will look at some of the diverse ways in which public investment also molds inequality. In the end, we will better understand the major reasons why inequality is historically so inconstant and why inequality in America is so high.

VISIBLE POLICY: REDUCING POVERTY THROUGH REDISTRIBUTION

Over the last century, American government has done much to help those left poor by the market. Public health programs, school lunches, food stamps, Aid to Families with Dependent Children (AFDC), and survivors' benefits have reduced the inequality left by earnings differences. Yet Americans have chosen not to pursue such programs as far as citizens in other affluent nations have (and the programs are being sharply cut back as we write). Most industrial societies provide "family allowances" to all families with children and some form of universal health care or health insurance to all residents. In such ways, the numbers and problems of the very poor are sharply reduced by government policies that are directed toward everyone and that do not single out the poor. Most American welfare programs, in contrast, are "means-tested"—available only to those who can prove that they are poor and that they are otherwise deserving. These targeted programs consequently lack wide political support and are vulnerable to budget-cutting. Only social security and Medicare, nearly universal entitlements for the elderly, have largely survived cutbacks in recent years. Most other nations, unlike the United States, also substantially subsidize housing for many moderate-income citizens, provide stipends for students who make it into higher education, and support the long-term unemployed.

Recent American antipoverty programs have had some success, but mostly in reducing poverty among the elderly, largely through social security and Medicare, and in taking the edge off misery. We can see the emphasis on the elderly by looking at the percentage of Americans who are pulled above the poverty line by all government financial programs (taxation, unemployment support, welfare, social security, etc.) put together. In 1992, 22 percent of Americans would have had incomes below the poverty line if all that had been available to them were their families' earnings. Government taxes and transfers reduced that to 12 percent, a drop of ten points in the proportion of poor Americans. For the elderly, taxes and transfers reduced the proportion by *forty points,* from the 50 percent who would have been poor based on nongovernmental income alone to the 10 percent who were poor after including governmental income and taxes. For children, however, the net effect of taxes and transfers was to reduce poverty rates by only *seven points,* from 24 percent to 17 percent. For young adults, the drop was merely five points, from 21 percent to 16 percent.[1] This generational imbalance is, in part, the outcome of policy changes during the 1980s that weakened the equalizing effects of taxes and transfers.[2] (As of yet, we have no data on the effects of the 1993 Clinton tax changes that raised the earned income tax credit for low-income families and raised the income tax rates for the very wealthiest households. Presumably, these laws shifted net incomes toward equality a little. But the changes enacted by the Republican Congress elected in 1994 will shift incomes away from equality.)

If we list all the programs that helped nonelderly Americans with low income—food stamps, AFDC, Women, Infants and Children (WIC—a nutrition program), Medicaid, SSI disability, the earned income tax credit, etc.—they sound like a lot. Adding together these programs and adding in as well a variety of federal, state, and local spending directed not just at the poor but also at many people who are above the poverty line, such as college loans, job retraining, and energy assistance, the total expenditures for "persons with limited income" in 1992 amounted to almost $290 billion. As sizable as that figure is, it represents less than 12 percent of all government expenditures at all levels that year. It comes to about $5,900 per low-income person. Almost half of this total, $134 billion, was for medical care, largely Medicaid. Nonmedical spending came to about $3,200 per limited-income person, of which about $2,100 was in the form of cash or food stamps. That $2,100 is roughly what the typical American family spent on eating out in 1992; it is within a few hundred dollars of what typical homeowners saved on their federal income taxes by being able to deduct mortgage interest. Even after this government spending—which is probably a high-end estimate of what America spent to aid low-income people in 1992—over 14 percent of Americans, 21 percent of American children, remained poor.[3]

We can best evaluate the effort to redress poverty comparatively. Low-income American children are worse off than low-income children in any other industrial nation. In the 1980s, for example, about 20 percent of American children lived in poverty, while 9 percent of Canadian children and of Australian children were poor, 7 percent of children in the United Kingdom, and even fewer in France, West Germany, and Sweden, respectively.[4]

Why are so many American children poor? Charles Murray claimed in an earlier book that American children are poor because welfare policies encourage poor women to have more children. He is wrong. Careful studies by demographers demonstrate minimal effects, if any, of AFDC on childbearing. Rather, young parents are more susceptible to poverty, and their poverty makes their children poor.[5] American children are more often poor, first, because American adults are more unequal in both wealth and income than people in any other industrial society. Second, children suffer especially because the incomes of young men have fallen so sharply since the mid-1970s. More young men cannot earn enough to keep their children out of poverty, and many then refuse to take on the responsibilities of marriage, leaving young mothers and children even poorer.

We can see how American government compares with others in dealing with poverty by turning to the Luxembourg Income Study. Lee Rainwater and Timothy Smeeding calculated, for eighteen nations, the percentage of children who were poor. (To be able to compare across countries, "poor" was defined as being in a household with real purchasing power less than half that of the median in the nation. Half the median is roughly what the poverty line in the United States was in the 1960s when it was first calculated.)[6] Figure 1 shows the percentage of children who were poor before and then after including taxes and government transfer payments in the calculations. Again, we look only at the populous nations. Before government intervention, a relatively high percentage of American children were poor, but not as high as in France and the United Kingdom. After counting taxes and government payments, however, the poverty rate for American children was substantially higher than that elsewhere (including nine other nations not shown in the figure). Even those countries with higher before-government child poverty than the United States managed to reduce their poverty levels to far below the level here.

Two objections might be raised to the evidence that America leaves so many of its children in poverty. One is that so many American children are poor because so many live in single-parent families. That is true. However, Rainwater and Smeeding also looked separately at children in two-parent and in single-parent families. In each case, the same pattern appears as in figure 1: American children were exceedingly likely to be left poor after government action.[7] The other objection is that being poor in America, being below 50 percent of the median, is in material terms not as terrible as being poor elsewhere. Unfortunately, that is not so. Rainwater and Smeeding calculated how much real purchasing power children at the 10th, 50th, and 90th percentiles

FIGURE 1. Percentage of Children Who Are Poor, Before and After Government Action, in Eight Nations

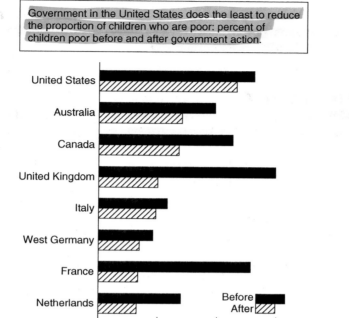

Government in the United States does the least to reduce the proportion of children who are poor: percent of children poor before and after government action.

Note: "Poor" is defined as children in households with incomes below 50 percent of the national median household income. Government action includes all taxes and all cash and "near-cash" transfers.

Source: Adapted from Rainwater and Smeeding, "Doing Poorly," table A-2

of the income distribution had available in each country. American children near the top and at the middle did, indeed, have more real income than did children near the top and at the middle elsewhere. But American children near the bottom had *less* real income than children in the other nations, 25 percent less than poor Canadian children and 40 percent less than poor West German children. And again, the researchers did not count some of the in-kind resources provided to poor children overseas.[8]

The United States does less than any other advanced nation to reduce poverty through government benefits.[9] In addition, our spending to aid the poor is precarious. Assistance is a donation; it is not a right, as it is elsewhere, and it is therefore politically vulnerable. For example, the main program that supports children, AFDC, has been repeatedly cut such that the monthly benefits dropped 25 percent in real value between 1980 and 1993.[10] And it will continue to decline as the federal government transfers responsibility for welfare to the state governments. Also, unlike aid to the poor in most other nations, these programs form an overlapping, conflicting, and sometimes impenetrable morass. One reason they do is that each program was targeted to a specific need and requires would-be clients to meet exacting qualifications. These features of American policies to help the unfortunate are consistent with Americans' belief that aid to the poor must be limited, conditional, and sufficiently unappealing so as to push people off assistance and into jobs.[11]

One of the newest and most ambitious efforts to redistribute income, one consistent with the American attitude toward aid, was the expansion of the earned income tax credit (EITC) that President Clinton, with bipartisan support, enacted in 1993. The EITC was originally established to refund low-income earners the money deducted from their paychecks to pay for federal insurance programs like social security. The 1993 expansion turned it into a general income support program for such workers, in which earners would get more money from the federal government the more they earned on their own, up to a ceiling. According to the 1993 law, workers filing income tax returns would have gotten, by 1996, credits worth 40 cents for every dollar they earned, up to a maximum refund of about $3,500. (That would have been for a family of four with earnings in the $8,400–$11,000 range; a fully employed worker earning the minimum wage grosses under $9,000.) Beyond $11,000 in earnings, the EITC would gradually shrink until reaching zero for families earning $27,000. Expansion of the EITC was initially popular among conservatives because it rewards working and among liberals because it provides the working poor with supplementary income in a nonstigmatizing way (applicants need only fill out an income tax return). Projections were that by the year 2000, EITC would have transferred $30 billion a year to poor and low-income families, more than either AFDC or food stamps.[12] However, the changes enacted by the 1995–96 Congress scaled back the expansion of the EITC.

The history of the EITC sheds light on the American approach to redistribution. First, the EITC provides no support at all for families whose head of household is, for whatever reason, not working. One must earn and *deserve* the help; the more you get in the marketplace, the more you get from government. Second, more generous than most programs, it is still limited. By one estimate, had it been fully implemented in 1996, EITC would have moved only about 25 percent of *working* poor families above the poverty line. Third, the design and discussion of the EITC has largely focused, not on how best to reduce poverty, but on how to aid only the deserving and to reward work effort. That is why, fourth, it encountered serious political trouble. Anger at unqualified recipients who fraudulently claimed the credit and concerns that the rebate structure may lead some workers near the top of the eligibility range to cut back on their work hours—together with efforts to balance the federal budget—propelled Congress to scale back the EITC.[13]

Overall, then, American government policy *does* reduce inequality by aiding the poor. The New Deal and the Great Society programs substantially helped the elderly and reduced some of the misery for others—all that the programs were ever designed to do.[14] This mix of policies may be what most American voters wish. There are prominent voices arguing that even this amount of redistribution to the nonelderly poor is too much, that it hurts the economy and even hurts the poor by undermining their self-reliance. Our point here is that in the case of our most visible policies, ones to aid the poor, Americans have *chosen* to do less rather than more, have designed greater inequality.

INVISIBLE POLICIES I: SUBSIDIZING THE MIDDLE CLASS

In contrast to the highly visible, if limited, direct aid given to the poor, American social policy tends to subsidize the middle class more generously, but indirectly and less visibly. The effects of these indirect policies have generally been to simultaneously *decrease* inequality between the middle class and the wealthy and to *increase* the gap between the middle class and low-income Americans.

Subsidizing Homeownership

The mortgage interest deduction is a quintessential example of the invisible ways American policy subsidizes the middle class and the wealthy and, indeed, offers a greater benefit the wealthier one is. A person too poor to buy a house receives no housing subsidy (unless he or she is so poor as to qualify for welfare), while a wealthy homeowner with a mansion and a vacation house may receive a subsidy worth tens of thousands of dollars. For example, someone carrying a million-dollar mortgage would get tax breaks worth over $33,000 *a year*.[15]

It might seem odd to think of the mortgage interest deduction as a "subsidy," because it is the taxpayer's own income that he or she keeps. But a subsidy it is, because it is a tax that the government forgoes in its effort to encourage homeownership. Had the taxpayer with the million-dollar mortgage rented the same home instead of buying it, he or she would have had to pay $33,000 more a year in taxes. If United States tax policy treated mortgage expenses the same way it treats other living expenses, like food, rent, cars, or clothes (for which no deductions can be taken), the government would have far greater revenues. Policy experts thus refer to deductions like mortgage interest as "tax expenditures," an awkward term, but one that accurately indicates that tax deductions cost the government money—which is to say that *they cost other taxpayers money*. Whatever one person saves on taxes, others must make up in taxes, or government debt, or reduced government services. By the early 1990s, the cost of the mortgage interest and property tax deductions amounted to more than $60 billion annually, over four times as much as was spent on direct housing assistance for low-income families.[16] (This expenditure was untouched in budget-balancing legislation of 1995–96.)

And even these figures do not fully measure the subsidy homeowners receive from the government. The government underwrites much of the real estate industry by insuring and regulating private mortgage lenders. Before the Great Depression, when the government first began guaranteeing and monitoring home loans, banks typically required a 50 percent down payment on homes and normally issued mortgages for only five or ten years. Not surprisingly, under those conditions, homeownership was beyond the means of many middle-class families. Only with government intervention in the housing finance system, through the Federal Housing Authority (FHA) and the Veteran's Administration (VA), did thirty-year mortgages at relatively low interest rates become common. And these long-term, low-rate mortgages, along with the mortgage tax deduction, are what has enabled so many middle-class Americans to buy their own homes.[17]

Another government aid to homeownership has been its massive road construction effort. For many years, but most especially in the 1950s, the federal government began ambitious projects to build tens of thousands of miles of new highways. Partly because of these highways, 85 percent of the new housing built after World War II was erected in the suburbs, where land was plentiful and relatively inexpensive.[18] Many of the new highways connected the suburbs to the downtown business districts of large cities, making it possible for middle-class Americans to buy a home in the suburbs and commute to work. Yet other government policies contributed to the expansion of middle-class homeownership in the postwar decades. Federal GI benefits allowed veterans to purchase their homes with a single dollar down. And government-funded research provided the plywood paneling, aluminum siding, and prefabricated walls and ceilings featured in the affordable housing of the 1950s and 1960s.[19]

Before World War II, many fewer Americans owned homes than do today. Nonfarm homeownership was confined primarily to the affluent. It was government policy that brought homeownership to large numbers of middle-class Americans.[20] Homeownership gave these middle-class Americans independence, real property to pass on to their children, and an opportunity to make the kind of financial investment that once only the wealthy had been able to afford.

Government subsidy of homeownership is a much-applauded policy that has shrunk some of the gap in the standard of living between wealthy Americans and middle-class Americans. But it has not yet worked that way for lower-income Americans who cannot afford to enter the housing market at all. Also, in recent years, this system has worked more to the advantage of the especially wealthy. After World War II and into the 1970s, tax expenditures for mortgage interest deductions helped the middle class about as much as they aided the wealthy. By the late 1980s, however, these tax expenditures benefited those at the top of the income distribution far more than those in the middle. The most recent statistics show that 44 percent of the mortgage subsidy goes to the 5 percent of taxpayers with incomes above $100,000 a year and that half of all homeowners receive no deductions at all.[21]

Other affluent nations have gone further than the United States in equalizing housing. Like the United States, they subsidize the middle class and the wealthy through tax deductions for mortgage interest payments. But elsewhere tax deductions are a part of comprehensive programs that also include relatively generous housing support for low- and moderate-income households.[22] In most European countries, for example, governments provide rent assistance for many working-class and poor families,[23] and in many of these countries governments also finance the construction of new housing.[24] By providing subsidies to a larger percentage of the population, and especially to those at the lower end of the income scale, European governments have tended to lessen inequality across the board.

Housing and Discrimination

American policies that promoted middle-class homeownership decreased the distance between the wealthy and the middle class. But these government programs, which made such an enormous difference to the security and well-being of generations of Americans, were essentially denied to black Americans.

Before the federal government would guarantee a loan through the FHA or the VA, it required a professional appraisal. Appraisers always rated black neighborhoods in the lowest of the four possible categories (indicated by the color red on the maps used by federal appraisers—hence the term "redlining") and usually rated neighborhoods near a black district in the next-to-worst category. Either designation was enough to render a property ineligible for FHA- or VA-guaranteed loans.[25] Other policies directly blocked African Americans from moving into white neighborhoods. Berkeley sociologist Troy Duster notes that "in 1939, the Federal Housing Authority's manual . . . stated that loans should not be given to any family that might 'disrupt the racial integrity' of a neighborhood. Indeed . . . the FHA manual went so far as to say that 'if a neighborhood is to retain stability, it is necessary that properties shall be continued to be occupied by the same social and racial classes.'" By the late 1940s, the FHA was recommending that developers use racially restrictive covenants as a way to ensure the financial viability of neighborhoods.[26]

Duster goes on to note that as a result of these policies, whites were able to get government-supported mortgages at 3 to 5 percent interest, "while blacks were routinely denied such loans. For example, of 350,000 new homes built in Northern California between 1940 and 1960 with FHA support, fewer than 100 went to blacks." By 1962 the VA and FHA had financed more than $120 billion in new housing, but less than 2 percent was available to nonwhite families, and most of that only in segregated neighborhoods.[27]

Other housing and development policies also widened class and racial divisions. Loan policies favored the expansion of suburbia, as did the building of the interstate highway system. The suburbs welcomed the jobs and stores that moved out with middle-class whites, while setting financial and racial barriers to city blacks who might try to move out. As a result, most blacks remained in urban ghettoes, far from growing centers of employment. Also, federal and local governments placed large-scale public housing projects, which concentrated the poor, in those same redlined neighborhoods. The contemporary isolation, concentration, and separation of poor blacks in inner cities is not simply the result of market forces, or even of market forces in combination with private racial discrimination. Rather, government poli-cies directly contributed to widening inequality between those who were able to buy homes and move to the suburbs during the postwar housing boom (almost exclusively whites) and those who were too poor to receive government help or who, like most minorities, were excluded from programs that subsidized new housing.

The ramifications of discriminatory policies and practices go beyond housing and segregation. Housing is most Americans' major financial asset; it can be used to lever-age credit from lenders; and it can be the major inheritance left to the next generation. While almost two-thirds of white households have home equity, at a median value of $45,000, only two-fifths of black households do, at a median value of $31,000. Blacks who have graduated from college earn 76 percent as much as whites who have gradu-ated from college, but they have only 23 percent as much net worth.[28] Part of the reason for these gaps is the legacy—and continuation, too—of housing discrimination.

* * *

PUBLIC INVESTMENTS: THE CASE OF HIGHER EDUCATION

Public investment decisions also shape inequality. Some investments, like clean water or public parks, improve everyone's quality of life up and down the income ladder. Other investments benefit some of us more than others. Roads that go from suburbs to downtown business areas of our large cities, for example, tend to advantage middle- and upper-class commuters more than they do central-city residents. One of the most important public investments that affects all of us, but in different ways, is public higher education.

In a crucial but not too visible manner, Americans a generation ago made a choice that moved the United States toward greater equality. From the 1950s to the 1970s, America invested enormously in higher education. In 1945 there were enough slots in postsecondary education for only one of five Americans aged eighteen to twenty-two. By 1992 the number had grown to about *four* for every five.[29] The expansion is espe-cially impressive because it happened while baby-boomers were entering their college years. Higher education expanded enough to serve an ever greater proportion of a growing population of young people.[30]

Expansion was achieved through a generous commitment of *public* resources. Indeed, private college and university enrollments grew only slightly faster than the eligible population, while enrollments in public colleges and universities soared. States like California and New York built elaborate systems of higher education: junior colleges, state colleges, and university campuses in California, and campus after campus of the State University of New York. Other public universities increased greatly in size—the University of Michigan from 20,000 to 45,000; Ohio State from 15,000 in 1955 to 62,000 in 1975. These political choices, made largely at state and local levels, expressed Americans' optimism and belief in opportunity, the aspirations of states and cities for prestige and economic expansion, and parents' desires to assure their children's futures.

Those who believed in the link between higher education and the expansion of opportunity were right. For those fortunate enough to earn one, a four-year-college degree levels out family advantages and disadvantages in a way that increases equal access to good jobs. Among college graduates, there is *no* connection between the occupational status of their parents and their own. Children of the working class are as likely to land prestigious jobs as are children of the middle class once they have a diploma.[31] So when higher education expanded from 1960 to 1980, the intergenerational inheritance of socioeconomic status dropped dramatically. How much a father's place on the economic ladder determined what his son's or daughter's place would be was cut by half, nearly all of this decline attributable to the rise in the proportion of the workforce with college degrees.[32] (The weakening of the connection between parents' and children's statuses directly contradicts Herrnstein and Murray's argument that a genetically based intelligence is becoming more important in the modern economy. If they were right, the correlation between parents' and children's statuses should have grown stronger during those years. There are signs, however, that, with increasing tuitions and stagnating investments in higher education, the pattern of expanding opportunity is beginning to reverse.)[33]

Expansion of higher education increased equality of *opportunity* by weakening the connection between parental and child status. But overall equality of *income* depends on whether expansion of higher education keeps pace with the economy's demand for educated workers. The great development of colleges in the 1950s and 1960s increased the supply of educated workers, reducing each graduate's claim on high wages. The number of managerial and professional jobs available fell from 2.2 for each college diploma-holder in 1952 to 1.6 in the mid-1970s.[34] Better-educated workers could still bump less-educated workers from jobs farther down the ladder, but overall income equality increased.

After the mid-1970s, however, the supply of educated workers that colleges provided rose more slowly than the demand for them. Thus, the wages of college graduates rose relative to those of nongraduates. And inequality of income between those who had and those who had not graduated college increased again.[35] Today, those who do not graduate from college—and even more so, those who have a high school education or less—face bleak prospects. The earnings of college graduates are rising at a time when the earnings of high school graduates who did not attend college are falling.[36] Between 1979 and 1989 the ratio of earnings for college graduates to earnings for high school graduates who did not go to college (the "B.A. premium") rose from 1.45 to 1.65. Growth in high-tech manufacturing, health services, legal services, and the like increased the demand for college graduates. Meanwhile the decline of traditional manufacturing, bookkeeping, and commerce reduced the demand for workers with a high school education. These shifts in the kinds of jobs available in the United States economy do not account for all of the increase in earnings inequality in the 1980s, but they do account for the increased B.A. premium.[37] It is a trend, we emphasize, that reversed an earlier one and that reflects not just the market demand for workers, but also the supply provided by our decisions about investing in higher education.

In addition, American policy regarding postsecondary education is distinctive. Most of our trading partners provide students who do not go to college with more vocational training than we do. Successful systems link schools and firms. Firms can explain their labor needs to schools, and schools can draw on firms for technology and job placement.[38] The United States has given little systematic attention to vocational education, although recent research shows that vocational programs tailored to the labor market notably increase workers' earnings.[39]

Overall, then, America's investment decisions about education have had important—if complicated—effects on inequality. The expansion of higher education after World War II reduced inequality, both because it gave more youngsters who were less affluent the opportunity to attain high-paying jobs and because the growth of the supply of educated workers tended to reduce the B.A. premium. Retreats since those days have increased inequality. At the same time, the failure of the United States to invest as generously in vocational training (or in primary and secondary education) has increased inequality here relative to other advanced countries where public investment in these kinds of education has been greater.

CONCLUSION: THE "FREE" MARKET AND SOCIAL POLICY

Influential commentator George Will, responding to headlines about growing inequality in America, voiced what many Americans believe: Inequality is not bad if it results from a free and fair market.

A society that values individualism, enterprise and a market economy is neither surprised nor scandalized when the unequal distribution of marketable skills produces
large disparities in the distribution of wealth. This does not mean that social justice
must be defined as whatever distribution of wealth the market produces. But it does
mean that there is a presumption in favor of respecting the market's version of distributive justice. Certainly there is today no prima facie case against the moral
acceptability of increasingly large disparities of wealth.[40]

However, "the market's version of distributive justice" results not from a natural
market but from complex political choices, many of them hidden. Some policies determine how unequal the starting points are of those who enter the market's competition;
other policies determine how the market selects winners and losers. For example,
African Americans in the 1950s were prevented by private discrimination and explicit
government policy from purchasing homes and thereby lost out on subsidized loans
and mortgage deductions. They were also unable to leave substantial assets to their
children. As another example, think of the businesses in industries that receive subsidies. The market is not a neutral game that distributes just rewards to the worthy; it is
a politically constructed institution with built-in biases.[41]

As we have shown here, the enormous prosperity and rising equality of post–
World War II America resulted in part from many government policies, some legacies
of the New Deal, policies that provided old-age security, encouraged homeownership,
gave labor increased bargaining power, built massive physical infrastructure, and
financed an enormous expansion of public education. Since the late 1970s, however,
public investment of these sorts has slowed and sometimes actually reversed. At the
same time, inequality has dramatically increased.

The kinds of inequalities we see reemerging in America are neither natural nor
inevitable, nor do they reflect the distribution of individual talents. Through our politics, Americans have chosen to increase equality of opportunity (expanding higher
education, for example) or equality of result (subsidies for homeownership, Medicaid,
and Medicare, for instance), but to do so to a far more limited extent than citizens in
other nations have chosen. We extend support to fewer of our citizens, largely the
elderly and the middle class; and we extend less support. For example, we provide
medical insurance for some residents; most nations provide medical care for all.
We provide a tax deduction for children of taxpayers; most nations provide family
allowances. Americans have also made choices that increased inequality, such as the
tax changes of the 1980s and the rules on unionization we have accepted. We have
structured many programs to help the well-off more than the less well-off, such as the
subsidies for homeownership and medical insurance.

What all this implies is that the inequality we see today in America is in great
measure a result of policy decisions Americans have made—or chosen not to make.
Generally, we have chosen to do far less to equalize life conditions than have other
Western people. We have chosen to reduce the inequality between the middle class

and the upper class somewhat, but to do far less to reduce the gap between the lower class and other Americans—with the notable exception of older people. And in the last couple of decades, our choices have moved us farther from equality. Some criticize these choices; others, like George Will, may applaud them. Either way, Americans constructed the inequality we have.

NOTES

1. U.S. Bureau of the Census, "Measuring the Effect of Benefits and Taxes," table 2, definitions 2 and 13. See also Smeeding, "Why the U.S. Antipoverty System Doesn't Work Very Well"; Smolensky et al., "The Declining Significance of Age in the United States." Another view of these effects is to examine the "gini coefficient," a measure of inequality. The coefficient runs from 0 to 1. The higher the number, the greater the inequality. The effects of government on this measure in 1992 are displayed below: One can see the great difference government makes for the elderly—a drop of 37 percent in the coefficient of inequality, from .649 to .409—compared with the minor effect it has on families with two parents and children—a drop of 15 percent, from .368 to .312.

GINI COEFFICIENTS

	All Households	Married Couples with Children	Households with Member Over 64
Market Income Inequality	.497	.368	.649
And the effect of taxes	.471	.340	.616
And non-means-tested transfers, plus Medicare	.404	.326	.418
And means-tested transfers	.385	.312	.409

Source: U.S. Bureau of the Census, "Measuring the Effects"; income definitions 4, 8, 10, and 14.

2. Smeeding, "Why the U.S. Antipoverty System Doesn't Work"; Gramlich, et al., "Growing Inequality in the 1980s." The latter estimate that 62 percent of the increase in inequality in the 1980s could be attributed to pretax, pretransfers economic changes, but 38 percent to the reduced effectiveness of taxes and transfers to correct for market inequality (p. 237).

3. The spending estimate is of "Cash and noncash benefits for persons of limited income," table 577 of U.S. Bureau of the Census, *Statistical Abstract 1994*. (The 1995 *Abstract* has the same data.) Other numbers come from tables 727, 464, 733, 703, and 510. The number of low-income Americans used for the per capita estimates is the number whose individual or family incomes were below 125 percent of the poverty line in 1992—49.2 million people.

4. Burtless, "Public Spending on the Poor."

5. See Garfinkel and McLanahan, *Single Mothers and Their Children;* McLanahan and Sandefur, *Growing up with a Single Parent;* Bumpass, "What Is Happening to the Family?"; Hoynes, "Does Welfare Play Any Role in Women's Family Decisions?"; Moffitt, "Incentive Effects of the U.S. Welfare System"; Schultz, "Marital Status and Fertility."

6. More specifically, Rainwater and Smeeding, "Doing Poorly," measured the "real" disposable incomes of households in which the children resided in the late 1980s and early 1990s.

They took household incomes and adjusted them, first, for the size of the households in which they lived and, second, for the different purchasing power in each nation (i.e., controlling the different costs of basic commodities across nations). The second adjustment was to enable them to compare living standards. They calculated incomes for children *before* taking into account any government taxes or transfer payments of cash or near-cash equivalents, and then the incomes *after* such government actions. (Not included are difficult-to-price services such as health care and day care.)

7. The following lists the percentage of children in poverty by number of parents:

	All Children		With Two Parents		With 1 Parent	
	Before	After	Before	After	Before	After
United States	26	22	14	11	70	60
Australia	20	14	12	8	73	56
Canada	22	14	15	7	68	50
United Kingdom	30	10	22	8	76	19
Italy	12	10	11	10	32	14
W. Germany	9	7	5	2	44	4
France	25	6	23	5	56	23
Netherlands	14	6	8	3	80	40

The numbers are from Rainwater and Smeeding, "Doing Poorly," table A-2. See also Garfinkel and McLanahan, "Single-Mother Families and Government Policy."

8. Rainwater and Smeeding, "Doing Poorly," table 1. Susan Mayer ("A Comparison of Poverty and Living Conditions") reports, based on examining surveys of consumption, that the American poor are no worse off than the poor in three other Western nations, even though their incomes are lower. She suggests that the American poor find ways, licit and illicit, of making up the difference. One way is by depending more heavily on family, friends, and charity. Questions remain about the methods of the study; also, many comparisons and many items are not included, such as child care and physical security. A deeper point is that the concept of poverty in that study simply considers it to be the lack of particular goods and services; poverty is more profoundly a matter of participation in the wider society—an issue of relativity (see, e.g., Rainwater, *What Money Buys*). In any event, a higher proportion of Americans are, in the end, poor than elsewhere, both materially and in the sense of cultural isolation.

9. Americans believe that they spend huge sums to support single mothers and their children. In fact, the entire budget for AFDC, the major program that supports poor women and children, was 1.6 percent of the federal budget in 1993. (Abolishing the entire $21 billion AFDC budget for the 1994–95 fiscal year would not have paid one $31 billion *monthly* premium for the interest on the national debt.) AFDC families typically receive other benefits, such as food stamps and Medicare, but AFDC is the cash allowance program that middle Americans most resent.

10. U.S. Bureau of the Census, *Statistical Abstract 1995*, tables 609, 762.

11. See, for example, Brock, *Welfare, Democracy, and the New Deal;* Katz, *In the Shadow of the Poor House;* and Trattner, *From Poor Law to Welfare State.*

12. Sources on the EITC include Holtzblatt et al., "Promoting Work through the EITC"; Scholz, "The Earned Income Tax Credit"; and Lerner, "Making Work Pay."

13. Peterson, "GOP Seeking to Curb Tax Break for Poor"; Novack, "The Worm in the Apple"; "IRS Appears Successful in Efforts to Curb Fraud," *Wall Street Journal*, June 9, 1995, p. 16; "The War on Work," *Newsweek*, October 2, 1995, p. 66.

14. Mayer and Jencks "War on Poverty."

15. This calculation assumes the taxpayer is at a 34 percent marginal tax rate and is paying a mortgage interest rate of 9 percent.

16. Grigsby, "Housing Finance and Subsidies in the United States"; Coontz, *The Way We Never Were*, p. 87. Dreier and Atlas, "Housing Policy's Moment of Truth," p. 70, lists the following expenditures (in billions):

> Mortgage interest and property tax deductions for homeowners—$64
> HUD subsidies to public agencies, private developers, and landlords—$26
> Tax breaks for investors in rental housing and mortgage bonds—$13
> Military subsidies to house personnel—$10
> Welfare payments—$7
> Rural subsidies—$3

17. These mortgage guarantees are now administered primarily through Ginnie Mae and Freddie Mac rather than through the FHA and the VA. On the growth of homeownership in the twentieth century, see Chevan, "The Growth of Home Ownership: 1940–1980"; Tobey et al., "Moving Out and Settling In."

18. Jackson, *The Crabgrass Frontier*, Coontz, *The Way We Never Were*, p. 24. See also Schneiderman, "The Hidden Handout."

19. See Jackson, *The Crabgrass Frontier*; Coontz, *The Way We Never Were*, p. 77. On the GI Bill, see Chafe, *The Unfinished Journey.*

20. Jackson, *The Crabgrass Frontier*; Coontz, *The Way We Never Were*; Chafe, *The Unfinished Journey.*

21. *Business Week*, May 11, 1992, p. 20; Dreier and Atlas, "Housing Policy's Moment of Truth," p. 74.

22. For good overviews of housing policies in other countries, see van Valet (ed.), *International Handbook of Housing Policies;* Husttman and Fava (eds.), *Housing Needs and Policy Approaches.*

23. Some rent subsidies are available in the United States under section 8 of the 1974 Housing Act, but this program has been very ineffective. Eligibility requirements are much more stringent than in other countries, and because the program is extremely underfunded, only an exceedingly small proportion of those eligible actually receive subsidies.

24. Heisler, "Housing Policy and the Underclass"; and Headey, *Housing Policy in the Developed Economy.* Coontz (*The Way We Never Were*, p. 87) points out that in the United States publicly owned housing accounts for only 1 percent of the housing market, while 37 percent of housing is publicly owned in France and 46 percent in England.

25. Jackson, "Race, Ethnicity, and Real Estate Appraisal" and "The Spacial Dimensions of Social Control"; Sugrue, "The Structures of Urban Poverty"; Massey and Denton, *American Apartheid.*

26. Duster, "The Advantages of White Males." See also Abrams, "The Housing Problem."

27. Duster, "The Advantages of White Males"; Quadagno, *The Color of Welfare*, p. 91.

28. Oliver and Shapiro, *Black Wealth/White Wealth*, tables 5.1, 5.2.
29. Technically these figures are not strict cohort measures. Rather they were arrived at by dividing total enrollments for a given year by an estimate of the population in the appropriate age group.
30. Hout, "The Politics of Mobility," p. 10.
31. Hout, "Expanding Universalism, Less Structural Mobility."
32. Mare, "Changes in Educational Attainment and School Enrollment"; Hout et al., "Making the Grade"; Hout, "Expanding Universalism, Less Structural Mobility."
33. See Lucas, "Educational Transitions of 1980 Sophomores."
34. Levy, *Dollars and Dreams*, p. 123.
35. Katz et al., "A Comparison of Changes in the Structure of Wages in Four OECD Countries," argue that wage differentials between more and less educated workers declined in the United States, Britain, Japan, and France in the 1970s. In the 1980s, when the relative supply of educated workers fell behind demand, educational wage differentials increased sharply in the United States and Britain and modestly in Japan. But inequality was held in check in France because of increases in the national minimum wage and the strength of French labor unions.
36. Levy, "Incomes and Income Inequality."
37. Ibid.
38. Müller and Karle, "Social Selection in Educational Systems in Europe."
39. Arum and Shavit, "Secondary Vocational Education."
40. Will, "What's Behind Income Disparity."
41. On this general point about markets, see Granovetter, "Economic Action and Social Structure."

STUDY QUESTIONS

1. Describe some of the subsidies and **government** monies that benefit the **middle class** and wealthy Americans.

2. Political commentator George Will argues that we should not be uncomfortable with a vast difference between the "haves" and the "have-nots," since our **society** values individualism, enterprise, and the free market. Why do the authors disagree?

3. Create a list of at least five ways that you have personally benefited from public policy decisions. If you are having trouble, remember to think broadly about your food, housing, transportation, and **education** and how each is touched by government intervention.

4. Before **Medicare** and **Social Security** were created, the elderly were in large part doomed to poverty. These two programs have helped support millions in their old age. Talk to older community members about how either program has supported their lives after retirement. What advantages do they describe? Do they describe any disadvantages of the programs?

GREGORY MANTSIOS

Class in America—2009

e hold these truths to be self-evident, that all men are created
equal, that they are endowed by their Creator with certain unalien-
able Rights, that among these are Life, Liberty, and the pursuit of
Happiness." So reads a famous portion of the United States' Declaration of
Independence. In theory, if you work hard you can succeed. But Gregory Mantsios points out that the American Dream is complicated by our distinct **social
classes**, he identifies four myths about class in contemporary America. Before
reading this article, think about how fair you perceive American life to be;
when you're finished, reconsider the question. Has Mantsios confirmed or
challenged your perceptions?

PEOPLE IN THE UNITED STATES DON'T LIKE TO TALK ABOUT CLASS.
Or so it would seem. We don't speak about class privileges, or class oppression, or the
class nature of society. These terms are not part of our everyday vocabulary, and in
most circles they are associated with the language of the rhetorical fringe. Unlike
people in most other parts of the world, we shrink from using words that classify along
economic lines or that point to class distinctions: phrases like "working class," "upper
class," and "ruling class" are rarely uttered by Americans.

For the most part, avoidance of class-laden vocabulary crosses class boundaries.
There are few among the poor who speak of themselves as lower class; instead, they
refer to their race, ethnic group, or geographic location. Workers are more likely to

"Class in America—2009," by Gregory Mantsios in *Race, Class, and Gender in the United States: An Integrated Study* (8th Edition), Paula S. Rothenberg, editor, Worth Publishers: 2010. Used by permission of the author.

identify with their employer, industry, or occupational group than with other workers, or with the working class.[1]

Neither are those at the other end of the economic spectrum likely to use the word "class." In her study of thirty-eight wealthy and socially prominent women, Susan Ostrander asked participants if they considered themselves members of the upper class. One participant responded, "I hate to use the word 'class.' We are responsible, fortunate people, old families, the people who have something."

Another said, "I hate [the term] upper class. It is so non-upper class to use it. I just call it 'all of us,' those who are wellborn."[2]

It is not that Americans, rich or poor, aren't keenly aware of class differences— those quoted above obviously are; it is that class is not in the domain of public discourse. Class is not discussed or debated in public because class identity has been stripped from popular culture. The institutions that shape mass culture and define the parameters of public debate have avoided class issues. In politics, in primary and secondary education, and in the mass media, formulating issues in terms of class is unacceptable, perhaps even un-American.

There are, however, two notable exceptions to this phenomenon. First, it is acceptable in the United States to talk about "the middle class." Interestingly enough, such references appear to be acceptable precisely because they mute class differences. References to the middle class by politicians, for example, are designed to encompass and attract the broadest possible constituency. Not only do references to the middle class gloss over differences, but these references also avoid any suggestion of conflict or injustice.

This leads us to the second exception to the class-avoidance phenomenon. We are, on occasion, presented with glimpses of the upper class and the lower class (the language used is "the wealthy" and "the poor"). In the media, these presentations are designed to satisfy some real or imagined voyeuristic need of "the ordinary person." As curiosities, the ground-level view of street life and the inside look at the rich and the famous serve as unique models, one to avoid and one to aspire to. In either case, the two models are presented without causal relation to each other: one is not rich because the other is poor.

Similarly, when social commentators or liberal politicians draw attention to the plight of the poor, they do so in a manner that obscures the class structure and denies any sense of exploitation. Wealth and poverty are viewed as one of several natural and inevitable states of being: differences are only differences. One may even say differences are the American way, a reflection of American social diversity.

We are left with one of two possibilities: either talking about class and recognizing class distinctions are not relevant to U.S. society, or we mistakenly hold a set of beliefs that obscure the reality of class differences and their impact on people's lives.

Let us look at four common, albeit contradictory, beliefs about the United States.

Myth 1: The United States is fundamentally a classless society. Class distinctions are largely irrelevant today, and whatever differences do exist in economic standing, they are—for the most part—insignificant. Rich or poor, we are all equal in the eyes of the law, and such basic needs as health care and education are provided to all regardless of economic standing.

Myth 2: We are, essentially, a middle-class nation. Despite some variations in economic status, most Americans have achieved relative affluence in what is widely recognized as a consumer society.

Myth 3: We are all getting richer. The American public as a whole is steadily moving up the economic ladder, and each generation propels itself to greater economic well-being. Despite some fluctuations, the U.S. position in the global economy has brought previously unknown prosperity to most, if not all, Americans.

Myth 4: Everyone has an equal chance to succeed. Success in the United States requires no more than hard work, sacrifice, and perseverance: "In America, anyone can become a millionaire; it's just a matter of being in the right place at the right time."

In trying to assess the legitimacy of these beliefs, we want to ask several important questions. Are there significant class differences among Americans? If these differences do exist, are they getting bigger or smaller, and do these differences have a significant impact on the way we live? Finally, does everyone in the United States really have an equal opportunity to succeed?

THE ECONOMIC SPECTRUM

Let's begin by looking at difference. An examination of available data reveals that variations in economic well-being are, in fact, immense. Consider the following:

- The wealthiest 1 percent of the American population holds 34 percent of the total national wealth. That is, they own over one-third of all the consumer durables (such as houses, cars, and stereos) and financial assets (such as stocks, bonds, property, and savings accounts). The richest 20 percent of Americans hold nearly 85 percent of the total household wealth in the country.[3]

- Approximately 338,761 Americans, or approximately eight-tenths of 1 percent of the adult population, earn more than $1 million *annually*.[4] There are nearly 400 billionaires in the U.S today, more than three dozen of them worth more than $10 billion each. It would take the typical (median) American (earning $49,568 and spending absolutely nothing at all) a total of 20,174 years (or approximately 298 lifetimes) to earn just $1 billion.

Affluence and prosperity are clearly alive and well in certain segments of the U.S. population. However, this abundance is in contrast to the poverty and despair that is also prevalent in the United States. At the other end of the spectrum:

- Approximately 13 percent of the American population—that is, nearly one of every eight people in this country—live below the official poverty line (calculated in 2007 at $10,590 for an individual and $21,203 for a family of four).[5] An estimated 3.5 million people—of whom nearly 1.4 million are children—experience homelessness in any given year.[6]

The contrast between rich and poor is sharp, and with nearly one-third of the American population living at one extreme or the other, it is difficult to argue that we live in a classless society. Big-payoff reality shows, celebrity salaries, and multimillion dollar lotteries notwithstanding, evidence suggests that the level of inequality in the United States is getting higher. Census data show the gap between the rich and the poor to be the widest since the government began collecting information in 1947[7] and that this gap is continuing to grow. In one year alone, from 2003 to 2004, the average after-tax income of the top 1 percent increased by 20 percent to $145,500 per year. This is the largest one-year increase going to the top 1 percent in fifteen years. On average the income of the bottom 80 percent increased only 2.7 percent.[8]

Nor is such a gap between rich and poor representative of the rest of the industrialized world. In fact, the United States has by far the most unequal distribution of household income.[9] The income gap between rich and poor in the United States (measured as the percentage of total income held by the wealthiest 10 percent of the population as compared to the poorest 10 percent) is approximately 5.4 to 1, the highest ratio in the industrialized world.[10]

Reality 1: There are enormous differences in the economic standing of American citizens. A sizable proportion of the U.S. population occupies opposite ends of the economic spectrum. In the middle range of the economic spectrum:

- Sixty percent of the American population holds less than 4 percent of the nation's wealth.[11]
- While the real income of the top 1 percent of U.S. families more than doubled (111 percent) between 1979 and 2003, the income of the middle fifth of the population grew only slightly (9 percent over that same 24-year period and its share of income (15 percent of the total compared to 48 percent of the total for the wealthiest fifth) actually declined during this period.[12]
- Regressive changes in governmental tax policies and the weakening of labor unions over the last quarter century have led to a significant rise in the level of inequality between the rich and the middle class. Between 1979 and 2005, the gap in household income between the top fifth and middle fifth of the population rose

by almost 40 percent.[13] From 1962 to 2004, the wealth held by most Americans (80 percent of the total population) increased from $40,000 to $82,000 (not adjusted for inflation). During that same period, the average wealth of the top 1 percent increased from $5.6 million to $14.8 million.[14] One prominent economist described economic growth in the United States as a "spectator sport for the majority of American families."[15] Economic decline, on the other hand, is much more "inclusive," with layoffs impacting hardest on middle- and lower-income families—those with fewer resources to fall back on.

The level of inequality is sometimes difficult to comprehend fully by looking at dollar figures and percentages. To help his students visualize the distribution of income, the well-known economist Paul Samuelson asked them to picture an income pyramid made of children's blocks, with each layer of blocks representing $1,000. If we were to construct Samuelson's pyramid today, the peak of the pyramid would be much higher than the Eiffel Tower, yet almost all of us would be within six feet of the ground.[16] In other words, the distribution of income is heavily skewed; a small minority of families take the lion's share of national income, and the remaining income is distributed among the vast majority of middle-income and low-income families. Keep in mind that Samuelson's pyramid represents the distribution of income, not wealth. The distribution of wealth is skewed even further.

Reality 2: The middle class in the United States holds a very small share of the nation's wealth and that share is declining steadily. The gap between rich and poor and between rich and the middle class is larger than it has ever been.

AMERICAN LIFE-STYLES

At last count, nearly 37 million Americans across the nation lived in unrelenting poverty.[17] Yet, as political scientist Michael Harrington once commented, "America has the best dressed poverty the world has ever known."[18] Clothing disguises much of the poverty in the United States, and this may explain, in part, its middle-class image. With increased mass marketing of "designer" clothing and with shifts in the nation's economy from blue-collar (and often better-paying) manufacturing jobs to white-collar and pink-collar jobs in the service sector, it is becoming increasingly difficult to distinguish class differences based on appearance.[19] The dress-down environment prevalent in the high-tech industry (what one author refers to as the "no-collars movement") has reduced superficial distinctions even further.[20]

Beneath the surface, there is another reality. Let's look at some "typical" and not-so-typical life-styles.

American Profile

Name:	Harold S. Browning
Father:	manufacturer, industrialist
Mother:	prominent social figure in the community
Principal child-rearer:	governess
Primary education:	an exclusive private school on Manhattan's Upper East Side

Note: a small, well-respected primary school where teachers and administrators have a reputation for nurturing student creativity and for providing the finest educational preparation

Ambition: "to become President"

Supplemental tutoring:	tutors in French and mathematics
Summer camp:	sleep-away camp in northern Connecticut

Note: camp provides instruction in the creative arts, athletics, and the natural sciences

Secondary education:	a prestigious preparatory school in Westchester County

Note: classmates included the sons of ambassadors, doctors, attorneys, television personalities, and well-known business leaders

Supplemental education: private SAT tutor

After-school activities: private riding lessons

Ambition: "to take over my father's business"

High-school graduation gift: BMW

Family activities:	theater, recitals, museums, summer vacations in Europe, occasional winter trips to the Caribbean

Note: as members of and donors to the local art museum, the Brownings and their children attend private receptions and exhibit openings at the invitation of the museum director

Higher education:	an Ivy League liberal arts college in Massachusetts

Major: economics and political science

After-class activities: debating club, college newspaper, swim team

Ambition: "to become a leader in business"

First full-time job (age 23):	assistant manager of operations, Browning Tool and Die, Inc. (family enterprise)

Subsequent employment:	*3 years*—executive assistant to the president, Browning Tool and Die
	Responsibilities included: purchasing (materials and equipment), personnel, and distribution networks
	4 years—advertising manager, Lackheed Manufacturing (home appliances)
	3 years—director of marketing and sales, Comerex, Inc. (business machines)
Present employment (age 38):	executive vice president, SmithBond and Co. (digital instruments)
	Typical daily activities: review financial reports and computer printouts, dictate memoranda, lunch with clients, initiate conference calls, meet with assistants, plan business trips, meet with associates
	Transportation to and from work: chauffeured company limousine
	Annual salary: $324,000
	Ambition: "to become chief executive officer of the firm, or one like it, within the next five to ten years"
Present residence:	eighteenth-floor condominium on Manhattan's Upper West Side, eleven rooms, including five spacious bedrooms and terrace overlooking river
	Interior: professionally decorated and accented with elegant furnishings, valuable antiques, and expensive artwork
	Note: building management provides doorman and elevator attendant; family employs au pair for children and maid for other domestic chores
Second residence:	farm in northwestern Connecticut, used for weekend retreats and for horse breeding (investment/hobby)
	Note: to maintain the farm and cater to the family when they are there, the Brownings employ a part-time maid, groundskeeper, and horse breeder

Harold Browning was born into a world of nurses, maids, and governesses. His world today is one of airplanes and limousines, five-star restaurants, and luxurious living accommodations. The life and life-style of Harold Browning is in sharp contrast to that of Bob Farrell.

American Profile

Name:	Bob Farrell
Father:	machinist
Mother:	retail clerk
Principal child-rearer:	mother and sitter
Primary education:	a medium-size public school in Queens, New York, characterized by large class size, outmoded physical facilities, and an educational philosophy emphasizing basic skills and student discipline
	Ambition: "to become President"
Supplemental tutoring:	none
Summer camp:	YMCA day camp
	Note: emphasis on team sports, arts and crafts
Secondary education:	large regional high school in Queens
	Note: classmates included the sons and daughters of carpenters, postal clerks, teachers, nurses, shopkeepers, mechanics, bus drivers, police officers, salespersons
	Supplemental education: SAT prep course offered by national chain
	After-school activities: basketball and handball in school park
	Ambition: "to make it through college"
	High-school graduation gift: $500 savings bond
Family activities:	family gatherings around television set, softball, an occasional trip to the movie theater, summer Sundays at the public beach
Higher education:	a two-year community college with a technical orientation
	Major: electrical technology
	After-school activities: employed as a part-time bagger in local supermarket
	Ambition: "to become an electrical engineer"

First full-time job (age 19):	service-station attendant
	Note: continued to take college classes in the evening
Subsequent employment:	mail clerk at large insurance firm; manager trainee, large retail chain
Present employment (age 38):	assistant sales manager, building supply firm
	Typical daily activities: demonstrate products, write up product orders, handle customer complaints, check inventory
	Transportation to and from work: city subway
Annual salary:	$45,261
	Ambition: "to open up my own business"
	Additional income: $6,100 in commissions from evening and weekend work as salesman in local men's clothing store
Present residence:	the Farrells own their own home in a working class neighborhood in Queens, New York.

Bob Farrell and Harold Browning live very differently: the life-style of one is privileged; that of the other is not so privileged. The differences are class differences, and these differences have a profound impact on the way they live. They are differences between playing a game of handball in the park and taking riding lessons at a private stable; watching a movie on television and going to the theater; and taking the subway to work and being driven in a limousine. More important, the difference in class determines where they live, who their friends are, how well they are educated, what they do for a living, and what they come to expect from life.

Yet, as dissimilar as their life-styles are, Harold Browning and Bob Farrell have some things in common; they live in the same city, they work long hours, and they are highly motivated. More important, they are both white males.

Let's look at someone else who works long and hard and is highly motivated. This person, however, is black and female.

American Profile

Name:	Cheryl Mitchell
Father:	janitor
Mother:	waitress
Principal child-rearer:	grandmother
Primary education:	large public school in Ocean Hill-Brownsville, Brooklyn, New York

Note: rote teaching of basic skills and emphasis on conveying the importance of good attendance, good manners, and good work habits; school patrolled by security guards
Ambition: "to be a teacher"

Supplemental tutoring: none

Summer camp: none

Secondary education: large public school in Ocean Hill-Brownsville
Note: classmates included sons and daughters of hairdressers, groundskeepers, painters, dressmakers, dishwashers, domestics
Supplemental education: none
After-school activities: domestic chores, part-time employment as babysitter and housekeeper
Ambition: "to be a social worker"
High-school graduation gift: corsage

Family activities: church-sponsored socials

Higher education: one semester of local community college
Note: dropped out of school for financial reasons

First full-time job (age 17): counter clerk, local bakery

Subsequent employment: file clerk with temporary-service agency, supermarket checker

Present employment (age 38): nurse's aide at a municipal hospital
Typical daily activities: make up hospital beds, clean out bedpans, weigh patients and assist them to the bathroom, take temperature readings, pass out and collect food trays, feed patients who need help, bathe patients, and change dressings
Annual salary: $16,850
Ambition: "to get out of the ghetto"

Present residence: three-room apartment in the South Bronx, needs painting, has poor ventilation, is in a high-crime area
Note: Cheryl Mitchell lives with her four-year-old son and her elderly mother

When we look at the lives of Cheryl Mitchell, Bob Farrell, and Harold Browning, we see life-styles that are very different. We are not looking, however, at economic extremes. Cheryl Mitchell's income as a nurse's aide puts her above the government's official poverty line.[21] Below her on the income pyramid are 37 million poverty-stricken Americans. Far from being poor, Bob Farrell has an annual income as an assistant sales manager that puts him well above the median income level—that is, more than 50 percent of the U.S. population earns less money than Bob Farrell.[22] And while Harold Browning's income puts him in a high-income bracket, he stands only a fraction of the way up Samuelson's income pyramid. Well above him are the 338,761 individuals whose annual salary exceeds $1 million. Yet Harold Browning spends more money on his horses than Cheryl Mitchell earns in a year.

Reality 3: Even ignoring the extreme poles of the economic spectrum, we find enormous class differences in the life-styles among the haves, the have-nots, and the have-littles.

Class affects more than life-style and material well-being. It has a significant impact on our physical and mental well-being as well.

Researchers have found an inverse relationship between social class and health. Lower-class standing is correlated to higher rates of infant mortality, eye and ear disease, arthritis, physical disability, diabetes, nutritional deficiency, respiratory disease, mental illness, and heart disease.[23] In all areas of health, poor people do not share the same life chances as those in the social class above them. Furthermore, lower-class standing is correlated with a lower quality of treatment for illness and disease. The results of poor health and poor treatment are borne out in the life expectancy rates within each class. Researchers have found that the higher your class standing, the higher your life expectancy. Conversely, they have also found that within each age group, the lower one's class standing, the higher the death rate; in some age groups, the figures are as much as two and three times as high.[24]

Reality 4: From cradle to grave, class standing has a significant impact on our chances for survival.

The lower one's class standing, the more difficult it is to secure appropriate housing, the more time is spent on the routine tasks of everyday life, the greater is the percentage of income that goes to pay for food and other basic necessities, and the greater is the likelihood of crime victimization.[25] Class can accurately predict chances for both survival and success.

CLASS AND EDUCATIONAL ATTAINMENT

School performance (grades and test scores) and educational attainment (level of schooling completed) also correlate strongly with economic class. Furthermore, despite some efforts to make testing fairer and schooling more accessible, current data suggest that the level of inequity is staying the same or getting worse.

In his study for the Carnegie Council on Children in 1978, Richard De Lone examined the test scores of over half a million students who took the College Board exams (SATs). His findings were consistent with earlier studies that showed a relationship between class and scores on standardized tests; his conclusion: "the higher the student's social status, the higher the probability that he or she will get higher grades."[26] Today, more than thirty years after the release of the Carnegie report, College Board surveys reveal data that are no different: test scores still correlate strongly with family income.

Average Combined Scores by Income (400 to 1600 scale)[27]

Family Income	Median Score
More than $100,000	1113
$80,000 to $100,000	1057
$70,000 to $80,000	1032
$60,000 to $70,000	1020
$50,000 to $60,000	1009
$40,000 to $50,000	994
$30,000 to $40,000	966
$20,000 to $30,000	936
$10,000 to $20,000	910
less than $10,000	886

These figures are based on the test results of 1,465,744 SAT takers in 2006.

In another study conducted thirty years ago, researcher William Sewell showed a positive correlation between class and overall educational achievement. In comparing the top quartile (25 percent) of his sample to the bottom quartile, he found that students from upper-class families were twice as likely to obtain training beyond high school and four times as likely to attain a postgraduate degree. Sewell concluded: "Socioeconomic background ... operates independently of academic ability at every stage in the process of educational attainment."[28]

Today, the pattern persists. There are, however, two significant changes. On the one hand, the odds of getting into college have improved for the bottom quartile of the population, although they still remain relatively low compared to the top. On the other hand, the chances of completing a college degree have deteriorated markedly for the bottom quartile. Researchers estimate the chances of completing a four-year college degree (by age 24) to be nineteen times as great for the top 25 percent of the population as it is for the bottom 25 percent.[29]

Reality 5: Class standing has a significant impact on chances for educational achievement.

Class standing, and consequently life chances, are largely determined at birth. Although examples of individuals who have gone from rags to riches abound in the mass media, statistics on class mobility show these leaps to be extremely rare. In fact, dramatic advances in class standing are relatively infrequent. One study showed that fewer than one in five men surpass the economic status of their fathers.[30] For those whose annual income is in six figures, economic success is due in large part to the wealth and privileges bestowed on them at birth. Over 66 percent of the consumer units with incomes of $100,000 or more have inherited assets. Of these units, over 86 percent reported that inheritances constituted a substantial portion of their total assets.[31]

Economist Harold Wachtel likens inheritance to a series of Monopoly games in which the winner of the first game refuses to relinquish his or her cash and commercial property for the second game. "After all," argues the winner, "I accumulated my wealth and income by my own wits." With such an arrangement, it is not difficult to predict the outcome of subsequent games.[32]

Reality 6: All Americans do not have an equal opportunity to succeed. Inheritance laws ensure a greater likelihood of success for the offspring of the wealthy.

SPHERES OF POWER AND OPPRESSION

When we look at society and try to determine what it is that keeps most people down— what holds them back from realizing their potential as healthy, creative productive individuals—we find institutional forces that are largely beyond individual control. Class domination is one of these forces. People do not choose to be poor or working class; instead, they are limited and confined by the opportunities afforded or denied them by a social and economic system. The class structure in the United States is a function of its economic system: capitalism, a system that is based on private rather than public ownership and control of commercial enterprises. Under capitalism, these enterprises are governed by the need to produce a profit for the owners, rather than to fulfill societal needs. Class divisions arise from the differences between those who own and control corporate enterprise and those who do not.

Racial and gender domination are other forces that hold people down. Although there are significant differences in the way capitalism, racism, and sexism affect our lives, there are also a multitude of parallels. And although class, race, and gender act independently of each other, they are at the same time very much interrelated.

On the one hand, issues of race and gender cut across class lines. Women experience the effects of sexism whether they are well-paid professionals or poorly paid clerks. As women, they are not only subjected to catcalls and stereotyping, but face discrimination and are denied opportunities and privileges that men have. Similarly, a wealthy black man faces racial oppression, is subjected to racial slurs, and is denied opportunities because of his color. Regardless of their class standing, women and members of minority races are constantly dealing with institutional forces that are holding them down precisely because of their gender, the color of their skin, or both.

On the other hand, the experiences of women and minorities are differentiated along class lines. Although they are in subordinate positions vis-à-vis white men, the particular issues that confront women and people of color may be quite different depending on their position in the class structure.

Power is incremental, and class privileges can accrue to individual women and to individual members of a racial minority. While power is incremental, oppression is cumulative, and those who are poor, black, and female are often subject to all of the forces of class, race, and gender discrimination simultaneously. This cumulative situation is what is meant by the double and triple jeopardy of women and minorities.

Furthermore, oppression in one sphere is related to the likelihood of oppression in another. If you are black and female, for example, you are much more likely to be poor or working class than you would be as a white male. Census figures show that the incidence of poverty varies greatly by race and gender.

Chances of Being Poor in America[33]

White male/ female	White female head*	Hispanic male/ female	Hispanic female head*	Black male/ female	Black female head*
1 in 12	1 in 5	1 in 5	1 in 3	1 in 4	1 in 3

*Persons in families with female householder, no husband present.

In other words, being female and being nonwhite are attributes in our society that increase the chances of poverty and of lower-class standing.

Reality 7: Racism and sexism significantly compound the effects of class in society.

None of this makes for a very pretty picture of our country. Despite what we like to think about ourselves as a nation, the truth is that opportunity for success and life itself are highly circumscribed by our race, our gender, and the class we are born into. As individuals, we feel hurt and anger when someone is treating us unfairly; yet as a society we tolerate unconscionable injustice. A more just society will require a radical redistribution of wealth and power. We can start by reversing the current trends that further polarize us as a people and adapt policies and practices that narrow the gaps in income, wealth, and privilege.

NOTES

1. See Jay MacLead, *Ain't No Makin' It: Aspirations and Attainment in a Lower-Income Neighborhood* (Boulder, CO: Westview Press, 1995); Benjamin DeMott, *The Imperial*

Middle (New York: Morrow, 1990); Ira Katznelson, *City Trenches: Urban Politics and Patterning of Class in the United States* (New York: Pantheon Books, 1981); Charles W. Tucker, "A Comparative Analysis of Subjective Social Class: 1945–1963," *Social Forces*, no. 46, June 1968, pp. 508–514; Robert Nisbet, "The Decline and Fall of Social Class," *Pacific Sociological Review*, vol. 2, Spring 1959, pp. 11–17; and Oscar Glantz, "Class Consciousness and Political Solidarity," *American Sociological Review*, vol. 23, August 1958, pp. 375–382.

2. Susan Ostander, "Upper-Class Women: Class Consciousness as Conduct and Meaning," in G. William Domhoff, *Power Structure Research* (Beverly Hills, CA: Sage Publications, 1980), pp. 78–79. Also see Stephen Birmingham, *America's Secret Aristocracy* (Boston: Little Brown, 1987).

3. Lawrence Mishel, Jared Bernstein, and Sylvia Allegretto, *State of Working America: 2006/2007* (Ithaca, NY: Cornell University Press, 2007), pp. 251, 253.

4. The number of individuals filing tax returns showing a gross adjusted income of $1 million or more in 2006 was 355,204 (Tax Stats at a Glance, Internal Revenue Service, U.S. Treasury Department, available at http://www.irs.gov/taxstats/article/0,,id=102886,00 .html).

5. Carmen DeNavas-Walt, Bernadette D. Proctor, and Jessica C. Smith, U.S. Census Bureau, Current Population Reports, P60–235, *Income, Poverty, and Health Insurance Coverage in the United States: 2007* (Washington, DC: U.S. Government Printing Office, 2008), pp. 12–19, available at http://pubdb3.census.gov/macro/032008/pov/new01_100_01.htm.

6. National Coalition for the Homeless, "How Many People Experience Homelessness?" NCH Fact Sheet #2 (June 2008), available at http://www.nationalhomeless.org/publications/facts/How_Many.html. Also see National Coalition for the Homeless, "How Many People Experience Homelessness?" NCH Fact Sheet #2 (June 2006), citing a 2004 National Law Center on Homelessness and Poverty study, available at http://www.national homeless.org/publications/facts/How_Many.pdf; U.S. Conference of Mayors, *Hunger and Homelessness Survey, 2008: A Survey Report on Homelessness and Hunger in American Cities* (Washington, DC: U.S. Conference of Mayors, 2008), pp. 13–23; Martha Burt, *What Will it Take to End Homelessness?* (Washington, DC: Urban Institute, September 2001); Martha Burt, "Chronic Homelessness: Emergence of a Public Policy," *Fordham Urban Law Journal*, 30, no. 3 (2003), pp. 1267–1279; and Kim Hopper, *Reckoning with Homelessness* (Ithaca, NY: Cornell University Press, 2002).

7. Mishel et al., op. cit., p. 253.

8. Arloc Sherman and Aviva Aron-Dine, "New CBO Data Show Income Inequality Continues to Widen" (Washington, DC: Center on Budget and Policy Priorities, January 2007), p. 3.

9. Based on a comparison of 19 industrialized states: Mishel et al., op. cit., pp. 344–349.

10. Mishel et al., op. cit., p. 345.

11. Derived from Mishel et al., p. 255, Table 5.3.

12. Mishel et al., op. cit., p. 64.

13. *Ibid.*, p. 59.

14. *Ibid.*, p. 255.

15. Alan Blinder, quoted by Paul Krugman, in "Disparity and Despair," *U.S. News and World Report*, March 23, 1992, p. 54.

16. Paul Samuelson, *Economics*, 10th ed. (New York: McGraw-Hill, 1976), p. 84.

17. DeNavas-Walt et al., op. cit., p. 12.

18. Michael Harrington, *The Other America* (New York: Macmillan, 1962), pp. 12–13.

19. Stuart Ewen and Elizabeth Ewen, *Channels of Desire: Mass Images and the Shaping of American Consciousness* (New York: McGraw-Hill, 1982).

20. Andrew Ross, *No-Collar: The Humane Work Place and Its Hidden Costs* (New York: Basic Books, 2002).

21. Based on a poverty threshold for a three-person household in 2007 of $16,650. DeNavas-Walt et al., op. cit., p. 1.

22. The median income in 2007 was $45,113 for men working full time, year round; $35,102 for women; and $50,233 for households. DeNavas-Walt et al., op. cit, p. 6.

23. U. S. Government Accountability Office, *Poverty in America: Economic Research Shows Adverse Impacts on Health Status and Other Social Conditions* (Washington, DC: U.S. Government Accountability Office, 2007), pp. 9–16. Also see E. Pamuk, D. Makuc, K. Heck, C. Reuben, and K. Lochner, *Socioeconomic Status and Health Chartbook, Health, United States, 1998* (Hyattsville, MD: National Center for Health Statistics, 1998), pp. 145–159; Vincente Navarro, "Class, Race, and Health Care in the United States," in Bersh Berberoglu, *Critical Perspectives in Sociology*, 2nd ed. (Dubuque, IA: Kendall/Hunt, 1993), pp. 148–156; Melvin Krasner, *Poverty and Health in New York City* (New York: United Hospital Fund of New York, 1989); U.S. Department of Health and Human Services, *Health Status of Minorities and Low Income Groups, 1985*; and Dan Hughes, Kay Johnson, Sara Rosenbaum, Elizabeth Butler, and Janet Simons, *The Health of America's Children* (The Children's Defense Fund, 1988).

24. E. Pamuk et al., op. cit.; Kenneth Neubeck and Davita Glassberg, *Sociology: A Critical Approach* (New York: McGraw-Hill, 1996), pp. 436–438; Aaron Antonovsky, "Social Class, Life Expectancy, and Overall Mortality," in *The Impact of Social Class* (New York: Thomas Crowell, 1972), pp. 467–491. See also Harriet Duleep, "Measuring the Effect of Income on Adult Mortality Using Longitudinal Administrative Record Data," *Journal of Human Resources*, vol. 21, no. 2, Spring 1986. See also Paul Farmer, *Pathologies of Power: Health, Human Rights, and the New War on the Poor* (Berkeley: University of California Press, 2005).

25. E. Pamuk et al., op. cit., fig. 20; Dennis W. Roncek, "Dangerous Places: Crime and Residential Environment." *Social Forces*, vol. 60, no. 1, September 1981, pp. 74–96. Also see Steven D. Levitt, "The Changing Relationship between Income and Crime Victimization," *Economic Policy Review*, 5, No. 3, September 1999.

26. Richard De Lone, *Small Futures* (New York: Harcourt Brace Jovanovich, 1978), pp. 14–19.

27. Derived from Viji Sathy, Sandra Barbuti, and Krista Mattern, "The New SAT and Trends in Test Performance," *College Board*, 2006, pp. 18–20.

28. William H. Sewell, "Inequality of Opportunity for Higher Education," *American Sociological Review*, vol. 36, no. 5, 1971, pp. 793–809.

29. The Mortenson Report on Public Policy Analysis of Opportunity for Postsecondary Education, "Postsecondary Education Opportunity" (Iowa City, IA; September 1993, no. 16).

30. De Lone, op. cit., pp. 14–19. Also see Daniel McMurrer, Mark Condon, and Isabel Sawhill, "Intergenerational Mobility in the United States" (Washington, DC: Urban Institute, 1997), available at http://www.Urbaninstitute.org/url.cfm?ID=406796; and Bhashkar Mazumder, "Earnings Mobility in the US: A New Look at Intergenerational Inequality" (March 21, 2001), FRB Chicago Working Paper No. 2001-18, available at SSRN: http://ssrn.com/abstract=295559, or DOI: 10.2139/ssm.295559.

31. Howard Tuchman, *Economics of the Rich* (New York: Random House, 1973), p. 15. Also see Greg Duncan, Ariel Kalil, Susan Mayer, Robin Tepper, and Monique Payne. "The Apple

Does not Fall Far from the Tree," in Samuel Bowles, Herbert Gintis, and Melissa Groves, *Unequal Chances: Family Background and Economic Success* (Princeton, NJ: Princeton University Press, 2008), pp. 23–79; Bhashkar Mazumder, "The Apple Falls Even Closer to the Tree than We Thought," in Bowles et. al., pp. 80–99. For more information on inheritance, see Sam Bowles and Herbert Gintis, "The Inheritance of Inequality," *The Journal of Economic Perspectives*, 16, no. 3 (Summer 2002), pp. 2–30, and Tom Hertz, *Understanding Mobility in America*, Center for American Progress, available at http://www.american progress.org/kf/hertz_mobility_analysis.pdf.

32. Howard Wachtel, *Labor and the Economy* (Orlando, FL: Academic Press, 1984), pp. 161–162.

33. Derived from U.S. Census Bureau, *Current Population Survey*, Tables POV01 and POV2, available at http://pubdb3.census.gov/macro/032008/pov/toc.htm.

FURTHER READING

Baird, Robert M., and Stuart E. Rosenbaum, eds. *Bigotry, Prejudice, and Hatred.* Buffalo, NY: Prometheus Press, 1992.

Bonilla-Silva, Eduardo. *Racism without Racists: Colorblind Racism and the Persistence of Racial Inequality in the U.S.* New York: Rowman & Littlefield, 2003.

——. *White Supremacy and Racism in the Post Civil Rights Era.* Boulder CO: Rienner, 2001.

Brandt, Eric, ed. *Dangerous Liaisons: Blacks, Gays and the Struggle for Equality.* New York: New Press, 1999.

Brown, Michael K., et al. *Whitewashing Race in America: The Myth of a Colorblind Society.* Berkeley: University of California Press, 2005.

Cose, Ellis. *The Rage of a Privileged Class.* New York: Collins, 1994.

DeMott, Benjamin. *The Trouble with Friendship: Why Americans Can't Think Straight about Race.* New York: Atlantic Monthly Press, 1995.

Dusky, Lorraine. *Still Unequal: The Shameful Truth about Women and Justice in America.* New York: Crown Books, 1996.

Dyer, Richard. *White.* London and New York: Routledge, 1997.

Faludi, Susan. *Backlash: The Undeclared War against American Women.* New York: Crown Publishers, 1991.

Feagin, Joe R. *Racist America: Roots, Realities, and Future Reparations.* New York: Routledge, 2000.

Harris, Leonard. *Racism.* New York: Humanities Books, 1999.

Kadi, Joanne. *Thinking Class: Sketches from a Cultural Worker.* Boston: South End Press, 1996.

Katznelson, Ira. *When Affirmative Action Was White: An Untold History of Racial Inequality in 20th C. America,* New York: W.W. Norton, 2005.

Kimmel, Michael. *The Gendered Society.* New York: Oxford University Press, 2000.

Lipsitz, George. *The Possessive Investment in Whiteness.* Philadelphia, PA: Temple University Press, 1998.

Perry, Barbara. *In the Name of Hate: Understanding Hate Crimes.* New York and London: Routledge, 2001.

Pharr, Suzanne. *Homophobia as a Weapon of Sexism.* Inverness, CA: Chardon Press, 1988.

Pincus, F. L., and H. J. Erlich. *Race and Ethnic Conflict: Contending Views on Prejudice, Discrimination and Ethnoviolence.* Boulder, CO: Westview, 1994.

Rhode, Deborah L. *Speaking of Sex: The Denial of Gender Inequality*. Cambridge, MA, and London, England: Harvard University Press, 1997.

Ronai, Carol R., et al. *Everyday Sexism in the Third Millenium*, New York and London: Routledge, 1997.

Shipler, David K. *A Country of Strangers: Blacks and Whites in America*. New York: Knopf, 1997.

Wellman, David T. *Portraits of White Racism*. Cambridge: Cambridge University Press, 1977.

Williams, Lena. *It's the Little Things: the Everyday Interactions That Get Under the Skin of Blacks and Whites*. New York: Harcourt, 2000.

STUDY QUESTIONS

1. What evidence does Mantsios present in support of his argument that **wealth** inequality is a problem in the United States?

2. What key differences do you think explain why Harold S. Browning and Bob Farrell have had such different trajectories? How do their aspirations and **work** ethics compare? Their achievements and salaries? What might their lives tell us about the idea of **meritocracy** in the United States?

3. Based on the known effect of **family income** on SAT scores, do you think standardized testing should be used as a basis of admission for institutions of higher learning? What might be a fairer, but still feasible, measure of a student's capacity to succeed at a given college or university?

4. Today, an overwhelming majority of Americans report that they are **middle class**. Based on your reading of this article, what do you think defines the middle class? Why might people be less likely to refer to themselves as **working class** or **upper class** than in the past?

HERBERT J. GANS

The Positive Functions of the Undeserving Poor: Uses of the Underclass in America

---

A nyone could make a list of the negative aspects of **poverty**, but it takes a **functionalist** sociologist to elaborate on the *positive* characteristics of poverty. In this 1994 article, Herbert J. Gans examines the **class** of people sometimes labeled the "undeserving poor"—a **group** criticized as lazy, shiftless, prone to giving birth out of wedlock, and liable to commit **crimes**—and considered undeserving of federal help. Gans discusses this group's positive functions in **society**—at least for those who aren't poor.

I. INTRODUCTION

POVERTY, LIKE ANY OTHER SOCIAL PHENOMENON, CAN BE ANA-lyzed in terms of the *causes* which initiate and perpetuate it, but once it exists, it can also be studied in terms of the consequences or *functions* which follow. These functions can be both *positive* and *negative,* adaptive and destructive, depending on their nature and the people and interests affected.

Poverty has many negative functions (or dysfunctions), most for the poor themselves, but also for the nonpoor. Among those of most concern to both populations,

---

"The Positive Functions of the Undeserving Poor: Uses of the Underclass in America" by Herbert J. Gans from *American Journal of Sociology* 78, No. 2, used by permission of Herbert J. Gans, Robert S. Lynd Professor of Sociology at Columbia University.

perhaps the major one is that a small but visible proportion of poor people is involved in activities which threaten their physical safety, for example street crime, or which deviate from important norms claimed to be "mainstream," such as failing to work, bearing children in adolescence and out of wedlock, and being "dependent" on welfare. In times of high unemployment, illegal and even legal immigrants are added to this list for endangering the job opportunities of native-born Americans.

Furthermore, many better-off Americans believe that the number of poor people who behave in these ways is far larger than it actually is. More important, many think that poor people act as they do because of moral shortcomings that express themselves in lawlessness or in the rejection of mainstream norms. Like many other sociologists, however, I argue that the behavior patterns which concern the more fortunate classes are *poverty-related,* because they are, and have historically been, associated with poverty. * * * They are in fact caused by poverty, although a variety of other causes must also be at work since most poor people are not involved in any of these activities.

* * *

Because their criminal or disapproved behavior is ascribed to moral short-comings, the poor people who resort to it are often classified as unworthy or *undeserving.* For example, even though the failure of poor young men (or women) to work may be the effect of a lack of jobs, they are frequently accused of laziness, and then judged undeserving. Likewise, even though poor young mothers may decide not to marry the fathers of their children, because they, being jobless, cannot support them, the women are still accused of violating conventional familial norms, and also judged undeserving. Moreover, once judged to be undeserving, poor people are then no longer thought to be deserving of public aid that is financially sufficient and secure enough to help them escape poverty.

Judgments of the poor as undeserving are not based on evidence, but derive from a stereotype, even if, like most others, it is a stereotype with a "kernel of truth" (e.g., the monopolization of street crime by the poor). Furthermore, it is a very old stereotype; Cicero[1] already described the needy of Rome as criminals. By the middle of the sixteenth century, complicated laws to distinguish between the deserving and undeserving were in existence. However, the term undeserving poor was first used regularly in England in the 1830s, at the time of the institution of the Poor Law.[2]

In America, a series of other, more specific, terms were borrowed or invented, with new ones replacing old ones as conditions and fashions changed. Such terms have included *beggar, pauper,* the *dangerous class, rabble, vagabond* and *vagrant,* and so on, which the United States borrowed from Europe. America also invented its own

---

[1] Roman philosopher and orator (106–43 BCE). [Unless otherwise indicated, as here, notes are those of the author; Ed.]

[2] However, the *Oxford English Dictionary,* compiled by J. A. Simpson and E. S. Weiner (New York: Oxford University Press, 1989), 19:996, already has a 1647 reference to beggars as undeserving, and the adjective itself was earlier used to refer to nonpoor people, for example, by Shakespeare.

terms, including *shiftless, tramp,* and *feeble-minded,* and in the late twentieth century terms like *hard-core, drifter, culturally deprived*—and most recently, *underclass.*[3] Nonetheless, in terms of its popular uses and the people to whom it is applied, the terms underclass differs little from its predecessors.[4]

It is not difficult to understand why people, poor and more fortunate, are fearful of street crime committed by poor people, and even why the jobless poor and welfare recipients, like paupers before them, may be perceived as economic threats for not working and drawing on public funds, at least in bad economic times. Also, one can understand why other forms of poverty-related behavior, such as the early sexual activity of poor youngsters and the dramatic number of poor single-parent families are viewed as moral threats, since they violate norms thought to uphold the two-parent nuclear family and related normative bases of the social order. However, there would seem to be no inherent reason for exaggerating these threats, for example, in the case of welfare recipients who obtain only a tiny proportion of governmental expenditures, or more generally, by stereotyping poor people as undeserving without evidence of what they have and have not done, and why.

One reason, if not the only one, for the exaggeration and the stereotyping, and for the continued attractiveness of the concept of the undeserving poor itself, is that undeservingness has a number of *positive* functions for the better-off population. Some of these functions, or uses, are positive for everyone who is not poor, but most are positive only for some people, interest groups, and institutions, ranging from moderate income to wealthy ones. Needless to say, that undeservingness has uses for some people does not justify it; the existence of functions just helps to explain why it persists.

My notion of function, or empirically observable adaptive consequence, is adapted from the classic conceptual scheme of Robert K. Merton. My analysis will concentrate on those positive functions which Merton conceptualized as *latent,* which are unrecognized and/or unintended, but with the proviso that the functions which are identified as latent would probably not be abolished once they were widely recognized. Positive functions are, after all, also benefits, and people are not necessarily ready to give up benefits, including unintended ones, even if they become aware of them.

* * *

---

[3] These terms were often, but not exclusively, applied to the poor "races" who arrived in the nineteenth and early twentieth century from Ireland, Germany, and later, Eastern and Southern Europe. They have also been applied, during and after slavery, to Blacks. Nonetheless, the functions to be discussed in this article are consequences of poverty, not of race, even though a disproportionate rate of those "selected" to be poor have always been darker-skinned than the more fortunate classes.

[4] The popular definition of underclass must be distinguished from Gunnar Myrdal's initial scholarly one, which viewed the underclass as a stratum driven to the margins or out of the labor force by what are today called the postindustrial and global economies. Gunnar Myrdal, *Challenge to Affluence* (New York: Pantheon Books, 1963), 10 and passim. Myrdal's definition viewed the underclass as victims of economic change, and said nothing about its moral state.

II. FUNCTIONS OF THE UNDESERVING POOR[5]

I will discuss five sets of positive functions: microsocial, economic, normative-cultural, political, and macrosocial, which I divide into 13 specific functions, although the sets are arbitrarily chosen and interrelated, and I could add many more functions. The functions are not listed in order of importance, for such a listing is not possible without empirical research on the various beneficiaries of undeservingness.

Two Microsocial Functions

1. *Risk reduction.* Perhaps the primary use of the idea of the undeserving poor, primary because it takes place at the microsocial scale of everyday life, is that it distances the labeled from those who label them. By stigmatizing people as undeserving, labelers protect themselves from the responsibility of having to associate with them, or even to treat them like moral equals, which reduces the risk of being hurt or angered by them. Risk reduction is a way of dealing with actual or imagined threats to physical safety, for example from people who might be muggers, or cultural threats attributed to poor youngsters or normative ones imagined to come from welfare recipients. All pejorative labels and stereotypes serve this function, which may help to explain why there are so many such labels.

2. *Scapegoating and displacement.* By being thought undeserving, the stigmatized poor can be blamed for virtually any shortcoming of everyday life which can be credibly ascribed to them—violations of the laws of logic or social causation notwithstanding. Faulting the undeserving poor can also support the desire for revenge and punishment. In a society in which punishment is reserved for legislative, judicial, and penal institutions, *feelings* of revenge and punitiveness toward the undeserving poor supply at least some emotional satisfaction.

   Since labeling poor people undeserving opens the door for nearly unlimited scapegoating, the labeled are also available to serve what I call the displacement function. Being too weak to object, the stigmatized poor can be accused of having caused social problems which they did not actually cause and can serve as cathartic objects on which better-off people can unload their own problems, as well as those of the economy, the polity, or of any other institutions, for the shortcomings of which the poor can be blamed.

   Whether societywide changes in the work ethic are displaced on to "shiftlessness," or economic stagnation on to "welfare dependency," the poor can be declared undeserving for what ails the more affluent. This may also help to

---

[5] For brevity's sake, I will hereafter refer to the undeserving poor instead of the poor-labeled undeserving, but I always mean the latter.

explain why the national concern with poor Black unmarried mothers, although usually ascribed to the data presented in the 1965 Moynihan Report,[6] did not gather steam until the beginning of the decline of the economy in the mid-1970s. Similarly, the furor about poor "babies having babies" waited for the awareness of rising adolescent sexual activity among the better-off classes in the 1980s—at which point rates of adolescent pregnancy among the poor had already declined. But when the country became ambivalent about the desirability of abortions, the issue was displaced on the poor by making it almost impossible for them to obtain abortions.

Many years ago, James Baldwin, writing in *The Fire Next Time,* illustrated the displacement function in racial terms, arguing that, as Andrew Hacker put it, Whites "need the 'nigger' because it is the 'nigger' within themselves that they cannot tolerate. Whatever it is that Whites feel 'nigger' signifies about Blacks—lust and laziness, stupidity or squalor, in fact exists within themselves. * * * By creating such a creature, Whites are able to say that because only members of the Black race can carry that taint, it follows that none of its attributes will be found in White people.[7]

Three Economic Functions

3. *Economic banishment and the reserve army of labor.* People who have successfully been labeled as undeserving can be banished from the formal labor market. If young people are designated "school dropouts," for example; they can also be thought to lack the needed work habits, such as proper adherence to the work ethic, and may not be offered jobs to begin with. Often, they are effectively banished from the labor market before entering it because employers imagine them to be poor workers simply because they are young, male, and Black. Many ex-convicts are declared unemployable in similar fashion, and some become recidivists because they have no other choice but to go back to their criminal occupations.

Banishing the undeserving also makes room for immigrant workers, who may work for lower wages, are more deferential, and are more easily exploitable by being threatened with deportation. In addition, banishment helps to reduce the official jobless rate, a sometimes useful political function, especially if the banished drop so completely out of the labor force that they are not even available to be counted as "discouraged workers."

---

[6] Report, also known as "The Negro Family: The Case for National Action," that argued that the decline of two-parent families would hinder economic and social progress in the African American community. [Ed.]

[7] Hacker is paraphrasing Baldwin. Andrew Hacker, *Two Nations: Black and White, Separate, Hostile, Unequal* (New York: Scribner, 1992), 61.

The economic banishment function is in many ways a replacement for the old reserve army of labor function, which played itself out when the undeserving poor could be hired as strikebreakers, as defense workers in the case of sudden wartime economic mobilization, as "hypothetical workers," who by their very presence could be used to depress the wages of other workers, or to put pressure on the unions not to make wage and other demands. Today, however, with a plentiful supply of immigrants, as well as of a constantly growing number of banished workers who are becoming surplus labor, a reserve army is less rarely needed—and when needed, can be recruited from sources other than the undeserving poor.

* * *

4. *Supplying illegal goods.* The undeserving poor who are banished from other jobs remain eligible for work in the manufacture and sale of illegal goods, including drugs. Although it is estimated that 80 percent of all illegal drugs are sold to Whites who are not poor, the sellers are often people banished from the formal labor market. Other suppliers of illegal goods include the illegal immigrants, considered undeserving in many American communities, who work for garment industry sweatshops manufacturing clothing under illegal conditions.

5. *Job creation.* Perhaps the most important economic function of the undeserving poor today is that their mere presence creates jobs for the better-off population, including professional ones. Since the undeserving poor are thought to be dangerous or improperly socialized, their behavior either has to be modified so that they act in socially approved ways, or they have to be isolated from the deserving sectors of society. The larger the number of people who are declared undeserving, the larger also the number of people needed to modify and isolate as well as control, guard, and care for them. Among these are the social workers, teachers, trainers, mentors, psychiatrists, doctors and their support staffs in juvenile training centers, "special" schools, drug treatment centers, and penal behavior modification institutions, as well as the police, prosecutors, defense attorneys, judges, court officers, probation personnel and others who constitute the criminal courts, and the guards and others who run the prisons.

Jobs created by the presence of undeserving poor also include the massive bureaucracy of professionals, investigators, and clerks who administer welfare. Other jobs go to the officials who seek out poor fathers for child support monies they may or may not have, as well as the welfare office personnel needed to take recipients in violation of welfare rules off the rolls, and those needed to put them back on the rolls when they reapply. In fact, one can argue that some of the rules for supervising, controlling, and punishing the undeserving poor are more effective at performing the latent function of creating clerical and professional jobs for the better-off population than the manifest function of achieving their official goals.

More jobs are created in the social sciences and in journalism for conducting research about the undeserving poor and producing popular books, articles, and TV documentaries for the more fortunate who want to learn about them. The "job chain" should also be extended to the teachers and others who train those who serve, control, and study the undeserving poor.

In addition, the undeserving poor make jobs for what I call the salvation industries, religious, civil, or medical, which also try to modify the behavior of those stigmatized as undeserving. Not all such jobs are paid, for the undeserving poor also provide occasional targets for charity and thus offer volunteer jobs for those providing it—and paid jobs for the professional fundraisers who obtain most of the charitable funds these days. Among the most visible volunteers are the members of "café" and "high" society who organize and contribute to these benefits.

Three Normative Functions

6. *Moral legitimation.* Undeservingness justifies the category of deservingness and thus supplies moral and political legitimacy, almost by definition, to the institutions and social structures that include the deserving and exclude the undeserving. Of these structures, the most important is undoubtedly the class hierarchy, for the existence of an undeserving class or stratum legitimates the deserving classes, if not necessarily all of their class-related behavior. The alleged immorality of the undeserving also gives a moral flavor to, and justification for, the class hierarchy, which may help to explain why upward mobility itself is so praiseworthy.

7. *Norm reinforcement.* By violating, or being imagined as violating, a number of mainstream behavioral patterns and values, the undeserving poor help to reaffirm and reinforce the virtues of these patterns—and to do so visibly, since the violations by the undeserving are highly publicized. As Emile Durkheim pointed out nearly a century ago, norm violations and their punishments also provide an opportunity for preserving and reaffirming the norms. This is not insignificant, for norms sometimes disparaged as "motherhood" values gain new moral power when they are violated, and their violators are stigmatized.

   If the undeserving poor can be imagined to be lazy, they help to reaffirm the Protestant work ethic; if poor single-parent families are publicly condemned, the two-parent family is once more legitimated as ideal. In the 1960s, middle-class morality was sometimes criticized as culturally parochial and therefore inappropriate for the poor, but since the 1980s, mainstream values have once more been regarded as vital sources of behavioral guidance for them.

   Enforcing the norms also contributes further to preserving them in another way, for one of the standard punishments of the undeserving poor for misbehaving—as well as standard obligation in exchange for help—is practicing the mainstream norms, including those that the members of the mainstream may only be preaching, and that might die out if the poor were not required to incorporate them in their behavior. Old work rules that can no longer be enforced in the rest of the economy can be maintained in the regulations for workfare; old-fashioned austerity and thrift are built into the consumption patterns expected of welfare recipients. Economists like to argue that if the poor want to be deserving, they should take any kind of job, regardless of its low pay or demeaning character, reflecting a work ethic which economists themselves have never practiced.

Similarly, welfare recipients may be removed from the rolls if they are found to be living with a man—but the social worker who removes them has every right to cohabit and not lose his or her job. In most states, welfare recipients must observe rules of housecleaning and child care that middle-class people are free to ignore without being punished. While there are many norms and laws governing child care, only the poor are monitored to see if they obey these. Should they use more physical punishment on their children than social workers consider desirable, they can be charged with child neglect or abuse and can lose their children to foster care.[8]

The fact is that the defenders of such widely preached norms as hard work, thrift, monogamy, and moderation need people who can be accused, accurately or not, of being lazy, spendthrift, promiscuous, and immoderate. One reason that welfare recipients are a ready target for punitive legislation is that politicians, and most likely some of their constituents, imagine them to be enjoying leisure and an active sex life at public expense. Whether or not very many poor people actually behave in the ways that are judged undeserving is irrelevant if they can be imagined as doing so. Once imagining and stereotyping are allowed to take over, then judgments of undeservingness can be made without much concern for empirical accuracy. For example, in the 1990s, the idea that young men from poor single-parent families were highly likely to commit street crimes became so universal that the news media no longer needed to quote experts to affirm the accuracy of the charge.

Actually, most of the time most of the poor are as law abiding and observant of mainstream norms as are other Americans. Sometimes they are even more observant; thus the proportion of welfare recipients who cheat is always far below the percentage of taxpayers who do so. Moreover, survey after survey has shown that the poor, including many street criminals and drug sellers, want to hold respectable jobs like everyone else, hope someday to live in the suburbs, and gen-

---

[8] Poor immigrants who still practice old-country discipline norms are particularly vulnerable to being accused of child abuse.

erally aspire to the same American dream as most moderate and middle-income Americans.[9]

8. *Supplying popular culture villains.* The undeserving poor have played a long-term role in supplying American popular culture with villains, allowing the producers of the culture both to reinforce further mainstream norms and to satisfy audience demands for revenge, notably by showing that crime and other norm violations do not pay. Street criminals are shown dead or alive in the hands of the police on local television news virtually every day, and more dramatically so in the crime and action movies and television series.

For many years before and after World War II, the criminal characters in Hollywood movies were often poor immigrants, frequently of Sicilian origin. Then they were complemented for some decades by communist spies and other Cold War enemies who were not poor, but even before the end of the Cold War, they were being replaced by Black and Hispanic drug dealers and gang leaders.

At the same time, however, the popular culture industry has also supplied music and other materials offering marketable cultural and political protest which does not reinforce mainstream norms, or at least not directly. Some of the creators and performers come from poor neighborhoods, however, and it may be that some rap music becomes commercially successful by displacing on ghetto musicians the cultural and political protest of record buyers from more affluent classes.

Three Political Functions

9. *Institutional scapegoating.* The scapegoating of the undeserving poor mentioned in Function 2 above also extends to institutions which mistreat them. As a result, some of the responsibility for the existence of poverty, slum unemployment, poor schools, and the like is taken off the shoulders of elected and appointed officials who are supposed to deal with these problems. For example, to the extent that educational experts decide that the children of the poor are learning disabled or that they are culturally or genetically inferior in intelligence, attempts to improve the schools can be put off or watered down.

To put it another way, the availability of institutional scapegoats both personalizes and exonerates social systems. The alleged laziness of the jobless and the anger aimed at beggars take the heat off the failure of the economy and the imagined derelictions of slum dwellers and the homeless, off the housing industry. In effect, the undeserving poor are blamed both for their poverty and also for the absence of "political will" among the citizenry to do anything about it.

---

[9] See Mark R. Rank, *Living on the Edge: The Realities of Welfare in America* (New York: Columbia University Press, 1994), 93.

10. *Conservative power shifting.* Once poor people are declared undeserving they also lose their political legitimacy and whatever little political influence they had before they were stigmatized. Some cannot vote, and many do not choose to vote or mobilize because they know politicians do not listen to their demands. Elected officials might ignore them even if they voted or mobilized because these officials and the larger polity cannot easily satisfy their demands for economic and other kinds of justice.[1] As a result, the political system is able to pay additional attention to the demands of more affluent constituents. It can therefore shift to the "right."

The same shift to the right also takes place ideologically. Although injustices of poverty help justify the existence of liberals and the more radical left the undeserving poor themselves provide justification and opportunities for conservatives to attack their ideological enemies on their left. When liberals can be accused of favoring criminals over victims, their accusers can launch and legitimate incursions on the civil liberties and rights of the undeserving poor, and concurrently on the liberties and rights of defenders of the poor. Moreover, the undeservingness of the poor can be used to justify attacks on the welfare state. Charles Murray understood the essence of this ideological function when he argued that welfare and other welfare state legislation for the poor only increased the number of poor people.[2]

11. *Spatial purification.* Stigmatized populations are often used, deliberately or not, to stigmatize the areas in which they live, making such areas eligible for various kinds of purification. As a result, "underclass areas" can be torn down and their inhabitants moved to make room for more affluent residents or higher taxpayers.

However, such areas can also be used to isolate stigmatized poor people and facilities by selecting them as locations for homeless shelters, halfway houses for the mentally ill or for ex-convicts, drug treatment facilities, and even garbage dumps, which have been forced out of middle- and working-class areas following NIMBY (not in my backyard) protests. Drug dealers and other sellers of illegal goods also find a haven in areas stigmatized as underclass areas, partly because these supply some customers, but also because police protection in such areas is usually minimal enough to allow illegal activities without significant interfer-

---

[1] In addition, the undeserving poor make a dangerous constituency. Politicians who say kind words about them or who act to represent their interests are likely to be attacked for their words and actions. Jesse Jackson was hardly the first national politician to be criticized for being too favorable to the poor.

[2] Charles Murray, *Losing Ground: American Social Policy, 1950–1980* (New York: Basic Books, 1984).

ence from the law. In fact, municipalities would face major economic and political obstacles to their operations without stigmatized areas in which stigmatized people and activities can be located.

Two Macrosocial Functions

12. *Reproduction of stigma and the stigmatized.* For centuries now, undeservingness has given rise to policies and agencies which are manifestly set up to help the poor economically and otherwise to become deserving, but which actually prevent the undeserving poor from being freed of their stigma, and which also manage, unwittingly, to see to it that their children face the same obstacles. In some instances, this process works so speedily that the children of the stigmatized face "anticipatory stigmatization," among them the children of welfare recipients who are frequently predicted to be unable to learn, to work, and to remain on the right side of the law even before they have been weaned.

If this outcome were planned deliberately, one could argue that politically and culturally dominant groups are reluctant to give up an easily accessible and always available scapegoat. In actuality, however, the reproduction function results unwittingly from other intended and seemingly popular practices. For example, the so-called War on Drugs, which has unsuccessfully sought to keep hard drugs out of the United States, but has meanwhile done little to provide drug treatment to addicts who want it, thereby aids the continuation of addiction, street crime, and a guaranteed prison population, not to mention the various disasters that visit the families of addicts and help to keep them poor.

The other major source of reproducing stigma and the stigmatized is the routine activities of the organizations which service welfare recipients, the homeless, and other stigmatized poor, and end up mistreating them. For one thing, such agencies, whether they exist to supply employment to the poor or to help the homeless, are almost certain to be underfunded because of the powerlessness of their clientele. No organization has ever had the funds or power to buy, build, or rehabilitate housing for the homeless in sufficient number. Typically, they have been able to fund or carry out small demonstration projects.

In addition, organizations which serve stigmatized people often attract less well-trained and qualified staff than those with high-status clients, and if the clients are deemed undeserving, competence may become even less important in choosing staff. Then too, helping organizations generally reflect the societal stratification hierarchy, which means that organizations with poor, low-status clients frequently treat them as undeserving. If they also fear some of their clients, they may not only withhold help, but attack the clients on a preemptive strike basis. Last but not least, the agencies that serve the undeserving poor are bureaucracies which operate by rules and regulations that routinize the work, encourage the stability and growth of the organizations, and serve the needs of their staffs before those of their clients.

When these factors are combined, as they often are, and become cumulative, as they often do, it should not be surprising that the organizations cut off escape routes from poverty not only for the clients, but in doing so, also make sure that some of their children remain poor as well.

13. *Extermination of the surplus.* In earlier times, when the living standards of all poor people were at or below subsistence, many died at an earlier age than the better off, thus performing the set of functions for the latter forever associated with Thomas Malthus. Standards of living, even for the very poor, have risen considerably in the last century, but even today, morbidity and mortality rates remain much higher among the poor than among moderate-income people. To put it another way, various social forces combine to do away with some of the people who have become surplus labor and are no longer needed by the economy.

Several of the killing illnesses and pathologies of the poor change over time; currently, they include AIDS, tuberculosis, hypertension, heart attacks, and cancer, as well as psychosis, substance abuse, street crime, injury and death during participation in the drug trade and other underworld activities, and intraclass homicide resulting from neighborhood conflicts over turf and "respect." Whether the poor people whose only problem is being unfairly stereotyped and stigmatized as undeserving die earlier than other poor people is not known.

Moreover, these rates can be expected to remain high or even to rise as rates of unemployment—and of banishment from the labor force—rise, especially for the least skilled. Even the better-off jobless created by the downsizing of the 1990s blame themselves for their unemployment if they cannot eventually find new jobs, become depressed, and in some instances begin the same process of being extruded permanently from the labor market experienced by the least skilled of the jobless.

* * *

The early departure of poor people from an economy and society which do not need them is useful for those who remain. Since the more fortunate classes have already developed a purposive blindness to the structural causes of unemployment and to the poverty-related causes of pathology and crime that follow, those who benefit from the current job erosion and the possible extermination of the surplus labor may not admit it consciously either. Nonetheless, those left over to compete for scarce jobs and other resources will have a somewhat easier time in the competition, thus assigning undeservingness a final positive function for the more fortunate members of society.

III. CONCLUSION

I have described thirteen of the more important functions of the undeserving poor, enough to support my argument that both the idea of the undeserving poor and the stigmas with which some poor people are thus labeled may persist in part because they are useful in a variety of ways to the people who are not poor.

This analysis does not imply that undeservingness will or should persist. Whether it *will* persist is going to be determined by what happens to poverty in America. If it declines, poverty-related crime should also decline, and then fewer poor people will probably be described as undeserving. If poverty worsens, so will poverty-related crime, as well as the stereotyping and stigmatization of the poor, and any worsening of the country's economy is likely to add to the kinds and numbers of undeserving poor, if only because they make convenient and powerless scapegoats.

The functions that the undeserving poor play cannot, by themselves, perpetuate either poverty or undeservingness, for as I noted earlier, functions are not causes. For example, if huge numbers of additional unskilled workers should be needed, as they were for the World War II war effort, the undeserving poor will be welcomed back into the labor force, at least temporarily. Of course, institutions often try to survive once they have lost both their reasons for existence and their functions. Since the end of the Cold War, parts of the military-industrial establishment both in the United States and Russia have been campaigning for the maintenance of some Cold War forces and weapons to guarantee their own futures, but these establishments also supply jobs to their national economies, and in the United States, for the constituents of elected officials. Likewise, some of the institutions and interest groups that benefit from the existence of undeservingness, or from controlling the undeserving poor, may try to maintain undeservingness and its stigma. They may not even need to, for if Emile Durkheim was right, the decline of undeservingness would lead to the criminalization, or at least stigmatization, of new behavior patterns.

Whether applying the label of undeservingness to the poor *should* persist is a normative question which ought to be answered in the negative. Although people have a right to judge each other, that right does not extend to judging large numbers of people as a single group, with one common moral fault, or to stereotyping them without evidence either about their behavior or their values. Even if a case could be made for judging large cohorts of people as undeserving, these judgments should be distributed up and down the socioeconomic hierarchy, requiring Americans also to consider whether and how people in the working, middle, and upper classes are undeserving.

The same equality should extend to the punishment of crimes. Today, many Americans and courts still treat white-collar and upper-class criminals more leniently than poor ones. The public excuse given is that the street crime of the undeserving poor involves violence and thus injury or death, but as many students of white-collar and corporate crime have pointed out, these also hurt and kill people, and often in larger numbers, even if they do so less directly and perhaps less violently.

Changes also need to be made in the American conception of deviance, which like that of other countries, conflates people whose behavior is *different* with those whose behavior is socially *harmful*. Bearing children without marriage is a long-standing tradition among the poor. Born of necessity rather than preference, it is a poverty-related practice, but it is not, by itself, harmful, or at least not until it can be shown that either the children—or the moral sensibilities of the people who oppose illegitimacy—are significantly hurt. Poor single-parent families are hardly desirable, but as the lack of condemnation of more affluent single-parent families should suggest, the major problem of such families is not the number of parents, actual or surrogate, in the family, but its poverty.

Finally, because many of the poor are stereotyped unjustly as undeserving, scholars, writers, journalists, and others should launch a systematic and public effort to deconstruct and delegitimate the notion of the undeserving poor. This effort, which is necessary to help make effective antipoverty programs politically acceptable again, should place the following five ideas on the public agenda and encourage discussion as well as dissemination of available research.

The five ideas, all discussed earlier in this article, are that (1) the criminal and deviant behavior among the poor is largely poverty related rather than the product of free choice based on distinctive values; (2) the undeservingness of the poor is an ancient stereotype, and like all stereotypes, it vastly exaggerates the actual dangers that stem from the poor; (3) poverty-related deviance is not necessarily harmful just because it does not accord with mainstream norms; (4) the notion of undeservingness survives in part because of the positive functions it has for the better-off population; and (5) the only certain way to eliminate both this notion and the functions is to eliminate poverty.[3]

STUDY QUESTIONS

1. What are the five sets of positive functions Gans ascribes to the undeserving poor?

2. How is poverty **normative**? That is, how does the presence and condition of poor people reinforce values that are considered **middle class** or mainstream?

3. Gans argues that the practice of labeling the poor "undeserving" should be stopped. Is he right? Who, if anyone, is "undeserving"? The poor? Wall Street? Congress?

---

[3] A fuller discussion of policy proposals appear[s] in my book, *Ending the War against the Poor.*

4. Much legislation and **political** rhetoric concerns what can be done to aid the needy in our **society**. Do some research on **government** programs to determine which programs are least likely to label the poor undeserving. Can you tell whether these programs are also the most successful at alleviating poverty?

MARY C. WATERS

Optional Ethnicities:
For Whites Only?

W "hat are you?" asks a person you've just met at a party. How would you respond to this question? Would you describe your ethnic background? Would you say American? Would you be offended and walk away? In this article Mary Waters suggests that inside your answer we can learn a great deal about your ethnic **identity**, how much it influences your day-to-day life, and how people of your ethnic identity are treated by **society** at large.

ETHNIC IDENTITY FOR WHITES IN THE 1990S

WHAT DOES IT MEAN TO TALK ABOUT ETHNICITY AS AN OPTION for an individual? To argue that an individual has some degree of choice in their ethnic identity flies in the face of the common sense notion of ethnicity many of us believe in—that one's ethnic identity is a fixed characteristic, reflective of blood ties and given at birth. However, social scientists who study ethnicity have long concluded that while ethnicity is based in a *belief* in a common ancestry, ethnicity is primarily a *social* phenomenon, not a biological one (Alba 1985, 1990; Barth 1969; Weber [1921] 1968, p. 389). The belief that members of an ethnic group have that they share a common ancestry may not be a fact. There is a great deal of change in ethnic identities across generations through intermarriage, changing allegiances, and changing social categories. There is also a much larger amount of change in the identities of individuals over their life than is commonly believed. While most people are aware of the phenomena known as "passing"—people raised as one race who change at some point and claim a different race as their identity, there are similar life course changes in ethnicity that happen all the time and are not given the same degree of attention as "racial passing."

White Americans of European ancestry can be described as having a great deal of choice in terms of their ethnic identities. The two major types of options White Americans can exercise are (1) the option of whether to claim any specific ancestry, or to just be "White" or American, [Lieberson (1985) called these people "unhyphenated Whites"] and (2) the choice of which of their European ancestries to choose to include in their description of their own identities. In both cases, the option of choosing how to present yourself on surveys and in everyday social interactions exists for Whites because of social changes and societal conditions that have created a great deal of social mobility, immigrant assimilation, and political and economic power for Whites in the United States. Specifically, the option of being able to not claim any ethnic identity exists for Whites of European background in the United States because they are the majority group—in terms of holding political and social power, as well as being a numerical majority. The option of choosing among different ethnicities in their family backgrounds exists because the degree of discrimination and social distance attached to specific European backgrounds has diminished over time.

The Ethnic Miracle

When European immigration to the United States was sharply curtailed in the late 1920s, a process was set in motion whereby the European ethnic groups already in the United States were for all intents and purposes cut off from any new arrivals. As a result, the composition of the ethnic groups began to age generationally. The proportion of each ethnic group made up of immigrants or the first generation began to gradually decline, and the proportion made up of the children, grandchildren, and eventually great-grandchildren began to increase. Consequently, by 1990 most European-origin ethnic groups in the United States were composed of a very small number of immigrants, and a very large proportion of people whose link to their ethnic origins in Europe was increasingly remote.

This generational change was accompanied by unprecedented social and economic changes. The very success of the assimilation process these groups experienced makes it difficult to imagine how much the question of the immigrants' eventual assimilation was an open one at the turn of the century. At the peak of immigration from southern and central Europe there was widespread discrimination and hostility against the newcomers by established Americans. Italians, Poles, Greeks, and Jews were called derogatory names, attacked by nativist mobs, and derided in the press. Intermarriage across ethnic lines was very uncommon—castelike in the words of some sociologists (Pagnini and Morgan 1990). The immigrants and their children were residentially segregated, occupationally specialized, and generally poor.

After several generations in the United States, the situation has changed a great deal. The success and social mobility of the grandchildren and great-grandchildren of that massive wave of immigrants from Europe has been called "The Ethnic Miracle" (Greeley 1976). These Whites have moved away from the inner-city ethnic ghettos to White middle-class suburban homes. They are doctors, lawyers, entertainers, academics, governors, and Supreme Court justices. But contrary to what some social science theorists and some politicians predicted or hoped for, these middle-class Americans have not completely given up ethnic identity. Instead, they have maintained some connection with their immigrant ancestors' identities—becoming Irish American doctors, Italian American Supreme Court justices, and Greek American presidential candidates. In the tradition of cultural pluralism, successful middle-class Americans in the late twentieth century maintain some degree of identity with their ethnic backgrounds. They have remained "hyphenated Americans." So while social mobility and declining discrimination have created the option of not identifying with any European ancestry, most White Americans continue to report some ethnic background.

With the growth in intermarriage among people of European ethnic origins, increasingly these people are of mixed ethnic ancestry. This gives them the option of which ethnicity to identify with. The U.S. census has asked a question on ethnic ancestry in the 1980 and 1990 censuses. In 1980, 52 percent of the American public responded with a single ethnic ancestry, 31 percent gave multiple ethnic origins (up to three were coded, but some individuals wrote in more than three), and only 6 percent said they were American only, while the remaining 11 percent gave no response. In 1990 about 90 percent of the population gave some response to the ancestry question, with only 5 percent giving American as a response and only 1.4 percent reporting an uncodeable response such as "don't know" (McKenney and Cresce 1992; U.S. Bureau of the Census 1992b).

Several researchers have examined the pattern of responses of people to the census ancestry question. These analyses have shown a pattern of flux and inconsistency in ethnic ancestry reporting. For instance, Lieberson and Waters (1986; 1988, p. 93) have found that parents simplify children's ancestries when reporting them to the census. For instance, among the offspring in situations where one parent reports a specific single White ethnic origin and the other parent reports a different single White origin, about 40 percent of the children are not described as the logical combination of the parents ancestries. For example, only about 60 percent of the children of English-German marriages are labeled as English-German or German-English. About 15 percent of the children of these parents are simplified to just English, and another 15 percent are reported as just German. The remainder of the children are either not given an ancestry or are described as American (Lieberson and Waters 1986, 1993).

In addition to these intergenerational changes, researchers have found changes in reporting ancestry that occur at the time of marriage or upon leaving home. At the ages of eighteen to twenty-two, when many young Americans leave home for the first time, the number of people reporting a single as opposed to a multiple ancestry goes up. Thus while parents simplify children's ancestries when they leave home, children themselves tend to report less complexity in their ancestries when they leave their parents' homes and begin reporting their ancestries themselves (Lieberson and Waters 1986, 1988; Waters 1990).

These individual changes are reflected in variability over time in the aggregate numbers of groups determined by the census and surveys. Farley (1991) compared the consistency of the overall counts of different ancestry groups in the 1979 Current Population Survey, the 1980 census, and the 1986 National Content Test (a pretest for the 1990 census). He found much less consistency in the numbers for northern European ancestry groups whose immigration peaks were early in the nineteenth century—the English, Dutch, Germans, and other northern European groups. In other words each of these different surveys and the census yielded a different estimate of the number of people having this ancestry. The 1990 census also showed a great deal of flux and inconsistency in some ancestry groups. The number of people reporting English as an ancestry went down considerably from 1980, while the number reporting German ancestry went up. The number of Cajuns grew dramatically. This has led officials at the Census Bureau to assume that the examples used in the instructions strongly influence the responses people give. (Cajun was one of the examples of an ancestry given in 1990 but not in 1980, and German was the first example given. English was an example in the 1980 instructions, but not in 1990.)

All of these studies point to the socially variable nature of ethnic identity—and the lack of equivalence between ethnic ancestry and identity. If merely adding a category to the instructions to the question increases the number of people claiming that ancestry, what does that mean about the level of importance of that identity for people answering the census? Clearly identity and ancestry for Whites in the United States, who increasingly are from mixed backgrounds, involves some change and choice.

Symbolic Ethnicities for White Americans

What do these ethnic identities mean to people and why do they cling to them rather than just abandoning the tie and calling themselves American? My own field research with suburban Whites in California and Pennsylvania found that later-generation descendants of European origin maintain what are called "symbolic ethnicities." Symbolic ethnicity is a term coined by Herbert Gans (1979) to refer to ethnicity that is individualistic in nature and without real social cost for the individual. These symbolic identifications are essentially leisure time activities, rooted in nuclear family traditions and reinforced by the voluntary enjoyable aspects of being ethnic (Waters 1990). Richard Alba (1990) also found later-generation Whites in Albany, New York, who chose to keep a tie with an ethnic identity because of the enjoyable and voluntary aspects to those identities, along with the feelings of specialness they entailed. An example of symbolic ethnicity is individuals who identify as Irish, for example, on occasions such as Saint Patrick's Day, on family holidays, or for vacations. They do not usually belong to Irish American organizations, live in Irish neighborhoods, work in Irish jobs, or marry other Irish people. The symbolic meaning of being Irish American can be constructed by individuals from mass media images, family traditions, or other intermittent social activities. In other words, for later-generation White ethnics, ethnicity is not something that influences their lives unless they want it to. In the world of work and school and neighborhood, individuals do not have to admit to being ethnic unless they choose to. And for an increasing number of European-origin individuals whose parents and grandparents have intermarried, the ethnicity they claim is largely a matter of personal choice as they sort through all of the possible combinations of groups in their genealogies.

Individuals can choose those aspects of being Italian, for instance, that appeal to them, and discard those that do not. Or a person whose father is Italian, and mother part Polish and part French, might choose among the three ethnicities and present herself as a Polish American. For instance, a nineteen-year-old college student, interviewed in California in 1986, told me he would have answered Irish on the 1980 census form that asked about ethnic ancestry. These are his reasons:

Q: Why would you have answered that?

A: Well my Dad's name is Kerrigan and my mom's name is O'Leary, and I do have some German in me, but if you figure it out, I am about 75% Irish, so I usually say I am Irish.

Q: You usually don't say German when people ask?

A: No, no, I never say I am German. My dad just likes being Irish. . . . I don't know I just never think of myself as being German.

Q: So your dad's father is the one who immigrated?

A: Yes. On his side is Irish for generations. And then my grandmother's name is Dubois, which is French, partly German, partly French, and then the rest of the family is all Irish. So it is only the maternal grandmother who messes up the line. (Waters 1990, p. 10)

Thus in the course of a few questions, this man labeled himself Irish, admitted to being part German but not identifying with it, and then as an afterthought added that he was also part French. This is not an unusual case. With just a little probing, many people will describe a variety of ancestries in their family background, but do not consider these ancestries to be a salient part of their own identities. Thus the 1990 census ancestry question, which estimated that 30 percent of the population is of mixed ancestry, most surely underestimates the degree of mixing among the population. My research, and the research of Richard Alba (1990), shows that many people have already sorted through what they know of their ethnic ancestries and simplified their responses before they ever answer a census or survey question (Waters 1990).

But note that this freedom to include or exclude ancestries in your identification to yourself and others would not be the same for those defined racially in our society. They are constrained to identify with the part of their ancestry that has been socially defined as the "essential" part. African Americans, for example, have been highly socially constrained to identify as Blacks, without other options available to them, even when they know that their forebears included many people of American Indian or European background. Up until the mid-twentieth century, many state governments had specific laws defining one as Black if as little as one-thirty-second of one's ancestors were defined as Black (Davis 1991; Dominguez 1986; Spickard 1989). Even now when the one drop rule[1] has been dropped from our legal codes, there are still strong societal pressures on African Americans to identify in a particular way. Certain ancestries take precedence over others in the societal rules on descent and ancestry reckoning. If one believes one is part English and part German and identifies in a survey as German, one is not in danger of being accused of trying to "pass" as non-English and of being "redefined" English by the interviewer. But if one were part African and part German, one's self identification as German would be highly suspect and probably not accepted if one "looked" Black according to the prevailing social norms.

This is reflected in the ways the census collects race and ethnic identity. While the ethnic ancestry question used in 1980 and 1990 is given to all Americans in the sample regardless of race and allows multiple responses that combine races, the primary source of information on people defined racially in the United States is the census race question or the Hispanic question. Both of these questions require a person to make a choice about an identity. Individuals are not allowed to respond that they are both Black and White, or Japanese and Asian Indian on the race question even if they know that is their background. In fact, people who disobey the instructions to the census race question and check off two races are assigned to the first checked race in the list by the Census Bureau.

In responding to the ancestry question, the comparative latitude that White respondents have does not mean that Whites pick and choose ethnicities out of thin air. For the most part people choose an identity that corresponds with some element of their family tree. However, there are many anecdotal instances of people adopting ethnicities when they marry or move to a strongly identified neighborhood or community. For instance Micaela di Leonardo (1984) reported instances of non-Italian women who married into Italian American families and "became Italian." Karen Leonard (1992) describes a community of Mexican American women who married Punjabi immigrants in California. Some of the Punjabi immigrants and their descendants were said to have "become Mexican" when they joined their wives' kin group and

---

[1] Reference to laws and customs defining a person as Black if he or she had "one drop" of Black blood—that is, any African ancestry at all.

social worlds. Alternatively she describes the community acknowledging that Mexican women made the best curry, as they adapted to life with Indian-origin men.

But what do these identities mean to individuals? Surely an identity that is optional in a number of ways—not legally defined on a passport or birth certificate, not socially consequential in terms of societal discrimination in terms of housing or job access, and not economically limiting in terms of blocking opportunities for social mobility—cannot be the same as an identity that results from and is nurtured by societal exclusion and rejection. The choice to have a symbolic ethnicity is an attractive and widespread one despite its lack of demonstrable content, because having a symbolic ethnicity combines individuality with feelings of community. People reported to me that they liked having an ethnic identity because it gave them a uniqueness and a feeling of being special. They often contrasted their own specialness by virtue of their ethnic identities with "bland" Americanness. Being ethnic makes people feel unique and special and not just "vanilla" as one of my respondents put it. For instance, one woman describes the benefits she feels from being Czech American:

> I work in an office and a lot of people in there always talk about their background. It's weird because it is a big office and people are of all different backgrounds. People are this or that. It is interesting I think to find out. Especially when it is something you do not hear a lot about. Something that is not common like Lithuania or something. That's the good part about being Czech. People think it is something different. (Waters 1990, p. 154)

Because "American" is largely understood by Americans to be a political identity and allegiance and not an ethnic one, the idea of being "American" does not give people the same sense of belonging that their hyphenated American identity does. When I asked people about their dual identities—American and Irish or Italian or whatever—they usually responded in a way that showed how they conceived of the relationship between the two identities. Being an American was their primary identity; but it was so primary that they rarely, if ever, thought about it—most commonly only when they left the country. Being Irish American, on the other hand, was a way they had of differentiating themselves from others whom they interacted with from day to day—in many cases from spouses or in laws. Certain of their traits—being emotional, having a sense of humor, talking with their hands—were understood as stemming from their ethnicity. Yet when asked about their identity as Americans, that identity was both removed from their day-to-day consciousness and understood in terms of loyalty and patriotism. Although they may not think they behave or think in a certain way because they are American, being American is something they are both proud of and committed to.

Symbolic ethnicity is the best of all worlds for these respondents. These White ethnics can claim to be unique and special, while simultaneously finding the community and conformity with others that they also crave. But that "community" is of a type that will not interfere with a person's individuality. It is not as if these people belong to ethnic voluntary organizations or gather as a group in churches or neighborhoods or union halls. They work and reside within the mainstream of American middle-class life, yet they retain the interesting benefits—the "specialness"—of ethnic allegiance, without any of its drawbacks.

It has been suggested by several researchers that this positive value attached to ethnic ancestry, which became popular in the ethnic revival of the 1970s, is the result of assimilation having proceeded to an advanced stage for descendants of White Europeans (Alba 1985; Crispino 1980; Steinberg 1981). Ironically, people celebrate and embrace their ethnic backgrounds precisely because assimilation has proceeded to the point where such identification does not have that much influence on their day-to-day life. Rather than choosing the "least ethnic" and most bland ethnicities, Whites desire the "most ethnic" ones, like the once-stigmatized "Italian," because it is perceived as bringing the most psychic benefits. For instance, when an Italian father is married to an English or a Scottish or a German mother, the likelihood is that the child will be reported to the census with the father's Italian ancestry, rather than the northern European ancestries, which would have been predicted to have a higher social status. Italian is a good ancestry to have, people told me, because they have good food and a warm family life. This change in the social meaning of being Italian American is quite dramatic, given that Italians were subject to discrimination, exclusion, and extreme negative stereotyping in the early part of the twentieth century.

RACE RELATIONS AND SYMBOLIC ETHNICITY

However much symbolic ethnicity is without cost for the individual, there is a cost associated with symbolic ethnicity for the society. That is because symbolic ethnicities of the type described here are confined to White Americans of European origin. Black Americans, Hispanic Americans, Asian Americans, and American Indians do not have the option of a symbolic ethnicity at present in the United States. For all of the ways in which ethnicity does not matter for White Americans, it does matter for non-Whites. Who your ancestors are does affect your choice of spouse, where you live, what job you have, who your friends are, and what your chances are for success in American society, if those ancestors happen not to be from Europe. The reality is that White ethnics have a lot more choice and room for maneuver than they themselves think they do. The situation is very different for members of racial minorities, whose lives are strongly influenced by their race or national origin regardless of how much they may choose not to identify themselves in terms of their ancestries.

When White Americans learn the stories of how their grandparents and great-grandparents triumphed in the United States over adversity, they are usually told in terms of their individual efforts and triumphs. The important role of labor unions and other organized political and economic actors in their social and economic successes are left out of the story in favor of a generational story of individual Americans rising up against communitarian, Old World intolerance and New World resistance. As a result, the "individualized" voluntary, cultural view of ethnicity for Whites is what is remembered.

One important implication of these identities is that they tend to be very individualistic. There is a tendency to view valuing diversity in a pluralist environment as equating all groups. The symbolic ethnic tends to think that all groups are equal; everyone has a background that is their right to celebrate and pass on to their children. This leads to the conclusion that all identities are equal and all identities in some sense are interchangeable—"I'm Italian American, you're Polish American. I'm Irish American, you're African American." The important thing is to treat people as individuals and all equally. However, this assumption ignores the very big difference between an individualistic symbolic ethnic identity and a socially enforced and imposed racial identity.

My favorite example of how this type of thinking can lead to some severe misunderstandings between people of different backgrounds is from the *Dear Abby* advice column. A few years back a person wrote in who had asked an acquaintance of Asian background where his family was from. His acquaintance answered that this was a rude question and he would not reply. The bewildered White asked Abby why it was rude, since he thought it was a sign of respect to wonder where people were from, and he certainly would not mind anyone asking HIM about where his family was from. Abby asked her readers to write in to say whether it was rude to ask about a person's ethnic background. She reported that she got a large response, that most non-Whites thought it was a sign of disrespect, and Whites thought it was flattering:

Dear Abby,

I am 100 percent American and because I am of Asian ancestry I am often asked "What are you?" It's not the personal nature of this question that bothers me, it's the question itself. This query seems to question my very humanity. "What am I? Why I am a person like everyone else!"

Signed, A REAL AMERICAN

Dear Abby,

Why do people resent being asked what they are? The Irish are so proud of being Irish, they tell you before you even ask. Tip O'Neill has never tried to hide his Irish ancestry.

Signed, JIMMY.

In this exchange JIMMY cannot understand why Asians are not as happy to be asked about their ethnicity as he is, because he understands his ethnicity and theirs to be separate but equal. Everyone has to come from somewhere—his family from

Ireland, another's family from Asia—each has a history and each should be proud of it. But the reason he cannot understand the perspective of the Asian American is that all ethnicities are not equal; all are not symbolic, costless, and voluntary. When White Americans equate their own symbolic ethnicities with the socially enforced identities of non-White Americans, they obscure the fact that the experiences of Whites and non-Whites have been qualitatively different in the United States and that the current identities of individuals partly reflect that unequal history.

In the next section I describe how relations between Black and White students on college campuses reflect some of these asymmetries in the understanding of what a racial or ethnic identity means. While I focus on Black and White students in the following discussion, you should be aware that the myriad other groups in the United States—Mexican Americans, American Indians, Japanese Americans—all have some degree of social and individual influences on their identities, which reflect the group's social and economic history and present circumstance.

Relations on College Campuses

Both Black and White students face the task of developing their race and ethnic identities. Sociologists and psychologists note that at the time people leave home and begin to live independently from their parents, often ages eighteen to twenty-two, they report a heightened sense of racial and ethnic identity as they sort through how much of their beliefs and behaviors are idiosyncratic to their families and how much are shared with other people. It is not until one comes in close contact with many people who are different from oneself that individuals realize the ways in which their backgrounds may influence their individual personality. This involves coming into contact with people who are different in terms of their ethnicity, class, religion, region, and race. For White students, the ethnicity they claim is more often than not a symbolic one—with all of the voluntary, enjoyable, and intermittent characteristics I have described.

Black students at the university are also developing identities through interactions with others who are different from them. Their identity development is more complicated than that of Whites because of the added element of racial discrimination and racism, along with the "ethnic" developments of finding others who share their background. Thus Black students have the positive attraction of being around other Black students who share some cultural elements, as well as the need to band together with other students in a reactive and oppositional way in the face of racist incidents on campus.

Colleges and universities across the country have been increasing diversity among their student bodies in the last few decades. This has led in many cases to strained relations among students from different racial and ethnic backgrounds. The 1980s and 1990s produced a great number of racial incidents and high racial tensions on campuses. While there were a number of racial incidents that were due to bigotry, unlawful behavior, and violent or vicious attacks, much of what happens among students on campuses involves a low level of tension and awkwardness in social interactions.

Many Black students experience racism personally for the first time on campus. The upper-middle-class students from White suburbs were often isolated enough that their presence was not threatening to racists in their high schools. Also, their class background was known by their residence and this may have prevented attacks being directed at them. Often Black students at the university who begin talking with other students and recognizing racial slights will remember incidents that happened to them earlier that they might not have thought were related to race.

Black college students across the country experience a sizeable number of incidents that are clearly the result of racism. Many of the most blatant ones that occur between students are the result of drinking. Sometimes late at night, drunken groups of White students coming home from parties will yell slurs at single Black students on the street. The other types of incidents that happen include being singled out for special treatment by employees, such as being followed when shopping at the campus bookstore, or going to the art museum with your class and the guard stops you and asks for your I.D. Others involve impersonal encounters on the street—being called a nigger by a truck driver while crossing the street, or seeing old ladies clutch their pocketbooks and shake in terror as you pass them on the street For the most part these incidents are not specific to the university environment, they are the types of incidents middle-class Blacks face every day throughout American society, and they have been documented by sociologists (Feagin 1991).

In such a climate, however, with students experiencing these types of incidents and talking with each other about them, Black students do experience a tension and a feeling of being singled out. It is unfair that this is part of their college experience and not that of White students. Dealing with incidents like this, or the ever-present threat of such incidents, is an ongoing developmental task for Black students that takes energy, attention, and strength of character. It should be clearly understood that this is an asymmetry in the "college experience" for Black and White students. It is one of the unfair aspects of life that results from living in a society with ongoing racial prejudice and discrimination. It is also very understandable that it makes some students angry at the unfairness of it all, even if there is no one to blame specifically. It is also very troubling because, while most Whites do not create these incidents, some do, and it is never clear until you know someone well whether they are the type of person who could do something like this. So one of the reactions of Black students to these incidents is to band together.

In some sense then, as Blauner (1992) has argued, you can see Black students coming together on campus as both an "ethnic" pull of wanting to be together to share common experiences and community, and a "racial" push of banding together defensively because of perceived rejection and tension from Whites. In this way the ethnic identities of Black students are in some sense similar to, say, Korean students wanting to be together to share experiences. And it is an ethnicity that is generally much stronger than, say, Italian Americans. But for Koreans who come together there is generally a definition of themselves as "different from" Whites. For Blacks reacting to exclusion, there is a tendency for the coming together to involve both being "different from" but also "opposed to" Whites.

The anthropologist John Ogbu (1990) has documented the tendency of minorities in a variety of societies around the world, who have experienced severe blocked mobility for long periods of time, to develop such oppositional identities. An important component of having such an identity is to describe others of your group who do not join in the group solidarity as devaluing and denying their very core identity. This is why it is not common for successful Asians to be accused by others of "acting White" in the United States, but it is quite common for such a term to be used by Blacks and Latinos. The oppositional component of a Black identity also explains how Black people can question whether others are acting "Black enough." On campus, it explains some of the intense pressures felt by Black students who do not make their racial identity central and who choose to hang out primarily with non-Blacks. This pressure from the group, which is partly defining itself by not being White, is exacerbated by the fact that race is a physical marker in American society. No one immediately notices the Jewish students sitting together in the dining hall, or the one Jewish student sitting surrounded by non-Jews, or the Texan sitting with the Californians, but everyone notices the Black student who is or is not at the "Black table" in the cafeteria.

An example of the kinds of misunderstandings that can arise because of different understandings of the meanings and implications of symbolic versus oppositional identities concerns questions students ask one another in the dorms about personal appearances and customs. A very common type of interaction in the dorm concerns questions Whites ask Blacks about their hair. Because Whites tend to know little about Blacks, and Blacks know a lot about Whites, there is a general asymmetry in the level of curiosity people have about one another. Whites, as the numerical majority, have had little contact with Black culture; Blacks, especially those who are in college, have had to develop bicultural skills—knowledge about the social worlds of both Whites and Blacks. Miscommunication and hurt feelings about White students' questions about Black students' hair illustrate this point. One of the things that happens freshman year is that White students are around Black students as they fix their hair. White students are generally quite curious about Black students' hair—they have basic questions such as how often Blacks wash their hair, how they get it straightened or curled, what products they use on their hair, how they comb it, etc. Whites often wonder to themselves whether they should ask these questions. One thought experiment Whites perform is to ask themselves whether a particular question would upset them. Adopting the "do unto others" rule, they ask themselves, "If a Black person was curious about my hair would I get upset?" The answer usually is "No, I would be happy to tell them." Another example is an Italian American student wondering to herself, "Would

I be upset if someone asked me about calamari?" The answer is no, so she asks her Black roommate about collard greens, and the roommate explodes with an angry response such as, "Do you think all Black people eat watermelon too?" Note that if this Italian American knew her friend was Trinidadian American and asked about peas and rice the situation would be more similar and would not necessarily ignite underlying tensions.

Like the debate in *Dear Abby*, these innocent questions are likely to lead to resentment. The issue of stereotypes about Black Americans and the assumption that all Blacks are alike and have the same stereotypical cultural traits has more power to hurt or offend a Black person than vice versa. The innocent questions about Black hair also bring up a number of asymmetries between the Black and White experience. Because Blacks tend to have more knowledge about Whites than vice versa, there is not an even exchange going on, the Black freshman is likely to have fewer basic questions about his White roommate than his White roommate has about him. Because of the differences historically in the group experiences of Blacks and Whites there are some connotations to Black hair that don't exist about White hair. (For instance, is straightening your hair a form of assimilation, do some people distinguish between women having "good hair" and "bad hair" in terms of beauty and how is that related to looking "White"?). Finally, even a Black freshman who cheerfully disregards or is unaware that there are these asymmetries will soon slam into another asymmetry if she willingly answers every innocent question asked of her. In a situation where Blacks make up only 10 percent of the student body, if every non-Black needs to be educated about hair, she will have to explain it to nine other students. As one Black student explained to me, after you've been asked a couple of times about something so personal you begin to feel like you are an attraction in a zoo, that you are at the university for the education of the White students.

Institutional Responses

Our society asks a lot of young people. We ask young people to do something that no one else does as successfully on such a wide scale—that is to live together with people from very different backgrounds, to respect one another, to appreciate one another, and to enjoy and learn from one another. The successes that occur every day in this endeavor are many, and they are too often overlooked. However, the problems and tensions are also real, and they will not vanish on their own. We tend to see pluralism working in the United States in much the same way some people expect capitalism to work. If you put together people with various interests and abilities and resources, the "invisible hand" of capitalism is supposed to make all the parts work together in an economy for the common good.

There is much to be said for such a model—the invisible hand of the market can solve complicated problems of production and distribution better than any "visible hand" of a state plan. However, we have learned that unequal power relations among the actors in the capitalist marketplace, as well as "externalities" that the market cannot account for, such as long-term pollution, or collusion between corporations, or the exploitation of child labor, means that state regulation is often needed. Pluralism and the relations between groups are very similar. There is a lot to be said for the idea that bringing people who belong to different ethnic or racial groups together in institutions with no interference will have good consequences. Students from different backgrounds will make friends if they share a dorm room or corridor, and there is no need for the institution to do any more than provide the locale. But like capitalism, the invisible hand of pluralism does not do well when power relations and externalities are ignored. When you bring together individuals from groups that are differentially valued in the wider society and provide no guidance, there will be problems. In these cases the "invisible hand" of pluralist relations does not work, and tensions and disagreements can arise without any particular individual or group of individuals being "to blame." On college campuses in the 1990s some of the tensions between students are of this sort. They arise from honest misunderstandings, lack of a common background, and very different experiences of what race and ethnicity mean to the individual.

The implications of symbolic ethnicities for thinking about race relations are subtle but consequential. If your understanding of your own ethnicity and its relationship to society and politics is one of individual choice, it becomes harder to understand the need for programs like affirmative action, which recognize the ongoing need for group struggle and group recognition, in order to bring about social change. It also is hard for a White college student to understand the need that minority students feel to band together against discrimination. It also is easy, on the individual level, to expect everyone else to be able to turn their ethnicity on and off at will, the way you are able to, without understanding that ongoing discrimination and societal attention to minority status makes that impossible for individuals from minority groups to do. The paradox of symbolic ethnicity is that it depends upon the ultimate goal of a pluralist society, and at the same time makes it more difficult to achieve that ultimate goal. It is dependent upon the concept that all ethnicities mean the same thing, that enjoying the traditions of one's heritage is an option available to a group or an individual, but that such a heritage should not have any social costs associated with it.

As the Asian Americans who wrote to *Dear Abby* make clear, there are many societal issues and involuntary ascriptions associated with non-White identities. The developments necessary for this to change are not individual but societal in nature. Social mobility and declining racial and ethnic sensitivity are closely associated. The legacy and the present reality of discrimination on the basis of race or ethnicity must be overcome before the ideal of a pluralist society, where all heritages are treated equally and are equally available for individuals to choose or discard at will, is realized.

STUDY QUESTIONS

1. What does Waters mean when she says ethnicity is largely **socially constructed** and not based on biology?

2. What is **symbolic ethnicity** and why does Waters argue that it is only available for white Americans?

3. Waters argues the experiences of students of color (she discusses African Americans specifically) on college campuses are different from those of their white counterparts. Waters believes that, because of this different treatment, students of color have a very different experience with their ethnic **identity** than white students do. Describe, using Waters's article, how the process of forming your ethnic identity is different for students of color and white students. Be sure to talk about both groups.

4. Write an essay or journal entry describing your ethnic identity. Based on what you learned reading this essay, do you think the way you describe yourself presents an accurate picture? Do you wish that you could describe your identity in a more complex—or a simpler—way? Why?

5. Hold a classroom discussion on whether your campus treats whites and people of color differently. Provide evidence or examples for your opinions. How would you describe racial and ethnic relations on your campus?

JUDITH LORBER

"Night to His Day": The Social Construction of Gender

From *Paradoxes of Gender*

Do you know what you are having?" is often the first question people ask when parents announced they're expecting. "It'll be a human, I think. At least it better be!" might be one standard response. From birth, we teach children to "do **gender**": flowered shoes for girls, ballcaps for boys, a future in nursing for girls and doctoring for boys. Judith Lorber provides evidence that the strictly defined two-gender system institutionalized in the West is not universal. She argues that "gender bending" individuals actually reinforce gender **norms**, and that **gender roles** serve to perpetuate inequality.

TALKING ABOUT GENDER FOR MOST PEOPLE IS THE EQUIVALENT of fish talking about water. Gender is so much the routine ground of everyday activities that questioning its taken-for-granted assumptions and presuppositions is like thinking about whether the sun will come up.[1] Gender is so pervasive that in our society we assume it is bred into our genes. Most people find it hard to believe that gender is constantly created and re-created out of human interaction, out of social life, and is the texture and order of that social life. Yet gender, like culture, is a human production that depends on everyone constantly "doing gender" (West and Zimmerman 1987).

And everyone "does gender" without thinking about it. Today, on the subway, I saw a well-dressed man with a year-old child in a stroller. Yesterday, on a bus, I saw

Chapter 1: "'Night to His Day': The Social Construction of Gender" from PARADOXES OF GENDER by Judith Lorber. Published by Yale University Press. Reprinted by permission of Yale University Press.

a man with a tiny baby in a carrier on his chest. Seeing men taking care of small children in public is increasingly common—at least in New York City. But both men were quite obviously stared at—and smiled at, approvingly. Everyone was doing gender—the men who were changing the role of fathers and the other passengers, who were applauding them silently. But there was more gendering going on that probably fewer people noticed. The baby was wearing a white crocheted cap and white clothes. You couldn't tell if it was a boy or a girl. The child in the stroller was wearing a dark blue T-shirt and dark print pants. As they started to leave the train, the father put a Yankee baseball cap on the child's head. Ah, a boy, I thought. Then I noticed the gleam of tiny earrings in the child's ears, and as they got off, I saw the little flowered sneakers and lace-trimmed socks. Not a boy after all. Gender done.

Gender is such a familiar part of daily life that it usually takes a deliberate disruption of our expectations of how women and men are supposed to act to pay attention to how it is produced. Gender signs and signals are so ubiquitous that we usually fail to note them—unless they are missing or ambiguous. Then we are uncomfortable until we have successfully placed the other person in a gender status; otherwise, we feel socially dislocated. In our society, in addition to man and woman, the status can be *transvestite* (a person who dresses in opposite-gender clothes) and *transsexual* (a person who has had sex-change surgery). Transvestites and transsexuals carefully construct their gender status by dressing, speaking, walking, gesturing in the ways prescribed for women or men—whichever they want to be taken for—and so does any "normal" person.

For the individual, gender construction starts with assignment to a sex category on the basis of what the genitalia look like at birth.[2] Then babies are dressed or adorned in a way that displays the category because parents don't want to be constantly asked whether their baby is a girl or a boy. A sex category becomes a gender status through naming, dress, and the use of other gender markers. Once a child's gender is evident, others treat those in one gender differently from those in the other, and the children respond to the different treatment by feeling different and behaving differently. As soon as they can talk, they start to refer to themselves as members of their gender. Sex doesn't come into play again until puberty, but by that time, sexual feelings and desires and practices have been shaped by gendered norms and expectations. Adolescent boys and girls approach and avoid each other in an elaborately scripted and gendered mating dance. Parenting is gendered, with different expectations for mothers and for fathers, and people of different genders work at different kinds of jobs. The work adults do as mothers and fathers and as low-level workers and high-level bosses, shapes women's and men's life experiences, and these experiences produce different feelings, consciousness, relationships, skills—ways of being that we call feminine or masculine.[3] All of these processes constitute the social construction of gender.

Gendered roles change—today fathers are taking care of little children, girls and boys are wearing unisex clothing and getting the same education, women and men are working at the same jobs. Although many traditional social groups are quite strict about maintaining gender differences, in other social groups they seem to be blurring. Then why the one-year-old's earrings? Why is it still so important to mark a child as a girl or a boy, to make sure she is not taken for a boy or he for a girl? What would happen if they were? They would, quite literally, have changed places in their social world.

To explain why gendering is done from birth, constantly and by everyone, we have to look not only at the way individuals experience gender but at gender as a social institution. As a social institution, gender is one of the major ways that human beings organize their lives. Human society depends on a predictable division of labor, a designated allocation of scarce goods, assigned responsibility for children and others who cannot care for themselves, common values and their systematic transmission to new members, legitimate leadership, music, art, stories, games, and other symbolic productions. One way of choosing people for the different tasks of society is on the basis of their talents, motivations, and competence—their demonstrated achievements. The other way is on the basis of gender, race, ethnicity—ascribed membership in a category of people. Although societies vary in the extent to which they use one or the other of these ways of allocating people to work and to carry out other responsibilities, every society uses gender and age grades. Every society classifies people as "girl and boy children," "girls and boys ready to be married," and "fully adult women and men," constructs similarities among them and differences between them, and assigns them to different roles and responsibilities. Personality characteristics, feelings, motivations, and ambitions flow from these different life experiences so that the members of these different groups become different kinds of people. The process of gendering and its outcome are legitimated by religion, law, science, and the society's entire set of values.

In order to understand gender as a social institution, it is important to distinguish human action from animal behavior. Animals feed themselves and their young until their young can feed themselves. Humans have to produce not only food but shelter and clothing. They also, if the group is going to continue as a social group, have to teach the children how their particular group does these tasks. In the process, humans reproduce gender, family, kinship, and a division of labor—social institutions that do not exist among animals. Primate social groups have been referred to as families, and their mating patterns as monogamy, adultery, and harems. Primate behavior has been used to prove the universality of sex differences—as built into our evolutionary inheritance (Haraway 1978a). But animals' sex differences are not at all the same as humans' gender differences; animals' bonding is not kinship; animals' mating is not ordered by marriage; and animals' dominance hierarchies are not the equivalent of human stratification systems. Animals group on sex and age, relational categories that are physiologically, not socially, different. Humans create gender and age-group categories that are socially, and not necessarily physiologically, different.[4]

For animals, physiological maturity means being able to impregnate or conceive; its markers are coming into heat (estrus) and sexual attraction. For humans, puberty means being available for marriage; it is marked by rites that demonstrate this marital eligibility. Although the onset of physiological puberty is signaled by secondary sex characteristics (menstruation, breast development, sperm ejaculation, pubic and underarm hair), the onset of social adulthood is ritualized by the coming-out party or desert walkabout or bar mitzvah or graduation from college or first successful hunt or dreaming or inheritance of property. Humans have rituals that mark the passage from childhood into puberty and puberty into full adult status, as well as for marriage, childbirth, and death; animals do not (van Gennep 1960). To the extent that infants and the dead are differentiated by whether they are male or female, there are different birth rituals for girls and boys, and different funeral rituals for men and women (Biersack 1984, 132–33). Rituals of puberty, marriage, and becoming a parent are gendered, creating a "woman," a "man," a "bride," a "groom," a "mother," a "father." Animals have no equivalents for these statuses.

Among animals, siblings mate and so do parents and children; humans have incest taboos and rules that encourage or forbid mating between members of different kin groups (Lévi-Strauss 1956, [1949] 1969). Any animal of the same species may feed another's young (or may not, depending on the species). Humans designate responsibility for particular children by kinship; humans frequently limit responsibility for children to the members of their kinship group or make them into members of their kinship group with adoption rituals.

Animals have dominance hierarchies based on size or on successful threat gestures and signals. These hierarchies are usually sexed, and in some species, moving to the top of the hierarchy physically changes the sex (Austad 1986). Humans have stratification patterns based on control of surplus food, ownership of property, legitimate demands on others' work and sexual services, enforced determinations of who marries whom, and approved use of violence. If a woman replaces a man at the top of a stratification hierarchy, her social status may be that of a man, but her sex does not change.

Mating, feeding, and nurturant behavior in animals is determined by instinct and imitative learning and ordered by physiological sex and age (Lancaster 1974). In humans, these behaviors are taught and symbolically reinforced and ordered by socially constructed gender and age grades. Social gender and age statuses sometimes ignore or override physiological sex and age completely. Male and female animals (unless they physiologically change) are not interchangeable; infant animals cannot take the place of adult animals. Human females can become husbands and fathers, and human males can become wives and mothers, without sex-change surgery (Blackwood 1984). Human infants can reign as kings or queens.

Western society's values legitimate gendering by claiming that it all comes from physiology—female and male procreative differences. But gender and sex are not equivalent, and gender as a social construction does not flow automatically from genitalia and reproductive organs, the main physiological differences of females and males. In the construction of ascribed social statuses, physiological differences such as sex, stage of development, color of skin, and size are crude markers. They are not the source of the social statuses of gender, age grade, and race. Social statuses are carefully constructed through prescribed processes of teaching, learning, emulation, and enforcement. Whatever genes, hormones, and biological evolution contribute to human social institutions is materially as well as qualitatively transformed by social practices. Every social institution has a material base, but culture and social practices transform that base into something with qualitatively different patterns and constraints. The economy is much more than producing food and goods and distributing them to eaters and users; family and kinship are not the equivalent of having sex and procreating; morals and religions cannot be equated with the fears and ecstasies of the brain; language goes far beyond the sounds produced by tongue and larynx. No one eats "money" or "credit"; the concepts of "god" and "angels" are the subjects of theological disquisitions; not only words but objects, such as their flag, "speak" to the citizens of a country.

Similarly, gender cannot be equated with biological and physiological differences between human females and males. The building blocks of gender are *socially constructed statuses*. Western societies have only two genders, "man" and "woman." Some societies have three genders—men, women, and *berdaches* or *hijras* or *xaniths*. Berdaches, hijras, and xaniths are biological males who behave, dress, work, and are treated in most respects as social women; they are therefore not men, nor are they female women; they are, in our language, "male women."[5] There are African and American Indian societies that have a gender status called *manly hearted women*—biological females who work, marry, and parent as men; their social status is "female men" (Amadiume 1987; Blackwood 1984). They do not have to behave or dress as men to have the social responsibilities and prerogatives of husbands and fathers; what makes them men is enough wealth to buy a wife.

Modern Western societies' *transsexuals* and *transvestites* are the nearest equivalent of these crossover genders, but they are not institutionalized as third genders (Bolin 1987). Transsexuals are biological males and females who have sex-change operations to alter their genitalia. They do so in order to bring their physical anatomy in congruence with the way they want to live and with their own sense of gender identity. They do not become a third gender; they change genders. Transvestites are males who live as women and females who live as men but do not intend to have sex-change surgery. Their dress, appearance, and mannerisms fall within the range of what is expected from members of the opposite gender, so that they "pass." They also change genders, sometimes temporarily, some for most of their lives. Transvestite women have fought in wars as men soldiers as recently as the nineteenth century; some married women, and others went back to being women and married men once the war was over.[6] Some were discovered when their wounds were treated; others not until they died. In order to work as a jazz musician, a man's occupation, Billy Tipton, a woman, lived most of her life as a man. She died recently at seventy-four, leaving a wife and three adopted sons for whom she was husband and father, and musicians with whom she had played and traveled, for whom she was "one of the boys" (*New York Times* 1989).[7] There have been many other such occurrences of women passing as men to do more prestigious or lucrative men's work (Matthaeï 1982, 192–93).[8]

Genders, therefore, are not attached to a biological substratum. Gender boundaries are breachable, and individual and socially organized shifts from one gender to another call attention to "cultural, social, or aesthetic dissonances" (Garber 1992, 16). These odd or deviant or third genders show us what we ordinarily take for granted—that people have to learn to be women and men. Men who cross-dress for performances or for pleasure often learn from women's magazines how to "do femininity" convincingly (Garber 1992, 41–51). Because transvestism is direct evidence of how gender is constructed, Marjorie Garber claims it has "extraordinary power . . . to disrupt, expose, and challenge, putting in question the very notion of the 'original' and of stable identity" (1992, 16).

GENDER BENDING

It is difficult to see how gender is constructed because we take it for granted that it's all biology, or hormones, or human nature. The differences between women and men seem to be self-evident, and we think they would occur no matter what society did. But in actuality, human females and males are physiologically more similar in appearance than are the two sexes of many species of animals and are more alike than different in traits and behavior (C. F. Epstein 1988). Without the deliberate use of gendered clothing, hairstyles, jewelry, and cosmetics, women and men would look far more alike.[9] Even societies that do not cover women's breasts have gender-identifying clothing, scarification, jewelry, and hairstyles.

The ease with which many transvestite women pass as men and transvestite men as women is corroborated by the common gender misidentification in Westernized societies of people in jeans, T-shirts, and sneakers. Men with long hair may be addressed as "miss," and women with short hair are often taken for men unless they offset the potential ambiguity with deliberate gender markers (Devor 1987, 1989). Jan Morris, in *Conundrum,* an autobiographical account of events just before and just after a sex-change operation, described how easy it was to shift back and forth from being a man to being a woman when testing how it would feel to change gender status. During this time, Morris still had a penis and wore more or less unisex clothing; the context alone made the man and the woman:

> Sometimes the arena of my ambivalence was uncomfortably small. At the Travellers' Club, for example, I was obviously known as a man of sorts—women were only allowed on the premises at all during a few hours of the day, and even then were hidden away as

far as possible in lesser rooms or alcoves. But I had another club, only a few hundred yards away, where I was known only as a woman, and often I went directly from one to the other, imperceptibly changing roles on the way—"Cheerio, sir," the porter would say at one club, and "Hello, madam," the porter would greet me at the other. (1975, 132)

Gender shifts are actually a common phenomenon in public roles as well. Queen Elizabeth II of England bore children, but when she went to Saudi Arabia on a state visit, she was considered an honorary man so that she could confer and dine with the men who were heads of a state that forbids unrelated men and women to have face-to-unveiled-face contact. In contemporary Egypt, lower-class women who run restaurants or shops dress in men's clothing and engage in unfeminine aggressive behavior, and middle-class educated women of professional or managerial status can take positions of authority (Rugh 1986, 131). In these situations, there is an important status change: These women are treated by the others in the situation as if they are men. From their own point of view, they are still women. From the social perspective, however, they are men.[10]

In many cultures, gender bending is prevalent in theater or dance—the Japanese kabuki are men actors who play both women and men; in Shakespeare's theater company, there were no actresses—Juliet and Lady Macbeth were played by boys. Shakespeare's comedies are full of witty comments on gender shifts. Women characters frequently masquerade as young men, and other women characters fall in love with them; the boys playing these masquerading women, meanwhile, are acting out pining for the love of men characters.[11] In *As You Like It*, when Rosalind justifies her protective cross-dressing, Shakespeare also comments on manliness:

> Were it not better,
> Because that I am more than common tall,
> That I did suit me all points like a man:
> A gallant curtle-axe upon my thigh,
> A boar-spear in my hand, and in my heart
> Lie there what hidden women's fear there will,
> We'll have a swashing and martial outside,
> As many other mannish cowards have
> That do outface it with their semblances.   (I, i, 115–22)

Shakespeare's audience could appreciate the double subtext: Rosalind, a woman character, was a boy dressed in girl's clothing who then dressed as a boy; like bravery, masculinity and femininity can be put on and taken off with changes of costume and role (Howard 1988, 435).[12]

M Butterfly is a modern play of gender ambiguities, which David Hwang (1989) based on a real person. Shi Peipu, a male Chinese opera singer who sang women's roles, was a spy as a man and the lover as a woman of a Frenchman, Gallimard, a diplomat (Bernstein 1986). The relationship lasted twenty years, and Shi Peipu even pretended to be the mother of a child by Gallimard. "She" also pretended to be too shy to undress completely. As "Butterfly," Shi Peipu portrayed a fantasy Oriental woman who made the lover a "real man" (Kondo 1990b). In Gallimard's words, the fantasy was "of slender women in chong sams and kimonos who die for the love of unworthy foreign devils. Who are born and raised to be perfect women. Who take whatever punishment we give them, and bounce back, strengthened by love, unconditionally" (D. H. Hwang 1989, 91). When the fantasy woman betrayed him by turning out to be the more powerful "real man," Gallimard assumed the role of Butterfly and, dressed in a geisha's robes, killed himself: "because 'man' and 'woman' are oppositionally defined terms, reversals . . . are possible" (Kondo 1990b, 18).[13]

But despite the ease with which gender boundaries can be traversed in work, in social relationships, and in cultural productions, gender statuses remain. Transvestites and transsexuals do not challenge the social construction of gender. Their goal is to be feminine women and masculine men (Kando 1973). Those who do not want to change their anatomy but do want to change their gender behavior fare less well in establishing their social identity. The women Holly Devor called "gender blenders" wore their hair short, dressed in unisex pants, shirts, and comfortable shoes, and did not wear jewelry or makeup. They described their everyday dress as women's clothing: One said, "I wore jeans all the time, but I didn't wear men's clothes" (Devor 1989, 100). Their gender identity was women, but because they refused to "do femininity," they were constantly taken for men (1987, 1989, 107–42). Devor said of them: "The most common area of complaint was with public washrooms. They repeatedly spoke of the humiliation of being challenged or ejected from women's washrooms. Similarly, they found public change rooms to be dangerous territory and the buying of undergarments to be a difficult feat to accomplish" (1987, 29). In an ultimate ironic twist, some of these women said "they would feel like transvestites if they were to wear dresses, and two women said that they had been called transvestites when they had done so" (1987, 31). They resolved the ambiguity of their gender status by identifying as women in private and passing as men in public to avoid harassment on the street, to get men's jobs, and, if they were lesbians, to make it easier to display affection publicly with their lovers (Devor 1989, 107–42). Sometimes they even used men's bathrooms. When they had gender-neutral names, like Leslie, they could avoid the bureaucratic hassles that arose when they had to present their passports or other proof of identity, but because most had names associated with women, their appearance and their cards of identity were not conventionally congruent, and their gender status was in constant jeopardy.[14] When they could, they found it easier to pass as men than to try to change the stereotyped notions of what women should look like.

Paradoxically, then, bending gender rules and passing between genders does not erode but rather preserves gender boundaries. In societies with only two genders, the gender dichotomy is not disturbed by transvestites, because others feel that a transvestite is only transitorily ambiguous—is "really a man or woman underneath." After sex-change surgery, transsexuals end up in a conventional gender status—a "man" or a "woman" with the appropriate genitals (Eichler 1989). When women dress as men for business reasons, they are indicating that in that situation, they want to be treated the way men are treated; when they dress as women, they want to be treated as women:

> By their male dress, female entrepreneurs signal their desire to suspend the expectations of accepted feminine conduct without losing respect and reputation. By wearing what is "unattractive" they signify that they are not intending to display their physical charms while engaging in public activity. Their loud, aggressive banter contrasts with the modest demeanor that attracts men.... Overt signalling of a suspension of the rules preserves normal conduct from eroding expectations. (Rugh 1986, 131)

FOR INDIVIDUALS, GENDER MEANS SAMENESS

Although the possible combinations of genitalia, body shapes, clothing, mannerisms, sexuality, and roles could produce infinite varieties in human beings, the social institution of gender depends on the production and maintenance of a limited number of gender statuses and of making the members of these statuses similar to each other. Individuals are born sexed but not gendered, and they have to be taught to be masculine or feminine.[15] As Simone de Beauvoir said: "One is not born, but rather becomes, a woman ...; it is civilization as a whole that produces this creature ... which is described as feminine" (1952, 267).

Children learn to walk, talk, and gesture the way their social group says girls and boys should. Ray Birdwhistell, in his analysis of body motion as human communication, calls these learned gender displays *tertiary* sex characteristics and argues that they are needed to distinguish genders because humans are a weakly dimorphic species—their only sex markers are genitalia (1970, 39–46). Clothing, paradoxically, often hides the sex but displays the gender.

In early childhood, humans develop gendered personality structures and sexual orientations through their interactions with parents of the same and opposite gender. As adolescents, they conduct their sexual behavior according to gendered scripts. Schools, parents, peers, and the mass media guide young people into gendered work and family roles. As adults, they take on a gendered social status in their society's stratification system. Gender is thus both ascribed and achieved (West and Zimmerman 1987).

The achievement of gender was most dramatically revealed in a case of an accidental transsexual—a baby boy whose penis was destroyed in the course of a botched circumcision when he was seven months old (Money and Ehrhardt 1972, 118–23). The child's sex category was changed to "female," and a vagina was surgically constructed when the child was seventeen months old. The parents were advised that they could successfully raise the child, one of identical twins, as a girl. Physicians assured them that the child was too young to have formed a gender identity. Children's sense of which gender they belong to usually develops around the age of three, at the time that they start to group objects and recognize that the people around them also fit into categories—big, little; pink-skinned, brown-skinned; boys, girls. Three has also been the age when children's appearance is ritually gendered, usually by cutting a boy's hair or dressing him in distinctively masculine clothing. In Victorian times, English boys wore dresses up to the age of three, when they were put into short pants (Garber 1992, 1–2).

The parents of the accidental transsexual bent over backward to feminize the child—and succeeded. Frilly dresses, hair ribbons, and jewelry created a pride in looks, neatness, and "daintiness." More significant, the child's dominance was also feminized:

> The girl had many tomboyish traits, such as abundant physical energy, a high level of activity, stubbornness, and being often the dominant one in a girls' group. Her mother tried to modify her tomboyishness: ". . . I teach her to be more polite and quiet. I always wanted those virtues. I never did manage, but I'm going to try to manage them to—my daughter—to be more quiet and ladylike." From the beginning the girl had been the dominant twin. By the age of three, her dominance over her brother was, as her mother described it, that of a mother hen. The boy in turn took up for his sister, if anyone threatened her. (Money and Ehrhardt 1972, 122)

This child was not a tomboy because of male genes or hormones; according to her mother, she herself had also been a tomboy. What the mother had learned poorly while growing up as a "natural" female she insisted that her physically reconstructed son-daughter learn well. For both mother and child, the social construction of gender overrode any possibly inborn traits.

People go along with the imposition of gender norms because the weight of morality as well as immediate social pressure enforces them. Consider how many instructions for properly gendered behavior are packed into this mother's admonition to her daughter: "This is how to hem a dress when you see the hem coming down and so to prevent yourself from looking like the slut I know you are so bent on becoming" (Kincaid 1978).

Gender norms are inscribed in the way people move, gesture, and even eat. In one African society, men were supposed to eat with their "whole mouth, wholeheartedly, and not, like women, just with the lips, that is halfheartedly, with reservation and restraint" (Bourdieu [1980] 1990, 70). Men and women in this society learned to walk in ways that proclaimed their different positions in the society:

> The manly man . . . stands up straight into the face of the person he approaches, or wishes to welcome. Ever on the alert, because ever threatened, he misses nothing of what happens around him. . . . Conversely, a well brought-up woman . . . is expected to walk with a slight stoop, avoiding every misplaced movement of her body, her head or her arms, looking down, keeping her eyes on the spot where she will next put her foot, especially if she happens to have to walk past the men's assembly. (70)

Many cultures go beyond clothing, gestures, and demeanor in gendering children. They inscribe gender directly into bodies. In traditional Chinese society, mothers bound their daughters' feet into three-inch stumps to enhance their sexual attractiveness. Jewish fathers circumcise their infant sons to show their covenant with God. Women in African societies remove the clitoris of prepubescent girls, scrape their labia, and make the lips grow together to preserve their chastity and ensure their marriageability. In Western societies, women augment their breast size with silicone and reconstruct their faces with cosmetic surgery to conform to cultural ideals of feminine beauty. Hanna Papanek (1990) notes that these practices reinforce the sense of superiority or inferiority in the adults who carry them out as well as in the children on whom they are done: The genitals of Jewish fathers and sons are physical and psychological evidence of their common dominant religious and familial status; the genitals of African mothers and daughters are physical and psychological evidence of their joint subordination.[16]

Sandra Bem (1981, 1983) argues that because gender is a powerful "schema" that orders the cognitive world, one must wage a constant, active battle for a child not to fall into typical gendered attitudes and behavior. In 1972, *Ms. Magazine* published Lois Gould's fantasy of how to raise a child free of gender-typing. The experiment calls for hiding the child's anatomy from all eyes except the parents' and treating the child as neither a girl nor a boy. The child, called X, gets to do all the things boys *and* girls do. The experiment is so successful that all the children in X's class at school want to look and behave like X. At the end of the story, the creators of the experiment are asked what will happen when X grows up. The scientists' answer is that by then it will be quite clear what X is, implying that its hormones will kick in and it will be revealed as a female or male. That ambiguous, and somewhat contradictory, ending lets Gould off the hook; neither she nor we have any idea what someone brought up totally androgynously would be like sexually or socially as an adult. The hormonal input will not create gender or sexuality but will only establish secondary sex characteristics; breasts, beards, and menstruation alone do not produce social manhood or womanhood. Indeed, it is at puberty, when sex characteristics become evident, that most societies put pubescent children through their most important rites of passage, the rituals that officially mark them as fully gendered—that is, ready to marry and become adults.

Most parents create a gendered world for their newborn by naming, birth announcements, and dress. Children's relationships with same-gendered and different-gendered caretakers structure their self-identifications and personalities. Through cognitive development, children extract and apply to their own actions the appropriate behavior for those who belong in their own gender, as well as race, religion, ethnic group, and social class, rejecting what is not appropriate. If their social categories are highly valued, they value themselves highly; if their social categories are low status, they lose self-esteem (Chodorow 1974). Many feminist parents who want to raise androgynous children soon lose their children to the pull of gendered norms (T. Gordon 1990, 87–90).

My son attended a carefully nonsexist elementary school, which didn't even have girls' and boys' bathrooms. When he was seven or eight years old, I attended a class play about "squares" and "circles" and their need for each other and noticed that all the girl squares and circles wore makeup, but none of the boy squares and circles did. I asked the teacher about it after the play, and she said, "Bobby said he was not going to wear makeup, and he is a powerful child, so none of the boys would either." In a long discussion about conformity, my son confronted me with the question of who the conformists were, the boys who followed their leader or the girls who listened to the woman teacher. In actuality, they both were, because they both followed same-gender leaders and acted in gender-appropriate ways. (Actors may wear makeup, but real boys don't.)

For human beings there is no essential femaleness or maleness, femininity or masculinity, womanhood or manhood, but once gender is ascribed, the social order constructs and holds individuals to strongly gendered norms and expectations. Individuals may vary on many of the components of gender and may shift genders temporarily or permanently, but they must fit into the limited number of gender statuses their society recognizes. In the process, they re-create their society's version of women and men: "If we do gender appropriately, we simultaneously sustain, reproduce, and render legitimate the institutional arrangements. . . . If we fail to do gender appropriately, we as individuals—not the institutional arrangements—may be called to account (for our character, motives, and predispositions)" (West and Zimmerman 1987, 146).

The gendered practices of everyday life reproduce a society's view of how women and men should act (Bourdieu [1980] 1990). Gendered social arrangements are justified by religion and cultural productions and backed by law, but the most powerful means of sustaining the moral hegemony of the dominant gender ideology is that the process is made invisible; any possible alternatives are virtually unthinkable (Foucault 1972; Gramsci 1971).[17]

FOR SOCIETY, GENDER MEANS DIFFERENCE

The pervasiveness of gender as a way of structuring social life demands that gender statuses be clearly differentiated. Varied talents, sexual preferences, identities, personalities, interests, and ways of interacting fragment the individual's bodily and social experiences. Nonetheless, these are organized in Western cultures into two and only two socially and legally recognized gender statuses, "man" and "woman."[18] In the social construction of gender, it does not matter what men and women actually do; it does not even matter if they do exactly the same thing. The social institution of gender insists only that what they do is *perceived* as different.

If men and women are doing the same tasks, they are usually spatially segregated to maintain gender separation, and often the tasks are given different job titles as well, such as executive secretary and administrative assistant (Reskin 1988). If the differences between women and men begin to blur, society's "sameness taboo" goes into action (G. Rubin 1975, 178). At a rock and roll dance at West Point in 1976, the year women were admitted to the prestigious military academy for the first time, the school's administrators "were reportedly perturbed by the sight of mirror-image couples dancing in short hair and dress gray trousers," and a rule was established that women cadets could dance at these events only if they wore skirts (Barkalow and Raab 1990, 53).[19] Women recruits in the U.S. Marine Corps are required to wear makeup—at a minimum, lipstick and eye shadow—and they have to take classes in makeup, hair care, poise, and etiquette. This feminization is part of a deliberate policy of making them clearly distinguishable from men Marines. Christine Williams quotes a twenty-five-year-old woman drill instructor as saying: "A lot of the recruits who come here don't wear makeup; they're tomboyish or athletic. A lot of them have the preconceived idea that going into the military means they can still be a tomboy. They don't realize that you are a *Woman* Marine" (1989, 76–77).[20]

If gender differences were genetic, physiological, or hormonal, gender bending and gender ambiguity would occur only in hermaphrodites, who are born with chromosomes and genitalia that are not clearly female or male. Since gender differences are socially constructed, all men and all women can enact the behavior of the other, because they know the other's social script: "'Man' and 'woman' are at once empty and overflowing categories. Empty because they have no ultimate, transcendental meaning. Overflowing because even when they appear to be fixed, they still contain within them alternative, denied, or suppressed definitions." (J. W. Scott 1988a, 49). Nonetheless, though individuals may be able to shift gender statuses, the gender boundaries have to hold, or the whole gendered social order will come crashing down.

Paradoxically, it is the social importance of gender statuses and their external markers—clothing, mannerisms, and spatial segregation—that makes gender bending or gender crossing possible—or even necessary. The social viability of differentiated gender statuses produces the need or desire to shift statuses. Without gender differentiation, transvestism and transsexuality would be meaningless. You couldn't dress in the opposite gender's clothing if all clothing were unisex. There would be no need to reconstruct genitalia to match identity if interests and life-styles were not gendered. There would be no need for women to pass as men to do certain kinds of work if jobs were not typed as "women's work" and "men's work." Women would not have to dress as men in public life in order to give orders or aggressively bargain with customers.

Gender boundaries are preserved when transsexuals create congruous autobiographies of always having felt like what they are now. The transvestite's story also "recuperates social and sexual norms" (Garber 1992, 69). In the transvestite's normalized narrative, he or she "is 'compelled' by social and economic forces to disguise himself or herself in order to get a job, escape repression, or gain artistic or political 'freedom'" (Garber 1992, 70). The "true identity," when revealed, causes amazement over how easily and successfully the person passed as a member of the opposite gender, not a suspicion that gender itself is something of a put-on.

GENDER RANKING

Most societies rank genders according to prestige and power and construct them to be unequal, so that moving from one to another also means moving up or down the social scale. Among some North American Indian cultures, the hierarchy was male men, male women, female men, female women. Women produced significant durable goods (basketry, textiles, pottery, decorated leather goods), which could be traded. Women also controlled what they produced and any profit or wealth they earned. Since women's occupational realm could lead to prosperity and prestige, it was fair game for young men—but only if they became women in gender status. Similarly, women in other societies who amassed a great deal of wealth were allowed to become men—"manly hearts." According to Harriet Whitehead (1981):

> Both reactions reveal an unwillingness or inability to distinguish the sources of prestige—wealth, skill, personal efficacy (among other things)—from masculinity. Rather there is the innuendo that if a person performing female tasks can attain excellence, prosperity, or social power, it must be because that person is, at some level, a man. . . . A woman who could succeed at doing the things men did was honored as a man would be. . . . What seems to have been more disturbing to the culture—which means, for all intents and purposes, to the men—was the possibility that women, within their own department, might be onto a good thing. It was into this unsettling breach that the berdache institution was hurled. In their social aspect, women were complimented by the berdache's imitation. In their anatomic aspect, they were subtly insulted by his vaunted superiority. (108)

In American society, men-to-women transsexuals tend to earn less after surgery if they change occupations; women-to-men transsexuals tend to increase their income (Bolin 1988, 153–60; Brody 1979). Men who go into women's fields, like nursing, have less prestige than women who go into men's fields, like physics. Janice Raymond, a radical feminist, feels that transsexual men-to-women have advantages over female women because they were not socialized to be subordinate or oppressed throughout life. She says:

> We know that we are women who are born with female chromosomes and anatomy, and that whether or not we were socialized to be so-called normal women, patriarchy has treated and will treat us like women. Transsexuals have not had this same history. No man can have the history of being born and located in this culture as a woman. He can have the history of *wishing* to be a woman and of *acting* like a woman, but this gender experience is that of a transsexual, not of a woman. Surgery may confer the artifacts of outward and inward female organs but it cannot confer the history of being born a woman in this society. (1979, 114)

Because women who become men rise in the world and men who become women fall, Elaine Showalter (1987) was very critical of the movie *Tootsie,* in which Dustin Hoffman plays an actor who passes as a woman in order to be able to get work. "Dorothy" becomes a feminist "woman of the year" for standing up for women's rights not to be demeaned or sexually harassed. Showalter feels that the message of the movie is double-edged: "Dorothy's 'feminist' speeches . . . are less a response to the oppression of women than an instinctive situational male reaction to being treated like a woman. The implication is that women must be taught by men how to win their rights. . . . It says that feminist ideas are much less threatening when they come from a man" (123). Like Raymond, Showalter feels that being or having been a man gives a transsexual man-to-woman or a man cross-dressed as a woman a social advantage over those whose gender status was always "woman."[21] The implication here is that there is an experiential superiority that doesn't disappear with the gender shift.

For one transsexual man-to-woman, however, the experience of living as a woman changed his/her whole personality. As James, Morris had been a soldier, foreign correspondent, and mountain climber; as Jan, Morris is a successful travel writer. But socially, James was far superior to Jan, and so Jan developed the "learned helplessness" that is supposed to characterize women in Western society:

> We are told that the social gap between the sexes is narrowing, but I can only report that having, in the second half of the twentieth century, experienced life in both roles, there seems to me no aspect of existence, no moment of the day, no contact, no arrangement, no response, which is not different for men and for women. The very tone of voice in which I was now addressed, the very posture of the person next in the queue, the very feel in the air when I entered a room or sat at a restaurant table, constantly emphasized my change of status.
>
> And if other's responses shifted, so did my own. The more I was treated as woman, the more woman I became. I adapted willy-nilly. If I was assumed to be incompetent at reversing cars, or opening bottles, oddly incompetent I found myself becoming. If a case was thought too heavy for me, inexplicably I found it so myself. . . . Women treated me with a frankness which, while it was one of the happiest discoveries of my metamorphosis, did imply membership of a camp, a faction, or at least a school of thought; so I found myself gravitating always towards the female, whether in sharing a railway compartment or supporting a political cause. Men treated me more and more as junior, . . . and so, addressed every day of my life as an inferior, involuntarily, month by month I accepted the condition. I discovered that even now men prefer women to be less informed, less able, less talkative, and certainly less self-centered than they are themselves; so I generally obliged them. (1975, 165–66).[22]

COMPONENTS OF GENDER

By now, it should be clear that gender is not a unitary essence but has many components as a social institution and as an individual status.[23]

As a social institution, gender is composed of:

Gender statuses, the socially recognized genders in a society and the norms and expectations for their enactment behaviorally, gesturally, linguistically, emotionally, and physically. How gender statuses are evaluated depends on historical development in any particular society.

Gendered division of labor, the assignment of productive and domestic work to members of different gender statuses. The work assigned to those of different gender statuses strengthens the society's evaluation of those statuses—the higher the status, the more prestigious and valued the work and the greater its rewards.

Gendered kinship, the family rights and responsibilities for each gender status. Kinship statuses reflect and reinforce the prestige and power differences of the different genders.

Gendered sexual scripts, the normative patterns of sexual desire and sexual behavior, as prescribed for the different gender statuses. Members of the dominant gender have more sexual prerogatives; members of a subordinate gender may be sexually exploited.

Gendered personalities, the combinations of traits patterned by gender norms of how members of different gender statuses are supposed to feel and behave. Social expectations of others in face-to-face interaction constantly bolster these norms.

Gendered social control, the formal and informal approval and reward of conforming behavior and the stigmatization, social isolation, punishment, and medical treatment of nonconforming behavior.

Gender ideology, the justification of gender statuses, particularly, their differential evaluation. The dominant ideology tends to suppress criticism by making these evaluations seem natural.

Gender imagery, the cultural representations of gender and embodiment of gender in symbolic language and artistic productions that reproduce and legitimate gender statuses. Culture is one of the main supports of the dominant gender ideology.

For an individual, gender is composed of:

Sex category, to which the infant is assigned at birth based on appearance of genitalia. With prenatal testing and sex-typing, categorization is prenatal. Sex category may be changed later through surgery or reinspection of ambiguous genitalia.

Gender identity, the individual's sense of gendered self as a worker and family member.

Gendered marital and procreative status, fulfillment or nonfulfillment of allowed or disallowed mating, impregnation, childbearing, kinship roles.

Gendered sexual orientation, socially and individually patterned sexual desires, feelings, practices, and identification.

Gendered personality, internalized patterns of socially normative emotions as organized by family structure and parenting.

Gendered processes, the social practices of learning, being taught, picking up cues, enacting behavior already learned to be gender-appropriate (or inappropriate, if rebelling, testing), developing a gender identity, "doing gender" as a member of a gender status in relationships with gendered others, acting deferent or dominant.

Gender beliefs, incorporation of or resistance to gender ideology.

Gender display, presentation of self as a certain kind of gendered person through dress, cosmetics, adornments, and permanent and reversible body markers.

For an individual, all the social components are supposed to be consistent and congruent with perceived physiology. The actual combination of genes and genitalia, prenatal, adolescent, and adult hormonal input, and procreative capacity may or may not be congruous with each other and with sex-category assignment, gender identity, gendered sexual orientation and procreative status, gender display, personality, and work and family roles. At any one time, an individual's identity is a combination of the major ascribed statuses of gender, race, ethnicity, religion, and social class, and the individual's achieved statuses, such as education level, occupation or profession, marital status, parenthood, prestige, authority, and wealth. The ascribed statuses substantially limit or create opportunities for individual achievements and also diminish or enhance the luster of those achievements.

GENDER AS PROCESS, STRATIFICATION, AND STRUCTURE

As a social institution, gender is a process of creating distinguishable social statuses for the assignment of rights and responsibilities. As part of a stratification system that ranks these statuses unequally, gender is a major building block in the social structures built on these unequal statuses.

As a *process,* gender creates the social differences that define "woman" and "man." In social interaction throughout their lives, individuals learn what is expected, see what is expected, act and react in expected ways, and thus simultaneously construct and maintain the gender order: "The very injunction to be a given gender takes place through discursive routes: to be a good mother, to be a heterosexually desirable object, to be a fit worker, in sum, to signify a multiplicity of guarantees in response to a variety of different demands all at once" (J. Butler 1990, 145). Members of a social group neither make up gender as they go along nor exactly replicate in rote fashion what was done before. In almost every encounter, human beings produce gender, behaving in the ways they learned were appropriate for their gender status, or resisting or rebelling against these norms. Resistance and rebellion have altered gender norms, but so far they have rarely eroded the statuses.

Gendered patterns of interaction acquire additional layers of gendered sexuality, parenting, and work behaviors in childhood, adolescence, and adulthood. Gendered norms and expectations are enforced through informal sanctions of gender-inappropriate behavior by peers and by formal punishment or threat of punishment by those in authority should behavior deviate too far from socially imposed standards for women and men.

Everyday gendered interactions build gender into the family, the work process, and other organizations and institutions, which in turn reinforce gender expectations for individuals.[24] Because gender is a process, there is room not only for modification and variation by individuals and small groups but also for institutionalized change (J. W. Scott 1988a, 7).

As part of a *stratification* system, gender ranks men above women of the same race and class. Women and men could be different but equal. In practice, the process of creating difference depends to a great extent on differential evaluation. As Nancy Jay (1981) says: "That which is defined, separated out, isolated from all else is A and pure. Not-A is necessarily impure, a random catchall, to which nothing is external except A and the principle of order that separates it from Not-A" (45). From the individual's point of view, whichever gender is A, the other is Not-A; gender boundaries tell the individual who is like him or her, and all the rest are unlike. From society's point of view, however, one gender is usually the touchstone, the normal, the dominant, and the other is different, deviant, and subordinate. In Western society, "man" is A, "wo-man" is Not-A. (Consider what a society would be like where woman was A and man Not-A.)

The further dichotomization by race and class constructs the gradations of a heterogeneous society's stratification scheme. Thus, in the United States, white is A, African American is Not-A; middle class is A, working class is Not-A, and "African-American women occupy a position whereby the inferior half of a series of these dichotomies converge" (P. H. Collins 1990, 70). The dominant categories are the hegemonic ideals, taken so for granted as the way things should be that white is not ordinarily thought of as a race, middle class as a class, or men as a gender. The characteristics of these categories define the Other as that which lacks the valuable qualities the dominants exhibit.

In a gender-stratified society, what men do is usually valued more highly than what women do because men do it, even when their activities are very similar or the same. In different regions of southern India, for example, harvesting rice is men's work, shared work, or women's work: "Wherever a task is done by women it is considered easy, and where it is done by [men] it is considered difficult" (Mencher 1988, 104). A gathering and hunting society's survival usually depends on the nuts, grubs, and small animals brought in by the women's foraging trips, but when the men's hunt is successful, it is the occasion for a celebration. Conversely, because they are the superior group, white men do not have to do the "dirty work," such as housework; the most inferior group does it, usually poor women of color (Palmer 1989).

Freudian psychoanalytic theory claims that boys must reject their mothers and deny the feminine in themselves in order to become men: "For boys the major goal is the achievement of personal masculine identification with their father and sense of secure masculine self, achieved through superego formation and disparagement of women" (Chodorow 1978, 165). Masculinity may be the outcome of boys' intrapsychic struggles to separate their identity from that of their mothers, but the proofs of masculinity are culturally shaped and usually ritualistic and symbolic (Gilmore 1990).

The Marxist feminist explanation for gender inequality is that by demeaning women's abilities and keeping them from learning valuable technological skills, bosses preserve them as a cheap and exploitable reserve army of labor. Unionized men who could be easily replaced by women collude in this process because it allows them to monopolize the better paid, more interesting, and more autonomous jobs: "Two factors emerge as helping men maintain their separation from women and their control of technological occupations. One is the active gendering of jobs and people. The second is the continual creation of sub-divisions in the work processes, and levels in work hierarchies, into which men can move in order to keep their distance from women" (Cockburn 1985, 13).

Societies vary in the extent of the inequality in social status of their women and men members, but where there is inequality, the status "woman" (and its attendant behavior and role allocations) is usually held in lesser esteem than the status "man." Since gender is also intertwined with a society's other constructed statuses of differential evaluation—race, religion, occupation, class, country of origin, and so on—men and women members of the favored groups command more power, more prestige, and more property than the members of the disfavored groups. Within many social groups, however, men are advantaged over women. The more economic resources, such as education and job opportunities, are available to a group, the more they tend to be monopolized by men. In poorer groups that have few resources (such as working-class African Americans in the United States), women and men are more nearly equal, and the women may even outstrip the men in education and occupational status (Almquist 1987).

As a *structure,* gender divides work in the home and in economic production, legitimates those in authority, and organizes sexuality and emotional life (Connell 1987, 91–142). As primary parents, women significantly influence children's psychological development and emotional attachments, in the process reproducing gender. Emergent sexuality is shaped by heterosexual, homosexual, bisexual, and sadomasochistic patterns that are gendered—different for girls and boys, and for women and men—so that sexual statuses reflect gender statuses.

When gender is a major component of structured inequality, the devalued genders have less power, prestige, and economic rewards than the valued genders. In countries that discourage gender discrimination, many major roles are still gendered; women still do most of the domestic labor and child rearing, even while doing full-time paid work; women and men are segregated on the job and each does work considered "appropriate"; women's work is usually paid less than men's work. Men dominate the positions of authority and leadership in government, the military, and the law; cultural productions, religions, and sports reflect men's interests.

In societies that create the greatest gender difference, such as Saudi Arabia, women are kept out of sight behind walls or veils, have no civil rights, and often create a cultural and emotional world of their own (Bernard 1981). But even in societies with less rigid gender boundaries, women and men spend much of their time with people of their own gender because of the way work and family are organized. This spatial separation of women and men reinforces gendered differentness, identity, and ways of thinking and behaving (Coser 1986).

Gender inequality—the devaluation of "women" and the social domination of "men"—has social functions and a social history. It is not the result of sex, procreation, physiology, anatomy, hormones, or genetic predispositions. It is produced and maintained by identifiable social processes and built into the general social structure and individual identities deliberately and purposefully. The social order as we know it in Western societies is organized around racial ethnic, class, and gender inequality. I contend, therefore, that the continuing purpose of gender as a modern social institution is to construct women as a group to be the subordinates of men as a group. The life of everyone placed in the status "woman" is "night to his day—that has forever been the fantasy. Black to his white. Shut out of his system's space, she is the repressed that ensures the system's functioning" (Cixous and Clément [1975] 1986, 67).

THE PARADOX OF HUMAN NATURE

To say that sex, sexuality, and gender are all socially constructed is not to minimize their social power. These categorical imperatives govern our lives in the most profound and pervasive ways, through the social experiences and social practices of what Dorothy Smith calls the "everyday / everynight world" (1990, 31–57). The paradox of human nature is that it is *always* a manifestation of cultural meanings, social relationships, and power politics; "not biology, but culture, becomes destiny" (J. Butler 1990, 8). Gendered people emerge not from physiology or sexual orientation but from the exigencies of the social order, mostly, from the need for a reliable division of the work of food production and the social (not physical) reproduction of new members. The moral imperatives of religion and cultural representations guard the boundary lines among genders and ensure that what is demanded, what is permitted, and what is tabooed for the people in each gender is well known and followed by most (C. Davies

1982). Political power, control of scarce resources, and, if necessary, violence uphold the gendered social order in the face of resistance and rebellion. Most people, however, voluntarily go along with their society's prescriptions for those of their gender status, because the norms and expectations get built into their sense of worth and identity as a think, the way we see and hear and speak, the way we fantasy, and the way we feel.

There is no core or bedrock human nature below these endlessly looping processes of the social production of sex and gender, self and other, identity and psyche, each of which is a "complex cultural construction" (J. Butler 1990, 36). *For humans, the social is the natural.* Therefore, "in its feminist senses, gender cannot mean simply the cultural appropriation of biological sexual difference. Sexual difference is itself a fundamental—and scientifically contested—construction. Both 'sex' and 'gender' are woven of multiple, asymmetrical strands of difference, charged with multifaceted dramatic narratives of domination and struggle" (Haraway 1990, 140).

NOTES

1. Gender is, in Erving Goffman's words, an aspect of *Felicity's Condition:* "any arrangement which leads us to judge an individual's . . . acts not to be a manifestation of strangeness. Behind Felicity's Condition is our sense of what it is to be sane" (1983, 27). Also see Bem 1993; Frye 1983, 17–140; Goffman 1977.
2. In cases of ambiguity in countries with modern medicine, surgery is usually performed to make the genitalia more clearly male or female.
3. See J. Butler 1990 for an analysis of how doing gender *is* gender identity.
4. Douglas 1973; MacCormack 1980; Ortner 1974; Ortner and Whitehead 1981a; Yanagisako and Collier 1987. On the social construction of childhood, see Ariès 1962; Zelizer 1985.
5. On the hijras of India, see Nanda 1990; on the xaniths of Oman, Wikan 1982, 168–86; on the American Indian berdaches, W. L. Williams 1986. Other societies that have similar institutionalized third-gender men are the Koniag of Alaska, the Tanala of Madagascar, the Mesakin of Nuba, and the Chukchee of Siberia (Wikan 1982, 170).
6. Durova 1989; Freeman and Bond 1992; Wheelwright 1989.
7. Gender segregation of work in popular music still has not changed very much, according to Groce and Cooper 1989, despite considerable androgyny in some very popular figures. See Garber 1992 on the androgyny. She discusses Tipton on pp. 67–70.
8. In the nineteenth century, not only did these women get men's wages, but they also "had male privileges and could do all manner of things other women could not: open a bank account, write checks, own property, go anywhere unaccompanied, vote in elections" (Faderman 1991, 44).
9. When unisex clothing and men wearing long hair came into vogue in the United States in the mid-1960s, beards and mustaches for men also came into style again as gender identifications.
10. For other accounts of women being treated as men in Islamic countries, as well as accounts of women and men cross-dressing in these countries, see Garber 1992, 304–52.
11. Dollimore 1986; Garber 1992, 32–40; Greenblatt 1987, 66–93; Howard 1988. For Renaissance accounts of sexual relations with women and men of ambiguous sex, see Laqueur

1990a, 134–39. For modern accounts of women passing as men that other women find sexually attractive, see Devor 1989, 136–37; Wheelwright 1989, 53–59.

12. Females who passed as men soldiers had to "do masculinity," not just dress in a uniform (Wheelwright 1989, 50–78). On the triple entendres and gender resonances of Rosalind-type characters, see Garber 1992, 71–77.

13. Also see Garber 1992, 234–66.

14. Bolin describes how many documents have to be changed by transsexuals to provide a legitimizing "paper trail" (1988, 145–47). Note that only members of the same social group know which names are women's and which men's in their culture, but many documents list "sex."

15. For an account of how a potential man-to-woman transsexual learned to be feminine, see Garfinkel 1967, 116–85, 285–88. For a gloss on this account that points out how, throughout his encounters with Agnes, Garfinkel failed to see how he himself was constructing his own masculinity, see Rogers 1992.

16. Paige and Paige (1981, 147–49) argue that circumcision ceremonies indicate a father's loyalty to his lineage elders—"visible public evidence that the head of a family unit of their lineage is willing to trust others with his and his family's most valuable political asset, his son's penis" (147). On female circumcision, see El Dareer 1982; Lightfoot-Klein 1987; van der Kwaak 1992; Walker 1992. There is a form of female circumcision that removes only the prepuce of the clitoris and is similar to male circumcision, but most forms of female circumcision are far more extensive, mutilating, and spiritually and psychologically shocking than the usual form of male circumcision. However, among the Australian aborigines, boys' penises are slit and kept open, so that they urinate and bleed the way women do (Bettelheim 1962, 165–206).

17. The concepts of moral hegemony, the effects of everyday activities (praxis) on thought and personality, and the necessity of consciousness of these processes before political change can occur are all based on Marx's analysis of class relations.

18. Other societies recognize more than two categories, but usually no more than three or four (Jacobs and Roberts 1989).

19. Carol Barkalow's book has a photograph of eleven first-year West Pointers in a math class, who are dressed in regulation pants, shirts, and sweaters, with short haircuts. The caption challenges the reader to locate the only woman in the room.

20. The taboo on males and females looking alike reflects the U.S. military's homophobia (Bérubé 1989). If you can't tell those with a penis from those with a vagina, how are you going to determine whether their sexual interest is heterosexual or homosexual unless you watch them having sexual relations?

21. Garber feels that *Tootsie* is not about feminism but about transvestism and its possibilities for disturbing the gender order (1992, 5–9).

22. See Bolin 1988, 149–50, for transsexual men-to-women's discovery of the dangers of rape and sexual harassment. Devor's "gender blenders" went in the opposite direction. Because they found that it was an advantage to be taken for men, they did not deliberately cross-dress, but they did not feminize themselves either (1989, 126–40).

23. See West and Zimmerman 1987 for a similar set of gender components.

24. On the "logic of practice," or how the experience of gender is embedded in the norms of everyday interaction and the structure of formal organizations, see Acker 1990; Bourdieu [1980] 1990; Connell 1987; Smith 1987a.

REFERENCES

Acker, Joan. 1990. Hierarchies, jobs, and bodies: A theory of gendered organizations. *Gender & Society* 4: 139–58.

Almquist, Elizabeth M. 1987. Labor market gendered inequality in minority groups. *Gender & Society* 1:400–14.

Amadiume, Ifi. 1987. *Male daughters, female husbands: Gender and sex in an African society.* London: Zed Books.

Ariès, Philippe. 1962. *Centuries of childhood: A social history of family life,* translated by Robert Baldick. New York: Vintage.

Austad, Steven N. 1986. Changing sex nature's way. *International Wildlife.* May–June, 29.

Barkalow, Carol, with Andrea Raab. 1990. *In the men's house.* New York: Poseidon Press.

Bem, Sandra Lipsitz. 1981. Gender schema theory: A cognitive account of sex typing. *Psychological Review* 88:354–64.

———. 1983. Gender schema theory and its implications for child development: Raising gender-aschematic children in a gender-schematic society. *Signs* 8:598–616.

———. 1993. *The lenses of gender: Transforming the debate on sexual inequality.* New Haven: Yale University Press.

Bernard, Jessie. 1981. *The female world.* New York: Free Press.

Bernstein, Richard. 1986. France jails 2 in odd case of espionage. *New York Times,* 11 May.

Bérubé, Allan. 1989. Marching to a different drummer: Gay and lesbian GIs in World War II. In Duberman, Vicinus, and Chauncey.

Bettelheim, Bruno. 1962. *Symbolic wounds: Puberty rites and the envious male.* London: Thames and Hudson.

Biersack, Aletta. 1984. Paiela "women-men": The reflexive foundations of gender ideology. *American Ethnologist* 11: 118–38.

Birdwhistell, Ray I. 1970. *Kinesics and context: Essays on body motion communication.* Philadelphia: University of Pennsylvania Press.

Blackwood, Evelyn. 1984. Sexuality and gender in certain Native American tribes: The case of cross-gender females. *Signs* 10:27–42.

Bolin, Anne. 1987. Transsexualism and the limits of traditional analysis. *American Behavioral Scientist* 31:41–65.

———. 1988. *In search of Eve: Transsexual rites of passage.* South Hadley, Mass.: Bergin & Garvey.

Bourdieu, Pierre. [1980] 1990. *The logic of practice.* Stanford, Calif.: Stanford University Press.

Brody, Jane E. 1979. Benefits of transsexual surgery disputed as leading hospital halts the procedure. *New York Times,* 2 October.

Butler, Judith. 1990. *Gender trouble: Feminism and the subversion of identity.* New York and London: Routledge.

Chodorow, Nancy. 1974. Family structure and feminine personality. In Rosaldo and Lamphere.

———. 1978. *The reproduction of mothering.* Berkeley: University of California Press.

Cixous, Helène, and Catherine Clément. [1975] 1986. *The newly born woman,* translated by Betsy Wing. Minneapolis: University of Minnesota Press.

Cockburn, Cynthia. 1985. *Machinery of dominance: Women, men and technical know-how.* London: Pluto Press.

Collins, Patricia Hill. 1990. *Black feminist thought: Knowledge, consciousness, and the politics of empowerment.* Boston: Unwin Hyman.

Connell, R. [Robert] W. 1987. *Gender and power: Society, the person, and sexual politics.* Stanford, Calif.: Stanford University Press.

Coser, Rose Laub. 1986. Cognitive structure and the use of social space. *Sociological Forum* 1:1–26.

Davies, Christie. 1982. Sexual taboos and social boundaries. *American Journal of Sociology* 87: 1032–63.

De Beauvoir, Simone 1953. *The second sex,* translated by H. M. Parshley. New York: Knopf.

Devor, Holly. 1987. Gender blending females: Women and sometimes men. *American Behavioral Scientist* 31:12–40.

———. 1989. *Gender blending: Confronting the limits of duality.* Bloomington: Indiana University Press.

Dollimore, Jonathan. 1986. Subjectivity, sexuality, and transgression: The Jacobean connection. *Renaissance Drama,* n.s. 17:53–81.

Douglas, Mary. 1973. *Natural symbols.* New York: Vintage.

Durova, Nadezhda. 1989. *The cavalry maiden: Journals of a Russian officer in the Napoleonic Wars,* translated by Mary Fleming Zirin. Bloomington: Indiana University Press.

Eichler, Margrit. 1989. Sex change operations: The last bulwark of the double standard. In Richardson and Taylor.

El Dareer, Asma. 1982. *Woman, why do you weep? Circumcision and its consequences.* London: Zed Books.

Epstein, Cynthia Fuchs. 1988. *Deceptive distinctions: Sex, gender and the social order:* New. Haven: Yale University Press.

Faderman, Lillian. 1991. *Odd girls and twilight lovers: A history of lesbian life in twentieth-century America.* New York: Columbia University Press.

Foucault, Michel. 1972. *The archeology of knowledge and the discourse on language,* translated by A.M. Sheridan Smith. New York: Pantheon.

Freeman, Lucy, and Alma Halbert Bond. 1992. *America's first woman warrior: The courage of Deborah Sampson.* New York: Paragon.

Frye, Marilyn. 1983. *The politics of reality: Essays in feminist theory.* Trumansburg, N.Y.: Crossing Press.

Garber, Marjorie. 1992. *Vested interests: Cross-dressing and cultural anxiety.* New York and London: Routledge.

Garfinkel, Harold. 1967. *Studies in ethnomethodology.* Englewood Cliffs, N.J.: Prentice-Hall.

Gilmore, David D. 1990. *Manhood in the making: Cultural concepts of masculinity.* New Haven: Yale University Press.

Goffman, Erving. 1977. The arrangement between the sexes. *Theory and Society* 4:301–33.

———. 1983. Felicity's condition. *American Journal of Sociology* 89:1–53.

Gordon, Tuula. 1990. *Feminist mothers.* New York: New York University Press.

Gould, Lois. 1972. X: A fabulous child's story. *Ms. Magazine,* December, 74–76, 105–06.

Gramsci, Antonio. 1971 *Selections from the prison notebooks,* translated and edited by Quintin Hoare and Geoffrey Nowell Smith. New York: International Publishers.

Greenblatt, Stephen. 1987. *Shakespearean negotiations: The circulation of social energy in Renaissance England.* Berkeley: University of California Press.

Groce, Stephen B., and Margaret Cooper. 1990. Just me and the boys? Women in local-level rock and roll. *Gender & Society* 4:220–29.

Haraway, Donna. 1978a. Animal sociology and a natural economy of the body politic. Part I: A political physiology of dominance. *Signs* 4:21–36.

——. 1990. Investment strategies for the evolving portfolio of primate females. In Jacobus, Keller, and Shuttleworth.

Howard, Jean E. 1988. Crossdressing, the theater, and gender struggle in early modern England. *Shakespeare Quarterly* 39:418–41.

Hwang, David Henry. 1989. *M Butterfly*. New York: New American Library.

Jacobs, Sue-Ellen, and Christine Roberts. 1989. Sex, sexuality, gender, and gender variance. In *Gender and anthropology*, edited by Sandra Morgen. Washington, D.C.: American Anthropological Association.

Jay, Nancy. 1981. Gender and dichotomy. *Feminist Studies* 7:38–56.

Kando, Thomas. 1973. *Sex change: The achievement of gender identity among feminized transsexuals*. Springfield, Ill.: Charles C Thomas.

Keller, Evelyn Fox. 1985. *Reflections on gender and science*. New Haven: Yale University Press.

Kincaid, Jamaica. 1978. Girl. *The New Yorker*, 26 June.

Kondo, Dorinne K. 1990b. *M. Butterfly*: Orientalism, gender, and a critique of essentialist identity. *Cultural Critique*, no. 16 (Fall):5–29.

Lancaster, Jane Beckman. 1974. *Primate behavior and the emergence of human culture*. New York: Holt, Rinehart and Winston.

Laqueur, Thomas. 1990. *Making sex: Body and gender from the Greeks to Freud*. Cambridge, Mass.: Harvard University Press.

Lévi-Strauss, Claude. 1956. The family. In *Man, culture, and society*, edited by Harry L. Shapiro. New York: Oxford.

——. [1949] 1969. *The elementary structures of kinship*, translated by J. H. Bell and J. R. von Sturmer. Boston: Beacon Press.

Lightfoot-Klein, Hanny. 1989. *Prisoners of ritual: An odyssey into female circumcision in Africa*. New York: Harrington Park Press.

MacCormack, Carol P. 1980. Nature, culture and gender: A critique. In *Nature, culture and gender*, edited by Carol P. MacCormack and Marilyn Strathern. Cambridge, England: Cambridge University Press.

Matthaei, Julie A. 1982. *An economic history of women's work in America*. New York: Schocken.

Mencher, Joan. 1988. Women's work and poverty: Women's contribution to household maintenance in South India. In Dwyer and Bruce.

Money, John, and Anke A. Ehrhardt. 1972. *Man & woman, boy & girl*. Baltimore, Md.: Johns Hopkins University Press.

Morris, Jan. 1975. *Conundrum*. New York: Signet.

Nanda, Serena. 1990. *Neither man nor woman: The hijiras of India*. Belmont, Calif.: Wadsworth.

Ortner, Sherry B. 1974. Is female to male as nature is to culture? In Rosaldo and Lamphere.

Ortner, Sherry B., and Harriet Whitehead. 1981. Introduction: Accounting for sexual meanings. In Ortner and Whitehead (eds.).

Paige, Karen Ericksen, and Jeffrey M. Paige 1981. *The politics of reproductive ritual*. Berkeley: University of California Press.

Palmer, Phyllis. 1989. *Domesticity and dirt: Housewives and domestic servants in the United States, 1920–1945*. Philadelphia: Temple University Press.

Papanek, Hanna. 1979. Family status production: The "work" and "non-work" of women. *Signs* 4:775–81.

Raymond, Janice G. 1979. *The transsexual empire: The making of the she-male*. Boston: Beacon Press.

Reskin, Barbara F. 1988. Bringing the men back in: Sex differentiation and the devaluation of women's work. *Gender & Society* 2:58–81.

Rogers, Mary F. 1992. They were all passing: Agnes, Garfinkel, and company. *Gender & Society* 6: 169–91.

Rubin, Gayle. 1975. The traffic in women: Notes on the political economy of sex. In *Toward an anthropology of women,* edited by Rayna R[app] Reiter. New York: Monthly Review Press.

Rugh, Andrea B. 1986. *Reveal and conceal: Dress in contemporary Egypt.* Syracuse, N.Y.: Syracuse University Press.

Scott, Joan Wallach. 1988. *Gender and the politics of history.* New York: Columbia University Press.

Showalter, Elaine. 1987. Critical cross-dressing: Male feminists and the woman of the year. In *Men in feminism,* edited by Alice Jardine and Paul Smith. New York: Methuen.

Sidel, Ruth. 1972. *Women and child care in China: A firsthand report.* New York: Hill and Wang.

Smith, Dorothy E. 1987. *The everyday world as problematic: A feminist sociology.* Toronto: University of Toronto Press.

———. 1990. *The conceptual practices of power: A feminist sociology of knowledge.* Toronto: University of Toronto Press.

van der Kwaak, Anke. 1992. Female circumcision and gender identity: A questionable alliance? *Social Science and Medicine* 35:777–87.

Van Gennep, Arnold. 1960. *The rites of passage,* translated by Monika B. Vizedom and Gabrielle L. Caffee. Chicago: University of Chicago Press.

Walker, Alice. 1992. *Possessing the secret of joy.* New York: Harcourt Brace Jovanovich.

West, Candace, and Don Zimmerman. 1987. Doing gender. *Gender & Society* 1:125–51.

Wheelwright, Julie. 1989. *Amazons and military maids: Women who cross-dressed in pursuit of life, liberty and happiness.* London: Pandora Press.

Whitehead, Harriet. 1981. The bow and the burden strap: A new look at institutionalized homosexuality in native North America. In Ortner and Whitehead (eds.).

Wikan, Unni. 1982. *Behind the veil in Arabia: Women in Oman.* Baltimore, Md: Johns Hopkins University Press, 1982.

Williams, Christine L. 1989. *Gender differences at work: Women and men in nontraditional occupations.* Berkeley: University of California Press.

Williams, Walter L. 1986. *The spirit and the flesh: Sexual diversity in American Indian culture.* Boston: Beacon Press.

Yanagisako, Sylvia Junko, and Jane Fishburne Collier. 1987. Toward a unified analysis of gender and kinship. In *Gender and kinship: Essays toward a unified analysis,* edited by Jane Fishburne Collier and Sylvia Junko Yanagisako. Berkeley: University of California Press.

Zelizer, Viviana A. 1985. *Pricing the priceless child: The changing social value of children.* New York: Basic Books.

REVIEW QUESTIONS

1. Do all **societies** have only two **genders**? Explain your answer in detail.

2. Lorber argues that **gender roles** have changed over the years with men and women being freer to engage in behaviors that used to be solely in the realm of the other gender. Do you agree with her?

3. If society has clearly defined gender expectations, then these expectations must be clearly communicated to the public at large. How do we communicate our gender expectations to boys, girls, men, and women? What happens when a female acts masculine or when a male acts feminine?

4. Watch a half hour of a children's television program. As you watch write down the basic plot of the story and describe which characters are driving the story (that is, moving it forward by initiating action). See if you see any **stereotypical** role assignments based on gender. Are boys displayed as active and girls passive? Explain in detail. (*Note*: If the show you pick doesn't have human characters you may want to pick another show).

PEPPER SCHWARTZ

Why Is Everyone Afraid of Sex?

n spite of the visibility of sex in the **media** and **popular culture**, despite a widespread acceptance of a variety of sexual practices, Americans still hold a deep-rooted fear of sex, according to Pepper Schwartz. In this article, she argues that Americans are more sexually constrained than liberated, more miserable than happy, and more misinformed than informed in American **society** than it appears. The acceptance of abstinence-only sexual **education** and **laws** outlawing sexual toys designed for women's sexual pleasure point to the existence of a **cultural** fear of sex. Schwartz explores reasons for this fear and suggests ways to overcome it.

WE ALL KNOW THAT SEXUALITY IS A PART OF COURTSHIP AND marriage. It goes without saying (I hope) to say it is critical, although I suppose not absolutely necessary, for reproduction. Eggs can be fertilized in a laboratory and inserted into a uterus, but most of us, if we can, prefer to become pregnant in the old-fashioned way. We flirt, we seduce, we touch, we make love in various ways, or sometimes we see sexuality as an appetite, which can be used merely to satisfy an urge. Most people think sex is most fulfilling when it is part of an expression of profound love. To put it another way, sexuality is an elemental aspect of being attracted to someone, choosing a partner, establishing or maintaining a relationship, and creating a family. It is part of our lives from childhood to old age. That said, *I believe sex is also something we are deeply afraid of.* Why is that so?

Before I begin my argument to support that statement and answer that question, I should admit that there is evidence to the contrary. Perhaps you think so too. You could, fairly, offer the following arguments.

First, look at popular culture. The media, print, Internet, movies, and television are saturated with sex. The Internet pushes the tolerance of community standards with access to exotic pornography and also allows smaller communities of people with specific sexual preferences (such as foot fetishists or swingers) to find and mingle with one another. Television titillates in almost every show, whether it is an adventure story, a soap opera ("is Brad *really* the long lost adopted brother of his lover?"), or just dancing (take a look at the costumes of the women competitors on *Dancing with the Stars,* for example). Advertising and marketing use sex both subliminally (such as showing a gorgeous woman stroking a car) or blatantly, such as Calvin Klein ads where sultry teenagers have their jeans unbuttoned to show just a little bit more of their long, lean torsos. And if that doesn't convince, you might remember the ads for Viagra and Cialis, where famous men endorse the erectile dysfunction product, or silver-haired men and women are able to be "ready when the time is right." The media doesn't seem too fearful, does it?

Second, what about actual behavior among young people? The statistics on premarital sexuality would seem to belie the title of this paper. A number of studies talk about the "decoupling of relationship status and sex" and the earlier entrance of young women into sexual intercourse, resulting in more sexual partners over a lifetime. Multiple short-term relationships and transitory cohabiting relationships[1] also help increase the number of sexual encounters in men's and women's premarital or nonmarital lives. Proponents of sexual freedom rather than restriction could also point out the relatively new phenomenon of "hooking up," a term adolescents and young adults use to describe brief and spontaneous interaction in noncommitted encounters that could encompass everything from just hanging out together to intercourse.[2]

Third, but isn't everyone doing everything? Yes, that's true too. There is a widening acceptance of different sexual behaviors, and a decrease in racial, age, class, and gender differences in terms of who is doing what.[3] There are many taboos that have been broached, not the least of which is the appearance of proudly "out" lesbians and gay men on national television, their relationships and sexual preferences interwoven into the story line of prime-time television (i.e., *Will and Grace*) and some indication that bisexual behavior is more acceptable and more common than it might ever have been, at least among young people.[4]

Still, while I agree with all these points, I still believe that we are more sexually constrained than liberated, more miserable than happy, and more misinformed than informed in American society than it would appear. And here are the issues and circumstances that support my position: (1) a national policy that underfunds or ignores comprehensive sex education and supports abstinence education, (2) a number of laws across our country that specifically outlaw sexual pleasure, and (3) our continued queasiness about homosexuality and continued insistence on a dichotomous view of sexuality.

ABSTINENCE EDUCATION

With any luck, this will change, but at the present time, Congress has systematically increased funding for programs and for a philosophy that is not supported by any credible research. Funding for abstinence started in 1997 at the cost of $9 million. At the time of this writing, the government has spent over $1 billion chasing a horse that left the barn so long ago that the manure has turned to topsoil.[5]

Complaints about the government's abstinence programs have come from Planned Parenthood, SIECUS (the Sexuality Information and Education Council of the United States), individual sex educators, state governments that resisted taking abstinence money but needed funding for sex education, and parents who want their children to hear more than "just say no." In 2004, Henry Waxman, a congressman from California, chaired congressional hearings on the efficacy of abstinence programs that, by definition, do not give any information on contraception, on sexual decision making once sexual behavior exists, or is desired, or in fact, accurate information on the consequences of sexual behavior. After reviewing the abstinence materials gathered from many states, Waxman concluded, "Over 80% of the Abstinence Only curricula used by $2/3$ of federally funded programs contain false, misleading or distorted information about reproductive health."

Waxman relied on some excellent research to come to his other conclusion: that the programs didn't accomplish their own goal—to keep young men and women (indeed, all men and women) abstinent until marriage. A well-done and well-publicized 2001 study by Bearman and Brückner looked at data on 20,000 students who had taken abstinence pledges and found that only 12 percent kept their promise. They did wait longer to have intercourse, but since they were significantly less likely than people who had had a comprehensive sex education to use condoms when they did have sex, they were as likely to get a sexually transmitted infection as people who had not made virginity pledges or had abstinence education.[6]

So here we have a paradox. The majority of unmarried people are having intercourse or some kind of genital sexuality before marriage. Only a small number of people intend to wait until marriage for sex, and most of them do not accomplish that goal. Still, legislators vote for programs that have been found to be ineffective because, I imagine, they believe this is the safest course for them to pursue. Why would they do this when there is a tidal wave of research indicating that abstinence education doesn't work? Why would they fund programs whose material is full of falsehoods such as teaching that premarital sexuality is likely to cause psychological and physical problems and that abstinence from sexual activity before marriage is the expected standard for all males and females in the United States!?

My answer is that *American parents are extremely uneasy with the idea of young people being sexual and acting sexually.* Even though the parents of teenagers were unlikely to have been sexually abstinent themselves, they are uneasy about endorsing any kind of sexual behavior for their children. If this were not true, they would be fighting tooth and nail to get their kids really good sex education that included the proper use of contraception. I think adults in America still think that sex is dangerous for youth—emotionally, physically, and morally. While they "handled it" (or not) themselves, they do not feel their sixteen-year-old is capable of good sexual choices. Meanwhile, of course, their sixteen-year-old is making sexual choices anyhow (about half of them will already have had intercourse) but without proper education about what kinds of information and self-knowledge should go into decision making or physical and mental safety. While there is a lot of sexiness on television (some of which is directed at *very* young people; for example, the 2008 singing group called Cliz, girls aged eleven to fourteen, sexily clad and coiffed, appearing on the *Today Show,* June 17, 2008), no network at this time will accept condom ads! Does this sound like a sexually sane or comfortable nation to you?

LAWS OUTLAWING SEXUAL PLEASURE

It is amazing that in this period that allows so much sexual license and freedom of choice, that there are laws that prohibit the way we become sexually excited. There are a number of ridiculous laws in this category, but for purposes of discussion, let me refer to the one that I find the most ludicrous. At present, though this may fluctuate since some of these laws are under attack, about six states outlaw the sale of vibrators. I know this is hard to believe, but legislators in the states of Alabama, Georgia, Texas, Mississippi, Arkansas, and Kansas have decided that vibrators are dangerous to American morality. I was an expert witness in cases in Alabama and Georgia, and I have followed the Texas case. Legislators denounced vibrators (or any nonhuman device used for sexual stimulation) as obscene and passed legislation to outlaw their sale. In these states, owners of small businesses that sold erotic toys, books, and lotions were persecuted and prosecuted. The Texas law was recently overturned, and after many twists and turns in court it looks like the Alabama law has also been overturned. (It is hard to know because some of these results are either under appeal or an appeal is being considered.) But the fact is that legally elected officials in these states felt that prosecuting sex shops would be a popular stance and legislators that disagreed (or were afraid to come out in favor of vibrators) were in the minority.

Isn't this more than a bit odd? When I testified in favor of vibrators, I could not base my testimony on the mere fact that vibrating devices felt great or that women deserved to have better or quicker orgasms any way they wanted to as long as their sexual pleasure was not endangering minors or pressuring an unwilling adult. No, the astute legal team felt the best approach was to defend vibrators as medical devices because they were useful for nonorgasmic women who had to learn how to have an orgasm. We took that approach and ultimately, had success with it. But it struck me, why would a sexually liberated society tolerate the control—and criminalization—of the lowly vibrator? Surely, this is in direct contradiction to other kinds of sexual license as portrayed in the media and as illustrated by sexual behavior. I could only come up with one hypothesis that seemed powerful enough to explain all the money and legal maneuvering that took place—a continuing fear of women's sexuality unless it related to either reproduction or men.

The idea of unpartnered sex is deeply frightening to many sectors of American society. Pleasurable sex is allowed if it is in the service of reproduction—or the attainment or maintenance of marriage. But when it allows women to have alternatives to men (or any partner) and, indeed, when there is the fear that the vibrator may not only be equivalent but perhaps superior to the pleasure produced by intercourse or other kinds of stimulation, then it becomes a public menace. We seem to believe in love and union, but not pleasure for its own sake. This prudish stance stands in the face of the obvious natural tendency of humans to masturbate and small children to touch themselves, unconsciously, and happily, unless criticized. Most boys and a significant number of girls teach themselves how to masturbate to orgasm, often before puberty.[7] And yet this has long been a tabooed activity. Even in the history of the last 100 years of Western civilization, children have had their hands tied to prevent touching themselves and, at the turn of the century, clitorectomies (surgical removal of the clitoris) were recommended by doctors who feared that masturbation or sexual interest by young women was a form of insanity.[8] One would think we had progressed far from those days, but perhaps we have not come as far as it would seem. Not so long ago, Joycelyn Elders, surgeon general under President Bill Clinton, was dismissed by Clinton because she said that she thought children should be taught about masturbation so that they would delay the complications that could ensue from precocious intercourse. Do you think the outcome would be different if a current surgeon general said the same thing?[9]

ATTITUDES TOWARD HOMOSEXUALITY

While there is much more acceptance of homosexuality and homosexuals than there has ever been, opinion is still split over whether or not homosexual relations between consenting adults should be legal. More encouraging is the fact that a clear majority of the public is comfortable with a gay doctor or teacher.[10] Debate has been particularly acrimonious, however, when it comes to the issue of gay marriage and gay union.

though somewhat less bitter for domestic partnerships, since rights for domestic partnership are not exactly the same as rights for heterosexual marriage and it is not called "marriage."[11] After decades of political activism by gay rights leaders and civil libertarians of various sexual orientations, there has been some political movement, such as fair housing and employment laws for homosexuals in various cities and states in the United States, and most recently, the legal right to get married in Massachusetts, Connecticut, Iowa, Vermont, and Maine. The Supreme Court of California had also ruled in favor of legalizing same-sex marriage, but this right was rescinded in California in November 2008 after the "yes" vote on Proposition 8 changed the state constitution to restrict marriage to opposite-sex couples. Personal feelings about homosexuality retain a kind of fear far beyond expectation, particularly as stereotypes about homosexual predatory behavior have been dismissed or diminished. One of the interesting ways we deal with this fear is to ignore what we know to be true about the extent of casual or intermittent attraction to members of our own sex and instead create a dichotomous category (either homosexual or heterosexual) of sexual orientation, regardless of this information to the contrary. In the late 1940s, the famous study by Alfred Kinsey[12] created the Kinsey scale, a 0 to 6 scale of sexual orientation, with 0 being people who had absolutely no experience with homosexual relations and 6 being people who had absolutely no heterosexual experience. Later academic books (for example, McWhirter, Sanders, Reinisch, 1990) have examined the scale and shown additional systematic ways to look at the breadth of same-sex experience (fantasy, love, identity). Still, the original contribution is important as created because it shows that there is a wide variety of homosexual experience that is not encapsulated in dichotomous terms. For example, Kinsey found that about a third of his male population had some kind of genital sexual experience with another man and about a fifth of the women had some kind of same-sex sexual contact.

Because homosexuality is stigmatized and used as a way of defaming individuals, it is not surprising that few men or women claim a middle place on the Kinsey continuum. Some women, particularly of late, have celebrated their bisexuality,[13] but few men feel safe in doing so. The politics of desire seems to offer some cover for female bisexuality but almost none for males. While females are conceived of being sexually labile, that is they can move back and forth between homosexuality and heterosexuality without having the latter impugned, men have quite the opposite situation. A man who has had one homosexual experience and fifty heterosexual ones is perceived to be in denial of his homosexuality. He is rarely seen as a bisexual or free sexual spirit.

The place of homosexuals in our society is still politically and personally unsafe; it can even be a life and death circumstance since strong fears and hatred of homosexuals have spawned violence and homicide. How can we begin to think of ourselves as a sexually secure nation when the mere mention of homosexuality or homosexual marriage ignites a firestorm of commentary, denial, or outrage?

SOURCES OF FEAR ABOUT SEXUALITY

These points lead me to turn to the bigger question: Why are so many individuals in the United States sexually frightened? I will discuss five of what I think are the main sources of fear: (1) religious indoctrination and tradition, (2) the double standard and patriarchal norms, (3) sexual transmission of disease, (4) cultural expectations about appearance and sexual competence, and (5) ostracism for not being masculine enough.

Religious Indoctrination and Tradition

Whatever the Bible says, (and scholars differ on their interpretations), the teachings of most religious institutions vary from conservative to extremely conservative views about sexual behavior.[14] Sex outside of marriage is often condemned, even if it is almost universal. Masturbation is not mentioned, or if it is, it is seen as sick or weak. The best most parishioners can hope for vis-à-vis homosexuality is a policy of tolerance and compassion. Usually any kind of same-sex sexual contact, or even just desire, is immediately condemned as immoral. The result of this generally negative or hushed approach toward sexuality is widespread guilt, shame, blame, horror, and anger at various populations of "sinners." At the individual level, many people trace their inhibitions, and inability to enjoy sexuality, to their religious training or background.[15]

While some religions are somewhat more supportive of marital sexuality (for example, orthodox Judaism clearly sees marital sexuality as a mitzvah, a blessing), there is still no toleration in ancient religious books for masturbation or homosexuality.

Double Standard and Patriarchal Norms

Our society has watched women's sexuality change to mirror men's sexuality. Women are now more likely to buy sex toys, to have sex before marriage, to "hook up," and to be overtly sexual in their presentation of self.[16] This drives a lot of people wild with apprehension and anger. To some, it puts the family, and even the nation, in jeopardy. Sexual freedom that includes sexual freedom for women is desired by men in the particular (i.e., personal access to sexually willing women), but it is decried in the general (social policy or public approval). In the United States, women are still threatened with the words "slut" or the amorphous "bad" reputation.[17] The double standard, greatly changed, still exists.[18]

In some parts of the world (particularly the Middle East), women are killed for sexuality outside of wedlock. These are called "honor killings" because the belief is that a woman who has had sex outside of marriage, even a woman who is raped against her will, creates a blot on the family name that can only be erased by her death. While this is not the practice in most of the world, it exists in Jordan, Egypt, Syria, Lebanon, Yemen, Iraq, Iran, Saudia Arabia, and a number of other countries, as well as among Israeli Arabs. For example, one 1995 government report in Egypt counted 52 honor killings out of a total of 819 murders. Yemen reported 400 such killings in 1997.[19] Until the mid-twentieth century in Texas, it was not illegal for a husband to kill his wife if he found her in bed with another man. No one suggested a reciprocal allowance for women. The idea of a free sexual life for women, equal to the privileges given to men, is still a very new, and to many people, troubling idea.

Association of Sexuality, Disease, and Death

Sexuality does require a certain amount of physical as well as emotional vulnerability. There is a sad history of sexually transmitted diseases.[20] Without prophylactic measures that could prevent transmission, centuries of sexually active men and women have suffered from debilitating and often fatal infections. Even when those prophylactic measures became more effective, availability, promotion, and consistent use of them has been limited.[21] When AIDS first emerged as a modern-day plague in the early 1980s, all the fears and hysteria of earlier periods of contagion reemerged, and frightened, angry moralists and policy makers reacted by blaming sex, gay men, and modern immorality for the deaths.[22] Influenza has also killed many people in its time, but when sexual transmission is added to a contagion, sex itself becomes the villain. Instead of concentrating on helping people avoid infection, policy makers, some religious leaders, and multiple moral entrepreneurs go on the attack, using the medical crisis to create a moral one. Instead of using the circumstances to create good public health initiatives such as helping sexually active people understand how to prevent most disease transmission, moral conservatives attack sex itself and condemn the very health practices that would make sex safer. Thus, in the very midst of an AIDS epidemic, government figures, religious leaders, and conservative action groups have condemned condoms, exaggerating their failure rate (which is actually quite small) and promoting the idea that condoms actually increase vulnerability to disease because they allow unmarried and gay people to have sex. Conservative forces do not want anyone but married, monogamous heterosexuals to have sex, and they refuse to accept the fact that teenagers, single adults, and gay and lesbian individuals are having sex, will continue to have sex, and need the best health protections they can get. The fact that sex is so obviously not restricted to the monogamously married anymore (if it ever was) has deepened the backlash of these morality police against all kinds of premarital and nonmonogamous sexuality.

Fear about Sexual Acceptability and Competence

We pretend that because sexuality is biological that it is easily accomplished. While some lucky people get sex education and, at a deeper level, advice and information about their own sexual quandaries and challenges, most of us learn, through trial and error, how to be what we hope is a good lover. At first it is just our attractiveness and acceptability that we worry about. Each period of recorded history has had normative evocations of what is beautiful, what is masculine or feminine, what is sexy or what is not.[23] The imagery is idealized, even iconic, rather than representative. Most female stars in movie scenes are tall, beautiful, and slim. Most male teenagers in ads have a "six pack," the name these days for chest and abdominal muscle definition. It is hard for the average person, however, to fit the media and model standard for sexual attractiveness, and a huge industry has grown up trying to make us recognize our imperfections so that we can buy goods and services to correct them. An enormous number of young men and women, and many people throughout the life cycle loathe their bodies, feel unlovable, and have no faith in their ability to make someone else sexually satisfied and emotionally faithful. As a result, there is often anger at all the sexual imagery—anger at how it makes us feel, anger at the standards we are oppressed by, and anxiety about whether or not we are sexually acceptable and whether or not we have a sex life that is "normal." As a result, we vacillate from condemning sex-saturated advertising and media content, to trying desperately to have a harder penis, more perfect breasts, or more instant orgasms.[24] So many people feel that cultural expectations about appearance and behavior are beyond their capacity or desire that many act out their fear by condemning the sexual behavior of others or personally retreating from sexual or romantic engagement.

Fears about Sexual Orientation

People have a variety of fantasies, sexual experiences, and crushes before they settle on a primary sexual identity. Because we are given only two categories of sexual being—heterosexual and homosexual—the presence of anything indicating homosexuality is extremely scary to people, particularly to men. Men are not only punished for anything that indicates femininity; they are also punished for not being heroically heterosexual (dating a lot, having sex with a succession of women, sporting a "six pack" chest, etc).[25] Anything, from being bad at athletics, to choosing not to have premarital sex with a girlfriend, could cause a man to be called a "fag" or some other nasty putdown. A teen does not have to be homosexual to be called a "fag." Rather, the word is often thrown at boys who are believed to be heterosexual but who are not enacting culturally adequate portrayals of masculine behavior in the way the peer group thinks "maleness" should look. Young men who not only fail at being heterosexual enough, but who are also believed to be homosexual, or who have stated that they are indeed homosexual, can still be in grave danger of ostracism.[26] Homophobic statements, and the fear that one might not be heterosexual, and the absence of any vision of another acceptable place on the Kinsey scale, creates a huge fear about one's sexual identity and performance of that identity. The literature on lesbians and gay men is consistent about how hard it is for young people with homosexual feelings to feel good about themselves and how much adult therapeutic work they often have to do to embrace their sexual selves. Fear about homosexuality and fear about any homosexual fantasies or experience creates fear in general about sexual identity, sexual preference, and sexual behavior.

CONCLUSION

For all the sexual imagery in American society, it seems clear that we are not at ease with our sexuality at either the policy or personal level. There are mixed signals in every realm. We sell everything from cars to toothpaste on television with sexual innuendo, but we cannot sell condoms during these same time slots. Women are now having almost as much sex as men before marriage, yet there is still a double standard. We have sex earlier, and it is normative to have sex before marriage, yet there is still guilt and shame and inadequate preparation for physical or emotional safety. We still have more trouble talking about sex than we do about doing it. We have a policy that does not fund comprehensive sexual education, even though half of all American teenagers are having intercourse by age sixteen and most parents are in favor of comprehensive sex education.[27] Fear, not comfort, lies only a few centimeters under our bravado and long lists of sexual partners.

The answer to all of this confusion and irrationality is clear but still oddly out of reach. We need to reduce sexual anxiety and ignorance through education. We can do that by using well-trained sex educators, researchers, and teachers to distribute scientific data and reassuring counsel to both children and their parents. This does not mean a sexual free-for-all. Far from it. It means giving valid sexual information and help in sexual decision making throughout the life cycle. It means recognizing that sexual desire is natural and that people of all ages need information and support to feel good enough about themselves, their bodies, and their sexual behavior, and to act responsibly and comfortably on their own behalf. It means legitimizing pleasure and giving people information about how to give it to themselves and others in honorable, honest, and safe ways. It means that we have to stop snickering about sex, or pontificating about it, and we need to make it part of our mental and social health curriculum from early childhood to late adulthood. This is not a new or brilliant idea; it is merely a rational one. Our culture is still afraid of sex, and it is in our individual interest, our family interests, and the interests of public health, to quash the toxic tactics that are aimed at creating sexual fears and instead to help make sexuality a source of happiness in our own life and in our intimate relationships.

NOTES

1. Laumann, Mahay, and Youm (2007).
2. Bogle (2008).
3. Laumann et al. (1994).
4. Baumgardner (2007).
5. Klein and Strossen (2006).
6. Bearman and Brückner (2001); Brückner and Bearman (2005).

7. Laumann et al. (1994).
8. Schwartz and Rutter (2000).
9. Klein and Strossen (2006).
10. Rom (2007).
11. Wilcox et al. (2007).
12. Kinsey, Pomeroy, and Clyde (1948).
13. Baumgardner (2007).
14. Campbell and Robinson (2007).
15. Reiss and Reiss (2002).
16. Kamen (2000).
17. Tannenbaum (1999).
18. Carpenter (2005).
19. Jehl (1999).
20. D'Emilio and Freedman (1988).
21. Brandt (1987).
22. Shilts (1987).
23. D'Emilio and Freedman (1988).
24. Tiefer (1995).
25. Schwartz (2007).
26. Pascoe (2007).
27. Boonstra (2009).

REFERENCES

Baumgardner, Jennifer. 2007. *Look Both Ways: Bisexual Politics.* New York: Farrar, Straus, and Giroux.

Bearman, Peter S., and Hannah Brückner. 2001. "Promising the Future: Virginity Pledges and the Transition to First Intercourse." *American Journal of Sociology* 106: 859–912.

Bogle, Kathleen A. 2008. *Hooking Up: Sex Dating and Relationships on Campus.* New York: New York University Press.

Boonstra, Heather D. 2009. "Advocates Call for a New Approach after the Era of 'Abstinence Only' Sex Education." Guttmacher Policy Review 12 (Winter).

Brandt, Allan. 1987. *No Magic Bullet: A Social History of Venereal Disease in the United States since 1880.* New York: Oxford University Press.

Brückner, Hannah, and Peter S. Bearman. 2005. "After the Promise: The STD Consequences of Adolescent Virginity Pledges." *Journal of Adolescent Health* 36: 271–278.

Campbell, D., and C. Robinson. 2007. "Religious Coalitions for and against Gay Marriage: The Culture War Rages On." Pp. 131–154 in *Politics of Gay Marriage.* Chicago: University of Chicago Press.

Carpenter, Laura M. 2005. *Virginity Lost.* New York: New York University Press.

D'Emilio, John, and Estelle B. Freedman. 1988. *Intimate Matters: A History of Sexuality in America.* New York: Harper and Row.

Jehl, Douglas. 1999. "For Shame: A Special Report; Arab Honor's Price: A Woman's Blood." *New York Times,* June 20.

Kamen, Paula. 2000. *Her Way: Young Women Remake the Sexual Revolution.* New York: New York University Press.

Kinsey, Alfred C., Wardell B. Pomeroy, and Martin, Clyde E. 1948. *Sexual Behavior in the Human Male.* Philadelphia: W. B. Saunders.

Klein, Marty, and Nadine Strossen. 2006. *America's War on Sex: The Attack on Law, Lust and Liberty.* Westport, CT: Praeger.

Lauman, Edward O., John H. Gagnon, Robert T. Michael, and Stuart Michaels. 1994. *The Social Organization of Sexuality: Sexual Practices in the United States.* Chicago: University of Chicago Press.

Laumann, Edward O., Jenna Mahay, and Yoosik Youm. 2007. "Sex, Intimacy, and Family Life in the United States." Pp. 165–190 in *The Sexual Self,* edited by Michael S. Kimmel. Nashville, TN: Vanderbilt University Press.

McWhirter, David P., Stephanie A. Sanders, and June M. Reinisch. 1990. *Homosexuality/Heterosexuality: Concepts of Sexual Orientation.* Kinsey Institute Series. New York: Oxford University Press.

Pascoe, C. J. 2007. *Dude, You're a Fag: Masculinity and Sexuality in High School.* Berkeley: CA: University of California Press.

Reiss, I., and H. Reiss. 2002. "The Role of Religion in Our Sexual Lives." In *Sexual Lives: A Reader on the Theories and Realities of Human Sexualities,* edited by Robert Heasley and Betsy Crane. New York: McGraw-Hill.

Rom, M. C. 2007. "Introduction." Pp. 1–38 in *The Politics of Same Sex Marriage,* edited by Craig Rimmerman and Clyde Wilcox. Chicago: University of Chicago Press.

Schwartz, Pepper. 2001. "The Social Construction of Heterosexuality." Pp. 80–92 in *The Sexual Self,* edited by Michael Kimmel. Nashville, TN: Vanderbilt University Press.

Schwartz, Pepper, and Virginia Rutter. 2000. *The Gender of Sexuality.* Lanham, MD: Alta Mira Press.

Shilts, Randy. 1987. *And the Band Played On.* New York: St. Martins Press.

Tannenbaum, Leora. 1999. *Slut! Growing Up Female With a Bad Reputation.* New York: Seven Stories Press.

Tiefer, Leonore. 1995. *Sex is Not A Natural Act and Other Essays.* Boulder, CO: Colorado Westview Press.

Wilcox, Clyde, P. Brewer, S. Shames, and C. Lake. 2007. "If I Bend This Far I Will Break? Public Opinion about Gay Marriage." Pp. 215–242 in *The Politics of Same Sex Marriage,* edited by Craig A. Rimmerman and Clyde Wilcox. Chicago: University of Chicago Press.

STUDY QUESTIONS

1. Why are Americans afraid of sex? Identify Schwartz's main arguments and give examples to highlight your response.

2. Schwartz lists three pieces of evidence that may support an argument that America has open and positive views about sex. Pick one of her examples and use evidence from her argument to analyze the ways in which these positive examples may falsely represent how America feels about sex.

3. What messages did you receive from your family about sex? Using examples from your own life or from television shows and movies, comment on Schwartz's argument.

4. Go to Norton's Everyday Sociology Blog (everydaysociologyblog.com) and search for "sexuality," "sex education," or another related topic. Find a post that interests you and do a critical evaluation of its content. Does it support or refute Schwartz's argument that Americans are afraid of sexuality? Use evidence from the reading to support your answer.

KARL MARX AND FRIEDRICH ENGELS

Bourgeois and Proletarians

From *Manifesto of the Communist Party*

Karl Marx and Friedrich Engels's *Manifesto of the Communist Party* is one of the most influential documents in history. First published in 1848, the manifesto describes the history of **class** struggle in **society**, from feudal serfs against their lords to the **proletariat**, or **working class**, against the **bourgeoisie**, or merchant class, of the mid-nineteenth century. Just as **capitalism** took over the means of production from feudalism, the authors argue, the proletariat will rise to retake the means of production from the bourgeoisie. As you read, consider whether you agree that the history of society *is* the history of class struggle.

THE HISTORY OF ALL HITHERTO EXISTING SOCIETY IS THE HIStory of class struggles.

Freeman and slave, patrician and plebeian, lord and serf, guild-master[1] and journeyman, in a word, oppressor and oppressed, stood in constant opposition to one another, carried on an uninterrupted, now hidden, now open fight, a fight that each time ended, either in a revolutionary re-constitution of society at large, or in the common ruin of the contending classes.

In the earlier epochs of history, we find almost everywhere a complicated arrangement of society into various orders, a manifold gradation of social rank. In ancient Rome we have patricians, knights, plebeians, slaves; in the Middle Ages, feudal lords,

---

[1] That is, a full member of a guild, a master within, not a head of a guild.

vassals, guild-masters, journey-men, apprentices, serfs; in almost all of these classes, again, subordinate gradations.

The modern bourgeois society that has sprouted from the ruins of feudal society has not done away with class antagonisms. It has but established new classes, new conditions of oppression, new forms of struggle in place of the old ones.

Our epoch, the epoch of the bourgeoisie,[2] possesses, however, this distinctive feature: it has simplified the class antagonisms: Society as a whole is more and more splitting up into two great hostile camps, into two great classes directly facing each other: Bourgeoisie and Proletariat.

From the serfs of the Middle Ages sprang the chartered burghers of the earliest towns. From these burgesses the first elements of the bourgeoisie were developed.

The discovery of America, the rounding of the Cape,[3] opened up fresh ground for the rising bourgeoisie. The East-Indian and Chinese markets, the colonisation of America, trade with the colonies, the increase in the means of exchange and in commodities generally, gave to commerce, to navigation, to industry, an impulse never before known, and thereby, to the revolutionary element in the tottering feudal society, a rapid development.

The feudal system of industry, under which industrial production was monopolised by closed guilds, now no longer sufficed for the growing wants of the new markets. The manufacturing system took its place. The guild-masters were pushed on one side by the manufacturing middle class; division of labour between the different corporate guilds vanished in the face of division of labour in each single workshop.

Meantime the markets kept ever growing, the demand ever rising. Even manufacture no longer sufficed. Thereupon, steam and machinery revolutionised industrial production. The place of manufacture was taken by the giant, Modern Industry, the place of the industrial middle class, by industrial millionaires, the leaders of whole industrial armies, the modern bourgeois.

Modern industry has established the world-market, for which the discovery of America paved the way. This market has given an immense development to commerce, to navigation, to communication by land. This development has, in its turn, reacted on the extension of industry; and in proportion as industry, commerce, navigation, railways extended, in the same proportion the bourgeoisie developed, increased its capital, and pushed into the background every class handed down from the Middle Ages.

We see, therefore, how the modern bourgeoisie is itself the product of a long course of development, of a series of revolutions in the modes of production and of exchange.

Each step in the development of the bourgeoisie was accompanied by a corresponding political advance of that class. An oppressed class under the sway of the

---

[2] Specifically, capitalists, or owners of factories and other means of production. *Proletariat*: here, wage laborers.

[3] That is, the cape of Good Hope, which provided an alternative trade route to the East.

feudal nobility, an armed and self-governing association in the mediaeval commune; here independent urban republic (as in Italy and Germany), there taxable "third estate" of the monarchy (as in France), afterwards, in the period of manufacture proper, serving either the semi-feudal or the absolute monarchy as a counterpoise against the nobility, and, in fact, corner-stone of the great monarchies in general, the bourgeoisie has at last, since the establishment of Modern Industry and of the world-market, conquered for itself, in the modern representative State, exclusive political sway. The executive of the modern State is but a committee for managing the common affairs of the whole bourgeoisie.

The bourgeoisie, historically, has played a most revolutionary part.

The bourgeoisie, wherever it has got the upper hand, has put an end to all feudal, patriarchal, idyllic relations. It has pitilessly torn asunder the motley feudal ties that bound man to his "natural superiors," and has left remaining no other nexus between man and man than naked self-interest, than callous "cash payment." It has drowned the most heavenly ecstasies of religious fervour, of chivalrous enthusiasm, of philistine sentimentalism, in the icy water of egotistical calculation. It has resolved personal worth into exchange value, and in place of the numberless indefeasible chartered freedoms, has set up that single, unconscionable freedom—Free Trade. In one word, for exploitation, veiled by religious and political illusions, it has substituted naked, shameless, direct, brutal exploitation.

The bourgeoisie has stripped of its halo every occupation hitherto honoured and looked up to with reverent awe. It has converted the physician, the lawyer, the priest, the poet, the man of science, into its paid wage-labourers.

The bourgeoisie has torn away from the family its sentimental veil, and has reduced the family relation to a mere money relation.

The bourgeoisie has disclosed how it came to pass that the brutal display of vigour in the Middle Ages, which Reactionists so much admire, found its fitting complement in the most slothful indolence. It has been the first to show what man's activity can bring about. It has accomplished wonders far surpassing Egyptian pyramids, Roman aqueducts, and Gothic cathedrals; it has conducted expeditions that put in the shade all former Exoduses of nations and crusades.

The bourgeoisie cannot exist without constantly revolutionising the instruments of production, and thereby the relations of production, and with them the whole relations of society. Conservation of the old modes of production in unaltered form, was, on the contrary, the first condition of existence for all earlier industrial classes. Constant revolutionising of production, uninterrupted disturbance of all social conditions, everlasting uncertainty and agitation distinguish the bourgeois epoch from all earlier ones. All fixed, fast-frozen relations, with their train of ancient and venerable prejudices and opinions, are swept away, all new-formed ones become antiquated before they can ossify. All that is solid melts into air, all that is holy is profaned, and man is at last compelled to face with sober senses, his real conditions of life, and his relations with his kind.

The need of a constantly expanding market for its products chases the bourgeoisie over the whole surface of the globe. It must nestle everywhere, settle everywhere, establish connexions everywhere.

The bourgeoisie has through its exploitation of the world-market given a cosmopolitan character to production and consumption in every country. To the great chagrin of Reactionists, it has drawn from under the feet of industry the national ground on which it stood. All old-established national industries have been destroyed or are daily being destroyed. They are dislodged by new industries, whose introduction becomes a life and death question for all civilised nations, by industries that no longer work up indigenous raw material, but raw material drawn from the remotest zones; industries whose products are consumed, not only at home, but in every quarter of the globe. In place of the old wants, satisfied by the productions of the country, we find new wants, requiring for their satisfaction the products of distant lands and climes. In place of the old local and national seclusion and self-sufficiency, we have intercourse in every direction, universal inter-dependence of nations. And as in material, so also in intellectual production. The intellectual creations of individual nations become common property. National one-sidedness and narrow-mindedness become more and more impossible, and from the numerous national and local literatures, there arises a world literature.

The bourgeoisie, by the rapid improvement of all instruments of production, by the immensely facilitated means of communication, draws all, even the most barbarian, nations into civilisation. The cheap prices of its commodities are the heavy artillery with which it batters down all Chinese walls, with which it forces the barbarians' intensely obstinate hatred of foreigners to capitulate. It compels all nations, on pain of extinction, to adopt the bourgeois mode of production; it compels them to introduce what it calls civilisation into their midst, *i.e.*, to become bourgeois themselves. In one word, it creates a world after its own image.

The bourgeoisie has subjected the country to the rule of the towns. It has created enormous cities, has greatly increased the urban population as compared with the rural, and has thus rescued a considerable part of the population from the idiocy of rural life. Just as it has made the country dependent on the towns, so it has made barbarian and semi-barbarian countries dependent on the civilised ones, nations of peasants on nations of bourgeois, the East on the West.

The bourgeoisie keeps more and more doing away with the scattered state of the population, of the means of production, and of property. It has agglomerated population, centralised means of production, and has concentrated property in a few hands. The necessary consequence of this was political centralisation. Independent, or but loosely connected provinces, with separate interests, laws, governments and systems of taxation, became lumped together into one nation, with one government, one code of laws, one national class-interest, one frontier and one customs-tariff.

The bourgeoisie, during its rule of scarce one hundred years, has created more massive and more colossal productive forces than have all preceding generations together. Subjection of Nature's forces to man, machinery, application of chemistry to industry and agriculture, steam-navigation, railways, electric telegraphs, clearing of whole continents for cultivation, canalisation of rivers, whole populations conjured out of the ground—what earlier century had even a presentiment that such productive forces slumbered in the lap of social labour?

We see then: the means of production and of exchange, on whose foundation the bourgeoisie built itself up, were generated in feudal society. At a certain stage in the development of these means of production and of exchange, the conditions under which feudal society produced and exchanged, the feudal organisation of agriculture and manufacturing industry, in one word, the feudal relations of property became no longer compatible with the already developed productive forces; they became so many fetters. They had to be burst asunder; they were burst asunder.

Into their place stepped free competition, accompanied by a social and political constitution adapted to it, and by the economical and political sway of the bourgeois class.

A similar movement is going on before our own eyes. Modern bourgeois society with its relations of production, of exchange and of property, a society that has conjured up such gigantic means of production and of exchange, is like the sorcerer, who is no longer able to control the powers of the nether world whom he has called up by his spells. For many a decade past the history of industry and commerce is but the history of the revolt of modern productive forces against modern conditions of production, against the property relations that are the conditions for the existence of the bourgeoisie and of its rule. It is enough to mention the commercial crises that by their periodical return put on its trial, each time more threateningly, the existence of the entire bourgeois society. In these crises a great part not only of the existing products, but also of the previously created productive forces, are periodically destroyed. In these crises there breaks out an epidemic that, in all earlier epochs, would have seemed an absurdity—the epidemic of over-production. Society suddenly finds itself put back into a state of momentary barbarism; it appears as if a famine, a universal war of devastation had cut off the supply of every means of subsistence; industry and commerce seem to be destroyed; and why? Because there is too much civilisation, too much means of subsistence, too much industry, too much commerce. The productive forces at the disposal of society no longer tend to further the development of the conditions of bourgeois property; on the contrary, they have become too powerful for these conditions, by which they are fettered, and so soon as they overcome these fetters, they bring disorder into the whole of bourgeois society, endanger the existence of bourgeois property. The conditions of bourgeois society are too narrow to comprise the wealth created by them. And how does the bourgeoisie get over these crises? On the one hand by enforced destruction of a mass of productive forces; on the other, by the conquest of new markets, and by the more thorough exploitation of the old ones. That is to say, by paving the way for more extensive and more destructive crises, and by diminishing the means whereby crises are prevented.

The weapons with which the bourgeoisie felled feudalism to the ground are now turned against the bourgeoisie itself.

But not only has the bourgeoisie forged the weapons that bring death to itself; it has also called into existence the men who are to wield those weapons—the modern working class—the proletarians.

In proportion as the bourgeoisie, *i.e.*, capital, is developed, in the same proportion is the proletariat, the modern working class, developed—a class of labourers, who live only so long as they find work, and who find work only so long as their labour increases capital. These labourers, who must sell themselves piece-meal, are a commodity, like every other article of commerce, and are consequently exposed to all the vicissitudes of competition, to all the fluctuations of the market.

Owing to the extensive use of machinery and to division of labour, the work of the proletarians has lost all individual character, and consequently, all charm for the workman. He becomes an appendage of the machine, and it is only the most simple, most monotonous, and most easily acquired knack, that is required of him. Hence, the cost of production of a workman is restricted, almost entirely, to the means of subsistence that he requires for his maintenance, and for the propagation of his race. But the price of a commodity, and therefore also of labour, is equal to its cost of production. In proportion, therefore, as the repulsiveness of the work increases, the wage decreases. Nay more, in proportion as the use of machinery and division of labour increases, in the same proportion the burden of toil also increases, whether by prolongation of the working hours, by increase of the work exacted in a given time or by increased speed of the machinery, etc.

Modern industry has converted the little workshop of the patriarchal master into the great factory of the industrial capitalist. Masses of labourers, crowded into the factory, are organised like soldiers. As privates of the industrial army they are placed under the command of a perfect hierarchy of officers and sergeants. Not only are they slaves of the bourgeois class, and of the bourgeois State; they are daily and hourly enslaved by the machine, by the over-looker, and, above all, by the individual bourgeois manufacturer himself. The more openly this despotism proclaims gain to be its end and aim, the more petty, the more hateful and the more embittering it is.

The less the skill and exertion of strength implied in manual labour, in other words, the more modern industry becomes developed, the more is the labour of men superseded by that of women. Differences of age and sex have no longer any distinctive social validity for the working class. All are instruments of labour, more or less expensive to use, according to their age and sex.

No sooner is the exploitation of the labourer by the manufacturer, so far, at an end, that he receives his wages in cash, than he is set upon by the other portions of the bourgeoisie, the landlord, the shopkeeper, the pawnbroker, etc.

The lower strata of the middle class—the small tradespeople, shopkeepers, and retired tradesmen generally, the handicraftsmen and peasants—all these sink gradually into the proletariat, partly because their diminutive capital does not suffice for the scale on which Modern Industry is carried on, and is swamped in the competition with the large capitalists, partly because their specialised skill is rendered worthless by new methods of production. Thus the proletariat is recruited from all classes of the population.

The proletariat goes through various stages of development. With its birth begins its struggle with the bourgeoisie. At first the contest is carried on by individual labourers, then by the workpeople of a factory, then by the operatives of one trade, in one locality, against the individual bourgeois who directly exploits them. They direct their attacks not against the bourgeois conditions of production, but against the instruments of production themselves; they destroy imported wares that compete with their labour, they smash to pieces machinery, they set factories ablaze, they seek to restore by force the vanished status of the workman of the Middle Ages.

At this stage the labourers still form an incoherent mass scattered over the whole country, and broken up by their mutual competition. If anywhere they unite to form more compact bodies, this is not yet the consequence of their own active union, but of the union of the bourgeoisie, which class, in order to attain its own political ends, is compelled to set the whole proletariat in motion, and is moreover yet, for a time, able to do so. At this stage, therefore, the proletarians do not fight their enemies, but the enemies of their enemies, the remnants of absolute monarchy, the landowners, the non-industrial bourgeois, the petty bourgeoisie. Thus the whole historical movement is concentrated in the hands of the bourgeoisie; every victory so obtained is a victory for the bourgeoisie.

But with the development of industry the proletariat not only increases in number; it becomes concentrated in greater masses, its strength grows, and it feels that strength more. The various interests and conditions of life within the ranks of the proletariat are more and more equalised, in proportion as machinery obliterates all distinctions of labour, and nearly everywhere reduces wages to the same low level. The growing competition among the bourgeois, and the resulting commercial crises, make the wages of the workers ever more fluctuating. The unceasing improvement of machinery, ever more rapidly developing, makes their livelihood more and more precarious; the collisions between individual workmen and individual bourgeois take more and more the character of collisions between two classes. Thereupon the workers begin to form combinations (Trade Unions) against the bourgeois; they club together in order to keep up the rate of wages; they found permanent associations in order to make provision beforehand for these occasional revolts. Here and there the contest breaks out into riots.

Now and then the workers are victorious, but only for a time. The real fruit of their battles lies, not in the immediate result, but in the ever-expanding union of the workers. This union is helped on by the improved means of communication that are created by modern industry and that place the workers of different localities in contact with one another. It was just this contact that was needed to centralise the numerous local struggles, all of the same character, into one national struggle between classes. But every class struggle is a political struggle. And that union, to attain which the burghers of the Middle Ages, with their miserable highways, required centuries, the modern proletarians, thanks to railways, achieve in a few years.

This organisation of the proletarians into a class, and consequently into a political party, is continually being upset again by the competition between the workers themselves. But it ever rises up again, stronger, firmer, mightier. It compels legislative recognition of particular interests of the workers, by taking advantage of the divisions among the bourgeoisie itself. Thus the ten-hours' bill[4] in England was carried.

Altogether collisions between the classes of the old society further, in many ways, the course of development of the proletariat. The bourgeoisie finds itself involved in a constant battle. At first with the aristocracy, later on, with those portions of the bourgeoisie itself, whose interests have become antagonistic to the progress of industry; at all times, with the bourgeoisie of foreign countries. In all these battles it sees itself compelled to appeal to the proletariat, to ask for its help, and thus, to drag it into the political arena. The bourgeoisie itself, therefore, supplies the proletariat with its own elements of political and general education, in other words, it furnishes the proletariat with weapons for fighting the bourgeoisie.

Further, as we have already seen, entire sections of the ruling classes are, by the advance of industry, precipitated into the proletariat, or are at least threatened in their conditions of existence. These also supply the proletariat with fresh elements of enlightenment and progress.

Finally, in times when the class struggle nears the decisive hour, the process of dissolution going on within the ruling class, in fact within the whole range of society, assumes such a violent, glaring character, that a small section of the ruling class cuts itself adrift, and joins the revolutionary class, the class that holds the future in its hands. Just as, therefore, at an earlier period, a section of the nobility went over to the bourgeoisie, so now a portion of the bourgeoisie goes over to the proletariat, and in particular, a portion of the bourgeois ideologists, who have raised themselves to the level of comprehending theoretically the historical movement as a whole.

Of all the classes that stand face to face with the bourgeoisie today, the proletariat alone is a really revolutionary class. The other classes decay and finally disappear in the face of Modern Industry; the proletariat is its special and essential product.

The lower middle class, the small manufacturer, the shopkeeper, the artisan, the peasant, all these fight against the bourgeoisie, to save from extinction their existence as fractions of the middle class. They are therefore not revolutionary, but conserva-

---

[4] Passed in 1847, the bill restricted the number of hours women and children could work in factories to ten hours a day, fifty-eight hours per week.

tive. Nay more, they are reactionary, for they try to roll back the wheel of history. If by chance they are revolutionary, they are so only in view of their impending transfer into the proletariat, they thus defend not their present, but their future interests, they desert their own standpoint to place themselves at that of the proletariat.

The "dangerous class," the social scum, that passively rotting mass thrown off by the lowest layers of old society, may, here and there, be swept into the movement by a proletarian revolution; its conditions of life, however, prepare it far more for the part of a bribed tool of reactionary intrigue.

In the conditions of the proletariat, those of old society at large are already virtually swamped. The proletarian is without property; his relation to his wife and children has no longer anything in common with the bourgeois family-relations; modern industrial labour, modern subjection to capital, the same in England as in France, in America as in Germany, has stripped him of every trace of national character. Law, morality, religion, are to him so many bourgeois prejudices, behind which lurk in ambush just as many bourgeois interests.

All the preceding classes that got the upper hand, sought to fortify their already acquired status by subjecting society at large to their conditions of appropriation. The proletarians cannot become masters of the productive forces of society, except by abolishing their own previous mode of appropriation, and thereby also every other previous mode of appropriation. They have nothing of their own to secure and to fortify; their mission is to destroy all previous securities for, and insurances of, individual property.

All previous historical movements were movements of minorities, or in the interests of minorities. The proletarian movement is the self-conscious, independent movement of the immense majority, in the interests of the immense majority. The proletariat, the lowest stratum of our present society, cannot stir, cannot raise itself up, without the whole superincumbent strata of official society being sprung into the air.

Though not in substance, yet in form, the struggle of the proletariat with the bourgeoisie is at first a national struggle. The proletariat of each country must, of course, first of all settle matters with its own bourgeoisie.

In depicting the most general phases of the development of the proletariat, we traced the more or less veiled civil war, raging within existing society, up to the point where that war breaks out into open revolution, and where the violent overthrow of the bourgeoisie lays the foundation for the sway of the proletariat.

Hitherto, every form of society has been based, as we have already seen, on the antagonism of oppressing and oppressed classes. But in order to oppress a class, certain conditions must be assured to it under which it can, at least, continue its slavish existence. The serf, in the period of serfdom, raised himself to membership in the commune, just as the petty bourgeois, under the yoke of feudal absolutism, managed to develop into a bourgeois. The modern labourer, on the contrary, instead of rising with the progress of industry, sinks deeper and deeper below the conditions of existence of his own class. He becomes a pauper, and pauperism develops more rapidly than population and wealth. And here it becomes evident, that the bourgeoisie is unfit any longer to be the ruling class in society, and to impose its conditions of existence upon society as an over-riding law. It is unfit to rule because it is incompetent to assure an existence to its slave within his slavery, because it cannot help letting him sink into such a state, that it has to feed him, instead of being fed by him. Society can no longer live under this bourgeoisie, in other words, its existence is no longer compatible with society.

The essential condition for the existence, and for the sway of the bourgeois class, is the formation and augmentation of capital; the condition for capital is wage-labour. Wage-labour rests exclusively on competition between the labourers. The advance of industry, whose involuntary promoter is the bourgeoisie, replaces the isolation of the labourers, due to competition, by their revolutionary combination, due to association. The development of Modern Industry, therefore, cuts from under its feet the very foundation on which the bourgeoisie produces and appropriates products. What the bourgeoisie, therefore, produces, above all, is its own grave-diggers. Its fall and the victory of the proletariat are equally inevitable.

STUDY QUESTIONS

1. How did the **bourgeoisie** gain power? Describe the previous system.

2. How is the bourgeoisie contributing to its own demise according to the *Manifesto*? How does competition among wage laborers slow the progress of the **proletarian** rise?

3. Considered within the context of the *Manifesto of the Communist Party*, what should the rise in electronic communication do for workers? Do you think worldwide electronic communication has improved the lot of workers? Why or why not?

4. In most places, the Communist system has not succeeded (in, for example, East Germany and the Soviet Union). Researching **communism** if necessary, discuss some reasons for its failure. Are "Communists" really practicing communism? Are there places where the proletariat rules?

RACHEL LOUISE SNYDER

Knock, Knock, Knockin'
on Factory Doors

From *Fugitive Denim: A Moving Story of People and
Pants in the Borderless World of Global Trade*

Those jeans you're wearing were most likely not made in the United States (even if they're Levi's!). They may have been made in a Chinese factory like the one Rachel Louise Snyder describes in this chapter from her book *Fugitive Denim*. Perhaps Lever Shirt is not the **sweatshop** you will be expecting, but you'll still learn much about **globalization** and free trade as you read Snyder's analysis.

SHENZHEN, CHINA, IS A CITY HARDLY MEANT TO BE. TWENTY-five years ago, it was no more than a fishing village. Now nearly eight million people live there, evidence of the central government's carefully planned economic strategy from the 1970s.[1] I try to imagine this in terms of an American city. It's as if Chicago went from a village with a handful of cornfields to the urban metropolis of today in just half of my current lifetime. Cities, to me, aren't established in two decades, but over generations, centuries. Shenzhen, less than an hour from Hong Kong by train, was established in 1980 by Deng Xiaoping as China's first special economic zone (the country created five in total). Establishing a business here meant tax relief and investment incentives. The Chinese government also invested heavily in the area's infrastructure and encouraged foreign companies to set up shop by reducing red tape.

Throughout the 1980s and 1990s, migrants from the countryside descended upon the area. In the beginning jobs were plentiful, even if salaries and conditions were far from ideal. Nearly from the time of the area's inception its economy averaged 28 percent growth annually, and in 2005 the city was responsible for 13 percent of China's total exports. The port is now the sixth biggest in the world.[2] Throughout the mid- to late 1990s however, property prices and start-up costs rose almost as fast as the city had, and low-skilled manufacturing was soon priced out of the special zone. Around the same time, China began to lose its seemingly endless low-skilled labor supply, for a variety of reasons. The one-child policy implemented in 1979 has led to an aging population. Increased demand for labor—new factories open daily in China—means migrants can be choosier about the jobs they take, and they can demand higher salaries and more benefits. Millions of young rural people are choosing to stay in school longer in the hopes of landing better jobs than merely low-skilled factory jobs many miles away from their homes and families.[3] And in 2005 China eliminated an agricultural tax, which induced many rural farmers to stay and farm their land rather than migrate to the country's manufacturing areas.[4] (On the other hand, some statistics suggest as many as one million manufacturing jobs are lost annually, mostly to technology advances.)

The earliest factories began to move farther and farther out from the city center, giving way to three- and four-star hotels, tourist attractions, and highrises. These days, technology parks dominate the inner circle of the special economic zone. But Shenzhen remains home to many of China's notorious factory sweatshops, the majority of them now in the surrounding suburbs of the city. As salaries have risen, however—by as much as 40 percent since 2000—workers have started to agitate for better conditions and higher wages. Though underreported by the Western press, strikes are frequent in China. Nearly every week thousands of workers protest their working conditions. Signs of improvement are slowly emerging. Minimum wage in China is set regionally, and for Shenzhen, in Guangdong province, it is US$100. China's suffering from its substantial labor shortage in low-wage industries like textiles and factories is forcing the country to recognize that creating conditions to keep workers around is simply sound economics. Most factories must agree to allow major buyers to dictate codes of conduct and acceptable working conditions, and for the past decade a new system of social compliance has begun to take shape both in multinational corporations and in their contracted manufacturing partners across the globe.

One morning, I took the train from Hong Kong to Shenzhen to meet a team of Vendor Compliance Officers (VCOs), as they're called, for Gap Inc. (which also owns Banana Republic and Old Navy). Like most major buyers these days, Gap has an extensive list of reforms that factories must follow in order to get contracts. Gap works with roughly 280 factories in the Southeast Asian region, including forty to fifty in Cambodia, and it's not above revoking contracts with factories that don't follow its protocol. It is no secret that extensive labor abuses and terrible conditions in a series of factories under contract with Gap, Nike, and others in the mid-1990s created public scandals resulting in significant revenue loss and consumer boycotts. Many people remember Kathie Lee Gifford's 1996 teary apology on national television after abuses were discovered in her Central American factories. A call for corporate reckoning and a new age of social responsibility by multinational firms soon emerged, though Levi's had an ethical workplace program in place long before the scandals, and companies like Patagonia and Esprit have built their brands on environmental prudence and ethical sourcing. International corporations, along with a handful of what are commonly called third-party auditors or certification groups, have now spent the past decade wending their way through this new reality. On one hand, it seems redundant even to *have* a corporate social responsibility, or CSR, department. Shouldn't CSR just naturally be in our business practices? Unfortunately, it seems, the abundance of terrible factory conditions that still exist today dictate the need for such administrative departments and activist groups.

While no one from any of the industry sectors claims sweatshops aren't still rampant, some companies are making substantial inroads. Like others, Gap has had a difficult time rehabilitating its corporate image, and perhaps as a result, the company is skirting a line between being naturally timid and increasingly transparent. In 1995, the National Labor Committee, led by Charles Kernaghan—a man who has probably done more to illuminate the horror of sweatshops than anyone else in the past century—organized a tour of the United States for two Central American teenage factory workers who were making clothes for Gap at 12 cents an hour. Their tour marked the beginning of the emergence of the sweatshop story. Gap responded by revamping their corporate guidelines, guaranteeing workers' rights in their factories around the world, and establishing independent monitoring by third-party auditors (and by their own VCOs). They were the first major buyer to list, in 2004, all the countries they operate in. In 2005 Nike went further by listing its factories, and others followed. Prior to this public disclosure, corporations had long maintained that this was proprietary information. Gap also was the only major brand that took great pains in scheduling me to go along on a factory audit (Levi's theoretically agreed, but we were never able to schedule it in time for my book deadline). Typically, no one is allowed on these audits, which can last anywhere from a few hours to a few days. Even the International Labour Organization and the Cambodian ministry of labor never allowed me to accompany their monitors. While Gap did have some requests—they asked me not to name the factory, or the VCOs, or any employee I spoke with directly—they were otherwise surprisingly open, particularly given that factories today continue to operate under shrouds of secrecy. It is a secrecy that brands are happy to exploit under the guise of "competition." Over and over I was told by various brands I contacted that they'd be happy to have me go into their factories, but it was the factory owners who were skittish (factory owners say the brands are skittish). Or I'd hear something about how they'd love to let me in if only their corporate competitors could be trusted not to swoop in and steal the factory contract out from under them—this was a particularly fun excuse, given that everyone involved in manufacturing already knows what factory makes what and for whom. Even I, in my limited experience, could walk a tourist down a street in Cambodia and point out factories that sew for Wal-Mart, Disney, Gap, Levi's, and H&M. The truth is that even in this age of burgeoning corporate social responsibility, factories operate inside fortresses behind concrete walls topped with razor wire and patrolled by armed guards. This is the transparency that exists today.

In the end, though, the factory I visited with Gap's VCOs asked that I use the facility's real name—Lever Shirt—and Gap agreed. The factory was understandably proud of the work they were doing. I don't want to suggest that I had free rein, but the VCOs I was embedded with, I came to learn, are far from seeing their role as merely a job. Instead, they believe they are, in one VCO's words, "on a mission."

Jerry, a forty-year-old VCO who exuded the air of a college student with his backpack, white golf shirt, and Gap jeans (relaxed fit, slightly faded), was charged with leading the audit the day I went. Short of stature, with close-cropped hair and a cheerful demeanor, Jerry wore the sort of funky round eyeglass frames I've seen in pictures of T. S. Eliot. We met at Shenzhen's main train station along with his boss, Peter, who also acted as a translator when necessary (Peter: pinstriped pants from a local designer and Gap button-down shirt. "Are you wearing Gap?" one of them asked me later in the day.) We drove an hour outside town in a minivan, well beyond the special economic zone.

On the way, we passed a tourist park where the world's greatest monuments stood in resplendent replica: the Eiffel Tower, slightly shorter, the Taj Mahal, slightly rounder. Skyscrapers gave way to concrete block apartment towers. Billboards lined the pristine highways, advertising luxury residences and manufacturing tools—forklifts, widgets, cranes. Blue trucks carrying goods to the port or returning for new loads inundated our periphery as we drove. Like a lot of China's factories, ours was a wholly unremarkable five-story white-tiled building inside a gated compound.

Monitoring has been criticized as merely a way for corporations to make consumers feel good about their purchases. It sometimes falls short when it comes to real change—a fact most managers acknowledge. The truth is that in the garment industry, layered as it is with subcontractors and vast interconnected geographies, monitoring may never allow multinational corporations, even those with the best of intentions, to fully know what goes on when they're not looking. Naysayers believe multinationals have only managed to create low-wage jobs in unskilled sectors while at the same time creating a whitewashed, Americanized global monoculture. Others believe these corporations have introduced technologies, management, and international business and cultural connections that would otherwise have remained unavailable to most in the developing world. In fact, corporations probably offer both. At a conference on corporate social responsibility in Hong Kong in September 2006 Paul Wolfowitz, the then head of the World Bank, said that corporate for-profit business is a greater poverty alleviator than donor funding. It's a belief that is fundamental to companies like Edun, who may not carry the economic weight of a corporation like Gap, Inc., but certainly influence the world's multinationals.

I had no illusions about being taken to a factory with sub-par conditions, but what I found was even beyond the best I'd seen in Cambodia. Later, I learned it was one of Gap's model factories (managers accuse Gap of having some of the strictest professional standards—a fact other buyers benefit from). Lever Shirt, a family-run outfit begun in Hong Kong in 1956, employed five thousand people between this factory and another compound several hours away. The CEO was a tall, funky Gen-Xer who'd graduated from the Wharton School at the University of Pennsylvania and returned to run the family business. When I met him, he was sheathed in premium denim and a button-down patterned shirt and looked as if he'd be well received on a nightclub junket with Lindsay Lohan. In fact, he'd just come from having lunch with five of his factory floor workers who'd been recognized for their productivity. They were awarded a meal away from the canteen in the trendy administrative offices with their boss. Not a bad incentive, overall. Such lunches apparently occurred a handful of times throughout the year.

The administrative offices had a series of glass-walled meeting rooms or managerial offices around the circumference. In the center of these meeting rooms were dozens of modern office cubes with half walls covered in electric blue cloth. Oversized artsy photos on the walls showed individual threads and shirt weaves magnified many thousands of times, as if you were viewing them through a microscope. Even the bathrooms featured natural slate and freestanding cobalt sinks. Later, when we walked through the factory, which of course didn't have quite the same funked-out feel of the offices, I felt air-conditioning. It remains the only air-conditioned factory I've ever visited.

Of course, it would be naïve to suggest that problems, generally termed noncompliance, were not still rampant in the industry as a whole. Numerous examples of child labor, forced labor, abhorrent conditions, and abysmal pay abound. In the spring of 2006, the National Labor Committee put out a report on widespread industry abuses in Jordan in factories that contract with Wal-Mart, Kmart, Kohl's, Gloria Vanderbilt, Target, and Victoria's Secret, among others. The report cites instances of forced labor, indentured servitude, physical and mental abuse, rape, mandatory pregnancy testing (mothers-to-be are often fired so the factory won't have to pay maternity costs), withholding payment, and unsanitary conditions. Of 60,000 factory workers in Jordan's export processing zone, more than half are immigrants (often illegal) and thus particularly vulnerable. Jordan also receives preferential access to the U.S. consumer market as part of the U.S.-Israel free-trade deal. The report told of workers locked in a single room at night and forced to work until 2:00 or 3:00 A.M.; factories had withheld meals and in one case punished a handful of workers by locking them for several hours in a deep freezer.

Levi's actually first drew my attention to the report as proof that they and their industry colleagues were looking closely at their own Jordanian contractors. Gap, too, has been up-front about the fact that noncompliance is an issue that they try to tackle as they discover it. "We're still in a mode of actually trying to teach our team to find as many issues in a factory as we can find," said Dan Henkle, Gap's senior vice president for social responsibility. "So we actually view success based on—this may sound strange—success to us would actually be increasing our findings of some of these harder-to-spot issues." In other words: the more problems they weed out, the more they believe their system is working. Gap killed contracts with over seventy factories in 2004 for not meeting its basic compliance requirements—including three in the Middle East—and more than one hundred the year before. In general, Henkle said that "philosophically, we do not like to move to what we call 'revocation.' We really believe [that] what's in the best interest of all concerned is to fix a problem that crops up." Each year, when Gap publishes its annual report, Henkle and his team are keenly aware of how increased noncompliance may look to the outsider, but it doesn't seem to faze him. What matters is that while problems may be on the rise, the kinds of problems they're seeing have to do with things like overtime policies or grievance procedures, as opposed to child or forced labor. "I really believe there's not a silver-bullet solution here," Henkle said. "It's more like a puzzle, and we're playing certain roles, certain pieces of the puzzle . . . Someone from the ILO did a presentation for our team and they said, 'You know, guys, this is all just one big bowl of spaghetti. Everything is tangled together.' You can't just fix one thing and not have some impact on the other things. And that's exactly what we're seeing."

––––––––––

My visit began with a brief presentation on the company, by a young Scottish-Chinese marketing manager just four months out of Edinburgh. It wouldn't be a stretch to see him in a Guy Ritchie movie. Urban hipsters who'd be at home in London's Brick Lane or New York's East Village are not exactly what comes to mind when I envision factory managers, but such is the pull of Shenzhen, migrants and managers alike are drawn to the place. Men's formal shirts are 45 percent of their business, he said, while a Power-Point presentation showed graphs of the company's annual revenue, along with stylish photos of their products. Behind the screen, real-life examples of those wares were folded and propped up like statues, each in its own white cube, and spotlighted individually; stars in their own tiny production. We sat in modern, blue-padded chairs around a circular table that separated into four parts. "In 2006," the marketing manager said, "sales will be eighty million. We hope to see an influx of orders after 2008."* Then he said: "We expect to double our business."

––––––––––

* When limits on how much China could export to the U.S. would run out.

For all the worrying I've heard in Cambodia and Italy and Azerbaijan, and all the other smaller countries I've followed on trade and industry Web sites, I never thought about just how much China is waiting for 2008 to end. While I've generally assumed Cambodia would be all right in the long run—one of the winners, to some degree—it wasn't until this moment that I began to understand just how terrified Cambodia and the others were, and why. The shift of business wasn't going to evolve slowly; nor would it happen in a vacuum. Everyone in China seemed wholly open not only about their expectations for 2008 but also about what they viewed as the rest of the world unfairly holding them back from their full capability. For all the dread that Cambodia and its industry allies felt, China was feeling similarly put out by trade rules and stopgaps. If the industry was a massive sand hill, China was a funnel at the bottom.

Gap has been Lever's longest-running contract, and 65 percent of what they made went to the States. The factory also made shirts for Abercrombie & Fitch, American Eagle, Miss Sixty, Ann Taylor, Land's End, Eddie Bauer, Next, Ben Sherman, Benetton, and a handful of others. "In the past twenty years, there's been very little growth," said Joe Yuen, the executive director, once the marketing presentation had finished. Very little growth in the context of China, presumably. He believed that the beginning of 2009 was really "when the playing field will be leveled."

For all the competitiveness, though, Joe and the Lever factory have done far more than most factories in Cambodia who comply with the strict labor codes. Recently, Lever became one of the roughly hundred and thirty factories in China to receive what is called an SA 8000 certification. SA 8000 is a relatively new program in the industry that seeks to certify individual factories. The program, whose name derives from a group called Social Accountability International (SAI), certifies companies as well. Eileen Fisher, which makes upscale women's fashions, was the first—and remains one of the only—brand to receive SA 8000 certification in the States, I was told. Lever hadn't received the SA 8000 rating for their other factory yet, but they told me they were planning to pursue it—probably a good thing, since many manufacturers with multiple factory locations have been accused of creating one model factory that they showed to the public while their other factories maintained poor conditions.[5] Gap contracts with thirty-five SA 8000 certified factories around the world, but it's not a requirement for them. "My wish is that it just becomes something [factories] bake into their overall system and process, and that they're doing it for the right reason, which is to improve overall working conditions, and hopefully to improve their whole business operation," Henkle said. "And they're not doing it because we're saying they have to."

Based on ILO and United Nations workplace conventions, SA 8000 has helped improve working conditions in factories and firms in more than forty countries around the world. To get such certification, a factory undergoes substantial auditing by trained professionals. In the case of Lever, the process took a year and a team of eleven auditors, and cost less than fifty thousand dollars. It's a sum Joe claimed wasn't substantial given the benefits, which he believed were a stable, happy workforce, credibility for international buyers, and increased productivity. Of course, even a well-regarded factory in Cambodia could never afford such fees. "We faced some challenges with SA 8000," Joe said. "Some workers didn't know about social compliance. There was a problem with controlling overtime, [but] we wanted to be among the pioneers for social compliance. In the long run, we see it as a competitive advantage."

SAI says they have created a global standard to improve the conditions of workers around the world through SA 8000. In some ways, what they do is the next phase of corporate social responsibility. It nullifies the common criticism that having a buyer do its own audits is like having the police policing themselves. SAI claims that once factories are certified the benefits are significant, including "improved staff morale, more reliable business partnerships, enhanced competitiveness, less staff turnover and better worker-manager communication."[6] Factories who sign on to participate in SA 8000 and who operate in a country where unions are outlawed—like China—are required to create alternatives to unions, much like Lever has done with a team of workers' representatives. The process can be arduous, even for a factory like Lever that was in decent shape before it received certification. Among others, factories are required to adhere to the United Nations charters on child labor, forced labor, women's rights, and debt bondage (when a factory worker is forced to pay a manager or agent for her job). Such "debt" can cost workers thousands of dollars, and arrangements like these permeate the garment industry.

SA 8000 organizes and vets consultants in the countries in which they work; the consultants then conduct ongoing audits. Factories are required, among other things, to appoint both a senior manager to be the point contact for all SAI-related materials, guidelines, and activities, and a workers' representative who understands the requirements for ongoing certification. In this way, SAI manages to include workers, a practice that Michael Kobori, the head of social compliance for Levi's, feels is the real key to change.

SA 8000 has certified factories in fifty-five countries and fifty-eight industries, the majority from apparel and textiles. Italy leads, with nearly four hundred certifications, followed by India, with 141. China is third, with 129. All told, roughly half a million people around the world work in factories under SA 8000's umbrella of good working conditions and respected workplace rights. In operation for a decade (SAI began in 1997), they are a good example of what can be accomplished.

Ironically, China's government is a great impediment to implementing the international codes that buyers are looking for, because it does not recognize the right to freedom of association. Joe believed that forced labor and child labor were still "quite common." These facts haven't stopped foreign firms from setting up shop in China, of course. The country does have one trade union—the ACFTU, or All-China Federation of Trade Unions—but it is widely viewed as an arm of the government. Though the ACFTU recently accomplished something their AFL–CIO counterparts in America have long failed to do by unionizing Wal-Mart employees in more than twenty of the big-box retailer's stores throughout China, such an effort must be taken with a grain of salt, given the organizing body. The ACFTU, for its part, of course has promised it will tirelessly seek better conditions and improved workers' rights. Individual factories like Lever recognize unions, and the right to collective bargaining, but, given the political situation, they've had to circumvent the rules by creating a three-person team of worker representatives for grievances and negotiations with management. There are only about a hundred and thirty factories with SA 8000 certification in China. One must presume that the overwhelming majority of manufacturers do not make grievance procedures and collective bargaining a priority.

Like the majority of countries around the world, China has a relatively detailed set of decent labor laws (in Cambodia's case, these labor laws compose about a half-inch-thick book; China's book more resembles the Bible). Around the world, the problem tends not to be creating labor laws to eradicate sweatshops but rather enforcing laws that exist. One of the surest incentives to keep monitors from taking bribes, for example, is simply to pay them well above market rates. The ILO pays its monitors in Cambodia $750–$1,000 a month—a phenomenally high salary for the country—claiming it offers a disincentive for graft.

Jerry began his audit of Lever by requesting a multitude of factory records. One of the common complaints from groups like Social Accountability International and its activist community, which includes other well-known groups like Verité and Fair Labor, is that many factories keep two sets of books: one for the auditors and another "real" one. Peter admits that this has been a problem in the past and outlines a number of ways they try to weed out this practice. They compare working dates, dates of fabric shipments logged in and finished garment shipments logged out, overtime records, production records versus factory capacity, public holidays and vacation days. Even weather can be telling—during rainy season, for example, some shipments that would otherwise go out on a working day may have to go out on a Sunday, and a determination must be made about whether or not employees were used for overtime and whether that falls within their acceptable overtime limit. Gap's 2004 corporate report admits monitoring is "more art than science" and that the best monitors are the ones who read beyond the page, extrapolating from a multitude of sources and records to create an accurate picture of what's really happening.

A woman named Joyce who heads the factory's three-person social compliance department began to produce large black binders for Jerry.[7] Peter explained what the binders were: records of personal protective equipment, or PPE, which included things like masks, metal gloves for the pattern cutting section (since a band knife, which, as noted earlier, cuts through dozens of layers of cloth at once, can go through a hand like it's mayonnaise), gloves if chemicals are used, eye protectors on button and rivet machines, finger protectors on sewing machines, and other gear. Because, as we have seen, fire safety is one of the biggest hazards in textile and garment production, the codes are stringent. Lever had binder after binder with records of their fire drills, each with dated pictures showing workers walking down lighted hallways and standing in lines on the pavement outside. Drills happened day and night. There were certain people designated to set off alarms, to count worker groups, to call the fire department and police, to work the extinguishers, and to give first aid—one in every fifty workers and one per sewing line must be first-aid-certified, with updated training every couple of years. Painted yellow boxes on the floor marked areas where fire equipment was stored, and emergency lights had lists of test dates taped to them. Doors opened out. Stairs required railings. Outer escapes were to be wide enough for two at a time. The detail was staggering, and as the hours passed, the binders and paperwork surrounding Jerry blossomed and spilled onto the surrounding tables like a time-lapse garden growing on a movie screen. Jerry began to look very small in contrast. "We need to spend time with the documents," Peter said, as if each record held the symbolic power of a line of poetry (which, in some ways, it does). After three hours, I was ready to leave. This is what separates marginally lazy people like me from people like Jerry, who believes he can make a difference in a worldwide corporate revolution. I never saw him yawn. I never saw him look up from his checklist or the garden of paper encircling him, and he maintained an air of respect and seriousness throughout the day. But he also seemed like the kind of guy you hope will audit you, someone who will understand the complexity and the difficulty and still demand, in the nicest way possible, that you do things his way.

Jerry had known the people at Lever, including Joyce, for the entire six years he'd been a compliance officer for Gap. He and Peter were among the pioneers of this painfully detailed style of audit—an audit that would have taken a whole second day if I hadn't been there (they sped things up for my limited schedule, but normally they spent the night in Shenzhen and took two full days to finish). They had learned by trial and error what to include, and while Gap had dictated the overall plan, the two spoke of monitoring as a sort of global collaboration. Different geographies dictate different safety and climate standards; different products require different machines and chemicals. In this regard, the kind of auditing Gap is doing is really in its infancy. Dan Henkle told me Gap had come up with a plan that they'd titled One-Plus-One. Basically, it meant one audit, one chance to fix the problems, and one follow-up visit. In the beginning, they found that they'd audit a factory, list a dozen problems, and each time they went back two or three more things would be better. It was a drain on everybody. "This is not a game we're playing," Henkle said. Gap's stance had had to get tougher. "If we tell you that there are fifteen problems, you need to fix those problems."

Every few minutes, Jerry pushed up his glasses and shifted in his seat, but otherwise he was wholly focused. He told me that before this job, he'd been an interior designer. In 1997, when the Asian economies crashed, no one cared about design anymore and he lost many of his clients. It was terrifying for him. He was already established in his career and he was afraid to change, afraid of what sort of sacrifice that might mean. He decided that the economic crisis might actually be offering him something entirely new. "It was a difficult time for me," he said. "I was not developing. But it was a good chance for me to take a risk." He interviewed for the newly created position of VCO at the Gap, and in the interview, he was asked what in his interior design experience could possibly have prepared him to be a factory auditor. He'd designed factories, of course, along with residential and commercial buildings, though designing a factory was, in his estimation, simply "construction." Still, he gave what may well be the greatest answer in the annals of job interview history.

"We both have the same goal, VCOs and interior designers," he told his interviewer. "To improve the living and working environments of people."

Later, he would refer to this as the single smartest moment of his life. "I don't know where this answer came from," he laughed.

Peter pulled out the binder that recorded accidents and picked several at random. Health costs were generally picked up by the factory, though there was no health clinic on site (they plan to build one next year). One woman was burned by hot water and sent to the hospital. Another was injured by a button-punching machine. The records showed the injury report, the hospital record and bill, and the payment. Jerry meanwhile had chosen a dozen or so random employees and asked for their records. Reviewing thousands of employee records would take several weeks, of course, so they tend to choose only a sampling. He looked at their work contract, their photocopied ID cards (using fake IDs has long been a problem in China), overtime and vacation records, payment history and attendance records. Their turnover rate was only 3 to 5 percent; clearly the factory was doing something right. Two young girls were called in to help locate files as Jerry asked for them. I imagined they would spend the bulk of tomorrow refiling the papers now filling the conference room.

It occurred to me that this factory, with its unbelievably good working conditions, its global certification, and its high-quality product, is exactly Italy's nightmare. Indeed, most of the fabric came from Italy, though there was talk of moving some fabric production to China or buying more locally from factories in China already producing the fabric they generally used.

Peter, Jerry, Joe, Joyce, another administrative staffer, and I took a break for lunch in the early afternoon. Peter and Joe walked ahead of the group and I overheard Peter saying quietly that Gap could not accept anything in the way of gifts from its vendors. I presumed this to mean he intended to pay for lunch. We walked first through the workers' canteen, as some employees were then on their (hour-and-fifteen-minute) lunch break. For about a quarter they could opt to eat here daily, and there were a dozen different dishes from which to choose. The two lunchroom areas were clean and bright, with long plastic picnic tables. Peter pointed out the emergency exit doors—"They open out, see?"—and the emergency lights, and he stood on his toes to hit the test button to make sure the system worked. The lights flickered on, then off. A side window with three or four dishes offered super-spicy food. Peter explained that one of the early complaints from workers was about the food. The migrants from the interior preferred spicy food to the bland seafood offerings in Shenzhen, and the factory created this separate culinary window for them. What I thought of when I saw this was whether or not such things could be replicated on a larger scale. Lever was undoubtedly a model factory, as is New Island, the Marks & Spencer factory in Cambodia, but if they're so wonderful, why *aren't* the others following in line? Were companies like Lever and New Island the equivalent of corporations in America who went into the red to build cafeterias and gyms for their employees? Even Stanley Szeto, Lever's CEO, said that changing the factory paradigm from sweatshop to archetype comes at a cost to the general business model: Earnings have not yet materialized in a way that suggests they've mastered the balancing act.

We ate in the café of a place called Mission Hills, a brand-new complex of ten golf courses designed by players like Ernie Els and Nick Faldo. It also had luxury residences, lush tropical gardens, and elegant restaurants, and covered such a vast area that it spilled into the boundaries of two separate cities and took more than half an hour to drive across. During lunch, Joe explained how he determined the capability of the factory. Overtime had been perhaps the factory's biggest impediment to getting the SA 8000 certification. Like many brands, Gap's corporate policy allowed up to a sixty-hour work week—or 80 hours of overtime a month—but China's labor law dictated that workers could not put in more than thirty-six hours of overtime in a month. The question was whether the government's or the employer's law had jurisdiction. It is a question repeated over and over in an age of globalization, where corporations and their mandates exist in one place with one set of rules, but the corporations establish offices or partnerships in another place with another set of rules. Lever had received a government waiver to follow Gap's code from the local authorities—a common practice among manufacturers in China. "A shirt takes thirty minutes to make, approximately," Joe said. "And in this one factory we can do four hundred thousand a month." Capacity is checked on a daily basis, and the production plan is adjusted only days in advance. In industry parlance, the big goal is "lean lines," meaning sewing lines that are not only efficient but running relative to one another. Having the front part of a pair of jeans arrive at the section of a sewing line where it is joined with the back part long before the back arrives is a common problem. The big challenge is accepting enough orders to keep the factory at full capacity without overtime and still getting the shipments to buyers on time. "If there is volatility in [our] daily productivity [or] we have excess orders, I may have to use overtime as a balance," Joe told me.

By contrast, overtime in a Cambodian factory is necessary for workers to make ends meet. If the minimum wage is $50 a month, but the average worker earns $69–$71, then overtime clearly plays a role more akin to, well, plain old work time. In Cambodia, I am eternally amused by people who say that Khmer girls just *like* to work till 6:00 or 8:00 or 10:00 P.M. They tend to be the same ones who think factory workers don't like air-conditioning anyway because it's too cold.

In the café, large tables of men on lunch breaks or golf breaks ate Chinese, Thai, or Singaporean dishes and smoked. I counted two other women in total among the patrons. After a while, Joe asked me about the expiration of all the safeguards. In particular, he wanted to know what I thought the United States might use to keep China in check. "Social compliance," he asked, "or anti-dumping?" Anti-dumping is basically a trade restriction to keep any one country from selling too much of one item, or dumping it, in another country very cheaply. His question suggested to me just how much economic power America still wields through its policies.

Joe said he thought the quota system might be indirectly responsible, to a degree, for some of the labor issues in China. It kept foreign investors—particularly those in Hong Kong who could have made a difference—from investing in the country. I told him I didn't quite buy that argument; it placed the blame for the abuses that are allowed to flourish on a group of people who weren't even there. The real blame, I said, should be on factories and governments willing to overlook rabid abuses. Hong Kong investors may well have created better working environments, but thousands and thousands of factories in China and elsewhere had still been built on the backs of a desperately impoverished citizenry. Joe didn't disagree with this. He suggested that politically China was making inroads to democracy, that the younger generation would eventually replace the elder statesmen and embrace democracy. Someday they would approve the right to establish unions, engage in collective bargaining, and enjoy freedom of association, all of which would be the key to honest economic growth in the country.

NOTES

1. Michael Schuman, "The Birth and Rebirth of Shenzhen," *Time*, Asia edition, August 14, 2006.
2. Ted C. Fishman, *China, Inc.* (New York: Scribner International, 2005), 93.
3. Thomas Fuller, "China Feels a Labor Pinch," *International Herald Tribune*, April 20, 2005.
4. See http://www.asianews.it/view.php?I=en&art=7688#, November 7, 2006.
5. Fishman, *China, Inc.*, 95.
6. SA 8000 Overview, www.sa-intl.org.
7. Her name has been changed.

STUDY QUESTIONS

1. Describe the job of a Vendor Compliance Officer.

2. What kind of factory is Lever Shirt? Do you think you would want to work there in any capacity? Why or why not?

3. How does Snyder's description of her visit to the factory change what you thought about clothing factories in China?

4. Visit the website of your favorite clothing line or shop. What can you find out about how and where its clothes are made from the website? Try a search engine. Does the information (or lack thereof) change your attitude toward the brand? Why or why not?

ROBERT D. PUTNAM

Thinking about Social Change
in America

from *Bowling Alone: The Collapse and Revival of
American Community*

For generations, Americans have been civic-minded. They've joined Rotary Clubs and the Shriners, softball teams and city councils. But, in this selection, Robert D. Putnam asks, "Where did everybody go?" Since the mid-1970s, Putnam argues, civic participation has steadily decreased. As the organizations in which "everyone" used to participate fade into obscurity, they also leave a real hole in the social safety net, since they provided a great deal of **social capital** for the communities they served. Without such **groups**, Putnam wonders, will **society** survive? As you read, think about whether you believe civic participation has dropped off—that is, whether people really are opting out of community service and participation—or if it is changing. If it's changing, where *have* all the people gone?

NO ONE IS LEFT FROM THE GLENN VALLEY, PENNSYLVANIA, Bridge Club who can tell us precisely when or why the group broke up, even though its forty-odd members were still playing regularly as recently as 1990, just as they had done for more than half a century. The shock in the Little Rock, Arkansas, Sertoma club, however, is still painful: in the mid-1980s, nearly fifty people had attended the weekly luncheon to plan activities to help the hearing- and speech-impaired, but a decade later only seven regulars continued to show up.

The Roanoke, Virginia, chapter of the National Association for the Advancement of Colored People (NAACP) had been an active force for civil rights since 1918, but during the 1990s membership withered from about 2,500 to a few hundred. By November 1998 even a heated contest for president drew only fifty-seven voting members. Black city councillor Carroll Swain observed ruefully, "Some people today are a wee bit complacent until something jumps up and bites them." VFW Post 2378 in Berwyn, Illinois, a blue-collar suburb of Chicago, was long a bustling "home away from home" for local veterans and a kind of working-class country club for the neighborhood, hosting wedding receptions and class reunions. By 1999, however, membership had so dwindled that it was a struggle just to pay taxes on the yellow brick post hall. Although numerous veterans of Vietnam and the post-Vietnam military lived in the area, Tom Kissell, national membership director for the VFW, observed, "Kids today just aren't joiners."[1]

The Charity League of Dallas had met every Friday morning for fifty-seven years to sew, knit, and visit, but on April 30, 1999, they held their last meeting; the average age of the group had risen to eighty, the last new member had joined two years earlier, and president Pat Dilbeck said ruefully, "I feel like this is a sinking ship." Precisely three days later and 1,200 miles to the northeast, the Vassar alumnae of Washington, D.C., closed down their fifty-first—and last—annual book sale. Even though they aimed to sell more than one hundred thousand books to benefit college scholarships in the 1999 event, co-chair Alix Myerson explained, the volunteers who ran the program "are in their sixties, seventies, and eighties. They're dying, and they're not replaceable." Meanwhile, as Tewksbury Memorial High School (TMHS), just north of Boston, opened in the fall of 1999, forty brand-new royal blue uniforms newly purchased for the marching band remained in storage, since only four students signed up to play. Roger Whittlesey, TMHS band director, recalled that twenty years earlier the band numbered more than eighty, but participation had waned ever since.[2] Somehow in the last several decades of the twentieth century all these community groups and tens of thousands like them across America began to fade.

It wasn't so much that old members dropped out—at least not any more rapidly than age and the accidents of life had always meant. But community organizations were no longer continuously revitalized, as they had been in the past, by freshets of new members. Organizational leaders were flummoxed. For years they assumed that their problem must have local roots or at least that it was peculiar to their organization, so they commissioned dozens of studies to recommend reforms.[3] The slowdown was puzzling because for as long as anyone could remember, membership rolls and activity lists had lengthened steadily.

In the 1960s, in fact, community groups across America had seemed to stand on the threshold of a new era of expanded involvement. Except for the civic drought induced by the Great Depression, their activity had shot up year after year, cultivated by assiduous civic gardeners and watered by increasing affluence and education. Each annual report registered rising membership. Churches and synagogues were packed, as more Americans worshiped together than only a few decades earlier, perhaps more than ever in American history.

Moreover, Americans seemed to have time on their hands. A 1958 study under the auspices of the newly inaugurated Center for the Study of Leisure at the University of Chicago fretted that "the most dangerous threat hanging over American society is the threat of leisure," a startling claim in the decade in which the Soviets got the bomb.[4] *Life* magazine echoed the warning about the new challenge of free time: "Americans now face a glut of leisure," ran a headline in February 1964. "The task ahead: how to take life easy."

> As a matter of fact, mankind now possesses for the first time the tools and knowledge to create whatever kind of world he wants. . . . Despite our Protestant ethic, there are many signs that the message is beginning to get through to some people. . . . Not only are Americans flocking into bowling leagues and garden clubs, they are satisfying their gregarious urges in countless neighborhood committees to improve the local roads and garbage collections and to hound their public servants into doing what the name implies.[5]

The civic-minded World War II generation was, as its own John F. Kennedy proclaimed at his inauguration, picking up the torch of leadership, not only in the nation's highest office, but in cities and towns across the land. Summarizing dozens of studies, political scientist Robert E. Lane wrote in 1959 that "the ratio of political activists to the general population, and even the ratio of male activists to the male population, has generally increased over the past fifty years." As the 1960s ended, sociologists Daniel Bell and Virginia Held reported that "there is more participation than ever before in America . . . and more opportunity for the active interested person to express his personal and political concerns."[6] Even the simplest political act, voting, was becoming ever more common. From 1920, when women got the vote, through 1960, turnout in presidential elections had risen at the rate of 1.6 percent every four years, so on a simple straight-line projection it seemed reasonable, as a leading political scientist later observed, to expect turnout to be nearly 70 percent and rising on the nation's two hundredth birthday in 1976.[7]

By 1965 disrespect for public life, so endemic in our history, seemed to be waning. Gallup pollsters discovered that the number of Americans who would like to see their children "go into politics as a life's work" had nearly doubled over little more than a decade. Although this gauge of esteem for politics stood at only 36 percent, it had never before been recorded so high, nor has it since. More strikingly, Americans felt increased confidence in their neighbors. The proportion that agreed that "most people can be trusted," for example, rose from an already high 66 percent during and after World War II to a peak of 77 percent in 1964.[8]

The fifties and sixties were hardly a "golden age," especially for those Americans who were marginalized because of their race or gender or social class or sexual orientation. Segregation, by race legally and by gender socially, was the norm, and intolerance, though declining, was still disturbingly high. Environmental degradation had only just been exposed by Rachel Carson, and Betty Friedan had not yet deconstructed the feminine mystique. Grinding rural poverty had still to be discovered by the national media. Infant mortality, a standard measure of public health, stood at twenty-six per one thousand births—forty-four per one thousand for black infants—in 1960, nearly four times worse than those indexes would be at the end of the century. America in *Life* was white, straight, Christian, comfortable, and (in the public square, at least) male.[9] Social reformers had their work cut out for them. However, engagement in community affairs and the sense of shared identity and reciprocity had never been greater in modern America, so the prospects for broad-based civic mobilization to address our national failings seemed bright.

The signs of burgeoning civic vitality were also favorable among the younger generation, as the first of the baby boomers approached college. Dozens of studies confirmed that education was by far the best predictor of engagement in civic life, and universities were in the midst of the most far-reaching expansion in American history. Education seemed the key to both greater tolerance and greater social involvement. Simultaneously shamed and inspired by the quickening struggle for civil rights launched by young African Americans in the South, white colleges in the North began to awaken from the silence of the fifties. Describing the induction of this new generation into the civil rights struggles of the 1960s, sociologist Doug McAdam emphasizes their self-assurance:

> We were a "can do" people, who accomplished whatever we set out to do. We had licked the Depression, turned the tide in World War II, and rebuilt Europe after the war.... Freedom Summer was an audacious undertaking consistent with the exaggerated sense of importance and potency shared by the privileged members of America's postwar generation.[10]

The baby boom meant that America's population was unusually young, whereas civic involvement generally doesn't bloom until middle age. In the short run, therefore, our youthful demography actually tended to dampen the ebullience of civil society. But that very bulge at the bottom of the nation's demographic pyramid boded well for the future of community organizations, for they could look forward to swelling membership rolls in the 1980s, when the boomers would reach the peak "joining" years of the life cycle. And in the meantime, the bull session buzz about "participatory democracy" and "all power to the people" seemed to augur ever more widespread engagement in community affairs. One of America's most acute social observers prophesied in 1968, "Participatory democracy has all along been the political style (if not the slogan) of the American middle and upper class. It will become a more widespread style as more persons enter into those classes."[11] Never in our history had the future of civic life looked brighter.

———————

What happened next to civic and social life in American communities? In recent years social scientists have framed concerns about the changing character of American society in terms of the concept of "social capital." By analogy with notions of physical capital and human capital—tools and training that enhance individual productivity—the core idea of social capital theory is that social networks have value. Just as a screwdriver (physical capital) or a college education (human capital) can increase productivity (both individual and collective), so too social contacts affect the productivity of individuals and groups.

Whereas physical capital refers to physical objects and human capital refers to properties of individuals, social capital refers to connections among individuals—social networks and the norms of reciprocity and trustworthiness that arise from them. In that sense social capital is closely related to what some have called "civic virtue." The difference is that "social capital" calls attention to the fact that civic virtue is most powerful when embedded in a dense network of reciprocal social relations. A society of many virtuous but isolated individuals is not necessarily rich in social capital.

The term *social capital* itself turns out to have been independently invented at least six times over the twentieth century, each time to call attention to the ways in which our lives are made more productive by social ties. The first known use of the concept was not by some cloistered theoretician, but by a practical reformer of the Progressive Era—L. J. Hanifan, state supervisor of rural schools in West Virginia. Writing in 1916 to urge the importance of community involvement for successful schools, Hanifan invoked the idea of "social capital" to explain why. For Hanifan, social capital referred to

> those tangible substances [that] count for most in the daily lives of people: namely good will, fellowship, sympathy, and social intercourse among the individuals and families who make up a social unit.... The individual is helpless socially, if left to himself.... If he comes into contact with his neighbor, and they with other neighbors, there will be an accumulation of social capital, which may immediately satisfy his social needs and which may bear a social potentiality sufficient to the substantial improvement of living conditions in the whole community. The community as a whole will benefit by the coöperation of all its parts, while the individual will find in his associations the advantages of the help, the sympathy, and the fellowship of his neighbors.[12]

Hanifan's account of social capital anticipated virtually all the crucial elements in later interpretations, but his conceptual invention apparently attracted no notice from other social commentators and disappeared without a trace. But like sunken treasure recurrently revealed by shifting sands and tides, the same idea was independently rediscovered in the 1950s by Canadian sociologists to characterize the club memberships of arriviste suburbanites, in the 1960s by urbanist Jane Jacobs to laud neighborliness in the modern metropolis, in the 1970s by economist Glenn Loury to analyze the social legacy of slavery, and in the 1980s by French social theorist Pierre

Bourdieu and by German economist Ekkehart Schlicht to underline the social and economic resources embodied in social networks. Sociologist James S. Coleman put the term firmly and finally on the intellectual agenda in the late 1980s, using it (as Hanifan had originally done) to highlight the social context of education.[13]

As this array of independent coinages indicates, social capital has both an individual and a collective aspect—a private face and a public face. First, individuals form connections that benefit our own interests. One pervasive strategem of ambitious job seekers is "networking," for most of us get our jobs because of whom we know, not what we know—that is, our social capital, not our human capital. Economic sociologist Ronald Burt has shown that executives with bounteous Rolodex files enjoy faster career advancement. Nor is the private return to social capital limited to economic rewards. As Claude S. Fischer, a sociologist of friendship, has noted, "Social networks are important in all our lives, often for finding jobs, more often for finding a helping hand, companionship, or a shoulder to cry on."[14]

If individual clout and companionship were all there were to social capital, we'd expect foresighted, self-interested individuals to invest the right amount of time and energy in creating or acquiring it. However, social capital also can have "externalities" that affect the wider community, so that not all the costs and benefits of social connections accrue to the person making the contact.[15] As we shall see, a well-connected individual in a poorly connected society is not as productive as a well-connected individual in a well-connected society. And even a poorly connected individual may derive some of the spillover benefits from living in a well-connected community. If the crime rate in my neighborhood is lowered by neighbors keeping an eye on one another's homes, I benefit even if I personally spend most of my time on the road and never even nod to another resident on the street.

Social capital can thus be simultaneously a "private good" and a "public good." Some of the benefit from an investment in social capital goes to bystanders, while some of the benefit redounds to the immediate interest of the person making the investment. For example, service clubs, like Rotary or Lions, mobilize local energies to raise scholarships or fight disease at the same time that they provide members with friendships and business connections that pay off personally.

Social connections are also important for the rules of conduct that they sustain. Networks involve (almost by definition) mutual obligations; they are not interesting as mere "contacts." Networks of community engagement foster sturdy norms of reciprocity: I'll do this for you now, in the expectation that you (or perhaps someone else) will return the favor. "Social capital is akin to what Tom Wolfe called 'the favor bank' in his novel *The Bonfire of the Vanities*," notes economist Robert Frank.[16] It was, however, neither a novelist nor an economist, but Yogi Berra who offered the most succinct definition of reciprocity: "If you don't go to somebody's funeral, they won't come to yours."

Sometimes, as in these cases, reciprocity is *specific:* I'll do this for you if you do that for me. Even more valuable, however, is a norm of *generalized* reciprocity: I'll do this for you without expecting anything specific back from you, in the confident expectation that someone else will do something for me down the road. The Golden Rule is one formulation of generalized reciprocity. Equally instructive is the T-shirt slogan used by the Gold Beach, Oregon, Volunteer Fire Department to publicize their annual fund-raising effort: "Come to our breakfast, we'll come to your fire." "We act on a norm of specific reciprocity," the firefighters seem to be saying, but onlookers smile because they recognize the underlying norm of generalized reciprocity—the firefighters will come even if *you* don't. When Blanche DuBois depended on the kindness of strangers, she too was relying on generalized reciprocity.

A society characterized by generalized reciprocity is more efficient than a distrustful society, for the same reason that money is more efficient than barter. If we don't have to balance every exchange instantly, we can get a lot more accomplished. Trustworthiness lubricates social life. Frequent interaction among a diverse set of people tends to produce a norm of generalized reciprocity. Civic engagement and social capital entail mutual obligation and responsibility for action. As L. J. Hanifan and his successors recognized, social networks and norms of reciprocity can facilitate cooperation for mutual benefit. When economic and political dealing is embedded in dense networks of social interaction, incentives for opportunism and malfeasance are reduced. This is why the diamond trade, with its extreme possibilities for fraud, is concentrated within close-knit ethnic enclaves. Dense social ties facilitate gossip and other valuable ways of cultivating reputation—an essential foundation for trust in a complex society.

Physical capital is not a single "thing," and different forms of physical capital are not interchangeable. An eggbeater and an aircraft carrier both appear as physical capital in our national accounts, but the eggbeater is not much use for national defense, and the carrier would not be much help with your morning omelet. Similarly, social capital—that is, social networks and the associated norms of reciprocity—comes in many different shapes and sizes with many different uses. Your extended family represents a form of social capital, as do your Sunday school class, the regulars who play poker on your commuter train, your college roommates, the civic organizations to which you belong, the Internet chat group in which you participate, and the network of professional acquaintances recorded in your address book.

Sometimes "social capital," like its conceptual cousin "community," sounds warm and cuddly. Urban sociologist Xavier de Souza Briggs, however, properly warns us to beware of a treacly sweet, "kumbaya"* interpretation of social capital.[17] Networks and the associated norms of reciprocity are generally good for those inside the network, but the external effects of social capital are by no means always positive. It was social capital, for example, that enabled Timothy McVeigh to bomb the Alfred P. Murrah

---

* African American spiritual (from the Creole language Gullah, meaning "Come by Here") that became a popular 1960s folk song and eventually a symbol of peaceful coexistence.

Federal Building in Oklahoma City. McVeigh's network of friends, bound together by a norm of reciprocity, enabled him to do what he could not have done alone. Similarly, urban gangs, NIMBY ("not in my backyard") movements, and power elites often exploit social capital to achieve ends that are antisocial from a wider perspective. Indeed, it is rhetorically useful for such groups to obscure the difference between the pro-social and antisocial consequences of community organizations. When Floridians objected to plans by the Ku Klux Klan to "adopt a highway," Jeff Coleman, grand wizard of the Royal Knights of the KKK, protested, "Really, we're just like the Lions or the Elks. We want to be involved in the community."[18]

Social capital, in short, can be directed toward malevolent, antisocial purposes, just like any other form of capital.[19] (McVeigh also relied on physical capital, like the explosive-laden truck, and human capital, like bomb-making expertise, to achieve his purposes.) Therefore it is important to ask how the positive consequences of social capital—mutual support, cooperation, trust, institutional effectiveness—can be maximized and the negative manifestations—sectarianism, ethnocentrism, corruption—minimized. Toward this end, scholars have begun to distinguish many different forms of social capital.

Some forms involve repeated, intensive, multistranded networks—like a group of steelworkers who meet for drinks every Friday after work and see each other at mass on Sunday—and some are episodic, single stranded, and anonymous, like the faintly familiar face you see several times a month in the supermarket checkout line. Some types of social capital, like a Parent-Teacher Association, are formally organized, with incorporation papers, regular meetings, a written constitution, and connection to a national federation, whereas others, like a pickup basketball game, are more informal. Some forms of social capital, like a volunteer ambulance squad, have explicit public-regarding purposes; some, like a bridge club, exist for the private enjoyment of the members; and some, like the Rotary club mentioned earlier, serve both public and private ends.

Of all the dimensions along which forms of social capital vary, perhaps the most important is the distinction between *bridging* (or inclusive) and *bonding* (or exclusive).[20] Some forms of social capital are, by choice or necessity, inward looking and tend to reinforce exclusive identities and homogeneous groups. Examples of bonding social capital include ethnic fraternal organizations, church-based women's reading groups, and fashionable country clubs. Other networks are outward looking and encompass people across diverse social cleavages. Examples of bridging social capital include the civil rights movement, many youth service groups, and ecumenical religious organizations.

Bonding social capital is good for undergirding specific reciprocity and mobilizing solidarity. Dense networks in ethnic enclaves, for example, provide crucial social and psychological support for less fortunate members of the community, while furnishing start-up financing, markets, and reliable labor for local entrepreneurs. Bridging networks, by contrast, are better for linkage to external assets and for information diffusion. Economic sociologist Mark Granovetter has pointed out that when seeking jobs—or political allies—the "weak" ties that link me to distant acquaintances who move in different circles from mine are actually more valuable than the "strong" ties that link me to relatives and intimate friends whose sociological niche is very like my own. Bonding social capital is, as Xavier de Souza Briggs puts it, good for "getting by," but bridging social capital is crucial for "getting ahead."[21]

Moreover, bridging social capital can generate broader identities and reciprocity, whereas bonding social capital bolsters our narrower selves. In 1829 at the founding of a community lyceum in the bustling whaling port of New Bedford, Massachusetts, Thomas Greene eloquently expressed this crucial insight:

> We come from all the divisions, ranks and classes of society . . . to teach and to be taught in our turn. While we mingle together in these pursuits, we shall learn to know each other more intimately; we shall remove many of the prejudices which ignorance or partial acquaintance with each other had fostered. . . . In the parties and sects into which we are divided, we sometimes learn to love our brother at the expense of him whom we do not in so many respects regard as a brother. . . . We may return to our homes and firesides [from the lyceum] with kindlier feelings toward one another, because we have learned to know one another better.[22]

Bonding social capital constitutes a kind of sociological superglue, whereas bridging social capital provides a sociological WD-40. Bonding social capital, by creating strong in-group loyalty, may also create strong out-group antagonism, as Thomas Greene and his neighbors in New Bedford knew, and for that reason we might expect negative external effects to be more common with this form of social capital. Nevertheless, under many circumstances both bridging and bonding social capital can have powerfully positive social effects.

Many groups simultaneously bond along some social dimensions and bridge across others. The black church, for example, brings together people of the same race and religion across class lines. The Knights of Columbus was created to bridge cleavages among different ethnic communities while bonding along religious and gender lines. Internet chat groups may bridge across geography, gender, age, and religion, while being tightly homogeneous in education and ideology. In short, bonding and bridging are not "either-or" categories into which social networks can be neatly divided, but "more or less" dimensions along which we can compare different forms of social capital.

It would obviously be valuable to have distinct measures of the evolution of these various forms of social capital over time. However, like researchers on global warming, we must make do with the imperfect evidence that we can find, not merely lament its deficiencies. Exhaustive descriptions of social networks in America—even at a single point in time—do not exist. I have found no reliable, comprehensive, nationwide measures of social capital that neatly distinguish "bridgingness" and "bondingness."

In our empirical account of recent social trends, therefore, this distinction will be less prominent than I would prefer. On the other hand, we must keep this conceptual differentiation at the back of our minds as we proceed, recognizing that bridging and bonding social capital are not interchangeable.

———————

"Social capital" is to some extent merely new language for a very old debate in American intellectual circles. Community has warred incessantly with individualism for preeminence in our political hagiology. Liberation from ossified community bonds is a recurrent and honored theme in our culture, from the Pilgrims' storied escape from religious convention in the seventeenth century to the lyric nineteenth-century paeans to individualism by Emerson ("Self-Reliance"), Thoreau ("Civil Disobedience"), and Whitman ("Song of Myself") to Sherwood Anderson's twentieth-century celebration of the struggle against conformism by ordinary citizens in *Winesburg, Ohio* to the latest Clint Eastwood film. Even Alexis de Tocqueville, patron saint of American communitarians, acknowledged the uniquely democratic claim of individualism, "a calm and considered feeling which disposes each citizen to isolate himself from the mass of his fellows and withdraw into the circle of family and friends; with this little society formed to his taste, he gladly leaves the greater society to look after itself."[23]

Our national myths often exaggerate the role of individual heroes and understate the importance of collective effort. Historian David Hackett Fischer's gripping account of opening night in the American Revolution, for example, reminds us that Paul Revere's alarum was successful only because of networks of civic engagement in the Middlesex villages. Towns without well-organized local militia, no matter how patriotic their inhabitants, were AWOL from Lexington and Concord.[24] Nevertheless, the myth of rugged individualism continues to strike a powerful inner chord in the American psyche.

Debates about the waxing and waning of "community" have been endemic for at least two centuries. "Declensionist narratives"—postmodernist jargon for tales of decline and fall—have a long pedigree in our letters. We seem perennially tempted to contrast our tawdry todays with past golden ages. We apparently share this nostalgic predilection with the rest of humanity. As sociologist Barry Wellman observes,

> It is likely that pundits have worried about the impact of social change on communities ever since human beings ventured beyond their caves.... In the [past] two centuries many leading social commentators have been gainfully employed suggesting various ways in which large-scale social changes associated with the Industrial Revolution may have affected the structure and operation of communities.... This ambivalence about the consequences of large-scale changes continued well into the twentieth century. Analysts have kept asking if things have, in fact, fallen apart.[25]

At the conclusion of the twentieth century, ordinary Americans shared this sense of civic malaise. We were reasonably content about our economic prospects, hardly a surprise after an expansion of unprecedented length, but we were not equally convinced that we were on the right track morally or culturally. Of baby boomers interviewed in 1987, 53 percent thought their parents' generation was better in terms of "being a concerned citizen, involved in helping others in the community," as compared with only 21 percent who thought their own generation was better. Fully 77 percent said the nation was worse off because of "less involvement in community activities." In 1992 three-quarters of the U.S. workforce said that "the breakdown of community" and "selfishness" were "serious" or "extremely serious" problems in America. In 1996 only 8 percent of all Americans said that "the honesty and integrity of the average American" were improving, as compared with 50 percent of us who thought we were becoming less trustworthy. Those of us who said that people had become less civil over the preceding ten years outnumbered those who thought people had become more civil, 80 percent to 12 percent. In several surveys in 1999 two-thirds of Americans said that America's civic life had weakened in recent years, that social and moral values were higher when they were growing up, and that our society was focused more on the individual than the community. More than 80 percent said there should be more emphasis on community, even if that put more demands on individuals.[26] Americans' concern about weakening community bonds may be misplaced or exaggerated, but a decent respect for the opinion of our fellow citizens suggests that we should explore the issue more thoroughly.

It is emphatically not my view that community bonds in America have weakened steadily throughout our history—or even throughout the last hundred years. On the contrary, American history carefully examined is a story of ups and downs in civic engagement, *not just downs*—a story of collapse *and* of renewal. Within living memory the bonds of community in America were becoming stronger, not weaker, and it is within our power to reverse the decline of the last several decades.

Nevertheless, my argument is, at least in appearance, in the declensionist tradition, so it is important to avoid simple nostalgia. Precisely because the theme of this book might lend itself to gauzy self-deception, our methods must be transparent. Is life in communities as we enter the twenty-first century really so different after all from the reality of American communities in the 1950s and 1960s? One way of curbing nostalgia is to count things. Are club meetings really less crowded today than yesterday, or does it just seem so? Do we really know our neighbors less well than our parents did, or is our childhood recollection of neighborhood barbecues suffused with a golden glow of wishful reminiscence? Are friendly poker games less common now, or is it merely that we ourselves have outgrown poker? League bowling may be passé, but how about softball and soccer? Are strangers less trustworthy now? Are boomers and X'ers really less engaged in community life? After all, it was the preceding generation that was once scorned as "silent." Perhaps the younger generation today is no less engaged than their predecessors, but engaged in new ways.

* * *

Before October 29, 1997, John Lambert and Andy Boschma knew each other only through their local bowling league at the Ypsi-Arbor Lanes in Ypsilanti, Michigan. Lambert, a sixty-four-year-old retired employee of the University of Michigan hospital, had been on a kidney transplant waiting list for three years when Boschma, a thirty-three-year-old accountant, learned casually of Lambert's need and unexpectedly approached him to offer to donate one of his own kidneys.

"Andy saw something in me that others didn't," said Lambert. "When we were in the hospital Andy said to me, 'John, I really like you and have a lot of respect for you. I wouldn't hesitate to do this all over again.' I got choked up." Boschma returned the feeling: "I obviously feel a kinship [with Lambert]. I cared about him before, but now I'm really rooting for him." This moving story speaks for itself, but the photograph that accompanied this report in the *Ann Arbor News* reveals that in addition to their differences in profession and generation, Boschma is white and Lambert is African American. That they bowled together made all the difference.[27] In small ways like this—and in larger ways, too—we Americans need to reconnect with one another. That is the simple argument of this book.

NOTES

1. David Scott and Geoffrey Godbey, "Recreation Specialization in the Social World of Contract Bridge," *Journal of Leisure Research* 26 (1994): 275–295; Suzi Parker, "Elks, Lions May Go Way of the Dodo," *Christian Science Monitor,* August 24, 1998; John D. Cramer, "Relevance of Local NAACP Is Up for Debate," *Roanoke Times,* January 24, 1999; Dirk Johnson, "As Old Soldiers Die, V.F.W. Halls Fade Away," *New York Times,* September 6, 1999. I am grateful to Professor David Scott for information about the Glenn Valley Bridge Club; "Glenn Valley" is a pseudonym for a college town in central Pennsylvania.

2. Christine Wicker, "A Common Thread of Decency," *Dallas Morning News,* May 1, 1999; David Streitfeld, "The Last Chapter: After 50 Years, Vassar Ends Its Famed Book Sale," *Washington Post,* April 28, 1999, C1; Caroline Louise Cole, "So Many New Uniforms, but So Few Musicians," *Boston Sunday Globe Northwest Weekly,* September 5, 1999, 1.

3. Jeffrey A. Charles, *Service Clubs in American Society: Rotary, Kiwanis, and Lions* (Urbana: University of Illinois Press; 1993), 157.

4. Eric Larrabee and Rolf Meyersohn, *Mass Leisure* (Glencoe, Ill.: Free Press, 1958), 359, as quoted in Foster Rhea Dulles, *A History of Recreation: America Learns to Play,* 2nd ed. (New York: Appleton-Century-Crofts, 1965), 390.

5. *Life,* February 21, 1964, 91, 93. I am grateful to Rob Paarlberg for spotting this remarkable issue in a Maine flea market.

6. Robert E. Lane, *Political Life: Why People Get Involved in Politics* (Glencoe, Ill.: Free Press, 1959), 94; Daniel Bell and Virginia Held, "The Community Revolution," *The Public Interest,* 16 (1969): 142.

7. In fact, turnout in 1976 was 53 percent and falling. See Richard A. Brody, "The Puzzle of Political Participation in America," in *The New American Political System,* ed. Anthony King (Washington, D.C.: American Enterprise Institute for Public Policy Research, 1978).

8. George H. Gallup, *The Gallup Poll: Public Opinion 1935–1971* (New York: Random House, 1972); Karlyn Bowman, "Do You Want to Be President?," *Public Perspective* 8 (February/March 1997): 40; Robert E. Lane, "The Politics of Consensus in an Age of Affluence," *American Political Science Review* 59 (December 1965): 879; and Richard G. Niemi, John Mueller, and Tom W. Smith, *Trends in Public Opinion* (New York: Greenwood Press, 1989), 303. The version of the "trust" question used in the 1940s, 1950s, and 1960s is not directly comparable to the one that has become standard in most recent years.

9. See Thomas R. Rochon, *Culture Moves: Ideas, Activism, and Changing Values* (Princeton, N.J.: Princeton University Press, 1998), xiii–xiv.

10. Doug McAdam, *Freedom Summer* (New York: Oxford University Press, 1988), 14–15.

11. James Q. Wilson, "Why Are We Having a Wave of Violence?" *The New York Times Magazine,* May 19, 1968, 120.

12. Lyda Judson Hanifan, "The Rural School Community Center," *Annals of the American Academy of Political and Social Science* 67 (1916): 130–138, quotation at 130. Ever the practical reformer, Hanifan was self-conscious about using the term *capital* to encourage hard-nosed businessmen and economists to recognize the productive importance of social assets. Having introduced the idea of social capital, he observes, "That there is a great lack of such social capital in some rural districts need not be retold in this chapter. The important question at this time is: How can these conditions be improved? The story which follows is an account of the way a West Virginia rural community in a single year actually developed social capital and then used this capital in the improvement of its recreational, intellectual, moral, and economic conditions." His essay, which included a list of practical exercises for community-based activists, was originally prepared in 1913 for West Virginia schoolteachers as "a handbook for community meetings at rural schoolhouses," and it was subsequently incorporated in L. J. Hanifan, *The Community Center* (Boston: Silver, Burdett, 1920). I am grateful to Brad Clarke for first spotting this usage of the term *social capital.*

13. John R. Seeley, Alexander R. Sim, and Elizabeth W. Loosley, *Crestwood Heights: A Study of the Culture of Suburban Life* (New York: Basic Books, 1956); Jane Jacobs, *The Death and Life of Great American Cities* (New York: Random House, 1961); Glenn Loury, "A Dynamic Theory of Racial Income Differences," in *Women, Minorities, and Employment Discrimination,* ed. P.A. Wallace and A. LeMund (Lexington, Mass.: Lexington Books, 1977), 153–188; Pierre Bourdieu, "Forms of Capital," in *Handbook of Theory and Research for the Sociology of Education,* ed. John G. Richardson (New York: Greenwood Press, 1983), 241–258; Ekkehart Schlicht, "Cognitive Dissonance in Economics," in *Normengeleitetes Verhalten in den Sozialwissenschaften* (Berlin: Duncker and Humblot, 1984), 61–81; James S. Coleman, "Social Capital in the Creation of Human Capital," *American Journal of Sociology* 94 (1988): S95–S120; and James S. Coleman, *Foundations of Social Theory* (Cambridge, Mass.: Harvard University Press, 1990). See also George C. Homans, *Social Behavior: Its Elementary Forms* (New York: Harcourt, Brace & World, 1961), 378–98. Except for a brief acknowledgment by Coleman of Loury's work, I can find no evidence that any of these theorists were aware of any of the preceding usages. For a comprehensive overview of the conceptual history of "social capital," see Michael Woolcock, "Social Capital and Economic Development: Toward a Theoretical Synthesis and Policy Framework," *Theory and Society* 27 (1998): 151–208.

14. Ronald S. Burt, *Structural Holes: The Social Structure of Competition* (Cambridge, Mass.: Harvard University Press, 1992); Ronald S. Burt, "The Contingent Value of Social Capital,"

Administrative Science Quarterly 42 (1997): 339–365; and Ronald S. Burt, "The Gender of Social Capital," *Rationality & Society* 10 (1998): 5–46; Claude S. Fischer, "Network Analysis and Urban Studies," in *Networks and Places: Social Relations in the Urban Setting*, ed. Claude S. Fischer (New York: Free Press, 1977), 19; James D. Montgomery, "Social Networks and Labor-Market Outcomes: Toward an Economic Analysis," *American Economic Review* 81 (1991): 1408–1418, esp. table 1.

15. In earlier work I emphasized this public dimension of social capital almost to the exclusion of the private returns to social capital. See Robert D. Putnam, "The Prosperous Community: Social Capital and Public Affairs," *The American Prospect* 13 (1993): 35–42, on which the present text draws. For a literature review that highlights the private returns almost to the exclusion of the collective dimension, see Alejandro Portes, "Social Capital: Its Origins and Applications in Modern Sociology," *Annual Review of Sociology* 22 (1998): 1–24.

16. Robert Frank in private conversation.

17. Xavier de Souza Briggs, "Social Capital and the Cities: Advice to Change Agents," *National Civic Review* 86 (summer 1997): 111–117.

18. *U.S. News & World Report* (August 4, 1997): 18. Fareed Zakaria, "Bigger Than the Family, Smaller Than the State," *New York Times Book Review,* August 13, 1995: 1, pointed out that McVeigh and his co-conspirators spent evenings together in a bowling alley and concluded that "we would all have been better off if Mr. McVeigh had gone bowling alone." Sometimes, as in certain cults or clans, even the *internal* effects of social capital can be negative, but these are less common than negative *external* effects.

19. In *Making Democracy Work: Civic Traditions in Modern Italy* (Princeton, N.J.: Princeton University Press, 1993), I ignored the possibility that social capital might have antisocial effects, but I recognized this possibility explicitly in "The Prosperous Community," published that same year.

20. So far as I can tell, credit for coining these labels belongs to Ross Gittell and Avis Vidal, *Community Organizing: Building Social Capital as a Development Strategy* (Thousand Oaks, Calif.: Sage, 1998), 8.

21. Mark S. Granovetter, "The Strength of Weak Ties," *American Journal of Sociology* 78 (1973): 1360–1380; Xavier de Souza Briggs, "Doing Democracy Up Close: Culture, Power, and Communication in Community Building," *Journal of Planning Education and Research* 18 (1998): 1–13.

22. As quoted in Richard D. Brown, "The Emergence of Voluntary Associations in Massachusetts," *Journal of Voluntary Action Research 2* (April 1973): 64–73, at 69. See also Ashutosh Varshney, *Ethnic Conflict and Civic Life: Hindus and Muslims in India* (New Haven, Conn.: Yale University Press, 2000).

23. Alexis de Tocqueville, *Democracy in America*, ed. J. P. Mayer, trans. George Lawrence (Garden City, N.Y.: Doubleday, 1969), 506. See also Wilson Carey McWilliams, *The Idea of Fraternity in America* (Berkeley: University of California Press, 1973), and Thomas Bender, *Community and Social Change in America* (Baltimore, Md.: Johns Hopkins University Press, 1978).

24. David Hackett Fischer, *Paul Revere's Ride* (New York: Oxford University Press, 1994).

25. Barry Wellman, "The Community Question Re-Evaluated," in *Power, Community, and the City*, Michael Peter Smith, ed. (New Brunswick, N.J.: Transaction 1988), 81–107, quotation at 82–83. Pamela Paxton, "Is Social Capital Declining in the United States? A Multiple Indicator Assessment," *American Journal of Sociology* 105 (1999): 88–127.

26. *The Public Perspective* 8 (December/January 1997): 64; Robert Wuthnow, "Changing Character of Social Capital in the United States," in *The Dynamics of Social Capital in Comparative Perspective*, Robert D. Putnam, ed. (2000, forthcoming); *The Public Perspective 10* (April/May 1999): 15; *Wall Street Journal*, June 24, 1999, A12; Mark J. Penn, "The Community Consensus," *Blueprint: Ideas for a New Century* (spring 1999). Respondents with no opinion are excluded.

27. Emma Jackson, "Buddy Had Kidney to Spare," *Ann Arbor News* (January 5, 1998). Thanks to Michael Dover for his elegant posting of this story in the Nonprofit and Voluntary Action listserv, www.arnova.org/arnova_1.htm, January 6, 1998.

STUDY QUESTIONS

1. What is **social capital**? It may help to compare social capital to human capital and physical capital in your answer.

2. What is the difference between the two types of social capital Putnam describes: bridging and bonding capital? Give an example of each that is *not* provided in the chapter.

3. Describe a situation in which you were able to achieve something (say, getting a job) because of a social connection. That is to say, when have you cashed in some of your social capital? Where did you get that social capital in the first place?

4. Use the Internet to find and list ten civic groups in your area that are open to you. What is the mission of each? Had you heard of any of them before? Contact one **organization** to ask about the work they do and their membership. Do you think they serve a vital function in your community?